SUSTAINED LEADERSHIP WBS

Endorsements

Tom Reid's *Sustained Leadership WBS* is the first comprehensive identification and assessment of the critical elements essential to lead people and organizations for sustained success. The graphic decomposition of the knowledge, skills and competencies makes this a practical learning tool for the seasoned leader as well as the aspiring novice. Thanks Tom.

—**Daniel M. Jacobs**, CPCM, CMC, PMP
Chairman/CEO
The Federal Market Group

I used a variety of leadership training materials and texts in my years as a college dean, but I have never seen anything even approaching *Sustained Leadership WBS*, with its encyclopedic view of all the various elements—229 of them—that contribute to becoming, sustaining, and developing oneself as a leader. Bravo to Tom Reid for producing a useful textbook on leadership!

— **Dr. David Stameshkin**
Associate Dean (retired)
Franklin & Marshall College

Sustained Leadership WBS is a scholarly, but easy to read treatment of various leadership principles and philosophies. Tom's concentration on "sustained" leadership, and his attendant work breakdown structure (WBS) to achieve "sustained" leadership, can be very useful tool for both those already in leadership positions and potential leaders. Well done.

— **Len Vincent** RADM USN (RET)
Formerly Commander, Defense Contract Management Command (DCMC)
and Commandant, Defense Systems Management College (DSMC)

SUSTAINED LEADERSHIP WBS

A Disciplined Project Approach
to Building You and Your Team
into Better Leaders

THOMAS G. REID
JD, CScM, CPCM

NEW YORK

NASHVILLE • MELBOURNE • VANCOUVER

SUSTAINED LEADERSHIP WBS
A Disciplined Project Approach to Building You and Your Team into Better Leaders

Published in New York, New York, by Morgan James Publishing. Morgan James is a trademark of Morgan James, LLC. www.MorganJamesPublishing.com

The Morgan James Speakers Group can bring authors to your live event. For more information or to book an event visit The Morgan James Speakers Group at www.TheMorganJamesSpeakersGroup.com.

ISBN 978-1-68350-593-8 paperback
ISBN 978-1-68350-594-5 eBook
Library of Congress Control Number: 2017907731

Cover Design by:
Rachel Lopez
www.r2cdesign.com

Interior Design by:
Bonnie Bushman
The Whole Caboodle Graphic Design

In an effort to support local communities, raise awareness and funds, Morgan James Publishing donates a percentage of all book sales for the life of each book to Habitat for Humanity Peninsula and Greater Williamsburg.

Get involved today! Visit
www.MorganJamesBuilds.com

The quotes and details concerning real people are believed to be accurate based on extensive research. When the character of "Ken" or Kenny" appears, this is a composite character based on real people and real events. The name and details were modified to protect the privacy of living persons.

www.SustainedLeadershipWBS.com

TABLE OF CONTENTS

Chapter 1

LEADERSHIP IN PERSPECTIVE

———————— ● ————————

I f you were to make the decision to set for yourself a personal goal of becoming a leader, how would you do that? Where would you start? Where would it end? How would you know whether you were making any progress? How would you know for a certainty that being a leader is even a goal you want to achieve? Quite simply, when making such a decision to pursue the goal of becoming a leader, into what, exactly, are you immersing yourself? Choosing to be a leader requires a great deal of work and concentration. It will require you to develop a strong ability to deal with ambiguity. And above all else, it will require a tremendous amount of self-discipline. This is one reason why good leaders are so hard to find. So few people will dedicate themselves to becoming one.

The available literature today is extensive, and unfortunately it is very often contradictory. The literature seems to focus on a narrow slice of leadership when in fact leadership is a very complex set of traits, practices, disciplines, and habits that interrelate with each other. So many elements comprise the concept of leadership that it is difficult to figure out what they are, let alone decide where to start to improve your leadership abilities. And just in case you haven't figured this part out yet, until a person learns to lead themselves, through discipline and hard work, they are not qualified to lead others. This is difficult, and finding strong leaders from whom to learn can be even more challenging. Accomplishing difficult tasks is part of what makes becoming a true leader worthwhile, and becoming a better leader of yourself is the important first step.[1] Those who do so are worthy of our admiration and, depending on their vision and moral center, worthy of being followed. When we seek leaders to follow, we look for someone who takes the role as seriously as we perceive it should be.

Being "in charge" does not make you a leader. Leadership is comprised of a great number of traits and characteristics, as well as habits, which cause people to *want* to follow you. You have seen those who are in positions of power who, due to a personal flaw, a critically bad decision, allowing improper influence to sway their judgment, or any number of other failures, were removed from that position. They did not sustain their leadership. One or more of the elements of leadership were missing or were not maintained. What we seek is "sustained leadership." By using this term we distinguish what is presented here from the many other writings on leadership.

When we refer to sustained leadership we intend to convey that a leader is constantly learning and improving themselves, preparing for every eventuality, and learning how to make better and better decisions. Their role as a leader is sustainable through good times and bad, from errors they might make to those situations that are thrust upon them. They become recognized as a leader by those who choose to follow them. They maintain and grow that following by continually demonstrating the things that people are seeking in their leaders. In social media circles you might see the term "influencer" (more often than not an aspirational desire rather than a demonstrable fact), which is really just one flavor of leader—hopefully a sustained leader.

Given that becoming a sustained leader is hard work and may require developing new habits (as well as breaking old ones), why would anyone pursue it? The first and most obvious reason is that it makes you a better you. You are the only you that will ever exist on this earth. What you do with that is completely a function of the choices you make. Have you made good choices in your life? If you could do it all

---

1   A. Harris, B. Harris, and C. Norris. *Do Hard Things: A Teenage Rebellion Against Low Expectations.* (US: Multnomah, 2008).

over, might you make different choices knowing what you know now? Improving your leadership ability starts with self-improvement. Even if you never want to be responsible for others or lead any type of team, you will find more satisfaction in your own life by developing your innate skills and traits.

The second reason is that by developing your leadership potential you will be positioned to help others, whether that is through a crisis (such as 9/11) or a more immediate emergency (a heart attack on the baseball field), a business predicament, or even a crisis faced by a family member. Leadership skills are applicable anywhere, but unless you have prepared yourself to act, you become one of the people wandering around wondering what happened rather than the person making things happen.

Organizational success is directly dependent on the leaders who guide it. Thus, any organization should be intensely interested in developing leaders at every level of the organization. By developing a team of strong leaders, the organization optimizes its performance and its opportunities for success of its mission.

Definitions of Leadership

There are more books on the market these days with "leadership" in the title than there appear to be grains of sand on a beach.[2] On the one hand, publishers would not keep pushing them into the market if they were not selling. On the other hand, hasn't enough been written on the subject that only the most cloistered hermit doesn't yet get what it means to be a leader? We have leadership secrets from George Patton, Colin Powell, George Washington, Abraham Lincoln, West Point, Jesus, Moses, Billy Graham, the Founding Fathers, Ulysses S. Grant, Jack Welch, Shakespeare, Attila the Hun, and even Santa Clause. Shouldn't every seeker of wisdom concerning leadership have been able to find some model to follow by now? A review of what passes for leadership in society today can be seen in the daily papers and online articles. Clearly our major institutions of business, government, and religion all suffer from serious leadership deficiencies. And yet every week some new title shows up in the market promoting the latest theory, designation, indispensable attribute, or natural talent that must exist before you are deemed a "leader."

---

2   Keith Grint, in *Leadership: A Very Short Introduction* (New York: Oxford University Press, 2010), notes that in 2003 there were 14,139 leadership books on Amazon (UK) and by 2009 there were 53,121. A search in 2016 found over 200,000.

The current literature provides no direct guidance on what makes a sustained leader. Various books and articles pretend to outline the three rules, the twenty-five rules, the top ten rules, the "one thing you need to know," and numerous permutations on these themes with no clear conclusion or magic formula that makes a leader.[3] One purpose of the *Sustained Leadership WBS* is to help with the language of leadership. The first step in understanding any field or discipline is to understand the jargon. If we are not all speaking the same language, we cannot communicate effectively.

The "solution" to perceived leadership problems is directly dependent on how you define leadership. In simplest terms, a leader is one who has followers. They might be subjects or slaves or prisoners or children, but if they are following you, you are their leader. And you might be an absolutely horrible leader.

Another popular definition tells us that leadership is an interpersonal influence directed toward the achievement of a goal. In this case, the leadership role includes the interpersonal element and directing the team toward a defined goal. The literature is full of such definitional examples, yet we never seem to get it quite right. There is always "one more thing" that must be considered. This causes some to suggest that leadership cannot be defined and must remain an amorphous "fuzzy skill." To define it in this way, however, is a great disservice. It suggests that leadership is either indefinable or that it can be whatever you want it to be. Perhaps this suggests why, despite the vast amount of literature on leadership, we still do not seem to get it right very often.

---

3   Kenneth H. Blanchard and Marc Muchnick, *The Leadership Pill: The Missing Ingredient in Motivating People Today* (New York: 2004).

Frances Hesselbein defines leadership in this way: "Leadership is a matter of how to be, not how to do. You and I spend most of our lives learning how to do and teaching others how to do, yet it is the quality and character of the leader that determines the performance, the results. Leadership is a matter of how to be, not how to do."[4] Ms. Hesselbein worked extensively with Peter Drucker and draws on his wisdom as well. She distills his wisdom on leadership into four concise points:

1. "The only definition of a leader is someone who has followers. Some people are thinkers. Some are prophets. Both roles are important and badly needed. But without followers, there can be no leaders.
2. An effective leader is not someone who is loved or admired. He or she is someone whose followers do the right things. Popularity is not leadership. Results are.
3. Leaders are highly visible. They therefore set examples.
4. Leadership is not rank, privileges, titles, or money. It is responsibility."[5]

In *On Becoming a Leader* Warren Bennis presents a number of leaders and distills four key points about leadership. Leaders, he observes, are committed to their mission, have a strong sense of self-knowledge, are capable of communicating a vision, and have great personal integrity.[6] In his other writings he has said, "Leadership is the capacity to translate vision into reality," and also, "Leadership is the capacity to create a compelling vision and translate it into action and sustain it. Successful leaders have a vision that other people believe in and treat as their own."

Tacitus

Reason and judgment are the qualities of a leader.

The literature is full of attempts to define leadership. It begins to seem that it is similar to what Supreme Court Justice Potter Stewart said regarding pornography:

---

4   Frances Hesselbein, *My Life in Leadership* (San Francisco: Jossey-Bass, 2011), 81.
5   Ibid., 122-23.
6   Ibid., 197.

"I shall not today attempt further to define [pornography].... But I know it when I see it...."[7] Another source suggests that leadership is "The skill of influencing people to work enthusiastically toward goals identified as being for the common good."[8] The author also notes "The role of the leader is a very high calling."[9] Jack and Suzy Welch observe that in discussing leadership, "we...present a new, holistic model we've developed from the entirety of our experience and observation, one that defines leadership as the relentless pursuit of truth and the ceaseless creation of trust."[10] They propose that leadership is simply about two things: "1. Truth and trust. 2. Ceaselessly seeking the former, relentlessly building the latter."[11]

Another definition suggests, "Anytime you seek to influence the thinking, behavior, or development of people in their personal or professional lives, you are taking on the role of a leader."[12]

Leadership is elsewhere defined as a dynamic relationship based on mutual influence and common purpose between leaders and collaborators in which both are moved to higher levels of motivation and moral development as they affect real, intended change.[13]

So what if you desire to be a leader, and further desire to be a good leader? What must you *do*? Or is the better question what must you *be*? The best answer seems to be—you must both do and be. There are many things that leaders do, and in most cases leaders are measured on their results. Whether it is winning a war, leading a country, or successfully completing a project—if they do not make something happen, what have they truly accomplished? There is also the issue of what leaders *are*. Generally, they must be people of high character and strong moral underpinning. They must have the ability to provide a vision and instill confidence. Along with these positive attributes, there are things a sustained leader must avoid. They must not be deceptive, duplicitous, or generally lacking in moral

---

7   *Jacobellis v. Ohio*, 378 U.S. 184 (1964).
8   James C. Hunter, *The Servant: A simple story about the true essence of leadership* (Rocklin, CA: Prima Publishing, 1998), 28.
9   Ibid., 27.
10 Jack and Suzy Welch, *The Real Life MBA: Your No-BS Guide to Winning the Game, Building a Team, and Growing Your Career* (New York: Harper Collins, 2015), 15.
11 Ibid., 123.
12 Ken Blanchard and Colleen Barrett, *Lead with Luv: A Different Way to Create Real Success* (Upper Saddle River, NJ: FT Press, 2011), 5.
13 Kevin Freiberg and Jackie Freiberg, *NUTS! Southwest Airlines' Crazy Recipe for Business and Personal Success* (US: Bard Press, 1996), 298.

fiber. Regardless of how you may decide to define a "leader," there is no single answer to the question of what makes a leader or how it should be defined. Thus, the path to leadership is strewn with the carcasses of those who failed to understand what the journey would entail and the level of commitment necessary to achieve it.

Where Are You Starting?

No two people will begin their pursuit of the goal of becoming a leader from the same starting point. The first precept that you must accept is that *it doesn't matter*. No two people are identically situated in terms of age, education, capabilities, experience, family, or any other factor that defines who you are. Your portfolio of traits, attributes, and abilities is totally unique to you. Thus, the path to the goal is going to be different for each person. Numerous people have also shown us that it is never too late. Grandma Moses did not start painting until she was already one hundred years old. Colonel Sanders started selling his special recipe for fried chicken when he was sixty-six and already collecting Social Security. There are numerous examples of people who got their lives sorted out and found great success after many years of experience, often many setbacks, and sometimes even personal or financial disasters. It doesn't matter. How do you sift through all the material that is available and focus on those specific things that your leadership portfolio lacks?

The reason that the *Sustained Leadership WBS* was developed was to provide anyone, starting from any point in their life, a framework against which they can compare their current status or situation and determine what areas need the most

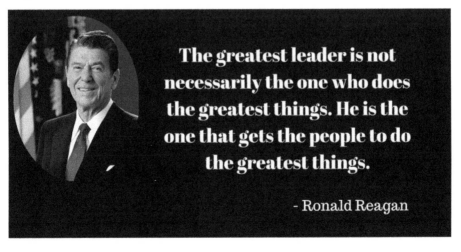

The greatest leader is not necessarily the one who does the greatest things. He is the one that gets the people to do the greatest things.

- Ronald Reagan

work. Simply saying that you have the goal to become a sustained leader provides you no direction, guidance, or path. The *Sustained Leadership WBS* is the guidance you need. You will still have to decide which aspects of leadership are reflected in your strengths and those that are lacking, thus highlighting your weaknesses. Only you can decide how much of your effort, time, energy, and resources will be devoted toward this goal. Thus, no matter your current starting point, the *Sustained Leadership WBS* resource will help you develop a plan to improve your leadership abilities. It does not matter one bit where you are today.

How do you take all the data and information that are available on the subject of leadership and construct a useful set of tools that has wide applicability to help motivated people better develop as leaders? The *Sustained Leadership WBS* borrows project management skills as a metaphor for building a leader and blends that with theories of leadership and personal development. This organization allows you to see the big picture of leadership development and easily identify those specific aspects of leadership where you excel and where you come up short. It will take a considerable effort and deep honesty to properly assess yourself against the criteria provided and determine YOUR specific path of improved leadership abilities.

A project, we are told by the Project Management Institute, is an endeavor that has a beginning, an end, and a unique product. All contracts are therefore projects, as are all construction efforts. What about you? Are you a project? You have a beginning and an end, and you are unquestionably unique. To restate a theme you see throughout the *Sustained Leadership WBS*, you are the only "you" there will ever be, and what you make of "you" is the most you will ever be. So what are you doing about it?

If you were to accept the responsibility for a project—the creation of some unique end product—and if you were versed in project management skills, you would start with a Work Breakdown Structure (WBS). What is a WBS? It is, in its simplest terms, a listing of all the requirements, all aspects for the end product with a focus on the deliverables.

The starting point for a useful WBS is what Covey told us—begin with the end in mind.[14] What exactly do you want to be? What would "You the Leader"

---

14   Stephen R. Covey, *The 7 Habits of Highly Effective People*, (Habit #2). But see, Jeffrey Gitomer, *Social Boom*, p. 179 actually goes the other way on this point.

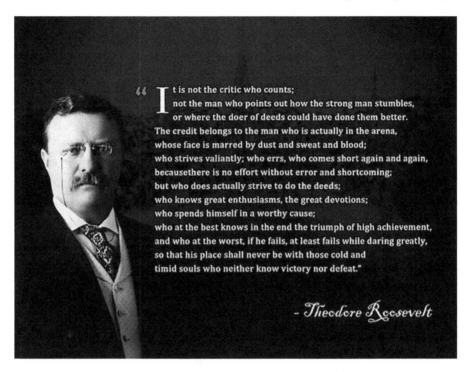

"It is not the critic who counts; not the man who points out how the strong man stumbles, or where the doer of deeds could have done them better. The credit belongs to the man who is actually in the arena, whose face is marred by dust and sweat and blood; who strives valiantly; who errs, who comes short again and again, becausethere is no effort without error and shortcoming; but who does actually strive to do the deeds; who knows great enthusiasms, the great devotions; who spends himself in a worthy cause; who at the best knows in the end the triumph of high achievement, and who at the worst, if he fails, at least fails while daring greatly, so that his place shall never be with those cold and timid souls who neither know victory nor defeat."

— *Theodore Roosevelt*

project look like? What traits, characteristics, innate abilities, training, education, or whatever would it take to make you a leader?

Unless you truly have a passion for any goal you might choose, you are unlikely to achieve it. Human nature is full of fears and things that will try to derail you. Even well-meaning friends and family will often be sources of discouragement. Becoming a leader requires real commitment, so you must be very comfortable with your "why" on your leadership journey. Becoming the best possible version of "you" should be enough, but for many it is not. And no one, absolutely no one, can give you that "why."

Our fear of failure, it seems, is more of an acquired trait than something innate. This means that it has been learned and can be unlearned. It is through the experience of setbacks that many leaders mature. In fact, in the *Sustained Leadership WBS* we have removed most references to "failure" and refer to such events as "setbacks" since you never truly fail until you give up. This reflects the fact that unless you are failing or experiencing setbacks in some manner, you are probably not active enough—you are not "doing" anything. Be bold. Be brave. Do not fear *fear*. If you allow this one thing to paralyze you, you will not succeed as a sustained leader. This is not to say that you need to be reckless and cavalier about risks. It simply means that sitting in your room engaging in omphaloskepsis[15] will not cause leadership to attack you and turn you into a leader. You must confront your fears and trepidations and actually DO something to be considered a leader. Leaders, after all, are measured by results.

One of the most popular books on leadership is *The Leadership Challenge*. The authors say, "…we firmly believe that leadership is not about position or title. It's about relationships, credibility, and what you *do*."[16] Only you can overcome your fears. Only you can dedicate yourself to becoming a better leader. Only you can learn to deal with your fears and commit yourself to becoming a leader. Merely holding a title of leadership, or being placed in a position of leadership, gives you positional power. And power alone is not sustained leadership.[17] The sustained leader will seek the relationships necessary to help them along the path. They will work toward improving their credibility among those who follow them. And most importantly, they will have a vision and a mission to bring their team together to do great things—to actually achieve something worthwhile.

Principles of Leadership

Leadership is often confused with power. Certainly leaders wield power, and they do so in a legitimate manner. Many people fill leadership positions because they were appointed to them. While someone in the hierarchy has determined that the person should hold the position, they may or may not be a true leader. The person holds what is known as positional power—they have leadership authority solely because they hold the position, not because they earned the position or are qualified for it. People certainly are placed in positions of leadership, but positional power is one of the weakest forms of power. Power is not leadership. It may be authority and it might be exercised in any number of inappropriate ways. Power is merely power. How that power is used will determine whether the person who wields it is truly a leader.

---

15 Big words can be fun. This one means "contemplating your navel."

16 James M. Kouzes and Barry Z. Posner, *The Leadership Challenge* (San Francisco: Jossey-Bass, 2002), 383. (Emphasis in original.)

17 Mark Sanborn, *You Don't Need a Title to Be a Leader: How Anyone, Anywhere, Can Make a Positive Difference* (New York: Currency Doubleday, 2006).

In *The Prince*, Machiavelli instructs a new prince on how to use the power of the realm to keep himself safe and his subjects in line. Much of what he says is good advice, but he includes enough of the use of kingly power to have gotten the reputation that someone who is manipulative and abuses power is being Machiavellian. Much can be learned from Machiavelli so long as you keep in mind a saying from Mark Twain: "No one is a complete waste; they can always serve as a bad example." Abusing your power, whether positional, legitimate, or any number of gradations of power, is wrong and not a trait of a sustained leader.

Certain personality types are also perceived as especially good or weak leaders. Creatives are viewed as less like leaders because creativity is messy. Creativity plus charisma, however, could be a winning combination. Introverts are also often overlooked as leaders, yet some of the best leaders are introverts—that does not mean recluse![18] While perceptions can define a person's reputation, they have little to do with capabilities or true leadership potential, and nothing to do with character. Many leaders who have performed an accurate self-assessment recognize either their own weaknesses or the perception of those weaknesses by others. Thus, sustained leaders know that they often must draw others around them who have stronger traits than they have in certain areas, thereby creating a synergy between the two. Bill Gates and Steve Ballmer from Apple are good examples, as are William Hewlett and David Packard. You will not be strong in every aspect of the *Sustained Leadership WBS*. Learning to identify your own weaknesses and drawing others around you who are strong where you are weak will enhance your leadership.

Leadership draws a distinction between variance and deviance. No two things are exactly alike. Variance is everywhere and is a characteristic of nature itself. In many parts of society extreme variances are accepted and not considered deviance. Many people enjoy decorating their bodies with various colors of permanent ink and piercing various body parts, often to insert obvious and oversized items. Rather than just a diamond stud earring, they insert a three-inch hoop into their earlobe. Other parts of society would suggest that this variance goes beyond the norm and becomes a deviant characteristic. Variance among us is a good thing and ensures preservation of the species in many respects. In this regard, different leaders will choose different courses of action. They will choose different visions and different

---

18   Susan Cain, *Quiet: The Power of Introverts in a World That Can't Stop Talking.* (US: Crown, 2012).

missions. They will lead differently and have different goals or ways of expressing themselves. This is actually a good thing. You, the sustained leader, will be a totally different work product than Joe, or Jim, or Sally, or whomever.

Judy Columbus

We can practice leadership principles, but the only way to learn to use them is to lead. Not knowing it all is no excuse not to start.

That's OK. There are variances, however, that do cross the line and become unacceptable deviance. For example, ethical lapses will often derail a leadership journey. Moral shortcomings, what used to be called moral turpitude, will not be tolerated by followers. Simple setbacks in achievements, or falling short of a bold goal, are acceptable variances. Learning from these setbacks is a normal process of leadership development. Deviant behavior, however, will not be tolerated, and the individual who exhibits such actions must commit to correcting them—and come back within society's norms—to continue on the leadership path. Some can do this quite readily, while others might need fifteen to twenty years in prison to properly reevaluate their conduct. Keep in mind that with leadership, variance is a good thing; deviance is not.

Leadership and Management

One popular quote, often attributed to Peter Drucker, is that managers do things right while leaders do the right things. What's wrong with doing the right things right? That should be the goal of any leader. A good leader may well be a good manager, but a good manager may or may not be a good leader. The skills are different, yet in many respects similar. Demonstrating your abilities as a manager may be an important steppingstone toward leadership. A manager is a boss; they have been put in a position of authority. They may or may not know how to have a positive vision and how to motivate a broad collection of people with different innate motivations and personality traits. When a manager can set a vision and begin to influence the team toward group performance rather than simply direct their performance, this is a sign that they are becoming a leader.

Change management and leadership authority John Kotter says both management and leadership are critical skills.[19] Management, as the *Sustained Leadership WBS* will explain, is comprised primarily of the tasks that are often remembered through the acronym POSDCoRB, which stands for Planning, Organizing, Staffing, Directing, Coordinating, Reporting, and Budgeting. Note that influencing, developing, and many other critical leadership elements are not included here. Managers tend to have more positional authority than actual authority. Managers are responsible for making sure the organizational goals are achieved, but they are often not included in the process by which such goals are set. Managers are perceived as being the "doers" of the organization and are expected to follow, and get others to follow, the direction provided by the SENIOR management (i.e. the presumed "leaders") of the organization. This misses a key point. An organization needs leaders at all levels, including those who serve as managers and those assigned to cubicles performing routine tasks.

The Difference between Knowing and Doing

In an extremely important book, Jeffrey Pfeffer and Robert I. Sutton discuss what they call *The Knowing-Doing Gap*.[20] We seem to know a great many things, whether as an individual or with a collective conscience. We don't, however, without some external stimulus, always do what should be done based on the knowledge we hold. That seems completely counterintuitive, yet we do it consistently. Consider your diet, the bad habits that you can't break, and the study you have made of your religious obligations. People know what to do but don't do it. The knowledge is out there; it simply isn't followed. We do not, as a society, seem to have sufficient self-discipline to control our actions and thus "what I want to do I do not do, but what I hate I do. ... For I have the desire to do what is good, but I cannot carry it out. For I do not do the good I want to do, but the evil I do not want to do—this I keep on doing."[21] The books, studies, and reports on leadership continue to flow, yet our collective demonstration of good leadership never seems to improve. All the

19   John P. Kotter, *A Force for Change: How Leadership Differs from Management* (US: The Free Press, 1990).

20   Jeffrey Pfeffer and Robert I. Sutton, *The Knowing-Doing Gap* (Boston: Harvard Business School Press, 2000).

21   Romans 7:15, 18-19 (NIV)

knowledge has no impact on the result. So quite clearly, they conclude, knowing what to do is not enough.[22]

Leadership suffers from this malady, and sadly, this lack of leadership permeates every level and function of society. Undertaking a study of the *Sustained Leadership WBS* will only provide you with more knowledge. Unless you take it to heart and actually *practice* true leadership, this additional knowledge will not make you a better you, or the world a better place. You must actually *do* the "leadership thing." British broadcaster and TV writer Sir Anthony Rupert Jay has said, "The only real training for leadership is leadership." Packing your head full of knowledge is a great start, but only by doing the activity will you truly understand how to apply all of this knowledge.

Too often when discussing leadership confusion also arises over the difference between what are sometimes called "hard" and "soft" skills or the "science of leadership" versus the "art of leadership." Orrin Woodward notes that there are leadership skills and traits that can be measured in an objective fashion while other areas may only be assessed subjectively.[23] And not everyone's opinion on the quality of the subjectively analyzed traits or skills is equal. Reasonable people can and do differ. Again, it is only by leading that you hone your skills, put all the knowledge into practice, and develop leadership wisdom. By preparing yourself with the knowledge of being a sustained leader you will find opportunities, or more accurately opportunities will find you, that will permit you to practice what you have learned to become a sustained leader.

Leaders Are Readers

Charlie "Tremendous" Jones, in his classic book *Life Is Tremendous*,[24] has a chapter titled "Leaders Are Readers." You, of course, are reading this and may be looking at the size of this volume and wondering—will I ever finish it? Many will, but most won't. Studies have shown that more people put a book down after the first chapter or two never to return. Other studies suggest that unless required to read, most people don't. And the most common genre of books is fiction. We contend that Charlie Jones is right. Leaders are readers, and the more they read the better leaders they become. They expose themselves to a great variety of thought and wisdom.

22 Op. Cit. *Knowing Doing Gap*. ix.
23 Orrin Woodward, *The Financial Matrix* (Cary, NC: Obstacles Press, 2015), 36.
24 Charles E. Jones, *Life Is Tremendous* (US: Executive Books, 1981).

They train their minds in critical thinking, not simply absorbing everything they read, but developing better discernment and making their own decisions about what they believe to be correct or incorrect in what they read.

If you seek to become a sustained leader, read everything you can and concentrate on those who provide the best advice. John Maxwell is excellent, and there are many others. Jack Welch, Norman Vincent Peale, Napoleon Hill, Og Mandino, Charlie "Tremendous" Jones, and Brian Tracy are just a few of the names that routinely top the list of recommended authors to read. Borrow from them. Put their wisdom into practice.

Biographies are also a great source of leadership training. When asked how people develop good business judgement, the most common answer is education and experience. Education is facilitated by reading. Experience, however, tends to be a form of trial and error. Face it; you can't live long enough to make every mistake from which you could possibly learn. It thus seems prudent to learn all you can from the mistakes of others. Prepare yourself, and when you least expect it you will suddenly discover that you are leading a team toward a worthwhile goal. Which would not have happened if you spent all your time trying to find those three rings or magic pill rather than preparing yourself to be the best "you" you can be. That is the only legitimate path to sustained leadership.

Measuring Success

The most common and definitive measure of success is results. A leader accomplishes things and moves the team toward the goal, the mission, and the vision. Is that the only measure? No. John Maxwell suggests "The true measure of success is succession—what happens after you're gone."[25] Thus, we have put the development of other leaders as an essential checkpoint of sustained leadership.

Others propose that successful leadership is reflected in the level and span of influence an individual wields. While influence can certainly be included in terms of measuring results, keep in mind that many influential people are very bad leaders because of a lack of character or other fatal flaw. The *Sustained Leadership WBS* contains a set of elements that are deemed critical toward success as a sustained leader (see Chapter 3). The legacy you leave behind will

---

25   John C. Maxwell, *Intentional Living: Choosing a Life That Matters* (New York: Center Street, 2015), 131.

reflect your leadership during your tenure. If it is not maintained, then despite many brave and noble accomplishments, you have failed in a significant item of sustained leadership.

John Maxwell suggests there are seven streams of influence which he defines as "arts, entertainment, sports, and culture; business; education; family; faith; government; and media."[26] Here we've condensed it to three, namely, religion, politics (and government), and business or industry as reflective of the three major institutions of society. The *Sustained Leadership WBS* is designed to make you a better you who can then influence these institutions. Regardless of how you delineate the categories, it is fair to say that success in each area is measured differently and success in one is not necessarily a predictor of success in any of the other areas. Leadership is, in this regard contextual. The true sustained leader should be able to lead in any of the areas described since leadership is a universal need. It is the application of leadership to the situation that will have a measurable impact on results, and each of those institutions has its own unique set of key performance indicators (KPIs). Even among elements within each of those institutions, the KPIs will vary. Success in leading a Johns Hopkins research lab might not translate to success in leading General Motors. The *Sustained Leadership WBS* is useful in both situations since the level of competence (WBS 2.0) will be different between those two similar, but different entities.

Peter Drucker

There may be such a thing as a natural born leader, but there are so few of them that they make no difference in the great scheme of things.

Born or Made

Much of the theoretical development of leadership stems from a search for the answer to the "born or made" question. Steven B. Sample notes that his long-term collaborator Warren Bennis observed, "The most dangerous leadership myth is that leaders are born. That's nonsense; in fact, the opposite is true. Leaders are made

---

26   Ibid., 258.

rather than born."[27] With due respect to these longstanding masters of leadership development, we would adjust that just a bit. If leaders were only born, then you may have no hope of developing into one. If they were only made, then why haven't we been successful in making more or better leaders? To say they are only made suggests that there is some magic formula to be discovered that will transform anyone into a perfect leader. All you have to do is read the right book, attend the right seminar, follow the right guru, find the right mentor, be offered the right project to pursue, or otherwise discover and possess the magic formula, and *poof* you are a leader. Clearly leadership is not that formulaic.

It is our view that leaders are both born and made. Some people are blessed with certain traits and characteristics naturally. No two people have the exact same traits and characteristics. Whether physical, mental, attitudinal, environmental, relational, spiritual, or any number of traits, everyone is different. For some, a lifetime of training might need to be undone before sustained leadership can take hold. For others, with no historical impediments and being blessed with many natural talents and abilities, developing into a sustained leader might be much easier. Regardless, sustained leadership can be learned and mastered by anyone wishing to embark on this self-improvement project.

The simplest answer is the most direct, specifically, that there are a number of traits, practices, and characteristics that, when combined in a single individual, cause us to consider them a leader. Some of them are naturally exhibited by certain individuals while others will exhibit a different set. In each case there is more that must be learned in terms of knowledge, habits, practices, or traits. People are differently endowed naturally and thus their leadership journey will be unique to them. Like any educational process, some people learn more quickly than others; some learn certain things well and struggle with other lessons. The point is that some people are drawn more naturally to leadership than others. Some, through upbringing or other experiences, have already learned critical lessons in leadership. Others have only had bad examples to follow and must first unlearn certain things before learning the correct skillset and adopting and manifesting favorable traits. All of the *Sustained Leadership WBS* elements can be learned and more finely honed. It will become a continuing journey.

---

27   Warren Bennis and Stephen B. Sample (with Rob Asghar), *The Art and Adventure of Leadership: Understanding Failure, Resilience, and Success* (Hoboken, NJ: John Wiley & Sons, 2015), xv.

Being the hierarchical leader is not the goal of sustained leadership. Too often people view a leadership role as a capstone to their career. This is the wrong perspective. Developing your leadership potential is the cornerstone of your career, not the capstone.

History of Leadership Theories

While we would like to believe we have long outgrown the ancient philosophy that "might makes right," the fact is that vestiges of this form of leadership persist today. Whether it is the bully on the playground, the psychological intimidators in college (including both fellow students and professors), or the bombastic ass at work (again including the arrogant coworker and the inept boss),[28] we still see various forms of might-makes-right playing out around us. From prehistoric times forward there are those who, because they are stronger and can inflict harm on others, are given their way. Even Attila the Hun followed this maxim, and it worked![29] And because it works, that form of leadership has not yet completely died out. In times long past (though interestingly still practiced in some forms around the world) the leader was the king. They were considered as gods on earth or sometimes actual gods. More frequently (then and now) their authority was considered as being derived from whatever god the people worshipped. The followers are exhibiting an extension of the might-makes-right philosophy.

The power and authority derived from might-makes-right was usually demonstrated as military prowess and was easily lost when another came along who was slightly more powerful, if not younger.[30] As technology advanced, personal power became less relevant as technology created a more level playing field among individuals. With the development of gun powder and continuing to the modern age of computers, technology has imposed a significant impact on our perceptions of leadership (and power and authority). Only more recently have we begun to perceive leadership as a social science where leadership is more a measure of influence over others gained when those who follow agree to do so voluntarily. Influence often is a form of knowledge, and first-world countries

---

28 Robert I. Sutton, *The No Asshole Rule: Building a Civilized Workplace and Surviving One That Isn't* (US: Business Plus, 2007).

29 Wess Roberts, *Leadership Secrets of Attila the Hun* (US: Business Plus, 1990).

30 For the biblically inclined, the rivalry between King Saul, King David, and David's son Absalom is very representative of this kind of leadership struggle (see 1 and 2 Samuel).

have evolved past the manufacturing era into a service economy where knowledge itself (even absent true wisdom) has become the "might" behind those who are in positions of power.

Leadership studies are a continuum of theories, many of which lead to dead ends, or are enhanced with short-lived fads. Likewise, individual case studies, while they may hold a particular lesson, are often not capable of universal application.[31] Just because someone reached a level of externally perceived success by leading in a certain fashion does not mean that a cookie-cutter approach will work for anyone else. This has led researchers to propose a variety of theories about leadership. Each has some merit and serves to explain some particular aspect of leadership, yet each also fails in providing a comprehensive view of leadership.

These theories are often based on some level of research, thus validating the outcome for which the test was designed, but not fully explaining leadership. Nonetheless each theory has predominated at least for a time, and each has its adherents who, to this day, believe that this one single theory of leadership does or should predominate. Thus, they all can exist simultaneously with a different class of adherents and will overlap in terms of timelines. Vestiges of all can be found in the literature today. For ease of discussion, we will review a few of the predominant theories that have been used to explain leadership.

The principal theories most often used to describe or define leadership include:[32]

- Trait
- Great Events
- Behavioral
- Contingency
- Situational
- Influence (including both Transformational and Servant-Leadership concepts)

---

31 See Jeffrey Pfeffer, *Leadership BS: Fixing Workplaces and Careers One Truth at a Time*. (New York: Harper Collins, 2015). Pfeffer observes that too often leadership training focus on the aberrations and not reproducible leadership characteristics.

32 For a description that provides greater granularity, see http://www.transformationalleadership. net/products/TransformationalLeadershipReport.pdf Accessed 04/23/17.

Trait Theory

From an historical perspective, an early measure of leadership was what became known as the Trait Theory. In research conducted in 1989 and 1990,[33] Bernard M. Bass proposed that there were three principal ways to explain how people became leaders. These have less to do with *being* a leader and more to do with being *identified* as a leader. The first is based on traits, primarily personality traits and including other physical attributes, and is appropriately called the trait theory. Through perceived personality and physical traits, whether innate or learned, leaders are identified and accepted by the followers. The personal traits tend to predominate, the primary ones involving physical and sociological traits. Thus, a strong, handsome man or a beautiful woman with a strong social presence would be selected by others as proper people to follow. Some of this extended to a form of hero-worship that drives the Hollywood "star" syndrome. Those who are viewed as leaders, for example in sports or movies, are not leaders within the sustained leadership construct because other than the ability to sink a basket or play a role (or make a sex tape), they exhibit very few of the aspects of leadership presented in the *Sustained Leadership WBS.*

By choosing which set of traits, or characteristics, were believed to indicate leadership potential, it was believed that the "right" leaders would be selected. This process fails on many levels. It assumes that the traits selected to discriminate among choices were in fact real indicators of leadership ability or potential. It assumes that the person so selected would choose to lead in a productive manner and would somehow be imbued with all of the many skills and attributes that successful leaders have. The physical traits that were commonly chosen might include youth, but tempered with a bit of experience, physically fit, and attractive based on that society's perception of beauty. Social attributes would vary based on the society, but might include coming from the right family line, having an education, particularly from an "acceptable" school, and fitting into the society across a broad spectrum of social strata. Those who were outgoing and charismatic were often seen as leaders, even if those characteristics were being used for more nefarious purposes such as frauds or scams. Being self-confident, diplomatic, tactful, and non-aggressive were also frequently viewed as positive traits for proposed leaders. Many of these traits

---

33   http://discoverthought.com/Leadership/References_files/Bass%20leadership%201990.pdf
     Accessed 04/23/17. See also https://scholar.google.com/citations?user=mr77kVoAAAAJ&hl=en
     Accessed 04/23/17.

are still used today in political contests to select the person for whom to vote. The problem remains, however, that the mere existence of these traits is not an accurate predictor of leadership success.

Thus, the trait theory fails under its own weight. People with similar traits do not maintain their positions of leadership similarly. Looking good takes precedence over results, and results are essential for a mission to succeed. It suggests that leaders are only born and cannot be developed. It focuses on the observable rather than the "how" of producing leadership results.

This leadership theory is so appealing to many that Hollywood continues to thrive regardless of the complete lack of sustained leadership exhibited in its operation and its products. Apart from the continuing hero-worship dynamic, some traits are still perceived as worthy of following such a pseudo leader. In the 2016 presidential primary, the Republican Party fielded seventeen major candidates. During several of the debates, the various Internet search engine companies reported that one of the most common searches on the candidates had to do with how tall they were. In brainstorming sessions where the various aspects of leadership were being proposed during research on the *Sustained Leadership WBS*, one of the suggestions was frequently "tall."

Oren Arnold

You don't make your character in a crisis, you exhibit it.

Consider a biblical example. The Hebrews had escaped Egypt and established their holy city of Jerusalem. They were led by judges and not kings as were the societies around them. As a theocracy, their true leader was the God of Moses, Jacob, and Abraham as interpreted by the priests from the tribe of Levi. Even so, the people began to insist that they be given a king like the societies around them. The priest/prophet Samuel had sons who were to assume his role, but they were not good men. They did not follow the ways of Israel. The people begged for a king, and Samuel even painted a very bleak picture of what a king would do to their society, forcing them to work the king's fields and taking their daughters to work in his kitchen. Still the people pleaded with Samuel to name a king who would lead them to battle and protect them with justice. Samuel continued to counsel against this, but the people insisted. And from this, King Saul was chosen to lead the Israelites. "There was a man of Benjamin [who] had a choice and handsome son whose name was Saul. There was not a more handsome person than he among the children of Israel. From his shoulders upward he was taller than any of the people."[34] Good breeding, good upbringing, physically attractive, and tall. Under the trait theory—a great choice.

If you study the history of the Jewish people, you know the outcome. Saul was a petulant, proud, emotionally unstable, fearful, and basically horrible leader. He failed his people and was ultimately killed in battle after trying for years to remove his rival, King David. As Alan Elliott has summarized, "It is great to be good-looking, but it is awesome to be both good-looking and useful."[35]

It is true that certain traits can be cited which characterize an effective leader. Having a vision and mission, the drive to succeed, a desire to lead, unimpeachable integrity, self-confidence, an appropriate level of intelligence, and job-relevant knowledge are all admirable traits and ones to be sought in any leader. These traits alone, however, are never enough.[36] There is much more to sustained leadership than just having the right package of attributes.

Great Events Theory

In the second primary theory proposed by Bass, leadership is shown when a crisis calls someone to rise to the occasion and demonstrate leadership. It is referred to as the Great Events Theory.

This theory of leadership has less to do with the development of leaders than with the measure of their capabilities. It suggests that when a need arises, something inside the leader just clicks and they sweep into action. It ignores the fact that someone who assumes a leadership role in crisis must prepare in some fashion. This theory offers no answer for this need. It does suggest that there are leaders-in-waiting, yet leadership is not needed solely in times of crisis. Certainly the measure of the leader can be taken more easily in such situations. In the midst of an arising

---

34 1 Sam 9:1-2. An excellent resource for those who follow the Bible is Maxwell's *Leadership Bible*.

35 Alan C. Elliott, *A Daily Dose of the American Dream: Stories of Success, Triumph, & Inspiration* (Nashville, TN: Rutledge Hill Press, 1998), 222.

36 John C. Maxwell, *Talent Is Never Enough: Discover the choices that will take you beyond your talent* (Nashville, TN: Thomas Nelson, 2007).

crisis, the situation must be assessed and the desired results targeted very quickly. Different types of leaders might take drastically different approaches that may or may not succeed. In fact, those that do not succeed might never be known since they may be lost in the crisis.

It is our view that leaders should not hide, waiting for the great event to reveal their superhero powers. That works in movies and comic books, but not real life. Or at least it should not. Given the need for leadership everywhere across society and in all levels of society, waiting just to be the hero is a form of hubris that should disqualify a sustained leader. Rudy Giuliani was mayor of New York City when the terrorists attacked the World Trade Center on September 11, 2001. He demonstrated great leadership during this crisis, much of which is documented in his book.[37] He was a leader before this event and had led New York to a greater standard of living and reduced crime than it had seen in many years. This crisis merely provided a demonstration of the leadership developed long before the event. Said Mr. Giuliani, "My father used to say to me, 'Whenever you get into a jam, whenever you get into a crisis or an emergency…become the calmest person in the room and you'll be able to figure your way out of it.'"

Winston Churchill
Character may be manifest in the great
moments, but it is made in the small ones.

Kouzes and Posner make the following observation:

When people think about their personal best they automatically think about some kind of challenge. Why? The fact is that when times are stable and secure, we're not severely tested. We may perform well, get promoted, even achieve fame and fortune. But certainty and routine breed complacency. In contrast, personal and business hardships have a way of making us come face to face with who we really are and what we're capable of becoming. Thus the study of leadership is the study of

---

37 Rudolph W. Giuliani and Ken Kurson, *Leadership* (US: Hyperion, 2002).

how men and women guide us through adversity, uncertainty, hardship, disruption, transformation, transition, recovery, new beginnings, and other significant challenges. It's also the study of how men and women, in times of constancy and complacency, actively seek to disturb the status quo and awaken to new possibilities. They search for opportunities to change, grow, innovate, and improve.[38]

Sustained leaders do not wait for the crisis. Sustained leaders know that change is inevitable and seek to guide that change rather than simply react to it. A crisis is generally a rapidly changing situation. Great-events leaders are only reactionary.

Behavioral

Stepping away from Bass for a moment, let's turn our attention to the Behavioral Theory. Behavior can be learned. If we accept this premise, then this theory forces us to look not at the inherent traits, or crisis confronted by a leader, but what we can learn about the behavior of both the leader and those they lead. It recognizes that there is a relational aspect to leadership and begins to move us away from forceful leadership to the relational aspects of persuasion rather than coercion. Thus, leaders can be trained, or "made" rather than just born, and in accomplishing goals and visions, the followers of the leader can be better guided once the leader understands more about the human side of these followers. This theory suggests that the ongoing dynamic between the leader and the team, and among the team members, can be managed for peak performance and thereby better results—the primary measure of success for a leader.

The key research in the behavioral theory of leadership is reflected in the work of Douglas McGregor, who pioneered Theory X and Theory Y in his book *The Human Side of Enterprise*. The "X" and "Y" reflect how the leader views the various members of the team. Theory X managers view team members as lazy with a poor work ethic. They are looking for a paycheck and will attempt to do the minimum to get that paycheck. They are uncooperative and often disruptive. They must be managed very rigidly and strictly. Theory Y managers believe that team members

---

38   James M. Kouzes and Barry Z. Posner, *The Leadership Challenge, Third Edition* (US: Jossey-Bass, 2002), 126-77.

have a high work ethic, enjoy their work, and exude a positive attitude toward the team and the task.

Certainly there are archetypes of each employee type. Some workers are lazy and uncooperative. Other workers are positive and hard-working. Because of these differences, the employees, workers, or team members should be managed differently. In today's society there is a strong push for equality of outcome rather than equality of opportunity. This tends to encourage Type X behavior and discourage Type Y behavior. The sustained leader must be aware of both these differences in team members and the current requirements of law.

One tendency of this dynamic is to have many more policies and procedures that everyone must follow. Policies and procedures are scars from past mistakes. When someone makes an error that causes harm to the team, senior management instructs that a policy be written to prevent this type of error ever again. And for the most part, it is successful. That error is not repeated. The downside of this is that those employees with good judgment, who would never have made the specific mistake, are now constrained from using their own discretion and must follow the policy, treating everyone, whether fellow team member, customer, or other stakeholder exactly the same, even when such treatment is not in the best interests of the stakeholders. And like scars, policies never seem to go away. They accumulate and over time are a severe burden on the entity. The older the entity, the more constrained they are by policy. This permits new upstarts who can take advantage of newer technology, a younger workforce, and greater flexibility in meeting customer needs to surpass the stodgy old firm and be more successful. In other words, strictly following the behavior theory can result in the prohibition of good leadership development and the demise of the entity.

When employees are free to exercise flexibility and use their ingenuity, institutional problems are more easily solved. The unnecessary impediment of arcane policies and procedures are avoided. The organizational and personal objectives align producing a synergy that can't be found in more rigid environments. This creates a natural conflict between interpersonal relationships and the solitary focus on achieving goals. Research is inconclusive on the dimensions of satisfaction and productivity. Productivity and higher job satisfaction are reported, however, for employee-centric leadership. Relationships seem to count.

Contingency

The Contingency Theory of leadership, as the name suggests, describes leadership on terms of a fluid and dynamic environment. It recognizes that one-size-fits-all leadership approaches don't work consistently, or often effectively. The contingency theory says that the leader must be adaptable—to their environment, to the participants, to the things they can control and the things they cannot, and a host of other variables. There is no one best way.

Fred E. Fiedler is credited with initially defining the contingency theory. His theory postulates that there is no best way for managers to lead. Situations will create different leadership style requirements for a manager. The solution to a managerial situation is contingent on the factors that create or affect the situation. Those situations that are very routine versus those that are very dynamic demand different leadership styles for greatest effectiveness. The contingency theory suggests, without providing fully accommodating strategies, that there is some type of measurable relationship between activities and the leadership methods that will be most effective. Since the theory is based on contingencies, it is impossible to adequately define all of the variables. While it may be instructive in certain situations, such as generally assigning an impersonal leader to a high task concentration effort and a more personable leader to situations that have lower task definition, it has less utility in general leadership situations.

Any situation is a combination of factors and variables that interact. Each situation is unique, and in most cases fluid. The solution to a managerial situation is contingent on the factors that impinge on the situation. Fiedler identified three primary variables that need to be assessed.

1. Leader member relations: This variable captures the relational aspects among the team and specifically as between the team members and the leader.
2. The task structure: Tasks tend to be defined as highly structured, as when a barista makes you a cup of coffee to the company's standards, unstructured, such as a research and development effort, or somewhere in between.
3. Position power: This question, in Fiedler's construct, looks only at the power held by the leader. He defined it as positional power, but as we

will see, in the *Sustained Leader WBS* there are many forms of power, and positional power is the weakest.

Among the possible combinations of these three variables, Fiedler believed that all leadership situations could be assessed. From this a weighted assessment would calculate whether the situation was favorable or unfavorable. At the extremes, strong task orientation styles worked best. In the middle, relational techniques from the leader were optimal. The solution to any mismatch was to either adjust the situation or change the leadership style.

One serious drawback to this theory is what might be considered collateral damage. When the job involves high task motivation, there is a natural tendency for leaders to congratulate themselves because of their great leadership through the task. When the issue is more relational, the entire team could share in the success of the mission. Thus, insecure leaders could force every situation into a task orientation even when relational attributes would prove more successful. This dichotomy causes many to dismiss the "touchy-feely" relational aspects and insist that all leadership is a function of power. While there is great merit to Fiedler's theories, they suffered greatly in implementation. As designed, both approaches can be appropriate, but if the established hierarchy rejects the relational half of the theory, the outcome cannot be successful more than 50 percent of the time.

Hersey-Blanchard Situational Leadership

Hersey and Blanchard pioneered situational leadership. The Hersey-Blanchard Situational Leadership Theory[39] is based on the amount of direction (task behavior) and socio-emotional support (relationship behavior) a leader must provide given the situation, and the "level of maturity" of the followers as related to the specific task to be accomplished. Task behavior is the extent to which the leader engages in spelling out the duties and responsibilities to an individual or group. This behavior includes telling people what to do, how to do it, when to do it, where to do it, and who's to do it. In task behavior the leader engages in one-way communication. Relationship behavior is the extent to which the leader engages in two-way or

---

39   http://situational.com/. See also Paul Hersey, *The Situational Leader* (US: Center for Leadership Studies, 1984).

multi-way communications. This includes listening, facilitating, and supportive behaviors. In relationship behavior the leader engages in two-way communication by providing socio-emotional support. Maturity is the willingness and ability of a person to take responsibility for directing their own behavior. People tend to have varying degrees of maturity, depending on the specific task, function, or objective that a leader is attempting to accomplish through their efforts. Self-discipline, self-confidence, and self-determination reflect high maturity levels, but that level is task specific. In other words, a person might be quite comfortable managing a major construction project, but arranging the celebration party upon completion might be beyond their comfort levels.

Hersey and Blanchard constructed a copyrighted chart to reflect their concepts. It has been widely used in organizational training. Starting with the maturity level of the team member vis-a-vis the specific task, the leader must assess where that aligns. If a high task orientation is required, the leader provides that. As the team member gains more confidence with the task, the leader reduces the task management approach and moves more toward a relational orientation. The curve on the chart guides the leader in adjusting their style to the needs of the team member as regards the specific task. Ideally the relationship starts with "telling" and progresses across the curve to the point that the leader can fully delegate the task to the team member.

The four leadership styles are telling, selling, participating, and delegating. High task/low relationship behavior is referred to as "telling." The leader provides clear instructions and specific direction. Telling style is best matched with a follower low readiness level. High task/high relationship behavior is referred to as "selling." The leader encourages two-way communication and helps build confidence and motivation on the part of the employee, although the leader still has responsibility and controls decision making. Selling style is best matched with a moderate follower readiness level. High relationship/low task behavior is referred to as "participating." With this style, the leader and followers share decision making and no longer need or expect the relationship to be directive. Participating style is best matched with a moderate follower readiness level. Low relationship/low task behavior is labeled "delegating." This style is appropriate for leaders whose followers are ready to accomplish a particular task and are both competent and motivated to take full responsibility. Delegating style is best matched with a high follower readiness level.[40]

Influence

The last theory we will review is the Influence Theory. Various aspects of this theory are still the subject of debate and definition in the literature. Essentially the issue for the influence leader is how to best persuade or motivate others to act, whether this is through the concept of the servant leader, or the social media concept of platform influencers, or transformational leaders who inspire the team to higher performance overall. Rather than simple transactional performance, the influential leader uses persuasion based on principle and inspiration to move the team in a desired direction. When the mission of an organization is altruistic—for example a charitable effort—such inspirational leadership may prove very successful. In other situations, the work may not inspire as well. Transformational, servant, and sustained leadership theories are discussed here.

Colin Powell

Leadership is the art of accomplishing more than the science of management says is possible.

Transformational

Returning to Bass, his third leadership theory, and the one subject to a great deal of literature and debate today, is the Transformational Theory. This theory attempts to treat leadership in a more comprehensive fashion, believes firmly that leadership can be learned by anyone, and is defined by those who demonstrate "leadership" as variously defined in the literature.

This theory of leadership begins to blend with several other popular ones that are found in the literature today. They all can be grouped broadly into the category of "Post-Situational Leadership" which includes Transformational Leadership,

---

40   Dr. Paul Hersey, *The Situational Leader,* (US: Center for Leadership Studies, 1984).

Influential Leadership, Servant Leadership, and Sustained Leadership. All of these, to somewhat varying degrees, recognize the role of influence over the old command-and-control leadership, encourage constant learning, and put considerable emphasis on personal improvement. Even with these similarities, their emphasis is different, so we will look at these in somewhat more detail.

Kenneth Blanchard
The key to successful leadership today is influence, not authority.

The transformational leader is charismatic and holds strongly to their vision. This combination can inspire their followers to rise above their own self-interest and work diligently toward the goals of the team, ideally achieving far more than could be expected. Transformational leaders are adept at framing the issues to maximize the perception of the team toward achievement of the goals.

Transformational theories seem to draw on their historical underpinnings to cull the best of each one. The prior theories were not wrong so much as they were incomplete. Unlike transactional leaders who work diligently toward task and skill alignment, transformational leaders tend to be more inspiring in their motivation. They are often charismatic and inspire the team to accept bold visions, motivating them to think in a more expansive way. Often playing off their moral values and ideals, transformational leaders use, according to the research, vision, framing, and impression management.

Vision is the creation of an ideal that is ambitious and inspiring. As John F. Kennedy said, "Some people look at things and say 'why?' I look at things as they could be and say 'why not?'"[41] In 1960 he set a vision of putting men on the moon and returning them safely within the decade. And we did. People were filled with national pride at seeing the dream come true. Framing relates to the manner in which the goals are expressed—giving the team a true sense of the meaningfulness of the goals. If John F. Kennedy had merely said, "Yeah, let's all figure out a way to get to the moon sometime," the motivation may not have been mustered to achieve such an amazing accomplishment.

---

41   But see where a similar quote is attributed to George Bernard Shaw at 5.1.4.

Impression management concerns how the team perceives the leader. Thus, the leader must demonstrate the appropriate leadership traits; they must act like the leader the team expects. Using these three tools of vision, framing, and impression management, the transformational leader, according to research, will create an environment that experiences lower turnover, greater productivity, and higher overall team satisfaction.

Transformational leaders are, by definition, inspirational. They are constant cheerleaders, inspiring the team toward greater achievement. They appeal to the moral fiber of the team and call on them to draw deeply from their intellect and innovation. The transformational leader is flexible and constantly presents a positive attitude.

On the downside, the transformational leader, especially the over charismatic one, can seem unrealistic, Pollyannaish, and disjointed from the team. Thus, the transformational leader must constantly strive to be authentic and to avoid pretension. The genuine transformational leader does tend to get more productivity from the team and is therefore perceived as creating a competitive advantage.

John Maxwell tells us "A transformational leader intentionally engages people to think and act in such a way that it makes a positive difference in their lives and the lives of others."[42] In today's literature the most prevalent approach is to emphasize the inspirational leader. Some of this comes from the idealistic desires of Generation X and Y, but demands that there be a big vision—a significant dream with defined goals. In some respects, this is a "save the world" perspective. People want to be involved in and are drawn to life-changing endeavors.

Servant Leadership

Theories surrounding the servant leader were popular in the literature in the 1970s through the early 2000s. Under this theory the leader was not a command-and-control model but a roll-up-your-sleeves contributor. The leader served to make the work of the followers easier and more productive. The leader's goal was to provide all the resources the team needed, run interference with the rest of the organization, and let the team do what they do best.

---

42   John C. Maxwell, *Intentional Living: Choosing a Life That Matters* (New York: Center Street, 2015), 234.

The primary contributor to this concept of leadership was Robert K. Greenleaf, who described it as "the servant as leader," thus making, as Peter B. Vaill noted, the idea of the servant being the subject and the leader as the predicate.[43] Greenleaf understood that the mission of the organization defined the nature of the service that was required and that the servant-leader's responsibility was to help the organization get its work done.

The primary model for servant leadership is, of course, Jesus, who said, "The one who is the greatest among you must become like the youngest, and the leader like the servant."[44] This was his response in settling an argument that had arisen among the apostles over who would be the greatest among them. His point was that you do not seek the highest position, you seek to serve, and the leadership position comes to you. Other writers such as James C. Hunter and Ken Blanchard have likewise pointed to Jesus as the model for servant leadership.[45]

―――――――――● ―――――――――

Margaret Thatcher

Being powerful is like being a lady.
If you have to tell people you are, you aren't.

―――――――――● ―――――――――

Sustained Leadership

The *Sustained Leadership WBS* neither adopts nor rejects any of these theories. There are meritorious arguments for and against them all. The person seeking to be a sustained leader seeks to improve themselves in all aspects of leadership; they assess themselves honestly and select specific areas for development or improvement including the ability to assess situations quickly. Rapid situational assessment and intense focus then permits the sustained leader to apply the appropriate tool,

---

43 Robert K. Greenleaf, Larry C. Spears and Peter B. Vaill, *The Power of Servant-Leadership* (US: Berrett-Koehler Publishers 1998), xi.

44 Luke 22:26

45 See James C. Hunter, *The Servant: A Simple Story about the True Essence of Leadership* (US: Prima 1998), and Kenneth H. Blanchard and Phil Hodges, *Servant Leader* (US: Thomas Nelson 2003).

technique, or decision process to deal with the situation and make progress toward the goal or vision.

That alone, however, is not enough. Maintaining a proper character, being a constant learner, being decisive, and developing new leaders are all essential elements of being a leader who can sustain themselves as a leader. Knowing what the situation requires and providing measurable results are hallmarks of a sustained leader. The *Sustained Leadership WBS* identifies 229 elements that contribute to leadership success. The sustained leader works to improve themselves in as many WBS elements as possible and apply what they learn to become a better individual, a stronger leader, and a positive contributor to the society in which they live.

A Note about Men and Women

Throughout the historical development of leadership theories, a continuing issue has been whether any of the definitions, and in some cases the underlying research, properly accounted for the differences between women and men. When the trait theory has predominated, unless you were a tall, fit, handsome white male, you could not be viewed as a leader. After all, you didn't have the right traits. And with the leaders of our three major institutions—business, government, and religion—ALL being headed by males for centuries and, recently, white males in the United States, this gave rise to the "good old boys network" thinking that created what was called the glass ceiling. Women could see above it to know there were higher positions to be filled, but they were kept under so as not to be able to fill them. In the case of both gender and race, women and non-whites were statistically under-represented, and in many respects still are.

Men, being the traditional leaders, have continued to trend toward being more transactional leaders with a task focus. Women trend toward being more transformational leaders. Even saying this, however, reflects a gender bias. Men go to work and accomplish tasks. Women stand on the sidelines and serve as cheerleaders. See the bias? Even when very accomplished women achieve great things in leadership roles, they are perceived as "less" than their male counterparts. Women, even in many traditional marriages, most often assume the role of social coordinator. After all, the men are too busy "working," which ignores the hard work and great importance to society of motherhood. Nonetheless research shows women in leadership roles share power more easily and engage in far more participative decision making.

Grace Hopper took on many leadership roles. In WWII she was an ensign in the navy and worked on the team with IBM that was developing the Mark I computer. In those days computers were a large collection of mechanical switches. When the computer failed to work one day, a careful review found a dead moth in one of the switches. The moth was removed and reportedly taped into the day's journal. Hopper noted that she had "debugged" the computer, thus coining a phrase in common use to this day. Hopper was a guiding force in computer and computer language development, leading many teams to succeed in their projects. In 1986 she retired from the navy as a rear admiral. Her contributions to computer development, and her extended service to America as a strong leader of men and women, serve as a role model to both. There was nothing stopping her from developing her leadership skills and abilities, least of all her gender.[46]

Jack Welch addressed the issue in May 2012 when he noted while speaking at a women's forum that results and performance were all that matter. A career track is created by results and performance. Programs that promote diversity, mentoring, or other allegiances[47] might be good, but it's not, he asserted, how women get ahead. "Over deliver....Performance is it." Many women who speak to such issues soundly criticized Welch. If it were only a performance issue, more than 3 percent of the Fortune 500 would be led by women. To suggest otherwise is to suggest that women, by nature, don't perform.

In a very useful book, *Leadership and the Sexes*,[48] the authors provide compelling scientific evidence that men and women use different parts of their brains when making decisions and serving in leadership roles. This is not an absolute, and they documented many cases of what they call "bridge brains" where a male seems to use those portions of the brain more commonly associated with women in similar roles, and vice versa. There are, however, clear distinctions between

---

46 Alan C. Elliott, *A Daily Dose of the American Dream: Stories of Success, Triumph, and Inspiration* (US: Thomas Nelson 1998), 174.

47 As quoted in *Wall Street Journal*, May 4, 2012, p. B1.

48 Michael Gurian and Barbara Annis, *Leadership and the Sexes: Using Gender Science to Create Success in Business* (US: Jossey-Bass 2008). See also *America's Competitive Secret: Women Managers* by Judy B. Rosener (US: Oxford University Press, 1997).

the average brain of the man and the woman. There are indisputable differences between men and women. But to suggest that one is exclusively qualified to lead while the other is not is simply crass sexism. Each person brings to the table their unique set of traits, tendencies, training, experiences, and everything else that makes them a unique individual. Deborah Tannen has clearly demonstrated[49] that men and women have different communication techniques, but "different" in no way implies "better." "Instead of different dialects, it has been said they speak different genderlects."[50]

The *Sustained Leadership WBS* is gender neutral. Anyone can review the many elements of leadership and identify those elements that do and do not describe their present position on the leadership journey. Armed with this information, anyone can make themselves a better leader.

Leadership Thinking Today

In an excellent book by Goffee and Jones, they ask the very pertinent question, *Why Should Anyone Be Led by You?* They summarize the current state of thinking quite concisely. "We have tried to resist a recipe—and we have included in our book men and women in very different places, all over organizations. Our central contention, then, is that leadership is **situational, nonhierarchical, and relational**. You might feel this is almost common sense, but you would be surprised how often it is forgotten."[51] The authors make a very compelling case that no single theory describes leadership fully. There are aspects of all the theories that come into play. There are so many variables that leadership cannot be simply defined or described. It is multidimensional, multifaceted, and does not come in a one-size-fits-all edition.

While often overlooked in much leadership writing, Dale Carnegie has done more than almost anyone else to guide people who want to be leaders. In his book *How to Win Friends and Influence People* he provides a complete roadmap to developing traits that are often seen as critical in a successful leader. In fact, much of what Carnegie promoted has come full circle, and we now see some of his

---

49 Deborah Tannen, *You Just Don't Understand: Women and Men in Conversation* (US: Ballantine Books 1991).

50 Id. @42.

51 Rob Goffee and Gareth Jones, *Why Should Anyone Be Led by YOU?* (Boston: Harvard Business School Press, 2006), 204. Emphasis in original.

principles reflected in current thinking about transformational and servant leaders. First published in 1937, the book now appears in more than thirty-six languages. It is viewed as the precursor to the work of Stephen Covey and Anthony Robbins, among others.

The first principle to Carnegie was learning how to handle people effectively. He presented several fundamental techniques for handling people, many of which are reflective of the Golden Rule. These included: Don't Criticize, Condemn, or Complain; Give Honest and Sincere Appreciation; and Arouse in the Other Person an Eager Want. The goal was to be the kind of person who attracts others toward them. Among his other encouragements were to become genuinely interested in other people, smile, and always remember that a person's name is the sweetest and most important sound in any language. Other traits that can be readily learned include the ability to be a good listener. This leads to an ability to encourage others to talk about themselves, and when you talk, to talk in terms of the other person's interests. You want the other person to think better of themselves and feel important, and to do so sincerely.[52]

Sustained leaders are encouraged to spend some time with Mr. Carnegie. Some of his examples are dated. You will probably not run into telegrams or typewriters in your career, but do not be distracted by that. Look to his principles—they are timeless.

The esteemed late Stephen Covey tells of a bicentennial research project he undertook in 1976 on the popular success literature during our country's history. He noted that for the first one hundred fifty years the literature focused on what he calls the *character ethic*. Focus was on various traits such "service, honesty, industry, charity, chastity, patriotism, integrity, benevolence, thrift, self-discipline, self-sacrifice, and so on."[53] He then notes that about fifty years ago (from a 1990 perspective), the *character ethic* began to be replaced by a *personality ethic*. This concentrates on "human relations techniques, on influence strategies, on image building, on getting what you want, on self-actualization, on assertiveness skills, on positive mental attitude, on success programming and people manipulation tactics." This personality ethic has led to self-centered

---

52 Some of the material here is derived from Christina Coffin, managing ed., *Business, The Ultimate Resource* (Cambridge, MA: Perseus Publishing, 2002), 908.

53 Stephen R. Covey, *Principle-Centered Leadership: Teaching Timeless Principles of Effectiveness* (US: Summit Books 1990, First Edition), Preface, xi.

cults and fads that "create an absolute distortion of life, an aberrant behavior and addiction."[54]

This shift tends to replace the moral with the secular; the natural law of a supreme God is supplanted by humanistic self-aggrandizement. We see the same in leadership theory. We can learn techniques and tricks fairly easily. It takes much more effort to develop virtue and establish a moral center, especially where none may have previously existed. True leadership, however, requires that the focus be not on technique but on a genuine shift to a moral center. Depending on how deeply such populist humanistic techniques have taken hold of you, your effort toward sustained leadership will vary in difficulty. If there is much you must first unlearn, the effort will be more difficult, yet all the more rewarding.

Post situational leadership, and where much of the literature is going today, looks more closely at the influence a leader wields. This is highlighted in the book *Leadership Is Dead: How Influence Is Reviving It* by Jeremie Kubicek.[55] John C. Maxwell described this in his *The 5 Levels of Leadership*. His starting point is one of position where people follow you because they are organizationally required to. Level 2 is permission where people voluntarily follow you. Level 3 leaders attract followers because they produce positive results. At level 4 followers are attracted to you because you know how to develop other leaders. Level 5 is what he calls the pinnacle or leadership that comes from respect—"People follow you because of who you are and what you represent.[56] He notes that very few people actually reach level five "because it requires a person to spend a lifetime developing others to their highest potential."[57]

As noted, the theories of leadership do not segregate neatly into nice little compartments. Many of them can coexist without conflict. Others are nearly diametrically opposed. Leadership is not a clean art or science. Given that it is situational, there are too many individual situations to permit easy categorization. The *Sustained Leadership WBS* does not attempt to address any other leadership

---

54 Ibid. See also, Jeffrey Pfeffer. *Leadership BS: Fixing Workplaces and Careers One Truth at a Time.* (New York: Harper Collins, 2015).

55 Jeremie Kubicek, *Leadership Is Dead: How Influence Is Reviving It* (US: Howard Books 2011).

56 John Maxwell, *The 5 Levels of Leadership: Proven Steps to Maximize Your Potential.* (US: Center Street, 2011).

57 John C. Maxwell, *How to Influence People* (Nashville, TN: Thomas Nelson, 2013), xiii, quoting from John C. Maxwell, *Developing the Leader within You* (Nashville, TN: Thomas Nelson, 1993), 5-12.

theories, nor to disparage the research that may have gone into the creation or promotion of such other theories. Many of them are widely accepted and may well have merit to explain leadership. The *Sustained Leadership WBS* does not attempt to explain leadership. Its goal is to introduce the many facets of leadership to those who wish to become better leaders. For those who wish to improve themselves personally and to position themselves to succeed in leadership opportunities, the *Sustained Leadership WBS* will help you start from wherever you are by offering you a guide, a roadmap, a personal mentor to assist in preparing you to be an outstanding leader.

Thus, we omit here the Vroom, Yetton, Jago Leader-Participation Model, Robert House's Path-Goal Model, the University of Iowa studies on the democratic, autocratic, and laissez-faire style of leadership, the Ohio State studies on the leadership styles of considerate and initiating structure, the University of Michigan study of leadership behaviors as being productive- or employee-centered, and the expansion of these studies by Robert Blake and Jane Mouton to create the Managerial Grid of leadership styles. Once you have begun to develop your leadership abilities through the *Sustained Leadership WBS*, learning more about these styles may be useful. Not everyone will naturally be adept at all of the possible styles. As reflected in the situational leadership theories, different situations will require the application of different leadership skills and styles. Understanding the different styles you can adopt will make your leadership more effective.

Henry L. Gantt

Without efficiency in management, efficiency of the workmen is useless, even if it is possible to get it. With an efficient management there is but little difficulty in training the workmen to become efficient. I have proved this so many times and so clearly that there can be absolutely no doubt about it. Our most serious trouble is incompetency in high places. As long as that remains uncorrected, no amount of efficiency in the workman will avail very much.

To review, earliest theories assumed that the primary source of leadership effectiveness lay in the personal traits of the leaders themselves. Yet traits alone cannot explain leadership effectiveness. Thus, later research focused on what the leader actually did when dealing with employees. These behavioral theories of leadership sought to explain the relationship between what the leader did and how the employees reacted, both emotionally and behaviorally. Yet behavior can't always account for leadership in different situations. Thus, contingency theories of leadership studied leadership style in different environments. Transactional leaders, such as those identified in contingency theories, clarify role and task requirements for employees. Yet contingency can't account for the inspiration and innovation that leaders need to compete in today's global marketplace. Newer transformational leadership studies have shown that leaders who are charismatic and visionary can inspire followers to transcend their own self-interest for the good of the organization.

Thomas J. Watson

Nothing so conclusively proves a man's ability to lead others as what he does from day to day to lead himself.

There is no single answer to the question of what makes a leader. The question you should ask is, What can I do to make myself the best leader possible so that when an opportunity to lead arises, I am prepared and can accept the mantle? The answer to that is much simpler. First, accept that leadership is not a destination but a journey that has no end. Leadership is built on experiences that mold you into a person capable of providing the vision and direction and guidance to your team to accomplish a particular objective and move on to the next level. Thus, the simple answer to the question "What must I do?" is to gain as much experience in as many dimensions as possible. Take on challenging tasks. Exercise discipline in all its many forms. Set goals and lay out tactics and plans to achieve them, and then achieve them. Develop the leaders around you (as John Maxwell tells us), and find ways to gain experience outside of the school of hard knocks.

Leaders must prepare. One way to do so is to read as much as you can on the subject. The mere use of this book demonstrates that you are actively working on yourself—learning to lead yourself. This alone pushes you far down the leadership path and gives direction to your journey. Russell Conwell noted the importance of preparing to lead. Being appointed (or elected) to a position of authority does not make you a leader. "You think you are going to be made great by an office, but remember that if you are not great before you get the office, you won't be great when you secure it."[58] Becoming a leader is a continuous journey, full of successes and missteps. You can become as great a leader as you choose. Be the exception. Choose to lead, and lead well.

---

58 Russell Conwell, *Acres of Diamonds* (Kansas City, MO: Hallmark 1968), 55.

Chapter 2

HOW TO BUILD A LEADER

———————●———————

The discipline of project management has evolved into a more formal structure than at any other time in human history. Through the efforts of the Project Management Institute, a detailed body of knowledge has been developed and the phases and activities of a project—any project—more clearly articulated. There are many excellent aspects to the discipline of project management. In a typical project, defined as a series of activities that have a beginning and an end with a unique product resulting, there is a project manager, or project leader. This is different from the project champion (typically the customer). Through the diligence of PMI, an increasingly rigorous exam is given to those who have prepared to become certified as a project management professional (PMP). They have, through their knowledge and study, demonstrated command of the Project Management Body of Knowledge (PMBOK, "pim-bock"). And while there are many leadership traits incorporated into the PMBOK, a PMP is not necessarily either a leader or a sustained leader. They are merely in charge.

Let's consider those aspects of project management that pertain to leadership. In typical fashion, when a project leader is named they hold the position by appointment. They may or may not be a true leader. A project is designed to create a unique product. In this case we are creating a metaphor of project management disciplines to create a unique product—you as a sustained leader. We will borrow some aspects of a project approach to develop a leader. The metaphor, by definition, will be inexact while providing a point of reference.

There are significant differences between a project as envisioned by the PMBOK and the journey on which you are about to embark. For example, your leadership journey will never end. You might decide to defer or delay the trek, but if you believe that there is some formula that says if you do A + B + C + D you will suddenly be a "leader," then you are reading the wrong book.

Project Scope Statement and the WBS

The project scope statement describes the goal, the unique product that will result from completion of the effort defined by this project. By deciding to pursue sustained leadership, you demonstrate that you want to be a better leader. It also shows that you desire to lead. What defines a leader? In simplest terms a leader is someone who has followers. These followers might exist due to organizational structure or because they are attracted to the leader. In other words, the leader might exist by position or because they have demonstrated those characteristics and traits that cause others to want to follow them. Only the latter describes authentic leadership or what we will call sustained leadership here. For purposes of using this book to its greatest advantage, we offer the following scope statement: This project will guide anyone who chooses to lead through the various considerations that define leadership and provide them a project guide for continuous improvement as a sustained leader. Those who follow the guidance contained here will improve as a leader, and as they work hard toward that goal they may become a sustained leader.

---

*The **Sustained Leadership WBS** will guide those who wish to learn more about being a leader to understand the skills, actions, and characteristics of successful leadership, offer a roadmap for assessing their current leadership acumen, and provide a personalized course of study and actions to improve their leadership.*

After defining the project scope, the next step is to create the Work Breakdown Structure. What exactly is a Work Breakdown Structure (WBS)? According to the PMBOK a WBS is "a deliverable-oriented hierarchical decomposition of the work to be executed by the team." It takes the entire scope of work to be accomplished and "breaks it down" into discrete, performable, measurable packages of effort.

The WBS is part of every project management plan. It organizes the many project components into a logical, delivery-focused set of objectives. It is the blueprint that defines the steps that will be required to meet the project objectives. At its lowest level the WBS contains work packages—discrete work elements that are well defined, separately costed, and which demonstrate progress on the project schedule. Each work package is a specific step toward the project objective. For the *Sustained Leadership WBS*, we will not rigidly follow the rules or guidelines for a WBS. Rather we will capture the concept of the various elements that a leader is required to master in order to earn the appellation of "sustained leader."

You will find that some WBS elements are easy for you. Perhaps you have already mastered them. With diligent effort there are others that you will master. There are some, however, that you might never personally master. Many of the elements will require constant attention and a dedicated effort to revisit them and further hone your leadership abilities. As you mature in life you will find that some elements take on more meaning or importance in your leadership journey. Once you embark on the *Sustained Leadership WBS* it will become part of your life.

There is no one correct draft to any particular WBS. It can be constructed in a variety of ways with the various efforts grouped differently. What is important is that the WBS includes EVERY necessary element that goes into the final product. For purposes of the sustained leader, as noted above, you are not likely to successfully complete every WBS element. This does not mean that you have failed. It merely means that you need to go back and revisit the various elements and work on them with more focus and vigor. In this WBS there are very few prerequisites to other WBS elements—a common characteristic of the typical WBS. Consequently, there is no "precedence diagram" or even a "critical path." There are, however, what we call Essential Leadership Journey Checkpoints (ELJC)—elements within the WBS without which you will ultimately fail in your leadership. You might find some immediate or short-lived success, but your failure to understand these essential elements, these ELJCs, will derail if not doom your leadership journey.

You might find yourself completely unbalanced in mastering any given part or parts of this WBS. Unlike a true project, there is no specific order in which you choose to approach the many elements of the WBS beyond the ELJCs. The key is to make sure that you ultimately address as many as you can since doing so will make you a better leader, a more well-rounded leader, and a more successful and happier person. Attempting to do too much at one time, however, will discourage you and provide minimal overall improvement. Significant identified deficiencies may point you to those areas that need your most focused attention.

Once a WBS is compiled, all of the various work packages define the "project baseline." The project baseline posits that if each work package is performed as defined, the entire project will be successfully completed and a unique product will result. In the case of the *Sustained Leadership WBS*, the unique project is an improved "you"—someone with better leadership skills and traits, and more knowledge about what it takes to be a leader. While it may seem a bit overly optimistic to say, the effort you expend in becoming a better leader will make you a better person. You will find that applying the tactics and disciplines described here will make you and those around you happier.

A WBS is a proven tool for successful projects. Without the WBS, project activity will merely be a disjointed set of activities with no clear beginning, end, or objective. Too often the result is that the participants confuse activity with progress. You can be very busy yet accomplishing nothing. If you look at your life honestly, this might well describe how you have approached self-improvement. "Perhaps I should go back to school," you might have thought, and the next week you were looking at the online catalog of the local college. The problem is that unless you know what you are trying to achieve by returning to a formal education, you are very unlikely to end up where you want to be. As baseball great Yogi Berra taught us, "You've got to be careful if you don't know where you're going 'cause you might not get there."[59]

The WBS gives you structure and focus. It also gives you confidence that if you do everything required by the WBS, you will achieve the desired project end-state. A WBS gives you a visual reference point, or in outline format, a word version if

---

59 Yogi Berra, et al., *The Yogi Book: "I Really Didn't Say Everything I Said"* (US: Workman Publishing Company, 1998), 102.

that helps you learn more effectively. A WBS avoids surprises and lets you know what to expect. The Project Management Institute notes that a WBS can be used to effectively decompose the project scope, improve estimating, better control the project execution, and accurately verify project completion.[60]

PMI also speaks to the use of past project structures to serve as lessons learned for future projects. You are likely to learn more than you intended and perhaps things you did not want to learn. These may have been stumbling blocks that, once cleared, will allow you to revisit the WBS and attack the leadership project once again. A WBS is a repeatable process.

Socrates

The beginning of wisdom is a definition of terms.

Work Breakdown Structure Dictionary

The Work Breakdown Structure is not complete until the WBS Dictionary is included. The WBS Dictionary includes an entry for each WBS element to define precisely what is included and what is excluded from that WBS component. Recall that in describing the WBS itself, we noted that there is generally not a single way to construct it. Different program managers will put their own structure on it. Thus, differences would be inevitable. Likewise, within a specific structure, it is important that the drafter explain to the team what each component is designed to attain. In this way there will not be confusion or redundancies, or even gaps in the project plan.

The WBS Dictionary will also define how the accomplishment of that task will be measured and when you will know that it is done—the acceptance criteria. The WBS provides the project structure and the dictionary provides the narrative. From this, the project plan will include the organizational entity responsible for achieving the progress on the element (which in this case falls entirely to you!), scheduled start and end dates, required resources, and other

---

60   Project Management Institute, *A Guide to the Project Management Body of Knowledge, 5th Edition (PMBOK Guides)* (US: Project Management Institute, 2013). See section 5.3, Create WBS.

information that will assist in communicating the element objective for those who will contribute.

In the case of the *Sustained Leadership WBS*, as a metaphor to a classic project, the primary contributor is you. The project is you. You are both the project manager and the project itself. The end result is an improved you. And the customer for whom this project is being undertaken—is you! The responsibility for success is squarely on your shoulders. To that end, the WBS Dictionary should communicate to you. It should contain the information that will motivate you to work toward accomplishing that skill or trait. The schedule for this project is entirely up to you. The desired end-state is entirely up to you. The most important thing is to get started on the journey.

Why This Project Is Not a Project

A project by definition has both a beginning and an end. It is unlikely that you will ever complete this journey of self-improvement. In his autobiography Ben Franklin talks about his self-improvement efforts.

It was about this time I conceiv'd the bold and arduous project of arriving at moral perfection. I wish'd to live without committing any fault at any time; I would conquer all that either natural inclination, custom, or company might lead me into. As I knew, or thought I knew, what was right and wrong, I did not see why I might not always do the one and avoid the other. But I soon found I had undertaken a task of more difficulty than I had imagined. While my care was employ'd in guarding against one fault, I was often surprised by another; habit took the advantage of inattention; inclination was sometimes too strong for reason. I concluded, at length, that the mere speculative conviction that it was our interest to be completely virtuous, was not sufficient to prevent our slipping; and that the contrary habits must be broken, and good ones acquired and established, before we can have any dependence on a steady, uniform rectitude of conduct.[61]

---

61 Benjamin Franklin, *The Autobiography of Benjamin Franklin & Selections from His Other Writings* (US: The Modern Library College Editions, 1950), 92-93.

After making a list of his faults (of which he says there were many) he realized that if he attempted to tackle them all at once he would not succeed. So he prioritized them and selected a single area of improvement and worked on that one and that one alone for one week. He kept meticulous records in a notebook of each transgression across his thirteen identified areas of focus. At the end of the week he selected another of his traits to improve and worked on that for one week. Once he completed his list, he went back to the beginning and started again. After successive passes through his list he was able to discern positive improvements. "I was surpris'd to find myself so much fuller of faults than I had imagined; but I had the satisfaction of seeing them diminish."[62]

As Franklin observed, the journey of self-improvement never really ends. While progress is made in one area our human nature causes us to backslide in other areas. It is a constant but rewarding battle. Becoming and remaining a sustained leader will take constant effort on your part. It is not for the faint of heart. No matter how good you are at anything, there will always be room to improve. Even concert pianists understand the need for continuous practice. Developing and maintaining your leadership potential is no different.

Psychologists tell us that it takes at least thirty days to develop new habits. Franklin might have cut himself a little short using the one-week approach. We are all different in that regard, and you will have to make your own management decision. How many areas of improvement can you work on at a time? If you choose too many perhaps you might look at WBS 2.3.10 (focus). If you do not actively work on improvement and you find yourself bogging down, you might want to look at WBS 2.3 (action) and perhaps look closely at one of the lower level elements. The point is that the *Sustained Leadership WBS* is intended to give you structure and definition. It is not designed as a magic wand that you wave to achieve leadership. There are also no leadership genies. Wishing does not make it so. As one author has said, hope is not a strategy.[63] Developing your leadership potential is hard work. It takes dedication and attention to detail. It takes being bluntly honest with yourself. In 1.3.3 we will discuss the need to be humble in

---

62 Ibid. at 99. See also Jeffrey Pfeffer, *Leadership BS: Fixing Workplaces and Careers One Truth at a Time* (New York: Harper Collins, 2015), 52 where he notes that a significant successful cultural or personal change often follows the precepts of a 12-step program.

63 Rick Page, *Hope Is Not a Strategy: The 6 Keys to Winning the Complex Sale* (US: McGraw-Hill, 2003).

order to put yourself in a learning mode. You may have many self-imposed hurdles to overcome and progress might seem slow at first. Like any project plan, however, the more attention you give to accomplishing the project goals, the sooner you will begin to see progress in realizing your leadership potential.

We recommend that you NOT try to accomplish the project of an improved you in one pass. That is not realistic. We recommend that you review the entire WBS and consider for each element how close you are to achieving mastery in that area and what resources you will need to apply to attain mastery, or at least noticeable progress.

We further recommend that you seek out one or more mentors to assist you and to hold you accountable. You might want to bring together a team of associates, a brain trust, or a board of directors or trustees to further guide you and get regular reports of your progress. More on mentoring can be found in element 1.3.12.

Review the Essential Leadership Journey Checkpoints (ELJC). These elements are designed to avoid the most prominent pitfalls and leadership failures. Without attending to these your odds of a sustained improvement will be greatly diminished. No matter how proficient you might be in any number of the areas, or WBS elements, exhibiting these fatal flaws will hinder your future opportunities and have been known to destroy careers and relationships. Depending on your personal experiences to date, you might determine that your ELJCs are somewhat different. There are any number of resources available that proclaim "The Ten Things Leaders Must do," or "Three Traits of a Leader." These are merely an effort to design a modified ELJC list. We encourage you, however, to consider where you are in conforming to each element of the *Sustained Leadership WBS*, and if there are significant issues with your current leadership practices or leadership goals, your focus might be on a different set of ELJC elements. Perhaps you can identify an element that will require extreme effort on your part and thus that element or those elements may be your "long pole" for sustained leadership. Then select an appropriate WBS element from your list and work to improve in that area. Make use of the resources identified and devote the necessary time.

It might seem overwhelming and, in truth, it is. The key to keep in mind is that so long as you are making ANY progress toward improving your leadership skills and understanding, you are outpacing 95 percent of your peers. Most people will never work toward self-improvement until forced to. Simply reading one book a month puts you among the top 5 percent (some say 1 percent) of leaders. It would be great if you could "change the world." Many have such noble objectives. Unfortunately, such monumental endeavors are beyond the capabilities of most individuals and seem to be more driven by circumstances than planning. That is not the goal of the *Sustained Leadership WBS*—at least not at first. The goal is simply to make you a better you. By improving just one leader's leadership abilities, the world is that much better off. Spreading that to an entire organization, the organization is that much better off along with the community within which it operates and the families of all those who have embarked on the path of self-improvement. Making voters better able to discern leadership in their representatives will put better leaders into office—from the local dog catcher to the president.

Will becoming a better leader help you keep the dishes clean? "Australian researchers Megan Oaten and Ken Cheng have even found some evidence of a halo effect around habit creation. In their studies, students who successfully acquired one positive habit reported less stress; less impulsive spending; better dietary habits; decreased alcohol, tobacco, and caffeine consumption; fewer hours watching TV; and even fewer dirty dishes. Sustain the discipline long enough on one habit, and not only does it become easier, but so do other things as well. It's why those with the right habits seem to do better than others. They're doing the most important thing regularly and, as a result, everything else is easier."[64]

You cannot do this singlehandedly. But you *can* make yourself a better leader, provide a positive example to a young leader, mentor others to develop their leadership abilities, enhance your ability to better discern the leaders around you, and before you know it you have, in fact, changed the world. For now you are only being asked to make the decision to improve your own leadership. Every project has a beginning.

The *Sustained Leadership WBS* is intended to improve the world one person at a time. Only you can make the decision to dedicate yourself toward becoming a better leader.

Consult the WBS and the dictionary often. It is your guide, mentor, and accountability matrix. Repeat the above approach when selecting a new area of emphasis. Things will change. Your opportunities will change. Your challenges

---

64   Gary Keller and Jay Papasan, The ONE Thing: The Surprisingly Simple Truth Behind Extraordinary Results (US: Bard Press, 2013), 59.

will change. You will develop new strengths and unfortunately either discover or regress into weaknesses. Make notes in the dictionary. Like any project these dynamics might demand or encourage a different approach or emphasis that is particular to you.

If you are "old school" you might pick up a composition notebook to record your progress. If you are more progressive toward technology, develop an APP! Review the entire WBS (Chapter 3). Use the assessment tool included with each element to indicate whether this element describes you or not, or to what degree it describes you. Make notes about those areas where you are weakest or simply don't understand what is expected. Perhaps you will start with the top-level elements of Character, Competence, Compassion, Communication, and Commitment. Perhaps you will choose one of them and do a deep dive to a lower-level element. Perhaps your self-assessment reflects that you have some very specific gaps in your leadership and you feel you must address that specific element immediately. This would be particularly true if it is an ELJC element. By gathering this data about yourself, you can begin to lay out your personal project plan.

Assess what will be required for you to do and what resources you will need to accomplish it. Then set a completion date—or at a minimum a reassessment date. The only difference between dreams and goals is that goals have deadlines. You can begin to replace your dreams with specific action plans which, diligently followed, will put you on the path of sustained leadership. Most will abandon the journey and seek a comfort zone. They will disqualify themselves to become leaders of many, but they will do so as a conscious choice rather than by neglect and default. What you do with this guide is entirely up to you. You have started the investment and only you can decide what you will become. You have the ability to become a sustained leader. What you do next will tell you whether sustained leadership is part of your future or not.

Leading Is a Choice

Choosing to be a leader is neither simple nor easy. The complexity is due to the fact that until a person learns to lead themselves, through discipline and hard work, they are not qualified to lead others. People certainly are placed in positions of leadership, but positional power is one of the weakest forms of power in leadership.

You want to become a sustained leader, and that starts with you—right now, right where you are.

Once you make the decision to be a better leader, even if just for your own self-improvement (that is, to become a better leader of yourself), you then must determine the scope of your leadership influence, whether it extends to your family, your church, your employer, your government, or your volunteer endeavors. Leaders must exist at all levels of the organization, and organizations come in a myriad of shapes, sizes, and purposes. Don't fall into the trap of believing that you must be at the top of the organizational chart to be a leader. Different situations call for differences in leadership tactics and techniques. Those you lead will have different needs. It is not easy to become a leader, in part because you must choose to discipline yourself to do and be the things that make a sustained leader. It is hard work and takes great strength of character.

You have to *want* to improve; you have to *decide* to improve. As you improve you will become a better leader of you and will qualify to lead others. This should illustrate for you what a leadership journey truly is. Right now, the only decision is: Do you want to be a better you?

Bad leadership, like stupidity, should be painful.[65] Sadly, it rarely is. There is no quick-fix to leadership. It takes hard work and commitment and a series of personal decisions. Some of the literature[66] has suggested that leadership has become disgraceful. This is not true. Leadership is never disgraceful. What is disgraceful is the immense lack of leadership that masquerades as sustained leadership. There is far more faux leadership than true leadership. This contributes to the overall confusion about what a leader is and what a leader does. Hitler was a leader. The head of a street gang is a leader. But they are not practicing sustained leadership. They each suffer from a fatal flaw that did or will result in their downfall, and the downfall of those around them. It is as important to become the best leader you can as it is to choose who your leaders will be. Again, not simple and not easy.

Some organizations issue to those appointed to leader positions a document referred to as an RAA. This stands for Responsibility, Authority, and Accountability. It is a process by which certain disciplines are imposed on a positional leader to determine if they are meeting their leadership responsibilities. This typically does

---

65 Arguably, bad leadership is an oxymoron since if it is bad, it isn't really leadership at all.
66 Vince Molinaro, *The Leadership Contract: The Fine Print to Becoming a Great Leader* (US: Wiley, 2013), 48.

nothing to improve the leadership abilities of the individual; it only serves to justify the ultimate removal of the non-leader from their appointed position. It is like a teacher who "teaches to the exam" rather than instilling the students with critical thinking and good communication skills. This is not to say that an RAA cannot be a useful tool, especially in communicating appropriate spans of control. It simply says that to rely on such a document to define the leader and train them in leadership is a misuse of a good tool. An RAA ≠ leader.

Where Should I Concentrate?

This effort is not like a classic project because it has no end. You are embarking on a lifelong journey. Given a long enough life, and a lucky set of leadership opportunities, you might have a chance to perfect all of your leadership skills and traits. That is not realistic. So the issue becomes one of balance versus focus. How do I reach a proper balance of leadership development while focusing on the most important areas of improvement? Where is that point where I am sufficiently well-rounded without wasting my time on things in which I will never excel?

The first step is to ensure that you have the ELJC elements covered. Even if you are not naturally adept at one or more of them, sustained leadership will require that you achieve some level of competence in those elements. An unethical leader will be found out and will fall. Some areas allow no margin for error. They must be 100 percent. Certain other areas, while not your forte, still need a minimal level of attention. Continual study and consideration of those elements will prove beneficial.

Andy Stanley has said, "The first thing that sometimes keeps next generation leaders from playing to their strengths is that the idea of being a balanced or well-rounded leader looks good on paper and sounds compelling coming from behind a lectern, but in reality it is an unworthy endeavor. Read the biographies of the achievers in any arena of life. You will find over and over that these were not 'well-rounded' leaders. They were men and women of *focus*."[67] He continues, "It is not realistic to strive for balance within the sphere of our personal leadership abilities. Striving for balance forces a leader to invest time and energy in aspects of leadership where he will never excel....When a leader attempts to become well-

---

67   Vince Molinaro, *The Leadership Contract: The Fine Print to Becoming a Great Leader* (US: Wiley, 2013), 22-23.

rounded, he brings down the average of the organization's leadership quotient—which brings down the level of the leaders around him. Don't strive to be a well-rounded leader. Instead, discover your zone and stay there. Then delegate everything else."[68]

---

68 Ibid., 24.

Chapter 3

HOW TO USE THE SUSTAINED LEADERSHIP WBS

———————————●———————————

A Work Breakdown Structure (WBS) can be structured as a hierarchical graph or as an outline. Following this introduction is the entire outline format of the *Sustained Leadership WBS*. Peruse it to your satisfaction while remembering that words can mean different things to different people. Simply reading the WBS might not clarify all the terms for you. Go to each section in Chapter 4 and read the WBS Dictionary entry for that WBS element. In this way you will understand the intent of the WBS words and begin to speak in terms that have a consistent meaning.

METHODOLOGY

The Leadership WBS is derived from an exhaustive review of the literature on the subject, detailed interviews with leaders of many types and at various stages of leadership development, and even a linguistic approach to understand the language we use to describe leaders, leadership traits, leadership talents, leadership capabilities, and leadership notions.

No leader will have every trait or even every trait in the same measure. As a result, every leader is different and comes to the table with a different set of skills, knowledge, traits, and preferences. Don't expect that you can follow this WBS, score 100 in every category, and suddenly you are the consummate leader for all situations and circumstances. Not going to happen. Doesn't matter how "type A" you are; you will always be a work in progress. Perhaps the "end" of this project is an improved you. And then you can go back to the beginning and develop a finer edge on a few items. Unlike a traditional project (beginning/end/unique product) the unique product here is an improved you, and you can cycle through this effort repeatedly. In fact, you are encouraged to do so. Situational awareness includes knowing those situations where you are the best leader in the group and when you are not. Even with all your weaknesses, however, you might still be the best in the group. Be prepared for all situations—improve yourself constantly.

You manage what can be measured. Leadership cannot be measured in the classic sense. It has more to do with overall comprehensive results, motivation of the workforce, and how the person makes you feel. What? Touchy/feely stuff in a leadership book? Yes. If there are no feelings, no compassion, no empathy, no sense of personal worth, there is an entire branch of the WBS (3.0) missing in your leadership toolbox.

Essential Leadership Journey Checkpoints

In every project there is a series of tasks that plot the longest path through the project. A delay on any item in the critical path is a day lost in the overall schedule. Since the path to leadership is a journey with no end and because you can start anywhere in the WBS, the analogy does not totally hold up. So to help the *Sustained Leadership WBS* to fit more comfortably within the project management construct, we have identified Essential Leadership Journey Checkpoints (ELJC) to highlight those elements that reflect the items without which a leader cannot be successful. In fact, it is fair to say that a failure in any of the ELJC elements will result, ultimately if not immediately, in a complete failure of your leadership journey. In other words, failing in an ELJC element prevents you from assuming or sustaining a leadership role. If you are placed in a leadership position, you will fail. Strong words? Yes. But totally and completely accurate. If you are just starting your leadership journey, focusing on the ELJC elements might be a good place to start.

Most apply to leaders at any level; others, such as developing other leaders (3.2), apply to leaders who have traveled further down the leadership path.

As you travel and grow you will encounter a great deal of data that will suggest a different set of critical items and identify them as essential to your success as a leader. You will find that others have identified some portion of the *Sustained Leadership WBS* that they believe to be the most critical items. These materials are not necessarily wrong. They have simply selected a different priority to sustained leadership. The *Sustained Leadership WBS* is more comprehensive. As you review the materials and the explanations (WBS Dictionary) for each element, you will find that your specific project plan for your development as a leader will have a unique set of critical items.

There are things you will need to work on that others might not. Thus, beyond the "must haves" as reflected in the ELJCs provided, you will find your own set of elements that need your attention—those things that are particularly difficult for you that are hindering your journey. Treat that list as your ELJCs toward successful leadership since each day you delay in resolving those issues is one more day that you are less qualified to lead or perhaps even disqualified from leading at all. Just don't think that developing any of the WBS elements is impossible. It is not. Any of them can be achieved with focus and perseverance. Your journey might be harder than others. It might take longer. Just don't lose confidence that it can be achieved. The more difficult the journey, the more rewarding the destination.

Why Read the *Sustained Leadership WBS*?

Everything you read is a tool. What you decide to do with the tool—what you decide to build—is totally your choice. Tools in the right hands can make masterpieces while others might only be able to carve a toothpick. The *Sustained Leadership WBS* is a tool. Robert Greene takes this perspective:

> The character you seem to have been born with is not necessarily who you are; beyond the characteristics you have inherited, your parents, your friends, and your peers have helped to shape your personality. The Promethean task of the powerful is to take control of the process, to stop allowing others that ability to limit and mold them. Remake yourself into a character of power. Working on yourself like clay should be one of your

greatest and most pleasurable life tasks. It makes you in essence an artist—
an artist creating yourself.[69]

For a graphical representation of the *Sustained Leadership WBS*, please visit
http://sustainedleadershipwbs.com/wbs/

Sustained Leadership WBS

1.0 Character
  1.1 Honesty/Trust/Loyalty
    1.1.1 Relationships
      1.1.1.1 Network
        1.1.1.1.1 Business
        1.1.1.1.2 Friendships and Acquaintances
      1.1.1.2 Followers/Subordinates/Superiors
      1.1.1.3 Family
        1.1.1.3.1 Immediate
        1.1.1.3.2 Extended
        1.1.1.3.3 Adoptive
    1.1.2 Traits
      1.1.2.1 Approachable
      1.1.2.2 Responsible
      1.1.2.3 Transparent
      1.1.2.4 Socially Adept
        1.1.2.4.1 Small Talk
        1.1.2.4.2 Networking
      1.1.2.5 Uses Influence Rather Than Authority
      1.1.2.6 Courage
      1.1.2.7 Foresight
  1.2 Integrity
    1.2.1 Values (Heart)
      1.2.1.1 Accept Responsibility
      1.2.1.2 Fact-Based
      1.2.1.3 Reliable/Consistent/ Delivers On Commitments
      1.2.1.4 Sincerity

---

69 Robert Greene, *The 48 Laws of Power* (New York: Penguin Books, 1998), 195.

1.2.1.5 Loyalty

1.2.1.6 Engenders Mutual Respect

1.2.1.7 Always Pursues Excellence

1.2.1.8 Authenticity

1.2.2 Spiritual (Anchor)

1.2.2.1 Strong Moral Compass

1.2.2.2 Nurture a Strong Conscience

1.2.2.3 Personal Life in Order

1.2.2.4 Respects Natural Law

1.2.2.5 Generous

1.2.2.6 Affirming

1.3 Know Yourself

1.3.1 Constant Learner

1.3.1.1 Reader

1.3.1.2 One Major with Lots Of Minors

1.3.1.3 Prepares

1.3.1.4 Wisdom Seeker

1.3.1.5 Inquisitive Mind

1.3.2 Self-Motivated

1.3.3 Humility

1.3.3.1 Assesses Self Honestly

1.3.3.2 Teachable

1.3.3.3 Handles Criticism

1.3.3.4 Unselfish

1.3.3.5 Understands Power and Shares Power

1.3.3.6 Aware Of Limitations

1.3.3.7 Controlled Ego

1.3.4 Models Behavior

1.3.5 Belief in Self

1.3.5.1 Confidence

1.3.5.2 Comfortable with Power

1.3.6 Maximizes Intelligence

1.3.7 Good Under Pressure

1.3.8 Is Conscious of Legacy

1.3.9 Thinking

    1.3.9.1 Critical Thinking

    1.3.9.2 Systems Thinking

    1.3.9.3 Strategic Thinking

1.3.10 Courage Of Convictions

1.3.11 Coping Ability

1.3.12 Has Mentors

1.3.13 Appreciates the Journey

1.3.14 Political Savvy

1.3.15 Risk and Fear Tolerance

1.3.16 Emotional Intelligence

1.3.17 Knows How to Have Fun and Celebrate

2.0 Competence

  2.1 Business Acumen

    2.1.1 Finance/Accounting/Bottom Line

    2.1.2 Legal

      2.1.2.1 Contracts

      2.1.2.2 Human Resources

      2.1.2.3 Regulatory

    2.1.3 Management

    2.1.4 Risk

    2.1.5 Global Perspective

    2.1.6 Situational Awareness

      2.1.6.1 Observant

      2.1.6.2 Order From Chaos

        2.1.6.2.1 Detail Sorting

        2.1.6.2.2 Relevance

  2.2 Technical Capability

    2.2.1 Excellence in One Primary Field

    2.2.2 Team Player

    2.2.3 Measures What Is Important

    2.2.4 Academic Achievement

    2.2.5 Strong Individual Contributor

    2.2.6 Stays Tech Savvy and Uses It Effectively

4.1.6 Write

4.2 Content and Audience

    4.2.1 Values and Mission

    4.2.2 Positions and Persuasion

    4.2.3 Proposals

    4.2.4 Clarity

    4.2.5 Conviction

    4.2.6 Consistency Of Message

    4.2.7 Credible

    4.2.8 Feedback

    4.2.9 Tact

    4.2.10 Negotiations

        4.2.10.1 Concessions and Compromise

        4.2.10.2 Alliances

    4.2.11 Enthusiasm

    4.2.12 Deals with:

        4.2.12.1 Employees or Those You Lead

        4.2.12.2 Press

        4.2.12.3 Other Stakeholders

        4.2.12.4 Regulators

        4.2.12.5 Customers and Beneficiaries

        4.2.12.6 Problems

    4.2.13 Diplomatic

    4.2.14 Understands Importance Of Sound Bite

    4.2.15 Saying "Sorry" and "Thanks"

4.3 Charisma

    4.3.1 Personable Warmth

    4.3.2 Direct

    4.3.3 Socially Adept

4.4 Techniques

    4.4.1 Good Questions

    4.4.2 Good Story Teller

    4.4.3 Able to Adjust Message to Audience Level

    4.4.4 Able to Simplify

4.4.5 Body Language

5.0 Commitment

  5.1 Do

    5.1.1 Passion

    5.1.2 Vision

    5.1.3 Consistency in Vision

    5.1.4 Creates a Legacy

    5.1.5 Adaptable

    5.1.6 Physically Fit

    5.1.7 Deals Effectively with Setbacks

    5.1.8 Gives Back to Profession/Industry/Society

    5.1.9 Knows When to Pull the Plug

  5.2 Don't Do

    5.2.1 Rigidity

    5.2.2 One-Dimensional Thinking

    5.2.3 Playing Politics

    5.2.4 Negativity and Cynicism

    5.2.5 False Promises and Deception

    5.2.6 Arrogance

    5.2.7 Hidden Agenda as a Strategy

    5.2.8 Willful Ignorance

    5.2.9 Authoritarianism

    5.2.10 Sense Of Privilege

    5.2.11 Gossip and Rumor

    5.2.12 Celebrity

    5.2.13 Anger/Emotional Extremes/Instability

    5.2.14 Imbalance in Positive Traits

    5.2.15 Integrity Enemies

      5.2.15.1 Self-Interest/Self-Dealing

      5.2.15.2 Self-Protection

      5.2.15.3 Self-Deception

      5.2.15.4 Self-Righteousness

Chapter 4

THE SUSTAINED LEADER PROJECT PLAN

———— ● ————

Essential Leadership Journey Checkpoint
1.0 Character

WBS Dictionary: Character is a reflection of the true quality of an individual. A popular aphorism notes that character is how you act when no one else is around. Character is comprised of the sub-elements honesty, integrity, and knowing yourself. Character is measured by the decisions you make. Choices are not always black and white, many are in shades of grey. Good character is reflected in good choices. This is not "luck" in circumstances, rather positive choices where alternative approaches are presented. Character is best reflected in moral choices. Deciding whether to wear the blue shirt or the red shoes is fairly inconsequential. Deciding to wear the extremely low cut top or revealing short skirt can be viewed as more of a moral choice that reflects character. In much of the literature, having good character is often called "authenticity." It means that there is no fake nature to the person; a person is exactly who they appear to be whether anyone is watching or not.

Application: Character is an essential leadership journey checkpoint for sustained leadership. It is one of those elements without which you can never excel as a leader. In fact, a lapse in character can manifest long into your career path and result in total derailment of your leadership objectives. It is a WBS element from which there is no rest. One lapse can undo decades of positive character demonstrations.

From the Judeo-Christian perspective, character flaws can disqualify you for greater service. For example, when David sinned with Bathsheba, (2 Sam 11), although a man of God, he disqualified himself from God's blessing and suffered family turmoil until his death. David's reign as king was forever hindered (2 Sam 12:10-12) and his family disrupted from that point on. (See WBS 1.2.2.3 and 2 Sam 13). News stories that reflect the fall of a great and powerful person due to a character flaw are so common as to almost become a cliché. Jimmy Swaggart was a popular preacher before being found out as an adulterer. Other preachers fell from grace for embezzling funds from their churches. Recognized men and women in responsible positions betrayed that trust and fell from their esteemed positions. Bernie Madoff, Ken Lay, Martha Stewart, and from the world of government procurement Darlene Druyen all fell prey to their character flaws and went to prison. Others fell victim to their vices and got derailed. Your vices are a direct reflection of your character.

Some sins against God are viewed by society as leadership derailment events. Others are not. For example, adultery is an accepted practice in some social circles; however, it is never acceptable in the Judeo Christian ethic. Embezzlement, on the other hand, while equally viewed as a sin to those of the Judeo Christian ethic, will get an employee summarily fired—even if they are the "big boss." Either way, these activities reflect serious character flaws. The question the sustained leader asks is, "Is this the right choice?" rather than "Will I go to jail for doing this?" True leaders must examine their character and work to strengthen it. Only in this way will temptation be resisted. When faced with temptation, there are only two ways out of it—complete resistance or giving in. Strengthen your character by continually making good choices. Giving in, while it immediately removes the temptation, is a choice that damages your character and makes it that much more difficult to make good decisions in the future.

Andy Stanley has made the following pronouncement: "Leading with character is not about doing right to avoid consequences. Leaders worth following do the right thing because it is the right thing. Virtue is not a means to an end. It is the end."[70] He goes on to say, "We will not allow ourselves to be influenced by men and women who lack moral authority. Inconsistency between what is said and what is done inflicts a mortal wound on a leader's influence. Consequently, the same inconsistency hampers a leader's ability to lead.

Helen Keller

Character cannot be developed in ease and quiet. Only through experience of trial and suffering can the soul be strengthened, ambition inspired, and success achieved.

"John Maxwell was right when he said that people have to buy into the leader before they will buy into the vision. It is your moral authority that opens the door for the people around you to buy into your vision. You can pay people to work for you based on your position alone, but you cannot involve people in a cause or a movement without moral authority."[71]

Aristotle noted that if a person trying to persuade you shows "common sense, virtue, and goodwill" (which for Aristotle was an ethical trifecta) then you are more likely to believe what the person says and be amenable to their point of view. Thus, persuasive attempts must work to "establish the speaker himself as being of a certain type—namely the type of person you'll believe." Yes, the logic of their argument must be unified. Simply reading or hearing the words of a person otherwise unknown to you might cause you to consider their position, but it is the combination of ethos, logos, and pathos that will influence you to concur with their point of view. That is, it is the character of the speaker, writer, or leader that convinces you, not their pretty words or apparent logic.

A lawyer once told his accountant boss that he should stop hiring friends, telling him, "Hire for character; you can train monkeys for most tasks." While that is a dose of hyperbole, the point is that you can train people to do most anything as a task. Unless they come to you with good character it is unlikely that you can

---

70 Andy Stanley, *The Next Generation Leader: 5 essentials for those who will shape the future* (Sisters, Ore.: Multnomah, 2003). 138.
71 Ibid., 140.

train character into them in an employer-employee relationship. This becomes very important when you begin to build teams (3.12). It is equally true when you are casting a vote for your political leaders.

Views on Character

Character is a diamond that scratches every other stone.
—Bartol

The conditions of success in life are the possession of judgment, experience, initiative, and character.
—Gustave Le Bon

In selecting men for office, let principle be your guide. Regard not the particular sect or denomination of the candidate—look to his character.
—Noah Webster, 1789

Nothing is more essential to the establishment of manners in a State than that all persons employed in places of power and trust must be men of unexceptionable characters.
—Samuel Adams, 1775

Most people say that it is the intellect which makes a great scientist. They are wrong: it is character.
—Albert Einstein

When you consider your character, an excellent question to ask is: "Am I committed to acting with character, or am I acting in this manner because I am required to do so?" When you accept personal responsibility for your actions you are demonstrating a commitment to character. If you are merely complying with orders or direction you are releasing personal responsibility. When people are asked why they acted in the manner they did, a common response is, "Well, I was just doing what I was told." Even in Nuremburg "I was just following orders" was not a successful defense. *Compliance* can be measured against an established standard. *Commitment* comes from within and is based on character.

Many laws are matters of compliance; whether it is the tax laws or speeding limits. We adjust our behavior in order to comply whether or not we agree with the law. Such things as morals and values are matters of commitment. Those who are not committed to their moral standard or established values will be trapped in a compliance mode. And such people will not be considered leaders.

Commitment is grounded in authentic behavior supported by an ethical framework which integrates our intellectual, emotional, spiritual, and physical selves. In a business environment commitment shifts expenditures from compliance, damage control, and penalties to a quality working environment and greater productivity. As a result, it becomes clear to see that commitment to a high moral standard becomes the apex of the ethical ladder; compliance is the bottom rung of the ethical ladder. While both behaviors will be considered correct, only one comes from a proper motivation. Thus, when you refuse to comply because of your commitment to your values, you are demonstrating good character.

The old standard of character was, "Is this legal?" In a more moderated way we might ask, is this specifically against company policy? You might even ask yourself, if I act in this way, will I be able to sleep at night? The problem with this mode of thinking is that your conscience, or your "gut," might not lead you in the right direction. If you have a history of good decision-making, your conscience may be clear and your "gut" might be trustworthy. It is possible, however, to harden your heart. Repeated misconduct, bad decision making, or allowing your moral standard to be influenced by the wrong people can result in a conscience that is not well grounded and should not be trusted. You may believe yourself to be more well-grounded, but consider even the extreme psychopathy of Jeffrey Dahmer, Charles Manson, or Nidal Hassan. Do you believe that they have or had any problem sleeping at night? Of course not. While stealing pencils from the office does not reduce you to that level of psychopathy, you do have to ask where the path to that position might start Know your moral standards. Review your value system. And act accordingly. Then when a situation arises where you must trust your "gut" you will have confidence in doing so.

Instead of asking whether your action is legal, ask "Is this how I would want someone I trust to act on my behalf?" It is a version of the golden rule, and every society, every religion, every tribe has its own version of it. That is not an accident.

John Maxwell provides an analysis of this perspective. "Retired general Norman Schwarzkopf asserted, 'Ninety-nine percent of leadership failures are failures of character.' So are ninety-nine percent of all other failures. Most people focus too much on competence and too little on character. How often does a person miss a deadline because he didn't follow through when he should have? How many times do people get lower grades on tests than they could have because they didn't study as much as they should have? How frequently do people fail to grow, not because they didn't have time to read helpful books, but because they chose to spend their time and money on something else that was less worthwhile? All of those shortcomings are the result of character, not capacity. Character growth determines the height of your personal growth."[72]

The sustained leader will think very seriously about the choices he or she makes and will make the choice that strengthens their character. They will do this whether anyone is watching or not; whether anyone will find out or not; and whether there is a law against it or not. The sustained leader understands that "right" means "right."

This sounds like me

A lot   **somewhat**   **just a little**   **not at all**

Additional Resources:

John Maxwell, *There's No Such Thing as "Business" Ethics.*

John MacArthur, *The Quest for Character.*

William Ury, *The Power of a Positive No.*

---

72   John Maxwell, *The 15 Invaluable Laws of Growth* (Center Street: New York, 2012), 144.

Personal Objective:

Specific Actions:

Due Date:

1.1 Honesty / Trust / Loyalty

WBS Dictionary: These three aspects of Character are strongly linked. Honesty has to do with seeing the facts, understanding the facts, and dealing with the facts. A quote attributed to Bernard M. Baruch and also used by Daniel Patrick Moynihan states that "you are entitled to your opinions, but you are not entitled to your facts." Facts are curious things in that they are provable. If they are not provable, they are either theories or opinions, but not facts. To hold on to things that have been shown to NOT be facts does not reflect a high quality of character. Trust is something that is built over time based on experience that shows that the party in whom you are placing trust has been honest with you. Loyalty, likewise, arises over time and is also rooted in honesty, based on trust, and linked to your vision (5.1.2). Loyalty means that people will continue to follow you when others raise doubts and will always provide you the benefit of the doubt, meaning that even when you err (and you will) those who are loyal will forgive and forget.

Application: Some people simply have trouble dealing with the facts. Some refuse to accept them. Some are just carelessly reckless about them, not really caring whether what they say or believe is accurate. There is no harm in being mistaken unless you are cavalier about it. What reflects poor character is the intentional misstatements of facts or being so unconcerned about the truth that you might say anything. "Little white lies" fall into this category. Some see no problem with that. As Thomas Jefferson said, "It is of great importance to set a resolution, not to be shaken, never to tell an untruth. There is no vice so mean, so pitiful, so contemptible; and he who permits himself to tell a lie once, finds it much easier to do it a second and a third time, till at length it becomes habitual; he tells lies without attending to it, and truths without the world's believing him. This falsehood of the tongue leads to that of the heart, and in time depraves all its good disposition."[73]

Unfortunately, as Jeffrey Pfeffer points out:

"Lying helps people attain powerful positions. Moreover, leaders are, by definition, people in positions of great power. And research consistently demonstrates that 'powerful people lie more often and with more ease.' Leaders prevaricate with greater aplomb because 'power…mitigates the impact of stress associated with dishonesty….. [and] high-power individuals are less sensitive to societal norms; e.g., norms that condemn the use of deception.' Thus, powerful people—leaders—are able to lie more successfully, and they do so."[74]

Andrew Breitbart

Truth isn't mean. It's truth.

Trust flows from an honest character. When people reliably tell you the truth, you place trust in them. Lies are a form of betrayal. When you are lied to you feel betrayed and sometimes vindictive. You have a sense of wanting to get even. You lose trust in people who lie. We are all imperfect and will, from time to time, let others down—sometimes we will even let ourselves down. Whether you have erred in one way or another is not the issue. Whether you learn from your errors and resolve never to err in that way again—that is the issue and the correct answer to that issue builds character.

---

73 Letter to Peter Carr — 1785
74 Jeffrey Pfeffer, *Leadership BS: Fixing Workplaces and Careers One Truth at a Time* (New York: Harper Collins, 2015), 115, (citations omitted).

Loyalty occurs at the intersection of honesty and trust under the streetlight of vision. In some studies, the single most reliable indicator of employee satisfaction was their trust and confidence in top leadership. Following close behind is the importance of communicating with employees (See 4.2.12.1)

To gain trust, you must trust. This puts you at risk that the trust you offer will be betrayed. It is, however, the sustained leader who understands that someone must act first. The sustained leader takes the initiative to trust and rely on their assessment of the person's character that the trust will not be betrayed. A risk worth taking.

Jefferson noted:

Galileo was sent to the inquisition for affirming that the earth was a sphere: the government had declared it to be as flat as a trencher, and Galileo was obliged to abjure his error. This error however at length prevailed, the earth became a globe, and Descartes declared it was whirled round its axis by a vortex. The government in which he lived was wise enough to see that this was no question of civil jurisdiction, or we should all have been involved by authority in vortices. In fact, the vortices have been exploded, and the Newtonian principle of gravitation is now more firmly established, on the basis of reason, than it would be were the government to step in, and to make it an article of necessary faith. Reason and experiment have been indulged, and error has fled before them. It is error alone which needs the support of government. Truth can stand by itself.[75]

---•---

Samuel Goldwin

*I don't want any yes-men around me. I want everybody
to tell me the truth even if it costs them their jobs.*

---•---

75 Thomas Jefferson, QUERY XVII: The different religions received into that state? http://xroads. virginia.edu/~hyper/jefferson/ch17.html Accessed 08/10/16.

Truth is objective, not subjective. We all lie to ourselves in one way or another. This is not healthy. As ugly as the truth might be on occasion, it must be faced. It causes people to trust us and over time engenders loyalty. The flow starts with honesty which leads you to trust which then leads to loyalty. Those you lead will never be loyal if they believe that you have not been honest with them.

The sustained leader must adhere to society's ethical norms. These can be defined as regular ways of doing things that everyone, or certainly most everyone, agrees are proper for a civilized society. Unlike other conventions in a society such as fashion or courtesy, however, ethical norms regulate all aspects of our lives in ways that are crucial for the existence of the society. Without them, it would self-destruct. This is why you will often hear some leaders speak to our "moral decline" or the debasement of our society. It is not easy to maintain high ethical norms unless most everyone agrees, and the society adopts common, ethical standards (the highest principle of which is the Rule of Law) to govern its actions.

When James Kouzes and Barry Posner conducted their surveys on leadership around the world, the most admired quality people sought in their leaders was honesty.[76] In the last half of the 1800's Russell Conwell relayed this view of honesty:

> "Oh," a young man says, "but I have been told that if a person has money he is dishonest and contemptible."
>
> My friend, that is the reason why you have none, because you have that idea. The foundation of your faith is altogether false. Let me say here clearly, and say it briefly: Ninety-eight out of one hundred of the rich men of America are honest. That is why they are rich. That is why they are trusted with money. That is why they carry on great enterprises and find people to work with them. It is because they are honest men.[77]

The sustained leader is scrupulously honest and works hard at earning the trust and loyalty of their followers. It is the single most important trait that followers seek in their leaders and that leaders seek in their followers.

---

76   James Kouzes & Barry Posner, *The Leadership Challenge, Third Edition* (US: Jossey-Bass, 2002). 23-28.

77 Russell Conwell, *Acres of Diamonds* (Kansas City, Mo.: Hallmark, 1968), 24.

This sounds like me

| A lot | somewhat | just a little | not at all |

Additional Resources:

Harry Frankfurt, *On Bullshit*.

Harry Frankfurt, *On Truth*.

Personal Objective:

Specific Actions:

Due Date:

1.1.1 Relationships

WBS Dictionary: Connecting with people is a critical leadership ability. While everyone has relationships, too often they are measured by quantity such as Facebook friends or Twitter followers rather than quality. This WBS element reflects the quality of relationships to the exclusion of quantity. Leaders tend to have three major categories of relationships—a social network; followers, subordinates, or those positionally above us in a hierarchy; and family. Each of these is unique as compared to the others. This network is important for social development, companionship, and social order.

Application: There is no requirement that leaders have specific relationships; what is important is that leaders understand social networks and the roles various parties might play in relation to the leader. Sociologists tell us that a healthy psyche depends on appropriate social relationships. Leaders who are introverts in the Meyers Briggs schema (1.3.3.1) may appear to have less need for social interaction.[78] This does not mean that the need is zero. Healthy relationships, as variable as the need may be among different leaders, are necessary for the development of a variety of leadership attributes.

The sustained leader will make a conscious effort to know their followers and take a sincere interest in them. On your lifetime journey you will encounter many people and develop relationships as casual as acquaintances and as intimate as marriage and family. And for better or worse, family knows you like no one else. Others will meet you as a mature member of society, but your parents will always know you as daddy's little girl, or mommy's baby boy. These are the people who changed your diapers. Siblings, both older and younger, grew up with you and you both know more about each other than anyone else ever will. Relationships come in an infinite number of shapes and sizes.

Stephen Covey speaks to developing an emotional bank account with your relationships—*all* relationships—across the entire spectrum of your roles. The investments you make into these bank accounts include treating people better than they treat you, walking the biblical second mile, offering help to those who are in no position to help you, doing right when it is natural to do wrong, and keeping your promises even when it hurts.

Stephen Covey's concept of an emotional bank account defined six types of deposits. These are:

1. Understand the individual—make the things that are important to them important to you

2. Attend to the little things—in relationships the little things are the big things

3. Keep commitments—keeping them is a major deposit; breaking them a major withdrawal.

4. Clarify expectations—"The cause of almost all relationship difficulties is rooted in conflicting or ambiguous expectations around roles and goals."

5. Show personal integrity—treat everyone with the same set of principles

---

78 Susan Cain, *Quiet: The Power of Introverts in a World That Can't Stop Talking* (US: Crown, 2012).

6. Apologize sincerely when you make a withdraw—the apology mitigates the withdraw.[79]

—————— ● ——————

General Colin Powell
Being responsible sometimes means pissing some people off.

—————— ● ——————

The sustained leader knows that before anyone will follow them there must be a connection. People do not tend to blindly follow someone, although they may be under their influence for many of the wrong reasons. Humans just tend to do that sometimes. It is in the establishment of the relationship that the sustained leader will give the follower a reason to follow. This is true in politics, in business, and in life generally. John Maxwell cites a source that has said, "Leadership is cultivating in people today a future willingness on their part to follow you into something new for the sake of something great."[80] A choice to follow a leader is solely that of the follower. Doing something new introduces change, which is another great source of fear for many people. The "something great" is the vision of the leader. (5.1.2). Thus, the vision must entice followers and overcome their innate fear of change. (2.3.7)

Stephen Spielberg first visited Universal Studios as a tourist. He sneaked away from the tour and spent the day on a movie set, acting as if he was right where he belonged. He found the head of the editorial department and struck up a friendship. The next day he went back, dressed in a suit, found an empty trailer and painted "Stephen Spielberg, Director" on it. He spent the summer associating with those involved in the movie industry, parlaying that into a phenomenal career making movies. He knew with whom to associate and with whom to build lasting beneficial relationships.

---

79 Stephen R. Covey, *The 7 Habits of Highly Effective People* (New York: Simon & Schuster, 1989), 190-97.

80 John Maxwell and J. Dornan, *How to Influence People: make a difference in your world* (Nashville: Thomas Nelson, 2013), 142 (unattributed quote).

This sounds like me

A lot   **somewhat**   **just a little**   **not at all**

Additional Resources:

Dale Carnegie, *How to Win Friends & Influence People.*

Susan Cain, *Quiet.*

Stephen Covey, *The 7 Habits of Highly Effective People.*

Jeffrey Gitomer, *Little Black Book of Connections.*

Personal Objective:

Specific Actions:

Due Date:

1.1.1.1 Network

WBS Dictionary: Network here is used as a noun rather than a verb (for the verb form see 1.1.2.4.2). The network is composed of both business and social connections. Sustained leaders appreciate the need for others on their team and value the relationships that stem from even casual acquaintances. Extroverts tend to adapt to networks more easily since they draw their strength from being around people. Introverts must work harder at their network since being around others is often a draining experience. In today's society it is often common to measure your network based on the number of friends on your Facebook page, the followers you have on Twitter, or the links you count on LinkedIn. While these newer social tools facilitate your network, for the most part the people are just names and do not seem real. Not until you choose to engage with others does a network truly begin to exist. Your network grows larger and stronger when you make the effort to reach out to people—to make a true human connection rather than just a digital one.

Application: A proper network suggests that you have actually made an emotional investment. Even then, however—unless it is reciprocated—it does not qualify as a relationship. A one-sided relationship is just that and is not a reciprocal relationship. The emotional investment might be as a mentor or mentee, or as a member of a family. It might be in a social or romantic situation. In each case you are not building a network if the emotional investment is not reciprocal.

Do you participate in social media groups? Do you initiate good discussions? Do you recommend your network connections? Do you write constructive and informative comments? Do you make introductions and referrals? Do you have a blog? Do you update it regularly? There is no requirement that you have 500 close personal friends, or even acquaintances, or even links or other social media followers. The social media environment is, however, where you have multiple opportunities to improve your communications (4.0). There is no magic number for your network. It should be large enough and broad enough to provide opportunities to grow and be supportive. It should be small enough that you can pay sufficient attention to the network and not let any of the relationships die due to neglect.

Kouzes and Posner note that, "Networking has value, value that goes far beyond anything monetary. It has to do with what really counts in our daily lives. We're helpless if left to ourselves. Socially and professionally, we need other people."[81]

The concept of team building and networking speaks to the concept of social capital. There are many who take pride in the number of friends or followers they have on various social media platforms. The sustained leader understands, however, that value is best measured in quality rather than quantity. It may be true that you have to kiss a lot of frogs to find your prince or princess. Thus, there may be some merit to numbers. Of equal importance is the combined intellectual capital, as compared to the social capital, that leaders draw towards themselves. It becomes the real manifestation of the adage that "it's not what you know but who you know." In reality it is both.[82]

---

81 Kouzes and Posner, *Leadership Challenge*, 260.
82 Cf. Malcolm Gladwell, *The Tipping Point: How Little Things Can Make a Big Difference* (US: Back Bay Books, 2002), and Seth Godin, *Linchpin: Are You Indispensable? Seth 2nd ed.* (US: Portfolio Hardcover, 2010).

Andrew Carnegie was able to build an extensive network of powerful businessmen while working at a telegraph office. He also learned a great deal about how business was conducted and what various commodities and consumer goods should cost. Later he plied the same trade at the Pennsylvania Railroad company which exposed him to the corporate titans of his day, many of whom took him under their wing and mentored him on the best business practices and techniques. He learned a great deal that served him well as he developed his own business and applied all that he had learned from his network. The sustained leader expends the effort necessary to draw in and nurture a positive network.

This sounds like me

A lot	**somewhat**	**just a little**	**not at all**

Additional Resources:

Susan Cain, *Quiet*.

Harvey Mackay, *Dig Your Well Before you're Thirsty*.

Sandy Vilas, et al., *Power Networking*.

Personal Objective:

Specific Actions:

Due Date:

1.1.1.1.1 Business

WBS Dictionary: The leader's business network includes those within their present organization at any level, those that are encountered through professional associations, those encountered through the conduct of business, and those met through any of the above. The point is that there is a commonality of interest with such a network, focused on the work performed or the profession practiced. When changing jobs, and especially when changing industries, this network is severely disrupted and requires special attention to rebuild it. Some avoid such a disruption by staying in the same job with the same company for too long, often becoming stale and less useful to the organization as well as plateaued professionally. Your business network is intended to assist in opening opportunities for additional growth. Your business network should include two or more mentors related to business matters. It should provide opportunities for stretch assignments to enhance growth. It should provide opportunities for a variety of business-related social encounters for exposure and growth. The business network provides unique challenges and opportunities, and presents you with new and different responsibilities toward this network.

Application: Every interaction in a business environment is an interview. It is one of the many bricks that goes into building a business relationship. Jeffrey Gitomer has said that all things being equal, people will do business with those they like. He goes on to say that all things NOT being equal, people will conduct business with those they like. This is an important principle for sustained leadership. One of the most compelling reasons for a sustained leader to develop a strong business network is simply because you learn to be likeable. See also 4.3.

The various business relationships we might foster can take many forms. They might be mentoring relationships or "best friend" relationships. They might be boss/supervisor or peer to peer. They might be romantic, as many intimate relationships begin in the workspace. Some of these are very appropriate, some perhaps less so. Tom Rath, in his book *Vital Friends* draws from extensive studies from the Gallup organization that tells us that those who have a best friend at work are 7 times more likely to be fully engaged in their jobs—a strong measure of retention.

Keith Ferrazzi notes the importance of having what he calls "lifeline relationships." From his experience he draws four needs that such relationships fulfill:

1. To help us identify what success truly means for us, including our long-term career plans.

2. To help us figure out the most robust plan possible to get there, through short-term goals and strategies that would tie us into knots if we tried to go it alone.
3. To help us identify what we need to stop doing to move forward in our lives. I'm referring to the things we all do that hold us back from achieving the success we deserve.
4. To have people around us committed to ensuring that we sustain change so that we can transform our lives from good to great.[83]

As noted by author Vince Molinaro, we all need these relationships with those few trusted individuals "who we can count on to offer encouragement, tough feedback when needed, and generous mutual support and to build resolve."[84]

C.E Woolman began as an agricultural agent who took to crop dusting to battle the boll weevil. In 1924 he joined a dusting company to do the seasonal crop dusting work. To fill in during slower times, he took on mail routes and eventually passenger service. This service soon took on the name of Delta Airlines. His motto for the company was, "Let's put ourselves on the other side of the ticket counter." He believed that dealing fairly and honestly with people was the true road to success. Alan Elliott summarized this philosophy as, "Never forget that businesses are made up of people with feelings, beliefs, and a hunger to belong to something that is good, honest, and worthwhile."[85] The sustained leader knows that the people they encounter in business are human beings 24 hours a day. They are not just "resources" to be exploited. Positive business relationships are fostered and work in both directions.

This sounds like me

A lot	somewhat	just a little	not at all

---

83 Keith Ferrazzi, *Who's Got Your Back* (New York, Broadway Books 2009), 27.
84 *Leadership Contract*, 129
85 Elliott, Alan C. *American Dream* 231.

Additional Resources:

Tom Rath, *Vital Friends.*

Keith Ferrazzi, *Who's Got Your Back.*

Joe Takash, *Results Through Relationships.*

Personal Objective:

Specific Actions:

Due Date:

1.1.1.1.2 Friendships and Acquaintances

WBS Dictionary: In the course of a day you encounter many people. In the course of a career you cross paths with many people with whom you've worked. Through your family and other friends, you meet additional people. All combined, these people become your friends/acquaintances network. Entrepreneurs understand that anyone and everyone has the potential to either become a customer/client or to lead to a new customer/client. Failing to acknowledge that everyone you meet is a potential opportunity to grow, learn, and lead can limit your potential. A person is often best known by the company they keep.

Application: Charlie Tremendous Jones tells us that the person we will be in five years is dependent on the people with whom we associate and the books we read. How do you choose your friends? How do you treat new acquaintances? Would they even WANT to become your friend? Do you attract appropriate people around you? Are your social interactions socially appropriate?

---•---

George Washington

Associate yourself with men of good quality if you esteem your own reputation; for 'tis better to be alone than in bad company. Rule 56.

---•---

Your circle of friends should be broad enough to matter while small enough to manage. Some people brag about the thousands of "friends" they have on social media. This is a serious misuse of the term "friend." These are not friends in the true sense. In most cases, you cannot recall how you even came to acknowledge this person, or they you. At best they are casual acquaintances.

It is important that your circle of friends and acquaintances hold some diversity as defined in 3.14. If you are an introvert, you may be completely comfortable NOT developing a wide circle of friends. There is no mandatory reason that the sustained leader do so. Developing friendships and nurturing acquaintances can be a significant part of developing a business. Some learned behaviors are essential to success in certain fields. Start small. Think of your hobbies and develop a neighborhood bridge club, or a fishing trip. Say yes to the next golf outing, and offer to host a dinner party or tailgate. Each of these can be an opportunity to develop a new aspect to your sustained leadership journey.

Multi-level marketing opportunities are often disparaged because they encourage you to treat every social or familial relation as an opportunity to grow your business. On one level, this is true in that there are those who might seek such an opportunity. On the other hand, too often the solitary focus on "growing your business" can become very tiresome to those around you and do not foster a long-term positive relationship. The sustained leader never abuses their relationships in this manner.

William Ury relates this story on how to build your circle of friends.

On one occasion in the White House when Lincoln was speaking sympathetically of the plight of the South, a Yankee patriot took him to task. "Mr. President," she decried, "how dare you speak kindly of our enemies when you ought to be thinking of destroying them?" Lincoln paused and addressed the angry patriot: "Madam," he asked, "do I not destroy my enemies when I turn them into my friends?"[86]

Robert Greene has written an intriguing book he titled "The 48 Laws of Power." It is extremely Machiavellian in tone and, in fact, presents arguments that are diametrically opposed to many of the principles put forth here. As to friendship he says, "All working situations require a kind of distance between people. You are trying to work, not make friends: Friendliness (real or false) only obscures that fact. The key to power, then, is the ability to judge who is best able to further your interests in all situations. Keep friends for friendship, but work with the skilled and competent."[87] What is important to see is that while leaders exercise power, simply having power does not make you a leader. In fact, Abraham Lincoln has cautioned us that if you wish to test a man's true character—give him power. If power is the sought goal, and power alone, the seeker is likely to never become a sustained leader. This is important to know that many people you encounter are not seeking leadership (or friendship) as much as power. Perhaps it is due to a mistaken perception of both power and leadership. Or perhaps it is more nefarious where a person is seeking power for the sake of power. Do not let such people derail your pursuit of leadership and the authentic power that comes from sustained leadership. You will encounter them. Choose your friends wisely.

This sounds like me

A lot   **somewhat**   **just a little**   **not at all**

Additional Resources:
Alan McGinnis, *Friendship Factor*.
Tom Rath, *Vital Friends*.

---

86 William Ury, *Getting to Yes with Yourself: And Other Worthy Opponents* (US: HarperOne. 2015) 128-9.
87 Robert Greene, *The 48 Laws of Power* (New York: Penguin Books, 1998). 13.

Personal Objective:

Specific Actions:

Due Date:

1.1.1.2 Followers/ Subordinates/Superiors

WBS Dictionary: Leaders are not just at the top of the organizational chart. Leaders appear, and are required, at all levels of an organization. Some leaders rise in a hierarchy, but not all do. It is important that leaders exist elsewhere so that team members who do not see the senior staff very often still have good models to follow. Having leaders dispersed also keeps the pipeline full for leadership development. And the modeling of leadership throughout an organization makes the entire organization healthier. A leader's network includes a great number of people. Those who report organizationally to the leader or those who choose to follow this person as a leader place a unique responsibility on the leader. Additionally every leader in every position has higher authority to whom they report and owe a duty of loyalty.

Application: Some people are put into positions of leadership. This makes them the boss, but not necessarily the leader. In fact, positional power is the weakest form of power (1.3.3.5). Even so, any organization requires that there be leaders at all levels. The organizational chart only reflects who the bosses are; it says little to nothing about who the leaders might be. A sustained leader can function in any position, and will often become the leader of their organizational superiors. In more recent times the concept of "reverse mentoring" has arisen where younger members of the team will mentor older members in areas such as technology. The sustained leader does not look at an org chart to determine who they are leading. They simply lead and the followers appear.

The sustained leader must acknowledge this network and its unique needs. The leader must actively choose to lead. He or she owes an obligation to inform their network if they lack the desire to lead. As a politician once said, "If nominated I will not run; if elected I will not serve." To pretend or give false assurances is a lack of character. When you discover that you have been placed in a position in which you do not choose to serve, or upon discovering that you are not capable or comfortable in that role, it is incumbent upon you to let the team know. The alternative is to simply fail, and such a failure is completely avoidable. It will hurt the team, the organization, and your reputation. It is not leadership.

Earlier we quoted Colin Powell who noted that "Leadership sometimes means pissing people off." It's not that you intentionally try to aggravate people or be rude to them, but that you will not be capable of pleasing everyone all the time. The sustained leader respects that relationship, whether toward organizational superiors or those assigned under their responsibility, while also recognizing that in most business/government/charitable entities, making friends is not the primary goal, or even possible to achieve.

Rear Admiral Grace Hopper understood this principle extremely well. "Somewhere along the line we lost our leadership. Quality of leadership is a two-way street. It is loyalty up and loyalty down. Respect your superior, keep him informed of what you're up to, and take care of your crew. When the going gets rough, you cannot manage a man into battle, you must lead him. You manage things, you lead people."[88] A good rule to follow is: Never let your boss be surprised by their boss.

J. Carla Northcutt has also contributed to the knowledge base in this area when she said, "The goal of many leaders is to get people to think more highly of the leader. The goal of a great leader is to help people to think more highly of themselves." Your network includes those within your organizational structure. These people may not become your friends, and not every leadership role occurs in business environments alone. Leadership, however, must be demonstrated wherever you are and to everyone within your circle of influence.

---

88 Quoted in Alan C. Elliott, *American Dream*. 174 from a CBS interview.

Great leaders—the truly successful ones who are in the top 1 percent—all have one thing in common. They know that acquiring and keeping good people is a leader's most important task. An organization cannot increase its productivity—but people can! The asset that truly appreciates within any organization is people. Systems become dated. Buildings deteriorate. Machinery wears. But people can grow, develop, and become more effective if they have a leader who understands their potential value.

"The bottom line ... is that you can't do it alone. If you really want to be a successful leader, you must develop other leaders around you. You must establish a team. You must find a way to get your vision seen, implemented, and contributed to by others. The leader sees the big picture, but he needs other leaders to help make his mental picture a reality.[89]

This sounds like me

A lot   **somewhat**   **just a little**   **not at all**

Additional Resources:

Roger Fisher, et al., *Getting It Done*.

Warren Bennis, et al., *Taking Charge Lessons in Leadership*.

Personal Objective:

Specific Actions:

Due Date:

---

89 John Maxwell, Developing *the Leaders around You* (Nashville: Thomas Nelson Publishers, 1995; Omnibus edition, 2000), 2.

1.1.1.3 Family

WBS Dictionary: It may seem odd to include your family within your network. When you realize there are probably no people on earth who know you as well as they do, you discover that they bring a perspective to your development that no one else can. Included are the groupings of your immediate family, your extended family, and what is called your adoptive family. This last category includes those you might consider closer than immediate family or as one person has said—the family you would have had if you got to pick them. Each of these share in, and perhaps may share some responsibility for, who you are and why you are the way that you are. Drawing on their experience and knowledge can be informative in developing your leadership style and capabilities as well as understanding why you choose certain reactions to situations. Some level of emotional investment is unavoidable even with those from whom you are estranged. The sustained leader has a family—one from which they were born, one with whom they were raised, and one that they may have built themselves through a network of friends. And of course, most people at some point leave their father and mother and begin to build a family of their own.

Application: Family relationships are difficult. They can be the source of the greatest joy in your life as well as the greatest distress and heartache. Every sustained leader is not expected to salvage the unsalvageable or to stay in familial relationships that are destructive. Nonetheless, there is a great deal that can be learned from such relationships, whether they are good or bad.

Today's families are much more diverse than in generations past. The traditional structure of a mom, a dad, and some number of rug rats, while still very popular, is not the only model. Certainly your view of the family structure from a moral or religious perspective will (and should) influence your perspective. Regardless, you will encounter a greater variety of family relationships and the sustained leader should be cautious in making assumptions that might be offensive to those in other family relationships.

Not all family relationships are positive. Children do not arrive with a complete instruction manual and will require upbringing that covers the physical, biological, societal, moral, and emotional aspects. Despite their best efforts, many parents will fail in one or more of these. This will affect the children, and in many cases—most likely subconsciously, the children will recreate the same situations in their later lives. Arresting that can be a significant challenge. The sustained leader will work diligently to correct any impediments that have been created in their lives, and will be sympathetic, if not empathetic, towards those they lead who are dealing with such issues. Family dynamics are incredibly instructive, but often not as intended.

This sounds like me

A lot   **somewhat**   **just a little**   **not at all**

Additional Resources:
Deborah Tannen, *You're Wearing That?*
Deborah Tannen, *That's Not What I Meant!*
Robert Wolgemuth, *She Still Calls Me Daddy*.

Personal Objective:

Specific Actions:

Due Date:

1.1.1.3.1 Immediate

WBS Dictionary: Your relationship with your immediate family has a direct bearing on many aspects of your personality. Understanding these relationships can assist you in understanding why you do some of the things that you do and why you react to certain stimuli as you do. As you work to develop your leadership potential, you can begin to adjust your responses and remove what might be considered self-destructive tendencies through these understandings. Your immediate family watched you grow and learn. They were there the first time you put your hand on the hot stove; they were there when you first got your heart broken; they were there when you got your first detention at school, had your first schoolyard fight, and dealt with your first bully. They even changed your diaper. They know you like no other person on earth. Some of their data might be "dated" in that it has less relevance than more current data, but that does not mean that the information is useless. In a more current vein, a leader is expected to have their personal life in order (1.2.2.3) and the relationship with your immediate family—both the one you were born into and the one you created through marriage—requires that you consider those relationships in the context of your leadership persona. A person who is not kind to their children, puppies, and aging parents is probably not spouse material. They are also not leadership material.

Application: Much is written on the impact of nature versus nurture and the long-term effects of either or both. The current consensus seems to be that both are relevant factors in different measures among individuals—even those raised in the same household. We are all born with natural abilities and talents as well as a lack of certain abilities or talents. Whether we cultivate them, and even when in our life we decide to seriously cultivate them, makes each of us the individual that we are. Those with whom we interact as children are the ones who have the most influence on us. It was in this way that Nazi Germany attempted to shape its Arian society by putting all children in state-run schools where they could be indoctrinated rather than educated. While some families are dysfunctional and some children are in situations that will not serve their best interests, it would be incorrect to assume that ALL children are better served by being removed from a healthy family environment.

When you choose a spouse, a close and intimate relationship is created that, according to most marriage vows, are to last "until death do us part." In today's society that vow seems to take on less and less validity, but it does not change the "vow" portion of that. Sadly, too often the vow is made in haste and later regretted. The marriage relationship creates a new family, a blending of genetics and the creation of new humans, parental responsibilities, and familial relationships.

Regardless of the environment within which you were raised, that environment had an influence on who you are today. Whether it was positive or negative or, as with most situations, a mixture, the fact remains that your immediate family—the one that raised you—is a part of your life and who you are. If the experience left scars that have not healed you might need professional assistance to help those scars heal as best they can. Allowing hard feelings or resentment to fester is not healthy for you and you are, in effect, allowing people toward whom you hold no positive feelings to continue to live in your head rent free. This is not the choice a sustained leader would make.

If your family relationships remain strong and positive, then you will continue to foster that. Over time it is very often the case that you will be called upon to assist with aging parents or other relatives. This may present both a time and financial challenge, but the sustained leader understands that it is the right thing to do. Our immediate family will affect us for the entirety of our life. Good or bad, long-term or short-term, the sustained leader will accept the history that is and make good decisions *today* that will further their leadership journey. That answer is not the same for everyone.

This sounds like me

A lot   somewhat   just a little   not at all

Additional Resources:

John MacArthur, *The Fulfilled Family*.

Stephen Covey, *The 7 Habits of Highly Effective Families*.

Personal Objective:

Specific Actions:

Due Date:

1.1.1.3.2 Extended

WBS Dictionary: Your extended family might be a few distant cousins or it might be 300 attendees at the annual family reunion. Either way, there are a great mix of personalities and perspectives that have contributed to your perception of family and familial relationships. Perhaps you share memories of being at the shore together as kids. Perhaps you had camping trips where you shared your deepest darkest childhood secrets. Or perhaps they were just strangers who showed up at your house from time to time with no explanation. While you might not be personally close to them, you are certainly close to people who felt these "strangers" were important to them. There is great interest today in exploring genealogy. For some, this provides a historical connection to their past. For others, it provides incentive to know of their ancestors' past deeds—or misdeeds. In times past it was common to have three or more generations living under one roof or on the same farm. Today, extended families are commonly geographically dispersed. Your extended family is still a part of your network even though the emotional attachment to an extended family doesn't always form the strongest of bonds.

Application: Whether or not the sustained leader has a close relationship with an extended family is less relevant than what that relationship or lack thereof causes the sustained leader to have with those who both do and do not have such a relationship. For example, you might never hear from a great niece on your birthday or holidays, but as soon as her school has a fundraiser, who do they call? Children need to learn the appropriate etiquette for such situations, and as we have seen in the adult world, some never do. The sustained leader learns that different people on the team will have different backgrounds. Some will mimic the leader's background; others will not. Appreciating the differences, understanding the similarities, and building a relationship with such a diverse set of team members can be an important part of building relationships with a more diverse set of people and understanding the breadth and depth of different networks.

Every family has their "weird Uncle Joe" or those who just don't fit in. Perhaps it's you. As you explore an extended family you begin to discover that there are those with some genealogical connection to you who have children with Down syndrome, muscular dystrophy, various forms of autism, and any number of things with which you have never had to deal personally. These situations become very real when you recognize the issues exist even within your own family. It is a process by which you can develop greater sensitivity to the issues confronted by others. While you might not be comfortable discussing the issues of an autistic child with a co-worker, learning firsthand from a family member can better prepare you to deal with others in similar situations.

An extended family may be an active or inactive part of your network. Whether or not your family relationships extend very far, there are many of your teammates, often driven by cultural differences, who will recognize a *very* extended family. This is not the lazy employee who attempts to get out of work by attending their grandmother's funeral (for the sixth time), but genuine family relationships that are respected by the individual. The sustained leader recognizes these differences and respects those with a genuine network of distant relatives whether the leader personally does so or not.

This sounds like me

A lot   **somewhat**   **just a little**   **not at all**

Additional Resources:
Dale Buss, *Family Man*.
Michael Josephson, et al., *The Power of Character*.

Personal Objective:

Specific Actions:

Due Date:

1.1.1.3.3 Adoptive

WBS Dictionary: In the context of this WBS, your adoptive family includes those people you are closest to today. To some, they might consider them their "BFF" or "Best Bud." Your relationships tell you, and those around you, a great deal about you. The people with whom you choose to spend time reflects on your character. Charlie "Tremendous" Jones has said that who you will be in five years is a direct result of the books you read and the people with whom you associate.[90] You have likely heard that "you are known by the company you keep," and your adoptive family are those people. Do you associate with people of equal ambition, education, and experience? While there is comfort in doing so, do you also expose yourself to those who are quite different from you in terms of age, experience, or ambition? As a leader you will be expected to lead people with a great diversity of attributes and backgrounds. Being too exclusive with those with whom you associate might not provide the network you should have and could deprive you of the experience of dealing with a greater diversity of cultures, people, habits, customs, and social settings. If the only group you see socially are those at the country club (unless you are the director of the country club!), your ability to lead others might be hindered.

Application: Blended families tend to be more the norm today than they used to. It is not unusual to have very extended families with whom you share little to no real genetic material. The relationship and familial affection that extends to these non-relatives is often stronger than those who are closely linked biologically. They become an important part of your emotional, and often physical support.

Close friendships, likewise, can become closer and more supportive than biological links. You would help out either group, but occasionally you do so with family more out of a sense of duty and obligation than genuine affection. Friends are the family you get to choose. And that raises an important point—you do not get to choose the family within which you are born. As you grow and mature you then get to select the people with whom you will most closely associate.

Many couples, and in the right circumstances, singles, will also open their home to foster children who live with them only a short while. These relationships can and often do become very close, lasting a lifetime. Similarly, adoptive

---

90   Charlie Jones, *Life Is Tremendous* (US: Tyndale Momentum, 1981).

relationships are made by choice. Some people make wise choices and others make poor choices that they come to regret. Some are bound by a vow and others are renewed every day as a relationship grows. Who you choose to have as an influence in your life, once you reach the age of legal majority, are clearly and simply your responsibility. The sustained leader learns to make good choices and to foster and nurture positive relationships.

The Gallup organization has done a great deal of research on employee engagement. In their survey they ask a question that many perceive as odd, yet Gallup insists it is one of the key predictors of employee engagement in the workplace. That question pertains to whether or not they have a "best friend" at work. The "adoptive" family that you build voluntarily and volitionally creates a strong sense of stewardship and engagement. Build these relationships.

What about pets? They can be closer than family members and we can have a deeper emotional attachment to them. We can learn a great deal from our pets, from responsibility to emotional investment, and with dogs (maybe not all cats) the concept of unconditional love. Pets can teach responsibility to younger children, yet it is fair to say that not everyone should have such responsibility. Our fellow earth dwelling species that we have domesticated can no longer take care of themselves. How people treat animals can be a good indicator of their character, and the sustained leader pays attention. If you cannot properly care for a pet, find a very low maintenance option, or simply spend more time in nature observing those that know how to care for themselves.

We also frequently choose to align ourselves with people of similar interests. This might be the local Rotary Club, the Knights of Columbus, the local political party, fraternal or sorority organizations, a book club, a knitting club, a hiking group, or a variety of non-profits or other charitable endeavors. Each of these is a statement of our desire to associate around common interests and many of these relationships are an integral part of our network for many years. A person can be stretched too thin by participating, or trying to participate, in too many such groups, yet each one provides a particular outlet for creativity, fulfillment, accomplishment, friendship, or even leadership. The sustained leader chooses wisely and allocates their time accordingly. Some relationships developed through these activities last a lifetime and produce favorable benefits throughout their life-cycle.

This sounds like me

A lot   **somewhat**   **just a little**   **not at all**

Additional Resources:

Markus Buckingham, et al., *First, Break All the Rules.*
Tom Rath, *Eat Move Sleep.*

Personal Objective:

Specific Actions:

Due Date:

1.1.2 Traits

WBS Dictionary: A trait is a particular quality or characteristic typical of a certain grouping of people. For leaders, there can be many traits that are attributed to them; not all of them are positive. The sustained leader knows that their actions reflect their character and a study of their character will reveal what traits they exhibit. The goal will be to get rid of the undesirable traits (5.2) and developed those traits that positively affect their leadership. This element includes a listing of those traits not covered elsewhere that best typify the sustained leader. The traits that most reflect character include the traits of being approachable, responsible, transparent, socially adaptable, having courage, using influence rather than authority, and developing foresight. There are others described in the literature that can be found in other parts of the WBS.

Application: A person's actions reflect their character. A person of good character exhibits certain traits commonly associated with good character. Those of weak character will likewise reflect that lack of character in their actions, thereby exhibiting undesirable traits. The Trait Theory of Leadership (Chapter 2) had some merit in that there was a consistent observation of successful leaders who exhibited similar traits. Unfortunately, people with similar traits did not perform equally successfully, thus the theory provides minimal predictive value on leadership potential.

It is true that people can be quite Machiavellian in that they may attempt to impersonate positive leadership traits that they do not truly possess or can't sustain for a long period of time. In some cases it may be a person who is attempting to "fake it 'til they make it" and that might be somewhat effective if the person is truly aspiring to improve their leadership abilities. The key to these traits, however, is that they reflect character and if you are not developing the character of a sustained leader you might be perceived as an imposter thus destroying your credibility and trustworthiness. It is like your first job—you can't get a job unless you have experience; you can't get experience until you get a job. This is a classic Catch-22 and applies equally to leadership. One scoffer is quoted as saying that sincerity is the key—once you can fake that you have it made. Thus, people exhibiting the classic traits of leadership might be imposters or those learning to be better leaders.

Sustained leaders should work to develop these traits, not as a subterfuge, but as a genuine effort to recognize that there are definite traits that identify leaders as leaders. Such perceptions instill confidence in those who are led. While some might perceive these traits as indicative of Charisma, that term is reserved for communication attributes rather than attributes of character. A person of good character—with no secrets to hide and no guilt—will naturally be more open.

This sounds like me

A lot **somewhat** **just a little** **not at all**

Additional Resources:
Marshall Goldsmith, et al., *What Got You Here Won't Get You There.*
Scott W. Ventrella, et al., *The Power of Positive Thinking in Business.*

Personal Objective:

Specific Actions:

Due Date:

1.1.2.1 Approachable

WBS Dictionary: A person is approachable when they greet people with a smile rather than a scowl, when they laugh easily, and when they take a personal interest in people. While some will speak to their "open-door policy," the facts suggest that they are less interested in actual visitors than they are on being perceived as approachable. Like the other traits listed here, these must be genuine. Not everyone takes to these traits naturally. Some must work very hard to *be* approachable rather than just *appearing* approachable. This element has much in common with 4.0 Communication in that approachable people have learned to communicate effectively with words and non-verbal signs. They spark communication and participate actively in the process. They understand active listening (4.4.5) and can lead a conversation through the use of good questions (4.4.1) and the ability to communicate with stories (4.4.2). Approachable people lower their guard even with strangers, and while this makes them more vulnerable, a sustained leader's self-worth is based on their own sense of self, not that imposed by others from the outside.

Application: Being approachable is more than a smile and a non-threatening demeanor. The sustained leader goes out of their way to approach people. Initiating contact is one of life's most frightening events. Some people simply refuse to do so most commonly due to a fear of rejection. If your self-worth is based on how others react to you, then you may have deeper issues than a lack of approachability. Remember back in high school when you were looking for a date to the prom or the

Sadie Hawkins dance? Out of a fear of rejection you hesitated to ask the one person with whom you would really like to attend the event. Then you hear that they are going with someone else—someone who had the gumption to simply ask. They went out of their way, they "put themselves out there" and made the approach. The sustained leader knows that taking the action sooner rather than later is a positive trait, (2.3) and that taking the action gives you valuable information. If the desired person says no, you now have information that lets you move on to another target for the event. Without taking the initiative, you might end up standing around the punch bowl with your buddies and not having a date at all. Given human nature, more than 80% of possible fruitful connections are never made because neither party took action. The sustained leader does not let that happen. It is *not* the responsibility of the follower to initiate the contact, although there is nothing wrong with them taking that role. It is the responsibility *and* the role of the leader to do so.

Being approachable means being accessible. You may be quite welcoming to those who find you; the goal is to make it easy for people to find you. Often, you need to seek out others to be present for them. Alan C. Elliott tells the story of J.B. Fuqua who firmly believed that doing business face to face and one-to-one was the *only* way to succeed. So convinced of this was he that on one occasion he jumped on a plane to catch two brothers before one of them left town. That led to a $20 million deal. Hearing of a businessman with tax problems, he showed up at the man's office at 8 AM to work out a leveraged buy-out. He always made a practice to answer his own phone and always present in his business. His goal was to be always available. Only then can you have the proper perspective to be able to see the opportunity before it passes away.[91]

This sounds like me

A lot   **somewhat**   **just a little**   **not at all**

Additional Resources:

Dale Carnegie, *How to Win Friends & Influence People.*

Spencer Johnson, *The Present.*

---

91   Alan Elliott, *A Daily Dose of the American Dream: Stories of Success, Triumph, and Inspiration* (US: Thomas Nelson, 1998), 271.

Personal Objective:

Specific Actions:

Due Date:

1.1.2.2 Responsible

WBS Dictionary: Being responsible means that you can manage the affairs of a normally adjusted member of society. You know when to call 911 and when it would be inappropriate. You can be trusted with money, children, maintaining a home, and other adult responsibilities. As simple as this sounds, it is more than can be expected from some people. A leader must, of course, exceed these minimal levels of responsibility. A leader must be able to take charge of a situation. They must have confidence in the actions they take and the maturity to accept the consequences of those actions. When the leader makes a mistake, they know how to accept the responsibility personally and to make amends, including an appropriate apology (4.2.15), when necessary. Even when the primary fault might lie with an employee or subordinate, a leader accepts the responsibility from the injured third party. A responsible person also keeps their word. This suggests that you should be very cautious when giving your word. If you have given a commitment to someone then you will move heaven and earth to make sure that commitment is met. If there are genuine intervening circumstances, then you give the other party as much notice as possible. You do not simply let the date pass. People are counting on you. Showing a lack of responsibility also shows a lack of credibility, honesty, and loyalty. A lack of responsibility destroys trust. Leaders must accept responsibility.

Application: Allowing others to take the blame, or overtly blaming someone else is a human characteristic as old as time. In the Garden of Eden, after Adam ate from the forbidden fruit, God confronted him and asked what he had done. God of course knew the answer. He was giving Adam an opportunity to take responsibility. Instead what does Adam say? "The woman whom you gave to be with me, she gave me of the tree, and I ate." (Gen 3:12). Interesting. It was not Adam's fault at all. First, it was God's fault for putting the woman there, and then it was Eve's fault for giving him the fruit. No responsibility accepted. Like Adam, it seems that no one wants to take responsibility. Just listen to any politician or failed business person. Passing blame, sadly, seems to have become a national pastime.

Malcolm Forbes

A man who enjoys responsibility usually gets it.
A man who merely likes exercising authority usually loses it.

The sustained leader understands the adage that rank has its privileges. As the leader, certain privileges can be taken and may have well been earned. That does not mean that the sustained leader should take undue advantage of those rights and privileges. On the contrary, the sustained leader pays far more attention to the incredible responsibilities they have undertaken rather than taking advantage of the rights whether deserved or not. Both humility (1.3.3) and the command to be a servant-leader (3.18) take precedence over any perceived rights.

The concept of responsibility is a natural human trait that has been recognized throughout the ages and in nearly every context. Businessman Donald trump has said, "Most of us need letters of recommendation now and then. I write them as well as receive them, and I always look for the words 'responsible, professional, and loyal.' If you can build your reputation on three words, those would be three at the top to choose from."[92] You can judge whether anyone actually practices what they preach. Responsibility is, nonetheless, a desired trait in business. John Deere, of tractor fame, has said, "I will never put my name on a plow that does not have in it the best that is in me." Taking responsibility for your actions, your words, your product, your services, or your reputation is a key sign of the sustained leader.

---

92   Donald Trump, and M. McIver, *Think Like a Champion: An Informal Education In Business and Life*. (US: Vanguard Press, 2009), 170.

Stephen R. Covey speaks to the taking of responsibility when discussing the emotional bank account. People who can't take responsibility cannot craft a sincere apology (4.2.15). "They feel it makes them appear soft and weak, and they fear that others will take advantage of their weakness.... In addition, they usually feel justified in what they did. They rationalize their own wrong in the name of the other person's wrong, and if they apologize at all, it's superficial."[93] And it is not taking responsibility.

Part of taking responsibility is to be vary circumspect when giving your word. Once you have given your word to someone it is a critical part of your integrity that you keep your word. You take the responsibility to follow through on whatever it is you promised to do. If you do not intend to follow through, then you should never pretend to give your word. As Napoleon Bonaparte has wisely said, 'The best way to keep your word is not to give it." Similarly, Ben Franklin advised, ""Resolve to perform what you ought. Perform without fail what you resolve."

The sustained leader is careful to take responsibility for those things they can reasonably control. If the situation is out of their control, they should not be making rash promises and taking responsibility unwisely. When the promise has been given, however, there is no recourse other than fulfilling the promise.

This sounds like me

A lot	**somewhat**	**just a little**	**not at all**

Additional Resources:

Allan Cohen, et al., *Influence Without Authority.*
Roger Martin, *The Responsibility Virus.*
Jeffrey Garten, *The Mind of The CEO.*

Personal Objective:

---

93 Stephen Covey, *The 7 Habits of Highly Effective Families: Building a Beautiful Family Culture in a Turbulent World* (US: Golden Books, 1997), 198.

Specific Actions:

Due Date:

1.1.2.3 Transparent

WBS Dictionary: Transparent means that the leader has no secret agenda and does not keep other operational secrets. There is no second set of books. There is no sharing of insider information. There is no self-dealing (5.2.15.1). No playing politics (5.2.3). No deception (5.2.5). Transparency suggests that you can see right through someone or a situation. Nothing is hidden. All organizations have certain matters that are not for publication, such as a human resources action or negotiations on mergers that would affect markets. Confidentiality is appropriate. Transparency is appropriate. And both can exist side by side without conflict.

Application: The Federal government has long had a law called the Freedom of Information Act (FOIA). The guiding principle behind that law is that the public has a right to know what its government is doing. Thus, any person can make a request of any federal agency and with some very limited exceptions, such as law enforcement investigations or confidential business data, the agency will release the records within ten days. The press of business, the man-power needed to search for the requested records, and a variety of other impediments have resulted in many requests not getting a response for years. The sense this has given the public is that its government is not being transparent. Believing none of the exemptions apply and the other excuses given by the agencies are not valid, the public and the press assumes that the government is hiding something. Unfortunately, as later events and disclosures have ultimately revealed, there is further evidence that, in fact, the government has kept things secret that it should not have been hiding. This is the epitome of *not* being transparent.

A person who is perceived as keeping secrets will be considered untrustworthy. Interestingly, this determination will be based on perceptions more often than actual fact. If a person in a leadership position is found to *actually* be untrustworthy, they will be removed from the position. The sustained leader must be perceptive about the way their actions and statements are viewed by those they lead as well as other stakeholders. It takes a great deal of effort to be transparent because you cannot control other peoples' perceptions. Further, any person who has been in a leadership role will attest to the fact that no matter how often you believe you have communicated information, there will be those on the team who never got the message. It becomes the leader's role to over-communicate (4.0) and to make the maximum amount of information readily available to the team as possible.

The sustained leader must avoid all deception, secretiveness, and misdirection. The sustained leader will make reasonable information available to the team and other stakeholders (4.2.12) as quickly as possible. Honesty and openness will be their goals. On an international level, sustained leaders will work to make bad actions of governments and organizations more transparent; shine a light issues, events, and people who take from society without any measurable positive return. This is not always easy or popular, but exposing the facts and dealing with them (1.2.1.2) is the role of the sustained leader.

Any attempt at deception, subterfuge, or lack of full and open communication will suggest a lack of transparency. Dishonesty, in any of its many forms (1.1), is rightfully and immediately viewed as a lack of transparency. What is the person attempting to hide by being less than truthful? The curious thing about lies is that the more you tell, the more you have to remember regarding those lies. Any error will reveal the web of deception that you have woven. The truth is far easier to remember.

People will be mistaken. It is an aspect of humanity that we are not all correct on all matters all of the time. Errors that are not made with intent are not dishonest, but this lays a trap for the inattentive. If you make a mistake, you correct the error and inform everyone of the correct information. When this happens occasionally, as it will to everyone, and the correct information is later provided, this does not affect the perceived transparency. If it happens frequently, the leader's competency might be questioned. When it happens regularly, or the correct information is not provided in a timely manner, then the person is either acting with careless disregard for the truth, or is inherently dishonest. The sustained leader never permits that perception to take root.

This sounds like me

A lot   **somewhat**   **just a little**   **not at all**

Additional Resources:

Dwight L. Johnson, et al., *The Transparent Leader*.

James M. Kouzes, et al., *The Truth about Leadership*.

Personal Objective:

Specific Actions:

Due Date:

1.1.2.4 Socially Adept

WBS Dictionary: Being socially adept means that you are sensitive to the social mores around you. Different circumstances will demand different mores, so it is important to have situational awareness (2.1.6) and be able to adjust. Part of this comes from gaining knowledge of the social (including cultural and ethnic parameters) of any situation in which the leader might find himself or herself. This requires a level of preparation when cultural shifts are to be expected, such as when planning to travel to a foreign country. In the more domestic situations the sustained leader must be able to distinguish between informal unstructured settings (attending a sporting event) and graduating levels of more formalized settings, such as a family dinner, or a wedding reception, or a White House dinner. The sustained leader must learn to be flexible in all such situations and to act accordingly.

Application: In his autobiography, General Norman Schwarzkopf tells the story of an honor he received as a young boy while traveling in the Middle East with his father. It was a high honor to be offered one of the roasted sheep's eyeballs. As the son of their honored guest, he was offered one after the adult dignitaries, including his father, had already been honored.

> With all the roasting and basting it didn't look like a staring eye—more like a brown fig. But it was still an eyeball as far as I was concerned. I said to my father, "I'm not going to eat that." He said out of the corner of his mouth, "You *will* eat it!" ... Holding my breath, I spooned the eyeball up and swallowed it whole, and everyone applauded. Afterward Pop said he was glad I'd done as I was told. "They were paying you a great tribute, and if you hadn't eaten the eye, you'd have insulted them," he said. "But instead you ate it, and by doing that you made a contribution to American-Iranian relations. I'm proud of you." Hearing him say these things made up for the fact that that I'd just had to swallow a sheep's eye.[94]

Being socially adept can require you to do things you may have thought you would never, under any circumstances, do. Certain mores are accepted conventions—such as grammar rules, fashion, and etiquette. The more important ones involve ethics and character. A sustained leader can adjust their speech, mannerisms, stories, and anecdotes to match the social segment in which they are engaged. The sustained leader should *never*, however, engage in situational ethics. Social mores are always situational; ethical mores are unchanging and are rooted in character (1.0).

The sustained leader understands the importance of social skill development. The management of relationships to move people in the desired direction is a key indicator of a leader. An unsocial or even anti-social person has little likelihood of drawing followers to their vision and is definitely incapable of being very persuasive.

Another aspect of being socially adept is something traditionally called deportment. If you arrive at a state dinner in Bermuda shorts, you will not be taken seriously and will probably be asked to leave. In certain establishments "appropriate attire," often meaning nice dresses for women and coats and ties

---

94 Norman Schwarzkopf, and P. Petre, *It Doesn't Take a Hero: The Autobiography* (US: Bantam Books, 1992), 32.

for men, is required. Your failure to comply will earn you an invitation to leave. Despite what many people perceive as a relaxation of these social norms, how you present yourself, particularly for a first impression, will absolutely have a significant impact on how you will be perceived. Traditional attire for the clergy, Wall Street Executives, keynote speakers, and the uniforms of blue collar workers all send a clear message to those who see you. Even accused criminals are encouraged to dress up in court. Appearance matters whether we think it should or it shouldn't. And just in case you were wondering whether you can present proper deportment when you are inebriated—you can't. You also do not "handle your liquor" as well as you think you can. Any overindulgence in a public setting is never a positive trait.

> Very wise advice in this area has been provided by religious evangelist and publisher F. Edson White: "Poise is a big factor in a man's success. If I were a young man just starting out, I would talk things over with myself as a friend. I would set out to develop poise—for it can be developed. A man should learn to stand, what to do with his hands, what to do with his feet, look his man straight in the eye, dress well and look well and know he looks well. By dressing well I don't mean expensively, but neatly and in taste."[95]

The sustained leader also treats all people from all social settings with respect. Whether it is the waiter who is struggling to provide good service, the beggar on the street, or the head of state. Each is due the respect of their humanity despite their social position, and this includes a person in a poor social position due to their own volition. The socially adept sustained leader respects all people in all stations of life.

The sustained leader exposes themselves to a variety of social settings and becomes an intense observer of the environment. They develop an understanding of the differences in social settings and their role in it. Sustained leaders do not dance on tables or draw undue attention to themselves. The sustained leader becomes adept at adjusting their appearance and demeanor to fit the social setting.

---

95   B.C. Forbes, *The Forbes Scrapbook of Thoughts on the Business of Life* (New York: Forbes, Inc., 1976), 352.

This sounds like me

A lot   somewhat   just a little   not at all

Additional Resources:

John Maxwell, *There's No Such Thing as "Business" Ethics*.

Colleen S. Clarke, *Networking*.

Personal Objective:

Specific Actions:

Due Date:

1.1.2.4.1 Small Talk

WBS Dictionary: "Small Talk" is the name given to socially required banter on trivial topics as a prelude to more substantive conversations. In a social setting it is important for a leader to master small talk to put people at ease and prevent the social event from turning out like a middle school dance with all the boys on one side of the room and all the girls on the other, or to use the example of negotiations, each side staking out opposite sides of the room. Small talk might be about the weather or local sports or current events. It is generally wise to follow the old adage about never talking about politics or religion on a first date when making small talk. In negotiations (4.2.10), small talk is commonly used prior to the negotiation sessions to make everyone comfortable and to build the relationship. When you accept that relationships are more important than transactions, small talk becomes easier because it is a means to an end—a positive relationship. Use small talk to get to know people. While the "talk" may be small, the rewards are great.

Application: Extroverts tend to adopt this trait more easily. They recharge by socializing. Introverts often must force themselves to (and often learn how to) engage in small talk. It is often helpful to research the attendees at an event. Learn as much about them as you can. Do they have a common interest, such as a local sports team, or are they divided, showing allegiance to different sports teams or college affiliations? Has the weather treated them especially kindly or especially harshly recently? Have there been any national news stories that emanated from their area? Any particular news related to their industry or profession? The success of small talk is based primarily on selecting the right subjects. Rest assured that no one wants to hear details about your latest prostate trouble or colonoscopy. Small talk, by definition, is on small matters of minimal consequence.

Make notes of your interactions, especially if you feel that you do not have a good memory. Notes about family members, birthdays or anniversaries, and even particular social views are worth remembering. Jot them down. Use index cards or your portable device. Review them before the next interaction. You will impress them with your "memory" when in fact it is just another way to learn how to take a genuine interest in others.

If you accept that in some respect you are always negotiating, the idea of small talk becomes more manageable. In negotiations you are always negotiating three things—the substance of the deal, the process, and the relationship (4.2.10). Small talk most often starts this process by orienting the participants and setting the framework in which the negotiations or discussions occur. Small talk also facilitates the negotiation of the substance, process, and relationship. Small talk involves no major investment or emotional involvement until the sense of trust is built. An old Chinese adage states that the journey of 1000 miles begins with the first step. Small talk is that first step.

The sustained leader works to become adept at small talk and to be an engaging conversationalist. They study their audience and remember important details about them. Their investment is targeted at the relationship, not the immediate conversation. Those who avoid the small talk will be perceived as anti-social and often this is interpreted as not being trustworthy. The goal is simply to be pleasant and likeable without being domineering. Small talk is a safe starting point for the novice, and a place to establish a strong social base while setting others at ease for the more experienced conversationalist.

This sounds like me

A lot   somewhat   just a little   not at all

Additional Resources:
Don Gabor, *Talking with Confidence for the Painfully Shy.*
Debra Fine, *The Fine Art of Small Talk.*

Personal Objective:

Specific Actions:

Due Date:

1.1.2.4.2 Networking

WBS Dictionary: Networking here is the activity (verb) involved in engaging with your network and taking actions to grow and strengthen it. This is distinguished from the network (noun) described in 1.1.1.1. Historically, networking was sending notes, paying visits, extending invitations, and engaging in purposeful social interaction. In the more modern world much of that occurs electronically, but that does not suggest that the old ways are inappropriate. What would it mean to you to receive a handwritten note from someone? You would consider it a significantly gracious act. Do you engage effectively on the social networks? Do you always try to put your best foot forward? Does your social networking site have pictures of your latest tattoo or of you receiving recognition? Are all of your "friends" bikers and people with a long rap sheet, or C-level corporate officers? You are known by the company you keep and you need to actively engage to keep your name in front of people in a positive light. Write posts. Make constructive comments. Do not be snide or rude. Don't pile on when a group denigrates one of its members. Reach out one-on-one to members of groups. Ask good questions (4.4.1) and practice good communication skills and techniques (4.0). You never know when you will need your network, so network effectively; make sure that you are a constant contributor so that everyone is willing to step up and help you when you ask.

Application: Networking is more than just developing a very large email list. It is more than collecting business cards and scanning them into a contact list. It is *not* a numbers game. It is intentionally engaging with a broad spectrum of people and exposing yourself to a myriad of social settings in which to build rapport with a very diverse selection of people. Certainly some of this can be automated and streamlined. A good calendar that contains birthdates and anniversaries can be very effective as a reminder. The sending of the congratulatory card or message, however, should be personal.

Introverts often struggle with networking. They shouldn't. Introverts are often drained by attempting to interact with a large number of people. They shun "networking events" and strive to become "wall flowers" at large gatherings. Networking, however, is nothing more than one-on-one relationship building. And even the most introverted introverts can handle that.

Networking might occur at a large event, but the actual interaction is directly person to person. Even when you are the presenter, you understand that the best presenters use a focal point toward which to direct their energy. It's still one-on-one.

The best approach to networking should be similar to making new friends. Ask more questions about the person and let them talk. The more they talk, the less you have to. In most cases people appreciate your interest in them. Those who simply talk about themselves incessantly are considered bores. In many cases you may not be called upon to say more than what is contained in your elevator speech. Nonetheless, be prepared to share some anecdotal stories about yourself—your background, your home town, your favorite sports team, your hobbies, and other points of interest about you personally. Just don't let your nervousness force you into talking too much, too loudly, or too giggly. Practice this and use a mirror or a trusted friend to coach you. The best extemporaneous speech is very well rehearsed (!) Making a real connection with one or two people is better than collecting two dozen business cards.

When you do obtain business cards, however, make sure you make a note or two on each one. Something you want to remember about the person or some point of interest or intersection with your own life. This will help you when you get back to your desk and have no idea who all these people were.

If food is served, be very careful what you eat. No one is attractive when stuffing their face. Food spilled down your shirt or dress is not going to attract the kind of attention you want. Drink moderately, if at all. And getting a piece of spinach from the dip stuck in your teeth is not something to which many people would alert you.

Like building any relationship, look for opportunities to give rather than take. You bring something to every engagement. Capitalize on it. Offer your view, or advice, or a recent resource such as a book. (1.3.1.1). If you are there only to take, others will notice you in a bad way. This does not mean that you should not soak up whatever is being offered by others. Make notes. People are drawn to you if they feel that you are genuinely absorbing what they are offering. Thank them for the gift they have given you—their time and advice. This is an excellent time to practice active listening. (3.4.1). Make eye contact and smile. Develop a proper handshake—neither too hard nor too soft. A good coach can help you calibrate in this area.

If the conversation lags, bring up an area of interest. Comments such as, "That last panel was rather intriguing, wasn't it?" will often spark a response that carries the conversation forward, or gets it going.

If you must, force yourself into networking situations. Crash a party where no one knows you and if you totally screw up, no one there will remember or care. This is an area where practice helps.

This sounds like me

A lot	somewhat	just a little	not at all

Additional Resources:
Colleen Clarke, *Networking*.
Donna Fisher, *People Power*.

Personal Objective:

Specific Actions:

Due Date:

1.1.2.5 Uses Influence Rather than Authority

WBS Dictionary: Influence is the persuasive power of a leader to cause people (who have options to choose who they follow) to follow this particular leader. Sustained leaders understand power (1.3.3.5) in all its many forms. To some, power is simply brute force. Authority is power granted by another over certain areas of conduct. Things can be accomplished through the use of authority, power, force, or influence. This element makes a clear distinction that the strongest and most lasting form of power is influence. With authority (or compulsion) people follow direction because the authority has the ability to mete out reward and punishment. Brute force works in some environs (consider maximum security prisons), but the greatest form of power is influence. With influence, people follow the leader because they choose to. They have options. They can leave and go elsewhere, but they choose to follow this leader. The sustained leader also knows that often people must be persuaded. With no influence, there is little possibility that any efforts of persuasion will be successful.

Application: Authority tends to exhibit a dictatorial aspect. Influence deals more with persuasion and using that with a deep sense of integrity. As Stephen Covey said, "If I try to use human influence strategies and tactics of how to get other people to do what I want, to work better, to be more motivated, to like me and each other—while my character is fundamentally flawed, marked by duplicity or insincerity—then in the long run, I cannot be successful. My duplicity will breed distrust, and everything I do—even using so-called good human relations techniques—will be perceived as manipulative."[96] He rightfully notes that duplicity or insincerity—to the sustained leader that includes any lack of honesty or integrity—will put up a complete roadblock in front of influence. You simply will not be able to get there from here.

Aristotle believed that persuasion was rooted in character and that the trifecta of ethos (ethics), pathos (passion), and logos (words) were the critical elements to successful persuasion. Without a positive character any attempt to influence others will fail. When the sustained leader chooses appropriate words, has demonstrated a high ethical standard, and expresses a view with passion, people are more likely to accept the view being presented. This is the crux of influence.

Political candidates often cross this line. They are seeking the authority of a political office. To obtain it they must influence the voters to turn out and cast their vote for them. The best political leaders who did the most to grow their nation's economy and earn respect for their country on the international stage were able to influence the voters to get into office, and then continue to influence those of all political parties to join with them in solving national issues.

In some circles, especially in social media environments, the popular phrase is to refer to "authenticity" and those who best reflect authenticity are referred to as "influencers." When people are rude or show other traits of a weak character they lose followers. They lose their influence. They are seen as inauthentic. Their abuse of authority disqualifies them from filling a leadership role. The sustained leader protects their influence by protecting their character, never abuses their legitimate authority, and thereby increase their leadership potential.

This sounds like me

A lot	somewhat	just a little	not at all

Additional Resources:

Jeremie Kubicek, *Leadership is Dead*.

Orrin Woodward, et al., *Launching a Leadership Revolution*.

---

96 Stephen R. Covey, *The Seven Habits of Highly Effective People: Restoring the Character Ethic* (New York: Simon and Schuster, 1989), xx.

Personal Objective:

Specific Actions:

Due Date:

1.1.2.6 Courage

WBS Dictionary: Courage is the ability to recognize your fears and take action anyway. It favors a bias for taking action (2.3). It does not mean that you have overcome all fears or that you act rashly; it simply means you have chosen not to let the fear control you and you act with due consideration of relevant factors. Many people fear failure and too often become paralyzed with fear and the result is that no action is taken at all. They are afraid to try for fear of failure. Fears come in many shapes and sizes; everyone has their fears. Most are rational (e.g. drowning, fires) while others are less so. Leaders demonstrate courage when dealing with risk (2.1.4), and in most cases it is not physical harm that is feared. It could be a particular business strategy. It could be a set of business tactics. It could involve a merger or a hiring/firing decision. It might be disagreement with the Board of Directors or with regulators. In some parts of the country, simply commuting to work takes courage. Taking foolish risks is not courage. It is foolishness. This element also includes having the courage of your convictions—knowing WHAT you believe and being able to articulate WHY you believe it. The sustained leader is disciplined in demonstrating courage of both actions and convictions.

Application: Children are read many stories that reflect aspects of courage. From *The Little Engine That Could* to the superheroes who fight for justice, we instill a sense of courage in our children as a positive trait. Childhood fears of a monster under the bed give way to fears of peer pressure and social rejection. Adults fear financial responsibility, the loss of a job, disrupted marital situations, safety of their children, and personal safety in travel situations. It is often an act of courage to simply leave the house and interact with others. The sustained leader steps up to these challenges—large or small—with courage in action (2.3) and in conviction (5.1.1).

------------•------------

Peter Drucker

Whenever you see a successful business,
someone once made a courageous decision.

------------•------------

Unless the action is dangerous or difficult, no courage is necessary. The nature of the danger or difficulty will certainly go into the risk equation and it might be a situation that requires moral courage, e.g. to stand up to a superior who is acting in an ethically challenged manner. It might be the action of donating a kidney, donating blood, or volunteering to enter closed spaces. Any phobia we might have could trigger a need for courage whether bugs, heights, blood, or spiders. While this may be a phobia to us, there are those who subject themselves to such environments or conditions every day. Courage might manifest in physical, mental, or moral situations. In each case, the level of commitment (5.0) is being tested.

The sustained leader always keeps in mind that courage is not reflected in truly unreasonable risks. That is not courage it is foolishness. Yet not everyone will have the same sense of courage or assess the risk similarly. Another word often used for courage is fortitude which brings resilience and determination to the discussion.

Failures in leadership are frequently failures in courage. The Catholic Church did not have the courage to acknowledge there were issues of pedophilia in its ranks. The failure of Enron was a failure of people to have the courage to come forward. The failure of many political careers flows from a lack of courage from the sycophants surrounding most politicians, resulting in no one telling the emperor that he has no clothes. Courage is an indispensable trait of the sustained leader and can manifest itself in a great variety of ways. The need for physical courage less often presents itself in today's society, but there are times when life and safety are an issue. Mental courage comes from dedicating the time and effort in applying critical thinking to issues and situations. Moral courage comes from knowing the right thing to do and actually doing it, despite the costs. The sustained leader develops courage in all three.

This sounds like me

A lot   **somewhat**   **just a little**   **not at all**

Additional Resources:
John Maxwell, *Failing Forward.*
Anthony L. Iaquinto, et al., *Never Bet the Farm.*

Personal Objective:

Specific Actions:

Due Date:

1.1.2.7 Foresight

WBS Dictionary: Foresight is the ability to assess a number of variables and predict with some level of confidence what those variables will do to affect future situations. This is different from Situational Awareness (2.1.6) in that foresight is predictive in approach and situational awareness is appreciating the circumstances as they actually exist. No one's crystal ball is perfect. A sustained leader should, however, understand the environment within which they are performing to a degree that they should rarely, if ever, truly be caught by surprise. They should be in a state of constant analysis on those data elements that are important to their vision (5.1.2) and mission. Leaders should rely on their trusted advisors and network (1.1.1.1) to stay informed of information that matters. They should be able to sift through the "noise" (2.1.6.2) and concentrate on significant drivers to their environment, considering all risks (2.1.4), to assess the most likely future scenarios for their operations.

Application: Foresight, when used correctly, will provide the sustained leader with the ability to be prepared for any number of future circumstances. It is not prescience or even precognition. You don't' want to stray into the arena of clairvoyance or holding a séance. Foresight is primarily a planning tool. By determining where you are (2.1.6), where you want to be (5.1.2), and what must be done to create the desired circumstances, (all elements of Strategic Thinking, 1.3.9.3) you can assess the many variables and potential outcomes to proceed with a level of confidence. To those unaware of the intense process that has been undertaken, you might well be perceived as clairvoyant! The better practiced you become in planning the better honed your foresight will become.

All entities go through a planning process. Similarly, but on a smaller scale, even family vacations require a bit of foresight. When is the best time to visit the locale? When are the rates the best? When is the weather usually best? When are the natural flora and fauna in their most appealing state? Even after compiling all the relevant data and making plans, vacations can still be disrupted by any number of unintended events from hurricanes to civil insurrection. Thus, there is the opportunity to purchase vacation insurance. Whether the vacation goes well or the insurance must be used, the person who planned the vacation will be credited with foresight.

Foresight, therefore also includes ability to not just plan, but to have back-up plans and options. Again, what is often viewed as foresight is really just good planning. Most entities also go through a process of forecasting. They evaluate markets and competitions. They view their strengths and weaknesses against the competition. They look for new or emerging opportunities. They consider various threats to the business environment and assess the impact and probability of each. From this accumulation of data, a forecast can be put forward. This is often done in terms of confidence levels. There might be high confidence that they can grow the market by 2% over last year; somewhat less confidence that it will grow by 5%; and if everything goes really well, a possibility, with much lower confidence that it might grow by 12%.

Planning and forecasting often use statistical forecasting models. It is also common to measure performance and provide feedback to the system to improve future results. The sustained leader learns how these systems work and uses them to good advantage (2.2.6). Foresight requires good judgement. Good judgement most commonly comes from experience. And the best learning experiences often come from—using bad judgement. The sustained leader recognizes that planning and forecasting are important tools of leadership and draws on the experience of those around them as well as the tools available and data available from many sources. The proper analysis of that data provides the baseline for planning and is, in effect, the ability to have foresight. It is a developed skill that the sustained leader learns.

This sounds like me

A lot	somewhat	just a little	not at all

Additional Resources:
Mark L. Herman, et al., *Wargaming for Leaders*.
William Duggan, *Strategic Intuition*.

Personal Objective:

Specific Actions:

Due Date:

1.2 Integrity

WBS Dictionary: Integrity reflects your sense of right and wrong. When you act, or fail to act, your actions suggest those things you find acceptable and those that you find unacceptable. Within different subcultures the sense of right and wrong can be diametrically opposed to each other. Thus, integrity has less to do with external judgements of your actions than it has to do with consistency with your values and source of those values. Thus, in a gang of murderers, your integrity is measured by those mores. For sustained leadership, however, the values and the anchor for those values is based on broadly based societal standards rooted in the natural law. Thus, success within this element is calibrated on those leadership aspects most common to demonstrated success and the values reflected in a capitalistic society. While much of that is rooted in the Judeo-Christian ethic, that is not a sine qua non of leadership success. Other ethical standards can be applied in different societal applications.

Application: Alan Elliot reports that in 1948 the Rev. Billy Graham met with fellow pastors and evangelists to discuss the fact that there were charlatans pretending to be men of God, (i.e., their lives did not reflect Christian values), thus placing all of them in a bad light. They were not able to control those who falsely preached, but they could control themselves. "The team prayed, discussed the problem, and came up with a list of actions they would take to avoid falling into moral problems. They would be paid by salary instead of depending on offerings. They would work through local churches and not independently. They also committed themselves to maintaining integrity in publicity and in the reporting of attendance figures for various religious services. Finally they pledged to avoid any appearance of sexual impropriety." Elliott concludes by saying, "Integrity doesn't just happen. You must pledge yourself to it and call on your closest associates to hold you to your standards."[97]

In sales you must often be quite persuasive. Sales and marketing master Zig Ziglar has said that, "The most important persuasion tool you have in your entire arsenal is integrity." If people do not trust that you are being sincere, they will not trust anything you say even if you are saying things that will greatly help them.

Any lack of integrity will cause potential teammates to look elsewhere for leadership.

"People will not follow people who they think have no integrity. This is not simply a moral matter—that followers won't like people who lack integrity—but a material one. When you follow people you follow their judgement. If it looks as if it can be moved around by events then

---

97 Alan Elliott, *Daily Dose,* 343.

it is dangerous to give them any credibility since you may find yourself following people who do odd things."[98]

Your integrity is a matter solely within your command. You demonstrate your integrity by the choices you make. The choices tend to lead to either high ethical standards or low ones. This arena of self-regulation requires that the sustained leader controls or redirects their disruptive emotions and impulses and adapt to changing circumstances with wise choices.

--- ◦ ---

Integrity Quotes

Guard your integrity as a sacred thing; nothing is as important as the integrity of your own mind.

—Brian Tracy

Integrity is the foundation upon which all of your other values are built.

—Brian Tracy

Integrity is the essence of everything successful.
—Richard Buckminster Fuller

If you want to take the meaning of the word integrity and reduce it to its simplest terms, you'd conclude that a man of integrity is a promise keeper. When he gives you his word. You can take it to the bank. His word is good.

—Bill McCartney

Integrity is not something that you should have to think about…nor consider doing…but something in the heart that is already done…then you will see long term success.

—Doug Firebaugh

---

98   Paul Corrigan, *Shakespeare on Management (US:* Kogan Page Ltd., 2000), 112.

The highest degree of wisdom is integrity.
—**Shimon Peres**

Knowledge without integrity is dangerous and dreadful.
–**Dr. Samuel Johnson**

———————●———————

Daniel Goleman tells the story of his good friend who, just before high school graduation, was seriously, almost fatally, hurt in an accident that destroyed his small sports car. Hot rods were his passion and far outstripped his studies in terms of what got his attention. After his recovery he attended a community college where he began to take a deep interest in filmmaking. He transferred to a film school where his projects caught the eye of some Hollywood folks, one of whom, a director, hired him as an assistant. He continued to hone his trade and get more attention from those who could help him. He got studio backing for one of his scripts, but the studio control over the creative process was a major drawback to this independently-minded creator.

Another of his scripts was offered a standard Hollywood deal, but based on his prior experience, he felt that his artistic integrity was more important so he refused the deal. Using his own funds he was nearly complete with the project when those funds ran out. Nine different banks turned him down. He was clearly dispirited and was likely wondering whether he had made the right decision to turn down the original Hollywood deal. Fortunately, a tenth bank came in at the last minute, and to the joy of science fiction lovers (and those who were and didn't yet know it), the first Star Wars film reached the big screen. George Lucas' integrity in putting forth the film he wanted the public to see was ultimately the right decision. Standing by your integrity always is.

To insist on the maintenance of your integrity despite tremendous financial disruption is a trait of the sustained leader who understands that nothing can replace or purchase your integrity. Once lost, it is gone. "Self-awareness [1.3]," says Goleman, "particularly accuracy in decoding the internal cues of our body's murmurs, holds the key. Our subtle psychological reactions reflect the sum total of our experience relevant to the decision at hand."[99]

This sounds like me

A lot   **somewhat**   **just a little**   **not at all**

Additional Resources:

John MacArthur, *The Power of Integrity.*

Michael Van Dyke, *Radical Integrity.*

Norman Vincent Peale, et al., *Power of Ethical Management.*

Personal Objective:

Specific Actions:

Due Date:

1.2.1 Values

WBS Dictionary: Your values reflect what is in your heart. Too often people are not honest with themselves and very often this is not by any conscious intent. They have simply fallen into a comfort zone from which they have not considered extracting themselves. Your values govern your actions, so a hard look at your actions and reactions will provide a broad window on your values. When a person exhibits sustained leadership values it can be seen that these values are centered outside of their selfish interests. They are focused on others, not on themselves.

---

99   Daniel Goleman, *Focus: The Hidden Driver of Excellence* (New York: Harper Collins, 2015), 61-2.

They reflect no self-serving or self-deceiving (5.2.15.3) traits. They are honest (1.1) with themselves and others. And they incorporate those values into their mission (See 4.2.1.)

Application: When someone says, "I have no idea why I did that," invariably the answer lies in their values. It is sometimes said that a particular person has no values. Perhaps they will cite to a criminal—whether armed robber or embezzler. These people have values—they are just very different than perhaps yours and diverge significantly from what we accept as proper societal values. Charlie Manson has values—just not ones we share. Your actions reflect your heart. If your heart is self-centered you do not have sustained leadership values. If your heart and actions are other-centered then you are showing sustained leadership values. Be careful. Pride is a great source of self-deception and can cause you to see (or rationalize) self-centered conduct as other-centered. See it for what it is even if it is painful. That is also a sustained leadership value.

Kouzes and Posner make the following observation on the importance of an organization having values that are shared among the various team members. "Recognition of shared values provides people with common language. Tremendous energy is generated when individual, group, and organizational values are in synch. Commitment, enthusiasm, and drive are intensified: people have reasons for caring about their work. When individuals are able to care about what they are doing, they are more effective and satisfied. They experience less stress and tension. Shared values are the internal compasses that enable people to act both independently and interdependently."[100]

They go on to note that research by Kotter, et al., demonstrates that organizations with shared values grew revenue, created jobs more quickly, grew their stock price, and generated profit at levels far above those organizations without shared values.[101]

David Allen notes that your values will drive those things you agree to take on as personal obligations, and the result is that you should take on fewer such obligations. "It has been a popular concept in the self-help world that focusing on your values will simplify your life. I contend the opposite: the overwhelming amount of things that people have to do comes *from* their values. Values are critical elements for meaning and direction. But don't kid yourself—the more you focus

---

100 Kouzes and Posner, *Leadership Challenge* p. 78

101 Ibid. at 80-81 citing Posner and Westwood, "A Cross-Cultural Investigation of the Shared Values Relationship."

on them the more things you're likely to feel responsible for taking on. Your values may make it easier for you to make decisions, but don't think they'll make things any simpler."[102]

When you conduct an honest self-assessment (1.3.3.1) a significant portion of that assessment will cause you to focus on your values. Try this exercise. Write at the top of a page "These Things I Believe." Then start a list. Shoot for ten items, but if the thoughts keep flowing, just keep writing. Some people have not stopped until they have written more than 100 things they believe. It might be a personal attribute such as "I am a good writer." It might be outwardly focused such as "My parents love me." It might be altruistic, "I think segregation is a national harm." Or it might be religious focused, "I believe in Jesus Christ as my lord and savior." Don't treat this as a checklist, rather treat it like a personal brainstorming session. What do you really believe? Write that down.

Now go back to each item and ask yourself this simple question: "Why?" Why do you think you believe that statement? Give your reasons, rationale, or whatever. Perhaps you will write, "Because my family always told me this." Perhaps you will write, "Because I witnessed segregation and it was a horrible experience I will never forget." You should always know what you believe and why you believe it. As you look at the things you believe, and often more importantly, the reasons you have chosen that belief, you begin to see where your true values lie. Perhaps you wrote something like, "I believe that making accommodations for the handicapped is a terrible inconvenience for the rest of us." Fine. Not the most altruistic thought, but if it is honest—write it down. You might want to reconsider that thought—or you might not. For now, you are just taking an inventory and engaging in some critical thinking about your beliefs. This can be very eye-opening. You might not like what you see. The sustained leader will be able to state their beliefs and explain why they hold those beliefs. They will assess what this says about their values and further assess whether those are values they truly wish to hold. These sessions can be very troubling. You might conclude you are a terrible person. Don't do that. Every day you make choices about your beliefs and you can work to change them if you believe you should. The starting point is, however, to do the assessment. Then you know your starting point for assessing your values.[103]

---

102 David Allen, *Getting Things Done* (New York: Penguin Group, 2001), 228.
103 Those who engage in blogging will find that this exercise will provide them a great wealth of starting material if they are brave enough to write about their self-discovery.

Albert Einstein has cautioned that we should, "Try not to become a man of success, but a man of value." The sustained leader is a person of high values. They assess their values and can articulate why they hold these values. You do have values, but until you conduct an honest assessment, and perhaps get some honest feedback from a mentor or two, you might not be fully aware of your values and you might want to raise your own standards.

This sounds like me

A lot	somewhat	just a little	not at all

Additional Resources:
John MacArthur, *The Quest for Character*.
William J. Bennett, *The Book of Virtues*.

Personal Objective:

Specific Actions:

Due Date:

1.2.1.1 Accept Responsibility

WBS Dictionary: In 1.1.2.2 we talked about being responsible as a trait. Here we are talking about taking on accountability in a conscientious and dependable manner. There is the acceptance of responsibility in terms of meeting commitments and the additional concept of taking the responsibility for the consequences of actions taken by the leader or other member of the team. Accepting responsibility includes accepting the accountability for outcomes (positive or negative) as well as accepting the mantle of authority. It is unfair for a leader to impose on others responsibility or accountability they would not undertake on their own behalf. It is also unfair to delegate responsibility unless the authority to manage the outcome is also granted. To do otherwise is setting up the team to fail.

Application: Responsible entities, run by responsible leaders, know to do the right thing no matter the consequences. Sustained leaders do not see this as moral dilemma; the bottom line must give way to treating people properly. When an error or accident is the result of the organization's action or inaction, the sustained leader fixes it. Most are aware of the response by Johnson and Johnson when its Tylenol product was the victim of tampering. Several people died. While there was never any evidence that the company held any direct responsibility, it immediately withdrew the entire product line from the market, at considerable expense. It redesigned the packaging to make it tamper proof and when assured that it had fixed the problem, reintroduced the product to the market. It's immediate and definitive response to the crisis earned it the returned loyalty of its many past customers and the Tylenol brand remains the top pain relieving medication on the over-the-counter market.[104]

Benjamin Franklin observed that, "He that is good at making excuses is seldom good at anything else." Making excuses or blaming someone else is not the hallmark of the sustained leader. Making excuses is not accepting responsibility.

Some bosses try to lay blame for bad outcomes at the feet of their employees. The sustained leader takes the opposite approach. Unless the team knows that their leader has their best interests at heart, they will quickly turn on each other in a defensive mode that will destroy the team. Dana Perino illustrates this from her time with President Bush.

Take the New Hampshire primary loss in 2000, for example. The Bush campaign was taken by surprise when it got stomped by Senator McCain, and the team was badly rattled. In Courage and Consequence, Karl Rove says that Bush had seen plenty "floundering campaigns" and that something he learned was that you can't "shoot at a wounded staff." So Governor Bush called everyone into his suite and said that he was fully

---

104 A similar story related to the response of a responsible company involves the Bissel carpet cleaning company. See Alan Elliott, *American Dream*, 293.

responsible for the loss. He asked them to project confidence and put their game faces on. His loyalty emboldened them and that was how he "got the best out of those around him." That's the hallmark of a good leader.[105]

Yes, Ms. Perino. Yes it is.

When in a position of leadership, regardless of where in the organization that might be, the sustained leader accepts the mantle of leadership and the responsibility that goes with it. If the intent is to bail out or find a scapegoat when things go awry, then the role of leader should not be accepted. A sustained leader will never do that.

This sounds like me

A lot   **somewhat**   **just a little**   **not at all**

Additional Resources:

Michael Van Dyke, *Radical Integrity*.

Peter Drucker, *Management*.

Jeffrey Gitomer, et al., *The Little Book of Leadership*.

Personal Objective:

Specific Actions:

Due Date:

---

105 Dana Perino, *And the Good News is…: Lessons and Advice from the Bright Side* (New York: Hachette Book Group 2015), 173.

1.2.1.2 Fact Based

WBS Dictionary: You are entitled to your opinions. You are not entitled to your facts. That thought has been variously attributed, and it is absolutely true. People are free to think whatever they choose, and their opinion may be an informed opinion or a completely uninformed opinion—or anything in between. Sustained leaders understand these vagaries in human nature and seek first to understand the facts. No decision will ever be based on having 100% of the facts (2.3.6.2). Nonetheless, you ignore facts at your own peril. Sustained leaders seek to understand the facts as best they are discernible. Sustained leaders test the facts that come to them to verify their veracity. While prevarication is often not present, mistakes, errors, misunderstandings, lack of understanding (intentional or situational), and other failures of communication are ubiquitous. They are unavoidable. The most successful leaders dig for the facts and sift opinion away. Managing by rumor or innuendo is damaging. Managing by fact is enlightening and fair. And while life has never promised that it will be totally fair, basing actions and decisions on provable facts tends to provide better decisions, greater acceptance, and more positive outcomes.

Application: Most corporate attorneys have investigated their share of sexual harassment complaints. In so many of the cases there were only two people present when the event occurred and while they experienced the EXACT same events, they PERCEIVED two vastly different experiences. It is the classic "He said/She said" situation that appear to be diametrically opposed. Both cannot be true. What often escapes us, however, is that NEITHER may be true.

Dorothy Leeds reflects on the role of assumptions in our life.

While I was writing this book, I kept asking myself, "Why do we make so many assumptions?" I realized that we have to make certain assumptions on our everyday lives, or all movement would stop. When we go into a store or office building, we assume it is well built and will not fall down around us. We assume that the water we drink is safe and the food we eat is not contaminated. If we did not make these assumptions, we would spend our lives worrying about everything that could possibly go wrong.[106]

The sustained leader does not waste time worrying, but strives to identify the facts and acts on those facts—not assumptions that might be based more on emotional factors than the reality of the situation. Ms. Leeds continues: "We also make assumptions about ourselves. We all have preconceived notions about what we can or cannot do—especially about what we cannot do. We suppose that the limitations we put on ourselves are facts and not beliefs."[107] The sustained leader makes no such assumptions. In fact, the sustained leader tends to assume that things will go right, rather than wrong. The sustained leader is a consummate optimist while tempering that optimism with a continuous search for the facts. Assumptions have their role when based on facts (local health departments continually test the water and we can generally assume that it is safe). Sustained leaders recognize when there is no quality assurance mechanism in place and seek to find the facts that will support a conclusion without making bold assumptions that may turn out to be wrong.[108]

Rely on Facts

You are not entitled to your opinion. You are entitled to your informed opinion. No one is entitled to be ignorant.

—Harlan Ellison

My opinions may have changed, but not the fact that I'm right.

—Ashleigh Brilliant

---

106 Dorothy Leeds, *The 7 Powers of Questions: Secrets to Successful Communication in Life and Work* (New York: Berkely Publishing, 2000), 83.
107 Id.
108 Alan Elliott shares the story of Carrier Air conditioning that had some difficulty getting a new, more efficient coolant approved by safety officials. Until, that is, they poured some out in the official's office and struck a match. It immediately removed the regulator's biases, replacing them with facts concerning the new coolant's flammability. *American Dream*, 317.

All opinions are not equal. Some are a very great deal more robust, sophisticated and well supported in logic and argument than others.
—Douglas Adams, *The Salmon of Doubt*

Our civil rights have no dependence on our religious opinions any more than our opinions in physics or geometry....
—Thomas Jefferson, *The Statute of Virginia for Religious Freedom*

Man seeks his inward unity, but his real progress on the path depends on his capacity to refrain from distorting reality in accordance with his desires.
—Goethe

Few people are capable of expressing with equanimity opinions which differ from the prejudices of their social environment. Most people are incapable of forming such opinions.
—Albert Einstein

Your assumptions are your windows on the world. Scrub them off every once in a while, or the light won't come in.
—Isaac Asimov

Jack Welch calls this the Reality Principle. This is, he says, "Seeing the world as it really is, not as you wish it would be."[109] It permits no wishes, fantasy, hopes, or assumptions. To those who remember the early days of television, it is Jack Webb on Dragnet saying, "The facts, ma'am. Just the facts."

The separation of fact from opinion is often difficult for those who have never learned to practice critical thinking (1.3.9.1). Critical thinking relies on the testing of the information at hand, separating fact from opinion, digging deeper for more facts or more revealing facts, and applying a rational assessment to these facts to draw a conclusion. The non-critical thinker is happy to determine a conclusion, and then seek only facts or half-facts that might support that

---

109 As quoted in Brian Tracy, *How the Best Leaders Lead* (New York: AMACOM, 2010), 22.

conclusion. Bertrand Russell made the following observation: "The opinions that are held with passion are always those for which no good ground exists; indeed the passion is the measure of the holder's lack of rational conviction. Opinions in politics and religion are almost always held passionately." While quite cynical, his point has factual foundation.

Peter Senge accurately notes that "An accurate, insightful view of current reality is as important as a clear vision. Unfortunately, most of us are in the habit of imposing biases on our perceptions of current reality."[110] It is extremely difficult to remove all our biases from our views. There are always difficult facts with which we must deal. The important thing is to not succumb to the temptation to change the facts, ignore some of the facts, or shade them into half facts, also known as half-truths. Another word for half-truths is lies, and now popular in political circles, false news.

Mark Twain was a consummate story teller and humorist. He observed the human condition and made some very pointed comments about it, often laced with humor. At one time he noted that, "I am not one of those who in expressing opinions confine themselves to facts." Like us, he observed that many people held opinions that were far removed from any facts to support that opinion. In support of this, at another time, he said, "Get your facts first, and then you can distort them as much as you please." He was, of course, expressing his humor. A Marine General once said, "I have to know the rules so that I know when to break them." Since the facts of any given situation might sufficiently vary from those that caused the rule to exist, he felt that a good leader must be sufficiently fact-based to properly apply even the rules of operations and engagement.

Thomas Starr King was a California minister during the Civil War. He was given the moniker of "the orator who saved the nation" due to his loyal support of the Union cause. He was an ardent believer in the need for facts on which to base opinion. He encouraged people to know what they believed and why they believed

---

110 Andy Stanley, *The Next Generation Leader: Five Essentials for Those Who Will Shape the Future* (US: Multnomah, 2003), p. 71 quoting from Peter M. Senge, *The Fifth Discipline* (New York: Currency/Doubleday, 1990), 155. See also Jim Collins, *Good to Great* p. 89. Stanley p. 73 quoting Collins: "Leadership does not begin just with vision. It begins with getting people to confront the brutal facts and to act on the implications."

it. He said, "Be sure of the foundation of your life. Know why you live as you do. Be ready to give reason for it. Do not, in such a matter as life, build an opinion or custom on what you guess is true. Make it a matter of certainty and science."[111] Similarly, Thomas Jefferson said, "If we are to guard against ignorance and remain free, it is the responsibility of every American to be informed." Dealing with the facts protects our very liberty.

The sustained leader is always fact based. There will be opinions, but only when based on facts. Knowing what you believe and why you believe it, along with the ability to articulate the reasons, supports the standard of the sustained leader and their respect for the facts.

This sounds like me

A lot   **somewhat**   **just a little**   **not at all**

Additional Resources:

James Kouzes, et al., *The Truth about Leadership*.

Harry Frankfurt, *On Bullshit*.

Harry Frankfurt, *On Truth*.

Jeffrey Pfeffer, *Leadership BS*.

Personal Objective:

Specific Actions:

Due Date:

---

111 B.C. Forbes, *The Forbes Scrapbook of Thoughts on the Business of Life* (New York: Forbes, Inc., 1976), 289.

1.2.1.3 Reliable/Consistent/Delivers on Commitments

WBS Dictionary: While somewhat related to being responsible (1.1.2.2) reliability pertains more to consistency in action. The sustained leader is very careful in making commitments and understands that once made, commitments MUST be met. Reliability and consistency build the trust (1.1.1) that is necessary for healthy productive relationships (3.0). Being reliable simply means that a leader comes through for their team in positive ways. While some people might be reliably undependable or simply untrustworthy, the sustained leader's reliability and consistency is always in a positive vein.

Application: Alexander Hamilton, back in 1790 said, "States, like individuals, who observe their engagements, are respected and trusted: while the reverse is the fate of those who pursue an opposite conduct." He equated countries with individuals in this regard. When you honor your commitments, or "engagements" you become respected and trusted. When you do not honor your commitments, you are not respected and not trusted. People need to know that when you commit to them, you are good for your word.

Certainly one way to avoid letting people down is to never make any commitments. The sustained leader, as a matter of personal integrity as well as simply being a leader, will not disengage from people entirely. They will make commitments and they will fulfill them. As is clear to see, however, you cannot say yes to everything. The sustained leader knows when to say yes to a commitment and when to say no. Sometimes it is necessary to say no.

Consistency in this context does not mean 100% duplication in all matters. Leadership is not a manufacturing process where raw material goes in one end and finished products come out the other. Leadership is people-driven and the many variables with all individuals simply do not permit such a cookie-cutter approach. What consistency *does* mean is that *when* commitments are made—they are fulfilled. Thus, the consistency is getting the job done, but not necessarily in exactly the same way. The sustained leader will rely on their ability to assess situations and develop innovative approaches to these situations to improve them and provide the most positive outcome possible. Simply going through the same motions without recognizing that situations are different or have changed since the last time action was taken is, as Einstein has told us, the height of stupidity. This is mindless consistency and in some cases what is called malicious compliance. The sustained leader should, however, set such consistency in outcome as a goal.

Ralph Waldo Emerson has one of the most famous quotes about consistency, and it is important to see it in context. He was writing about self-reliance when he said:

> A foolish consistency is the hobgoblin of little minds, adored by little statesmen and philosophers and divines. With consistency a great soul has simply nothing to do. He may as well concern himself with his shadow on the wall. Speak what you think now in hard words, and to-morrow speak what to-morrow thinks in hard words again, though it contradict everything you said to-day. — 'Ah, so you shall be sure to be misunderstood.' — Is it so bad, then, to be misunderstood? Pythagoras was misunderstood, and Socrates, and Jesus, and Luther, and Copernicus, and Galileo, and Newton, and every pure and wise spirit that ever took flesh. To be great is to be misunderstood.

This does not mean that you seek to confuse. It means that when new facts come to light, the situation has changed and it may require a new approach. Do not let rigid adherence to consistency lead you down a path of no return. Be flexible. Be adaptable. Certainly stay true to your principles and values, but that does not mean that all situations remain the same. The sustained leader is reliable in their commitments and is consistent in applying principles and values. The sustained leader is careful when making commitments, but once made, invariably meets those commitments.

This sounds like me

A lot	somewhat	just a little	not at all

Additional Resources:

Genie Z. Laborde, *Influencing with Integrity*.

Rick Brandon, *Survival of the Savvy*.

Personal Objective:

Specific Actions:

Due Date:

1.2.1.4 Sincerity

WBS Dictionary: George Burns is quoted as saying, cynically, "Sincerity—if you can fake that, you've got it made." The word was more popular in the era of handwritten letters where everyone ended with "Sincerely" or "Sincerely Yours." Many learned in grade school, when cursive letter writing was still taught, what that word meant. Unfortunately, today it has become a perfunctory statement with little meaning. Sincerity suggests that what is being conveyed is free from deceit or hypocrisy. It reflects an honesty of expression with warmth and genuine caring about the person. It is intended to be a relationship-facilitating term. It suggests a direct forthrightness to what is being communicated without duplicity, prevarication, or hidden agenda (5.2.7).

Application: When we say someone is sincere we mean that they are acting without any pretense, deceit, or hypocrisy. They are telling the truth, being honest, and can be trusted to act in your best interests. Sincere people are truthful and genuine. They are acting in a way that is true to themselves. The sustained leader should be sincere in all of their actions and words. Anything less will ultimately be seen as deceitful and will affect the trust others place in them.

Insincere people will often say what they believe is expected to please another when the sentiment is not truly felt. To some, there is no harm in the "little white lies" but others disagree. This does not mean that you should go out of your way to offend. It is better to just remain silent than to tell a lie of any color.

Sincerity is a virtue, like patience. Sincerity comes from the heart and encompasses true feelings and beliefs. The thoughts and desires of the speaker are actually made subservient to the needs of the other. When we speak of virtues, it always seems that we must draw on the wisdom of Aristotle who spoke frequently on sincerity. It is a word derived from the Latin *sincerus* which means clean or pure. It relates to "first growth" as being fresh.[112] Aristotle viewed virtues as positive traits while recognizing that a deficiency of the virtue or an excess of the virtue were vices and not virtues at all. The deficiency of sincerity he referred to as irony or self-deprecation. The excess vice was boastfulness. Thus, sincerity lies between those two vices.

Aristotle noted how the concept of sincerity fit within the concept of excellence and how your choices will affect your destiny most directly. "Excellence is never an accident. It is always the result of high intention, sincere effort, and intelligent execution; it represents the wise choice of many alternatives—choice, not chance, determines your destiny."

In discussions on sincerity many other words arise with a similar meaning. Other common words include authenticity, candor, honesty, realism, legitimacy, faithfulness, and validity. Some of these are addressed in other elements of the Sustained Leader WBS. There is overlap among many of these words and concepts as, perhaps, there should be. Each reflects a slightly different positive aspect of character traits within the concept of integrity.

One important point remains in our discussion. Sincerity can be misdirected in that the person may genuinely believe they are acting in another's best interest, but it is not, in fact, helping that person. When a parent helps a child too much with their homework, or is a bit vocally loud in their disciplinary communications, the intent might be sincere, but the effect may not be helpful. In business, a boss might volunteer a team member for a particular assignment without realizing that it might negatively affect that person's home life. A person might make a donation in another's name—to a purpose that the person would not voluntarily support. All good intentions and sincere, but misdirected.

---

112 There is a popular legend that "sincere" derives from Latin words meaning "without wax." To cover up flaws, it's been alleged, sculptors would fill the flaws with wax. Thus, a "true" piece of art would be without wax fillers. The best linguists seem to believe that this is legend and that the "first growth" is the best etymology.

It might be difficult to separate the actions from the intent. The caution is to be aware that you cannot always read another's heart. When sincerity is misdirected, the sustained leader pauses to consider the intent behind the action and to appreciate the intent. Such graciousness is a good trait for a sustained leader as well.

This sounds like me

A lot	somewhat	just a little	not at all

Additional Resources:
William Bennett, *The Moral Compass*.
John MacArthur, *The Quest for Character*.

Personal Objective:

Specific Actions:

Due Date:

1.2.1.5 Loyalty

WBS Dictionary: Loyalty is a faithfulness to commitments or obligations. It includes obligations to people with whom we share trust and being faithful to our values. Loyalty may also involve tough love when our values are being trounced (by others or ourselves) or people are being disparaged. Loyalty is a strong sense of fidelity—adherence to the facts, and especially the ugly ones. Loyalty can be measured by the actions of the sustained leader. Loyalty can be enhanced or hurt by both action and non-action. Failure to act when you should is as culpable as acting inappropriately. Loyalty is often measured by the perception of others in observing the degree to which a person will go to support a friend or deeply held value.

Application: Benedict Arnold was a traitor. There is no question that he attempted to shift his loyalties in the midst of the Revolutionary War. He was found out and escaped. Some of his British handlers were not so fortunate. His actions could have turned the tide of the war. Like all traitors, he is universally considered disloyal.

When you say, "I am loyal" you have to define what it is to which you are expressing strong support or allegiance. It is, in its essence, a feeling or sentiment. It is sufficiently strong to cause you to take action that expresses the feeling. If you are loyal, then you will spring to the defense of the person or cause toward which you feel the loyalty. You might express this toward your country, school, individual, or other identified group that might include a company, a political party, a religion, a social objective, or any other identifiable entity. Loyalty can also be expressed toward causes and beliefs. People often are loyal to their vegan principles, or green initiatives, or racial parity, or any other cause toward which you feel strongly. If you look at where you invest your time, talent, and riches you will quickly determine where your loyalties lie.

Loyalty tends to be long-lasting. When someone identifies a charity they wish to support, it is often the case that they continue to support that charity or cause for many years. Fidelity is another term for loyalty that is often applied in marriages. A lack of fidelity means that one member of the pair has shared intimacies with someone other than the spouse. This is a breach of fidelity; it is the violation of a vow ("to have and to hold…until death do we part"); it is a failure of loyalty.

There is no requirement that the sustained leader be intensely loyal to the point of devotion to anything in particular. While followers will seek out those who have demonstrated loyalty in some capacity, the more important aspect is the absence of disloyalty. You do not have to be passionately loyal to anything in particular, but one act of disloyalty will destroy the confidence others might place in you. The minimal levels of loyalty would include, for example, a refusal to breach confidences whether under a business non-disclosure agreement or the confidence shared by a friend. If you do not wish to keep such confidences you must not allow yourself to be invited into such positions. In this way you remain loyal to your personal principle not to breach any confidences. Like giving your word, if you give it you must honor the commitment. With loyalty, if you allow confidences to come to you, you must maintain them as confidences. It was Ben Franklin who said, "Three may keep a secret if two of them are dead."

When you adopt this minimalist approach, however, you are depriving yourself of more intimate relationships and the ability to have the mutual trust and loyalty that comes from close personal friendships. Loyalty must be a two-way street, so while you might attempt an isolationist approach, you will not be called upon to lead. Once tapped to serve as a leader, you *must* be loyal to the team, its mission, its vision, and its goals. The refusal to accept such responsibility does not make you a bad person, just not a strong leader. Conversely, being disloyal will disqualify you from your leadership roles. The sustained leader will identify where their loyalties lie and remain faithful to them.

This sounds like me

A lot	somewhat	just a little	not at all

Additional Resources:

Brian Kilmeade, et al., *George Washington's Secret Six*.

Dennis G. McCarthy, *The Loyalty Link*.

Personal Objective:

Specific Actions:

Due Date:

1.2.1.6 Engenders mutual respect

WBS Dictionary: Mutual respect among team members indicates that each member of the team can place reliance on the other team members with confidence that the team member will do as expected. It expects the other team members to live up to their commitments and meet their obligations. Teambuilding is a structural necessity and involves those who are demonstrably team players (2.2.2). Today's workforce must be multidisciplinary and the only way to achieve that is through the formation of teams that brings a diversity of talent together. A team consists of those who have a sense of shared values, complimentary capabilities, and a focus on a common mission. The mutual respect that derives from the shared values extends to the recognition that each team member brings a unique set of capabilities which, when combined with the rest of the team capabilities, creates a unique team. The whole becomes greater than the sum of the parts. This creates a defined, although perhaps small, society with a common sense of values and constructs that enhance performance of the team as a whole. This is the mutual respect among the team members to which all sustained leaders adhere.

Application: When you respect someone you treat their confidence with deference. You do not use information you may have gleaned from confidential encounters in a manner that would hurt them. As counterpoint, Robert Greene suggests, in Law #33, that you should discover each person's "thumbscrew," i.e. the one thing you can use against them successfully. "'Tis the art of setting their wills in action," he says quoting Baltasar Gracian. "It needs more skill than resolution. You must know where to get at anyone. Every volition has a special motive which varies according to taste. All men are idolaters, some of fame, others of self-interest, most of pleasure. Skill consists in knowing these idols in order to bring them into play. Knowing any man's mainspring of motive you have as it were the key to his will."[113] This point of view is clearly Machiavellian, meaning that it is intentionally cunning, deceptive, and opportunistic, done solely for personal gain or advantage. It is dishonest and manipulative. It is, in other words, something a sustained leader would never do. It is raised here as an example of one of the primary ways in which trust can be destroyed. People do not respect those who act in such a fashion and would never voluntarily follow them.

---

113 Robert Greene, *The 48 Laws of Power* (New York: Penguin Books, 1998), 281.

George Orwell, in his novel *1984*, addresses a similar concept. In the controlled society where Big Brother is always watching, those in control learn the one thing that will break every individual. And when needed, they use that against the individual.

> "You asked me once," said O'Brien, "what was in Room 101. I told you that you knew the answer already. Everyone knows it. The thing that is in Room 101 is the worst thing in the world."
>
> ———————
>
> "The worst thing in the world," said O'Brien, "varies from individual to individual. It may be burial alive, or death by fire, or by drowning, or by impalement, or fifty other deaths. There are cases where it is some quite trivial thing, not even fatal."[114]

Quality authority Phillip B. Crosby notes that quality is only one thing that deteriorates as morality in business erodes. While the integrity of most people is strong, it can diminish over time if the team sees the leader setting a bad example. Team members will not respect their leaders if they see them shaving the numbers, removing company property, or fudging their expense reports. Community standards are maintained only to the level of the leaders; certainly no higher. This is why the Rule of Law is so important in a civilized society. No one is above the law; the laws are fair and administered fairly, the laws are clear and people can understand what the laws are. Whether we are talking about the laws of a society, the corporate policies and procedures, or the rules applicable to your team, the standards must not only be set high, but maintained at that level by everyone on the team. Any diminution of those rules will affect the entire team negatively. The first sign of such a failure is when the team loses its mutual respect for each other.

There are many ways to destroy the trust between or among people. This is only one of them, albeit a rather severe one. It is naive to believe that some people do not do this. They do. They consider it a particular talent. You will see it in business, in politics, and yes, even in religion. The sustained leader understands the level of respect due all people, whether part of their team or

---

114 George Orwell, *1984*. (New York: Penguin Group, 1949), 283.

part of the competition. There is a sense of human dignity that the sustained leader respects at all times and in all places. Mutual respect takes time to develop and must be protected by both sides of the arrangement. Either one can take an action, say something, or fail to act or speak which in a mere heartbeat destroys a lengthy process of building respect for each other. Constant vigilance is required.

This sounds like me

A lot   somewhat   **just a little**   not at all

Additional Resources:
Patrick Lencioni, *The Five Dysfunctions of a Team.*
William Bennett, *The Book of Virtues.*
Personal Objective:

Specific Actions:

Due Date:

1.2.1.7 Always Pursues Excellence

WBS Dictionary: The pursuit of excellence is a never-ending process. Most organizations have continuous improvement programs, six sigma/lean improvement programs, and tout their use of best practices. Physical operations can always be improved. This element is more focused on personal achievement. A pursuit of high quality excellence is generally a commendable trait; like most traits, carried to an extreme it becomes a detriment. That ugly side is perfectionism. Perfectionism prevents progress. It prevents accomplishment of tasks. It can impact the keeping of commitments and can cause failure throughout the organization. Thus, this element becomes one of balance—at some point "good enough" has to be acceptable, while the constant pursuit of excellence should be reflected in the improvement of the processes in order to continue the pursuit of excellence.

Application: On the concept of excellence Aristotle wrote, "Excellence is an art won by training and habituation. We do not act rightly because we have virtue or excellence, but we rather have those because we have acted rightly. We are what we repeatedly do. Excellence, then, is not an act but a habit." In other words, you don't "do" excellence, you perform whatever tasks you choose and in the performance choose to do the best you possibly can. This yields excellence. Keep in mind that everyone everywhere who tries something new for the first time, will not produce excellence. When you watch the Olympics, do you think about how many times the net or floor mats had to catch these stunning performers? You know they have fallen. Even now at the Olympic level of their performance they sometimes fail. And then they get up and they try it again, with just a little bit more excellence.

What is excellent for you may mean nothing to others. Excellent for you might be to bench press 100 pounds. For the gym rat, it's 400 or nothing. Thus, you should not be comparing yourself to others and what might be a standard of excellence for them. Abraham Lincoln said, "I do the very best I know how, the very best I can, and I mean to keep doing so until the end." Excellence comes from doing your best each time.

In element 2.2.1 we talk about being excellent in one primary field. And with sufficient focus, study, practice, and determination you should attempt to be the best in your field—whatever that field might be. You will not, however, be capable of being the best in all things. You should still pursue excellence in everything you do, but do not refuse to do something just because you will not get it exactly right on the first try. Everyone was an amateur at everything the first time they tried.

Set your standards high. Expect the best from yourself and your team. "It's a funny thing about life," said author W. Somerset Maugham, "if you refuse to accept anything but the best, you very often get it." So seek the best, pursue the best, search out excellence wherever you can find it. But don't beat yourself up over it so long as you have done your best.

Alan C. Elliott tells the story of baseball great Hank Aaron who had a very sick baby. Father Seblica came into his life and showed great caring and compassion. Whatever he did, he did vigorously and tirelessly. Hank asked him what kept him going, Father Seblica said, "I do what I can, and then some." If you were to apply this to your life, you would quickly begin to see a clear move to greater productivity and excellence.[115] George Allen has noted that "The difference between mediocrity and greatness is extra effort." Always make the effort.

There is a caution to this element. When you are a perfectionist you will quickly discover that nothing you ever do will truly reach the point of perfection. No matter what sports record gets broken, someone, somewhere, sometime will break that record as well. Seth Godin has written many blogs on the point of being "good enough." When you will only accept perfection, you will ultimately not accomplish anything. So where is that balance between getting product out the door and insisting only on perfection?

The sustained leader understands that perfection is a laudable goal, albeit not often achievable. Even where six sigma standards apply (that's 3.4 defective features per million opportunities) such as airplane landings, anyone who has flown with any regularity knows there are hard and soft landings. Everyone is safe, and as many military pilots have said, any landing you can walk away from is a good landing. So while you may want to fly with a pilot who has the exact same number of takeoffs and landings, very few landings are considered "perfect."

Nonetheless, you should not let the sense of perfection dissuade you from pursuing excellence. Do not let perfect be the thing that keeps you from being "good enough" and indeed, as excellent as you can be. Even the best batters only get on base about 1/3 of the time. They are considered excellent players, but not perfect.

The sustained leader always pursues excellence. If perfection can be achieved, all the better. If you have done the best you possibly can, accept that and move on. Each time, try to improve and be even more excellent. If you do not achieve perfection, however, it is not the end of the world.

This sounds like me

A lot	somewhat	just a little	not at all

115 Alan C. Elliott, *American Dream* p. 260

Additional Resources:

James D. Murphy, *The Debrief Imperative*.

Tom Peters, et al., *In Search of Excellence*.

Robert Pirsig, *Zen and the Art of Motorcycle Maintenance*.

"Barking up the Wrong Tree" http://www.bakadesuyo.com/2014/08/most-organized-people/?utm_source=%22Barking+Up+The+Wrong+Tree%22+Weekly+Newsletter&utm_campaign=a550ed2dc2-expert_8_21_2016&utm_medium=email&utm_term=0_78d4c08a64-a550ed2dc2-57230737

Personal Objective:

Specific Actions:

Due Date:

1.2.1.8 Authenticity

WBS Dictionary: Authenticity of anything is based on an assessment that suggests that it is genuine and not false or copied. It is original. Authenticity is a complete lack of phoniness. It is entitled to deference and acceptance because its evidence is in agreement with known facts or experience. People place their trust in authentic leaders because of a belief, based on evidence and facts, that assures them that this leader will not mislead, prevaricate, self-aggrandize, or otherwise seek personal interests (5.2) rather than organizational interests. The authentic leader places their loyalty within their own organization and never betrays that loyalty. An authentic leader is considered "the real thing." They are not resting on past laurels, borrowed credibility, false pretense, or pretending to be guided by one set of values when the facts and experiences of those around them suggest that there is a falsity, at worst, or a hidden agenda, at best, to their claims and positions.

Application: The pretender will try to exhibit a genuine sense of caring. Such pretenders are most often found out because they lack the genuine caring that is paramount to this element. Their falsity is discovered eventually and sadly there are many who participate in the political arena for whom it can never be said that they are authentic. A movie starring Leonardo DiCaprio and Tom Hanks called "Catch Me if You Can" told the story of Frank Abagnale who took on a variety of personas as he lived a string of false lives. At times he pretended to be an airline pilot, a doctor, and a legal prosecutor. His cons netted him millions of dollars. He was successful for many years in his cons and was particularly successful in bank forgery. His lack of authenticity finally brought his crime spree to an end and he went to prison, only to ultimately end up working for the FBI. His ability at forgery had taught him so much that he was particularly adept at spotting other forgeries. Frank Abagnale was an authentic forger. He was inauthentic as a pilot, doctor, and lawyer.

Nicolo Machiavelli lived in the 1500's where he advised local politicians. He lived in a different time and counseled the aristocracy. His values were, by today's standards, a bit questionable. For example he said, "For a long time I have not said what I believed, nor do I ever believe what I say, and if indeed sometimes I do happen to tell the truth, I hide it among so many lies that it is hard to find."[116] This is what is meant when someone refers to another as being Machiavellian—expressing ways to gather power without any necessary underlying value system. There are many who believe this to be a proper way to gather power; it is not, however, how a sustained leader demonstrates their authenticity. Machiavelli, was authentic in his own right, not hiding behind a value system to which he did not subscribe. Being authentic is being true to yourself—to your own nature. It is not fake, false, or pretentious. Being authentic is being genuine and of undisputed origin. This is not to say that the sustained leader does not work to continually improve themselves, and thereby, in a way, re-invent themselves, creating a new authenticity about who they are.

---

116 In a letter to Francesco Guicciardini, May 17, 1521, quoted in Robert Greene, *The 48 Laws of Power* (New York: Penguin Books, 1998), 321.

Abraham Lincoln

I am not bound to win, but I am bound to be true. I am not bound to succeed, but I am bound to live by the light that I have. I must stand with anybody that stands right, and stand with him while he is right, and part with him when he goes wrong.

For example, it is often said that you should dress for the position you aspire to, not the position you hold. If your peers are the jeans and a t-shirt kind of folks, walking in with a coat and tie simply because you want to be CEO some day is not authentic. You should care about your appearance and make sure that if you are going to dress like your peer group you do not show up with dirty jeans, holes in inappropriate spots, T-shirts with questionable legends (or those of a competitor), or other attire that might offend or set you apart too much. When you dress authentically you wear what is comfortable to you, perhaps similar to your peer group. If your aspirations are to get the corner office, you should try to dress somewhat similar to those who occupy those offices. This is not being pretentious or in-authentic; it is establishing your own authenticity for who you are and who you aspire to be. Ideally it would show that you care about your appearance, the reflection you have on your employer, and your desire to continually grow and improve. Many millennials who got tattoos and visible piercings discovered that their peer group often found them to be authentic within their cultural. It does not often make them stand out in a positive way, however, to those who hold decision-making authority over certain career opportunities. If tattoos and piercings are the real you, by all means, be true to yourself. Accept, however, that this authenticity is not always going to be acceptable to other peer groups and may limit your leadership opportunities.

At the same time, pretending to be what you are not, and are not comfortable being, is not authentic. Self-improvement requires not only that you learn new habits and customs, but also work to rid yourself of your less desirable traits. The sustained leader knows who they are, the journey they are on, and what advancement means to them. They are authentic to themselves and to the peer group with which they choose to identify. Falseness, phoniness, pretensions, affectations, and deception are too easily seen through and will damage the leader's credibility. The authentic leader learns to be the best "you" you can ever be; there will never be another you.

This sounds like me

A lot   **somewhat**   **just a little**   **not at all**

Additional Resources:
Bill George, et al., *Authentic Leadership*.
Ron Jenson, *Achieving Authentic Success*.
Robert W. Terry, et al., *Seven Zones for Leadership*.

Personal Objective:

Specific Actions:

Due Date:

1.2.2 Spiritual

WBS Dictionary: The spiritual side of a leader reflects where they have set their anchor. Their values (1.2.1) may or may not be set from a spiritual perspective, but they are nonetheless set by something, even if that something is total randomness. For our purposes, we consider this element from two perspectives. The first is from the Judeo Christian perspective that recognizes the God of Abraham and Jacob and accepts the Bible as the revelation of God. We also provide an alternate view of pure humanism where there is no god, no afterlife, and all man has, or is, is what he has made of and for himself in this life. In either instance, all men, and anthropologically all societies, recognize some form of deity. Spirituality, even if humanistic, is a constant, and it does provide the anchor by which the sustained leader acts.

Application: William Ury writes, "In the end, each of us must answer the question 'Who is responsible for meeting my core psychological needs?' If we answer 'someone else,' we will give our power away to them. But, if we answer, 'ourselves,' we can reclaim the power to change our life and our future."[117] In other words, what is the source of your convictions? The sustained leader knows what they believe and why they believe it. Everyone has a spiritual center—it is part of the human condition. Some try to destroy it; some align with bad influences (e.g. gangs, thugs, and perverts). Others have a strong moral center based on religious convictions and a firm understanding of their role in the world created by God. It is key that the sustained leader recognize that their psychological needs are best met within their religious convictions. The sustained leader with a strong moral center commands self-leadership. They do not despair that their sins disqualify them from many things; they rejoice in the knowledge of their salvation. They know that all have sinned and fall short of the glory of God. They recognize that blame, and guilt, and yes even shame, are tools of control that are not healthy—for them or those they lead. They accept their faults and setbacks, not as a steady diet, but as a natural condition of man. Thus, they seek a higher power to confess and improve. And with each error, false step, and even failure they learn and improve. Making errors is not failure. Making the same error over and over may suggest a great need to reassess whether true confession (which means to agree with God) and repentance has occurred. In the Judeo Christian ethic, false confession does not necessarily disqualify you from salvation but violates a command given by the God they claim to love.

Maya Angelou notes that forgiving yourself for your mistakes is crucial. "If we all hold on to the mistake, we can't see our own glory in the mirror because we have the mistake between our faces and the mirror."[118]

---

117 William Ury, *Getting to Yes with Yourself: And Other Worthy Opponents* (US: HarperOne, 2015), 59.
118 Quoted in Ury, 102.

Abraham Lincoln said, "I have been driven many times to my knees by the overwhelming conviction that I had nowhere else to go." This is a common lament of many Christians, but it is a bit curious. Why is falling to your knees to pray—to ask forgiveness, to honor God's glory, to petition—the LAST thing we humans tend to do. If we practice true Christianity, we should "pray without ceasing." Jesus prayed all the time. He told us to do so as well. The spiritual sustained leader does not appeal to prayer as a last resort.

When you adopt a humanistic approach to your spirituality you do not recognize any god. You might be an atheist or agnostic. If you adopt agnosticism, to the degree you might believe there is a god, you perceive them as irrelevant to your day-to-day life. Regardless, the rejection of the Judeo-Christian ethic and the God of Abraham simply takes that ethical structure out of your frame of reference. Most people do not leave a void; they fill their spiritual need with a sense of doing good, being kind, being one with nature, or some other sense of spirituality. This then becomes their moral imperative. The sustained leader will take to heart the concepts of character and integrity as described in this WBS with or without the moral anchor of any scripture, or a scripture that is different than the Judeo-Christian ethic. In all cases, our perception of our spirituality is fundamental to our existence and shapes our perception of ourselves and the world around us.

Growing as a sustained leader requires that you recognize your moral anchor and remain true to that fundamental precept of your humanity.

This sounds like me

| **A lot** | **somewhat** | **just a little** | **not at all** |

Additional Resources:

Your preferred religious reference.

Robert Mandrou, et al., *History of European Thought.*

Personal Objective:

Specific Actions:

Due Date:

1.2.2.1 Strong Moral Compass

WBS Dictionary: A compass works because the earth has a molten center that creates a magnetic field as the earth spins. This creates magnetic poles that cause a compass to point to magnetic north, providing a world-wide reference point that is the same in all times, places, and circumstances. Having a strong moral compass says that you have a set of values that will be maintained regardless of the time, place, or circumstances. It is objective and external. You reject situational ethics and have accepted a reference point for your morals against which you measure every action you take. While you are not perfect and sometimes act contrary to that compass, you recognize the shortcoming and take appropriate remedial actions. Among those are to learn from the experience, vow to make every effort not to let it repeat, and from the Judeo-Christian perspective, confess the sin. A strong moral compass requires that you understand the philosophical principles on which your beliefs rest. You have studied them, researched them, and made a personal commitment to adhere to them. You accept them as unchanging based on circumstances, time, place, temptation (in nature or magnitude), or consequences. You have made this moral compass your determining guidepost in all decisions and actions. You are not boastful about it, yet those who are around you for any length of time will be able to discern that you follow a set of standards and hold yourself accountable to those standards.

Application: Stephen Covey has written about the importance of having a moral compass and notes that principles are the "true north" to which the moral compass should point. Values, he has said, are the maps; principles are the actual territory. Maps become outdated; principles are permanent and derive directly from natural law. You can violate natural law, but you cannot escape the consequences of violating that law. Covey has said:

Principles are not practices. Practices are specific activities or actions that work in one circumstance but not necessarily in another. If you manage by practices and lead by policies, your people don't have to be the experts; they don't have to exercise judgment, because all of the judgment and wisdom is provided them in the form of rules and regulations.

If you focus on principles, you empower everyone who understands those principles to act without constant monitoring, evaluating, correcting or controlling. Principles have universal application. And when these are internalized into habits, they empower people to create a wide variety of practices to deal with different situations.[119]

In other words, you want people to develop a proper moral compass. It will guide everything they do. If your only requirement is for compliance, you might get them to comply, but once the maps change, they will be lost without the principles against which to measure their actions.

Elizabeth Dole served as Secretary of Transportation in the Reagan Administration and Secretary of Labor in the Bush administration. From 2003 to 2009 she served as North Carolina's first female Senator. She later headed the American Red Cross. Clearly an intelligent and highly accomplished woman. She was asked to present the commencement address to Duke University, her alma mater, in 2000. In that address she said, "In the final analysis, it is your moral compass that counts far more than any bank balance, any resume, and yes, any diploma." She understands that doing right is far more important than any other accomplishment you might achieve or even aspire to achieve.

Too often today we see arguments put forward advocating a relative standard to right and wrong. Many of these argue against natural law and in fact will often deny that any natural law exists. The American founding fathers recognized the importance of natural law (both the Declaration of Independence and the US Constitution are natural law documents), often appealing to "providence" as the source. In the Declaration they even said that "We hold these truths to be self-evident: That all men are created equal; that they are endowed *by their*

---

119 "Messages from the Masters" Covey, Steven R. MORAL COMPASSING (Part Two, 2006). No longer available on the web.

Creator with certain unalienable rights...." It is interesting that some who argue against natural law misquote that phrase by deleting the "by their Creator" clause. If there is no creator there is no god. If there is no god there can be no God-given law. If there is no God-given law, then man is free to make up the rules as they go along. It might be couched in terms of fairness or equality, but in every case it establishes a relative view of right and wrong. It is difficult to establish an accurate sense of your moral compass without the necessary reference point of true north, i.e. absolute sense of right and wrong. As General Patton reminded us, "Moral courage is the most valuable and usually the most absent characteristic in men"

The sustained leader has a strong moral compass and a clear view of right and wrong. When they violate those principles their compass tells them that they have gone off course and must readjust to get back on the right path.

This sounds like me

| **A lot** | **somewhat** | **just a little** | **not at all** |

Additional Resources:

John Maxwell, *Ethics 101*.

Judith A. Boss, *Analyzing Moral Issues*.

James Rachels, *The Elements of Moral Philosophy*.

Personal Objective:

Specific Actions:

Due Date:

1.2.2.2 Nurture a Strong Conscience

WBS Dictionary: All people have an inherent sense of right and wrong that seems to stem from their very nature of being human. At the same time, all people have free will and can make whatever choices they decide to make, whether good or bad. Most people will hear a voice inside of them when they do something they know to be wrong and we refer to this as our conscience. Despite this apparent in-built sense of right and wrong, if it is ignored consistently, it will sit down and shut up (or alternatively, join the other side and encourage you to continue making bad choices—choices that you will perceive as "correct.") On the other hand, a consistent record of making good choices nurtures your conscience and strengthens its ability to be heard and followed. Sustained leaders are often required to make decisions quickly and without having access to all of the facts to fully understand the situation. Good situational awareness (2.1.6) coupled with a strong, well-developed conscience results in better decision making (2.3.6). A poorly developed conscience most often leads to a series of increasingly bad decisions that can ultimately result in the disqualification of the person as a leader.

Application: Many people make decisions based on their gut. It just feels right. Some end up making good decisions. More often, the decision is no better than random choices. Occasionally, even worse. Given free will, as man has been given, you have the option of listening to that voice inside of you or not. If you don't listen often enough, it is possible to sear your conscience. A history of poor choices makes reliance on your conscience very problematic. Since it can be trained, it can be trained to make bad (from a moral perspective) choices. A history of bad choices tends to lead to more bad choices. It's like the little white lie that causes more lies. Once you start, it becomes easier and easier to tell lies. In a letter to Peter Carr in 1785, Thomas Jefferson made the following observation about the human tendency to tell lies:

> It is of great importance to set a resolution, not to be shaken, never to tell an untruth. There is no vice so mean, so pitiful, so contemptible; and he who permits himself to tell a lie once, finds it much easier to do it a second and a third time, till at length it becomes habitual; he tells lies without attending to it, and truths without the world's believing him. This

falsehood of the tongue leads to that of the heart, and in time depraves all its good disposition.

Conversely, dealing with the truth, making good decisions, listening to your conscience, and paying attention to your moral compass trains your conscience in a positive way. Only then can you say that your "gut" is reliable. Examine yourself and assess whether your conscience can be trusted. The Greek playwright Euripides said, "There is one thing alone that stands the brunt of life throughout its course: a quiet conscience." Similarly, George Washington advised us to, "Labour to keep alive in your Breast that Little Spark of Celestial fire Called Conscience."[120]

So is guilt a good thing? Guilt is that feeling that comes from acting against what your conscience is telling you. Christians believe this is the voice of the Holy Spirit chastening you. Research published in the Harvard Business Review shows that "People who are prone to guilt tend to work harder and perform better than people who are not guilt-prone. They are also perceived to be more capable leaders."[121] Why might this be the case? If you feel guilt you are honing your ability to discern right and wrong. You know, and want to act, in a right manner. Your team will perceive this. If, on the other hand, you act capriciously or cavalierly toward others and the decisions you make without concern or guilt toward those who are affected negatively, your team will perceive this as well. In the Harvard study, it was found that superiors also noted these tendencies, reflecting them in performance reviews. You can incapacitate yourself by being excessively guilt-ridden, but studies show that a bit of guilt can be a good thing. It seems to nurture a strong conscience.

The sustained leader will take to heart the words of Nido Qubein, a noted author and speaker who has said, "Whether you are a success or a failure in life has little to do with your circumstances; it has much more to do with your choices."[122] Make good choices.

---

120 George Washington, *Rules of Civility & Decent Behaviour In Company and Conversation.* (Mount Vernon Ladies Association, Mount Vernon, VA: Mount Vernon Ladies Association, 1989). (Rule 110)

121 "Barking Up the Wrong Tree." http://www.bakadesuyo. com/2012/03/do-guilt-ridden-people-make-great-leaders/?utm_ source=%22Barking+Up+The+Wrong+Tree%22+Weekly+Newsletter&utm_ campaign=abd8201f6a-guilt_11_15_2015&utm_medium=email&utm_term=0_78d4c08a64- abd8201f6a-57230737 Accessed 08/20/16

122 Cited in John C. Maxwell, *The 15 Invaluable Laws of Growth* (New York: Center Street, 2012), 86.

This sounds like me

A lot   **somewhat**   **just a little**   **not at all**

Additional Resources:

George Washington, *Rules of Civility & Decent Behaviour In Company and Conversation.*

John MacArthur, *The Book on Leadership.*

Personal Objective:

Specific Actions:

Due Date:

1.2.2.3 Personal Life in Order

WBS Dictionary: A leader must have their personal life in order. This means that there are no secrets within the family structure. No affairs, no financial mismanagement, taxes paid, and no avoidable lawsuits or investigations. Some believe that this includes having "perfect" children, but that is not included here insofar as children, upon reaching the age of majority tend to follow their own paths—sometimes temporarily; sometimes more permanently. Parents cannot be held fully responsible for their children's choices. Even so, having your own personal life in order—those things that a person can reasonably control, reflects well on their leadership. Having your personal life in order suggests that you are not carrying around great guilt over your past actions, that you know how to control your temper and libido, and do not engage in other destructive behaviors. You do not have a drinking or gambling problem, are hospitable to friends and strangers, and have the capacity to teach others. You are not violent, given to too much wine, not greedy, quarrelsome, or covetous. A leader must be gentle, experienced, not full of pride, and he must be well reputed. And a leader MUST have their financial affairs in order and not be tempted to engage in activities because of financial distress or even blackmail. This is a very tall order, but sustained leaders understand this and work diligently on a day to day basis to ensure that they maintain that positive reputation.

Application: Money does not solve every problem. In truth, money often creates more problems than it solves. This seems counter-intuitive to many, especially those who fail to understand the proper role of money in their lives. Money is not "good" or "bad." Money is, in itself, amoral. It is what you *do* with the money entrusted to you that makes it good or bad. That is why it is perceived that your character is reflected in how you handle money—your own and others. From a biblical perspective, many people misquote the lesson by saying that money is the root of all evil. The proper quote, however, is that the ***love*** of money is the root of all kinds of evil.[123] Again, the money is neutral. It is your reaction to it that creates the good or evil. The sustained leader is clear on this point and strives to teach others its importance. In fact, financial problems are most often an indicator of other personal issues. They simply manifest themselves in a financial environment.

Survey after survey has demonstrated that having more money does not create happiness. Most research suggests that those who make more money are more prone to affairs, cheating on taxes, and are less generous than those with less. Having more money breeds selfishness and self-centeredness. Yes, there are generous philanthropists, but that seems to be the exception. Even those who give their money away too often do it for selfish reasons—having a building at a college named after them, for example.

Why the focus on money amidst a discussion on having your personal life in order? Because it is the most common manifestation of *not* having your life in order. People do not save enough for retirement. They squander what money they have and begin gambling or drinking. Perhaps even buying escorts for more than escorting. Lotteries are clearly shown to be a tax on the poor since most lottery tickets are sold to those at lower income levels.

The sustained leader is scrupulous about their handling of money and they are insistent that those they mentor understand that precept as well. They have every

---

123 1 Tim 6:10. See also Malachi 5:10

aspect of their personal life in order and above reproach—and this is reflected in how they view and handle the money entrusted to them.

Similarly, sexual fidelity is a strong indicator of moral integrity. If a person is going to lie and betray the oath they made to their spouse, how loyal will they be to the team? Admittedly, the later breach of such an oath might be due to it being given too imprudently in the first instance, but that merely highlights two aspects to the issue of fidelity. Don't give your word unless you ABSOLUTELY intend to keep it, and once given, stand by it. Whether it is within the marriage vows or another matter entirely. The failure to do so will cause your personal life to fall out of order.

It was not too long past in our development as a society when questioning a woman's virtue was actionable in court. Russell Conwell noted in 1877 that "You cannot trust a man in your family who is not true to his own wife. You cannot trust a man in the world who does not begin with his own heart, his own character, and his own life."[124] Many of us probably read The Scarlet Letter by Nathaniel Hawthorne while in high school. A woman's purity and virtue were prized possessions and not to be impugned. Today we, as a society, have lowered the bar considerably such that urban wisdom is that the third date often means sex. With fidelity being "no big deal" to so many, the focus on having your personal life in order may seem irrelevant. Yet we still sense, collectively, that there is a moral breach that occurs with infidelity and legitimately calls into question the person's integrity and good sense. On the other hand, given the pervasiveness of such actions, it could perhaps, disqualify everyone from serving as a leader. Consider David from the Bible who not only sinned with Bathsheba, but then went on to arrange her husband's death. Even so, he was considered a great leader and a man chosen by God. His sinfulness (here and in other respects) did ultimately disqualify him from building the temple in Jerusalem, a task that was left for his son Solomon, and left his entire family in turmoil.

To say that having your personal life in order is not a significant matter is to suggest that there are no moral laws at all. Any transgression becomes acceptable. And while God does forgive, the voting public often does not. As seen in many elections, the scandal of an affair can be a quick way to derail a campaign.

---

124 Russell Conwell, *Acres of Diamonds*, 33.

This sounds like me

A lot	somewhat	just a little	not at all

Additional Resources:

Stephen Covey, *Principle-Centered Leadership*.

Dave Ramsey, *Financial Peace Revisited*.

Orrin Woodward, *The Financial Matrix*.

Personal Objective:

Specific Actions:

Due Date:

1.2.2.4 Respects Natural Law

WBS Dictionary: Natural law is, as the name suggests, a law of morality derived from human beings' inherent sense of right and wrong. As such, it is not subject to vagaries of man-made laws or the customs of a society (known as "positive law"). Natural law is a view that certain rights or values are inherent in or universally cognizable by virtue of human reason or human nature. Your perspective on this will depend on how you perceive nature, but this natural law is universal (since it is determined by nature) and appeals to the conscience of man as a creation inferior to his creator. Under this view of natural law, man discovers those principles and understands himself to have been born with a free will and subject to the laws of God (or in more humanist terms, a god). The sustained leader respects that there are natural laws that govern the universe. Actions will have consequences and the complexity of our world, whether our natural world, our business world, our personal world, or the intersection of any of these, will not always make those interactions predictable with exactitude. Nonetheless, a full understanding of natural law will assist the sustained leader in developing foresight, making forecasts, and understanding the possible results of a series of actions or complex situations.

Application: Going back to the first century, Decimus Junius Juvenal (c. 60–127 A.D.) noted that "Never does nature say one thing and wisdom another." The idea that our world is controlled by some natural law has been clear to man since before recorded history. If you choose to develop your own sense of "wisdom," you are certainly free to do so. Any violation of natural law will show your "wisdom" to be flawed. That's simply not the way things work. Understand that if you step off a 20 story building NOT believing in gravity, natural law will still pull you to your death.

Steven Covey, in his paradigm-shifting work *Principle-Centered Leadership*, addresses the nature of natural law. He says that "Individuals and organizations ought to be guided and governed by a set of proven principles. These are the natural laws and governing social values that have gradually come through every great society, every responsible civilization over the centuries. They surface in the form of values, ideas, norms, and teachings that uplift, ennoble, fulfill, empower, and inspire people."[125]

Similarly, John C. Maxwell notes that "Inside victories precede outside ones."[126] He notes that some people seem to be doing all the right things, yet success escapes them.

> The right motions outwardly with the wrong motives inwardly will not bring lasting progress. Right outward talking with the wrong inward thinking will not bring lasting success. Expressions of care on the outside with a heart of hatred or contempt on the inside will not bring lasting peace. Continual growth and lasting success are the result of aligning the inside and the outside of our lives. And getting the inside right must come first—with solid character traits that provide the foundation for growth.[127]

What he is observing is the action of natural law.

---

125 Stephen R. Covey, *Principle Centered Leadership*, 5.
126 John C. Maxwell, *The 15 Invaluable Laws of Growth*, 146.
127 Id.

William J. Bennett clearly shows how choices have consequences. You can always make your own choices, but you cannot avoid the consequences of those choices. That is fundamental to the concept of natural law.

> National prosperity, as it happens, is largely dependent upon lots of good private character. If lying, manipulation, sloth, lack of discipline, and personal irresponsibility become commonplace, the national economy grinds down. A society that produces street predators and white-collar criminals has to pay for prison cells. A society in which drug use is rampant must pay for the drug treatment centers. The crack-up of families means many more foster homes and lower high school graduation rates. A society that is parsimonious in its personal charity (in terms of both time and money) will require more government welfare. Just as there are enormous benefits to moral health, there are enormous financial costs to moral collapse. [128]

If you reject natural law, does this mean that you can't be a sustained leader? No. Your values may be "good" and your actions reflect compassion, empathy, and competence. You can still adopt leadership traits. There will simply be a dynamic around you that will influence things that will not quite make sense. You might also be prone to adopt a weak or even demonstrably bad value system, or to follow bad influences. Too often pop culture examples are followed, which almost invariably leads to a distortion, if not a full adulteration, of good values.

Thomas Edison worked with the laws of nature to create many useful inventions. He knew that natural law was exactly that—the law of nature that could not be violated. Following those laws, whether the laws of physics or the laws of right action, led to advances in man's understanding of the world in which he exists. He said, "I know this world is ruled by infinite intelligence. Everything that surrounds us—everything that exists—proves that there are infinite laws behind it. There can be no denying this fact. It is mathematical in its precision." Benjamin Franklin also weighed in on the fundamental concepts of natural law when he said, "Freedom

---

128 William J Bennett, *The Death of Outrage: Bill Clinton and the Assault on American Ideals.* (New York: Free Press, 1998), 35-36.

is not a gift bestowed upon us by other men, but a right that belongs to us by the laws of God and nature."

The sustained leader accepts and respects that natural law exists and that actions taken in contravention of natural law will have consequences. Your free will allows you to fight it all you wish, and you might perceive temporary victories. Ultimately, natural law will prevail. The better approach is to learn its rules and follow them.

This sounds like me

A lot   **somewhat**   **just a little**   **not at all**

Additional Resources:

Steven R. Covey, *Principle-Centered Leadership*.

Charles E. Rice, *50 Questions on the Natural Law*.

Personal Objective:

Specific Actions:

Due Date:

1.2.2.5 Generous

WBS Dictionary: Generosity comes in a variety of forms. People tend to perceive this as the sharing of treasure, and that is an important thing to share. It is also important to include the sharing of time and talent as well. It should also not be reflected solely in church or charitable settings. Sharing your time with a younger team member in a mentoring or coaching relationship can be just as valuable. Assisting at a conference where attendees can benefit from your experience counts. Yes, time is at a premium and there are many other demands on your time. Sharing of your time, talent, and treasure is an important aspect of a sustained leader. It assists in the developing of other leaders (3.2) and in preserving your legacy (1.3.8 and 5.1.4). It also allows you to demonstrate walking the talk, and avoids perceptions that you are engaging in leadership "don't do" elements (5.2).

Application: Some will attempt to masquerade behind apparent generosity while not portraying any other leadership element. This is not an element that can be faked or covered over. Often there are objections that there is simply no time or resources with which to be generous. In almost all cases this has more to do with the mismanagement of the time, talent, and treasure that has been given to you. The first step in accomplishing success in this element might be to obtain the training and guidance to better manage the resources you have. Keep in mind that "to whom much is given, much is expected" and "to he who manages what he has, more will be given." This is not a case of "give me more and I'll manage that well." It is clearly a case of "manage what you have and more will be given."

Master negotiator Bill Ury explains how important it is to be a "giver" rather than a "taker."

Whatever the perceived challenges, there are enormous benefits in adopting a basic attitude of giving for our negotiations as well as our lives. In his groundbreaking book *Give and Take*, Professor Adam Grant of Wharton Business School presents an impressive array of evidence from academic studies that the most successful people in life, perhaps surprisingly, are 'givers,' not 'takers.' It is, of course, important to be intelligent in one's giving and mindful of those who merely take, otherwise you may end up doing yourself a disservice. But the research on the tangible benefits of giving is eye-opening.[129]

Where do you devote your time, treasure, and talent? An honest answer to this question will tell you where your heart truly is. Without conscious thought you will discover that your time, or treasure, or talents are focused or concentrated in a particular area of your life. Is it a self-serving area? Are you spending time

129 William Ury, *Getting to Yes with Yourself,* 145.

on the golf course rather than with your children at a miniature golf course? Are you buying the latest gadgets or a car every two years, or are you investing in your children's education?

Remember as well that your charitable efforts should generally NOT be done in public. Giving a large gift to a college is a generous act. Doing so just so you can get your name on a building might diminish the generous heart that this element is targeting. Remember too that simply "paying your taxes" with full knowledge that much of these funds will be going to support various social objectives and welfare programs, is not what this element is addressing. Your giving should be targeted toward specific goals and objectives that are calling to you from the deepest recesses of your heart. Give to the beggar at the stop light if you choose. Serve food at the local soup kitchen (and not just on the holidays). Support your local humane society. Money can only be used once. Where you spend it, whether on yourself or others, will reflect your true motivation. The sustained leader has a generous heart.

John Maxwell paints a great metaphor by suggesting that we think of ourselves "as a river instead of a reservoir."[130] Rather than simply storing up our gifts and wisdom, we are called upon to share them; to let things flow through us to benefit others. As Maxwell notes, this requires an abundance mindset that allows you to give with confidence that whatever you give will return to you and that you will keep receiving as you give.

You should also be very careful to identify the charlatans and those who hide their greed behind the shell of a "foundation." Several of these came to light in the mid 2010's. There are organizations that review how charitable entities actually spend their money. If you are giving to such an organization and it turns out the 92 or 96% of the donated funds are not going to the charitable intent but to the salaries and "expenses" of those who run it, it is not worthy of your donation. Do your homework. Be a good steward of your time, treasure, and talent. Associate yourself with worthy causes.

This sounds like me

A lot	somewhat	just a little	not at all

---

130 John C. Maxwell, *The 15 Invaluable Laws of Growth* (New York: Center Street, 2012), 246.

Additional Resources:

Dave Ramsey, *Financial Peace Revisited*.

Larry Burkett, *Financial Freedom Library Vol. 1*.

Robert T. Kiyosaki, et al., *Rich Dad's Rich Kid, Smart Kid*.

Personal Objective:

Specific Actions:

Due Date:

1.2.2.6 Affirming

WBS Dictionary: Affirming means to state or assert positively. In the context of the *Sustained Leadership WBS* there are two aspects to this. The first is that the sustained leader knows what he or she believes and can articulate with clarity their values and beliefs. They affirm their beliefs through both their words and actions. Thus, the sustained leader is consistent in their words and actions because both are based on their value system. The other part of affirming is the encouragement the leader gives others to know their values and encourages them to stick to them. It is a strong and focused encouragement toward establishing and maintaining a strong value system for themselves.

Application: In the 70's there was a popular t-shirt slogan that said, "Everyone should believe in something. I believe I'll have another beer." Sadly, as funny as it seemed at the time, some peoples' sense of affirmation truly runs only that deeply.

Positive self-talk is an important aspect of this element. Too often people are heard saying, "Oh, I could never do what you do." Or "It's too late for me." These are the exact opposite of affirmations and the sustained leader trains themselves to identify and root out such negative thoughts and actions. The leader knows the importance of encouraging their team to be the best they can possibly be. Mark

Twain had the right perspective on this when he said, "Keep away from people who try to belittle your ambitions. Small people always do that, but the really great make you feel that you, too, can become great."

William James noted that the core of the human personality, what he referred to as the spiritual self—the most permanent and concrete of the "selves" he identified, was the need to be appreciated. "The deepest principle in human nature is the craving to be appreciated." When the sustained leader affirms their team members, he or she is addressing that need in the true manner of a servant-leader (3.18). Hare has also told us that "What a person praises is perhaps a surer standard, even, than what he condemns, of his character, information and abilities. No wonder, then, that most people are so shy of praising anything."[131]

Kouzes and Posner offer the following observation:

> "[E]xemplary leaders make other people feel strong. Thy enable others to take ownership and responsibility for their group's success by enhancing their competence and their confidence in their abilities, by listening to their ideas and acting upon them, by invoking them in important decisions, and by acknowledging and giving credit for their contributions. Long before empowerment was written into the popular vocabulary, exemplary leaders understood how important it was that their constituents felt strong, capable, and efficacious. Constituents who feel weak, incompetent, and insignificant consistently underperform; they want to flee the organization, and they're ripe for disenchantment, even revolution."[132]

Napoleon Hill

The person who sows a single beautiful thought in the mind of another, renders the world a greater service than that rendered by all the faultfinders combined.

---

131 B.C. Forbes, *The Forbes Scrapbook of Thoughts on the Business of Life* (New York: Forbes, Inc., 1976), 159.
132 Kouzes and Posner, *The Leadership Challenge*, 281

John Maxwell tells us that we should always associate with those who are "larger" than ourselves. People of integrity, who are positive, who are ahead of us professionally, and who lift us up are all good candidates. Find those who always take the high road and continue to grow. "They should be like Ralph Waldo Emerson and Henry David Thoreau, whose question for each other whenever they met was, 'What have you learned since we last met?'"[133] People who challenge us while encouraging us are excellent models of this element.

One of history's most affirming individuals was an employee of Andrew Carnegie. In fact, Carnegie was so impressed with this man that he made him the first employee to earn over $1 million in salary a year. This man, it seems, had an amazing ability to get the most out of his team. His formula was simple: "First, he aroused enthusiasm in people; he developed the best in a person through genuine appreciation and encouragement; and third, [he] never criticized anyone."[134]

A man once said, "I have yet to find a man, however exalted his station, who did not do better work and put forth greater effort under a spirit of approval, than under a spirit of criticism." His tombstone carries the inscription, "Here lies one who knew how to get around him men who were cleverer than himself." That man was Charles Schwab who started an investment company that bears his name to this day. The sustained leader knows how to affirm the team. It pays great dividends.

This sounds like me

A lot   **somewhat**   **just a little**   **not at all**

Additional Resources:
Norman Vincent Peale, *Inspirational Writings of Norman Vincent Peale.*
Zig Ziglar, et al., *See You at the Top.*

Personal Objective:

---

133 John Maxwell, *The 15 Invaluable Laws of Growth* (New York: Center Street, 2012), 92-3.
134 Alan C. Elliott, *American Dream*, 81

Specific Actions:

Due Date:

1.3 Know Yourself

WBS Dictionary: Self-awareness causes you to understand yourself, what motivates you, what your priorities might be, how you learn, how you interact with others, and what behaviors you model. You understand what risks you are willing to take and which ones you avoid; you know the difference between work and play and where you have confidence and where you don't. Most importantly, you have a good grasp of what you know and what you do not know, and actively seek to convert both "unknown unknowns" and "known unknowns" into "known knowns." For each person, that catalog will be different—often VERY different. Thus, the importance of knowing yourself and enhancing your leadership abilities, maximizing the things you do well and minimizing and changing those that you do less well. Everyone is comprised of a unique set of values, traits, skill, abilities, and temperaments. Without a proper inventory and honest evaluation, you will not be able to focus your attention on further development. Additionally, part of being self-aware causes you to be aware of how others respond to you. This leads to greater self-management which in turn leads to greater influence; the essence of leadership.[135]

Application: Knowing yourself requires a high level of self-awareness, which has been defined as the ability to know one's emotions, strengths, weaknesses, drives, values, and goals; and to recognize their impact on others while developing the ability to use gut feelings to guide decisions.

A key aspect of knowing yourself is to be temperate in your traits and responses. For example, being aggressive and goal oriented is generally a good thing. Taken to an extreme, however, this aggressive nature may drive people

---

135 See generally Daniel Goleman, *Focus: The Hidden Driver of Excellence* (New York: Harper Collins, 2015), 231-32.

away rather than draw them in. This concept of calibration runs through the entire *Sustained Leadership WBS*. You naturally have many positive traits. Take any of them to an extreme and you have developed a negative trait or habit. Conversely, if you hide your positive trait under a barrel and do not exercise it, it is worse than not having the trait at all. The measure of the response will always be determined by the leader's assessment of the situation (2.1.6). Successful sustained leaders know themselves well enough to know when to go all out with a reaction and when to pull it back. This is an extremely difficult balance, in part because there will always be critics. Sustained leaders do not calibrate on popular opinion but on being true to themselves. And until you know yourself fully, you cannot accomplish this balance.

The sum of your experiences creates your mindset—the filter through which everything you perceive is strained. All of your biases, your sense of perspective, your perceptions, and your preconceptions. Everyone has them, and all of their information intake is run through those filters. The effect can be that you are blind to certain things and misperceive others. Your idea of "facts" (1.2.1.2) may be distorted with the result being that you make bad decisions and lead poorly. If you are aware of your mindset, you can adjust and compensate for the margin of error that you introduce to your own thought processes. If you do not know yourself, your potential for errors and mistakes in leadership is greatly enhanced.

———————•———————

Knowing Yourself

Let him who would move the world first move himself.
—Socrates

He that would govern others, first should be Master of himself.
—Philip Massinger

Men can starve from a lack of self-realization as much as they can from a lack of bread.

—Richard Wright

This above all: to thine own self be true, And it must follow, as the night the day, Thou canst not then be false to any man.
—Spoken by Polonius: *Hamlet Act 1, scene 3, 78–82*

Knowing thyself is the height of wisdom.
—Socrates

Everything that irritates us about others can lead us to an understanding of ourselves.

—C.G. Jung

The greatest thing in the world is to know how to belong to oneself.
—Michel de Montaigne,

———————— ◆ ————————

Daniel Goleman provides this insight on self-awareness:

Leaders who inspire can articulate shared values that resonate with and motivate the group. These are the leaders people love to work with, who surface the vision that moves everyone. But to speak from the heart, to the heart, a leader must first know her values. That takes self-awareness.

Inspiring leadership demands attuning both to an inner emotional reality and to that of those we seek to inspire. These are elements of emotional intelligence, which I've had to rethink a bit in light of our new understanding of focus.

Attention gets talked about only indirectly in the emotional intelligence world: As "self-awareness," which is the basis of self-management; and as "empathy," the foundation for relationship effectiveness. Yet awareness of our self and of others, and its application in managing our inner world and our relationships, is the essence of emotional intelligence.[136]

---

136 Daniel Goleman, *Focus: The Hidden Driver of Excellence* (New York: Harper Collins, 2015), 225-26.

Various studies have shown that absolute IQ is a poor predictor of success in business and life. "[O]nce you are at work among a pool of colleagues who are about as smart as you are, your cognitive abilities alone do not make you outstanding—particularly as a leader."[137] The one trait that causes the best among equals to stand out is self-awareness. It is the meta-ability of leadership.

We have all been in discussions with people who take very dogmatic positions on a subject, and when asked to explain their views, say something to the effect of, "I can't explain why. I just know that it is true." The sustained leader should *never* say such things. Always know what you believe and why you believe it. Only then can you begin the long journey of knowing yourself.

A useful adage is: *never second guess; always reassess.* What this means is that if you are confident in your beliefs and knowledge you can act more decisively. Don't second guess your decisions. On the other hand, new facts are constantly coming to light and circumstances are constantly in flux. It is important to reassess everything from time to time and to be open minded enough to make mid-course corrections or change direction altogether. Only by knowing yourself can the sustained leader act with confidence in such matters.

This is also an area where it can be difficult to be honest with yourself. We all have flaws and the sustained leader does not shy away from learning what theirs are. The help of a trusted friend, mentor, or coach will often be necessary to decipher all of the inputs that we give ourselves. Andy Stanley makes this point very directly. "To be the best next generation leader you can be, you must enlist the help of others. Self-evaluation is helpful, but evaluation from someone else is essential. You need a leadership coach."[138]

Part of knowing yourself comes from understanding your own dreams and goals. Philosophically, it is like asking the question, "Why am I here?" Whether you answer that from a spiritual or humanistic perspective, everyone must understand their "why." As John Maxwell states it:

Your *why* is the life's blood of intentional living.

---

137 Ibid., 233-36.
138 Andy Stanley, *The Next Generation Leader: Five Essentials for Those Who Will Shape the Future* (US: Multnomah, 2003), 106.

If you know your *why* and focus on going there with fierce determination, you can make sense of everything on your journey because you see it through the lens of *why*. This makes the *way* so much more meaningful and complete because you have context to understand the reason you're on the journey in the first place.... I [have] made the following statement: "Once you find your *why*, you will be able to find your *way*." How do these things differ? *Why* is your purpose. *Way* is your path. When you find your *why*, your path automatically has purpose.[139]

The sustained leader works diligently to understand what makes them tick. They work to be self-aware about their strengths, weaknesses, traits, and beliefs. The various sub-elements presented here gives considerable guidance to those wishing to know themselves and improve their leadership abilities.

This sounds like me

A lot	somewhat	just a little	not at all

Additional Resources:

Simon Sinek, *Start with Why*.

William Ury, *Getting to Yes with Yourself*.

John Maxwell, *The 360 Degree Leader*.

Personal Objective:

Specific Actions:

Due Date:

---

139 John C. Maxwell, *Intentional Living: Choosing a Life That Matters*. (New York: Center Street, 2015), 79-80.

Essential Leadership Journey Checkpoint
1.3.1 Constant Learner

WBS Dictionary: Arborists tell us that a tree is either growing or dying. There is no status quo for trees. The same is true of the human mind. You are either growing and expanding it, or it is shrinking. Regardless of your field, background, education, or profession, nothing is static. The sustained leader recognizes this dynamic and works to stay current. This starts by being a constant learner. All learning begins with the gathering of facts and enough humility (1.3.3) to recognize that there is something you need to learn. Facts are provable. They can be verified. One key fact about yourself is the things that you know and you are aware that you know them. Another fact is the things that you do not know. The most dangerous "facts," however, are those about which you are mistaken and you are not aware of your error. These are the hardest ones to identify and fix. The only solution is to be in a constant learning mode, to be open to learning new things, and be open-minded enough to change your views or positions based on new facts. A proper self-assessment (1.3.3.1) informs this and guides you toward a learning plan. Much learning comes from being observant (2.1.6.1), a great deal from reading, and even more from life experiences. This element also means that you retain what you learn; it is genuine learning and not just rote memorization. It must be available to you to apply when the appropriate situation arises. The sustained leader strives constantly to build on their prior knowledge and experience in every way possible.

Application: Some people seem to thirst for new knowledge. Some become "professional students" as they accumulate degrees and certificates. Unless, however, this education is put to some practical use, the effort of accumulating knowledge seems a bit wasted. The sustained leader has a curiosity and likes to apply what is learned.

There are many different ways to learn, and as adults, nearly everyone has identified their preferred learning method. Rather than review these educational theories, however, the sustained leader applies their preference to a variety of learning goals—whether directed or general learning. Directed learning pertains to a specific body of knowledge, such as learning a foreign language. General learning comes from exposing yourself to a wide diversity of information sources—from the daily news to the local ballet, to opera, to a divergent political view. Sustained leaders recognize their need to be constant readers—of everything: blogs, newspapers, editorials, position papers, books, textbooks, street signs. It is truly amazing how many people simply fail to pay attention to the words around them.

Frances Hesselbein under a heading of "Life-Size Learning" notes how important constant training and education is to the team and the organization as a whole. "It is the continuing study, the research into what is just over the horizon, that places the board and staff in a very positive position to help everyone in the movement be part of that future and not just react to it. We invested heavily in the training and development of our people, and the money was peanuts compared to the results. The first item in your budget should be learning, education, and the development of your people."[140]

Always be Learning

[A] good moral character is the first essential in a man, and that the habits contracted at your age are generally indelible, and your conduct here may stamp your character through life. It is therefore highly important that you should endeavor not only to be learned but virtuous.
—George Washington (1790)

Leadership and learning are indispensable to each other.
—John Fitzgerald Kennedy

Once you stop learning, you start dying.
—Albert Einstein

Look, everyone knows something you don't. Everyone.
—Jack and Suzy Welch

---

140 Frances Hesselbein, *My Life in Leadership* (San Francisco: Josey Bass, 2011), 95.

If a man empties his purse into his head, no man can take it away from him.
An investment in knowledge always pays the best interest.
—Benjamin Franklin

————————— ● —————————

Learning is a curious thing. There are things we have learned and forgotten. There are things we learned that simply were or are no longer correct. There are things that are learned by us that contradict other things we have learned. And no matter how much discipline we exhibit, over time our memories will fade and without directed discipline, we lose sight of the journey. A process of critical thinking (1.3.9.1) is crucial for the leadership journey. You must also be constantly aware of how you may be being seduced or deceived either by yourself or others. We view our life through a variety of filters and not all of these filters lead to truth. Many filters are designed to cloud our perception. Some information purveyors work to their own agenda, and unless you apply critical thinking, you might believe every news cast or TV show produced. Biases are everywhere.

Leadership guru Steven R. Covey has noted that principle-centered leaders are characterized by the fact that they are continually learning.[141] Noted quality guru Philip B. Crosby has said, "There is a theory of human behavior that says people subconsciously retard their own intellectual growth. They come to rely on clichés and habits. Once they reach the age of their own personal comfort with the world, they stop learning and their mind runs on idle for the rest of their days. They may progress organizationally, they may be ambitious and eager, and they may even work night and day. But they learn no more."[142] Jack and Suzy Welch also say, "… stop learning at your peril! Better yet, embrace learning, and watch what happens to your organization, your team, and your career. Excitement. Growth. Success."[143]

Mentors (1.3.12) are another source of learning. How important is having and being a mentor? John Maxwell tells us that "In an article published by the Harvard Business Review, author Joseph Bailey examined what it took to be

---

141 Covey, *Principle-Centered Leadership*, 39.
142 Quoted in Maxwell, *How to Influence People*, 109-10.
143 Jack and Suzy Welch, *The Real Life MBA: Your No-BS Guide to Winning the Game, Building a Team, and Growing Your Career.* (New York: Harper Collins, 2015), x.

a successful executive. In conducting his research, he interviewed more than thirty top executives and found that every one of them learned firsthand from a mentor. If you want to raise up leaders who reproduce other leaders, you need to mentor them."[144]

Your most important asset is yourself. You are the only "you" that will ever exist and you will have your time on earth to achieve what you can. Your health and your abilities will determine, in large measure, how long you have and what you can accomplish. Clearly, everyone starts with a different underlying set of skills and different propensity toward good health or biological impediments. That's no excuse not to make yourself the best "you" that is possible. And it makes sense to enhance those assets. Health is addressed in 5.1.6. This element focuses on constantly finding ways to enhance the asset of your brain and your ability to apply what you learn. In today's ever-increasing rate of scientific and technical advancement, you will need to find an increasing ability to adapt and learn, or you will be relegated to the ranks of the dinosaurs, suitable only for display in a museum. In case you hadn't guessed, you can't lead as a mounted display. In 1.3.13 we talk about appreciating the journey. Being a constant learner makes it that much easier to appreciate the journey.

Kouzes and Posner make the following observation:

There's one other important lesson here. Nothing in our research even hints that leaders should be perfect. Leaders aren't saints. They're human beings, full of the flaws and failings of the rest of us. They make mistakes. Perhaps the very best advice we can give all aspiring leaders is to remain humble and unassuming—to always remain open and full of wonder. The best leaders are the best learners.[145]

This sounds like me

A lot	somewhat	just a little	not at all

144 John Maxwell, *How to Influence People*, 171-72, citing Joseph Bailey, "Clues for Success in the President's Job," Harvard Business Review (special edition), 1983.

145 James M. Kouzes and Barry Z. Posner, *The Leadership Challenge* (San Francisco, CA: Jossey-Bass, 2002), 398.

Additional Resources:

Stephen R. Covey, *Principle Centered Leadership*, Principles #1 and #8.

John Kotter, *Leading Change*.

Benedict Carey, *How We Learn*.

Personal Objective:

Specific Actions:

Due Date:

1.3.1.1 Reader

WBS Dictionary: Leaders are readers. There is an increasing level of information available everywhere and the rate of increase grows ever higher. Readers vicariously experience the lives of others, whether that is in the form of fiction/fantasy, biographies, or accumulations of data and knowledge, but knowledge is only the beginning of wisdom (1.3.1.4). It has been suggested that wisdom comes from experience and no one can live long enough to make every mistake. We must therefore learn from others. And reading is a key process for gaining the knowledge of the ages. Reading also is part of the cultural heritage. The so-called classics are classic *because* they are the key components of the culture. They transmit knowledge, they preserve recorded history, and they create a common base of understanding. The challenge for the leader of today is that so much knowledge is being gathered at such an incredible rate that the sustained leader must work diligently to at least remain familiar with all the advances, while filling in gaps of their cultural and historical perspective. It is difficult, but the sustained leader accepts the challenge.

Application: In today's society a person need only mimic a raspy, slightly squeaky voice and say "the force is strong in that one" and everyone will understand the reference. There is hardly a soul on earth who does not know of Yoda and his unique form of phrasing sentences. Without such common points of reference, each such comment must be preceded with a detailed context. "As the guide to young Luke Skywalker said to Obi Won as he referred to the young Padawan…" You see the reference becomes far too awkward to make the simple point. We rely on our common sense of cultural literacy to communicate.

Bennis and Sample note that some of this literature becomes "super texts" and provide a timeless perspective that helps the leader avoid a herd mentality. "And the super texts, more than contemporary literature, do an excellent job of helping us understand this timelessness of human nature. Moreover, they are important not only for what they say but also for how they say it. Because these texts have been read by so many people over such a long period, they have exerted, and continue to exert, an extraordinary influence on the language effective leaders use, often unbeknownst to the leader themselves."[146]

How does a sustained leader know what to read? One excellent source is the *Wall Street Journal's* weekly list of best business books. Many of these best sellers remain on, or return frequently to the list. This tells you what other leaders are reading. Over time, you are likely to have read 6 to 8 of the top ten. Keep reading.

Leaders also make use of other resources. Both books on tape (preferably unabridged), and services that provide a 20 minute synopses of top business books, expand the leader's exposure to the most current literature on their subject. The linkage between reading and those who lead has a long and consistent history. From student W. Fusselman who, in 1926, is credited with coining, "Today a reader, tomorrow a leader," to Charlie Tremendous Jones who in 1968 titled a chapter in his book *Life is Tremendous*, "Leaders are Readers."

Extensive reading has often been shown to provide motivation and education. Ewing M. Kaufman was stricken with an illness at the age of 11 in 1908 that damaged a heart valve. He was confined to constant bed rest for a year, not being permitted to even sit up. To absorb the time, he became a voracious reader, reportedly consuming 100 books month. Many were fiction, many were non-fiction, thus

---

146 Warren Bennis and Stephen B. Sample (with Rob Asghar), *The Art and Adventure of Leadership; Understanding Failure, Resilience, and Success.* (Hoboken, NJ: John Wiley & Sons, Inc., 2015), 82.

exposing the lad to some of the greatest minds of his day. He later excelled in most everything in which he engaged, especially sales. When his commissions at one position made him the highest paid person at the company, his commissions were cut, causing him to form his own $100 million business.

Kaufman could have allowed his mind to waste away while his body healed. Instead, he took every opportunity to keep his mind alert and full of useful information. When his body healed, he put all of that knowledge—perhaps even wisdom at that point—to good use, and built a sizeable business and fortune.

The sustained leader takes advantage of every opportunity to read and learn. They do not let minutes waste away, rather, they carry reading material with them either in printed or electronic form. The sustained leader also capitalizes on the opportunity presented by what others would consider misfortune. A year of bed rest might be perceived as a massive inconvenience and interruption to life. Well used, however, the time can prepare the mind for wonderful accomplishments.

What should leaders read? As noted, there is insufficient time to read everything that is written, and sadly, just because a book is published does not necessarily suggest it should be read. Certainly the leader should stay current in their field (2.0) by reading material in their area of expertise. General business topics are consistently popular, and of course books on leadership. Most leaders find time to stay current on popular culture and current events, and as time permits, blogs, postings, and news online.

A variety of statistics have been published concerning our reading habits. John Maxwell provides us the following facts and figures. "Sadly, a third of high school graduates never read another book for the rest of their lives, and 42 percent of college graduates similarly never read a book after college. And publisher David Godine claims that only 32 percent of the U.S. population has ever been in a bookstore. I don't know if people are aware of the gap between where they are and where they could be, but relatively few seem to be reading books to try to close it."[147]

Mo Siegel founded Celestial Seasonings in 1969 after his many hikes in the Colorado Mountains outside of Boulder brought him into contact with a great variety of herbs, petals, and leaves which he blended into teas. He worked hard, but as a college drop-out, he did not have the formal business education that might have helped. Instead, he focused on reading the biographies of his heroes to develop a sense of business, work ethic, and drive to succeed. These included biographies of Tom Watson (IBM), Walt Disney, Abe Lincoln, and Jesus (from the bible). In 1984 the company was sold to Kraft foods for $40 million, bought back in 1989 at an estimated value of $60 million, and eventually merged with Hain Food Group in 2000. Reading can be financially rewarding.

Historian Thomas Carlyle said, "What we become depends on what we read after all the professors are finished with us. The greatest university of all is the collection of books." As proof of this, John Brooks Fuqua created a series of businesses that became Fuqua Industries, Inc. He credits his ability to have created

147 John C. Maxwell, *The 15 Invaluable Laws of Growth* (New York: Center Street, 2012). 161, citing Craig Ruff, "Help, Please," *Dome Magazine*, July 16, 2010, accessed October 25, 2011, http://domemagazine.com/craigsgrist/cr0710, and Dan Poynter, "Book Industry Statistics," Dan Poynter' Parapublishing.com, accessed October 25, 2011, http://parapublishing.com/sites/para/resources/statistics.cfm.

the conglomerate that bears his name by borrowing the brains of many others by reading books he borrowed by mail from Duke University.

The sustained leader develops a thirst for knowledge and satisfies that thirst in great measure by reading as much as possible. If direct reading from books is difficult or simply a drudge, you are not likely to retain what you read. Find other ways to read such as eBooks or audio books. This aspect of being a continuous learner is simply too important to ignore. Leaders are readers. Sustained leaders are prolific readers.

This sounds like me

A lot   somewhat   just a little   not at all

Additional Resources:
Burke Hedges, *Read & Grow Rich*.
Walter Anderson, *Read With Me*.

Personal Objective:

Specific Actions:

Due Date:

1.3.1.2 One Major with Lots of Minors

WBS Dictionary: This element suggests that a leader must be proficient in at least one primary area related to the leadership role, and also must have a strong working knowledge of many other areas. It does not mean that the leader must know everything; that is eminently impractical. A review of many large businesses will reveal that there is a preferred background for the CEO. A person who has achieved a level of professionalism by obtaining their discipline's terminal degree, in some cases a Ph.D., in others a Masters, in law a JD, and medicine an MD, shows that they have demonstrated the discipline to learn all they can about the specific profession and achieve a level of academic success. It is less usual to hold multiple professional levels, although JD/CPA's, MD/JD's, and Engineers with JD's are fairly common. More importantly, sustained leaders round out their education either formally or informally by engaging in hobbies, targeting their reading (1.3.1.1), and seeking opportunities outside of their specific training, sometimes called "stretch opportunities." A novice leader is well advised to learn to ask good questions (4.4.1) and to deal effectively with people. In this way they can engage with others in their organization and maximize their exposure to all phases and aspects of the organization. In any position in which you find yourself, make it a point to learn everything there is to know about the business—how it operates, who does what, what skills are necessary to succeed in the different departments, and how success is measured. It is not important to asses or critique any of these things, only to absorb the critical information. In effect, the leader must become the proverbial "renaissance man (or woman)" with a wide variety of interests and knowledge. One major—lots of minors.

Application: Each industry or charity may have a preference for a particular field of concentration. For example, many defense and aerospace firms are headed by an engineer. A Southwest Airlines CEO previously served as their general counsel—which makes sense in a highly-regulated industry that is very tied to its union contracts as the airlines are.

When Ken started his business he recognized that he needed a website. He was able to go through the basic registration process to capture a domain, and then set about building the website. Feeling reasonably intelligent and seeing people less educated and experienced than he successfully building websites, he purchased expensive software and two books on the subject. What he found was that the software he selected was not very intuitive and even less user friendly. Every time he tried to work with the software and build his site it was like learning all over again. One day, as he booted up his software to take another run at building his site, he got a pop-up notice that the software was out of date. It was, in fact, two versions behind the current release. It dawned on Ken that the technology was advancing faster than he was learning. This was not a winning path.

The experience was not wasted, however. He learned a lot about the language of web design and had a greater appreciation for what was good and what was less useful. With this knowledge, he was able to sift through a great many people who tried to obtain his business who in fact knew little more than he did. He was able to ask very good questions (4.4.1) and ultimately found the webmaster he needed. While he bears no illusions that he might go into the web designing business, he understands what he needs to in order to have a current, useful website for his clients.

Robert Greene, while addressing power, tells the story of an astrologer who, standing before King Louis XI, prophesied his death as occurring "just three days before Your Majesty." Whereupon King Louis made sure that the astrologer was well cared-for for the rest of his long life. Greene notes:

> The astrologer survived Louis by several years, disproving his power of prophecy but proving his mastery of power. This is the model: Make others dependent on you. To get rid of you might spell disaster, even death, and your master dares not tempt fate by finding out. There are many ways to obtain such a position. Foremost among them is to possess a talent and creative skill that simply cannot be replaced.[148]

It is sometimes difficult when reading Greene to tell whether he is as Machiavellian as his writing suggests, but there is no denying the key point he makes—be completely outstanding in one thing; be the best you can possibly be and apply that skill and talent to the benefit of the team. While it has been said that you should not make yourself indispensable since, while it does suggest you can't be fired, it also suggests that you can't be promoted. Thus, if ALL you can do is one thing extremely well, and you are quite content to do that for the rest of your working career, then by all means, become that absolutely superlative individual contributor. Do not expect to become a leader beyond your selected field unless you have also rounded yourself out with the other elements of the *Sustained Leadership WBS*.

---

148 Robert Greene, *The 48 Laws of Power* (New York: Penguin Books, 1998), 86.

St. Francis of Assisi
Do few things, but do them well.

As an exercise, look up the biography of William McGowan one of the leaders of the Microwave Communications, Inc. You might know the company as MCI that revolutionized telecommunications. He held many jobs, studied pre-med, served in the Army, studied chemical engineering, and eventually got an MBA from Harvard in 1954. He then went on to start several businesses before the MCI adventure. Remember to balance this element with 2.2.1, to excel in one primary area, but still keep yourself well rounded. The sustained leader can hold that ambiguity without confusion or uncertainty.

This sounds like me

A lot	somewhat	just a little	not at all

Additional Resources:
Daniel Goleman, *Focus*.
Benedict Carey, *How We Learn*.

Personal Objective:

Specific Actions:

Due Date:

1.3.1.3 Prepares

WBS Dictionary: Nothing compares to doing your homework. Preparation comes in many forms from dutifully attending school and completing assignments to receiving a diploma or degree. Your preparation might be to seek expansive opportunities such as joining the military or Peace Corps, to seeking stretch assignments within an employment situation, or to reading and researching the necessary background information before a meeting, an encounter with a mentor, or for negotiations. The sustained leader prepares themselves, generally and specifically, for their chosen profession, and also prepares to meet the day-to-day obligations and commitments. They will typically go above and beyond the immediate needs and will adhere to the principle that knowledge is power—gaining more knowledge in order to be better positioned to serve. This level of being a constant learner (1.3.1) focuses on gathering facts, data, and information to be applied in furtherance of the organization's vision, mission, and goals.

Application: Dana Perino speaks to her time as a deputy press secretary where she got to know President Bush by working holidays and weekends. She notes that she "always recommends that young people take the deputy job—no matter what industry or organization. Being second in command is where you learn how to be the leader, and it's when you establish a good relationship with the boss."[149] While in college, Kenny followed a similar approach. He was fully qualified to be president of any number of organizations in his senior year and opted instead to take the second position in order to get a broader base of experience and satisfy his insatiable urge to be as diverse as possible. He was vice president of the English club, vice president of his fraternity, Assistant GM of the radio station, and expanded his role in choir to join a small song and dance troupe. Had he taken any one of the top positions in any of these activities, participation in most of the others would have been precluded entirely.

Different people and different situations will require different approaches for optimal preparedness. The Boy and Girl Scout mottos are to "Be Prepared" and the great variety of merit badges available to scouts allows them to prepare in a vast number of ways.

---

149 Dana Perino, *And the Good News is…: Lessons and Advice from the Bright Side* (New York: Hachette Book Group, 2015), 95.

A very key way in which the sustained leader prepares is by spending a fair amount of time in self-reflection. This is a form of the habit advocated by Stephen Covey to spend time "Sharpening the Saw."[150] It is important that the sustained leader not simply move rashly through life, but takes time to reflect on the events and people they have encountered. The lessons that can be learned from life will not be retained unless some time is spent on reflection and consideration of the implications. John Maxwell observes that, "If you are a leader, you can probably take the normal busyness of life and multiply it by ten. Leaders are so action oriented and have so many responsibilities that they are often guilty of moving all the time and neglecting to stop and take time to think. Yet this is one of the most important things leaders can do. A minute of thought is worth more than an hour of talk."[151]

The sustained leader considers two aspects of preparation—practice and experience. As A.B. Zu Tavern wisely tells us, "Some people confuse practice with experience. Practice consist of doing the same thing over and over. Experience comes from applying accumulated knowledge, observing results, and making improvements." Developing a skill requires practice. Malcolm Gladwell has posited that it takes 10,000 hours of practice to become an expert.[152] A lifetime of experience might still not lead to wisdom for some. Believing you have 17 years of experience when you have performed the same task over and over is probably a misleading statement. You have one year of experience 17 times over. The sustained leader practices and seeks out new experiences, broadening their knowledge and experience base with each year of practice. Both prepare the leader for greater responsibility.

———————— ◦ ————————

Abraham Lincoln
I will study and get ready, and perhaps my chance will come.

———————— ◦ ————————

---

150 Stephen Covey, *The 7 Habits of Highly Effective People* (US: Free Press, 1990), x.
151 John C. Maxwell, *The 15 Invaluable Laws of Growth* (New York: Center Street, 2012), 56 (citation omitted).
152 Malcolm Gladwell, *Outliers: The Story of Success* (US: Little, Brown and Company, 2008). Other research has questioned the accuracy of this assertion.

A fable is told of a wild boar that stood under a tree and rubbed his tusks against the trunk. A Fox was passing by and asked him, "Why do you waste time sharpening your teeth when there is no danger about? Neither hunter nor hound is near." The boar responded to his wily friend, "I do it to prepare; for it would never do to have to sharpen my weapons just at the time I ought to be using them." The sustained leader prepares, and in fact, works very hard to over-prepare.

This sounds like me

A lot   somewhat   **just a little**   not at all

Additional Resources:
Benedict Carey, *How We Learn*.
Napoleon Hill, *The Law of Success in Sixteen Lessons*.
Og Mandino, *Og Mandino's University of Success*.

Personal Objective:

Specific Actions:

Due Date:

1.3.1.4 Wisdom Seeker

WBS Dictionary: Training and education are important. Learning to apply that training and education is also important. None of it, however, leads directly to wisdom. Wisdom is the direct application of positive values to everyday situations. It applies judgment anchored in truth and righteousness to actions. It includes the concepts of discernment and insight. A person with wisdom has the right values (1.2.1) and applies these values to all decisions (2.3.6). Discernment is a rare commodity; Madison Avenue advertisers have tried for decades to sway our purchasing decisions and in the process have destroyed discernment. In religious, political, and life choices, bad decisions are being made constantly. Just look around. Bad decision-making seems to be a national pastime. The sustained leader seeks wisdom and strives diligently to apply it in every situation.

Application: The most widely known example of wisdom is Solomon who was granted one gift from God. When Solomon chose wisdom, God granted him wealth and power as well since, with wisdom, he would use those appropriately. Victor Frankl said, "The last of the human freedoms is to choose one's attitudes." There is a lot of wisdom there. Winston Churchill observed that, "All the great things are simple, and many can be expressed in a single word: freedom, justice, honor, duty, mercy, hope." Again—a lot of wisdom in that thought. And Mary Crowley noted that, "Real Wisdom is looking at the world from God's point of view."

Twentieth century journalist Peter Richard Calder put some of this in perspective when he noted that "Science at best is not wisdom; it is knowledge. Wisdom is knowledge tempered with judgment." Many people are extremely knowledgeable and yet lack wisdom. The Jeopardy Game show winner may take home a lot of money and not have the wisdom to invest it properly. Occasionally, this is phrased as a difference between "book smarts" and "street smarts." Knowledge is great. Start there and gain as much as you can. But do not stop there. Apply that knowledge "tempered with judgment" to begin to approach real wisdom. See also 1.3.9.

Psychiatrist Theodore Isaac Rubin observed that "Kindness is more important than wisdom, and the recognition of this is the beginning of wisdom." As valuable and important as wisdom is, it is not the ultimate goal. If Solomon was wise, why did he ultimately begin making so many bad decisions? Wisdom must be actively practiced. Bad choices disrupt wisdom and as humans we are too often drawn to bad decisions (1.2.2.2). Charles Spurgeon, a preacher who lived in the 1800's said, "The doorstep to the temple of wisdom is a knowledge of our own ignorance." Are you aware of your areas of ignorance? (1.3.3.6)

Wisdom is also not popular opinion. Right and wrong is not a function of majority rule. A commonly seen wall plaque says, "Never confuse the will of the people with the will of God." Anatole France, an author, observed that "If 50 million people say a foolish thing, it is still a foolish thing." Wisdom rises above popular opinion. Wisdom is reflected in the choices made. Perhaps David Starr Jordan said it best when he offered this perspective: "Wisdom is knowing what to do next, skill is knowing how to do it, and virtue is doing it."

This sounds like me

A lot   **somewhat**   **just a little**   **not at all**

Additional Resources:
The Bible, Book of Proverbs.
James Allen, *As a Man Thinketh*.
Daniel Goleman, *Emotional Intelligence*.

Personal Objective:

Specific Actions:

Due Date:

1.3.1.5 Inquisitive Mind

WBS Dictionary: A sustained leader wonders about a lot of things. They ask questions, seek answers, and then test the answers they receive. They are either curious by nature or they develop a sense of curiosity. They are never quite satisfied with the answers given. They want to dig deeper; to understand more. They will occasionally ask questions to which they already know the answer just to see if someone has a different perspective. They will also pose more philosophical questions just to see where the discussion will lead. They would have enjoyed the discussions at the Greek Forum—argument in the classic sense.

Application: Children are so naturally inquisitive. It is a shame that so many people lose that quality. Of course, by the 27th time a child says "why?" most adults have reached their limit of patience with such things. Some children are also constantly taking things apart just to see how they work. Not all of them know how to put them back together, however. As frustrating as these childhood activities are to most adults, this is *exactly* the type of inquisitiveness that the leader must develop. Albert Einstein said, "I have no particular talent. I am merely inquisitive."

Being inquisitive means that you have a desire, perhaps even a burning desire, to investigate. Some such endeavors might seem nosy to others; there are boundaries in being too inquisitive about the personal affairs of others. It is the right sentiment, just a bit misdirected. The sustained leader wants to know how things work. They want to know why.

This is linked to critical thinking (1.3.9.1), questioning (4.4.1), and systems thinking (1.3.9.2). Again from Einstein, "Intellectual growth should commence at birth and cease only at death." Regardless of your age or experience in any of these related elements, you can always start today to develop an inquisitive mind. First, set an immediate goal to learn one new thing every day. Keep a journal to document your new-found knowledge. Journaling, in itself, helps to develop an inquisitive mind. Then set a longer-term goal to learn something significant. Perhaps you might return to school to either gain some college credits or get a degree. There are many free classes you can take, often sponsored by local schools or charities. Many community colleges will let local residents audit (sit-in-on) most of their classes. You are not taking it for the grade or the credit; you are developing your mind and learning something useful. There are also groups or clubs that meet regularly on a particular subject—a hobby. Maybe you like coin collecting or genealogy, or quilting, or you don't know whether you like it or not. Get involved and find out. Another worthwhile project is to take classes on a language. Learn a new one. Language and music are two of the best mind trainers there are. The inquisitive mind sees life as an adventure. Always ask why and seize the day.

Curiosity keeps your mind active; work on being observant (2.1.6.1). This is another way a journal can help. Simply record what you observe. Perhaps most importantly of all, read, read, and read. Read everything you can across all genres.

Science tells us that helpful activities include doing puzzles, crosswords, Sudoku, or anything else that exercises and stretches your mind. Science also says that exercise, meditation, travel, and learning new recipes are excellent mind trainers. No matter your physical age, maintain an inquisitive mind. It keeps you young.

John Maxwell promotes what he calls "The Law of Curiosity." He says, "I believe curiosity is the key to being a life-long learner, and if you want to keep growing and developing, you must keep on learning."[153] It is terribly unfortunate that we have stopped asking "why?" How often have you posed that simple question this week? Make a commitment to ask that question daily of someone. You do not need to get into a protracted conversation, or even agree with the person answering your question. The important part is that you ask the question.

Maxwell also provides the following warning: "Anytime a person is answering more than asking, you can be sure they've slowed down in their growth and have lost the fire for personal growth."[154]

The sustained leader takes this additional quote from Albert Einstein to heart: "Learn from yesterday, live for today, hope for tomorrow. The important thing is not to stop questioning."

This sounds like me

A lot	somewhat	just a little	not at all

Additional Resources:
Dorothy Leeds, *The 7 Powers of Questions*.
John Maxwell, *How Successful People Think*.
Gerald Nierenberg, *The Art of Creative Thinking*.

Personal Objective:

---

153 John C. Maxwell, *The 15 Invaluable Laws of Growth* (Center Street: New York, 2012), 193.
154 Ibid. p. 196. See also, Ibid @ 203-06 where he shares the story of Richard Feynman and his desire to have "fun" with math and physics which led ultimately to his participation in the Manhattan project and winning a Nobel Prize.

Specific Actions:

Due Date:

1.3.2 Self-Motivated

WBS Dictionary: External motivators can be effective in getting people to engage in desired behaviors. The threat of imprisonment for thieves, loss of driving privileges for those who drink and drive, and loss of TV accessibility for kids are all examples of negative external motivators, also known as discipline. Positive external motivators include raises and promotions, being able to drive in the HOV lanes, and being taken out to dinner. The problem with each of these is that the external source of the motivator puts control of the situation in the hands of the external party. The sustained leader controls their own destiny by creating their own motivation. Whether that is believing that hard work is its own reward, treating yourself to a frozen yogurt after a hard week of workouts, or the satisfaction that comes from doing a charitable work, being self-motivated says that you make things happen (2.3); you accomplish results based on an internal drive and desire—a passion (5.1.1). You do not require external drivers because you are already doing what needs to be done based on your own determination to reach a goal or to progress toward an objective. Self-motivation says that you do not engage in non-productive time-wasting activities or procrastination. That is not to suggest that you do not take appropriate time off to recharge and relax, but that you focus on the task at hand and engage in the activities that will push it to completion.

Application: Behavioral theorists suggest that the McGregor studies of type X and type Y employees put all of us in one of only two buckets. Thus, this suggests, you are either self-motivated or you are not. If so, then great! Go do something you are motivated to do. If not, well, there is no hope for you. Give up now and don't waste your time and effort. Obviously, the *Sustained Leadership WBS* believes no such thing. Some people do discover that they have a natural motivation, at least in certain areas. For others, developing a sense of self-motivation might require considerable effort.

Self-motivation begins with a goal (2.3.1) about which you feel passionately. From the goal, you specify particular actions you will take toward achieving that goal. Ideally, you will find something you can do each day toward achieving that goal—toward achieving the accomplishment of the daily activity. If you do not find yourself motivated to accomplish today's task, you have to reassess whether the ultimate goal is truly drawing on your passions. Alternatively, you have not sufficiently figured out the connection between the daily activity and the achievement of the goal. For some, you may need to set smaller goals that are more easily and quickly achieved just to prove to yourself that you can, in fact, set goals and achieve them. This level of self-confidence, and the increased passion for believing that the goal you have set is achievable, is often all you need to begin to see self-motivation take hold.

Many other elements of the *Sustained Leadership WBS* begin to come into play. Keeping true to your moral center (1.2.2.1) while working on smaller goals (2.3.1), being a constant learner (1.3.1), associating with like-minded people (whether mentors (1.3.12), or simply friends and associates (1.1.1.1)), understand the things (1.3) that truly motivate you, and celebrating your successes (1.3.17). Following these elements will cause you to make progress on your goals and gradually develop an internally generated motivation toward achieving your goals. The sustained leader comes from a center of self-motivation and does not rely solely on external motivation to guide them.

This sounds like me

A lot   **somewhat**   **just a little**   **not at all**

Additional Resources:

Noel M. Tichy, et al., *Control Your Destiny or Someone Else Will.*
Mark Victor Hansen, et al., *The Master Motivator.*

Personal Objective:

Specific Actions:

Due Date:

1.3.3 Humility

WBS Dictionary: Humility is characterized by modesty. It rejects and avoids arrogance or prideful talk or actions. It must also be genuine rather than characterized by a false humility that engages in self-deprecation in order to have others brag on your behalf. It reflects a courteous and respectful approach to everyone—both those perceived as your superiors and as your inferiors. In fact, true humility recognizes no inferiors.

Application: Humility is often lacking in those in positions of power. True humility is, in essence, a recognition that you are not the smartest, best, prettiest, (or whatever other superlative you wish to express) person in the room or organization. There is always someone better in some aspect of the evaluation. A person who is not humble is not capable of learning—their perception is that since they are the smartest (or whatever) person, there is nothing that another person could teach them. The pride reflected by a lack of humility transcends their ability to grow as a person, and as a result prideful people become stunted in their growth.

Interestingly, in ancient Greek society emphasis was put on honor and reputation, so much so that "In the 147 pithy maxims of the Delphic Canon (6th century BC), considered by the ancient Greeks to be the sum and substance of the ethical life, there is no mention of the theme of, let alone the word, 'humility.'"[155]

Pride, it has been said, is the deadliest of the seven deadly sins (the others being lust, greed, sloth, gluttony, anger, and envy) because it is incapable of recognizing itself. The prideful person is so self-centered that they lose the ability to recognize facts and reality that are obvious to others. Their self-imposed delusion prevents them from honestly assessing themselves, learning.

---

155 John Dickson, *Humilitas: A Lost Key to Life, Love, and Leadership* (Grand Rapids, MI: Zondervan, 2011) 88.

Benjamin Franklin

In reality there is perhaps no one of our natural Passions so hard to subdue as Pride. Disguise it, struggle with it, beat it down, stifle it, mortify it as much as one pleases, it is still alive, and will now and then peek out and show itself.

---

feeling compassion, understanding real power, accepting that they have limitations, or controlling their own ego. These limitations can be overcome with extensive effort and usually external counseling with a trusted mentor. The solution to shortcomings in this area requires at least SOME level of self-recognition of the issue. As noted above, pride cannot recognize itself and some are eternally lost in their own ego and self-interest, which disqualifies them from serving as a sustained leader. Ted Turner, when speaking of himself, said, "A full moon blanks out all the stars around it."[156] The better axiom to follow is from Rabindranath Tagore who said, "We come nearest to the great when we are great in humility."[157]

John Maxwell speaks to the importance of moving from success to significance. Being successful does not necessarily determine whether you will be significant. When Donald Trump was asked who should play him in a biographical movie he said, "It should be someone incredibly handsome."[158] Success and humility are often mutually exclusive, but they don't need to be for the sustained leader. The sustained leader understands that significance is measured more by the lives you have touched in a positive way. Mother Theresa was significant. Abraham Lincoln was significant. George Washington and the founding fathers were significant. The egotistical person puts themselves first, and lacking humility, they are a less significant person/leader. "Publisher Malcolm Forbes said, 'People who matter most are aware that everyone else does, too.' Think about this. Self-centeredness is the root of virtually every problem—both personally and globally. And whether we want to admit it or not, it's a problem all of us have."[159]

---

156 Jeff Parietti, *The Book of Truly Stupid Business Quotes*, 3.
157 B.C. Forbes, *The Forbes Scrapbook of Thoughts on the Business of Life*. (New York: Forbes, Inc., 1976), 352.
158 Jeff Parietti, *The Book of Truly Stupid Business Quotes*, 4.
159 John C. Maxwell, *Intentional Living: Choosing a Life That Matters* (New York: Center Street, 2015), 110.

Later Maxwell shares the story of an executive who recognized that he was missing out on his daughter's formative years. He left his high-powered position and opted for a portfolio of part-time jobs that offered him more flexibility and less travel. This was a significant alteration of priorities. Maxwell observes that this individual "acknowledges that not everyone can afford to quit their job to spend more time at home. But that's not the key change. What needs to change are our hearts. What must transform are our attitudes. What must be purified are our motives. We can't allow our lives to be all about us. That's not the way to do something that makes a difference. If we want to choose significance, we must put other people first."[160] The sustained leader knows that putting others first and demonstrating genuine humility are important keys to success.

Sometimes a leader arrives with great natural abilities and characteristics. Sir Walter Raleigh is one such example. While serving in the court of Queen Elizabeth he demonstrated proficiency in the sciences and the arts. He led men, captained ships and businesses, wrote poetry that is still recognized for its beauty today, and was a naturally charismatic person who attracted supporters and detractors everywhere he went. His supporters were many and fed his ego; his detractors were more subtle and ultimately were successful in bringing his downfall. Unaware of the power of those he had offended, he was charged with treason, imprisoned, and beheaded, and this outcome was probably a cause of great surprise and confusion to him. He was simply trying to be the best he could be and put his many talents to their proper use. While seeming to charm people with his charisma, he was offending those less talented and accomplished to the point that they wished to remove him from their society entirely. Sustained leaders do not flaunt their talents and abilities. They understand that jealousy can be a powerful motivator in others and they stay aware of when such feelings are being raised. They are sensitive to the feelings of others and do not "show them up," which places retaliation at the forefront of their enemies' thoughts.

The sustained leader is also cautioned about being excessively humble toward their convictions. When you are standing for a principle, regardless of the opposition confronting you, it does not mean that you should equivocate on those principles. Dickson says, "Humility applied to convictions does not mean believing things any less; it means treating those who hold contrary beliefs with respect and

---

160 Ibid. 126.

friendship."[161] Later he concludes that there is a way to deal with those whose views are diametrically opposed to ours. "It's where we learn to respect and care even for those with whom we profoundly disagree. We maintain our convictions but choose never to allow them to become justification for thinking ourselves better than those with contrary convictions. We move beyond mere tolerance to true humility, the key to harmony at the social level."[162]

This sounds like me

A lot	somewhat	just a little	not at all

Additional Resources:

John Dickson, *Humilitas*.

Andy Stanley, *The Next Generation Leader*, chapter 11.

Personal Objective:

Specific Actions:

Due Date:

---

161 John Dickson, *Humilitas: A Lost Key to Life, Love, and Leadership* (Grand Rapids, MI: Zondervan, 2011), 167.

162 Id at 170. See also William J. Bennett, *The Death of Outrage: Bill Clinton and the Assault on American Ideals* (New York: Free Press, 1998), 121-23. "So tolerance is a great social good, which is precisely why it needs to be rescued from the reckless attempt to redefine it. For it is a social good only up to a point, and only when its meaning is not massively disfigured. But 'tolerance' can be a genuinely harmful force when it becomes a euphemism for moral exhaustion and a rigid or indifferent neutrality in response to every great moral issue—when in G.K. Chesterton's phrase, it becomes the virtue of people who do not believe in anything. For that paves the road to injustice."

1.3.3.1 Asses Self Honestly

WBS Dictionary: Socrates said the unexamined life is not worth living. A sustained leader takes stock of what they have available to them and determines to improve. This means both enhancing those positive things that are weak or lacking, and ridding themselves of those things that are detrimental. The sustained leader deals with the honest, sometimes brutal, facts about themselves and seeks continuous improvement. This element includes the use of valid assessment tools and the proper interpretation of the results. It provides facts on which decisions can be based. What a person chooses to do with the information, once obtained, is entirely their choice. This element deals only with learning as much about yourself as objectively as possible; gathering the facts, assessing them with complete candor, and then deciding what actions you should take to deal with what you have learned.

Application: There are a number of very valid assessment tools. Each will shine a light on a different aspect of you. One of the basic tools is the Meyers-Briggs Type Inventory. This will tell you how you prefer to interact with people and process information. Another one is the Gallup Strengths survey, informing you of the areas where you have strengths in approaching and solving problems. Others include the 360 degree assessment, Keirsey Temperament Sorter, Big Five personality assessments, Predictive Index Behavioral Assessment, MAPP Test, and others.

Napoleon Hill

No man has a chance to enjoy permanent success until he begins to look in the mirror for the real cause of all his mistakes.

The *Sustained Leadership WBS* is another such tool. Each element of the WBS invites you to perform a self-assessment for each element, and then to fill in the blanks to create a personal project plan. By making this commitment to yourself, look to the additional resources, and then set forth your personal objective for improvement, the specific actions you will take to reach that objective, and a due date. A project is defined as a set of activities with a beginning and an end, resulting in a unique product. (See chapter 2). For the *Sustained Leadership WBS* **YOU** are the unique output—at least a more improved you as a sustained leader. The starting point is the honest self-assessment. Any assessment that is not comprehensive and honest will cause you to start at the wrong point, which is a pretty good indicator that you will not end up where you intended.

John Maxwell tells us of the importance of knowing your personality type in order to align the methods we use to motivate ourselves. "Use whatever personality profile you prefer to study your personality type. (If you haven't used one before, then find one. Examples include Meyers-Briggs Type Indicator, DiSC, and Personality Plus.) Once you have a good handle on what makes your personality type tick, then develop a daily growth system that is simple and plays to your strengths."[163]

Aesop tells us in "The Fable of The Two Bags" that every man, according to an ancient legend, is born into the world with two bags suspended from his neck—a bag in front full of his neighbors' faults, and a large bag behind filled with his own faults. Hence it is that men are quick to see the faults of others, and yet are often blind to their own failings.[164] The sustained leader turns those two bags around and takes a serious look at the bag filled with their own faults.

James C. Hunter, in reference to an article in *Psychology Today* cites the following figures. [165]

Fully 85 percent of the general public see themselves as "above average." Asked about their "ability to get along with others," 100 percent put themselves in the top half of the population, 60 percent rate themselves in the top 10 percent, and fully 25 percent rated themselves in the top 1 percent of the population. Asked about their "leadership ability," 70 percent rated themselves in the top quartile and only 2 percent rated themselves as below average. And check out men. When males were asked about their "athletic ability compared to other males," 60 percent rated themselves in the top quartile and only 6 percent said they were below average athletically.

163 John C. Maxwell, *The 15 Invaluable Laws of Growth* (New York: Center Street, 2012), 83.
164 http://aesopfables.com/cgi/aesop1.cgi?4&TheTwoBags Accessed 10/19/14
165 James C. Hunter, *The Servant: A simple story about the true essence of leadership* (Rocklin, CA: Prima Publishing, 1998), 138.

---•---

Benjamin Franklin

There are three things extremely hard:
steel, a diamond, and to know one's self.

---•---

Clearly, there are some mathematical impossibilities buried in those numbers. The same is true if you ask a group of people if they believe themselves to be more ethical than average. Nearly every hand will go up. When you then mention that, statistically, half of them are wrong, the reaction is generally one of disbelief. It seems to be human nature to assess ourselves as better than we really are. This is why an honest self-assessment is an important starting point. Unless we know the magnitude between the current condition and the desired condition it is difficult to plot an effective and efficient path between the two, and most of us are not really capable of seeing ourselves as we really are. A good mentor, coach, or trusted friend who will be brutally honest with us is essential in making this assessment. Any level of dishonesty, hyperbole, or "shading" that is done, whether intentionally or through willful ignorance, will be a serious disservice to the sustained leader and the team as a whole.

This sounds like me

A lot   somewhat   just a little   not at all

Additional Resources:
John C. Maxwell, *The 360 Degree Leader.*
David Keirsey et al., *Please Understand Me.*

Personal Objective:

Specific Actions:

Due Date:

1.3.3.2 Teachable

WBS Dictionary: Unless a person is receptive to being taught, there is little possibility that they will learn anything. A failure to learn will be a failure to progress. The sustained leader must be receptive to the subject matter, focused on learning, and confident in the instructor. If any of these elements are missing, learning will not occur. The sustained leader will ensure that all parts are present when a teaching opportunity arises—whether they are serving as the student or the teacher. This is not always a given, so the leader must be open to adjusting the circumstances to ensure that they, and the other students, are within the criteria. Being receptive to the subject matter includes having a fair dose of humility (1.3.3). Unless the student will humble themselves and recognize that they need to learn the subject, they will not be receptive and any learning experience will be blocked.

Application: Many organizations send people to "required" training. Many laws, across all jurisdictions, require such training, or the mitigation of legal risk mandates such training or awareness. When such training is derived from a bureaucratic sense of social engineering, the participants' receptiveness is often at its lowest. When such efforts move from the training arena to the education arena the proper term is indoctrination rather than education.[166] Being teachable means that the paramount objective is the gaining of knowledge, the application of critical thinking, and the ultimate attainment of wisdom.

You may be familiar with the adage that "experience is the best teacher." John Maxwell expands on that concept. "According to one expert, the earliest recorded version of this saying came from Roman emperor Julius Caesar, who wrote, 'Experience is the teacher of all things,' in *De Bello Civili*. With all due respect, I

---

166 Training, as used here refers to instruction that relates to the performance of specific tasks. Education refers to the gathering of knowledge and its application to specific scenarios that involve a process of critical thinking.

have to disagree with that statement. Experience is not the best teacher. Evaluated experience is! The only reason Caesar was able to make that claim was because he had learned much by reflecting on his life and writing about it."[167]

Being teachable means that the leader is receptive to absorbing new ideas and experiences. This requires that they have an open mind to these new ideas and are willing to put the new information to good use as soon as possible. The more quickly you put new information or training to use, the more firmly it will be cemented into your repertoire.

The sustained leader develops a thirst for knowledge and knows themselves well enough to know how they learn. They then maximize the use of the preferred learning method for themselves, and then apply the new knowledge as soon as possible. Unless you are willing to change by gaining new information and using it, you will not learn. Learning is a process of change for the better. Sustained leaders make themselves teachable.

This sounds like me

A lot   **somewhat**   **just a little**   **not at all**

Additional Resources:
John C. Maxwell, et al., *Sometimes You Win--Sometimes You Learn.*
Benedict Carey, *How We Learn.*

Personal Objective:

Specific Actions:

Due Date:

---

167 John C. Maxwell, *The 15 Invaluable Laws of Growth* (New York: Center Street, 2012), 53-54.

1.3.3.3 Handles Criticism

WBS Dictionary: No one is perfect, and if you think you are the exception, refer to WBS element 1.3.3. Many people reject criticism either because they do not wish to admit the truth, they do not respect the opinions of those offering the criticism, or they are incapable of recognizing their own short comings. Occasionally, people will suggest that it is "constructive criticism" and only designed to help. When any criticism is offered the sustained leader knows that the proper response to this gift is a simple "thank you." As humans, our nature is to become defensive and one common reaction is to attack the person who is offering their assessment. Too often this becomes an ad hominem attack. The person offering the criticism might be well-informed, or not. The criticism might be fair, or not. The criticism might be well-intentioned, or not. The point is that there are too many variables to immediately assess and determine the validity, accuracy, or intent (although sustained leaders continually work to become better at situational assessments) of any criticism. The sustained leader will accept the gift with a thank you, and then catalog it for future review and consideration. The sustained leader does not simply collect the criticism; they conscientiously return to the criticism and assess it and where necessary make the appropriate personnel adjustments. This element does not address how the sustained leader deals with excessively critical or opinionated people.

Application: Criticism is the passing of judgment on something or someone. Not everyone's judgment is accurate and in matters of pure opinion, it is just that—opinion on which reasonable people might differ. Often the suggestion is not to do "better" but rather to simply do something "differently." Different might or might not be better. The sustained leader recognizes that not everything they do will be perfect. There will always be room for improvement. There will also be many setbacks (See 5.1.7); the absence of setbacks suggests that the leader is taking the safe approach and is not trying hard enough to stretch their horizon. Setbacks are learning experiences, if treated properly. Criticism is the delivery method for suggestions on solutions and failure mode analysis.

One remarkable thing about criticism is that it is a gift. The person offering it is not compelled to do so. And like any gift, upon receipt, you simply say "thank you" (4.2.15). What you do with the gift, subsequently, is purely your choice, but unless you wish to shut down the communication conduit, you simply say "thanks." As retired Lockheed Martin chairman Norm Augustine has noted, "You should never shoot the messenger. It dries up the supply of messengers."

Criticism is typically an expression of disapproval. It attempts to point out perceived faults or mistakes. It may also point out the merits as in the case of a critical review. Thus, it may be balanced. More often than not, it is aimed at describing the flaws as a matter of judgement. While the critic may feel that they are being reasonable or justified in their comments, all criticism is an opinion with which reasonable people might not agree. Thus, the sustained leader will assess the judgement through their own filters to decide whether the criticism has merit. If so, then a decision must be made whether to accept the criticism and make adjustments, or reject the criticism and make no changes. For the sustained leader, accepting the criticism with a gracious *thank you* is the purpose of this element.

As Ben Franklin wisely noted, "We must not in the course of public life expect immediate approbation and immediate grateful acknowledgement of our services. But let us persevere through abuse and even injury. The internal satisfaction of a good conscience is always present, and time will do us justice in the minds of the people, even those at present the most prejudiced against us."

This sounds like me

| **A lot** | **somewhat** | **just a little** | **not at all** |

Additional Resources:
Kerry Patterson, et al., *Crucial Confrontations*.
Kerry Patterson, et al., *Crucial Conversations*.
Thomas F. Gilbert, *Human Competence*.

Personal Objective:

Specific Actions:

Due Date:

1.3.3.4 Unselfish

WBS Dictionary: The world is full of consumers and givers. Depending on the circumstances, a person will occasionally find themselves being both. The true dividing line between the two is the motivation behind the giving and the taking, and the only place that is found is in the heart where the anchor of your values rests. It is often difficult for a person to determine what is in another's heart, but a good self-assessment will assist you in determining your own motives. Everyone has control over their time, treasure, and talent. The question becomes how much of each will you keep for yourself to consume and how much of each will you give away to others? Don't be confused by the question of "do they deserve it?" Certainly you do not cast pearls before swine. The measure, however, is not what you give or how much, but whether you have what is known as a "giving heart." Only you will know if that appellation applies to you. The sustained leader has a giving heart.

Application: You do not engage in giving, whether it is credit, appreciation, or wisdom for what it gives you or to make others think better of you. You also do not give so that others are indebted to you. That is selfish. Being unselfish means that you do not concern yourself with who gets the credit—only that good is done. You do not need to be a full-blown philanthropist. If you are in a position to do so, that's great. Everyone can and should give in measure to what they have.

Watching the nature of people on social media is an interesting study in being unselfish. When asked how a person becomes an influencer—a person others go to for reliable information—the most common sentiment is that an influencer has learned to give before taking. Participate in Twitter chats and offer sound advice. Support others who host the chats. Offer to work with someone offline to assist them. If you only come to the table looking to take the free advice of others, make a sale, or to have them help you without a fee, you will quickly be seen as a taker. Others will be less willing to help you.

Similarly, marketers understand that simply telling someone they need to buy a particular product or service is generally not persuasive. If, however, you give away samples, whether it be food, trial sizes, or sample chapters of a book, people are more inclined to purchase the full product or service. You cannot give everything away for free, obviously, yet the more generous you are without expecting more in return, the more likely people are to call on you and promote you.

Some people also crave attention. They become very narcissistic and think only of themselves. Often you can discern this just by hearing them speak. Rather than focus on others, their consistent use of "I" brings the focus repeatedly back on themselves. Even in environments where the focus should be on others, such as in a eulogy, all they talk about is how the event affects them–even when there are others more tragically affected. It is almost a sickness in their heart, rather than having a heart of giving.

Author and founder of *Success* magazine, Orison Swett Marden said, "Sweeter than the perfume of roses is a reputation for a kind, charitable, unselfish nature; a ready disposition to do to others any good turn in your power." What do you have the power to do? How have you used that power lately? Are you confident enough with your time, talent, and treasure to be generous with what you have and are you willing to use them to promote others, to make their life more comfortable, or to encourage them?

The sustained leader is unselfish and works hard to be other-centered rather than self-centered. They avoid any indicators of narcissism and place others ahead of themselves. They develop an unselfish heart and are generous with their time, talent, and treasure.

This sounds like me

A lot	somewhat	just a little	not at all

Additional Resources:
John P. Dickson, *Humilitas*.
Ken Blanchard, *The Heart of a Leader*.
Todd G. Gongwer, *LEAD . . . for God's Sake!*
Joyce Meyer, *A Leader in the Making*.

Personal Objective:

Specific Actions:

Due Date:

1.3.3.5 Understands Power and Shares Power

WBS Dictionary: This element highlights some key aspects of power that the sustained leader must understand. First, power is neither good nor bad, it simply is. It is how power is used that makes it either good or bad. Second, everyone has power of one form or another and very often they are not conscious of the type and amount of power they hold. Third, the more power is shared, the more of it is created. Like a smile, the more you give away the more you get in return. Power is often misunderstood and often abused. This element is different from 1.3.5.2 Comfortable with Power/Wants to Lead in that this element explores power in all of its dimensions, whether being used for good or evil. All aspects of power and its use need to be understood, even the abusive uses, because there are those who can and will use their power against you. The sustained leader must be able to identify when someone holds power, what type of power they hold, and how they intend to use it. Only then can the sustained leader use their legitimate power to gather the team on a focused vision and deal with the power abusers.

Application: Understanding power requires an appreciation of the sources of power, namely force, guile, influence, and coercion. James C. Hunter defines power as "The ability to force or coerce someone to do your will, even if they would choose not to, because of your position or your might."[168] This is a rather obtuse view in that the power exists whether used or not and does not address the most

---

168 James C. Hunter, *The Servant: A simple story about the true essence of leadership* (Rocklin, CA: Prima Publishing, 1998), 30.

common form of power in today's digital world—that of influence. The weakest form of power is positional power—power you can wield solely because you are in a position of power. In other words, the power vests with the position, not the individual. Some who hold positional power may grow into it and ultimately gain influential power, but others will not use the power properly and will never gain a following. They lead solely because of their position, not because others have chosen to follow them. Short of using "might" (for example appealing to HR to mete out discipline) the positional power holder must learn how to gain and use other forms of power.

It is important to understand types and forms of power, develop an ability to identify them, and to have tactics to avoid, blunt, or defeat the misuse of power. Abraham Lincoln said, "Nearly all men can stand adversity, but if you want to test a man's character, give him power." It seems that one of the first things a person does who obtains power is to misuse it. This certainly will quickly show them just how limited their power is; hopefully, it will not corrupt them or destroy their credibility. It is a dangerous but essential tool; dangerous when abused, essential since it is necessary to accomplish great visions.

War, all wars, are examples of this. There are those who seek to oppress and those who seek to liberate. These factions arise from different moral centers and the oppressors seek to eradicate their opponents. The liberators seek to constrain the avarice of the oppressors and free those who are subject to this illegitimate power. As we have learned throughout human history, the "good guys" do not always win. War is, of course, an extreme example, but it does exemplify the adage that "Might makes right." In our prehistoric days, this was the universal law. In our civilized societies of today, we do not adhere to that, preferring to use the power that is centered primarily in influence. Nonetheless, there are those elements of the global society who still permit power to corrupt them, thus making constant vigilance by sustained leaders a requirement.

Every failure is a failure in leadership, whether of the individual or the team. Very often this failure can be traced to a misunderstanding of power, an abuse of power, or the failure to use legitimate power when it is necessary to do so. In every leadership failure, whether in our societal system of religion, government, or commerce, the abuse of power, i.e. using power for negative or evil purposes, or alternatively failing to use the power one holds for good while letting evil prevail at all, thus permitting the evil efforts to succeed, is at the root of the failed leadership effort.

The sustained leader must understand how power can and should be used productively, including the power necessary to overcome evil. Political discussions often polarize over whether to use diplomacy or force (warfare). Each side labels the other as a "hawk" or a "dove" when in fact such monikers are very misleading. Both diplomacy and warfare are uses of power, the former being one of influence or possibly coercion and the latter of force or guile. It was Edmund Burke who said, "The only thing necessary for the triumph of evil is for good men to do nothing." The sustained leader sees where power needs to be balanced and exercises the power they hold to accomplish good things or prevent bad things. American author Josiah Gilbert Holland observed that, "Calmness is the cradle of power." Brute power need not be your first tool, or your loudest, or even your most often used. The greatest power comes from influence, persuasion, competence, and compassion.

Sharing power can be difficult, especially for the leader who lacks humility or is narcissistic. As Denis Waitley has noted, however, "Real power comes by empowering others." When a leader shares power he or she is demonstrating trust. The person receiving the power is being trained in its use. When combined, the power of the team is increased because the power was shared. When power is closely held, the lack of trust is evident and the team becomes frozen while they constantly ask for permission. The insecure leader holds tightly to the power they have, and over time, even that power is lost. "Power consists," said Woodrow Wilson, "in one's capacity to link his will with the purpose of others, to lead by reason and a gift of cooperation." Power should be shared and the team mentored in its proper use.

Australian author, Bryce Courtenay notable for his book *The Power of One,* said, "The power of one is above all things the power to believe in yourself. Often well beyond any latent ability previously demonstrated. The mind is the athlete, the body is simply the means it uses." The first source of power is the power you hold over yourself. If you do not use it wisely, it can be taken from you and others will see that where power is concerned, you are not to be trusted. The sustained leader understands power and uses what they have to good ends, which might include defending those with less power.

This sounds like me

A lot   somewhat   just a little   not at all

Additional Resources:

Robert Greene, *The 48 Laws of Power*.

Niccolo Machiavelli and Daniel Donno, *The Prince*.

Max DePree, *Leading Without Power*.

Personal Objective:

Specific Actions:

Due Date:

1.3.3.6 Aware of Limitations

WBS Dictionary: The sustained leader accepts that they will not excel in everything. There may be people who seem to have the Midas touch and appear to be successful in everything they do. Closer analysis will suggest that they have developed their senses and worked to enhance their skills. They have sought improvement and prepared themselves so that when opportunity was presented they could capitalize on it. The uninformed call this luck. The sustained leader, however, does not rely on luck; the sustained leader is aware of their limitations and seeks every opportunity to overcome those limitations. The sustained leader has conducted an extensive self-assessment (1.3.3.1), has approached the results with humility (1.3.3), and has reached a point of acknowledging their limitations. Only then can the leader decide whether they wish to do anything with that knowledge, including the avoidance of situations where those limitations present an undue risk.

Application: The first step is to understand, in humility, where your limitations lie. No one is good at everything. Understanding where your limits are is important for knowing how to lead. Some things can be learned through trial and error; to excel in some areas may require a greater investment than you are willing or capable of making. If you have never skied throughout your life, and then at age 60 decide to compete for the Olympics, it is fair to say that you have a few limitations in reaching that goal. This is an extreme example, but the point is simple. When you can recognize your limitations you can make a choice to diminish or overcome those limitations or to accept and live with them. No one can do everything. Choices must be made, and understanding true limitations—not lies you have told yourself, help you make better choices.

It is important for a person who seeks to be a sustained leader to be very, very honest with themselves about limitations. For some people, they see limitations where there are none in a misguided effort to provide an excuse for not trying. This is not the way of a sustained leader. The sustained leader will often not accept limitations, working very hard to overcome any of them while *never* creating false ones to serve as an excuse.

Helen Keller was confronted with a great number of limitations that would have dissuaded many others. Blind, deaf, basically robbed of all her senses except touch, and yet she did more with her life than most other people who had none of her limitations. She found joy in overcoming her limitations and is a model for the sustained leader. She said, "The marvelous richness of human experience would lose something of rewarding joy if there were no limitations to overcome. The hilltop hour would not be half so wonderful if there were no dark valleys to traverse." If not for the bad times, you lose the ability to appreciate the good ones. Thus, overcoming limitations makes life all the more rewarding and satisfying.

Everyone has a learning curve to overcome when starting anything new. Depending on your talents, your abilities, and where you start, this curve might be steep or somewhat flat. To be good at anything you have to start at a point where you are really terrible. Everyone does. Everyone is an amateur at everything at first. You then must work to learn what you need and develop your skills and abilities. The same is true about your leadership journey. Zig Ziglar has said, "Some of us learn from other people's mistakes and the rest of us have to be other people."

Sustained leaders work hard not to be "other people" but to be the one who learns from others and how they overcame their limitations.

This sounds like me

A lot   **somewhat**   **just a little**   **not at all**

Additional Resources:

Helen Keller, *The World I Live In and Optimism*.

Dan Jacobs, *The Art of the Possible*.

Anthony Robbins, et al., *Unlimited Power*.

Personal Objective:

Specific Actions:

Due Date:

1.3.3.7 Controlled Ego

WBS Dictionary: Controlling your own ego is important in understanding how to be humble, but a controlled ego has more benefits than just avoiding narcissism. Too often people allow their ego to control their actions, including their words, and thus appear to others as braggarts and unworthy of being emulated. Everyone has an ego, which is that part of us that reacts to the world external to the self. It is that internal voice that identifies you as separate from everyone else—the ultimate "I". People with a controlled ego tend to not use the word "I" very often. They identify with the team or organization and more often use the word "we." Even when a particular accomplishment was achieved because of you and you alone, the sustained leader tends to use the word "we" in a sharing of credit. It is, from a psychoanalytical perspective, that part of you that controls the baser animal instincts and prevents you from reacting anti-socially to the external environment. So it is not all bad—it simply must be controlled. It avoids self-importance, but allows positive self-esteem and proper self-image, calibrated against the reality of the facts. See 1.2.1.2. If the facts do not support a positive self-image, then it is necessary to change the facts, i.e. adjust your behavior to more closely match the societal norms and generate self-improvement. Create the facts that make you the sustained leader that you know you can be.

Application: Most people have encountered the narcissist.[169] This is the person who is firmly convinced that the entire world revolves around them. The word "we" is not part of their vernacular and whatever credit is due, is due to them. The team? Well, they were just impediments to even greater achievements by the narcissist. This attitude is often revealed in the narcissist's communications. They are often laced with a lot of "I's" and "me's." Even when the subject is (or should be) another person, they cannot help themselves. They must talk about themselves and how the situation affects them. As a boss, all staff meetings are about them. And no matter what story or accomplishment is told, the narcissist will have a better story. One-upmanship is a game to them and they play to win.

Being around a narcissist is never fun. Whether it is a boss, a co-worker, or a family member, they tend to suck the air out of a room and make everyone else miserable. Narcissists are also excellent blame-shifters. Nothing is ever their fault. When dealing with a narcissist, the best advice is to put as much distance as you can between you and them. Do not join their team voluntarily. Do not let their braggadocio go without comment or correction. Certainly you must be tactful, but more importantly, be factual (1.2.1.2). Do not engage in their games and be very careful not to cross them unless you have a plan to remove yourself from the situation.

What does this mean to the sustained leader? First and foremost, if you see yourself in any of these scenarios, take a hard look at your tendencies. Get help. Seriously. This is probably not something you can handle on your own. Pride, it is said, is the worst of the deadly sins because it cannot identify itself. Being a

---

169 Jeffrey Pfeffer. *Leadership BS: Fixing Workplaces and Careers One Truth at a Time.* (New York: Harper Collins, 2015). Chapter 2.

narcissist, not having your ego under control, will derail your leadership journey. If you begin to sense that things are changing, and that you might be starting to exhibit such tendencies again—ask for help. Call on a mentor. In serious cases, get professional help. No one will want to work with you and without followers, you have nothing to lead.

To prevent yourself from falling into the traps of an uncontrolled ego, listen to yourself. Are all your stories about you? Do you say "I" a lot? Does every conversation eventually turn out to be about you? And do not justify it on the basis that someone else brought you into it as the focus. The sustained leader is adept at turning the conversation away from themselves. There are times to be bold and brash, but never forget that, "Timid is how the deer stay alive."[170]

This sounds like me

A lot	somewhat	just a little	not at all

Additional Resources:

Roger L Martin, *The Responsibility Virus*.

Michael Maccoby, "Narcissistic Leaders," Harvard Business Review, January 2004, PP. 92-101.

Personal Objective:

Specific Actions:

Due Date:

---

170 Jack Elder, editor of Citibank Economic week, quoted in Sarah Myers McGinty, *Power Talk: Using Language to Build Authority and Influence* (US: Warner Business Books, 2001), 33.

1.3.4 Models Behavior

WBS Dictionary: A sustained leader understands the social mores and acceptable etiquette that is expected from a leader and models the appropriate behavior. The sustained leader knows that the team will be watching them constantly (just as children do with their parents), and will remain conscious of the impression their actions will leave on those who are watching. The sustained leader will live by appropriate standards. In the colloquial parlance, a leader "walks the talk." This means that they do not just preach or pontificate. They actually live in accordance with the standards they require of others and hold themselves accountable. Achievement of this standard requires that the leader understands what acceptable conduct is and in fact lives to those standards. Through this active practice, the leader develops the ability to attract other talent (3.1.2) and influence them (1.1.2.5). Failures in this area will result in being disqualified for leadership positions until the behavior is modified and demonstrated over a sufficient period to convince others that the old actions have been fully abandoned.

Application: Albert Schweitzer said, "Example is not the main thing in influencing others, it is the only thing." It is amazing what sort of conduct can be forgiven. So many people in leadership positions have been found out to be adulterers, drunkards, embezzlers, and guilty of so many sins and crimes against the public. Sometimes they go to prison; often they do not. Society too often seems to grant blanket amnesty to such persons. As sustained leaders, however, shouldn't we hold our leaders to a higher standard?

When ethical standards are not upheld at the highest level, others on the team believe that they can get away with the same conduct. Sometimes it's a function of group-think where deviant behavior is not an aberration, but becomes the new standard and often celebrated. Under the law, a failure to uphold such standards universally can prevent it ever being enforced, since occasional enforcement will be perceived as discriminatory conduct.

When an entire society becomes lawless, or simply accepts it, anthropologists say that it reflects a society in decline. Whether it was the Roman Empire or any other well-established society, a failure to enforce the rule of law affects the entire fiber of the society. Similarly, conduct that is unethical, yet perhaps not illegal, will cause the entire organization to accept such conduct. Ultimately, it will cause the team to fail. A recent example in America was when Enron failed and its accounting firm Arthur Anderson ceased to exist; such examples can be found where bad behavior at the top permitted bad behavior throughout the organization. The sustained leader understands the importance of modeling proper behavior. Only by doing so can they legitimately enforce proper behavior throughout the team.

As children, we adopt the behavior of our parents. As we grow and move into society, we model the behavior of our peers. If that means we set our sights on existing within "high society" or believe that the best choice is to join a street gang, we model what we see. More recently, there seems to be a sense that when someone does something you don't like, you should burn down local businesses and loot them. To many, there is a cognitive dissonance in that logic. Yet, this is what has been modeled in certain segments of society, it is often not punished, and thus it continues as an acceptable model.

Training is often based on modeling techniques, showing a person how a process is to be performed and having them repeat it. Without delving into neurolinguistics theories or developmental psychology, much of which is based on modeling behavior, the sustained leader understands the concepts and knows that their followers will mimic the behavior they see. If the leader is not behaving in accordance with established norms, or societal standards, or ethical standards, or even the law, they can expect that other members of the team who do not have a strong moral compass (1.2.2.1) will copy the leader's behavior. The team will suffer.

A common saying asserts that "Character is how you act when no one is watching." The sustained leader always assumes that someone somewhere is watching and behaves accordingly.

This sounds like me

A lot	somewhat	just a little	not at all

Additional Resources:
John C. Maxwell, et al., *Becoming a Person of Influence.*
John MacArthur, *The Quest for Character.*
Max DePree, *Leadership Is an Art.*

Personal Objective:

Specific Actions:

Due Date:

1.3.5 Believes in Self

WBS Dictionary: This element includes the sub-elements of confidence and being comfortable with the power that comes with leadership roles. It is a legitimate sense of your capabilities as well as your limitations. It is understanding that you have your values in order and attempt, to the best of your ability, to adhere to those values. When you fail, and you will, you adjust, make amends if appropriate, and resolve to do better next time. You resist temptations to violate your principles and embark on efforts that, while not guaranteed to succeed, give you a sense that with appropriate focus and hard work, you will have a reasonable opportunity to succeed. You know that your weaknesses will find you out, and often at the most inopportune times. Nonetheless, based on your experience and conditioning, you will overcome your weaknesses or find another way to compensate for them—again without compromising your principles. You have certitude about your abilities and assurance that you will always strive to do your best. And if you cannot commit to doing your best, you will not engage in the activity at all. You are trustworthy and faithful to your friends and associates and resolve never to betray a confidence or assume a role that is beyond your legitimate abilities.

Application: This element is all about being the best you you can possibly be. John Maxwell provides this perspective: "Pastor and radio broadcaster Tony Evans says, 'If you want a better world, composed of better nations, inhabited by better states, filled with better countries, made up of better cities, comprised of better neighborhoods, illuminated by better churches, populated by better families, then you'll have to start by becoming a better person.' That's always where it starts—with me, with you. If we focus on personal character, we make the world a better place. If we do that our entire lives, we've done the best things we can do to improve our world."[171] Later he quotes Rabbi Nachman of Bratslav who said, "If you won't be better tomorrow than you were today, then what do you need tomorrow for?"[172] Great question. You are either growing or dying. It's part of the natural law (1.2.2.4).

Mary Crowley practiced her sales technique during severe economic times and was confident enough to tell a prospective employer that she would work one Saturday, and if she did not earn enough to pay her salary, she would not return. She reportedly outsold everyone that day and earned herself a sales position in the store. She was a woman of strong Christian convictions and a teetotaler. Even though she was a top producer, she got into a disagreement with her boss over a planned cocktail party for the top producers. This ended that relationship, but she had enough confidence by then to start her own business which became known as Home Interiors. At each step of the process, Mary had enough self-confidence to sell herself and succeed while remaining true to her principles.

The sustained leader knows themselves well enough to have confidence in their abilities and principles to comfortably wear the suit of leadership power. By constantly learning and improving, he or she can have the confidence that, while fully acknowledging in all humility that they are not perfect, they can make amends when appropriate and continuously improve, becoming a better person day by day. Acknowledge your God-given abilities. Be prepared (1.3.1.3), take action to accomplish something (2.3), be aware of your body language (4.4.5) by projecting a positive attitude, and speak with certainty (4.3.2) which is much easier if you have properly prepared. When you are confident in yourself and comfortable with power all of these elements come together.

This sounds like me

A lot	somewhat	just a little	not at all

---

171 John C. Maxwell, John C. *The 15 Invaluable Laws of Growth* (Center Street: New York, 2012), 152.
172 Ibid. 168.

Additional Resources:

William Ury, *Getting to Yes with Yourself.*

Napoleon Hill, *The Law of Success In Sixteen Lessons (2 Volume Set).*

Dale Carnegie, *How to Develop Self-Confidence.*

Personal Objective:

Specific Actions:

Due Date:

1.3.5.1 Confidence

WBS Dictionary: A sustained leader must know themselves sufficiently to know the limits of their abilities. Only by knowing these limits can a leader act with confidence in their decision making and actions. Too often people adopt a "fake-it-til-you-make-it" philosophy with confidence, but that is a false confidence and can lead to tragic mistakes. This does not, however, require that you act with 100% assurance of anything. You must constantly strive to stretch your challenges and thereby push your abilities. Only by constantly stretching a bit beyond what you KNOW you can do will you be able to grow. As you grow, things that at one time were stretch assignments become routine and matters which you can now approach with great confidence. A failure to stretch is a failure in your leadership. Confidence is not limited to skills and capabilities. A sustained leader must also have confidence in their character (1.0), power (1.3.5.2), trustworthiness (1.1.2.2), and reliability (1.2.1.3). They must know themselves (1.3) and acknowledge with complete honesty the results of their self-assessment (1.3.3.1).

Application: When President Kennedy announced the initiative in 1961 to go to the moon within the decade there were a lot of people who questioned the wisdom of that vision. It was something that had never been attempted, much less achieved. While there was great confidence in our abilities generally, there were immediate discussions about what we knew that we knew, what we knew that we didn't know, and how to find out what we didn't know and were unaware we needed to know it. There were many technological advances in many areas of science by the time Neil Armstrong set foot on the moon. We learned many things, and by the time Gene Cernan was the last person to walk on the moon, we were approaching the moon missions with great confidence. The same was true with the Space Shuttle. By the time the last shuttle flew the launches and landings, while not perfect, were fairly routine. We had great confidence in our spaceflight abilities.

Times have changed. If we were to set a new vision to return to the moon, it would not be as simple as pulling the old Apollo blueprints out of the drawer and building new rockets. We no longer have the confidence we once had. Putting another human on the moon or the first person on Mars would require a whole new set of knowns and unknowns. We would have to rebuild our confidence.

A leader must act with certitude and self-reliance. This comes from consistent attention to the development of your abilities and testing them often. Will you sometimes fall short? Of course. Setbacks are an integral part of developing your abilities. The key is to try to never fail in the same way twice. Thomas Edison is reported to have been asked by a reporter about is many failures in trying to find a suitable filament for his proposed light bulb. Edison's response reportedly was, "I have not failed. I've just found 10,000 ways that won't work." He had confidence that he would succeed and quite obviously he did. With each test that did not provide the desired solution, he learned a little more until eventually he succeeded. Without the self-confidence in his and his team's abilities he would have given up.

Here's a useful exercise. Write down ten things that you believe. It might be religion based or society focused. Just list ten things that you believe to be true. Now go back and write a paragraph on WHY you believe that statement is true. The sustained leader must know what it is they believe, AND be able to articulate why they believe it. If you are unable to articulate the "why", then you have to consider that you do not have as much confidence in the belief as you initially thought. When you can state your belief and then state why you hold that belief, you have confidence in the belief system you have chosen.

Kouzes and Posner make the same point. "People expect their leaders to speak out on matters of values and conscience. But how can you speak out if you don't know what to speak about? How can you stand up for your beliefs if you don't know what you stand for? How can you walk the talk if you have no talk to walk? How can you do what you say if you don't know what you want to say? To speak effectively, it's essential to find your own true voice. To earn and sustain personal credibility, you must be able to clearly articulate your deeply held beliefs."[173]

This sounds like me

A lot   **somewhat**   **just a little**   **not at all**

Additional Resources:

Les Giblin, *How to Have Confidence and Power in Dealing with People.*
Dale Carnegie, *How to Develop Self-Confidence.*

Personal Objective:

Specific Actions:

Due Date:

1.3.5 2 Comfortable with Power/ Wants to Lead

WBS Dictionary: Power is the ability to make things happen. Power is neither good nor bad within itself—it simply is. The real question that a leader should ask is, "What power do I have and what do I intend to do with it?" Too often leaders

---

173 James Kouzes and Barry Posner, *The Leadership Challenge, Third Edition* (US: Jossey-Bass, 2002), 46.

seek power for the sake of power. This is more prominent in political and commerce environments, but is found across all types of leaders. This element addresses the idea of using power in order to lead effectively. It is distinguished from 1.3.3.5 Understands Power where the leader must gain an appreciation for those who wield power inappropriately. This is important because there will be those who will attempt to usurp the leader's role in order to achieve their own personal selfish ends and will use whatever power they hold to do so. In this element the leader is vested with power and has a choice of whether to use that power for good or evil. The sustained leader is comfortable with that situation and overtly makes the choice to lead with a proper moral underpinning rather than for selfish or self-serving motives. They are comfortable in the role of "leader" and all that it entails; they want to serve in that role.

Application: The sustained leader seeks legitimate power. It is important to note that positional power, although the weakest form of power, is still legitimate. Often positional power is the first form of power that all leaders, great and weak, are given. What they do with that power tells a great deal about what kind of leader they will ultimately become. They will learn through trial and error. It is often asked how a person develops good judgement. The most popular answer is that it comes from education and experience. Unfortunately, the life span of any person is insufficient for them to make every possible mistake and learn from it (although there are some who seem to give it a valiant try!) Thus, a leader must learn from the mistakes of others. George Santayana said that "Those who do not learn history are doomed to repeat it."[174]

Johann von Goethe

Beware of dissipating your powers; strive constantly to concentrate them. Genius thinks it can do whatever it sees others doing, but it is sure to repent of every ill-judged outlay.

---

174 There is some debate over the origin of this quote. Edmond Burke was known to have said, "Those who don't know history are doomed to repeat it." And Santayana has also been quoted as saying, in a slightly modified form, "Those who cannot remember the past are condemned to repeat it."

The sustained leader engages in study and constant learning to prepare themselves to lead. General Patton was a great student of history, and studied very ancient battles and warfare tactics, delving deep into recorded history to understand warfare and its tactics. This was what made him such a strong military leader.

Warren Bennis and Stephen B. Sample suggest that everyone is born with an innate desire for respect; to feel important. They go so far as to say, "The drive for importance is today commonly called leadership."[175] They go on to say that man, as unique in the animal kingdom, alone seeks to "mold the collected facts and institutions into a sophisticated and ever-evolving art of moving others in new directions. Of course, the ability to move others in new directions isn't solely a practical concern: It is a piece of our inner drive to matter, to be of value and significance."[176] If everyone so strongly desires to lead, why does it seem so scarce? Why are good leaders so hard to find? Why aren't the necessary leadership skills and traits automatically imbued in us so that we all aspire, desire, and rise to leadership? Quite simply, because too few people exercise the discipline to understand leadership and enhance their skills, develop the traits, and take the actions to put them in a leadership role. They never become comfortable with the power of leadership and either fail as leaders or, more wisely, simply choose not to accept the responsibility. Sustained leaders recognize the on-going journey that is leadership and accept it.

Robert Greene says in his book on power:

In the world of power you will constantly need help from other people, usually those more powerful than you. The fool flits from one person to another. Believing that he will survive by spreading himself out. It is a corollary of the law of concentration, however, that much energy is saved, and more power is obtained, by affixing yourself to a single, appropriate source of power.[177]

---

175 Warren Bennis and Stephen B. Sample (with Rob Asghar) *The Art and Adventure of Leadership; Understanding Failure, Resilience, and Success* (Hoboken, NJ: John Wiley & Sons, Inc. 2015), 11.
176 Ibid, 11-21.
177 Robert Greene, *The 48 Laws of Power* (New York: Penguin Books 1998), 175.

He writes from a considerably Machiavellian viewpoint, yet his point has much merit.

The sustained leader uses their power in a comfortable and relaxed manner. They can identify those who are misusing whatever power they have and can confront that abuse with their own power to put the team on a proper trajectory. They are comfortable with the necessary confrontation, correction, and if necessary, discipline to lead the team in the direction and manner that is necessary. While everyone may aspire to leadership, or significance, or importance, the proper use of power calibrates them to the appropriate span of control

We note elsewhere that good judgement comes from education and experience. And where does much of that experience originate? From exercising bad judgement. This includes the use, or abuse, of power.

This sounds like me

| A lot | somewhat | just a little | not at all |

Additional Resources:

Daniel Goleman, *Emotional Intelligence.*
James Hillman, *Kinds of Power.*
Robert J. Danzig, et al., *The Leader within You.*
Jeffrey Pfeffer, *Managing With Power.*

Personal Objective:

Specific Actions:

Due Date:

1.3.6 Maximizes Intelligence

WBS Dictionary: We are told that to whom much is given, much is expected. Whether you are gifted with an extraordinary IQ, or a relatively low IQ, there is a much greater level of "smarts" that can mean much more than raw intelligence. Some might call it "street smarts" or "savvy." Intelligence does not limit itself to book knowledge, formal education, or high standardized test scores. Many very inventive people lack all of these things and yet have contributed considerably to society while making very comfortable livings. This element requires the sustained leader to recognize their natural abilities and find ways to make the most of them. Some research suggests that Alzheimer's and certain other later-life illnesses can be helped by continuing to engage in mentally challenging tasks—even things as simple as crossword puzzles or Sudoku. Regardless of your natural abilities, this element requires that you find ways to take what your natural talents may be and make the most of them.

Application: Can you volunteer at a local shelter and advocate for the rights of those less fortunate? Then do so. Are you a practicing attorney with a large corporate practice? What pro bono work have you done that genuinely helps those with less access to our system of justice? Are you a trained medical professional? Have you volunteered for a blood drive or a health fair? In each of these cases it might seem that you are on the giving end, but those who routinely engage in these activities will tell you that what they learn benefits them in many unexpected ways. Can you write a blog? There are no longer the impediments to publishing and reaching a very broad audience as was once the case with book publishing. What books have you read? Have you considered learning another language? What if you learned sign language so you could interpret for a co-worker or a student at the local community college? Yes, this would ultimately help others, but in the process you would be working toward maximizing your intelligence. If you need more formal education, go get it. If you have thought of getting an advanced degree, go get it. If you have not read a book since high school (a description of 87% of Americans), go to the local library and hang out for a while. What is your hobby? Have you joined a local group of people with the same hobby who, working together, might put on a sewing class, or a train show, or a genealogical help group? Take what you have and use it to its maximum potential.

Sustained leaders do not allow themselves to stagnate. They have a constant drive to achieve and attain. They understand that to do so they must stretch themselves. As John Maxwell tells us, "If you are always at the head of the class, then you're in the wrong class."[178]

The sustained leader is a constant learner (1.3.1). Applying your learning endeavors to a variety of areas broadens your knowledge base. Sustained leaders know that drawing on the mistakes of others, the lessons learned, the lessons of history, and stories of where CEO's have made bad decisions, where religious advocates have sinned very publically, and where generals have led successful campaigns all contribute to the wealth of knowledge held by the leader. Drawing on these lessons will help sustained leaders make better decisions, have a greater vision, and better define their mission.

And a final note to those who are advancing in their age. Modern science has many things that help to keep your mind sharp and balance out your brain chemistry. Games and puzzles (e.g. crossword, Sudoku, word-search have been shown to keep an aging mind sharp. It seems to work like a muscle and must be regularly exercised to stay in shape. Advances in understanding brain chemistry have also advanced. Even if you have reached a point in your life where you have the maximum level of knowledge and experience, continue to maximize what your brain can do. Share it. Mentor someone. Learn a new technology, language, or musical instrument.

This sounds like me

A lot	somewhat	just a little	not at all

Additional Resources:

Morgan Jones, *The Thinker's Toolkit*.

Marilyn Vos Savant, *The Power of Logical Thinking*.

Personal Objective:

---

178 John C. Maxwell, *The 15 Invaluable Laws of Growth* (New York: Center Street, 2012), 85.

Specific Actions:

Due Date:

1.3.7 Good under Pressure / Composed

WBS Dictionary: Some people contend that they work best under pressure. While on a practical level that may be true, it is rarely true that people do their best work when in a rush or without enough time to consider and act rather than acting quickly. Most hasty undertakings are described accurately as rash. It is also true that many people fold very quickly when even slight pressure is applied to their lives. Some people will not drive on freeways (thankfully) because of their inability to deal with such pressures. Some retreat into an emotional cocoon at the slightest provocation. Sustained leaders do not succumb to this. They prepare for situations by expanding their training, education, and experience to maximize their abilities and perceptions of perplexing or seemingly intractable problems. They know themselves well enough to control their emotions; they control their physical reaction to stress; they recognize their natural reaction to stress; they assess the situation objectively and accurately (and preferably quickly); and then they apply wisdom to their decisions. From an external perspective, this may seem "cool-headed" or, "good under pressure." In fact, it is the combination of specific leadership traits and attitudes to a specific situation to yield the best outcome. The sustained leader does not seek out pressure situations, or create them falsely. But the sustained leader can deal with them effectively when they arise.

Application: In ancient Macedonia there was a town known as Gordium. It was led by Gordius the father of Midas (he of the golden touch). Midas had arrived in town when the elders were reviewing a prophecy from an oracle that predicted their salvation would come from a man pulling a wagon. Upon being fortuitously made king of Phrygia, Midas commemorated his ascension to the throne by constructing a shrine that included his wagon. He tied it to a pole in the center of the acropolis with a knot of bark from the cornel tree. This shrine ultimately made its way to

Gordium where it became quite the tourist attraction. It was considered bad luck not to visit the shrine and at least *try* to untie the complicated Turkish knot with no exposed ends. Many had tried and all had failed. As the lore continued to grow, an oracle foretold that whoever loosed the Gordian knot would lord over the whole of Asia. It was, in effect, the same story as the Sword in the Stone that brought King Arthur to power.

Alexander, known as "The Great," had been born into aristocracy, the son of King Philip II of Macedon. He grew up in privilege and even studied under Aristotle. He had studied deeply the art of war from within his father's court, and then proceeded to conquer most of the then-known world. At one point, with his troops depleted and demoralized, he rested near Gordium and sought guidance from the gods. Having decided to continue his conquests, his personal seer cautioned him that proceeding without attempting the knot would cause him to encounter bad luck. So Alexander proceeded to the shrine, making quite a spectacle before all of the townspeople as their esteemed king attempted their famous knot. After two hours of puzzling over the knot with no ends, and seeing that the solution would not lie within the realm of manual dexterity, Alexander took out his sword and sliced the knot in half, revealing the hidden ends inside. Alexander, standing before his people and under considerable pressure to "perform," did exactly that—with a completely unique solution. And, as the oracle foretold, Alexander went on to conquer all of Asia and even parts of India.

In business, politics, or religion today we often refer to what seems to be an intractable problem as a Gordian knot, suggesting that the problem has no solution. The sustained leader, when under pressure, knows that every problem has its solution and that a variety of tools are available to them to apply to the situation. They are well trained, educated, and practiced. They know how to muster their resources and apply them to even the most difficult problem—and often NOT with the wisdom previously applied by others. Under pressure, the sustained leader can still perform, and occasionally do so in an outstanding and unpredictable way.

Alexander was well trained in war and experienced in conquest. He approached his Gordian knot in a unique and innovative way. His training in strategy and logical argument provided him a different way to approach the problem he encountered. How does one untie a knot that has no ends? While everyone else had seen the knot and just "knew" that the solution to any knot was to "untie" it. He knew that the goal was to release the knot—not just untie it. He used a contrary line of thinking to solve a long-standing and perplexing problem. Using all of his education, training, and experience, and with so many of his subjects looking on, he found his victory, despite the pressure, in an innovative way. The sustained leader of today does the same thing –even under, and perhaps especially under, pressure. Henry Kissinger reminds us that "A diamond is a chunk of coal that is made good under pressure." The sustained leader knows how to keep their cool when others around them are losing theirs.

Maintain your composure in all situations. Bite your tongue, snap a wrist band, count to ten—whatever it takes to maintain your composure under pressure or when you are goaded to lose it. The sustained leader remains composed—always. Einstein reminds us that "No problem can be solved from the same level of consciousness that created it." Raise your level of consciousness.

This sounds like me

A lot	somewhat	just a little	not at all

Additional Resources:
Robert Goffee, et al., *Why Should Anyone Be Led by You?*
Daniel Goleman, *Focus.*

Personal Objective:

Specific Actions:

Due Date:

1.3.8 Conscious of Legacy

WBS Dictionary: What you do and who you are will survive your earthly life. A sustained leader understands this and pays attention to the legacy he or she is creating. The legacy might be the raising of God-fearing children who have strong spiritual anchors; or opening your home to those without a home; or creating great wealth that is guided toward charitable purposes; or creating the better mousetrap that makes everyone's life more comfortable or productive; or perhaps their legacy will be to fulfill Mark Twain's prediction that "No one is a complete waste; they can always serve as a bad example." A sustained leader, in humility (1.3.3), should not be seeking fame or self-aggrandizement as their legacy. Sadly some do. A sustained leader knows that they will be remembered by their family, friends, and co-workers. Some are remembered fondly; others less so. A sustained leader seeks the betterment of everyone through their efforts and the legacy they leave behind.

Application: Charlie Manson, Jeffrey Dahmer, and Adolf Hitler have legacies. Not good ones, of course, but legacies nonetheless. This element is like the proverbial class exercise to write what you want to appear on your tombstone. Others such as Andrew Carnegie left their fortunes to many varied philanthropic initiatives.

Arab Proverb

If you have much, give of your wealth; if you have little, give of your heart.

Enoch Pratt was born in Massachusetts, graduating Bridgewater Academy at the age of 15. He started his working career in a hardware store, and at age 23 moved to his adopted city of Baltimore to open a hardware store. Enoch was a successful businessman and soon had interests in railroads, banking, and shipping. He and his wife were unable to have children of their own, so they initially opened their home to orphans in Baltimore. His many philanthropic endeavors included refurbishment of his church, installing a new organ, art that remains on exhibit to this day in various Baltimore locales, and the Peabody Institute. He was constantly involved in benefitting children, especially members of minority groups and the deaf. Any of these would individually be a remarkable legacy, and collectively reflected his position, for a time, as one of the wealthiest men in America. His most notable contribution, however, was none of these. In 1882 he offered to the city of Baltimore a central library with six branch libraries and a financial endowment of well over $1,000,000. It was his goal to create a facility that "shall be for all, rich and poor without distinction of race or color, who, when properly accredited, can take out the books if they will handle them carefully and return them." Thus was created in Baltimore a facility known to this day as the Enoch Pratt Free Library. Despite all of this, Enoch Pratt was not done.

After his death, he left a large portion of his fortune to the trustees of the Moses Sheppard endowment who, in Pratt's opinion, were the "only Board of Trustees in Baltimore who have carried out exactly the directions of the founder." That contribution led to the renaming of a hospital as the Sheppard Pratt Hospital that also continues to serve the community more than 100 years after Pratt's death. Here is a man who was very conscious of his legacy. He contributed to specific purposes and sought to control the outcomes even after his death. He contributed to an existing charity *because* the trustees had demonstrated a loyalty to the original founder. It makes you wonder if the founders of most charities would believe that the current trustees of that institution are fulfilling the purposes for which it was founded.

The reach of a legacy is often unpredictable. Andrew Carnegie also contributed extensively to libraries. He once said, "Pratt was my guide and inspiration." What are you doing to leave a positive legacy? Who are you influencing in regard to their legacy? Few will have the resources to leave the legacy of an Enoch Pratt or Andrew Carnegie, but the issue here is not quantity but quality. What will be on your tombstone?

President Bush had a healthy view of his legacy. As reported by Dana Perino, President #43 noted that "Last year I read three books about George Washington. So if they're still analyzing the first president, then the forty-third doesn't have a lot to worry about."[179]

John Maxwell shares the story of his heart attack in 1998. At the age of 51 his two primary thoughts were a concern that those close to him knew how much

---

179 Dana Perino, *And the Good News is…: Lessons and Advice from the Bright Side* (New York: Hachette Book Group, 2015), 107.

he loved them and that there was still a lot that he wanted to accomplish. This certainly encourages a bias for action (2.3). Maxwell then tells us that David Rae of the Young President's Organization reports that most CEO's are less afraid of dying than they are of not making a contribution to their world.[180] The sustained leader is conscious of their legacy.

Will people be sorry when you leave? As an anonymous speaker noted, "Anyone can please a room, some by entering others by leaving." You will have a legacy; it's up to you whether it is favorable or unfavorable.

This sounds like me

A lot | **somewhat** | **just a little** | **not at all**

Additional Resources:

James Kouzes, et al., *A Leader's Legacy.*

Les Wallace, et al., *A Legacy of 21st Century Leadership.*

Personal Objective:

---

180 John C. Maxwell, *The 15 Invaluable Laws of Growth* (New York: Center Street, 2012), 245.

Specific Actions:

Due Date:

1.3.9 Thinking

WBS Dictionary: Thinking implies that there is some reasonable and rational level of reasoning going on. The sustained leader must exercise their abilities in being thoughtful and reflective. In this process, the sustained leader develops judgment in all areas of leading. Thinking is different than acting on instinct or predisposition. It assesses variables and chooses the appropriate framing for the issues under consideration. To suggest "I wasn't thinking" is a mischaracterization of what was going on. We are always thinking. The better question is: How can I think more clearly, more critically, more systemically, or more strategically? Clear thinking is reflected in 4.0 Communication where the point is made that muddled communications stem from muddled thinking. There are times when visceral or involuntary actions are taken that relate to self-preservation and the ability to bypass rational thought in those circumstances is important. Most situations faced by a leader, however, do not rise to that level of survival. They require the application of the best brain-power the leader can bring to the situation. Leaders should always be thinking and thinking about why and what they are thinking. The brain is the leader's most formidable tool. Used well, it will serve them well. A failure to develop their thinking abilities will limit a leader's influence.

Application: We are all victims of our habits and proclivities. Assessing yourself properly allows you to see and understand how you are most likely to act in a variety of situations. How you think, how you more normally react, how you typically process information, and how your biases affect the actions you take are all tempered by how you think. And how you think can be trained and developed. Recall as a child when you were responsible for an accident a parent might ask, "What were you thinking?" That was an instructive question to ask a young developing mind. Somewhere along the way, we have lost our ability to ask ourselves that very question.

Tom Watson of IBM challenged his employees by using an office poster that just said, "THINK."[181] Simply performing the same task over and over yields no creativity or innovation. Stop. Think. Ask "why?" Challenge yourself to ask incisive and often difficult question of yourself. Why did I do that? Why did I react in that way? What triggered my anger in that situation? What could I have done differently? How would a different action or reaction have changed the outcome? What thinking tools can I bring to bear on a current problem, risk, or situation?

A poster found in an office said, "Think or Thwim". This is a creative play on the combination of Watson's "Think" poster and a popular saying of "Sink or swim." When a leader takes time to think and not react viscerally, they will discover new relationships and concepts. They will be creative and spur their team to become more creative. They will discern the situations that require lifesaving self-preservation and those that call up the deepest reflection on reasonable and rationale progress. Thinking is a critical function for the sustained leader. The world could use more thinking.

Graphic—This sounds like me

A lot	somewhat	just a little	not at all

Additional Resources:
Morgan Jones, *Thinkers Toolkit*.
Malcolm Gladwell, *Blink*.

Personal Objective:

---

181 IBM continues to sponsor a poster series, available on the web, encouraging people to think.

Specific Actions:

Due Date:

1.3.9.1 Critical Thinking

WBS Dictionary: Our brains work continuously, 24/7, even if we are not aware of it (such as when sleeping). What we are thinking is driven by many factors. We can, however, control our thoughts and guide them in a particular direction. A critical thinker is open-minded and leaves themselves open to alternatives to what they might initially think about a situation. They do not immediately accept the obvious, but they think clearly about the alternatives in order to assess them rationally. Rather than blindly accepting a posited position, rational analysis is applied to set the beliefs of the critical thinker. They develop a fine sense of discernment. The sustained leader uses critical thinking and applies discernment to know with a certainty not only *what* they believe, but *why* they believe it.

Application: Too many people act more like sponges than humans. Sponges do not think much at all. They respond from instinct. Their cells and parts just seem to know what to do to survive. They absorb what comes their way and digest it without processing it in any critical way. Some leaders may function like a sponge in absorbing data, but they then fail to apply any form of analysis. They might be storing data like a simple flash drive, but they are not adding any value to the data. Sustained leaders process the information received in a disciplined manner that takes the facts (1.2.1.2) (not opinion or conjecture or hype) and approaches those facts in a clear and rational manner.

Some people seem capable of only parroting back data they have accumulated. It is, in some respects, no different than the person who spends their time on twitter sending retweets. When people speak to the idea of "thought leaders" they are referring to those who do not simply toss out facts, but apply a level of critical thought to those facts and find the interrelationships that link them and distinguish them. In the political arena people sometimes refer to "low information voters" who are those who hear the news broadcast or the single campaign ad and base their opinion (and their vote) on that limited data set without thinking through the ramifications of the position.

Robert H. Ennis has posited 12 elements of a critical thinker[182]:

1. Is open-minded and mindful of alternatives
2. 2Desires to be, and is, well-informed
3. Judges well the credibility of sources
4. Identifies reasons, assumptions, and conclusions
5. Asks appropriate clarifying questions
6. Judges well the quality of an argument, including its reasons, assumptions, evidence, and their degree of support for the conclusion
7. Can well develop and defend a reasonable position regarding a belief or an action, doing justice to challenges
8. Formulates plausible hypotheses
9. Plans and conducts experiments well
10. Defines terms in a way appropriate for the context
11. Draws conclusions when warranted—but with caution
12. Integrates all of the above aspects of critical thinking.

    Clearly, critical thinking is more than just accumulating data. A person with an encyclopedic-mind might do well on "Jeopardy™," though they should not be confused with a critical thinker. The critical thinker must make the effort to analyze the information gathered and determine the weight to be given each piece of data. All data are not equal. The critical thinker makes judgments or conducts an analysis of the data, reaching for the facts behind the facts rather than simply applying emotion or opinion (e.g. "I like this."). The critical thinker is open-minded and willing to adjust their presently-held view of the data gathered. The critical thinker will also ask themselves what data they are lacking or simply don't know. The critical thinker will also know themselves (1.3) and be able to filter out of their analysis their own prejudices or preconceived ideas. As Aristotle said, "It is the mark of an educated mind to be able to entertain a thought without accepting it." Critical thinking turns knowledge into wisdom.

---

182 http://criticalthinking.net/ Accessed 07/23/14

Sadly, it seems that critical thinking is no longer taught in our schools, from kindergarten through college. What is taught is the exact opposite of critical thinking, sometimes referred to as indoctrination or rote memorization. While knowledge is the starting point of wisdom, it is only the starting point. In order to become a critical thinker, you might need to un-learn certain habits of your thought processes. And old habits, especially favorite ones, are hard to break.

Ralph Waldo Emerson has noted that "A foolish consistency is the hobgoblin of little minds, adored by little statesmen and philosophers and divines."[183]

Educators have long known that critical thinking is much more than rote memorization. They also know that when challenged, almost all students will rise to the challenge. Too often educators have a set curriculum that is followed, and whether the individual student is excelling or lagging, they get the same curriculum. Thus, the ones who could excel are never given the opportunity, and those who are lagging eventually fall so far behind that recovery becomes impossible.

Marva Collins understood this well. She challenged her students and they did well—better than other classes. This created animosity and she eventually was forced out of her position. Opening a private school, Marva, who was educated in the south, pressed her views that children would excel when challenged. Catering to "problem" students, she taught them Shakespeare, Dickens, real-world math problems, and encouraged discussions on philosophy and life in general. When the students were tested, they scored well above the national average.[184] The students were challenged. They did not just memorize (although they did memorize a great deal). They developed the skills of critical thinking—the one thing that HR representatives today say is most lacking in candidates who apply for positions in their companies. What Ms. Collins said about all this was, "You can't weep or talk your way through a mess. When you come up against a problem, you have to work your way through it."

This sounds like me

A lot   **somewhat**   **just a little**   **not at all**

---

183 See 1.2.1.3 for the full quote in context.
184 Alan C. Elliott, *A Daily Dose of the American Dream: Stories of Success, Triumph, and Inspiration* (US: Thomas Nelson, 1998), 255.

Additional Resources:

"Critical Thinking: A Streamlined Conception" from *Teaching Philosophy*, (1991).

Sylvan Barnet, et al., *Critical Thinking, Reading, and Writing*.

M. Neil Browne, et al., *Asking the Right Questions*.

Personal Objective:

Specific Actions:

Due Date:

1.3.9.2 Systems Thinker

WBS Dictionary: A systems thinker can perceive the intricate interaction of all the variables involved in any system. Any organization is such a system, but the approach applies to any environment. The dynamic interactions of all the components of a whole interrelate in unique ways. Even the smallest of elements can have an extreme effect, perhaps not as extreme as is suggested by the "Butterfly Effect," but a pronounced and measurable effect nonetheless. In an organization, the people, processes, procedures, politics, finances, and other inputs to the system all affect the outcome. Understanding them is critical to success as a leader. A sustained leader is able to "fine tune" the system by making timely and often small adjustments to improve the effectiveness or efficiency of the organization. Occasionally a more drastic adjustment is necessary, including the scrapping of the entire, or large segments of, the system. Bankruptcy, death of a principle in the organization, and failure to stay current with technology would be examples of such significant events. Events from a small reorganization to a large merger or acquisition will have a significant impact on the organizational systems.

Application: The sustained leader grasps that nearly everything in life is a type of complex system. Whether it is a large organization, a manufacturing process, a customer service process, or a new system for delivering astronauts to the space station, moons, or planets, no system functions effectively unless there are leaders who understand all aspects of the system. This element demands that the best leaders understand the systems involved in their area of leadership. It also demands that they gather around them followers who better understand those systems, or parts of systems, than they do (3.12).

Consider the trajectory of a planetary mission—minor adjustments early in the trajectory have an extreme effect on the ultimate position of the spacecraft in relation to its destination. NASCAR cars and drivers compete most weekends in their season constantly looking for that tiny adjustment to the many intricate systems, both mechanical and human, that will give them an edge. In races of five hundred miles or more, the win can sometimes be measured in the hundredths of an inch.

Peter Senge in *The Fifth Discipline* tells us that "Systems thinking is a discipline for seeing wholes. It is a framework for seeing interrelationships rather than things, for seeing patterns of change rather than static 'snapshots.' It is a set of general principles—distilled over the course of the twentieth century, spanning fields as diverse as the physical and social sciences, engineering, and management….During the last thirty years, these tools have been applied to understand a wide range of corporate, urban, regional, economic, political, ecological, and even psychological systems. And systems thinking is a sensibility—for the subtle interconnectedness that gives living systems their unique character."[185]

There is a discipline within engineering called "systems engineering." Its purpose is to take the disparate parts of a system and integrate them into a working whole. People are not the same as

inanimate objects. While both must adhere to the laws of physics, humans make choices that might be based on a myriad of factors—logic and emotion being two of the primary ones. A sustained leader appreciates these differences and recognizes that as a leader, the only followers that count are the human ones, and their systems are more complex than the mechanical or chemical ones. It is interesting to see how

---

185 Peter M. Senge, *The Fifth Discipline*, 68-69.

much science is devoted to trying to understand the complexities of humans in an engineering system construct.

Dee Hack

Simple clear purpose and principles give rise to complex and intelligent behavior. Complex rules and regulations give rise to simple and stupid behavior.

"The best leaders have system awareness...." So says Daniel Goleman.[186] Quoting scientist Larry Brilliant, he continues, "If you think in a systems way ... that drives how you deal with values, vision, mission, strategy, goals, tactics, deliverables, evaluation, and the feedback loop that restarts the whole process."[187]

The sustained leader develops a sense of systems thinking to understand the myriad interactions that occur under their leadership. The mechanical and scientific systems tend to yield absolute answers and measurable results that are repeatable. The human factor in systems is far more complex, less well understood, and not usually repeatable. That, however, provides no excuse for not working to understand it. In the final analysis outcomes are determined by people, not systems and processes.

This sounds like me

A lot	somewhat	just a little	not at all

Additional Resources:
Peter M. Senge, *The Fifth Discipline.*
Stephen R. Covey, *Rethinking the Future.*

Personal Objective:

---

186 Daniel Goleman, *Focus: The Hidden Driver of Excellence* (New York: HarperCollins, 2015), 214.
187 Ibid., 214-15.

Specific Actions:

Due Date:

1.3.9.3 Strategic Thinking

WBS Dictionary: A strategy is an overall plan to manage change in order to achieve a desired result. Strategic thinking, therefore, is the disciplined thought process that allows a leader to assess current situations, determine appropriate goals, formulate a plan to achieve these objectives (including the assignment of responsibilities), and establish metrics to assess whether the chosen strategy and tactics are succeeding. It is not overstatement to say that an absence of strategic thinking will guarantee that the leader will have nothing to lead—no goals, no vision, no mission to implement—and thus no followers. Strategic thinking is a dynamic process and requires an iterative approach to assess changes as they occur and determine any impact to desired goals.

Application: The goal of strategic thinking is the development of a strategic plan. If you only desire to maintain the status quo, no strategy is needed. Things will certainly change, but you will be following those changes and being managed by them rather than leading and managing the change. Strategic thinking allows you to anticipate changes, manage risk, and be prepared to adjust as plans unfold. It is, in part, a combination of both critical thinking and systems thinking applied to specific objectives.

Strategies can be applied to any aspect of leadership. Whether the application of the strategy has to do with the organizational structure, the marketing, the political environment, the temporal or schedule issues, or any other aspect of leading, the application of strategic thinking is a necessary component of leading.

You cannot just sit back and wait to win the lottery. Strategic thinking allows you to define your own life journey. It is required of all leaders at all levels of an organization. It is not limited to "management". The better the entire team thinks strategically, the better the organization will function. By understanding the five questions of a strategic thinking process, each member of the team is better focused on the team objectives. It allows them to know unequivocally that the team is doing the right thing.

The Strategic Planning Process described in the chart below reflects the five essential questions, or steps, to strategic thinking. By applying strategic thinking you assess where you are and where you want to be, (see also 2.3.1). You assess the gap between these two and lay out a series of actions that will get you from the "is" to the "desired" state. You apply the correct resources, assign responsibility and accountability for achieving the desired results, and have defined that end state with the metrics by which you will determine success.

STRATEGIC THINKING/PLANNING

1. WHERE ARE WE NOW?
1. Internal/External Assessment
2. SWOT Analysis
3. Core Capabilities
4. Market Drivers

2. WHERE DO WE WANT/NEED TO BE?
1. Vision
2. Values
3. Mission
4. Value Proposition
5. SMART Goals
6. Metrics

3. HOW DO WE GET THERE?
1. Customers
2. Strategies
3. Programs
4. Priorities

4. WHO WILL TAKE US THERE?
1. Key Personnel & Stakeholders
2. Most Effective Organization (MEO)
3. Leveraged Networks
4. Delegation/Accountability

5 HOW ARE WE DOING?
1. Monitoring
2. Consistency
3. Discipline
4. Reviews
5. Accountability

Copyright © Daniel M. Jacobs

© 2009 Daniel M. Jacobs Used with permission.

The sustained leader applies strategic thinking to situations that indicate a change is necessary. They allow for directed thinking toward specific goals and objectives within a construct that facilitates the successful attainment of those goals. Without the structure of strategic thinking, results will be left to chance which does not favor sustained leadership. The entire *Sustained*

Leadership WBS process is an exercise in strategic thinking applied to your self-improvement.

This sounds like me

A lot   **somewhat**   **just a little**   **not at all**

Additional Resources:
Daniel M. Jacobs, *The Art of the Possible.*

Personal Objective:

Specific Actions:

Due Date:

1.3.10 Courage of Convictions

WBS Dictionary: Once a leader has honestly considered the many possible positions and adopted the one they believe to be most appropriate, the one most solidly consistent with their moral center (1.2.2), the sustained leader maintains this position unless and until circumstances clearly demonstrate that they have changed and a different position is more suitable. The sustained leader will be confronted with pressure to modify their decisions, position, or views. This pressure can be extreme and can be a challenge to the fundamental beliefs of the leader. Quite often this pressure may be couched in terms of critical thinking (1.3.9.1) or being open-minded. Sometimes holding firm to your convictions will be labeled intolerant, racist, sexist, or some type of phobia towards particular groups. When a leader is sure of their moral center and natural law, when they are certain that they have assessed the parameters of right and wrong, especially when there is no bright line distinction, and have reached a decision, there is no deviation from this conviction. It will take courage to maintain it in the face of these accusations. Having the courage of your convictions is to act in accordance with your fundamental beliefs despite actions that go against popular opinion or criticism—even extreme criticism. It embodies a sense of fearlessness and a firm conviction of knowing right from wrong. Elements of courage, bravery, and fortitude are involved. The leader must have enough determination to pursue their goals because of the underlying belief system that might run contrary to those surrounding him or her.

Application: The sustained leader acts in accordance with their beliefs. They do not give into pressure, even if extreme. Their character must withstand that pressure. The sustained leader will say and do what they believe is right regardless of the disagreement of others. The sustained leader will not act in an intentionally hurtful manner or express opinions for the desired effect of stirring up trouble, but upon being asked a direct question the sustained leader will not sugarcoat the truth.

Kouzes and Posner address this issue. "Leadership and challenges are inextricably linked. Leadership and principles are inextricably linked. The implication is very clear. The leaders most people admire are ones who have the courage of their convictions. What's just as important to constituents as having leaders with values is having leaders who stand up for those beliefs during times of intense challenge and radical change." [188]

Followers are looking for leaders who are steadfast in their beliefs. Those whose opinions or views shift with the wind are not reliable leaders. Kenny once served on a board with a president who was a very personable and conscientious person. The issue was that this president was so personable that he never wanted to upset people. While one group would talk with him and he would agree with their approach, all it took was another group to talk with him later to sway him to their view. This lack of firm conviction and his desire to please everyone led to serious rifts in the team and a tremendous amount of rework. From the team's perspective, no decision was ever final and thus very little was actually accomplished even though many projects were reworked. And reworked. And reworked, depending on today's decisions.

---

188 James Kouzes and Barry Posner, *The Leadership Challenge, Third Edition* (US: Jossey-Bass, 2002), 182.

Sir Winston Churchill noted that, "You have enemies? Good. That means you've stood up for something, sometime in your life." You will not please everyone all the time, thus the need to be true to your own convictions. Sustained leaders do not act rashly and they are conscientious to consider the views of others. They do not hold a superiority complex believing that they are always right. That is an act of extreme hubris. They simply have the determination and confidence to push forward to their goals and vision based on their honest assessment of doing the right thing. Your convictions do not make you stubborn or bullheaded; you must retain an open mind as new facts come to your attention. Your convictions, to be valid, must be based on a prior detailed analysis based on facts, not conjecture or, worse, indoctrination. The assessment is based on your moral compass and best judgement. The sustained leader then fully commits to their convictions by taking action.

This sounds like me

A lot	somewhat	just a little	not at all

Additional Resources:

R. Albert Mohler, *The Conviction to Lead*.

Theodore Wilhelm Engstrom, et al., *Integrity*.

John C. Maxwell, *There's No Such Thing as "Business" Ethics*.

Personal Objective:

Specific Actions:

Due Date:

1.3.11 Coping Ability

WBS Dictionary: The sustained leader recognizes that things do not always work out as planned and situations cannot be changed or rectified on a desired schedule, e.g. "overnight." Sometimes there are simply facts and circumstances that are outside of our control. Consequently, the sustained leader must engage in some struggle to overcome the undesirable condition. During that struggle we may have no choice but to deal with the situation, i.e. to cope with it. Sustained leaders develop a strong coping ability; the ability to exercise patience even in the face of some urgency. Coping is not acceptance. The mere fact that it is perceived as coping suggests that the situation has NOT been accepted, but must be brooked until the situation can be changed or overcome. Coping involves dealing with the responsibility of leadership during problem solving in a calm and considered manner. Excessive emotionalism will hinder coping, although in some circumstances emotional reactions are part of the healing process in learning to cope with a situation that cannot be changed. Even in those situations, getting stuck in the emotional phase will prevent final acceptance and prolong the need for coping which can, long term, be unhealthy.

Application: Some life events are irreversible. No matter how much patience you have, your children will never return to their cute innocent selves and aunt Bertha is not going to return from the grave. Certain life events are completely outside of our control. Call it fate, Karma, Providence, or God as your faith dictates. Things will change and not always in a way you might prefer.

Other life events are within your control even if it will take a great deal of effort on your part to control them to the best of your ability. Until you can make the change occur, or accept the things you can't, you must cope with the situation. An inability to cope will considerably hinder your performance as a leader. Coping is a psychological device used to master, minimize or tolerate stress and conflict. An inability to do so can cause a variety of ill effects that can lead to death. Literally.

Humor is often a useful coping mechanism. Numerous office plaques have used this approach to make daily stress factors seem less stressful. For example, "The difficult we do immediately; the impossible takes a little longer," while variously attributed in many forms over 200 years, this version was adopted by the Army Ordinance Department in WWII. Another with no specific source is, "I'm sorry, but your failure to plan does not constitute an emergency on my part."

Ultimately, coping is facilitated by understanding the length of the stress. Prisoners of War often give up hope simply because their prison life seems interminable. For most situations, knowing how long it will persist eases the stress. You can withstand almost anything if you know how long it is going to last. The sustained leader uses goal setting and a bias for action to bring unpleasant circumstances to a quicker resolution. For those things that have permanently changed, accepting that they will never return places a stamp of finality on it which also assists in coping with the change.

Somewhat less humorous sayings, perhaps more with a philosophical bent, are often used to ease the stress. Sayings such as, "Don't be sad because it's over; smile because it happened" and "Don't curse the darkness, light a candle" provide some solace. Perhaps the wisest words are attributed to American theologian Reinhold Niebuhr who offered the prayer: God, grant me the serenity to accept the things I cannot change, courage to change the things I can, and the wisdom to know the difference. Popularly known as the Serenity Prayer it was later adopted by a variety of 12-step programs including Alcoholics Anonymous to assist those recovering from various addictions to cope with their condition while working to take better control of their lives.

The sustained leader develops effective coping mechanisms that preserve their health, and in many respects, their sanity. Effectively dealing with stress and conflict is a crucial tool to maintain both physical and mental health.

This sounds like me

A lot	somewhat	just a little	not at all

Additional Resources:
Roger Fisher, et al., *Beyond Machiavelli*.
Mark Towers, *Reinventing Your Self*.

Personal Objective:

Specific Actions:

Due Date:

1.3.12 Has Mentors

WBS Dictionary: Every great leader had mentors who helped them get to a leadership opportunity. This element is expressed in the plural because it is wise to have several mentors. No one is great at everything; each mentor has their own mix of capabilities, traits, and talents and just because someone exhibits such characteristics, it doesn't mean they can train or guide others. A sustained leader chooses their mentors wisely, has a specific purpose for asking this person to mentor them, and lays out a specific plan on how to use each mentor to achieve the desired result. It is important to keep in mind that mentoring is a two-way path and it is inappropriate to simply become a consumer of mentoring. It is important that you give back to the mentor. Certainly this requires expressing appreciation, but might also include referring business opportunities, sharing information, and actually putting the mentoring to practical application. No one will continue mentoring if they feel that their guidance is being ignored.

Application: The selection of mentors is an extremely important step in your leadership development. Select the wrong ones and you will waste time being misled or learning the wrong things. As you grow as a leader, you will develop a better sense of leadership. You will know it when you see it and miss it when it is absent. You will be able to discern real leadership from faux leadership. Too often we have spent our lives experiencing poor leadership rather than sustained leadership. We adopt those traits and habits as conventional when in fact they are detrimental to your development as a leader. You must occasionally unlearn some things. We suffer from the disease of bad examples. Until you develop a higher level of discernment and critical thinking (1.3.9.1), you could be misled by this disease. Choose your mentors wisely.

Andy Stanley suggests the following as guidelines in selecting your mentors or, as he calls them, leadership coaches.

Find someone to observe you in a variety of leadership settings. Outside input is critical. Even if you could watch yourself in a mirror twenty-four hours a day, you would never see yourself as others see you.

Select a coach who has no axe to grind and no reason to be anything except brutally honest. He need not be an expert in your field. What your coach must be able to do, however, is put himself in the shoes of those who are influenced by your leadership.

Try to find someone who can articulate his thoughts with clarity and precision. You don't need glaring generalities; you need to know exactly what needs to be repeated and deleted in your leadership.[189]

Having a team of coaches is not a bad idea if you can manage them. You must be a good mentee and actually be willing to follow the advice given. You have to trust the advisor. Another approach that can be effective, especially when you are sure that you are not sufficiently familiar with sustained leaders who can mentor you, is to establish a study group, much as you may have done in college in order to prepare for an exam. Put a team of people together who are at different stages of their leadership development. Borrow their experiences and share your successes and failures. In areas where you are weak they may be strong, and vice versa. The team approach to leadership can be effective in some circumstances. This is not, however, a one-semester task. Remember, this is a life-long journey.

Tea Leoni is a very accomplished actress. She says, "I sort of thought I wanted to be an anthropologist. But my father suggested I go to a cocktail party full of anthropologists first. I did. He's a very wise man."[190] One excellent reason to find a mentor, and especially as a summer internship while you continue your education, is to expose yourself to a variety of career choices that you MIGHT like. It's only a summer. Hang out with those who are doing what you think you might enjoy. Pick their brains. See if it is a profession to which you would readily adapt. A mentor does not have to be for long periods or for a particular crisis. Simply exposing yourself to a variety of people, skills, and professions will help you focus on what really excites you and will engender passion for a lifetime.

---

189 Andy Stanley, *The Next Generation Leader: Five Essentials for Those Who Will Shape the Future* (US: Multnomah, 2003), 128.
190 Jeff Parietti, *The Book of Truly Stupid Business Quotes* (US: Harper Paperbacks, 1997), 139.

After leaving her post as presidential press secretary, Dana Perino recognized the important role that mentors had played in her life. One of her mentors, Susan Molinari, noted that the only thing mentors ask in return for their role as mentor is that the mentee pay it forward. Perino took this to heart and, with the help of others, created what she describes as "a version of speed dating, but with mentoring instead of romance." In these sessions, a team of mentors would meet with a small group of mentees and share their wisdom and answer question. Once the designated time had passed, they moved on to the next mentee. Most got to see six different mentors, then were invited to a cocktail party to further hone their networking skills. These "Minute Mentoring" sessions were then essentially syndicated across the country in order to keep up with demand.[191] Even a minute or two with a good mentor can pay dividends. A sustained leader knows the incredible value of mentors. No single person is the "best" at all things. A sustained leader knows themselves (1.3) well enough to have identified their weaknesses and found people who have excelled, or at least achieved a high level of success, in those areas. The sustained leader has approached these candidate mentors and arranged to be mentored by them, with all of the investment in time and respect that a mentor deserves. The sustained leader takes their wise counsel and learns and grows.

While this element is promoting the use of living mentors, John Maxwell encourages us to consider the many excellent biographies that are available. "Most people who decide to grow personally find their first mentors in the pages of books."

You can learn a wealth of knowledge and wisdom by exposing yourself to people you will never meet. Through books, and especially biographies, you will discover the very flawed nature of man (1.3.1.1). You will not live long enough to make every possible mistake from which to learn (although we may all know someone who seems to be trying to accomplish that record), so you must learn from the mistakes of others. Everyone is flawed, regardless of how they might be portrayed in history. Despite being gifted or talented, a person's flaws will eventually come to light. This does not mean that you can't learn from them. Cynicism aside, everyone has something to offer, and you can learn from anyone.

---

191 Dana Perino, *And the Good News is…: Lessons and Advice from the Bright Side* (New York: Hachette Book Group 2015), 160-61.

This sounds like me

A lot   **somewhat**   **just a little**   **not at all**

Additional Resources:

Andy Stanley, *The Next Generation Leader*, Chapter 12.

John C. Maxwell, *The 15 Invaluable Laws of Growth*, Chapter 13 "The Law of Modeling."

Tony Dungy, et al., *The Mentor Leader*.

Personal Objective:

Specific Actions:

Due Date:

1.3.13 Appreciates the Journey

WBS Dictionary: It is important to be focused on goals and to have a vision. Reaching goals provides a great sense of satisfaction and accomplishment. The sustained leader understands the need for the small or interim victories and the importance of celebrating them (1.3.17). These small victories comprise the journey toward success—a point that does not really exist. The sustained leader has a deep felt appreciation for the journey itself. No team or situation is static. This particular part of the journey will never be replicated, and conversely, has never existed previously. Some aspect will be different next time. This gives truth and credence to the aphorism that every day is a new day. In the same way the sustained leader knows how precious each minute of each day is. Too often a great deal of time is wasted on non-productive or non-beneficial activities. This is not to say that the sustained leader is not entitled to their down-time and even frivolous activities. It's merely noting that the journey of time will pass with or without your consent. It is the sustained leader's choice how that journey will be filled. Essentially, it will either be filled by the leader's volition or by yielding to the volition of someone else.

Application: It has been previously pointed out that while we are using the metaphor of the Work Breakdown Structure from the disciplines of project management, this particular effort is not really a project. The PMBOK® defines a project as having a beginning, an end, and a unique product. You begin the process of making yourself a better you whenever you choose, and hopefully, your dedication to that will create a unique product—a better you. This process, however, never really ends. You never reach a point of "success" and you can always find ways to continuously improve yourself. This journey has no end, so you might as well enjoy it!

Today will never be repeated. The minutes lost are gone forever. How will you be different tomorrow (or even in the next ten minutes)? Will it be because of actions you take today to manage these future situations, or will you simply wait for circumstances to overwhelm you? The choice is yours. The train is leaving the station whether you are on it or not. Will you regret the inconvenience or be excited about the journey? Rabbi Nachman of Breslov observed that "If you are not going to be any better tomorrow than you were today, then what need have your for tomorrow?" Excellent question. You should be on a thoroughly enjoyable journey of continuous self-improvement.

Oliver Wendell Holmes posited that "The great thing in this world is not so much where we are, but in what direction we are moving." Are you making progress toward your goals? Is the achievement of your vision another day closer to happening? Thomas J. Watson, the founder of IBM observed that "Whenever an individual or a business decides that success had been attained, progress stops." You never want progress to stop. Even Yogi Berra, the master of malapropisms noted that "You've got to be careful if you don't know where you're going 'cause you might not get there!"[192] Sometimes getting lost and discovering new places is part of the adventure. Wandering aimlessly is never good. The sustained leader has a sense of direction as dictated by their goals and vision.

---

192 Yogi Berra, *The Yogi Book: "I Really Didn't Say Everything I Said"* (US: Workman Publishing Company, 1998), 102.

Wherever you are in your journey, take time to look back and celebrate your progress, or identify where you have not achieved as much as you had hoped. Class reunions, for example, are often difficult because of the realization of your lack of progress. Rather than lament the lost time, celebrate the accomplishments you can identify and celebrate the realization of your commitment to continue the journey, improving from this day forward.

This sounds like me

A lot somewhat just a little not at all

Additional Resources:
Josh Waitzkin, *The Art of Learning*.
Frances Hesselbein, *My Life in Leadership*.
Brian Tracy, *Success Is a Journey*.

Personal Objective:

Specific Actions:

Due Date:

1.3.14 Political Savvy

WBS Dictionary: Politics is a dangerous sport. In its simplest terms, a sustained leader understands that others do not share their values, goals, passions, or objectives. This requires that the leader identify those differences and address them in terms the audience can understand and appreciate. The sustained leader seeks those areas of common understanding and builds from there. The leader can couch positions and views in a manner that addresses the listener's viewpoints and interests to gain their support. Some abhor the use of "politics," especially in the corporate or institutional setting, but the leader understands that these situations exist whether they acknowledge them or not. Thus, the answer is not to ignore them, but to use them in a productive manner. There are some who will never be convinced to adopt your views or values. That is not necessarily the goal. The goal is to find ways to harness the energy of the entire team toward a mutually agreed objective *despite* the differences in opinion and views. This takes political savvy.

Application: Politics are ubiquitous. Every interaction of people carries a sense of politics. Local parochial interests will often reflect political power struggles, even down to the level of schoolboard or dog-catcher. Wherever there are people there will be those seeking to gain political power, and thereby advantage, over their fellow humans.

The sustained leader understands the dynamics of persuasion (4.2.2) and its role in political environments. Politics invades nearly all situations so it is important to understand how to manage the interpersonal relationships in an astute manner. At its extreme politics can often cloud the issues and introduce irrelevant material into the discussion. In fact, being obscure and "spinning" conversations are part of the political game. This is what Kathleen Kelly Reardon refers to as "pathologically political environments. Much of what goes on in these types of organizations involves less than up-front behavior."[193] The sustained leader never permits such an extreme to be practiced by them or the team.

Having political savvy includes a large amount of discernment. "And what's discernment? Good judgment, basically. Or more precisely in this context [globalization], it's the combination of business savvy, cultural sensitivity, and good old wisdom. It's the ability and self-confidence to know when to push forward the company's will and ways, and when not to, out of respect for local customs and mores."[194]

All organizations have an organizational chart that, for the most part, reflects the reporting lines of those in the organization. The sustained leader respects these formally established lines and conducts another exercise to discover where the

---

193 Kathleen Kelly Reardon, *It's All Politics: Winning in a World Where Hard Work and Talent Aren't Enough* (New York: Currency Doubleday, 2005), 43.
194 Jack and Suzy Welch, *The Real Life MBA: Your No-BS Guide to Winning the Game, Building a Team, and Growing Your Career* New York: Harper Collins, 2015), 68.

true leaders are—those who hold leadership power because of their influence, not just because of where they appear on the org chart. By asking as many people as possible the question similar to the following: "When you have a particular issue, to whom do you go for help and advice?" The answer to this question will show who the real influencers are. From this information you can construct a different organizational chart reflecting the real leaders. The sustained leader associates with these influencers and respects the advice and guidance they can provide. This is not to say they abuse the relationship or take unfair advantage. Being political savvy means, in part, that you recognize and respect the real performers in the organization while also respecting those who hold power based on their position in the organization. Like it or not, people in positions of power can affect your development and ability to gain leadership roles.

Nearly all offices have receptionists, which the politically savvy leader understands are some of the most important people in the office. They are the gatekeepers. They control access to those with either positional or genuine power in the organization. If you make the gatekeepers your enemy, your access to the people who can help and guide you will be limited. The gatekeepers also interact with a broad range of people in the organization and can be excellent guides to the real performers and those who are just "filling space." Rather than make these influential people your enemy, make them your friend.

Those who hold political savvy tend to share information more readily, especially information that reflects positively on their accomplishments. This doesn't mean that you become an insufferable braggart, only that you find useful and factual information and share it with others. Part of showing political savvy also suggests that you are perceived as a team player. You have the best interests of the organization and other team members as your focus. You support the vision and mission established by the leader. You express genuine interest in support of the organization and fellow team members.

Some methods of demonstrating political savvy can be Machiavellian and should be avoided. The political savvy person does not become a sycophant, groveling toady, or backstabbing manipulator. Taken to an extreme, all attempts at being political savvy can be read this way. Part of being successful in navigating the political minefields in any organization is understanding the acceptable limits of such activities. The sustained leader learns and respects these environments.

This sounds like me

A lot   **somewhat**   **just a little**   **not at all**

Additional Resources:

Jeffrey Pfeffer, *Managing With Power*.

Patrick Lencioni, *Silos, Politics and Turf Wars*.

Kathleen Kelley Reardon, *It's All Politics*.

Personal Objective:

Specific Actions:

Due Date:

1.3.15 Risk/Fear Tolerance

WBS Dictionary: Each leader has their own level of tolerating risk. In effect, they become afraid at different points on different matters. Some are quite low; others are quite high. The sustained leader must learn their level of risk tolerance based on a variety of factors and circumstances. Certain industries carry their own risk levels, but nothing is ever completely risk free. The sustained leader develops a tolerance for reasonable risk, develops sound risk assessment skills, and is adept at implementing risk mitigation strategies. They understand fear as a warning sign, not a sign of immanent disaster or injury, and builds confidence in their abilities to manage through the risk and the fear. Sustained leaders view any setback as a temporary situation and an opportunity for a learning moment. This element differs from 2.1.4 Risk. There, risk addresses the competence of assessing and mitigating business and performance risks. Here, risk pertains to knowing yourself and understanding risk, your fears, and the emotional reaction of worrying in a more general sense rather than taking positive action to manage the risk and your fear reaction. The sustained leader must understand the risks that are specific to the business in which they are involved (2.1.4) and also the risks that relate to them personally and their ability to deal with their fears. When facing fear, conveying confidence to the team is a role of the sustained leader.

Application: On a per-capita basis, teenagers in Chicago are safer in Afghanistan during military operations than they are on the streets of Chicago. More people are killed on our highways than from sky-diving accidents. Pedestrians, motorcyclists, and bicyclists are in greater danger than drivers of cars. Aside from physical safety, some are willing to risk their reputation and fortunes for a cause they believe in. The Founding Fathers said in the Declaration of Independence, "And for the support of this Declaration, with a firm reliance on the protection of divine Providence, we mutually pledge to each other our Lives, our Fortunes and our sacred Honor." That's lying it all on the line. Such risks require great rewards, and more than 200 years of religious freedom and political liberty bear truth to the faith of our founding fathers. Sustained leaders have a relatively high tolerance to risk and fear, but they are also adept at managing that risk and the fear that comes with it. They do not engage in extreme risk unless their assessment suggests extreme rewards. Alternatively, when things are very dire, taking the extreme risk might be the only solution. Each situation is different.

Let's take an extreme example and assume that you are a local drug dealer. Why? Because you can make a lot of money and have a lot of nice things. Despite the risk of getting caught by the civil authorities and the risk of incarceration, there is also the risk of death from rival drug dealers seeking the same buyers. You have, however, weighed all of these risks and have decided that you are willing to take that risk in order to reap the rewards. Most others, fortunately, have no such risk tolerance and would never consider dealing drugs no matter the possible rewards. Many people will never even exceed a speed limit for fear of getting stopped and receiving a traffic ticket. Everyone's tolerance is different.

Management and leadership expert Max DePree has observed, "An unwillingness to accept risk has swamped more leaders than anything I can think of."[195] Andy Stanley has noted that "Leaders know that the best way to ensure

---

195 Max De Pree, *Leadership Jazz* (New York: Doubleday, 1992), 144.

success is to take chances. While the average man or woman fears stepping out into a new opportunity, the leader fears missing out on a new opportunity. Being overly cautious leads to failure because caution can lead to missed opportunities."[196] General George S. Patton similarly said, "Take calculated risks. That is quite different from being rash." And Ralph Waldo Emerson astutely perceived that "Fear defeats more people than any other one thing in the world."

The sustained leader does not deny risk or fear. They learn to accurately assess the risk and the possible reward and make an informed decision based on their personal or organizational risk tolerance. "No power is strong enough to be lasting if it labors under the weight of fear."[197]

A team will most often adopt the view of its leader. Very often the leader is unaware what specific observations are being made and what conclusions the team, or individual team members, are drawing from their observations. Not everyone deals with fear in the same way and many do not do so effectively. Thus, part of a sustained leader's obligation is to help the team deal with fear whether well founded or not. One key way of doing this is to make sure that the facts are well presented and well communicated. (See 1.2.1.2 and 4.2.12.1) Jack and Suzy Welch report that they have observed a particular "thief" within organizations that is very insidious. Specifically, these are "employees who steal your time and energy, underperformers and inveterate conflict-creators" and the "thief" they refer to is the feeling of fear. "Fear of job loss, fear of industry collapse, fear of economic decline. If you are a leader, part of your job is acknowledging that many of your people live with worry as their constant companion. And it's your job, too, to face it straight on."[198] This is also an important thing to remember when mentoring others and being mentored. See 3.2 and 1.3.12.

This sounds like me

A lot   somewhat   **just a little**   not at all

---

196 Andy Stanley, *The Next Generation Leader: 5 essentials for those who will shape the future* (Sisters, Ore.: Multnomah, 2003), 56.

197 Cicero, quoted in B.C. Forbes, *The Forbes Scrapbook of Thoughts on the Business of Life* (New York: Forbes, Inc., 1976), 434.

198 Jack and Suzy Welch, *The Real Life MBA: Your No-BS Guide to Winning the Game, Building a Team, and Growing Your Career* (New York: Harper Collins, 2015), 159.

Additional Resources:
John C. Maxwell, *Failing Forward.*
Ben Carson, et al., *Take the Risk.*

Personal Objective:

Specific Actions:

Due Date:

1.3.16 Emotional Intelligence

WBS Dictionary: The most popular current proponent, Daniel Goleman, proposes a broad set of competencies and skills that drive and are predictive of leadership ability. Goleman identifies five EI constructs that include self-awareness (1.3), self-regulation (1.2), social skill (1.1.2.4), empathy (3.4), and motivation (2.3). In effect, Goleman combines these five WBS elements into alternative essential leadership journey checkpoints. Whatever the theory or driving determiners, the element of emotional intelligence for sustained leaders suggests that the leader holds a relatively high level of certain attributes. Goleman also suggests that all of these can be learned and developed to a higher maturity level. To demonstrate emotional intelligence, the sustained leader must also be able to quickly assess situations (2.1.6) including their EI and the EI of those who will be affected by the leader's action or inaction.

Application: The immaturity displayed by some leaders is truly amazing. Displays of anger, petulance, stubbornness, vindictiveness, and selfishness have no place in a leader's repertoire. Such displays are a lack of maturity, put the rest of the team at an inappropriately high emotional level, and generate fear within the team. The leader should never be the source of disruptive actions. The leader's job, in part, is to bring the team together. Even on a personal level, sulking is not positive. Some of the literature[199] suggests that it is the leader's responsibility to be tough without being rough. There is rarely any reason to be hard on your people, and especially not rude or demeaning. The sustained leader controls their emotions and has prepared themselves through self-awareness, self-regulation, social skill, empathy, and motivation to demonstrate emotional intelligence.

"Interpersonal ineptitude in leaders lowers everyone's performance: It wastes time, creates acrimony, corrodes motivation and commitment, builds hostility and apathy."[200]

Kouzes and Posner refer to this ability to resist interpersonal ineptitude as being psychologically hardy. "This situation has two important implications for leaders. First, people can't lead if they aren't psychologically hardy. No one will follow someone who avoids stressful events and won't take decisive action. Second, even if leaders are personally very hardy, they can't enlist and retain others if they don't create an atmosphere that promotes psychological hardiness. People won't remain long with a cause that distresses them. They need to believe that they can overcome adversity if they're to accept the challenge of change. Leaders must create the conditions that make all of that possible."[201]

Jon Gordon tells us that "Research says [emotional intelligence is] responsible for 80 percent of adult success." He then goes on to say "[What] emotional intelligence really is all about is tapping the power of your heart when you are leading, selling, and communicating. EI and heartfelt leadership are one and the same. It's all about communicating effectively and contagiously with others. And you know what this means when you really simplify it? It means that people like you, respect you, and they want to follow you."[202]

Elsewhere Kouzes and Posner cite the research of Claudio Fernandez-Araoz who noted that he "had the opportunity to conduct research that… clearly demonstrated that the classic profile organizations look for in hiring a senior executive (relevant experience and outstanding IQ) is much more a predictor of failure than success, unless the relevant emotional intelligence competencies are also present. In fact,

199 Vince Molinaro, *The Leadership Contract: The Fine Print to Becoming a Great Leader* (US: Wiley, 2013), 117-18.
200 Daniel Goleman, *Working with Emotional Intelligence* (US: Bantam, 2000), 3 and 32.
201 Kouzes and Posner, *Leadership Challenge*, 222.
202 Jon Gordon, *The Energy Bus* (Hoboken, NJ: John Wiley 2007), 104.

serious weaknesses in the domain of emotional intelligence predict failure at senior levels with amazing accuracy."[203]

Kouzes and Posner continue their thoughts concerning success predictors. "This is serious stuff. Senior executives can graduate at the top of the best business schools in the world, reason circles around their brightest peers, solve technical problems with wizard-like powers, have the relevant situational, functional, and industry experience, and still be more likely to fail than succeed—unless they also possess the requisite personal and social skills. Boards of directors beware! Do not hire that brilliant turnaround artist with decades of experience in your industry and three degrees from the most elite universities—and a track record of not working and playing well with others. The appointment is likely to get you into more trouble than you were in in the first place."[204]

"No doubt, emotional intelligence is rarer than book smarts, but my experience says it is actually more important in the making of a leader. You just can't ignore it," says Jack Welch.

This sounds like me

A lot	somewhat	just a little	not at all

Additional Resources:
Daniel Goleman, *Emotional Intelligence.*
Hendrie Weisinger, *Emotional Intelligence at Work.*

Personal Objective:

Specific Actions:

Due Date:

---

203 Kouzes and Posner, *Leadership Challenge*, 264-65.
204 Ibid, 265.

1.3.17 Knows How to Have Fun and Celebrate

WBS Dictionary: As social creatures we seek enjoyment. The old adage that "all work and no play makes Jack a dull boy" carries a great deal of truth. Too many people are suffering from burnout and excessive stress. They have forgotten how to relax and shut down to regenerate. Even the Borg had to regenerate, and we all know that resistance is futile. Similarly, office parties and celebrations have a positive effect on the workforce. A key element of maintaining a cohesive team (3.12) is to achieve some quick wins and celebrate them. Such events bring team members together, even the introverts. Have a cigar; sip a good port wine. Slap each other on the back and shake hands. Congratulate each other for a job well done and hand out some form of recognition that is meaningful to the team. Then get back to work.

Application: There are exactly as many special occasions in life as we choose to celebrate. Sustained leaders know that humor and joyfulness elicit positive attitudes and better results. There is, certainly, a down side to excessive celebrations, or celebrating the extremely trivial. It demeans the things that are truly worth celebrating and exhausts the team. Too much ice cream and cake is not healthy.

Research has shown that laughter, while maybe not the best medicine, is absolutely good for you. Eric Barker cites to those who have been in extremely stressful situations, such as being a prisoner of war, or simply surviving Ranger school who understand the importance of humor in just getting through another day. Said one ranger,

> "You know what? If I can laugh once a day, every day I'm in Ranger School, I'll make it through." Said a Navy trainee, "You've got to have fun and be able to laugh; laugh at yourself and laugh at what you're doing. My best friend and I laughed our way through [training]."[205]

---

205 Eric Barker http://www.bakadesuyo.com/2013/08/fearlessness/?utm_source=%22Barking+Up+The+Wrong+Tree%22+Weekly+Newsletter&utm_campaign=8e3c612e4e-SF_03_29_2015&utm_medium=email&utm_term=0_78d4c08a64-8e3c612e4e-57230737 Accessed 08/24/16

Medical research from the Mayo Clinic has shown that laughter and a positive attitude make a difference on recovery results.[206] When a team celebrates and enjoys a good laugh together, the comradery rises and productivity goes up. The sustained leader understands the importance of relaxing, celebrating, and sharing a good laugh. But not at another's expense.

Humor, by its nature, can be offensive to certain groups to the point that under many laws it can create a "hostile workplace." You do not make fun of blondes, or a particular nationality, or ethnic group. (Apparently, you can still disparage lawyers, however.) All humor in the workplace must be tasteful. What is acceptable in a comedy club or on cable TV may well be inappropriate at work. This has caused many workplaces to become very dour and un-fun locations. Effectively, all humor is discouraged. The sustained leader understands these rules and why they exist, yet still finds a way to laugh and share humor in an appropriate way. As George Washington said, "Let your Recreations be Manfull not Sinfull."[207] A proverb reflects the need for this balance: "A joyful heart is good medicine, but a broken spirit dries up the bones."[208]

Jon Gordon reflects the importance of team celebrations in his parable *The Energy Bus*.

"But interestingly enough when George told his team they could all go home and enjoy the day off, none of them wanted to leave. They all wanted to celebrate with the team and George. They wanted to savor the sweet smell of victory and soak up the energy of the moment together. George began to understand that a team who puts their heart and soul into a project and works hard toward a shared purpose wants to celebrate together. They had accomplished something amazing and they deserved to bask in the light of a job well done. He couldn't deny them that."[209]

---

206 http://www.mayoclinic.org/healthy-lifestyle/stress-management/in-depth/stress-relief/art-20044456 Accessed 08/24/16
207 George Washington, *George Washington's Rules of Civility & Decent Behaviour in Company and Conversation* (US: Mount Vernon Ladies Association of the Union, 1989), Rule 109.
208 Proverbs 17:22
209 Jon Gordon, *The Energy Bus* (Hoboken, NJ: John Wiley 2007), 149.

Even Andrew Carnegie noted that, "There is little success where there is little laughter," and Roald Dahl observed that "A little nonsense now and then is cherished by the wisest men."

Jack and Suzy Welch note that innovation thrives when people are recognized, even for the small improvements. It is not "speeches by the boss."

> No, this kind of mindset requires a culture of recognition, in which the leaders celebrate the heck out of incremental improvements. Sam in the call center figured out a way to increase customer retention rates by 5 percent—time for an office party toasting his discovery, with the very public reward of two tickets to a great new show in town. Marie came up with a way to avoid downtime in the factory by a small shift in scheduling that everyone liked better anyway. Send her family to Disney World. Whatever—the details aren't important. Just celebrate in a way that feels right and makes sense. (Knowing, of course, that celebration never, and we repeat never, means dinner with the boss. Because no matter how wonderful and fun the boss is—and a few are—dinner with the boss is still work.)[210]

Celebrating success is an important social dynamic. The sustained leader balances all of the interests, celebrates the victories, and shares a good laugh, with appropriate humor, and stays attuned to the preferences of the one being celebrated. "Play doesn't just help us to explore what *is* essential. It is essential in and of itself."[211]

This sounds like me

A lot	somewhat	just a little	not at all

Additional Resources:

Barking Up the Wrong Tree http://www.bakadesuyo.com/2016/05/way-to-improve/?utm_source=%22Barking+Up+The+Wrong+%22+

---

210 Jack and Suzy Welch, *The Real Life MBA: Your No-BS Guide to Winning the Game, Building a Team, and Growing Your Career* (New York: Harper Collins, 2015), 53.
211 Greg Mckeown, *Essentialism: The Disciplined Pursuit of Less* (New York: Crown Business, 2012) 89.

Weekly+Newsletter&utm_campaign=8b016c775e-titans_12_18_2016&
utm_medium=email&utm_term=0_78d4c08a64-8b016c775e-57230737
Adrian Gostick, et al., *24-Carrot Manager*.
Clint Swindall, *Engaged Leadership*.
Doug Jensen, et al., *The Manager's Guide to Rewards*.

Personal Objective:

Specific Actions:

Due Date:

2.0 Competence

WBS Dictionary: Competence is the ability to make things happen and reach a desired objective within a given physical or intellectual discipline. Competence suggests that a person has made some effort to learn and develop a particular skill that has practical application (see 1.3.1.2). Certain types of competence relate to entertainment and amusement but do not provide more than transient value. Others, such as the skill evidenced by performers in Cirque du Soleil, involve the development of special skills that provide superior entertainment value (see 2.2.1).

While all competence can be said to have some value even if intangible, only certain competence can add value and generate revenue directly or indirectly, and in many cases the ability to generate income, if that is the objective, applies only in defined circumstances. Competence must be demonstrated in terms of furthering the organizational mission. People who demonstrate competence are perceived to be credible and can be trusted, thus drawing a team toward themselves. Competence requires at least some minimal level of achievement in each of the sub-elements, and there has to be a balance among them. Business acumen, technical ability, and taking action must be balanced to be a sustained leader. Another word that is sometimes used in the literature to describe competence or some aspect of competence is the word "capacity."

Application: A leader might serve in a position by appointment, and the team members will quickly decide whether they will remain as followers. The first thing that team members seek is a person of demonstrated competence. What has the newly appointed boss accomplished? What do they know about the business or mission of the organization? What value-add do they bring to the table in accomplishing the organizational mission? Do they have a vision for the organization? These questions go to the issue of competence.

In most business settings there is a requisite level of business acumen as well as a requisite level of technical capability. With no identifiable exceptions, organizational leaders demonstrate strong business competence and technical competence in at *least* one primary area related to the organization's mission. For example, many leaders of aerospace companies were initially competent engineers. In a highly regulated industry like airlines, one president of Southwest Airlines was previously their general counsel. It is not required that a leader have competence in every area related to the business; they do not have to be able to perform every job in the organization. If that were the requirement, no one would be qualified. They must, however, be able to identify the competence of those who follow them so that the organization does not fail for a lack of competence in any significant area.

This WBS element is made up of three components, namely, business acumen (2.1), technical ability (2.2), and a strong bias for action (2.3). Having any ability but not applying it toward a defined end (see 5.1.2 and 2.3.1) is worse than useless. Leaders understand the business they undertake and can perform one or more of the critical functions. They then apply that toward defined ends with activity that produces measurable results.

More so today than in times past, leaders must be good at many things. Being a good technician, being a good bookkeeper, or being a good cab driver requires that you know a few things very well. In the professional disciplines, such as being a doctor, a lawyer, or an astronaut, the requirements of having a wider breadth and depth of knowledge, the ability to perform well (physically, mentally, or both), and having the ability to stay current in a rapidly evolving field of study become much more important. It's not enough to know where to apply the leeches. You have to be willing to study and practice your trade or profession in accordance with the most current institutional knowledge and best practices. More is required today.

Orrin Woodward reflects on "Project Oxygen" at Google where it was demonstrated that out of eight identified important skills for leadership, technical competence ranked last. He notes that this merely reflects statistically what has been known viscerally since 1936 when Dale Carnegie wrote that "15 percent of one's financial success is due to one's technical knowledge and about 85 percent is due to skill in human engineering—to personality and the ability to lead people."[212] While it might rank last among other important aspects of leadership, it is still on the list and constitutes a significant percentage of the necessary abilities. In many, if not most, cases, technical competence is the one thing that opens the door to the organization so that a leadership journey can begin. You have to be able to do something—to make a contribution—just to get in the door.

Competency reflects a sense of ability. When people achieve they gain confidence. Confidence in turn leads to future success. This success will lead to greater confidence in related areas. Serving in the role of a leader likewise requires a level of competence in leadership traits, skills, and attributes. By building on the elements of the *Sustained Leadership WBS*, greater competence, confidence, and achievement will be possible.[213]

This sounds like me

A lot	somewhat	just a little	not at all

Additional Resources:
Thomas F. Gilbert, *Human Competence.*
Marcus Buckingham and Donald O. Clifton, *Now, Discover Your Strengths.*
Personal Objective:

---

212 Orrin Woodward, *The Financial Matrix* (Cary, NC: Obstacles Press, 2015), 37.
213 See generally James M. Kouzes and Barry Z. Posner, *The Leadership Challenge* (San Francisco, CA: Jossey-Bass, 2002), 308-09.

Specific Actions:

Due Date:

2.1 Business Acumen

WBS Dictionary: Business principles are ubiquitous whether you are running a business, a charity, a homeowners association, or a lemonade stand. Any leader in a capitalistic society must understand basic business principles and, if conducting business globally (or anywhere other than the US), will require an understanding of business principles in the other society as well. There is no reason that all business leaders must be CPAs (or lawyers, or whatever). It is important, however, that basic accounting and relevant basic legal principles be understood. A leader who lacks business acumen will quickly alienate followers and other stakeholders derailing their leadership journey.

Business acumen also reflects risk assessment and management, a global perspective, and a fundamental appreciation of the classic management principles reflected in the acronym POSDCoRB (2.1.3). More importantly, a sustained leader must have a strong appreciation for situational assessment. A failure to observe a situation and quickly and accurately assess its impact will delay decision making (2.3.6), can foster a lack of trust (1.1), and may negatively affect communication (4.0) and commitment (5.0). For this reason, situational awareness (2.1.6) is one of the essential leadership journey checkpoints for the sustained leader. Failure in this one area will adversely affect so many other leadership attributes that the leadership will not be sustainable. Industry, government, and religion all require an appreciation for the "business" side of things. Having a strong sense of this business side will assist tremendously in being able to quickly assess situations. And lead.

Application: The organizational chart does not identify the leaders, only the bosses. Leaders are required at every level of the organization, and the person who is waiting to be "put in a leadership role" will wait a long time. Unless you demonstrate your leadership abilities where you are right now, your odds of being put in a more responsible position are slim. Part of being a leader is to understand the business you are in. Every employee at every level of the organization should be provided with sufficient information to know how to make good business decisions. This should include understanding how the company makes money, its sales cycle, its competitive discriminators, and clarity on the vision and mission. Jack Stack notes that "The best, most efficient, most profitable way to operate a business is to give everybody in the company a voice in saying how the company is run *and* a stake in the financial outcome, good or bad....Financial education of the workforce—we call it open-book management—is the key to extraordinary and sustained success....Everyone at SRC...understands how they personally affect the income and profitability of the company."[214]

There are many ingenious people who come up with amazing ideas. Some of them actually capitalize on those ideas and manage to get them into production or to begin to provide the service. It is also true that most businesses fail within a few years of their start. These two thoughts are not completely unrelated. Inventive people do not always understand what it takes to run a business. Rudolf Diesel invented the engine that carries his name. His utter failure at business led ultimately to his suicide. Who was James Murray Spangler? He invented a wonderful time-saving and health-improving device. You would think you would have heard of its inventor. Instead, you might be more familiar with the person who made it a commercial success: William Hoover. Yes, the vacuum cleaner company Hoover. The sustained leader either holds the necessary skills and knowledge or knows how to find someone who does. The sustained leader does not have to know everything, but enough to know how to make a business success from a bold new idea. A successful idea is only one piece of the puzzle. Without all the other pieces, you will be very disappointed in the outcome.

A major division of an aerospace company gave its senior staff desk plaques that read, "If you think something is more important than the customer, think again." Too few employees appreciate the importance of the customer to the existence of the business and their job. They fail to take into consideration that unless you

---

214 Kouzes and Posner, *Leadership Challenge*, p. 293 citing J. Stack with B. Burlingham, *The Great Game of Business* (New York: Currency Doubleday, 1994), 3. Kouzes and Posner go on to note, "At SRC, 86 percent of the training budget is spent on educating everyone to be a businessperson. Jack believes that when everyone has the same information about what's happening in the business, then everyone starts thinking and acting like a CEO—regardless of their organizational position."

> ### IF YOU THINK SOMETHING IS MORE IMPORTANT THAN THE CUSTOMER, THINK AGAIN.

take care of the customer, someone else will. The leader of a business, a charity, a social organization, a political party or government, and, yes, even a religion must know how the entity fits within the overall sociological scheme of society. All of them have customers regardless of the name used to describe them (constituents, stakeholders, interested parties, citizens, parishioners, etc.) Failing to understand that, the leader will soon be replaced and the entity may soon cease to exist. It is not hyperbole to say that everything depends on the leader. A sustained leader gets that.

This sounds like me

A lot   **somewhat**   **just a little**   **not at all**

Additional Resources:
Jae Shim, Joel G. Siegel, and Abraham J. Simon, *The Vest-Pocket MBA.*
Jack P. Friedman, *Dictionary of Business Terms.*
Ram Charan, *What the CEO Wants You to Know.*

Personal Objective:

Specific Actions:

Due Date:

2.1.1 Finance/Accounting/Bottom Line

WBS Dictionary: The sustained leader must gain an understanding of the financial aspects of a business operation, including the sales cycle, the risk profiles, and the financial understanding and development of the team, among others. A leader in business must recognize that a business exists to make a profit while every government and charity must minimally remain solvent. Every employee should understand how the entity generates its revenue. A leader in a non-profit is not interested in "making" money since by definition there is no profit, yet an understanding of the business side of the organization is necessary to maintain it as a going concern. The leader still must understand the costs of operating the non-profit and maximize the funds available to promote the mission of the organization.

A leader in government is similar to the non-profit but tends to operate with large sums and is required to account for the funds entrusted. Further, the use of public monies requires that the leaders act with transparency to the public so that there is confidence in their expenditure. The rules related to the handling of public funds tend to be far more complicated and comprehensive and thus require an understanding of the byzantine nature of such rules. If you are serving as a leader in any respect, one thing to keep in mind is that funds for your salary must come from some source regardless of the organizational mission. If that source dries up, you will be out of your position or working as a volunteer. Understanding the bottom line is an important aspect of your leadership. Learn the numbers. Business acumen means that you pay attention to the numbers and have educated yourself on what the numbers mean.

Application: Ken spent several years with the government before joining industry. He had minimal financial background, but serving on the senior staff caused him to be in all the review meetings. In that day presentations were made with view-graphs, and in every presentation there was the proverbial "eye-chart"— that one chart put up by the finance people that had the little numbers in all those tiny blocks that could not be read unless you were right up close to the chart. Like others in the room, Ken would lean back and just wait for the next chart to be presented. He noticed, however, that there were a couple of people who would pull their chairs up to the front of the room, study the numbers, and actually ask insightful questions about what the numbers were showing.

As Ken progressed in his field, it dawned on him that the people who were getting promoted were those "nerds" who used to ask questions about the numbers. He realized that a proper understanding of the numbers was crucial in any business. He then embarked on an intensive self-study of the numbers and what they meant. He made friends in accounting and finance. He took them to lunch and asked questions. He learned about overhead rates, G&A, management reserves, and contract funding modification. He learned what ROI was intended to show, and he learned what data, in what level of detail, were required to be passed up the management chain. He took classes on financial matters and volunteered to be on financial review teams, proposal teams, and even to teach financially related classes. Before Ken left industry, he landed a position as a VP of finance and administration, capitalizing on an opportunity that never would have been open to him without his independent efforts. Ken later went on to manage his own successful consulting business. Learn the numbers. It is too important an aspect of leadership regardless of the forum.

It is important to understand the numbers from a practical organizational perspective. Gaining only academic perspectives might not serve you as well; while academia can provide a significant background, it is not enough. As management and leadership author Noel Tichy has noted, "Most professors of finance can't hold an intelligent conversation with a vice president of finance."[215]

In *The Real Life MBA*, Jack and Suzy Welch have an entire chapter devoted to finance, appropriately titled "Fear of Finance...No More."[216] They note that those who fear finance are legend. It is a common characteristic. In fourteen short pages they describe a few key concepts, provide memorable stories, and show how understanding variance analysis while digging deeply for the truth will help you "to make good business decisions. Decisions based on sound assumptions, decisions that have examined all the options, decisions that have looked under the hood.... making good business decisions is your job."[217]

Andrew Carnegie honed his cost accounting skills while serving twelve years within the Pennsylvania Railroad operations. One of the first things he discovered when he began running steel mills was that they were not at all aware of their

---

215 Jeff Parietti, *Stupid Business Quotes*, 69.
216 Jack and Suzy Welch, *The Real Life MBA: Your No-BS Guide to Winning the Game, Building a Team, and Growing Your Career* (New York: Harper Collins, 2015), chapter 5.
217 Ibid., 89.

cost structures. With careful attention to the cost details, he reduced the cost of steel from $56 per ton to $11.50 per ton and implemented across-the-board efficiency initiatives. By calculating the costs going into production, he was able to run his mills twenty-four hours a day. While that did wear out his machines more quickly, as his competitors laughingly said, he had already calculated that cost into his equations and was therefore ready to buy new upgraded equipment while his competitors' outdated equipment forced them to charge even more for their steel.[218]

The sustained leader must either understand the numbers that drive their operation or hire those who do. Even if the tasks are delegated, the sustained leader must understand them well enough to ask the right questions, know what data to trust, and know how to hire the right cost managers.

This sounds like me

A lot	**somewhat**	**just a little**	**not at all**

Additional Resources:
William G. Droms, *Finance & Accounting for Nonfinancial Managers.*
Jae Shim and Joel G. Siegel, *Dictionary of Accounting Terms.*

Personal Objective:

Specific Actions:

Due Date:

---

218 Alan C. Elliott, *A Daily Dose of the American Dream: Stories of Success, Triumph, and Inspiration*, Rutledge Hill Press, Nashville: 1998, 288.

2.1.2 Legal

WBS Dictionary: All businesses and organizations are subject to legal constraints and requirements. The leader of any organization must pay attention to those requirements and, for the success of the organization, remain vigilant over the business operations so as to avoid legal entanglements. The leader who does not pay attention to such matters will lead their organization down the same path as Enron, the IRS, or the many banks involved in the mortgage mess of the 2000s. Many people went to jail; many lost fortunes; many lost their jobs and reputations. And many sacrificed their stakeholders—stockholders, employees, families, suppliers, etc.—on the altar of their ego. There are very high costs for failure to comply with the law. This element involves three key areas to which a leader must pay attention, those being contracts, human resources, and regulations. Depending on your leadership role, each of these will take on different levels of significance. Every leader should have at least a fundamental knowledge of these areas and, perhaps most importantly, a network on which to draw when specific legal issues arise.

Application: There is an old saying that you can't legislate morals, and yet our law books are full of laws, rules, and regulations that purport to provide guidance to society on how it can most effectively and efficiently operate. Seems almost silly when you figure that we started with just the Ten Commandments and the Golden Rule. What the sustained leader recognizes, however, is that if there were no laws they would still lead in a way that maximizes the greatest good to the most people. Sustained leaders don't need laws, but they must follow the ones that exist. They might advocate for changes in the laws while following the ones that are there. Alexander Hamilton said that if all men were angels we would need no laws. Men are not angels—none of them. And neither are sustained leaders. They are as flawed as the rest of us; they have simply embarked on a voyage to be a better person and thereby a better leader.

Because we are a nation of laws and not of men,[219] there must be an acceptance of these rules. This is known as the rule of law. The laws that exist should comply with the rule of law which, in its primary formation, says that laws must be enacted in accordance with an established process by a legitimate legislature, be clear enough to be followed by the average person, and be evenly and uniformly enforced. If that

---

219 Variously attributed.

statement sounds strange, it is probably because the media today highlights how often these simple precepts are not followed. Without a lengthy discourse on the subject, suffice it to say that the sustained leader must follow the laws that exist to the best of their ability and understanding and, when appropriate, argue through the political process to change the laws or the people who pass them, enforce them, or interpret them.

This portion of the WBS reviews the various types of rules that the sustained leader must recognize and follow to consider themselves competent in their specific field, discipline, or vocation. Each will apply to any endeavor at some level and intensity. There are both heavily and lightly regulated activities, and very few that find little to no regulation at all. Interacting with governmental bodies of one form or another is a fact of modern life, and the sustained leader should know how to do so competently and adeptly.

But it doesn't mean that you can't laugh about it!

A MAN died leaving a large estate and many sorrowful relations who claimed it. After some years, when all but one had had judgment given against them, that one was awarded the estate, which he asked his attorney to have appraised.

"There is nothing to appraise," said the attorney, pocketing his last fee.

"Then," said the successful claimant, "what good has all this litigation done me?"

"You have been a good client to me," the attorney replied, gathering up his books and papers, "but I must say you betray a surprising ignorance of the purpose of litigation."[220]

This sounds like me

A lot   **somewhat**   **just a little**   **not at all**

Additional Resources:

Marianne Jennings, *Business.*

Margaret Jane Radin, *Boilerplate.*

---

220 Attributed to Ambrose Bierce.

Personal Objective:

Specific Actions:

Due Date:

2.1.2.1 Contracts

WBS Dictionary: Business is conducted through contracts. Whether this is the simple verbal agreement reached at retail stores or the complicated, multi-volume agreement related to a merger or acquisition, it is still a contract. And contracts have rules. There are rules regarding formation, rules regarding interpretation, rules related to authority, and rules related to rules! You do not need a legal degree to be adept at managing a contract, but it does require a level of study and expertise to effectively understand and comply with your contracts. Many industries and markets have their own unique aspects regarding contracts. For example, in government contracting, the rules are somewhat different because of the foundational law on which such contracts are based. These contracts are nearly always written and contain a myriad of required clauses, terms, and conditions. Many of them also comply with a uniform format, with specifically lettered sections containing certain types of information related to the contract. Your business acumen must include an understanding of contracts and especially the aspects that might be unique to the industry or market within which you are leading. Experience and study will provide you with this basic understanding.

Application: Ideally you want to learn the rules of contracting with other parties in a place *other than* the school of hard knocks. A failure to understand your business relations as reflected in the contracts and arrangements that are entered into will invariably lead to unpleasant surprises.

There are numerous business classes you can take at a community college or extension university. The Small Business Administration along with SCORE offers a number of free seminars on the subject. Portions of the Project Management Institute Body of Knowledge, especially the section on subcontract management, will prove enlightening.

Most commercial deals today are governed by the Uniform Commercial Code, which sets forth the rules for forming, ending, and performing contracts related to the sale of goods. While there are differences in the alleged uniformity due to each state having a right to modify the basic document, the rules are relatively consistent and should be understood by the sustained leader.

In the government environment, contracts are governed by a completely different set of rules, including the law on which the rules are based. If you are leading in a government environment you will need to understand these differences. Since public contracts use public funds, there must be greater accountability and transparency to the transactions. All eligible parties must have an ability to compete, and the contracts are required by law and regulation to follow formal formats and contain a great deal of specific content that in part implements social policy not typically found in commercial deals. Many of these rules flow down to the subcontractors who assist the prime contractors in performing the work for the government. These hybrid contracts are commercial in that they are governed by the UCC, but contain a great deal of the government-required content, making them substantially different from pure commercial contracts. Contracts between international parties often use the UN Convention on the International Sale of Goods, which is also a separate body of laws related to such agreements. Charities and religions often use a contract vehicle known as a grant, which will have its own rules. While the sustained leader need not know all these intricacies, it is important that they understand the uniqueness of such contracts and the effect they will have on their mission and operations.

This sounds like me

A lot   **somewhat**   **just a little**   **not at all**

Additional Resources:
Lawrence Hsieh, *The Small-Business Contracts Handbook*.
Margaret Jane Radin, *Boilerplate*.

Personal Objective:

Specific Actions:

Due Date:

2.1.2.2 Human Resources

WBS Dictionary: Historically an employer would agree to hire a worker on terms and conditions negotiated between the parties. Unequal bargaining power and employer abuses led to the creation of unions and an entire body of law related to labor relations. Many laws and regulations have been passed by various governments, down to the municipal level, that affect your treatment of employees. Minimum wage laws, safety regulations, non-discrimination policies, benefit rules, and many more directly affect the relationship between employers and employees, making this an extremely complicated area of law. Additionally, union contracts strongly influence this relationship whether or not a collective bargaining agreement applies to your specific workforce. Your business acumen must include a basic understanding of all these rules and most often a wise counsel to assist you. A leader who does not follow these complicated and overlapping laws will not be perceived as a trustworthy leader and will most likely not be considered a sustained leader. Proper treatment of your employees and other stakeholders is covered in more detail in 3.0.

Application: Employees have a variety of rights that must be honored. Some of them apply only to large employers, and many do not kick in until you have fifty or more employees, but the rules exist and your ability to attract the right cadre of qualified team members can be affected by the perception of how you follow the laws.

HR management is a specialty area, and having such an advisor on your team is crucial to successful leadership. Many of the rules are not intuitive, and with the many layers of rules and regulations, from the federal government to the local municipality, a specialist in this area is strongly encouraged. Even so, you must have a sufficient grasp of all this to manage effectively day to day.

The truly sustained leader does not need any of these laws. They would understand their team's needs and address them in a fair and equitable manner without government oversight. Such is not the present condition of the world; thus the laws must be understood and followed.

This sounds like me

A lot   **somewhat**   **just a little**   **not at all**

Additional Resources:

Adrian Gostick and Chester Elton, *24-Carrot Manager.*

Curt Coffman and Gabriel Gonzalez-Molina, *Follow This Path.*

Personal Objective:

Specific Actions:

Due Date:

2.1.2.3 Regulatory

WBS Dictionary: All businesses and organizations are regulated. Whether it involves the formation, management, operation, or dissolution of the organization, federal, state, and local laws will apply. Not every regulation applies to every operation. For example, food handling regulations apply only to those who handle food, flight safety to those who fly, and compliance with product safety rules to those who introduce products into commerce. Other rules, such as safety (Occupational Safety and Health Administration), traffic rules, minimum insurance requirements, and consumer protection rules, apply to most operations. The sustained leader will gain an understanding of the scope and framework of those regulations that apply to the operations of the entity they lead. Even non-profits have such rules to follow. And, of course, everyone pays taxes, which is the most convoluted and complex set of regulations governing any single activity known to man.

Application: Under the rule of law a legitimate legislature makes the rules and an executive branch implements these laws. Once Congress has established a policy on a topic, it is the responsibility of the executive branch to establish the means and processes by which that policy will be followed. Over time, the United States Congress has delegated to a great variety of executive branch agencies, each one established by Congress in the first place, more and more of the legislative authority to set policy. Congress reserved to itself the ability to undo regulations put forth by these agencies, but the authority is rarely used.

The result is a myriad of many agencies sometimes with overlapping authority, each attempting to fulfill the intent of Congress as best they interpret it. And sometimes trying to stretch their authority and power beyond congressional intent. This has given rise to a large body of law known as administrative law and a constant political struggle among the three branches of government that often does not provide clarity as much as intentional ambiguity so that each political entity can argue that things are being done "their way." While you might argue that this is no way to run a country, or that this discussion is too "political," yet it reflects the regulatory environment within which business, government, and religious entities must operate. The sustained leader does not need to like it, but they must be able to competently guide their team through the morass of administrative regulation that applies to their business.

The first step is to identify which rules apply that may require the advice and counsel of an expert in the area or from the government entity itself. Many regulatory agencies offer help in making sure their rules are followed. The next step is to establish compliance mechanisms to ensure the rules are followed and the costs of compliance are properly considered in the operations. While it is often a requirement of the regulatory body, the sustained leader also establishes an internal audit mechanism to ensure that the entity or any of its operational units does not become complacent and fail to exercise the operational discipline necessary to stay in compliance. Many regulatory agencies can literally shut down your operations or prohibit you from doing business of a certain type or in a certain area for failure to maintain compliance. When you operate internationally, you then become subject to a similar environment and a completely different set of rules and procedures for compliance. Again, the sustained leader is not responsible for knowing HOW to do all of this so much as to know how to get the right people in the right positions to protect the team's interest and ability to continue their mission.

This sounds like me

A lot   **somewhat**   **just a little**   **not at all**

Additional Resources:

Wesley B. Truitt, *Power and Policy.*

Ernest Gellhorn and Barry B. Boyer, *Administrative Law and Process in a Nutshell.*

Personal Objective:

Specific Actions:

Due Date:

2.1.3 Management (POSDCoRB)

WBS Dictionary: Management, it has been said, is doing things right while leadership is doing the right things.[221] It has also been said that management is done with things while leadership is done with people. Regardless of your perspective, leadership includes a significant dose of management. You can be a good manager and a good leader, or a good manager and a terrible leader. Conversely it is somewhat more difficult to be a terrible manager and a good leader. If you have not mastered management skills, your leadership will be hindered in both opportunity and quality. Thus, competence in a variety of management disciplines is important for the sustained leader to hold. This does not suggest that you need to know how to perform the details of every function within your sphere of leadership, but it does suggest that you have to know enough about each of them to know if your followers are doing their job and enough knowledge to ask insightful questions about the work products you see. You have to understand the basic operations of an organization.

Application: **P**lanning, **O**rganizing, **S**taffing, **D**irecting, **C**oordinating, **R**eporting, and **B**udgeting (POSDCoRB) are often cited in the literature as the elements of good management. These relate to the management of a business's operations and are the focus of much of the education and training involved in a master's in business administration or public administration degree. Routinized operations tend to focus around these elements of business activities. The sustained leader must understand these basic tools and understand how to interpret the data they generate.

Many, if not most, business operations tend toward a stable state where employees perform these operations almost by rote, and the data are then reviewed by the bosses. Sustained leaders understand how the data are generated and the value-added aspects of each business process or operation. Systems can fail and become outdated. Unless the sustained leader tracks the processes and the data emanating from them, they will most likely miss early warning signals and the opportunity to make midcourse corrections to these activities. As ubiquitous as these activities are, the methods are in a constant state of flux. Hopefully this pressure to

---

221 This idea has been variously attributed to a number of management experts. Both Warren Bennis (in *On Becoming a Leader*) and Peter Drucker are cited as the originator of the expression.

change is toward the positive, but this is not always the case. Sustained leaders must constantly monitor all the business processes to ensure that they are still measuring the right things and providing the most relevant data for the operation.

Robert Green provides the example of Douglas MacArthur.

> When General Douglas MacArthur assumed command of American forces in the Philippines during World War II, an assistant handed him a book containing the various precedents established by the commanders before him, the methods that had been successful for them. MacArthur asked the assistant how many copies there were of this book. Six, the assistant answered. "Well," the general replied, "you get all those six copies together and burn them—every one of them. I'll not be bound by precedents. Any time a problem comes up, I'll make the decision at once—immediately." Adopt this ruthless strategy toward the past: Burn all the books and train yourself to react to circumstances as they happen.[222]

Kouzes and Posner reflect a similar sentiment.

> Leaders must destroy routines because routines get us into ruts, dull our senses, stifle our creativity, constrict our thinking, remove us from stimulation, and destroy our ability to compete. Once-useful routines can sap the vitality of an organization and cause it to atrophy. Yet there's a paradox: some routines are essential to a definable, consistent, measureable, and efficient operation. We get annoyed when we can't figure out who reports to whom. We get confused when our employers keep changing the strategy. We get absolutely livid when we're taken off one project and put on another just when we're beginning to get the hang of things. There are no economies in *always* changing; constant changes in direction and in the ways things are done are confusing and costly to everyone.[223]

What is the sustained leader to learn from this? There is merit to doing things based on precedent. When things work—they work. Can they be improved?

---

222 Robert Greene, *The 48 Laws of Power*, 354.
223 Kouzes and Posner, *The Leadership Challenge*, 190.

Always. The sustained leader must know when to make changes and when to let things lie.

This sounds like me

A lot   **somewhat**   **just a little**   **not at all**

Additional Resources:
John P. Kotter, *On What Leaders Really Do.*
Jack and Suzy Welch, *The Real-Life MBA.*

Personal Objective:

Specific Actions:

Due Date:

2.1.4 Risk

WBS Dictionary: All business endeavors involve risk. From a capitalistic perspective, it is the assumption of risk that generates profit. The higher the risk assumed, the higher the profit. The sustained leader, therefore, requires a deep and comprehensive understanding of risk as it relates to the mission of the organization. It will affect the opportunities sought, the pricing of the effort, the management attention to the project, and the coordination of the deliverables. Providing office paper is fundamentally different than producing rocket engines or delivering a satellite to space. As identified by the Project Management Institute, risk can also be positive, such as opportunities that arise unexpectedly for which the sustained leader should be prepared. Risk, properly managed, can remove a great deal of pain in your leadership journey.

Managing risks requires that you manage based on facts (1.2.1.2) and that you prepare properly (1.3.1.3). Risk events should never be a surprise, and the leader confronted with risk should not fear it but rather understand it and develop their own level of tolerance for risks related to their endeavors (1.3.15). Furthermore, fear of risk should never paralyze a leader, who should be focused on a strong bias for action (2.3). Risk can appear in any endeavor and exists in all elements of this WBS. Properly managed, it will be identified, mitigated, or removed. A sustained leader knows how to handle that.

Application: This is not the book to teach you how to manage risk. Its purpose is solely to identify that risk management is a critical skill for sustained leaders. The ability to tolerate risk varies considerably among people. Some people love the thrill of a fast rollercoaster. Others will never get on one. Some people play the stock market every day; others stay away entirely or try to find "safe" investments. What the sustained leader needs to understand is that there are no truly risk-free endeavors. The issue is one of assessing the risk and determining when the assumption of risk becomes unreasonable.

There is no formula for this. Reasonable people will differ on acceptable and unacceptable risk. Understanding risk requires that the maximum level of facts related to the risk be gathered and given due consideration. NASA engineers convinced themselves that the risks were acceptable to launch Challenger in January 1986. They were wrong. There were some engineers who cautioned against the launch in such cold temperatures, unusual for the Florida coast, and their management decided to view the exact same facts differently.

When assessing risks, a risk matrix is often useful to categorize the known facts and better identify the potential unknown facts. Both the likelihood of occurrence and the magnitude of the damage the risk event will cause are assessed. From an engineering perspective, a formal Failure Modes and Effects Analysis might be performed to consider all the possible failures, in combination and alone, and the possible outcome. Identified failures are prioritized based on the likelihood and seriousness of the possible consequences, how often they will be observed, and, very importantly, whether the detection of the failure is easy or difficult. From this analysis, resources can be allocated to eliminate the failure or minimize its effect. And insurance merely shifts the financial burden—it has nothing to do with risk mitigation.

Engineering failures are not the only risks confronted by the sustained leader. There are business risks, personnel risks, legal risks, financial risks, and a host of other normal activities that hold risk. Some flight attendants like to joke at the end of a flight that the safest part of the traveler's journey has ended so they should be more careful driving home. Statistically, they are correct— more people die in auto accidents than in plane crashes. Merely walking across the street carries risks, eating food can have bad consequences, and at least one person has been hit (but not killed) by a falling meteor. In America you are most likely to die from a heart attack, yet the marketers for other debilitating diseases and conditions collect far more money to find their cure. This is not to say such efforts are misguided, only that they do not necessarily reflect where the greatest risk may exist.

The sustained leader understands risk, especially as it relates to their team's activities. They constantly assess the risk, assess the situation, and assess the factors that affect the risk profiles, and they take action to eliminate or mitigate the risk. The sustained leader demonstrates competence in managing risk.

This sounds like me

A lot	somewhat	just a little	not at all

Additional Resources:

Ben Carson and Gregg Lewis, (Contributor). *Take the Risk.*

Tom Kendrick, *Identifying and Managing Project Risk.*

Personal Objective:

Specific Actions:

Due Date:

2.1.5 Global Perspective

WBS Dictionary: Most things today are affected and influenced by global issues. A popular saying suggests that all politics are local, but even those issues have a global overtone. Industry, government, and religious entities must be aware of global events and dynamics, from simple monetary exchange rates to government subsidies to foreign competition. Few supply chains are bereft of international implications, and the sustained leader must understand how these circumstances might affect their operations. See 2.1.2 and 2.1.3. No one is immune and the sustained leader will be aware of these issues, their dynamics, and how they affect their operations. These are often mixed with both economic and political elements as well as sociological and cultural dynamics. To remain socially adept (1.1.2.4) the sustained leader must be aware of these differences across cultures in which the organization operates. Generally spending time in these environs immerses the leader in relevant matters. Learning quickly, adopting to the customs, and learning the language are all important parts of this element.

Application: There exists a type of treaty among many nations called the United Nations Convention on the International Sale of Goods. As an international agreement, it takes precedence over local law such as the laws of a particular state regulating commerce. Many business executives have been surprised to discover that while they believed they were contracting under the laws of a particular state, the UNCISG was the controlling body of law. The failure to appreciate this global perspective has resulted in some very unfortunate outcomes.

Having a global perspective also means that the sustained leader appreciates that we have but one world on which to live. This introduces a certain global sociological perspective into every action taken by a leader. The sustained leader applies that to every situation they encounter, large or small, physical, spiritual, or mental. John Maxwell relates the following story.

> Recently I had dinner with an advertising executive and author Linda Kaplan Thaler. You may not know her name, but I'm sure you know her work. She is the creative person who came up with the duck for AFLAC. During our dinner conversation as we talked about acts of significance, she mentioned the Hebrew phrase *tikkun olam*, and told me it means "repairing the world." She said it was part of her faith tradition and it meant that no

one should live in this world without trying to find a way to make it better. What a wonderful way to think about living a life that matters.[224]

The sustained leader does not retreat to their comfort zone; they cannot afford to do that. And while they may have no control over exchange rates, political upheaval, or supply chain disruptions, the sustained leader makes themselves aware of these possibilities and prepares backup plans or other risk-mitigation (2.1.4) strategies to protect their team and its mission. Without a global perspective, they will be unprepared to deal with both the risks and opportunities that might jeopardize their mission.

Regardless of where in the world the sustained leader chooses to live and work, global implications will affect their actions. Among their competencies is the need to appreciate these dynamics over which they have no direct control.

This sounds like me

A lot	**somewhat**	**just a little**	**not at all**

Additional Resources:
Wall Street Journal.
Lan Liu, *Conversations on Leadership.*
Rosabeth Moss Kanter, *World Class.*

Personal Objective:

Specific Actions:

.

Due Date:

---

224 John C. Maxwell, *Intentional Living: Choosing a Life That Matters* (New York: Center Street, 2015), 95.

Essential Leadership Journey Checkpoint
2.1.6 Situational Awareness

WBS Dictionary: One marked sign of a leader is the ability to properly assess the circumstances in which they find themselves. This may be local and temporary circumstances or broader in scope and duration. A sustained leader should be able to walk into a room and identify those with whom they must speak, understanding almost intuitively the proper social protocols, and perceiving whether there is tension—and if so its nature—in the room. In business, the sustained leader knows the market, knows their people, and knows their objectives. In government, the sustained leader can read the crowd and the opposition. They are adept at understanding the issues that are important to the constituency and determining the course of action that will best serve the needs of those governed—even if not the popular path. Their vision is clear and their priorities straight. With minimal input, the sustained leader perceives what is important in the situation and what is not. They can identify red herrings and the personal, sometimes hidden, agendas of those with whom they interact.

The sustained leader can read body language and knows when someone is lying or being deceptive. They perceive what is motivating those around them, and especially those who stand in opposition to the leader. The sustained leader displays almost a sixth sense about the surroundings, and with situational awareness, makes quick decisions based on that awareness. The sustained leader is rarely if ever surprised. To others they seem to have prescience about how things will unfold. It can be almost eerie to those watching, as if the leader could predict the future. In fact, it is a keen sense of observation coupled with the ability to sort order from chaos—both of which can be learned and mastered.

Application: Dana Perino notes that at a particular point in her career she began to pick up on the subtleties of communications, being sensitive to tension and having a natural tendency to be the peacemaker.[225] The earlier you can assess a situation, the more quickly you can gather the necessary information to assist those who are in dispute. Coupled with that is a post-facto assessment of what was said in prior situations to learn and improve on the process of message manipulation so as to ease tensions and improve on successful resolutions. Gaining the most

---

225 Dana Perino, *And the Good News Is…: Lessons and Advice from the Bright Side* (New York: Hachette Book Group, 2015), 53-54.

information as quickly as possible provides an information differential that puts the person with the most information in a more powerful position. Being able to assess any situation quickly puts the sustained leader ahead of the pack.

When a crisis arises, there is usually no time to conduct a full assessment to determine the most appropriate response. As Warren Bennis and Steven B. Sample note, "A true leader must have done the mental math beforehand and must be able to step up and intuitively take the appropriate action."[226] Decisiveness (2.3.6) is enhanced by knowing without question the morality of the situation in advance. This element of situational awareness is an essential leadership journey checkpoint because of its importance in making quick and correct decisions. Several of the other elements are dependent on the ability to quickly assess situations correctly. When a sustained leader has a proper moral center (1.2.2.1) and can assess situations quickly, they have the ability to implement appropriate action quickly. By being decisive (2.3.6) and acting on that decision, the sustained leader never says, "What should I do now?" They know. Even in crisis, quick decisive action demonstrates leadership probably better than any other trait or quality, so long as the action turns out to have been correct.

Charles Gow

Observation is more than seeing, it is knowing
what you see and comprehending its significance.

Daniel Goleman observes that our brains have great control over our reaction to situations. Fortunately, we can also control which part of our brain controls the reaction. He tells of studies where volunteers were told stories about those who were experiencing physical pain. This caused the pain centers of the listeners' brains to react. Interestingly, for stories of psychological suffering, "it took relatively longer to activate the higher brain centers involved in empathetic concern and compassion. As the research team put it, it takes time to tell 'the psychological

---

226 Warren Bennis and Stephen B. Sample (with Rob Asghar), *The Art and Adventure of Leadership: Understanding Failure, Resilience, and Success* (Hoboken, NJ: John Wiley & Sons Inc., 2015), 47-48.

and moral dimensions of a situation.'"[227] The sustained leader trains themselves to assess situations quickly, including both the obvious physical issues and the less obvious psychological or sociological issues. Being aware of the situation facilitates a better reaction more quickly, avoids missteps, and demonstrates both situational- and self-control—traits that followers seek in those they choose as leaders.

How important is situational awareness to a sustained leader's acumen? Let's consider two quotes. David Darst was vice president at Goldman Sachs, the investment banking firm. He was asked a question about predicting the success of leveraged buyout (LBO) transactions and the success of any one of them, in particular surviving a recession. He said, "You can't tell who's swimming naked until after the tide goes out." Even when there are great sums of money and many jobs at stake, some situations are difficult to assess until after the risk event has occurred. Regardless of your experience, competency, or raw knowledge, all aspects of a situation cannot always be assessed accurately. In another example, a spokesperson for the New York establishment Tavern on the Green stated simply, "[He] was just doing his job." What situation was incorrectly assessed? The doorman had merely called a cab—for two thieves. Very often assessments are no better than (hopefully educated) guesses. Some situations must develop further before accurate assessments can be made. In other cases, a failure to gather as many relevant facts as possible will cause an errant assessment. The sustained leader who truly hones the skill of situational assessment will make better decisions and will be a more successful leader.[228]

---•---

George Bernard Shaw

People are always blaming their circumstances for what they are.
I don't believe in circumstances. The people who get on in this
world are the people who get up and look for the circumstances
they want, and, if they can't find them, make them.

---•---

227 Daniel Goleman, *Focus: The Hidden Driver of Excellence* (New York: Harper Collins, 2015), 107.

228 Both quotes are taken from Jeff Parietti, *The Book of Truly Stupid Business Quotes*, pages 122 and 140.

Change is a constant (2.3.7), and the sustained leader recognizes this natural law (1.2.2.4). Thus, any set of circumstances, any situation the sustained leader encounters, is temporary and will change. The sustained leader will continue to assess any situation and identify the changes. This will help in projections and estimates of outcomes. More importantly, however, for the sustained leader there is a recognition that there is no such thing as perfect circumstances. Given that they will inevitably change, the sustained leader will work to modify the situation in a manner that suits their objectives. Certainly this can be a bit Machiavellian if taken to an extreme, but it is nonetheless a legitimate and often important aspect of a leader's abilities and development.

This sounds like me

A lot   **somewhat**   **just a little**   **not at all**

Additional Resources:
Paul Hersey, *The Situational Leader.*
Robert Goffee and Gareth Jones, *Why Should Anyone Be Led by You?*

Personal Objective:

Specific Actions:

Due Date:

2.1.6.1 Observant

WBS Dictionary: The sustained leader develops their sense of observation. To observe is to see, but more than that it is to assess and register the memory. The observant leader walks into a room and immediately assesses who is there, where they are standing, with whom they are standing, to whom they are talking, and who is trying to get away from whomever is talking to them. They assess body language, dress, and comfort level and distinguish among the "tribes" (in the Seth Godin sense). More than this, they collect data on a variety of subjects, observing the market, what the competition is doing, and what the international situations are doing to exchange rates and commodity pricing. The sustained leader pays attention, acts like a sponge, and catalogs the information mentally. Similarly, they pay attention to the team and the dynamics going on among them. Through this process the leader hones the skill of observation and improves their ability to accurately assess the situation. Being observant will assist you in becoming more socially adept (1.1.2.4 and 4.3.3) and a better networker (1.1.1.1).

Application: "You can observe a lot by watching."[229] Yogi Berra often fractured phrases, but there was always a lot of truth beneath what he said. When a case is tried in court each party calls its witnesses. A witness is one who has seen and therefore has knowledge. Whether you are called as a "witness" in court or not, you are a witness to everything that has happened in your presence. It is always interesting during investigations to interview the witnesses. Law students are taught that if there is an accident on the corner where ten people are waiting for the bus, you do not, as you might expect, have one accident with ten witnesses. You will discover that you have ten very different accidents with one witness each. The car will be green, gray, blue, and black. The light will be red, yellow, and green— apparently simultaneously. And the driver will be an old man, a young woman, a black teenager, and an Asian grandmother. The point is that most people simply don't pay attention. Their minds play tricks on them, and they fail to retain what it was they saw.

Start small where the risks are low. If you must, guess what the observation is suggesting. An improved sense of empathy (3.4) helps tremendously. Did you ever try the "Where's Waldo?" game? It is a game of observation. Have you ever looked at someone and then turned away and tried to describe them—their facial structure, what they were wearing, their jewelry, and their eye color? There are very simple exercises you can do to improve your powers of observation. And the

---

229 Yogi Berra, et al. *The Yogi Book: "I Really Didn't Say Everything I Said"* (1998), 95.

starting point is to simply pay attention. The sustained leader makes sure that they are "present" in the situation. If your mind is preoccupied with other matters, you will not be absorbing what is going on right in front of you. Being focused is a good thing, yet focusing solely on the speaker will cause you to be oblivious to things that might be happening on the periphery. Train yourself to widen your aperture and absorb more than just the main event. Even a circus has three rings where exciting things are happening. Take it all in.

In 1999 cognitive psychologists Daniel Simons and Christopher Chabris created a film where six people, three in white shirts and three in black, passed a ball around. The observers were asked to silently count the number of passes made by those in the white shirts. After viewing the video the participants were asked about the gorilla. You see, "a gorilla strolls into the middle of the action, faces the camera and thumps its chest, and then leaves, spending nine seconds on screen." Fully half of the people who viewed the video and counted the passes never consciously saw the gorilla. In later experiments, because the film had become quite popular, the psychologists added other peripheral action that was also missed. Some of the later observers were probably looking for the gorilla, who never appeared in those later versions![230]

Thus, psychologists have shown that we are not as observant as we think we are. Pay attention. It is a sign of a sustained leader.

This sounds like me

A lot	somewhat	just a little	not at all

Additional Resources:
Spencer Johnson, *The Present.*
Seth Godin, *Tribes.*

Personal Objective:

---

230 http://www.theinvisiblegorilla.com/gorilla_experiment.html Accessed 08/27/16

Specific Actions:

Due Date:

2.1.6.2 Order from Chaos

WBS Dictionary: A keen observer takes in a great deal of data, most of which is of no practical value. People are messy; their lives are messy. It is difficult to attribute any single change to a single cause. At the same time, people are sending out a multitude of signals—from their word choice, their phrasing, their accent (assumed or natural), their body language, their sense of personal space (or lack thereof), and countless other observable signals. Assessing everything on everyone would put you on overload. This element suggests that of all the signals your brain is trying to process, you have developed the skill to sort through all the details and place a prioritized relevance on each one. The sustained leader systematizes the data gathered and organizes it, at least mentally, into a more comprehensible data set. From here, the leader can respond in an appropriate manner and often assists others in clarifying their view of the situation as well. It can be a very important persuasive tool (4.2.2).

Application: Fuzzy writing reflects fuzzy thinking. Communicating clearly and effectively is not a skill everyone has. A sustained leader must develop their ability to express themselves clearly while simultaneously dealing with the lack of clarity in communication by many others (4.2.4). Often this is another application of finding order in chaos. Verbal communications can have the same issue. Some people seem unable to leave out the irrelevant and tangential matters. They are the kind of person who, when you ask the time, insists on telling you how to build a clock. You are often tempted to ask these people whether their train of thought has a caboose. What you must ask yourself, however, is, "Am I one of these people?"

Disciplining yourself in this way improves your ability to do the same with others. Sometimes games as simple as word search and Sudoku help you sort things. Using tools such as a fishbone diagram, outline, matrix, or decision tree or even brainstorming with others can help you orient your thinking in a more organized manner. Organized thinking tends to lead to breakthroughs in thought and direction and allows you to express yourself more clearly.

Similarly, however, it is the cross-relation of ideas that often leads to innovation. While clarity of thinking will mandate that you compartmentalize the vast torrent of information that flies at you, it is occasionally important to allow some time for reflection on these areas of division. Allow some cross pollination of these narrower compartments and see what relationships become more obvious. Creating order from this chaos will often provide you insights that others have missed. The sustained leader understands this.

This sounds like me

A lot	somewhat	just a little	not at all

Additional Resources:

Morgan Jones, *The Thinker's Toolkit.*

Gary Keller and Jay Papasan, *The ONE Thing.*

Personal Objective:

Specific Actions:

Due Date:

2.1.6.2.1 Detail Sorting

WBS Dictionary: The information age in which we live is constantly increasing the amount of information to which we are exposed. Most of it is useless and unnecessary, but that is not obvious until you have assessed it. The sustained leader can quickly sort through great amounts of data and sort out the important details from the less important and even unimportant details. The first part of this is the ability to absorb and digest lots of information. The second part is to condition themselves to identify things that are important, generally with a glance or quick review. The third part is to apply that conditioning to the massive amounts of data to quickly focus on the important details and, where possible, remove the source of the irrelevant data entirely. With practice, it can be learned.

Application: Consider the daily newspaper or newsfeed. A tremendous amount of data comes through these sources. As you skim these pages your eye spots particular words. Maybe you are a big sports fan, and on the financial page you are skimming a sports figure's name pops up. You pause. You take an interest. You read past the headline and into the article. Or perhaps you like a particular editorial writer. As you skim the editorial pages, your eye catches on the reporter's name. You pause. That is this element in action. You are already conditioned to spot things that you have previously told yourself are important. The real question becomes, as you work toward being a sustained leader, are you focusing on the important things related to your leadership responsibilities? Most people have to answer that with a no. To improve in this area, spend a little more time reviewing the details of your organization and the market within which it functions. Pick up on key words. Some of this might come from your training and education. Some might just be "current events." Some might be new buzzwords or changing trends. If you are interested in the subject, you will absorb the key details. Perhaps you simply need to take a greater interest in the subjects related to your leadership role. Making sure that you keep current with technology also helps in this area (2.2.6).

Robert Reich

Averages don't always reveal the most telling realities. You know Shaquille O'Neal and I have an average height of six feet (Reich is four-foot-ten).

The Wall Street Journal has a left-hand column on the front page. It contains the major business and political headlines from around the world. Make a habit of reading that every day. Consider some of the newsfeeds you currently get. You probably get too many and are making your job harder by daily reading things that do not enlighten, engage, or entertain. The same can usually be said about the blogs to which you subscribe. Or perhaps you focus too much on the entertainment side of that ledger rather than the enlightening or engaging sides. Fix that. Find the sources that provide you the relevant details in the shortest fashion. Subscribe to a business book summary service. You can't possibly read every book on business that is published; with such a service you can get reviews of three to five books a month. Perhaps some of them will interest you sufficiently to go buy the book and read it, but at least you will have been exposed to the topics found in the current literature.

This sounds like me

A lot	somewhat	just a little	not at all

Additional Resources:

Wall Street Journal.

David Allen, *Getting Things Done.*

Greg McKeown, *Essentialism.*

Personal Objective:

Specific Actions:

Due Date:

2.1.6.2.2 Relevance

WBS Dictionary: Facts are facts, opinions are opinions, and data are data. Yet they are not equal. Some facts are more important than others; some opinions carry more weight or are based on more valid data, and data—well, as Mark Twain said, "There are lies, damn lies, and statistics." Amid the absolute torrent of information that flows to us, the pace seems to increase without end. What do you do with all of that? The sustained leader finds a way to sort it out and assign a proper level of relevance to all this information. They do not clutter their mind with useless information, although that can be a very subjective term. The sustained leader exposes themselves to a great deal of information and then determines where the most reliable sources exist. Their focus is then on those sources to the exclusion of others. The sustained leader trains themselves to actively remove the irrelevant and retain the relevant. In the flood of information that is our current society, the sustained leader is decisive and explicit in terms of what they retain and on what they focus. Everything else is just noise.

Application: Some people think it is important to know the batting averages of everyone playing in the major leagues. Or perhaps just their home team. Others find the waste of brainpower on such matters a terrible thing. Most people with common stock in their retirement plan have no idea how the market really works or how to make good investments—often jumping on a "hot stock" long after it has cooled, or selling at the slightest dip, before it starts another rapid increase. You would think that with so much riding on their retirement they would pay more attention to the data that are relevant and the data that are not, or would value the opinion of someone who had steered them right in the past, or simply do their own research and gather the facts.

In the field of engineering there is a concept called "signal to noise ratio." In the discipline of electronic broadcast all intended signals get cluttered with a variety of noises, almost all of which are irrelevant. If you are tuning a radio to a particular station, you will find that the signal you are trying to capture might become weak and then get stronger. Other stations on the same or nearby frequency will bleed into the signal you are trying to capture. The atmosphere, sunspots, and broadcast tower locations (geography) will all introduce various sources of noise or will diminish the desired signal. For engineers the challenge is to increase the signal and diminish the noise. This is as true when communicating with satellites that have left our solar system as it is on a social media discussion site. What is relevant is the signal. Everything else is just noise. The sustained leader works to increase the signal of their communication and the information they are receiving while, to the best of their ability, reducing the noise.

If a leader is to engage in small talk and work their network, some level of incidental information is necessary. So while one leader might not particularly follow college sports, a meeting with an executive at a firm with whom they wish to do business might cause a bit of studying on the local team. It comes from the desire to relate better to the other party and show interest in what interests them. Draw resources to you that contain data and opinions that you find relevant. Read articles that consistently contain reliable facts. Reading comic books was a fun entertainment as a child, but carries little relevant information unless you are in the entertainment industry or collect vintage comics. Be decisive about what you let through the filter, and then filter it all again against things that are relevant to you now or in the near future. Let everything else slide by. Do not clutter your brain with anything you can look up. And you know what? With the Internet you can look up almost anything!

This sounds like me

A lot   **somewhat**   **just a little**   **not at all**

Additional Resources:
Chris McChesney and Jim Huling, *The 4 Disciplines of Execution.*
Marcus Buckingham, *The One Thing You Need To Know.*

Personal Objective:

Specific Actions:

Due Date:

2.2 Technical Capability

WBS Dictionary: A leader must demonstrate competency in at least one significant technical discipline. Technical, as used here, does not relate solely to what is generally defined as technology; it also includes any craft or trade where the person has demonstrated particular skill or competence. No person can be expected to be able to competently perform every position or function in an organization, although many who choose a path of entrepreneurship feel as though they must. What it does mean is that every leader has clearly demonstrated competence in one or more areas. Typically this is demonstrated through some level of academic achievement, or the leader has a track record of making an individual contribution in their field, or both. A sustained leader must stay current with technology insofar as it relates to their particular field, not necessarily as an early adopter, but one who engages in recent technology and translates its use into a productive tool.

In some fields this is much more important than others. The craftsman who fashions furniture from hand tools is no less technically competent than the computer programmer using the latest programming tools and languages. This also includes the aspect of versatility. One way to view this is to say that the leader need not know everything, but must know something relevant to the organizational mission and goals and how each of the systems' parts contribute to the vision and mission of the organization. This also means that the leader can appreciate what is truly important, understands the role of data on business operations, and thinks systematically.

Application: R.S. Reynolds Sr. operated the Reynolds Metals Company. In operation since 1919, it produced a variety of foils and packaging materials and purchased all its supplies of aluminum. By watching the market of this critical component, Mr. Reynolds was able to determine that Germany was buying massive quantities of aluminum allegedly to make doorknobs and truck bodies. The year was 1939 and Reynolds quickly deduced that the large purchases of aluminum were for airplanes to fight the coming war. He knew that aluminum would become a critical item where the demand would outstrip the supply. At first he could not get the attention of Congress, but eventually he was able to obtain the necessary financing to develop his own aluminum production. Other experts predicted that it would take five years to fully develop the production. Reynolds did it in six months.

Other experts predicted that domestic production would serve the country's needs for two years. Ninety days later aluminum was the first metal declared to be in shortage, thus directing all production to the war effort.

After the war, Reynolds saw that aluminum would become the metal of the future. When the government sought to dispose of its aluminum production assets, Reynolds bought them and, anchored on the sale of aluminum foil, he built a very successful business selling a variety of aluminum products commercially.[231]

Napoleon Hill

Successful men, in all callings, never stop acquiring specialized knowledge related to their purpose, business, or profession.

Reynolds knew his business. Reynolds understood better than any other "experts" what would be required to produce vast quantities of aluminum quickly. His technical knowledge was a significant factor in the successful war effort. Without his technical knowledge, his leadership in persuading someone to listen, and his defiance of all the other "experts" because he *knew* what was required, the war might not have been won by the Allies. If you are not a student of history (and the sustained leader almost always is), you might not know that for many years the Allies were not winning. Even in victory, the Allied losses far exceeded those of the Axis. Knowing the technology necessary to run his business, R.S. Reynolds was a war hero. And an industrial leader.

The sustained leader always has a craft, skill, trade, or profession—not "to fall back on" but as a critical component of their accomplishments. The sustained leader has a definite proficiency in some area. From that base, they learn the many other aspects of technical and managerial competence that improve their leadership capabilities.

This sounds like me

A lot	somewhat	just a little	not at all

---

231 Alan C. Elliott, *A Daily Dose of the American Dream: Stories of Success, Triumph, and Inspiration* (1998), 302.

Additional Resources:

Marsha Sinetar, *Do What You Love, the Money Will Follow.*

Zig Ziglar, *Top Performance.*

Personal Objective:

Specific Actions:

Due Date:

2.2.1 Excellence in One Primary Field

WBS Dictionary: This element differs from 1.3.1.2 in that the element regarding mastering a particular field with a good exposure to many others encompasses a well-rounded individual with a strong focus. This one focuses solely on having a particular technical proficiency that relates to the area of leadership. Every successful leader is extremely well versed in a field that relates directly to their particular field of study. Its direct relationship to the business at hand might be somewhat tangential. What is important is that the leader has shown that they can pursue a particular course of study and successfully complete it. They have achieved a measure of success in a defined area. Such an accomplishment suggests—note it does not prove; it merely suggests—that the person holds a level of capability that can be transitioned to the specific needs of the organization. It is then the responsibility of the organization to teach the potential leader the specifics of the organization's mission and goals, which might not be possible if the person were being trained beyond their abilities. Pick a field and get as familiar as you can with its jargon, its conventions, and its principles. Demonstrate command of a particular field of study and then work to translate that to the material related to your leadership opportunity. The sustained leader pursues a specialized field in as much detail as they possibly can. They train intensely to fully understand a subject to the very end of the current state of the art or limit of human understanding. You have to be good at something, and that something must have some relationship to the organization's vision. This element is further distinguishable from 1.3.1.2 in that the self-assessment shows you where you are. This element directs you toward where you are going.

Application: This element attempts to focus you on selecting that area in which you wish to excel. You might try a variety of disciplines before settling on one, or you might see yourself in a progression from, for example, an emergency medical technician to nurse to doctor to specialist.

How many times have you heard that a job you sought required a degree? In many cases the specific degree is not relevant; the important aspect is that you have completed a level of education that demonstrates an ability to communicate and retain knowledge. In the field of government contract administration certain positions require a degree. There are certain minimal business class requirements, but no *specific* degree is required. Very few colleges offer a degree in government contract management. Thus, the entry ticket is a degree—any degree; a demonstrated competence in being able to learn. The same is true for those who pursue a JD. Almost any degree qualifies you for law school admission. The important parts are how well you excelled in that course of study and your score on the LSAT—designed to measure your aptitude for thinking like a lawyer. The sustained leader will demonstrate that they have an appropriate level of education and accomplishment by demonstrating excellence in a particular field.

While this discussion thus far centers on college achievements, there are countless leadership roles that do not require any college study at all. That does not change the requirement. As a truck driver, you need to show a clean driving record which demonstrates your adherence to traffic laws, which presupposes that you know them! If you are working in warehousing, you can demonstrate your ability to handle the forklift or similar material handling equipment. You might even demonstrate your organizational skills with the items in the warehouse. The point, again, is not a degree requirement—that only applies where a degree is required. There are other ways to demonstrate excellence in a primary field. The sustained leader will do so.

Ken's father told him that he really didn't care what his son did, so long as he worked to be the absolute best in whatever he did. He sincerely did not care if his son chose to be the local garbage man so long as he was the best garbage man that town had ever seen.

Law students find themselves drawn to particular areas of the law. Some wish to represent plaintiffs, others defendants; some focus on white-collar crimes, others on family relations or corporate work. Engineers likewise at some point in their formal education decide to pursue mechanical or electrical or civil or some other engineering discipline. Even doctors specialize. A dermatologist once noted that she selected her discipline because she was unaware of any skin condition emergency that would call her out of bed in the middle of the night. And, puzzling to some who are nonetheless grateful, some doctors decide to be proctologists.

Specialization is critical to an organized and functional society. Even in the era of hunters and gatherers, specialization was a necessary part of society. Those who are specialists may or may not choose to develop the capabilities of being a leader. We have all seen people who get promoted and then fail in the new position. The wise organization will return them to the role of an individual contributor and thereby not violate the Peter Principle. Do what you do best. This is true in all circumstances. If you aspire to be a leader, this is just one element of that journey.

This sounds like me

A lot   **somewhat**   **just a little**   **not at all**

Additional Resources:

Laurence J. Peter and Raymond Hull, *The Peter Principle.*

Tom Rath, *StrengthsFinder 2.0.*

Marcus Buckingham and Donald O. Clifton, *Now, Discover Your Strengths.*

Personal Objective:

Specific Actions:

Due Date:

2.2.2 Team Player

WBS Dictionary: While everyone must find a way to contribute, it is the exception where a person does everything totally on their own in completing a project—in producing the result. Even Michelangelo had a cadre of students who assisted in painting the Sistine Chapel. Thus, a leader must understand the dynamics of being part of a team. This is why you often hear the saying that a leader must first be an effective follower. They must understand the dynamics of team interactions and be able to make their contribution. With the technical and business acumen they bring to the team, and their base of experience, a leader has to be able to make a substantive contribution as part of the team. In the process of being a team member, the leader learns what type of leadership best facilitates their temperament. The sustained leader learns what leaders do and how they do it in leading the team in which they are participating. They catalog, even if subconsciously, the positive and negative traits of leaders. They decide which ones they choose to emulate and those they wish to avoid (5.2). They learn that different members of the team bring different talents to the team, and each in their own way makes a contribution. They each have their own way of responding to leadership, thus educating the sustained leader on matching leadership style and techniques to each of the team members.

Application: Members of a team often assume various constructive roles such as facilitator, champion, coach, sponsor, initiator, gatekeeper, harmonizer, and summarizer. They also might fall into disruptive roles such as blocker, aggressor, withdrawer, dominator, and topic jumper. These disrupters can also be negative stakeholders (those who desire that the team fail in its mission) even while not acting intentionally. Identifying which team members belong in which group can often tell whether the person might be a good leader or needs some additional maturity and training.[232]

Team dynamics are often dictated by the nature of the task to be performed.

The MIT research also made the significant discovery that when organizations employ the hierarchical model, the person atop the hierarchy reports the greatest satisfaction whereas others report far less satisfaction. In the collaborative model, the satisfaction was greater all around, although no one person enjoyed the supreme delight of being in charge.

The research confirmed an old maxim: None of us is as smart as all of us. When a task is simple and unambiguous, the most efficient way to handle it is for one person to take charge.

But what if the task is vague, nebulous, and open to multiple interpretations and solutions? In such a case, no one dominant player, no matter how smart, makes choices that are as effective as a group of people.[233]

There are occasions, however, when the availability of the potential leader will also dictate the dynamics. Less experienced leaders may not have the full toolbox to use in their expanded role. The team structure might result less from the task than from the abilities of the leader or even the availability of team members with specific skills. This is why the sustained leader works diligently to expand their competence and that of each team member. Greater versatility (2.2.8) and leadership ability draws more followers and higher quality followers to the team.

This sounds like me

A lot	somewhat	just a little	not at all

---

232 One version of these roles is summarized at http://www.maxwideman.com/issacons3/iac1363/ tsld006.htm and http://www.maxwideman.com/issacons3/iac1363/tsld007.htm. Another version of the disruptive list can be found at https://www.linkedin.com/pulse/destructive-team-roles-project-management-rahul-gupta

233 Warren Bennis and Stephen B. Sample (with Rob Asghar), *The Art and Adventure of Leadership: Understanding Failure, Resilience, and Success* (Hoboken, NJ: John Wiley & Sons Inc., 2015), 100.

Additional Resources:

Patrick Lencioni, *The Five Dysfunctions of a Team.*

Stanley McChrystal, *Team of Teams.*

Personal Objective:

Specific Actions:

Due Date:

2.2.3 Measure What Is Important

WBS Dictionary: A sustained leader knows what is important and what is just noise. We have the capability today to measure just about anything, and it is widely acknowledged that what gets measured gets done. Some feel a need to measure everything and to collect data on everything. Collecting data is not free, however. There is a cost in gathering, analyzing, and ultimately storing data. While there may be some gems hiding in there, a detailed cost/benefit analysis should consider whether the cost is worth it. In other organizations, it is important to limit the data collected to what might have a significant impact on the organization. The sustained leader brings to the table the knowledge of what is important to the organization and limits the measurement to those aspects of the mission. It is related to the need to be focused (2.3.11) insofar as different organizations will require the gathering of different data sets. The need for specific data will also change over time and with external conditions that will require the collection of different data. Collecting data for the sake of collecting data is neither good business nor sustained leadership.

Application: Management literature of today often uses the term KPI, which stands for key performance indicators. Ideally (and no situation is ever ideal) the leader will identify those few things that should be measured that will provide the most accurate leading indicator of the processes and systems that most directly affect the KPIs.

Peter M. Senge, in his seminal work on learning organizations, *The Fifth Discipline*, said:

> Because service quality is intangible, there is a strong tendency to manage service businesses by focusing on what is most tangible: such as numbers of customers served, cost of providing the service, and revenue generated. But focusing on what is easily measured leads to "looking good without being good"—to have measurable performance indicators that are acceptable yet not providing quality service. Work gets done but at a steadily poorer standard of quality, by servers who are increasingly overworked, underpaid, and under-appreciated.[234]

Sometimes it is very difficult to either measure a particular metric or to appropriately analyze what the metric is saying. Just because it is difficult does not mean it should not be attempted. Every indicator has a beginning. Over time the sustained leader will mature the collection and analytical process to improve what the metric is attempting to indicate. The sustained leader also does not automatically adopt all previous metrics. Doing things "the way we've always done it" is not leadership.[235] Apart from the obvious that change is a constant, thus making past metrics potentially irrelevant, new technology, new data collection methods, and better analysis can all be adjusted to make sure that the effort in collecting data is not wasted. The sustained leader measures what is important and properly analyzes the data to provide legitimate and valid KPIs to the team.

Senge also tells us:

> While traditional organizations require management systems that control people's behavior, learning organizations invest in improving the quality of thinking, the capacity for reflection and team learning, and the ability to develop shared visions and shared understandings of complex business

---

234 Peter M. Senge, *The Fifth Discipline: The Art & Practice of the Learning Organization* (New York: Currency, 1990), 333.

235 John Kotter, and Rathgeber, H. *That's Not How We Do It Here!: A Story about How Organizations Rise and Fall--and Can Rise Again.* (US: Portfolio, 2016).

issues. It is these capabilities that will allow learning organizations to be both more locally controlled *and* better coordinated than their hierarchical predecessors.[236]

The sustained leader understands that measuring the right things also helps develop new leaders.

This sounds like me

A lot　　　　**somewhat**　　　　**just a little**　　　　**not at all**

Additional Resources:

Robert S. Kaplan and David P. Norton, *The Balanced Scorecard.*
Peter M. Senge, *The Fifth Discipline.*

Personal Objective:

Specific Actions:

Due Date:

2.2.4 Academic Achievement

WBS Dictionary: The maintenance of technical capability requires that there be a solid functional base on which to build. One pillar of that is a level of academic achievement appropriate to the mission. This element does not require that every sustained leader obtain a PhD. In some disciplines, that may well be the expectation, but as discussed elsewhere any organization requires leaders at all levels of the organization. High academic achievement is not motivating to

---

236 Peter M. Senge, *The Fifth Discipline: op cit.* 289. Emphasis in original.

some; to many it is not required to demonstrate sustained leadership. What is important is to have the necessary foundation for the mission of the organization and the leadership role. As times change, the need for additional academic achievement may also change. That's not what is important about this element. The critical factor is to obtain that level of academic achievement appropriate to the leadership role assumed.

Application: Academic achievement suggests that you can achieve, that you can lay out a plan, perform the necessary tasks to accomplish the mission, and collect the credential that reflects the achievement. The specific field of study is less relevant than the mere fact that you have demonstrated the competence and discipline to achieve a specific goal. Many jobs require a degree; very few jobs require a specific degree. Professions often require an advanced degree or licensure that will require a basic level of education and, commonly, continued education in the field. The accomplishment of an academic degree shows that you know "something" and that you have some ability to learn. It says nothing of character (1.0) but does speak well to the fact that you know how to learn (1.3.1).

An inherent problem with this element is that too often academic achievement has far less to do with learning the critical body of knowledge related to your field, or even with learning how to think critically (1.3.9.1). It is wrongly measured by the time of butts-in-seats. Too many high school "graduates" are functionally illiterate, and even those with a college degree may have found a diploma mill or what used to be called "Grade 13" in which you put in sufficient time to walk out with a piece of paper masquerading as a diploma. These do not truly reflect any academic achievement, and those who attempt to pretend that they do show poor character and will be found out. Academic achievement, like any achievement, must by definition demonstrate some advancement. Doing the same thing repeatedly does not show progress.

Succeeding in an academic environment should reflect that the student has developed an ability to think critically (1.3.9.1) and communicate clearly. In a survey of human resource professionals, they cited the lack of critical thinking ability as the single greatest deficiency in new employees. Unfortunately, too many academic institutions have come to believe that being comfortable and perpetually protected from experiencing any offense is their goal. This is not the path to developing strong critical thinking skills or effective communication. The sustained leader ensures that their academic achievement reflects that they have been challenged and have learned to think critically without any particular indoctrination.

This sounds like me

| A lot | somewhat | just a little | not at all |

Additional Resources:

Benedict Carey, *How We Learn.*

John C. Maxwell, and John Wooden, (Foreword), *Sometimes You Win--Sometimes You Learn.*

Personal Objective:

Specific Actions:

Due Date:

2.2.5 Strong Individual Contributor

WBS Dictionary: A sustained leader will eventually demonstrate different characteristics than a person who remains an individual contributor. An individual contributor might simply choose not to lead and be very comfortable contributing from a set position for their entire career. There is absolutely no problem with that choice. Sustained leaders must both choose and desire to lead (1.3.5.2). To be a successful sustained leader some level of demonstrated competence must exist and have been exhibited. The person who has never contributed to a team effort, has not been in the forefront of production or improving organizational capability, or otherwise made a measurable contribution is rarely considered for leadership positions. An individual contributor must have a track record of positive results.

This is not to ignore the importance of learning from setbacks (5.1.7); the important thing is that they have actually learned and have not been repeating the same error (3.17). A leader will be unable to engage others in accomplishing goals if they have never demonstrated the capability as an individual. And anyone who attempts to rest on the laurels of the team without making any individual contribution lacks sufficient character (1.0) to be a sustained leader.

Application: Everyone must pull their own weight, as the old saying goes. Or as the Bible tells us, he who doesn't work doesn't eat. Certainly everyone is differently equipped with capabilities, whether they be mental or physical. Nonetheless they should be encouraged to do what they can. There is a great sense of personal value and self-satisfaction in having accomplished anything, whether it is a woodworking project, an academic degree, or stopping smoking. Personal accomplishment is critical for success in any field. The sustained leader appreciates the benefits that come from hard work, whether physical or mental, and capitalizes on the opportunity to achieve and excel.

The failure to reach for the stars and make the largest contribution possible will most likely result in a clear application of the Peter Principle where a person is promoted to their highest level of incompetence and then just stays there. They may have been a strong individual contributor at a lower level and when promoted discovered they are simply not cut out for the larger position to which they were promoted. Sustained leaders have a track record of accomplishment—of working toward a goal and achieving it. Those who have never really accomplished anything are incapable of rolling up their sleeves and contributing to the team's efforts.

Where does one learn to be a strong individual contributor? It must start early in life, even as young as a grade school. Children learn that performing usual household chores benefits the family and provides an allowance for discretionary benefits. Later the individual obtains an entry-level position where he or she develops a proper work ethic and can demonstrate achievement. Internships are often useful for the same purpose. Eventually the leader must be able to self-initiate and pitch in where effort is needed, now being able to identify for themselves what needs to be done and begin to develop the ability to set their own vision and mission and ultimately do the same for an entire team. It starts with the person being an individual contributor—accomplishing something worthwhile.

The sustained leader will have served as an individual contributor and will recognize that the success of any organization relies on the contributions of all its individuals. Whether those individual contributors choose to remain in their selected area of contribution or seek a broadening of their leadership role, it does not diminish their role as a leader in their chosen field of contribution. The organization needs leaders at all levels. The sustained leader will respect those choices.

This sounds like me

A lot	somewhat	just a little	not at all

Additional Resources:
Tom Rath, *Are You Fully Charged?*
Marcus Buckingham, *Go Put Your Strengths to Work.*

Personal Objective:

Specific Actions:

Due Date:

2.2.6 Stays Tech Savvy and Uses It Effectively

WBS Dictionary: The sustained leader understands that technology will continuously advance. This requires that the sustained leader learn what the new technology can do and adapt these advances to improve their leadership. This does not suggest that a leader must be an early adapter, although some are, and it does not mean that a sustained leader must stay on the bleeding edge of technology, although some do. It simply suggests that a sustained leader never permits themselves to become a dinosaur with technology. Advances in all areas of science and technology occur at an ever increasing pace. Things that baby boomers learned in college are now taught in high schools. Classes on social media, web design, and PC repair were not even subjects for the baby boomer in high school or college. Now handheld devices are operated by toddlers and many cell phones contain more computing power than the astronauts had in their capsule that took them to the moon and back. The point is that where you are with technology is often driven by where you started. What is familiar to you as a child is often considered the "norm," and progress beyond that is uncomfortable to many.

Application: This is an area where reverse mentoring can be useful. Younger members of society tend to adapt to new technologies more quickly. An older member can enlist their aid. With the information available on the Internet, anyone can research a particular product or technology. Yes, it takes time and attention, but regardless of other leadership attributes or qualities, a positional leader who is perceived as a non-adapter of technology will not long retain many important followers. Listen to your technical team. Consider appropriate upgrades to systems and technologies. Accept that change will occur (2.3.7), and guide it. Technology will advance. Systems must adapt. Sustained leaders understand this.

In the mid-2000s Kenny worked with a man who refused to use email. Each morning his administrative assistant would print out all his emails and present them to him in a folder. Throughout the day he would review the emails, make notes about the type of response he wished to give, and then hand them back to his assistant to type in and send the response. The man did not even know how to log onto his account. While he was not truly a Luddite, he was not comfortable with technology. This aspect of his performance was observed by both those above and below him in the organization. He lost the respect of his followers and eventually took an early retirement. His failure to use technology unquestionably stunted his career.

Just ask any boomer about why the "12:00" continued to flash on nearly every VCR in America. They will laugh. Too few people ever learned to program it. Now such things are linked to the atomic clock in Boulder, Colorado, and never need to be manually set. The sustained leader seeks to understand technology and apply it promptly and effectively to those situations in which they lead.

The sustained leader is extremely pragmatic with technology, finding a way to use it to improve efficiency or effectiveness. If the technology does not have a measurable improvement in either of those areas, the sustained leader will hesitate to adopt. The sustained leader also understands that technology has a cost. There is the cost of the technology, the cost of adoption, lost productivity during the learning curve, and the cost of disposal of old technology. New technology gets old surprisingly fast; thus the cost-benefit analysis has to account for all of these variables (2.1).

Much technology can become a phenomenal time waster. Many of the social media platforms have only marginally improved communications while more often causing a reduction in efficiency. The immediacy of the communication has also served to derail many leaders due to posting before thinking.[237] The basest of thoughts, including those that are hateful, prejudicial, or just uncaring, can cause a backlash that places the potential leader in a poor light and reflects negative character traits. And too few keep in the forefront of their mind that what gets posted to the Internet has the potential, if not the probability, that it will exist there forever. Youthful indiscretions live forever and can have a negative impact much later in life.

Jack and Suzy Welch emphasize the importance of staying current with rapidly evolving technologies, specifically addressing "anyone who's decided to leave technology expertise to the 'kids.' Big mistake. Not being tech-current is a surefire way to lose your seat at the table where any and all important organizational and strategic issues are being discussed. It's purgatory glue."[238]

They also address this from the other direction. They share the story of an associate of theirs named Joey Levin.

"The best tech people are bilingual," Joey explains. They speak fluent tech; they're the real thing. But they also speak fluent business. They embrace the company's mission and values. They understand what activities drive revenues and costs. They worry about the competition. They feel strong ownership of the numbers.[239]

---

237 See, e.g. http://www.huffingtonpost.com/2011/06/15/10-careers-derailed-by-tweet_n_877894.html?slideshow=true#gallery/29809/0 Accessed 08/27/16

238 Jack and Suzy Welch, *The Real Life MBA: Your No-BS Guide to Winning the Game, Building a Team, and Growing Your Career* (New York: HarperCollins, 2015), 206.

239 Ibid., 161.

Robert Greene provides a more ominous perspective:

The Powerful are often people who in their youth have shown immense creativity in expressing something new through a new form. Society grants them power because it hungers for and rewards this sort of newness. The problem comes later, when they often grow conservative and possessive. They no longer dream of creating new forms; their identities are set, their habits congeal, and their rigidity makes them easy targets. Everyone knows their next move. Instead of demanding respect they elicit boredom; Get off the stage! We say, let someone else, someone younger, entertain us. When locked in the past, the powerful look comical—they are overripe fruit, waiting to fall from the tree.[240]

The sustained leader does not let their knowledge and talent go stale. They stay current. They stay tech savvy. They stay relevant. To do anything less is to abdicate the role of leader.

This sounds like me

A lot   **somewhat**   **just a little**   **not at all**

Additional Resources:
Maribeth Kuzmeski, *And the Clients Went Wild!*
Jeffrey H. Gitomer, *Social BOOM!*

Personal Objective:

Specific Actions:

Due Date:

---

240 Robert Greene, *48 Laws of Power*, 425.

2.2.7 Understands Corporate Processes

WBS Dictionary: Corporate processes relate to the institutional functions of the organization. Whether the organization is a small charitable entity or a Fortune 500 corporation, there are processes that constitute the system of operations. They might involve the establishment and recognition of a hierarchy, rules of authority, concepts of responsibility, and mandates of accountability. Often the processes are either completely informal (and too often subject to loss of any "corporate memory" that resides with the team members) or so formally structured that it is impossible to follow them all. Such rigidity does tend to remove the human factor of discretion which, depending on the circumstances, may be a positive or negative attribute. It is unusual that they are all correctly sized and formalized although that should be the goal of the sustained leader. Leadership requires an understanding of values espoused by the organization, in line with its vision and mission, to be able to ascertain the correct level of formality for systems in terms of both implementation and interpretation. This element also includes the concept of continuous improvement.

Application: Tracey and Weirsema in *The Discipline of Market Leaders* speak to three choices for market leaders. They may either be focused on process excellence, technology excellence, or total solution excellence. Each of these demands a different type of corporate process for success. Those who demand process excellence, such as Starbucks and McDonald's, know that their customers expect that a caramel macchiato or a Big Mac® will be exactly the same at each and every store in the system. Customers expect no less—complete fungibility for each of the various products. Those who pursue technological excellence recognize that whatever they are placing in the market today will be made obsolete. Their goal is to ensure that it is they who replace their own products. The iPhone and BlackBerry are good comparisons here. There have been several iterations of the iPhone, effectively replacing all the prior versions. The BlackBerry struggles in the marketplace due in part to its static technological improvement.

The total solution provider deals with the external systems of the client more directly since the "fix" will most likely require the adjustment to a variety of systems, and sometimes the people involved in the system, including training or replacement. The total solution providers charge a premium and deliver a final product that enhances whatever the subject of the consulting engagement may have been. In each case, the values, vision, and mission, as understood and reflected by the team members, drive the assessment of the various systems.

As Thomas Edison noted, "There ain't no rules around here! We're trying to accomplish something!" It is the creative mind that functions well in that environment, and the sustained leader who can totally and completely trust their team, who in turn knows how to exercise their discretion in an environment bereft of rules. The 100 percent human system contains a unique set of risks.

Jim Collins observes that "Most companies build their bureaucratic rules to manage the small percentage of wrong people on the bus, which in turn drives away the right people on the bus, which then increases the percentage of wrong people on the bus, which increases the need for more bureaucracy to compensate for incompetence and lack of discipline, which then further drives the right people away, and so forth.... [A]n alternative exists: Avoid bureaucracy and hierarchy and instead create a culture of discipline. When you put these two complimentary forces together—a culture of discipline with an ethic of entrepreneurship—you get a magical alchemy of superior performance and sustained results."[241] Policies are scars from past mistakes and like scars, they never go away. Most mature organizations become moribund in their policies and procedures.

The sustained leader must recognize and accept that change will occur and that true sustained leadership requires that all parts of the system must undergo adjustment to adapt to changing circumstances (2.3.7). As discussed with technology (2.2.6), there will always be advances in science and art. The sustained leader anticipates and adapts in a continuous flow. Continuous improvement is part of the organizational psyche and is championed by every member of the organization. Such dedication exists only when the leader has made that an important precept of the organization. And such change is not limited to technology or systems. Changes in personnel will also occur as they are replaced, added, or as they mature. Each of these will cause disruption or change that the sustained leader will seek to move in a direction that improves the organization and the team's effectiveness and efficiency. Efforts to systematize this element have taken many shapes and forms. Quality Circles, Six Sigma, and Lean Manufacturing are all attempts to better define and quantify parts of processes that are, in many respects, unquantifiable.

---

241 Jim Collins, *Good to Great: Why Some Companies Make the Leap...And Others Don't* (Harper Business, 2001), 121-22.

The sustained leader recognizes the existence and role of corporate or institutional systems. Through assessment and continuous improvement, they continually seek improvements and simplification.

This sounds like me

A lot   **somewhat**   **just a little**   **not at all**

Additional Resources:

Michael Treacy and Fred Wiersema, *The Discipline of Market Leaders.*

Jim Collins, *Good to Great.*

Spencer Johnson, *The Present.*

John P. Kotter, *Leading Change.*

Michael L. George, David Rowlands, and Bill Kastle, *What is Lean Six Sigma?*

Personal Objective:

Specific Actions:

Due Date:

2.2.8 Versatility

WBS Dictionary: The sustained leader is not permitted to be a "one-trick pony." This means that while excellence in a primary field is necessary, limiting your knowledge and expertise to that area alone is inappropriate. A sustained leader develops sufficient acumen and familiarity with the jargon of a number of fields. This does not require a master's degree in each area, but a level of understanding that would permit the structuring of excellent questions (4.4.1) to those better versed in the discipline. The skills and disciplines of leadership are universal, but the environments within which they are practiced are never the same. The dynamics of the mission, team, values, and chosen target market of an organization will dictate how leadership must be practiced. The sustained leader can serve as a leader in any environment, supplementing their skills and knowledge related to the specific goals of the organization as necessary. This also suggests that the sustained leader cultivates, and actively engages in, hobbies and civic activities that expand their versatility.

Application: Paul was a senior executive at a medical device company. A family situation required that he relocate across the country. He then became the CEO of a small company that made high-precision, high-reliability components for the space program. None of them were related to the medical field at all, but the technical knowledge and the great need for leadership at this new company allowed him to make the transition with ease and serve in a very effective and successful way. He demonstrated versatility as a sustained leader.

The sustained leader never seeks to be the "Jack of all trades but master of none." On the contrary, they seek to have a strong knowledge in a specific field and as broad a base of knowledge, flexibility, and adaptability as possible. The sustained leader is capable of turning from one task to another quite easily. This is not the same as multitasking, or attempting to do multiple tasks simultaneously. Versatility relates more to the longer term ability of changing careers, focus on particular projects, or leading different types of organizations.

One thing that is very common among sustained leaders is that they have interesting hobbies that most commonly have no direct link to their career or vocation. It is another way that sustained leaders show their many interests and abilities. The sustained leader is characterized by many of the traits normally attributed to the "Renaissance Man (or Woman)"—one who has acquired insightful knowledge or broad proficiency in multiple fields of study or disciplines.

This sounds like me

A lot	somewhat	just a little	not at all

Additional Resources:
Eric Chester, *Bring Your A Game to Work*.
Patrick Lencioni, *The Three Signs of a Miserable Job*.

Personal Objective:

Specific Actions:

Due Date:

2.3 Bias for Action

WBS Dictionary: Leadership without active accomplishment is not leadership. On the other hand, never confuse activity with progress. In its simplest terms, leadership is demonstrated only through the results produced. One way to view this element is to understand that you cannot steer a ship that is dead in the water. It must be moving before the rudder has any effect on a ship's direction. Both procrastination and perfectionism can negatively impact this element and must be avoided. Sustained leaders set goals and work toward their achievement. They demonstrate persistence and manage their time effectively. They make decisions that move progress along and solve problems or impediments to achieving goals. Sustained leaders are change agents and actively manage change rather than letting it manage them. They are, to use a popular term, proactive. They have an intensity or urgency about them and execute effectively. They have a clear vision (5.1.2) of the goal and work to get tangible progress across the finish line. Sustained leaders are measured by their contribution and quickly identify those activities that are unnecessary, allowing them to refocus on the specific goal. This does not mean they run off madly in every direction; quite the contrary, they maintain focus and discipline, sometimes with a measure of audacity based on their accomplishments—not on their future promises.

Application: This is how you demonstrate to the world that you are in fact a leader. You actually accomplish something. Your success as a leader will be measured in large part by what was accomplished under your watch. It is hard to imagine how many great ideas were lost because the person who had it never acted on it. Having a great imagination, or having great empathy that generates good feelings, are important leadership traits, but they become meaningless if there is no evidence of progress toward defined goals.

Harvey S. Firestone

A business won't stand still and wait while
you dally around, wondering what to do.

A bias for action shows that the sustained leader is motivated to achieve, to accomplish something. While motivation may have an external impetus, it very often consists of a drive to achieve just for the sake of achievement. Since leadership is most often measured by results, this suggests that the sustained leader knows they have to actually *do* something. Leadership is not passive. The key is to get your ship moving. Then a minor turn of the rudder will aim the ship in the desired direction. The first necessary element is movement. Everything else flows from that.

ACT NOW!

Leadership is action, not position.
—Donald H. McGannon

Leadership is practiced not so much in words as in attitude and in actions.
—Harold S. Geneen

You have to pretend you're 100% sure. You have to take action; you can't hesitate or hedge your bets. Anything less will condemn your efforts to failure.
—Andrew Grove, Intel co-founder

Vision is not enough; it must be combined with venture.
It is not enough to stare up the steps; we must step up the stairs.
—Vaclav Havel

If you are thinking about starting tomorrow, just know that
someone who wants it more than you do is starting right now.
—Anonymous

Do not wait to strike til the iron is hot, but make it hot by striking.
—William Butler Yeats

Do you want to know who you are? Don't ask.
Act! Action will delineate and define you.
—Thomas Jefferson

John Maxwell provides some excellent advice on the importance of taking action. "People who develop systems that include action steps are almost always more successful than people who don't. Even less talented people with fewer resources accomplish more if they have developed the habit of taking action. That's one of the reasons I've developed the habit of asking myself three questions every time I learn something new:

- Where can I use this?
- When can I use this?
- Who needs to know this?"[242]

Taking action takes courage. The first one who sticks their neck out is taking the greatest risk. As the cynic notes, it is the tallest blade of grass that gets cut down first. When the first Mercury astronauts were named, they were perceived as heroes—willing to risk their lives to achieve something momentous in the entire story of mankind. Andy Stanley has noted that:

---

242 John C. Maxwell, *The 15 Invaluable Laws of Growth* (New York: Center Street, 2012), 114.

Courage is essential to leadership because the first person to step out in a new direction is viewed as the leader. And being the first to step out requires courage. In this way, *courage establishes leadership.*

We saw this principle at work when we were children. Remember standing around with your friends, daring each other to do something? Then suddenly, somebody went first and everybody followed. The person who goes first is generally viewed as the leader. Courage to act defines the leader, and in turn the leader's initiative gives those around him courage to follow.[243]

This willingness to act first is often called initiative. Sustained leaders consistently take the initiative and encourage others to do so as well. The higher the risk, however, the less initiative people tend to show. Sustained leaders, through the development of their leadership qualities as reflected in the entire *Sustained Leadership WBS*, tend to gain more confidence (1.3.5.1) in taking the initiative. They fully recognize the risks, the possibility of failure (or setbacks), and the perception of others who want to see them fail (3.11.2). And they take action anyway. This element subsumes some of the same concepts as promoted by Stephen R. Covey in his seminal work, *The 7 Habits of Highly Effective People*, when he promotes his first habit: Be Proactive.

――――――― ● ―――――――

Napoleon Hill

Create a definite plan for carrying out your desire and begin at once, whether you're ready or not, to put this plan into action.

――――――― ● ―――――――

The use of the word "bias" in the context of taking action means that there is a preference toward taking action rather than waiting. This is not an absolute; it is definitely a matter of degrees. If you are too prone to action without some minimal level of information you might be guilty of the "ready-fire-aim" approach to situations. Such an approach will destroy your credibility and cause your followers

---

243 Andy Stanley, *The Next Generation Leader: Five Essentials for Those Who Will Shape the Future* (2003, 51).

to question your judgment. A complete lack of bias toward action might be better characterized as "ready-aim-aim-aim-aim…." This is the debilitating characteristic of procrastination, or more colloquially, paralysis by analysis.

Procrastinators forego action for a variety of reasons. Some say the time is not right, or they will take action after a certain event or condition is met. All these are excuses for inaction. There is no better time than the present to begin acting. Start where you are with what you have no matter how inadequate that might seem. As Russell Conwell noted:

> Let every man or woman here, if you never hear me again, remember this, that if you wish to be great, you must begin where you are and with what you are, now. He who can give to his city any blessing, he who can be a good citizen while he lives here, he who can make better homes, he who can be a blessing whether he works in the shop or sits behind the counter or keeps house, whatever be his life, he who would be great anywhere must first be great in his own community. Right here. Right now.[244]

For every management adage, there is an opposite one that can be equally quoted. Most people have heard the caution of "Haste makes waste."[245] There are occasions where caution is warranted.

———————— ● ————————

Act Toward Results

You can't build a reputation on what you are going to do.
—Henry Ford

During a very busy life I have often been asked, "How did you manage to do it all?" The answer is very simple: It is because I did everything promptly.
—Sir Richard Tangye

---

244 Russell Conwell, *Acres of Diamonds*, 60.
245 For an excellent example see Robert Greene, *The 48 Laws of Power* (New York: Penguin Books, 1998), 296.

Some of us will do our jobs well and some will not,
but we will be judged by only one thing: the result.
—Vince Lombardi

So what do we do? Anything. Something. So long as we don't just
sit there. If we screw it up, start over. Try something else. If we
wait until we've satisfied all the uncertainties, it may be too late.
—Lee Iacocca

———————— • ————————

Kouzes and Posner provide this example: "Legendary Hollywood superagent Irving ('Swifty') Lazar once said, 'Sometimes I wake up in the morning and there's nothing doing, so I decide to make something happen by lunch.'"[246]

Another interesting aspect of having a bias for action is this: perceived failures are not true failures until you give up. In fact, setbacks are an important part of a leader's development. By learning from these setbacks, leaders grow and mature. Having a bias for action means that you get moving on making all those errors from which you will learn. This doesn't mean that you act rashly. You should still be deliberate in your actions. You should plan and execute effectively. Even so, many efforts will fail. Get to it. Start failing, or rather learning.

Ben Franklin noted, "If time be of all things most precious, wasting time must be the greatest prodigality; since lost time is never found again; and what we call time enough always proves little enough. Let us then be up and doing, and doing to a purpose; so by diligence shall we do more with less perplexity." And football coaches have been known to say, "We don't talk this game, we play it."[247]

A bias for action also prevents regrets. "At the conclusion of their exhaustive research, Gilovich and Medvec in 1994 wrote, 'When people look back on their lives, it is the things they have not done that generate the greatest regret…. People's actions maybe troublesome initially; it is their inactions that plague them most with long-term feelings of regret.'"[248]

---

246 Kouzes and Posner (p. 178) citing M. Korda, "The King of the Deal," *New Yorker* (29 March 1993), 43. See generally their material on pages 173—204.
247 Variously attributed, and quoted in Jon Gordon, *The Energy Bus*, 16.
248 Gary Keller and Jay Papasan, *The ONE Thing: The Surprisingly Simple Truth Behind Extraordinary Results* (US: Bard Press, 2013), 214.

This sounds like me

| A lot | somewhat | just a little | not at all |

Additional Resources:

Simon Sinek, *Start with Why.*

Duke Corporate Education, *Translating Strategy into Action (Leading from the Center).*

Personal Objective:

Specific Actions:

Due Date:

2.3.1 Goal Setting

WBS Dictionary: It has been said that the difference between goals and dreams is that goals have deadlines. When a leader demonstrates a bias for action, this is not simply mindless activity, or filling the square, or getting your ticket punched, or (as in training) demonstrating time of "butts in seats." Every activity should be focused on the achievement of a goal, and this involves two primary elements: actually having a goal and understanding the activities that contribute toward that goal. This in turn requires that there are metrics that can be applied toward that goal. The process of goal setting demands that the goals have certain traits. The most popular formulation of this is the SMART criteria. Goals must be Specific, Measurable, Attainable, Realistic, and Time-limited.[249] The sustained leader is adept at setting goals that work toward the achievement of the vision (5.1.2). The sustained leader

---

249 There are several variations on the acronym "SMART." For a more detailed explanation, see https://www.mindtools.com/pages/article/smart-goals.htm. Accessed 04/08/17.

knows how to demonstrate the passion (5.1.1) to inspire (3.5) the team (3.12) to apply their competence (2.0) with integrity (1.2) toward achieving SMART goals. And all of this revolves around setting the right goals, managing the progress toward those goals, and demonstrating the necessary bias for action to achieve those goals within the defined time.

Application: Goals can be formed in the abstract, but more typically they are centered on a vision—a grand objective. Sustained leaders hold strong visions (5.1.2). Goals most often start as dreams. They are then tempered with a dose of realism and must cover long- and short-term endeavors. If we define a goal as a dream with a deadline, the goals must be concrete and tangible. Too often people set a goal of "happiness" or "success." These are not appropriate goals because they are too ill-defined and subject to temporal distortions. You can't be happy all the time or successful at everything. Some of the best business leaders have ruined their family lives. John Condry is quoted as saying, "Happiness, wealth, and success are by-products of goal-setting; they cannot be the goals themselves."[250] In other words, your level of happiness, wealth, and even success are not tangible measures so much as the feelings that result from accomplishing worthwhile goals.

---◦---

Ralph Waldo Emerson
The ancestry of every action is a thought.

---◦---

There is, however, a different perspective. Bob Bly, a well-known copywriter, has observed that setting goals is too self-centered. His approach is to simply focus on the project in front of him and to complete that project as best he possibly can. He does not set future goals; only immediate ones. He appeals to Matt Furey who calls such people "unconsciously successful." Goal setting is, to them, a waste of time that could be better spent completing the project before them. [251]

---

250 Quoted in Maxwell, *How to Influence People*, 119.
251 From Bob Bly Newsletter 12/11/14; used with permission of the author, Bob Bly at www.bly. com.

Joe Vitale

A goal should scare you a little, and excite you a lot.

So do we abandon goals and all of the wisdom that has been put forth supporting the importance of setting goals? Absolutely not. There are, however, certain people whose goals tend to be more immediate. They attack the problem in front of them knowing that it is a worthwhile project. Any other goal they might set is furthered by the immediate focus (2.3.11). They already have a strong bias for action, and they are off and running. Others, most of us perhaps, do not have that natural focus and must, repeat MUST, consider our goals and objectives and set down in writing what those goals are. We must then lay out a specific set of actions that will work toward achieving those goals.

Boyee

The method of the enterprising is to plan with audacity, and execute with vigor; to sketch out a map of possibilities; and then to treat them as probabilities.

The *Sustained Leadership WBS* is designed to assist you in achieving the goal of becoming a sustained leader. In each element of the WBS you are given specific information on what that element means and how it can be applied. You are then asked to assess how well you already believe you meet that standard. You are cautioned repeatedly to make sure you are making an honest self-assessment and to request feedback from others on their perception of you as compared to that element. If you then choose to make an active decision to work on that element as an area of personal improvement, you are provided with a set of possible resources. You are then asked to do two things. The first is to identify **specific** actions that you will take and write them down. You are then asked to set a deadline to achieve those specific actions. What you have just done is create a goal, with a deadline that meets the SMART criteria. You must then hold yourself accountable to meet that goal and do something *every day* that moves you toward completing that goal. Start small if you must, but keep in mind the old saying that the journey of a thousand miles begins with the first step. Setting goals is an excellent first step.

Frances Hesselbein tells of her friend Rose Hawkins who had occasion to say to her, "You have to carry a big basket to bring something home." Hesselbein then says, "I have never forgotten Rose's well-turned metaphor. Through all the years, I have carried many big baskets of different types, materials and shapes. The small basket with its small vision, small scope, small expectations, and small impact is woefully inadequate. When we carry a big basket, what we bring home can change lives and build community. It can transform organizations and societies. In the end, it is we ourselves who are transformed."[252]

Start small. Think big. Set goals and work toward achieving them.

This sounds like me

A lot	somewhat	just a little	not at all

Additional Resources:
Daniel M. Jacobs, *The Art of the Possible.*
Brian Tracy, *Goals!*

Personal Objective:

Specific Actions:

Due Date:

---

252 Frances Hesselbein, *My Life in Leadership* (San Francisco: Jossey-Bass, 2011), 54.

2.3.1.1 Realist

WBS Dictionary: Goals must be realistic, and the sustained leader will be adept at setting goals that are attainable by the team that has been gathered within the organization. Realism includes neither pessimism not optimism, per se. A goal that does not stretch the individual or the organization is perhaps not a proper goal. In many respects an audacious goal will instill some elements of fear. Realism contains elements of a practical understanding and acceptance of how the world, or nature if you prefer, actually functions. It eschews those views often considered idealized or romantic. It is accurate and reproducible because the laws of nature are unchangeable. It accepts the concept of incrementalism—achieving large goals in small bites. Given the constant of change (2.3.7), the perception of what is realistic will also change over time. Some things will move into the realm of realistic while others move out of it. The sustained leader sets goals in support of the vision (5.1.2) that are realistic when considering all the variables within the team, further managing those variables to achieve the desired outcome.

Application: What if we don't make it? This is always a possibility with a challenging goal. It has been said that it is better to shoot for the stars and only reach the moon than to have shot for the ground and hit it. It is realistic for a five-year-old who loves ice skating to believe they might one day compete in the Olympics. It is not realistic for a sixty-year-old man to seek the same goal. Many considered John F. Kennedy's national goal of reaching the moon in a decade as unrealistic—but it was achieved.

Studies by the Gallup organization have supported the notion that not everyone should be "well-rounded" and required to participate in all aspects of an organization before being eligible for promotion. This is commonly called "getting your ticket punched." Their studies say that a completely different approach is more appropriate. Once a person's strengths are identified, they should be given assignments that focus on those strengths. Forcing people to engage in activities in which they are not as adept will result in poor results and personal dissatisfaction. Certainly people should be encouraged to understand all aspects of an organization and seek improvement in all areas. The primary focus, however, should be on their inherent strengths. Andy Stanley makes this point as well by stating, "Only do what only you can do." He goes on to explain, "This might seem unrealistic from where you sit today. You might even laugh out loud. But once you get past the seeming improbability of this axiom, write it down and work toward it.... Identify the areas in which you are most likely to add unique value to your organization—something no one else can match—then leverage your skills to the absolute max. That's what your employer expected when he put you on the payroll! More importantly, leveraging yourself generates the greatest and most satisfying return on your God-given abilities."[253]

Realists sit between the poles of optimism and pessimism. Being excessively optimistic may be setting yourself up for failure, but do not erect barriers that don't really exist due to an overly pessimistic view. You are not likely to win the lottery this week. That's not a realistic expectation. It happens—but not to everyone and not when they feel they need it. On the other hand, some people erect their own barriers. They create labyrinthine and byzantine plans that, in themselves, assure that the goal will never be met. Some plans appear more like Rube Goldberg contraptions than executable plans. So realism apples on both sides of the goal-setting coin. Do not ignore the realities of life, but do not create barriers where none truly exist.

———————————— • ————————————

E.W. Howe

Some people storm imaginary Alps all their lives, and die in the foothills cursing difficulties that do not exist (from Success Is Easier Than Failure).

———————————— • ————————————

This sounds like me

A lot	somewhat	just a little	not at all

Additional Resources:
Marcus Buckingham and Curt Coffman, *First, Break All the Rules.*
Marcus Buckingham and Donald O. Clifton, *Now, Discover Your Strengths.*
Larry Bossidy and Ram Charan, *Confronting Reality.*

---

253 Andy Stanley, *The Next Generation Leader: Five Essentials for Those Who Will Shape the Future* (2003, 19-21).

Personal Objective:

Specific Actions:

Due Date:

2.3.1.2 Dreamer

WBS Dictionary: Some of the best goals are audacious, and audacious goals are the direct products of big dreams. Only a sustained leader has the ability (and confidence) to propose truly audacious goals. While always tempered with realism (2.3.1.1), the large goals of dreamers set them apart from those who practice a much more conservative approach to their goals. It is important to recognize that what is a large goal for one may be a small goal to another. The size of the goal, in an absolute sense, is not what separates the dreamer's goals from those more tied to realistic approaches. The goal must be understood in the context of the starting point of the one setting the goal. Taking a dream and setting specific timeframes around it, establishing the metrics, and starting on the path toward achievement (2.3) comprise the essence of goal setting. The dream is properly measured from the perspective of the dreamer, not some external barometer. Nonetheless, it is fair to say that everyone has dreams. The sustained leader knows how to turn them into goals and set out to achieve them.

Application: A woman who made a choice to carry her child to full term and raise it herself, foregoing her continued education, may at times consider the attainment of her college degree an unachievable dream. Setting such a goal could be a very large dream to her. A student with good grades and strong family support may cruise through high school and on to college without hesitation. Achieving his or her degree is more of a foregone conclusion than the goal of a dreamer. This context is important. If you only dream of something and take no action to see that dream come true, you are lying to yourself. It is not really a dream at all. It is just a safety net that makes your day-to-day life more palatable by thinking about "someday." Someday will never come.

Napoleon Hill

Cherish your visions and your dreams as they are the children of your soul; the blueprints of your ultimate achievements.

Dreams can be easily turned into goals. All it takes is a commitment to set a due date and to outline for yourself the necessary steps. You then must be committed to a bias for action (2.3) to motivate yourself to work ***every day*** on those steps necessary to achieve the goal.

Jim Collins, in both of his important works, talks about the importance of establishing Big Hairy Audacious Goals (BHAGs). By definition these are BIG ideas—dreams. "A BHAG…is a huge and daunting goal—like a big mountain to climb. It is clear, compelling, and people 'get it' right away. A BHAG serves as a unifying focal point of effort, galvanizing people and creating team spirit as people strive toward a finish line….[A] BHAG captures the imagination and grabs people in the gut."[254]

Woodrow Wilson

Every great man of business has got somewhere a touch of the idealist in him.

Very often the large goal must be broken down into smaller components, each of which in itself may not seem to be so great a goal. When you engage in proper goal-setting techniques, you discover that all goals are an accumulation of smaller goals, each of which is achieved primarily by starting down the right path. It is

---

254 Jim Collins, *Good to Great: Why Some Companies Make the Leap…And Others Don't* (Harper Business, 2001), 202.

the action toward the goal that is critically important. Think of the ship metaphor referenced earlier. If it is just sitting in the harbor, moving the rudder back and forth accomplishes nothing. Once the ship is under way and moving through the water, a very minor change in the very small (relative to the ship) rudder points the ship in a completely different direction. Get moving on your dreams. Convert them to goals and action steps. Start moving. You will amaze yourself on what you will be able to accomplish. And when a midcourse correction is necessary, adjust the rudder and keep moving.

This sounds like me

A lot   **somewhat**   **just a little**   **not at all**

Additional Resources:

Jim Collins, *Good to Great.*

John C. Maxwell, *Put Your Dream to the Test.*

Personal Objective:

Specific Actions:

Due Date:

2.3.1.3 Long- and Short-Term Goals

WBS Dictionary: Human nature dictates that enthusiasm be maintained toward specific goals. Having only long-term goals prevents the necessary celebration of short-term victories (1.3.17). Proper goal setting demands that there be an appropriate mix of both long- and short-term goals in the portfolio. For the most audacious goals (2.3.1.2) it is necessary to break them down into their components—a practice often referred to as incrementalism. The sustained leader adjusts the organizational goal portfolio to include ultimate goals of short duration, ultimate goals of long duration, interim goals of both long and short duration, and proper definition of penultimate goals—the last step before final achievement. The proper mix of dreamer and realistic goals, properly defined by their sequence of achievement within realistic and measurable timeframes, will provide the most progress and greatest achievement in realizing all the goals.

Application: It is important for the sustained leader to set SMART goals that have both long-term and more immediate realization. For some the goal may be as simple as going online to look up the course offerings at the local community college. The longer-term goal is to obtain a degree, but that goal might be two to seven years in the future. So several interim goals should be set. For example, the completion of a set number of credits each semester, or working enough overtime to get the funds to pay for the tuition and books. By breaking it down into these interim goals, the accomplishments of which are individually celebrated, the ultimate goal does not seem so distant and the confidence built by achieving goals allows for the setting of even greater goals and realizing their accomplishment. The same concept of incrementalism applies to goals of physical fitness and weight control. I'm not depriving myself of all doughnuts forever. I'm simply not going to have *this* doughnut today.

A corporate turnaround expert might assume the helm of a company that is bleeding money, failing to meet financial goals, losing people, and falling behind in technology. If the sole goal is "save the company," he or she is unlikely to be very successful. That certainly is the ultimate goal; there will be many more shorter-term and interim goals toward achieving that major goal. Based on the vision set by the leader, based on what loyalty the new leader engenders, based on what talent the leader can gather around himself or herself, and based on how well the team is motivated, immediate goals that arrest the downfall and the hemorrhaging of money are put into place. Interim goals of gaining back customer support, employee loyalty, and the confidence of the financial supporters would then be appropriate. By building on the success of these goals, the team will be positioned to reach that initial larger goal of "save the company" (and the investors' money and the employees' jobs and the community tax base, and many other positive things that come from the achievement of business success).

Sidney J. Harris

An idealist believes that the short run doesn't count. A cynic believes the long run doesn't matter. A realist believes that what is done or left undone in the short run determines the long run.

The sustained leader knows the importance of long- and short-term goals and the necessity to have a mix of them. Some goals are smaller and more immediately achieved. Others are larger, more audacious, and take longer. Sometimes *much* longer. The point is, however, that the sustained leader sets goals and has a strong bias for action toward achieving them. If you never take action on any of your goals, or worse, keep them only as dreams and never define them as goals, you are likely to achieve nothing. And a sustained leader knows the importance of achievement.

This sounds like me

A lot	somewhat	just a little	not at all

Additional Resources:

Brian Tracy, *Focal Point.*

Robert A. Neiman, *Execution Plain and Simple.*

Personal Objective:

Specific Actions:

Due Date:

2.3.2 Problem Solving

WBS Dictionary: Problems are an everyday occurrence. There is no avoiding them. Perhaps having no goals or ambitions seems to be a way to have no problems, but lethargy and sloth will ultimately create their own problems. Problems are unavoidable. Thus, it should be obvious that it is necessary to be proactive in seeking out problems and conquering them. This element assumes the ubiquity of problems and recognizes that a leader must seek to solve them. The sustained leader will develop a toolbox of problem-solving techniques. The starting point of each is to frame the problem properly, to ask the right initial question. By properly defining the problem to be solved, the solution is often clearly framed. Sustained leaders practice this art. They then muster the proper resources to attack the problem, direct the team, and create a positive outcome. This element includes the identification of a problem, the framing of the problem, and the definition of an acceptable outcome. The outcome may not be perfect; it might only be satisficing behavior. Even so, the sustained leader seeks to solve problems and recognizes that a particular crisis might provide the appropriate opportunity to solve a larger or more complex problem.

Application: General Colin Powell (Ret.) noted the importance of problem solving when in a leadership role. He said, "The day soldiers stop bringing you their problems is the day you have stopped leading them. They have either lost confidence that you can help them or concluded that you do not care. Either case is a failure of leadership."

When "Kenneth"[255] started his consulting business he recognized that people without problems would not become clients. He had to be the Saint George slaying the dragons for clients to be attracted to him. He had to be a problem solver. Starting a business has many perks and responsibilities. One of them is to establish a title for yourself. Many people use the term "Principal" or "Managing Director." Others choose the title of "President" (even if the company has only the president as its sole employee). And there is the full span of "C-level" titles—CEO, COO, CAO, CFO, etc. In each case the "C" stands for "Chief" of something. So Kenneth decided that his title needed to be "Chief Problem Solver." He had it printed on his cards, and people remembered him by his title. Kenneth's view was that without problems people did not need a consultant.

---

255 In the interest of full disclosure (and a little confession) this is the author's own story.

Knowing that problems are ubiquitous, he merely had to decide what sorts of problems he was best equipped to solve and seek out people with those types of problems, building for himself a very successful business.

Covey's Habit #2 is to "Begin with the end in mind."[256] In solving a problem, the problem solver must be able to recognize what exactly a correct solution might be. There must be a target. In many instances the solution is not perfect. It might create other problems, or only solve a portion of the initial problem. Sometimes that's good enough, for now. It is not enough to identify that there is a problem. The sustained leader must seek to understand the problem fully and know when it is sufficiently solved.

In the field of customer service, well-trained representatives are trained to ask the customer what they feel an appropriate remedy might be. Simply slapping a remedy on a problem without input from the person who feels aggrieved, the "solution" could very well create more problems than it solves. This is especially true if the solution is phrased in terms of "company policy."

John Maxwell appeals to Ken Blanchard to summarize a proven problem-solving approach. "Management expert Ken Blanchard recommends a four-step problem-solving process that includes (1) thinking about the problem in order to make it specific, (2) forming theories for solving it, (3) forecasting the consequences of carrying out the theories, and (4) then choosing which method to use based on the big picture."[257]

As simplistic as this sounds, it is a completely effective problem-solving approach. The sustained leader becomes adept at seeking problems to solve. Like a Six Sigma approach to process improvement, the goal is to identify the source of the problem. First-blush guesses are often wrong. Having properly defined the problem, making it specific, and thinking about possible solutions, the sustained leader will then assess which proposed solution has the highest probability of success and implement the proposed solution. Unsolved problems fester, and that's not good for the health of any person or organization.

A further comment on gender differences in problem solving is warranted. Generally speaking, women tend to explore problems more completely than men.

---

256 Stephen R. Covey, *The 7 Habits of Highly Effective People* (1990).
257 John C. Maxwell and Jim Dornan, *How to Influence People: make a difference in your world* (Nashville, TN: 2013), 126.

Men tend to rush to a solution. As Deborah Tannen has noted,[258] women are more comfortable discussing a problem or situation, not so much to solve it as to fully understand it. Men, on the other hand, tend to rush to conclusion to "solve" the issue. Women will often suggest that as long as the problem is being discussed, progress toward a solution is being made. Men will say, "If we have to keep talking about it, it must still need an immediate solution." As Tannen notes, "Boys and girls grow up in different worlds, but we think we're in the same one, so we judge each other's behavior by the standards of our own."[259] Different approaches do not suggest different methods or even that only one is preferable. The sustained leader knows that different approaches are not just okay but may well be a significant benefit with problem-solving efforts.

------ o ------

Nancy Reagan

A woman is like a teabag: you cannot tell how strong she is until you put her in hot water.

------ o ------

This sounds like me

A lot	somewhat	just a little	not at all

Additional Resources:

Max DePree, *Leadership Is an Art.*

Morgan D. Jones, *The Thinker's Toolkit.*

Michael Gurian and Barbara Annis, *Leadership and the Sexes.*

Deborah Tannen, *You Just Don't Understand.*

Benedict Carey, *How We Learn.*

Personal Objective:

---

258 Deborah Tannen, *You Just Don't Understand: Women and Men in Conversation* (1991), 279. "[F]rom the earliest ages through adulthood, boys and girls create different worlds, which men and women go on living in…. We try to talk to each other honestly, but it seems at times we are speaking different languages—or at least different genderlects."

259 Deborah Tannen, *You Just Don't Understand: Women and Men in Conversation* (1991), 254.

Specific Actions:

Due Date:

2.3.3 Persistent / Patient / Tenacious

WBS Dictionary: Few efforts see perfect results in the first attempt. Successive tries are necessary. No one ever stepped onto the ice for the first time and did a triple axel perfectly. The sustained leader understands the importance of persistent pursuit of noble objectives. The sustained leader develops the patience necessary to permit things to develop, often in their natural course, to see them through to a successful conclusion. The sustained leader develops a sense of tenacity in pursuit of the defined goals. This is not to say that it should be to a foolish extreme, and the sustained leader must also know when it is time to change direction or even abandon prior goals (2.3.15). Nonetheless, the proper balance of persistence and the reality of the situation form the matrix within which the sustained leader judges the appropriate use of resources toward a goal. Too often goals are abandoned prematurely, most commonly due to unreasonable fear (1.3.15). Leaders develop a stronger sense of tenacity and patience to achieve worthy goals; they overcome the fear (1.3.15) that causes others to give up, and they persist toward the goal.

Application: It's like the perfect cup of coffee at Starbucks. Have you heard people go into the store and order the double shot expresso, skinny superlight, three pumps, venti, extra hazelnut, no foam, extra hot "crappochino"? Seriously, how many cups of coffee did they have to buy before they settled on that combination as the perfect cup of coffee? Mindboggling. But persistent. You have to admire that.

Warren Bennis notes that "leaders learn by leading, and they learn best by leading in the face of obstacles. As weather shapes mountains, problems shape leaders. Difficult bosses, lack of vision and virtue in the executive suite, circumstance beyond their control, and their own mistakes have been the leaders' basic curriculum."[260] These obstacles may seem formidable. If the goal is worthy,

---

260 Warren Bennis, *On Becoming a Leader* (Reading, MA: Addison-Wesley, 1988).

the sustained leader will be persistent in overcoming the obstacles and succeeding in spite of them.

Persistence Quotes

Only the weak rest on their laurels and dote on past triumphs;
in the game of power there is never time to rest.
—Robert Greene

Few things are impossible to diligence and skill.
—Samuel Johnson Rasselas

The harder you work, the harder it is to surrender.
—Vince Lombardi

Let me tell you the secret that has led me to my goal:
my strength lies solely in my tenacity.
—Louis Pasteur

It's not that I'm so smart, it's that I stay with problems longer.
—Albert Einstein

The sustained leader will not live long enough to make every possible mistake from which they can learn. While experience is the best teacher, the lesson comes after the fact and usually after the bad consequence of a bad decision has occurred. The sustained leader, therefore, maximizes what they can learn from the mistakes of others. Every situation is different, and the sustained leader must assess the situation (2.1.6) and determine what next action is appropriate. This includes knowing both when to persist and when to change direction. Throwing more money down a failed effort is never wise, regardless of the lost sunk costs. Stopping just before a major breakthrough can be equally disastrous.

Calvin Coolidge

Nothing in the world can take the place of Persistence. Talent will not; nothing is more common than unsuccessful men with talent. Genius will not; unrewarded genius is almost a proverb. Education will not; the world is full of educated derelicts. Persistence and determination alone are omnipotent. The slogan 'Press On' has solved and always will solve the problems of the human race.

Russell Conwell's *Acres of Diamonds* is a parable of someone who left his home and searched far and wide for his fortune, only to learn that he left such a fortune back in his hometown. During the gold rush era, there were examples of those who gave up and abandoned their mines only to have a subsequent miner come along and quickly discover that had the original team persisted they would have found a motherlode that now belonged to the new miner.

Few people remember that the Hula Hoop was a financial failure for its manufacturer—at least initially. When Wham-O first started making the fad item, they promoted it heavily and even gave away many in parks, beaches, and college campuses. While they had trademarked the name, they had not yet gotten the patent, and many other manufacturers started making the popular gadgets and capitalizing on the promotion that Wham-O had done at its own expense. From this costly lesson, Wham-O adjusted its roll-out process for its next "big thing"—the Frisbee flying disc. The Frisbee flying disc was very successful for the company, and with its rights now firmly in place on the Hula Hoop, they reintroduced it years later and were able to make money this time around. One lesson from being persistent is that no effort is totally wasted if you learn from it and do not repeat the same mistake.

The sustained leader understands that failing to learn from your experiences is one definition of failure. Certainly a leader must recognize when it becomes necessary to stop beating your head against the wall (5.1.9 and 2.3.15). The sustained leader knows the difference and captures the lessons that any short-term setback can teach you, using these lessons on future endeavors to ensure greater success.

The films of Charlie Chaplin are classics. Many people do not realize, however, that most of them never had a script. Chaplin's genius would point the actors in a particular direction and film what happened. As the story took shape in his head, he would re-film a scene many times, often hundreds of times, until he got it just the way he wanted it. The final product that the audience saw was actually a series of shots meticulously developed over many, many "takes." His financiers and studio bosses crossed swords with him often due to the expense of repeated shots and, in some cases, the cast and crew having nothing to do until he came up with his next idea. His final products are classics in the film industry and inspired many others to pursue a filmmaking career. Our film heritage would be much less impressive without the "Little Tramp's" persistence and tenaciousness in getting it "just right," not the first time, but by repeatedly fine tuning the product he saw in his head until it was right on film.

Gail Borden failed many times in finding ways to keep milk fresh and unadulterated. His condensed milk was revolutionary and provided healthy nourishment to the troops in the Civil War. He could have easily given up long before he succeeded at the age of fifty-six.

Henry Ford was perceived as a hardheaded individual, and he was. Very much so. While many examples could be given, his relentless pursuit of the V8 engine, which his best engineers maintained could not be built, is just one example. He insisted that it be built anyway. After more than a year of no success, his engineers finally created a working V8 engine. This level of persistence and determination in pursuit of his vision led to many "impossible" improvements in his products.

More recently Steve Jobs has noted, "I'm convinced that about half of what separates successful entrepreneurs from the non-successful ones is pure perseverance." The sustained leader understands the need to stick to a vision and persevere in the face of obstacles. Worthy goals must be pursued vigorously, with tenacity, patience, and persistence.

This sounds like me

A lot   **somewhat**   **just a little**   **not at all**

Additional Resources:

Russell Conwell, *Acres of Diamonds.*

Seth Godin and Hugh Macleod, *The Dip.*

Peter B. Kyne, et al., *The Go-Getter.*

Personal Objective:

Specific Actions:

Due Date:

2.3.4. Time Management

WBS Dictionary: The management of time includes both the wise use of time and the ability to prioritize among the many competing items that call for our attention. The sustained leader has an innate sense that each moment of each day is precious and once spent is gone forever. Too often people learn this valuable lesson too late in life when too many moments have already been wasted. Even so, it is never too late to start making good decisions about how you spend your time. The sustained leader chooses the most productive use of each moment of the day. The sustained leader also understands the importance of balanced health (5.1.6) and the need for certain amounts of "downtime," relaxation, family time (1.1.1.3), and the pursuit of charitable and hobby activities. Each can and should be the first priority at appropriate times. The sustained leader discovers and adapts tools that best suit their personality to maximize the efficient use of time. These might include to-do lists, electronic scheduling applications, a live or virtual administrative assistant, and decision-making tools to assess cause and effect and priorities. Equally important, the sustained leader recognizes that many things conspire to distract from the efficient use of time. An excellent leader will also construct a "don't do" list to keep themselves from being tempted to engage in unnecessary time wasters.

Application: For any task to fail to be accomplished does not require that it be number twenty-three on your list of things to do. It need only be item number two. Most people will put their attention to task number one, and by the time it is accomplished a new number one has arisen, thus keeping number two at number two—or lower. The less efficient among us will actually engage in more mundane if not menial tasks rather than respect the established priority.

Occasionally this makes sense. When you are overwhelmed and can't seem to accomplish anything, or the work has piled up so high that you can no longer find a space in which to work, there is a good argument for simply picking up any task or piece of paper and pushing it to completion, regardless of priority. This permits an immediate "win" that will set up the necessary momentum to continue. The key is to not permit yourself to remain in this mode of operation for long else it becomes a habit.

———————— ● ————————

Peter F. Drucker
Until we can manage time, we can manage nothing else.

———————— ● ————————

One way to help you prioritize is to use a process known as matched pairs. The process is simple. Make a vertical list of your top ten action items. Then compare item one on your list to item two. Which of the two is the more urgent? It might be by the smallest of margins, but one of them will be more important. Put a hash mark next to that one. Then compare number one to number three. Which of those is more important? Place the hash mark. Continue to compare number one to each item on the list, placing the appropriate hash mark next to the more important of the two. Then go back to number two on your list. Since you have already compared it to your number one, just compare it to each of the items below it, placing the hash mark next to the one that is more important. Then look at number three, comparing it to each item below it in the list. When you have compared number nine to number ten, you are done. See which of the items has the most hash marks. That is your most important task. Perhaps it is the one you thought; perhaps not. You have your prioritized list of top ten actions. Get to work on number one.

You should also prepare a "stop doing" list. As described by Jim Collins, "Most of us lead busy but undisciplined lives. We have ever expanding 'to do' lists, trying to build momentum by doing, doing, doing—and doing more. And it rarely works. Those who built the good-to-great companies, however, made as much use of 'stop-doing' lists as the 'to do' lists. They displayed a remarkable discipline to unplug all sorts of extraneous junk … They displayed remarkable courage to channel their resources into only one of a few arenas."[261]

Whether your favorite distraction is solitaire, video gaming, or TV, you need to regain your focus and tend to the important tasks that further your goals. Stop partaking of time wasters. Remember, however, that planned recreation and breaks are not time wasters. They are an important part of maintaining good physical and mental health. As Aristotle has reminded us, "What lies in our power to do lies in our power not to do." Stop doing things that do not enhance your leadership.

The Pareto principle was first described by Italian mathematician Vilfredo Pareto. He determined a consistent ratio between various inputs and outputs. In practice this tells us that 20 percent of our efforts result in 80 percent of our production. As Richard Koch noted in *The 80/20 Principle*, "for all practical purposes, four fifths of the effort—a dominant part of it—is largely irrelevant."[262] Thus, it becomes the responsibility of the sustained leader to identify the key inputs and eliminate the unnecessary. By focusing on that 20 percent of our truly productive effort, we become more productive and free up a great deal of time that was, for all intents and purposes, wasted. You should construct a "don't do" list, and that list should be about four times longer than your "to do" list. Never confuse activity with progress (or production.) The truth is that what you most enjoy doing is probably what you are best at doing anyway. If you allocate your time more appropriately you will find that you produce more, enjoy it more, and free up a great deal of time. Find others who have strengths where you don't and delegate.

---

261 Jim Collins, *Good to Great* (New York: HarperCollins, 2001), 139-40. Also found in *Next Generation Leader*, p. 70. Ellipses in original. See also Greg Mckeown. *Essentialism: The Disciplined Pursuit of Less* (US: Greg Mckeown, 2012).

262 Richard Koch, *The 80/20 Principle* (New York: Currency/Doubleday, 1998), 4.

David Allen identifies one of the key disrupters to effective time management. "Defining what real doing looks like, on the most basic level, and organizing placeholder reminders that we can trust, are master keys to productivity enhancement."[263] He continues, "Often the simplest things are stuck because we haven't made a final decision yet about the next action."[264] The "next action" is very key to Allen's system. Too often we have not yet figured out the very next action to take, and as a result we do nothing. Consider any project that has been "hanging around" on your to-do list. What is the VERY NEXT action that needs to be taken? Is it a phone call, an email, the acquisition of specific information, a specific tool that needs to be acquired? The point is that there is SOMETHING standing in the way of progress. What is that one thing?

---•---

Anonymous

Time is the quality of nature that keeps events from happening all at once. Lately it doesn't seem to be working.

---•---

Sometimes you have to trace the trail back a considerable distance. You typically do not walk out of your house one day and go buy a new car. You do research. You look at other cars, you visit car lots. And even if you have settled on a specific make and model, you will continue to seek the best financing, you will check on insurance rates, you will consider options and "extras" that you might want to include. This is a long and somewhat complex process for many. The view at the beginning of the path appears impossible, especially if you have never been through it before. The sustained leader understands that any decision that involves multiple interrelated aspects must have a starting point. There is that ONE thing that will get the process moving. And along the path there will be various obstacles and impediments. For each one the sustained leader will say, "What is *the* next thing that has to happen?" Mark Twain said, "The secret of getting ahead is getting started. The secret of getting started is breaking your complex overwhelming tasks into small manageable tasks, and then starting on

---

263 David Allen, *Getting Things Done* (New York: Penguin Group, 2001), 239.
264 Ibid.

the first one." Unfortunately, too many people fail to think sufficiently deeply about a goal or vision or even a task to identify the *very next* step. Knowing that piece of information allows you to then prioritize the many tasks related to the various activities in your life, personal and professional, and know exactly what has to happen to move each one along.

Gary Keller and Jay Papasan note that things do not matter equally. The sustained leader must identify and segregate the most important thing to tackle first. "Sometimes it's the first thing you do. Sometimes it's the only thing you do. Regardless, doing the most important thing is always the most important thing."[265]

This sounds like me

A lot	**somewhat**	**just a little**	**not at all**

Additional Resources:

Stephen R. Covey, *The 7 Habits of Highly Effective People.*

David Allen, *Getting Things Done.*

Larry Bossidy, Ram Charan, and Charles Burck, *Execution.*

Gary Keller, and Jay Papasan, *The ONE Thing.*

Greg McKeown, *Essentialism.*

Personal Objective:

---

265 Gary Keller and Jay Papasan, *The ONE Thing: The Surprisingly Simple Truth Behind Extraordinary Results* (US: Bard Press, 2013), 42.

Specific Actions:

Due Date:

2.3.5 Tackles the Difficult

WBS Dictionary: The sustained leader appreciates a challenge and seeks out opportunities to excel. There is often a strong argument for "playing it safe," but the sustained leader knows that with great challenges come great victories. Even so, there is no sense in tilting at windmills or chasing a fool's errand. While difficult challenges lead to great victories, the sustained leader must exercise the wisdom necessary to discern those that are not worth the risk (1.3.15). Tackling the difficult is also not something that is generally accomplished in great leaps. A measured response that takes on increasingly challenging tasks develops the leader. Jumping too far ahead at one time can over stress the leader's abilities and result in a setback. The sustained leader recognizes that a setback is not a failure; it is not a failure until you give up. Even then, there are lessons to be learned. The sustained leader enjoys the spoils of tackling the difficult even if those spoils consist entirely of gaining knowledge or wisdom.

Application: Many great leaders of our history were recognized as leaders due to their conquests in war. Military leaders are some of the most recognized; we currently refer to the generation of Americans who won the Second World War as the "Greatest Generation." Military conquests, by definition, are difficult. There is an aggressor and a defender. Each battles to the death of many of their society. And the conqueror gets to write the history. Interestingly, there are always two great leaders that go into battle, each with their followers. Only one exits the conflict victorious, even if it is a Pyrrhic victory.

John Maxwell has, among his many laws related to leadership, one he calls "The Law of Pain." To those who fear taking action, even difficult action, or fear failure in the attempt, he says, "Inventor Charles F. Kettering, who was the head of research at General Motors, said, 'you will never stub your toe standing still. The faster you go, the more chance there is of stubbing your toe, but the more chance you have of getting somewhere.' In other words, where there is no struggle, there is no progress. Facing difficulties is inevitable. Learning from them is optional. Whether you learn is based on if you understand that difficulties present opportunities to learn and treat them accordingly."[266]

It was Irish statesman and supporter of both the French and American Revolutions, Edmond Burke, who said, "The only thing necessary for the triumph of evil is for good men to do nothing." It is important that the "something" that is done in lieu of "nothing" be a properly measured response. Otto von Bismarck viewed war as glorious, not unlike Star Trek's Klingons. He said, "The great questions of the time will be decided, not by speeches and resolutions, but by iron and blood." This is captured in the Klingon society by the Tenth Precept within the Klingon Art of War, which says "Guard Honor Above All." The dictum adds, "Scaling the cliffs demands strength, will, and courage, and it exacts a toll of sweat and blood and pain. But standing at the utmost height of honor, a warrior has conquered demons."[267] Tackling the difficult may take extraordinary effort, or effort not contemplated at the inception of the great task, or both. The sustained leader accepts this potentiality and undertakes the difficult anyway. Especially when there is evil to be overcome.

Often people feel that they can't succeed because they feel victimized, that life did not deal them a fair hand and they are thus forever constrained to live under the cloud of their handicap. If that is you, you are challenged to look up the biographies of authors O. Henry and John Bunyan who both started writing while in prison. Charles Dickens was crushed by the love of his life and used the experience to write David Copperfield. Milton was blind. Beethoven became deaf. Helen Keller was deaf, mute, and blind. This is not designed to make you feel sorry for them, but to get you to stop feeling sorry for yourself. The sustained leader accepts that they have talents and perceived handicaps and gets over themselves. It doesn't matter what you believe might be holding you back. The only thing holding you back is your own view of yourself. Assess yourself honestly (1.3.3.1) so that you are aware of your real limitations (1.3.3.6), but don't lie to yourself and hold yourself back from tackling the difficult.

---

266 John C. Maxwell, *The 15 Invaluable Laws of Growth* (New York: Center Street, 2012), 131-32.
267 Keith R. DeCandido, *The Klingon Art of War* (Pocket Books/Star Trek, 2014), 126-27.

---◆---

When life gives you lemons, make lemonade.
–Unknown

When life gives you melons, you might have dyslexia. Get over it.
–Also Unknown, but better advice.

---◆---

This sounds like me

A lot   **somewhat**   **just a little**   **not at all**

Additional Resources:

John C. Maxwell, *Failing Forward.*

Stephen R. Covey and Breck England, *The 3rd Alternative.*

Alex Harris, et al., *Do Hard Things.*

Personal Objective:

Specific Actions:

Due Date:

Essential Leadership Journey Checkpoint
2.3.6 Decisive

WBS Dictionary: Being decisive means that you choose a course of action and execute it. Decisiveness avoids procrastination and perfectionism and understands that "good enough" most often is. The process of making a decision has a great many variables, and while it is often easy to determine if a decision was "good" or "bad" such things may be couched in considerable shades of gray. A decision is a choice among multiple alternatives. Using judgment, the sustained leader applies their decision-making authority across a nearly infinite number of situations. Some decisions are purely fact-based. The numbers either work or they don't. Many decisions are based on less concrete data. In any organization, decisions *will* be made. The question becomes more a matter of who will make the decision and what will form the basis of that decision. If it is rumor, innuendo, false facts, or emotion, then the organization is not incorporating sustained leadership principles.

Application: Do you think that Jeffrey Dahmer or Charlie Manson had trouble sleeping at night? Of course not. Their actions did not affect their consciences the way they might affect you. They had seared their consciences to the point that what we find repulsive was normal behavior to them. Martha Stout PhD tells us that 4 percent of the population suffers from the mental disorder of having no conscience.[268] They are not all violent criminals; they simply feel no shame, guilt, or remorse at all. Such people should never trust their gut, but they are probably incapable of realizing that. They are inherently unable to make good decisions.

While it would be comforting to suggest that "things always work out in the end," it is even more verifiable that the best batters only get on base less than a third of the time and that well over 50 percent of marriages, based on a personal vow of "until death do we part," end in divorce. We, as individuals and as a society, do not have a great track record on making good decisions. The cynics among us will consider the choices and results in recent elections to see the proof of this point.

It is unwise to rely strictly on "the law" in making decisions. To simply ask "Is it legal?" will too often lead to bad choices. Our Western society has historically tended to set our legal standard below our ethical standard. This standard is not always followed in other societies. The American law does not necessarily impose a liability on a person for not acting in a manner that would positively affect others. Generally, the laws prohibit us from doing wrong to others.

This element is an essential leadership journey checkpoint and is deeply related to other essential leadership journey checkpoints, most notably situational awareness (2.1.6) and moral center (1.2.2.1). As reflected there, a strong moral

---

268 Martha Stout, *The Sociopath Next Door* (Harmony, 2006).

center plus situational awareness plus a bias for action yields good decisions, which is a key hallmark of sustained leadership. Without deciding what to do, it is difficult to take action.

Decision Quotes

I am not a product of my circumstances. I am a product of my decisions.
—Stephen Covey

When I've heard all I need to make a decision,
I don't take a vote. I make a decision.
—Ronald Reagan

When your values are clear to you, making decisions becomes easier.
—Roy Disney, executive

Leaders sense when difficult decisions must be taken, and that is a rare quality in an age too often defined by narcissism. No leader will fight for values, for principles, if their government is a value-free vacuum. Moral relativism is morally wrong.
—Rupert Murdoch

Some people make decisions "from the gut." They explain that it simply "feels right." This can be dangerous because such decision making is contingent on proper "gut guidance." Simply stated, if you have trained your "gut" through a series of good decision making, then when less data is available it might make sense to rely on your gut. If, on the other hand, you have a history of making bad choices, it is possible that your conscience has been seared and you are no longer capable of making good decisions. A history of good decision making suggests that you have an innate ability to discern variables and assess their outcome. A history of making bad decisions suggests that your ability here is less finely honed. In those cases, DO NOT rely on your conscience (or your "gut") for decisions. Be more careful in making decisions, particularly life-changing ones. Return to your moral center to assess which factors should be given priority.

Daniel M. Jacobs in his book *The Art of the Possible* talks about how you can measure a quality decision. The first analysis ensures that any decision aligns with the organizational vision, principles, mission, and goals. He offers the following checklist against which all decisions should be measured.

- Incorporates credible, honest information from appropriate experts
- Appropriate in scope and perspective
- Includes market and competitive insight
- Focuses on what's important, not on what you know how to do
- Includes analysis of uncertainty and risk
- Compares several real options, not just justification of a predetermined decision
- Uses a systematic decision process
- Appropriate balance of cost versus benefits; risk versus return
- Logical Analysis that is comprehensive, insightful, but focuses on critical questions
- Organization has "buy-in" and is committed to implementing the final recommendation[269]

Bob Lewis

There are also many leaders, at all levels, who exhibit more psychopathy than you might personally fiuld be measured. laws. ctices toward customers, assignements or explanations given to you that dnd comfortable, but who don't express it in ways that break laws or harm shareholders. If you report to them, you might find yourself dealing with abusive behavior, unreasonable demands on your staff, shoddy practices toward customers, assignments or explanations given to you that deliberately conflict with those given to other managers, or any of a number of other circumstances that break no laws.

---

269 Daniel M. Jacobs, *The Art of the Possible: Create an Organization with No Limitations* (2010).

Copywriter Bob Bly makes the following observation about making decisions:

One of the most unappreciated and valuable business skills you can possess is the ability to make quick decisions—and the smaller the decision, the quicker you should make it.

The longer you agonize over decisions, the more likely it becomes that you will never make them at all—and so you won't move forward and progress toward your goal.

As the saying goes: money loves speed. Successful people are able to make quick decisions and take action swiftly.

Those who agonize over every little move rarely get much done, make much money, or accomplish more than a tiny fraction of their goals and dreams. ***

Too many people I hear from are held back by 'analysis paralysis.' ***

Busy and successful people don't spend hours making minor decisions, because they have other things to do and the decisions are just not that difficult or important.

They just aren't.[270]

This sounds like me

A lot   somewhat   **just a little**   not at all

Additional Resources:

Daniel M. Jacobs, *The Art of the Possible.*

Robert Heller, *Making Decisions.*

Daniel Kahneman, *Thinking Fast and Slow.*

Martha Stout, *The Sociopath Next Door.*

Personal Objective:

---

270 From Bob Bly Newsletter; used with permission of the author, Bob Bly at www.bly.com.

Specific Actions:

Due Date:

2.3.6.1 Considers Options

WBS Dictionary: We are the sum of our decisions. This includes those that determined where we went to school, where we work, where we live, and what we wore to work today. Clearly some of these decisions are more important than others, but nonetheless when they are all combined they represent our life and have determined where we are today. For each of these decisions, in fact any decision, there were options. More than one choice must exist before a decision is required. Decisions are either passive or active. Passive decisions are those that occur by default. A good decision maker looks at the alternatives and assesses the most probable outcomes. A comparison is then made as to the costs and benefits of each, as filtered through our values, and a final decision is made. This is active decision making. Importantly, once the decision is made, action is taken to implement the decision. Without immediate action, the decision is not really made. The sustained leader trains themselves to make good decisions by fairly evaluating various options. The failure to evaluate options suggests that the decision is either predetermined or decisions are being made passively and not based on the best objective data.

Application: What you decide to wear today may seem like an inconsequential decision. Consider what would happen, however, if you wore your pajamas to work. Or an evening gown to the grocery store. Each of those would make a statement and is a decision that the statement needs to be made. But generally such decisions are pretty much inconsequential.

Active decisions are always the preferable course of action and are crucial for the sustained leader to manage change. In these matters there are choices to be made. This says that there are different courses to take and each will have its own outcomes. The consideration of options is crucial to the effective decision making of sustained leaders. This consideration must be on an objective basis. Passive decisions are a function of the passage of time—just letting things happen. Good decision making is difficult. It involves hard work.

Since any decision must be a choice between or among options, the sustained leader must have tools that permit the weighing of options. Certainly some choices, such as fight or flight, are automatic to most humans. To the sustained leader, any other decision must be carefully considered based on relevant and available data. The leader gets to choose which data to consider and how to weigh that data, much as a jury is instructed to do. The leader also must consider how certain they must be of the decision. Consider the jury: must the decision be based on a preponderance of the evidence (something more than 50 percent), or must it be "beyond a reasonable doubt" (closer to 100 percent)? The combination of the available relevant data compared against the level of certainty required (all of which are variables among individuals) creates our decisions.

In the landmark book *Getting to Yes*,[271] the authors explain the use of a BATNA, or the best alternative to a negotiated agreement. Too often in negotiations people fail to prepare adequately. By preparing a BATNA the negotiator has a clear understanding of what the best option is if the current negotiation does not result in an agreement. Without working on a BATNA, the negotiator may feel they have no choice but to accept a bad deal. The development of your BATNA creates other choices. If none are obvious, work to create alternatives.

In many cases, to develop other leaders or to place decision-making at a proper level in the organization, the leader can and should delegate the decision, which is an important decision in itself. See 3.8.

The sustained leader recognizes both the choices to be made and the weight of the consequences of those choices. Unimportant decisions are made more quickly and often on less data. Important or consequential decisions require greater consideration and carry weightier consequences.

This sounds like me

A lot	**somewhat**	**just a little**	**not at all**

---

271 Roger Fisher, et al., *Getting to Yes: Negotiating Agreement Without Giving In* (1991).

Additional Resources:

Roger Fisher and William Ury, *Getting to Yes.*

Mikael Krogerus, *The Decision Book.*

Personal Objective:

Specific Actions:

Due Date:

2.3.6.2 Does Not Require Complete Data

WBS Dictionary: No decision is ever made with absolute certainty of the outcome. Decisions are based on probabilities. Life and leadership are composed of too many variables for there to be absolute certainty. The question becomes, what level of data is necessary to act on a particular decision? The sustained leader accepts that decisions will be based on incomplete data and perhaps even false data. The goal should be to make the best possible decision at the time and act on it. As the situation evolves, more data will become available and, if necessary, midcourse corrections can be made to the initial decision. There are a variety of techniques that decision-makers use to evaluate decisions and determine what midcourse corrections would be appropriate. Sustained leaders must get comfortable making decisions based on incomplete data and reach a comfort level of acting on decisions before all the data are in. This does not imply that sustained leaders act rashly or make decisions to act before the time is appropriate to act. Decisions must be fully considered and based in rationality. They need not, however, be based on absolute certainty of outcome. Additionally, the best decisions allow for "midcourse corrections" as additional data become available.

Application: When a decision can be made based on a complete set of data, there is relative assurance that the decision will turn out to be correct. In life, however, such assurance is almost never possible. There are too many variables and much of life, or business, or government, or religion is too complex to be reduced to simplistic predictions that will most likely be correct. The sustained leader must be able to make decisions and take action even when some uncertainty of success remains. As Warren Buffet has said, "It is better to be approximately right than precisely wrong." Or too late.

The sustained leader will seek as much data as possible but will not require repeated analysis, thus setting up a setback for failing to make a decision due to paralysis by analysis. Jack Welch was speaking of making decisions concerning company strategy. He believed that the decision was easy. "You pick a general direction and then implement like hell." In other words, take action. Get the ship moving at least in the general direction. As more data become available, make the midcourse corrections. But do not stay dead in the water while you wait for more data. Accept what you have and make the decision.

This sounds like me

A lot	somewhat	just a little	not at all

Additional Resources:
Stuart Crainer, *The 75 Greatest Management Decisions Ever Made.*
Michael A. Roberto, *The Art of Critical Decision Making.*

Personal Objective:

Specific Actions:

Due Date:

2.3.7 Change Agent

WBS Dictionary: This much-overused phrase properly pertains to a person who watches trends and notes the immediate and future changes that flow from the current trajectory of an organization. This includes the internal shifts, the external forces, and the macro-level dynamics of global-scale changes. The sustained leader makes sure that the changes are anticipated, and they can then manage the change rather than being managed by it. Change is inevitable, and only a fool fails to prepare for the inevitable nature of change. To say that the sustained leader is a change agent is to say that even the surprises that arise are not generally very far afield from the other changes that the sustained leader has anticipated due to their analysis of current trends and situations. As used here, a change agent is one who prepares for the inevitable changes and has the foresight to predict the short- and long-term consequences, thus positioning themselves to appear to be prescient about the future and, to the degree possible, guide those changes in ways that are favorable to the team. Constant preparation and analysis, along with plans that can be implemented, quickly if necessary, are the hallmark of the sustained leader serving as the change agent. This element also includes the ability to bring together any other WBS elements necessary to effectively create needed change.

Application: In simplest terms a "change agent" is a person who encourages others to change their behavior, opinions, or positions. Situations change, and both people and societies evolve. Technology advances, politics shift, climates goes through cycles, populations grow and shift, and even people's tastes change. This will all happen. The sustained leader prepares for both the anticipated and unanticipated changes that will affect their environment. Orrin Woodward has noted that "Achievers hate losing enough to change, while the rest hate changing enough to lose."[272] The sustained leader guides these changes and prepares their team for the necessary adjustments.

Taken to an extreme, however, change can be needlessly disruptive. Kouzes and Posner note that "Change for change's sake can be just as demoralizing as complacency."[273] The sustained leader knows the difference between needed change and simply creating drama to "shake things up."

---

272 Orrin Woodward, *The Financial Matrix* (Cary, NC: Obstacles Press, 2015), 67.
273 James M. Kouzes and Barry Z. Posner, *The Leadership Challenge* (San Francisco: Jossey-Bass, 2002), 396.

Change Is Inevitable

The measure of intelligence is the ability to change.
—**Albert Einstein**

Incredible change happens in your life when you decide to take control of what you do have power over instead of craving control over what you don't.
—**Steve Maraboli**

If you want to make enemies, try to change something.
—**Woodrow Wilson**

One of the things I learned when I was negotiating was that until I changed myself I could not change others.
—**Nelson Mandela**

People don't resist change. They resist being changed!
—**Peter Senge**

Every great dream begins with a dreamer. Always remember, you have within you the strength, the patience, and the passion to reach for the stars to change the world.
—**Harriet Tubman**

A corporation is a living organism; it has to continue to shed its skin. Methods have to change. Focus has to change. Values have to change. The sum total of those changes is transformation.
—**Andrew Grove**

Change is the process by which the future invades our lives.
—**Alvin Toffler**

Even when significant changes are necessary, the sustained leader understands that moving in a disciplined manner will result in greater sustainment of the change. John Maxwell notes that "Trying to make a huge change overnight often creates fear, uncertainty, and resistance, because the change appears unachievable. The idea of making small changes is less threatening and helps us overcome our hesitation and procrastination."[274]

Malcolm Gladwell tells us that "We need to prepare ourselves for the possibility that sometimes big changes follow from small events, and that sometimes these changes happen very quickly."[275] Unless the sustained leader stays closely tuned to the changes that are happening and works to manage those changes in a particular, desirable direction, they will effectively be left in the dust. Gladwell goes on to explain that many changes are precipitated by reaching the tipping point. For example, precipitation is rain above 32 degrees Fahrenheit. Once the temperature falls below that, it will be snow. The laws of physics don't change day-to-day. Thirty-two degrees is the tipping point, and no amount of leadership will change that.

The sustained leader searches for these points of inflection, predicts the consequences, and determines what actions the team can take to adjust or, even better, capitalize on these changes. They are going to happen. The sustained leader is never surprised.

In being a change agent, the sustained leader has a clear vision and has articulated how the coming changes will affect that vision. Occasionally they may need to persuade the team that the change is coming and that preparations need to be made. This will often take a great deal of patience since constantly screaming "The sky is falling" will either cause the team to panic or make them immune to the needed changes.

Thus, the sustained leader articulates a vision, observes the environment, and predicts the changes. They then assess whether they can manage the change in a desirable direction, or must ride the wave over which they have no control. This is the essence of being a change agent.

This sounds like me

A lot	somewhat	just a little	not at all

---

274 John C. Maxwell, *Intentional Living: Choosing a Life That Matters* (New York: Center Street, 2015), 66.
275 Malcolm Gladwell, *The Tipping Point*, 11.

Additional Resources:

John P. Kotter, et al., *Our Iceberg Is Melting*.

Ed Oakley and Doug Krug, *Enlightened Leadership*.

Personal Objective:

Specific Actions:

Due Date:

2.3.8 Organizational Growth

WBS Dictionary: The sustained leader understands that an organization is similar to a living organism in that it is either growing or dying. Since many organizations are designed for perpetual existence, the growth has to be managed with a long-term perspective. Even for short-term projects, the team will have a natural growth cycle. This may include the ultimate dissolution of the team when the project is completed—successfully or otherwise. The sustained leader understands these phases of organizational development and leads their team through these natural cycles, enhancing the positive aspects and diminishing the effect of the negative aspects. Being prepared for this growth and having a plan to implement the necessary organizational adjustments is a clear indication of sustained leadership.

Application: Unmanaged growth will cause an organization to be unbalanced. Growth for the sake of growth will cause an organization to lose its focus, occasionally defeating the accomplishment of its expressed mission and preventing the realization of its vision. Many companies have suffered from rapid over-expansion—some having disappeared completely or having been absorbed into a company better equipped to handle the growth. Failure to properly plan for organizational growth may well defeat the leader and remove them from the leadership role.

For these reasons the sustained leader pays close attention to organizational growth. A failure to grow can cause stagnation and provides team members limited ability to advance within the organization. A failure to provide new challenges and meaningful work can cause the organization to shrink involuntarily.

Starbucks grew phenomenally fast under Howard Schultz. When he stepped aside the new management team introduced an array of non-coffee products like books and CDs. Profits sank. Schultz returned, cleaned out all the extraneous merchandise, and brought Starbucks back to being the fifteen-minute vacation experience that made it popular in the first place. Simply seeking sales growth, for example, might not be sustainable and could very well imbalance the organization. When growing quickly alternative metrics can become more important. For example, making sure you are bringing the right people onto the team, developing your supply chain, and meeting the financial needs can be priorities.

Krispy Kreme took a hard-to-find specialty treat and made it available in numerous outlets as well as prepackaged in grocery stores and convenience stores. Too many outlets caused franchisees to compete with each other and the corporation. Saturation reduced profits and discouraged customers from standing in line when a new store opened. After all, you could get the treat (just a doughnut) at the corner store.

And even the dot com companies are not immune. Pets.com quickly opened up a vast distribution network and spent extensively on sock-puppet commercials. With a grand opening in 1998, by late 2000 it closed and cost its investors an estimated $300 million. Growing receivables are not cash flow. Growing too quickly can outstrip your usual cash needs, and not all banks are friendly in this regard. KIND Snacks and Zynga are two other "grew too fast" companies. While both survived, they struggled.

Growth is good, and for most entities necessary. But to have sustainable growth you need a sustained leader with all the necessary leadership abilities. When you plan to lead the team on a wild ride, make sure they are all on board and the necessary decisions are backed with facts and capital.

This sounds like me

| **A lot** | **somewhat** | **just a little** | **not at all** |

Additional Resources:

John Kotter, John and Holger Rathgeber, *That's Not How We Do It Here!*

Steven Kelman, Steven, *Unleashing Change.*

Warren G. Bennis and Robert Townsend, *Reinventing Leadership.*

Personal Objective:

Specific Actions:

Due Date:

2.3.9 Intensity

WBS Dictionary: Great accomplishments are not achieved with minimal effort. It takes extreme focus and intense concentration for significant progress to occur. Lackadaisical approaches lead to incomplete solutions, and occasionally significant disasters. The sustained leader understands the importance of intensity of thought, belief, and action. Sustained leaders know what they believe and why they believe it. They are intense in their beliefs, think through the morass of daily issues, and focus their actions on moving toward a proper vision. A lack of intensity will thwart even the best of plans.

Application: Intensity is broadly defined as anything that exhibits an extreme level of strength, force, or energy. This can often be reflected in both activity and feeling. An extreme level of activity may reflect great intensity. Whether that activity contributes to any measurable progress is a different question. Sustained leaders never confuse activity with progress. Likewise, an extreme level of feeling can show great compassion (3.0) but can also be debilitating if the empathy interferes with effective performance. Thus, any discussion of intensity must consider it in context and be balanced to fit that context.

Intensity also assumes that the intensity is exhibiting the right focus. Some people, it seems, are intensely irritating. Some are intensely intrusive. In those contexts, intensity is not a positive trait. If it can be focused in a proper direction, however, the sustained leader can improve overall team performance.

Occasionally a lack of intensity can cause paralysis. What if we do the wrong thing? Seth Godin has an excellent daily blog, and he has made this observation:

"You've permitted magical to walk on by. Not to mention good enough, amazing and wonderful.

"Waiting for the thing that cannot be improved (and cannot be criticized) keeps us from beginning.

"Merely begin."[276]

Thus, the start of intensity is to simply—start! Certainly there will be critics, as Godin notes. The sustained leader does consider a variety of views and opinions, but is certain enough within themselves to know they are doing what needs to be done. As you progress through the *Sustained Leadership WBS*, you will need to muster a great deal of intensity. Regardless of where you start, what leadership roles you might have had, or what natural talents and abilities you have, the leadership journey has no end. To improve yourself you will need to be very intense and act as if the world needs you as a sustained leader *now*. In fact, it does.

This sounds like me

A lot	somewhat	just a little	not at all

Additional Resources:
Rich Horwath, *Deep Dive.*
Michael Treacy and Fred Wiersema, *The Discipline of Market Leaders.*

Personal Objective:

---

276 While Waiting for Perfect, 3/14/16 http://sethgodin.typepad.com/seths_blog/2016/03/while-waiting-for-perfect.html Accessed 07/18/16

Specific Actions:

Due Date:

2.3.10 Effective Execution

WBS Dictionary: The sustained leader never confuses activity with progress. When executing a plan, the sustained leader clearly sees the goal and focuses activity toward the achievement of that goal. They will eliminate activity that is not useful in achieving the goal and will measure those aspects of execution that provide meaningful data about progress. This is the essence of effective execution. Simply engaging in activities that do not add value is a waste of time and resources. The sustained leader is not oblivious to the need to perform certain things in the interest of keeping a program sold, addressing the unavoidable political interference, and satisfying certain stakeholders or constituencies. These will be eliminated to the degree appropriate, but not avoided since the failure to maintain the support of these constituencies could result in greater costs later in regaining their support. The sustained leader, however, will not let the unreasonable demands of those constituencies affect the need for effective execution of the program plan.

Application: "I do the very best I know how—the very best I can; and mean to keep doing so until the end. If the end brings me out all right, what is said against me won't amount to anything. If the end brings me out wrong, ten angels swearing I was right would make no difference." These words from Abraham Lincoln speak deeply to the need for effective execution.

The sustained leader understands the importance of both proper planning and execution. Leonardo da Vinci observed that "Oysters open completely when the moon is full; and when the crab sees one it throws a piece of stone or seaweed into it and the oyster cannot close again so that it serves the crab for meat. Such is the fate of him who opens his mouth too much and thereby puts himself at the mercy of the listener."[277] How does the crab know to do this? Let's call it instinct for survival so that it can eat. This does not serve the oyster very well, but you have also

---

277 Robert Greene, *The 48 Laws of Power* (New York: Penguin Books, 1998), 33.

heard the adage that the early bird gets the worm, suggesting that an early start can improve success of the endeavor. This ignores, however, the fact that the early worm gets eaten and the second mouse gets the cheese. Context is everything.

Napoleon Hill

A good encyclopedia contains most of the known facts of the world, but they are as useless as sand dunes until organized and expressed in terms of action.

The sustained leader understands that taking action is meaningless unless it is directed action. Simply going through the motions, or filling the square, does not further the vision of the team. It is not enough to execute against a plan; the execution must be effective in furthering the objectives of the team and account for the many ancillary actions that must be taken to support the primary initiative. The more objectives an action affects, the more effective that action can be. Thus, the measurement of "effective" includes both the progress toward the objectives and not backsliding against any of the other elements. "Effectiveness" must take into account both the three steps forward *and* the two steps back. While opinions may differ on the absolute measure of effectiveness, the sustained leader will consider all aspects of an action to determine its ultimate effectivity on the team's objectives.

This sounds like me

| A lot | somewhat | just a little | not at all |

Additional Resources:
Larry Bossidy, Ram Charan, and Charles Burck, *Execution.*
Chris McChesney, Jim Huling, and Sean Covey, *The 4 Disciplines of Execution.*

Personal Objective:

Specific Actions:

Due Date:

Essential Leadership Journey Checkpoint
2.3.11 Focused and Disciplined

WBS Dictionary: Many people live their lives in a very haphazard manner. They flit from one thing to another, justify it as "multitasking," and in reality never get anything accomplished. Very capable people have succumbed to this malady. They are good at many things and as a result try to do many things. Too many things. This causes them to lose their focus and be less productive. Such activities also tend to introduce errors. Avoiding this requires discipline. The sustained leader masters their ability to focus on a single item. The sustained leader must learn the necessary discipline to stay focused. This skill can be developed, but depending on your personality type and predilections this might be an extremely difficult skill to master. It is essential; thus it is an essential leadership journey checkpoint. Your failure to gain this discipline will significantly impact your leadership influence, to the point of perceived failure in leadership.

Application: Andy Stanley reminds us that it is necessary to say no more often than we say yes. When you try to do too much, you dilute your energy and thereby your effectiveness. Al Ries says, "It's been my experience that great leaders, in spite of a multitude of distractions, know how to keep things focused. They know how to inspire and motivate their followers to keep pushing 'the main chance.' They don't let side issues overwhelm them."[278]

Russell Conwell served as a captain in the Civil War. He had occasion to petition the president on behalf of a soldier.

I never was so afraid when the shells came around us at Antietam as I was when I went into that room that day; but I finally mustered the courage—I

---

278 Andy Stanley, *The Next Generation Leader: Five Essentials for Those Who Will Shape the Future* (2003), 70, quoting from Al Ries, *Focus* (New York: Harper Business, 1996), 78.

don't know how I ever did—and at arm's length tapped on the door. The man inside did not help at all, but yelled, "Come in and sit down!"

Well I went in and sat on the edge of a chair, and wished I were in Europe. The man at the table did not look up. He was one of the world's greatest men, and was made great by one single rule. Abraham Lincoln's principle for greatness can be adopted by nearly all. This was his rule: Whatever it was he had to do, he put his whole mind into it and held it all there until it was done. That makes men great almost anywhere. He stuck to those papers at that table and did not look up at me, and I sat there trembling. Finally, when he had put a string around his papers, he pushed them over to one side and looked at me, and a smile came over his face.[279]

Daniel Goleman, promoter of the importance of emotional intelligence, has noted, "For leaders to get results they need all three kinds of focus. Inner focus attunes us to our intuitions, guiding values, and better decisions. Other focus smooths out connections to the people in our lives. And outer focus lets us navigate in the larger world. A leader tuned out of his inner world will be rudderless; one blind to the world of others will be clueless; those indifferent to the larger systems within which they operate will be blindsided."[280]

———— • ————

The Importance of Focus

You don't have to focus on everything to be successful.
But you have to focus on something.
—Al Ries

What is the essence of kingship? [It is] to rule oneself well,
and not be led astray by wealth or fame.
—Apocrypha, letter of Aristeas, No. 178.

279 Russell Conwell, *Acres of Diamonds*, 48-49.
280 Daniel Goleman, *Focus: The Hidden Driver of Excellence* (New York: HarperCollins, 2015), 4. Later Goleman reviews the success of investor Steve Tuttleman and his extensive quest for information on his successful investments, noting that "leaders need the full range of inner, other, and outer focus to excel—and that a weakness in any one of them can throw a leader off balance" (221-24).

A primary reason for business failure is a loss of focus.
—Brian Tracy

I was going to invent Velcro, but I just couldn't stick to it.
—Anonymous

———————— ◆ ————————

There are some Meyers-Briggs types that tend to lose tfocus more easily than others. Those who are strong perceivers, and especially those who are intuitives, tend to have a very active mind and flit from one thought to another easily. While this could be diagnosed as a form of ADD, studies have shown that the most creative people often exhibit strong adult ADD tendencies. On the creative side, this can be a big plus; to an extreme it prevents clarity of focus.

———————— ◆ ————————

John D. Rockefeller Jr.

Singleness of purpose is one of the chief essentials
for success in life, no matter what may be one's aim.

———————— ◆ ————————

Our minds naturally wander, and this is not necessarily a bad thing. Many great discoveries are made by people who take what appear to be disparate thoughts and link them in a way that has never been done before. Some might call this "insight," and it is a positive trait. It becomes a problem when you fail to pull yourself back to the immediate circumstances. This of course is completely dependent on those circumstances. Goleman also reports that a random survey of thousands of people found that their focus was highest, and by a significant margin, while they were making love. A lagging second was exercising, followed by conversing and what he describes as "playing." Our minds seem to wander the most while working, using a computer, and commuting.[281]

Interestingly, though not surprising if you think about it, our internal distractions are far more disruptive and constant than external ones. We have a strong ability to tune out many external distractions. The undisciplined mind,

---

281 Ibid., 47.

 Schwerpunkt – The power of focus

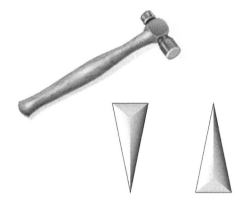

Which wedge will make a deeper hole?
Why? Focus.

© 2016, Bob Lewis. Used with permission.

however, allows our internal self-talk (bottom-up) to run wild without any override from the top-down. When you must concentrate, you must exercise the top-down discipline to shut yourself up. The unfocused leader has not trained themselves to do so. This often leads to muddled thinking that is aptly reflected in both muddled writing and muddled conversation. Lack of discipline. Lack of focus.

In today's world of constant electronic stimulation of news, information, data, and amusement the task of maintaining focus has only become more difficult. Perhaps some people's brains can adapt to that more readily than others. There is no question, however, that a flood of stimuli unknown to any past generation is currently bombarding us in a volume and quantity never before seen. Focus has not become easier; it has become much more difficult.

Jim Collins offers this insight from J.W. Marriott Sr.: "Discipline is the greatest thing in the world. Where there is no discipline, there is no character. And without character, there is no progress."[282] And as Robert Greene has advised, "Concentrate on a single goal, a single task, and beat it into submission."[283]

---

282 James C. Collins and Jerry I. Porras, *Built to Last: Successful Habits of Visionary Companies* (New York: HarperCollins, 1994), 186. Citing Robert O'Brian, *Marriott* (Salt Lake City, UT: Deseret, 1987).

283 Robert Greene, *The 48 Laws of Power* (New York: Penguin Books, 1998), 175.

A final caution in this area comes from David Allen. "I suggest that you use your mind to think *about* things, rather than think *of* them. You want to be *adding* value as you think about projects and people, not simply reminding yourself they exist."[284]

The sustained leader should adopt the Winchester Philosophy. On the MASH TV series, a talented surgeon joins MASH 4077 in season six. Ivy-League trained and coming from Boston's upper crust, Charles Emerson Winchester III ends up getting assigned to the unit permanently. As it turns out, although he is an extreme narcissist coming from a life of privilege, he is a talented surgeon and is knowledgeable about all the latest surgical techniques. Hawkeye Pierce asks, "What's so great about him?" To which Charles responds, "I do one thing at a time, I do it very well, and then I move on."[285] That's the focus of a sustained leader.

This sounds like me

A lot	somewhat	just a little	not at all

Additional Resources:

Brian Tracy, *Focal Point.*

Daniel Goleman, *Focus.*

Spencer Johnson, *The Present.*

Personal Objective:

Specific Actions:

Due Date:

---

284 David Allen, *Getting Things Done* (New York: Penguin Group, 2001), 233.

285 M*A*S*H Season 6 Episode 1, "Fade Out, Fade In," aired 9/20/1977. http://www.tv.com/shows/mash/fade-out-fade-in-43322/ Accessed 08/28/16

2.3.12 Thorough

WBS Dictionary: Some jobs can be done in a partial manner and you get partial benefit. Others must be performed completely or they are useless. The sustained leader understands the need to complete tasks thoroughly and not just halfway. A thorough job ensures that all the different pieces and tangential matters are addressed and, if necessary, completed as well. Doing the whole job is more efficient and effective than trying to do it only partially and then picking it up later and restarting. The sustained leader will understand all parts of a task and make certain that the appropriate resources are applied to ensure the overall project is performed thoroughly. The sustained leader knows where the finish line is and makes sure the project gets across the finish line (2.3.14) intact and thoroughly complete.

Application: An old adage asks, "Why is it we never have time to do it right, but we always find time to do it over?" A sustained leader understands the efficiency of doing a complete job the first time through. There are some activities that, with partial performance, you can achieve partial rewards. An example of that might be filling the gas in the car to the halfway point. You will be able to go a long way, but not as far as with a full tank. On the other hand, if you are building a bridge and you fail to complete the last ten feet across the river, you do not have a functional bridge. You have a very long fishing pier. In that case, there is no "almost" that can ever be considered good enough.

To be thorough means that nothing has been left out or omitted. The ideal leader, from the perspective of the *Sustained Leadership WBS*, would score well in each of the elements, but we suspect that is not humanly possible. Each time you find a way to improve in one of the elements, you become a better leader and better qualified to train new leaders. If you conduct a very thorough self-assessment and identify those specific WBS elements that need your greatest attention, you will be increasingly able to take on larger leadership roles. Since the journey will never really end, your goal should be one of continuous improvement. Being thorough in your assessment is the important part. With each pass through the WBS you are filling your gas tank just a little bit more. You will be able to go further each time. You will be able to lead a larger team; you will be able to accomplish larger tasks. You will grow to the point where you can lead teams that have less well-defined missions. If, however, you fall short in any of the essential leadership journey checkpoints, you will discover that you are an incomplete bridge and cannot serve as a sustained leader.

The sustained leader must approach most tasks with an intent to be as thorough as possible. Remember that leaders are measured by results. The best results come from leaving nothing out and completing the tasks as thoroughly as possible. Any failure to pay attention to the details will result in a less than thorough result against which the team will be measured and for which the leader will be responsible.

This sounds like me

A lot   **somewhat**   **just a little**   **not at all**

Additional Resources:

Carey Lohrenz, *Fearless Leadership*.

Mark Sanborn, *The Encore Effect*.

Marcus Buckingham, *Go Put Your Strengths to Work*.

Personal Objective:

Specific Actions:

Due Date:

2.3.13 High Energy

WBS Dictionary: Like enthusiasm (4.2.11), high energy reflects a personal emotional attachment to the vision (5.1.2) and the goals (2.3.1). It reflects attention to physical well-being (5.1.6) and an ability to focus (2.3.11). High energy can be contagious. It can also foster burn-out. Everyone's capacity for demonstrating high energy is not the same. Often this energy must be calibrated since it makes no sense to burn out unnecessarily. It also must be focused toward the proper objectives. Exhibiting high energy inspires the team.

Application: Long-haul truck drivers often drive late at night. Fatigue is a constant concern. When they feel sleepy they open the window, turn up the radio, or stop for coffee. The goal is to turn up the energy to overcome the danger of sleepy driving. The same can apply in a boring meeting or training session. Stand up. Stretch your legs. Start taking copious notes. Practice your active listening skills. Get the blood flowing. In a phrase, turn up the gain. Draw more energy to yourself.

Donald Trump is a high-energy person. He has said, "When I run a meeting, I'm in charge and I need people to keep up with me. People who work with me know my tempo, and they've adjusted. New people learn how. No matter what situation or business you are in, be alert to the level of energy around you—it will help you through every day. So if you are not in charge yet, realize it's your responsibility to take the cue and respond accordingly."[286]

Early in the 2016 presidential campaign, Trump was heard to criticize other candidates, both Jeb Bush and Ben Carson, for their "low energy," even chiding them about being asleep at the podium. Energy levels among individuals vary, and there is no one set standard by which these things can be measured. Nonetheless there are those who need to dial their energy up a bit, while others need to tone it down or at least refocus it. The sustained leader, in conducting their own self-assessment (1.3.3.1), should take care to assess their energy, their drive, and their motivation. In all likelihood, they will discover great inconsistencies. There are some things they pursue with genuine passion; other tasks are avoided and little energy is devoted to them.

There is no absolute answer to this element. Occasionally what appears to be low energy is more than compensated by great intensity and focus. Other times great energy, un-tempered by focus, can appear to others that a person is flying off in all directions—confusing activity with progress.

One way the sustained leader can adjust their energy level, and bring up the level of others on the team, is to give each member a specific task with a specific deadline. It might be something small, yet significant. And then hold them

---

286 Donald Trump with Meredith McIver, *Think Like a Champion* (New York: Vanguard Press, 2009), 118.

accountable. The ability to focus on a specific task with a firm deadline usually sparks a higher level of energy.

This sounds like me

A lot   **somewhat**   **just a little**   **not at all**

Additional Resources:

Stephen R. Covey, *Principle Centered Leadership*, Principle #3.
James E. Loehr and Tony Schwartz, *The Power of Full Engagement*.

Personal Objective:

Specific Actions:

Due Date:

2.3.14 Pushes Results across the Goal

WBS Dictionary: The sustained leader understands that effort alone can be worthwhile but is essentially meaningless unless the effort is translated into tangible results. A book that is written but remains unpublished is not a book—it is a manuscript. A garage full of all the parts necessary to build a car does not have a car inside it—it is a warehouse of parts. The sustained leader sees the goal and does not rest until the goal is achieved. "Almost" just doesn't count. A leader is measured by results. A person who produces no complete results is not a leader—yet.

Application: An old adage says that hard work is its own reward. While true in many respects, many efforts are less meaningful until they cross a predetermined goal. When a football team gets the football down to the one-yard line, it nets them no points. Their failure to carry the ball across the goal line results in no points, and since each opportunity to score can be determinative of the outcome, a failure to score can alter the game outcome. The best teams know that they must capitalize on every scoring opportunity. Likewise, the sustained leader has to understand that typically it is not sufficient to just get close (as they say, "close" only counts in horseshoes and atom bombs) but to actually cross the finish line. The football team might kick a field goal and get less than half the points they would get from a touchdown, but they have failed in maximizing their return for moving the ball the other ninety-nine yards.

Seth Godin often blogs about shipping once the product is "good enough." Too often we fall prey to the paralysis that sets in when we allow "excellent" to be the enemy of "good." Certainly you want to put your best effort forward, and you want to make sure the output is quality. Getting something out into commerce is really the goal, once it is sufficiently good. Waiting until it is perfect may seem to be a better move. It isn't. Getting a product across the finish line and celebrating the victory (1.3.17) are important parts of sustained leadership.

Says Godin, "So, just about everything that can be improved, *is* being improved. If you define 'improved' to mean more features, more buttons, more choices, more power, more cost.

"The washing machine I used this morning had more than 125 different combinations of ways to do the wash… don't get me started about the dryer. Clearly, an arms race is a good way to encourage people to upgrade.

"I wonder, though, if 'good enough' might be the next big idea. Audio players, cars, dryers, accounting… not the best ever made, not the most complicated and certainly not the most energy-consuming. Just good enough.

"For some people, a clean towel is a clean towel."[287]

The sustained leader must decide whether the analogy is better to football or commerce. In football there is only one winner, and scoring the touchdown rather than the field goal may be the only measure of victory. In commerce, the first to market has a large advantage against the competition. Successive iterations of a product can be introduced serially in commerce. Thus, clearly defining the goal is critical to understanding the best approach when implementing this element.

---

287 Good Enough, 8/23/06 http://sethgodin.typepad.com/seths_blog/2006/08/good_enough. html Accessed 7/18/16

---◆---

Napoleon Hill

Anyone can "START," but only a thoroughbred will "finish!"

---◆---

Some personality types find themselves more adept at thinking a problem to death than actually solving it. That is no excuse. The sustained leader recognizes this tendency and takes this element to heart. Eventually the decision has to be rendered. The article has to be submitted to the publisher. The filing deadline must be met. The report has to be delivered to the client. Whatever the objective happens to be, the sustained leader can see the goal and gets the team effort across that line.

Ken Blanchard and Colleen Barrett have noted that "Leadership is about going somewhere—If you and your people don't know where you are going your leadership doesn't matter."[288]

---◆---

Col. Dandridge M. Malone

The very essence of leadership is its purpose. And the purpose of leadership is to accomplish a task. That is what leadership does–and what it does is more important than what it is or how it works.

---◆---

Similarly, Mary Kay Ash has said, "Those who are blessed with the most talent don't necessarily outperform everyone else. It's the people with follow-through who excel."

And if none of the others motivate you to excel in completing tasks, here is Jack and Suzy Welch's advice: "Let's turn…finally to the most common reason that careers stall. Performance. Or more precisely, underperformance. Now, underperformance doesn't mean you're not trying hard at work. You might very

---

288 Ken Blanchard and Colleen Barrett, *Lead with Luv: A Different Way to Create Real Success* (Upper Saddle River, NJ: FT Press, 2011), 26.

well be giving it your all. But the last place effort counted more than results was in elementary school. This is real life."[289]

This sounds like me

A lot   **somewhat**   **just a little**   **not at all**

Additional Resources:
Seth Godin, *Linchpin.*
Tony Dungy and Nathan Whitaker, *Uncommon.*

Personal Objective:

Specific Actions:

Due Date:

2.3.15 Knows When to Quit

WBS Dictionary: Quitters never win and winners never quit. This phrase has been used, often in sports and lottery contests, and is very misguided advice. Even in wrestling there is a sign to give that you yield, usually before serious injury is inflicted. The point is that there is wisdom in knowing when to cease the "bias for action" and withdraw. A retreat and regrouping can be very effective. The sustained leader understands that, despite sunk costs, there is a time to stop the hemorrhaging and cease the activity. This element is different from 5.1.9 regarding knowing when to pull the plug. While similar, that element pertains to shutting things down completely. This element is focused on particular actions within a

---

289 Jack and Suzy Welch, *The Real Life MBA: Your No-BS Guide to Winning the Game, Building a Team, and Growing Your Career* (New York: HarperCollins, 2015), 200.

comprehensive strategy. Both require a level of discernment and the ability to be decisive. Quitting too soon defeats the idea of persistence, and waiting too long will only waste precious resources.

Application: One way to know when to quit is to understand that there are some ventures that should not be started. If the cost-benefit analysis says it is a losing venture, perhaps the sustained leader should not embark on the venture in the first instance. This requires a proper analysis and a large amount of discretion and discernment. This analysis is also helpful when making decisions (2.3.6). If the opportunity does not show positive projections, honest projections, then the wise leader will not embark. Certainly some matters of principle and right must be started and pressed to completion, even if the prospects are glum. As Winston Churchill said, "What is the use of living, if it be not to strive for noble causes and to make this muddled world a better place for those who will live in it after we are gone?"

A variation of this is knowing when to allow other experts to take the ball and run with it. The inventors of both Monopoly and Scrabble board games turned down opportunities to capitalize on their inventions. Instead they licensed their games to an experienced company with both the resources and experience to produce and market the games. This wise decision made the inventors very wealthy.

In other cases the task has been started. In various elements of this section of the WBS, that has been the message—get started. And that is good advice. Depending on the uncertainties involved in any venture, however, there is a point in time where it makes sense to stop what you are doing and either choose a new direction or abandon the effort entirely. Consider the Blockbuster story. When nearly every American bought a VHS player, pre-recorded VHS tapes were sought by the millions. Blockbuster grew by being the go-to location to rent almost any movie that existed. Over time, however, new online services began to grow. Cable TV systems offered on-demand movies. Netflix challenged both the Blockbuster and the cable TV models. Blockbuster went bankrupt and closed. Cable TV providers struggle on many fronts. The shareholders of Blockbuster would have fared better if it had closed long before it did. They did not know when to quit.

Jack Welch, who led GE for so many successful years, approached this from the other side of the equation. "Contrary to reputation, I've often been too cautious. I waited too long to get rid of managers who weren't willing or able to face reality.

I was hesitant with some acquisitions, slow to embrace the Internet, even timid about blowing up all the rituals and traditions of what once had been a bureaucracy. Almost everything should and could have been done faster."[290]

The sustained leader considers exit strategies at the inception of a new venture. How will we know that the long-term prospects are diminishing? What metrics will we use? How reliable are those metrics? What bellwether event might occur? What technological advances might be on the horizon that will obviate the need for our product or service? A full analysis of any venture requires such considerations. Knowing when to pull the plug is an important consideration of the sustained leader. It is important for the sustained leader to be heavily invested in any venture they start. They must not, however, be so personally invested that its lack of success causes them to view themselves as a failure. Such personal attachment is inappropriate for the sustained leader.

This sounds like me

A lot	somewhat	just a little	not at all

Additional Resources:
Anthony L. Iaquinto and Stephen Spinelli Jr., *Never Bet the Farm.*
Jack Welch and John A. Byrne, *Jack: Straight from the Gut.*

Personal Objective:

Specific Actions:

Due Date:

---

290 Jack Welch and John A. Byrne, *Jack: Straight from the Gut* (Business Plus, 2001), 431-32.

2.3.16 Hard Work, "Luck," and Timing

WBS Dictionary: Very often, observers of successful leaders attribute that success to luck or "being in the right place at the right time." When a leader considers the path to success, they recognize that hard work and preparation were necessary prerequisites. This element recognizes that what people call luck and good timing are most likely the intersection of preparation with opportunity. The sustained leader does not rely on, or attribute success in leadership to, either luck or timing. Sustained leaders do have a sense of timing and can patiently wait for the right time to act on an opportunity. And a sustained leader makes themselves available so that they are in the right place and well prepared when opportunities arise. This has nothing to do with what people call luck or good timing. It has everything to do with the hard work and preparation that the sustained leader pursues to be ready to capitalize on the opportunities that arise.

Application: Russell grew up in the Berkshire Hills of Massachusetts. His father was fanatically religious, ultimately turning his young son away from any religious beliefs. He grew into a very charismatic man, and in 1862 he organized a Massachusetts militia company for which he was elected captain. He and his company served honorably, and about ten years after the war he was asked to present at a regimental reunion. He chose to tell a story he had heard from a Turkish guide while working as a foreign correspondent. The story was of a Persian farmer who wasted his life chasing wealth. Shortly after the farmer died a pauper, diamonds were discovered on his farmland. The moral Russell took from this was that "Your diamonds are not in far-distant mountains or in yonder seas; they are in your own back yard, if you but dig for them." Russell was asked to speak about this story over six thousand times between 1877 and his death in 1925.

Russell made several million dollars from telling this story, ultimately giving away every penny to promote higher education. Throughout his life he recognized the importance of hard work serving as a soldier, school teacher, lawyer, lecturer, newspaper correspondent, and Baptist minister. Russell Conwell also founded Temple University. His message that "Money is power, and you should be reasonably ambitious to have it…because you can do more good with it than you could without it"[291] reflects that those who go chasing after quick riches, lottery

---

291 Russell Conwell, *Acres of Diamonds* (Kansas City, MO: 1968), 25.

winnings, or any get-rich-quick scheme are chasing rainbows while riding unicorns. Hard work from wherever you are today offers you the best opportunity, if you will only work for it.

How "Lucky" Are You?

Luck is a dividend of sweat. The more you sweat, the luckier you get.
—**Ray Kroc**

Plans get you into things but you've got to work your way out.
—**Will Rogers**

The higher men climb the longer their working day....
There are no office hours for leaders.
—**Cardinal Gibbons**

In the Project Management Body of Knowledge (PMBOK) there is a section on risk management. Element 11.5.2.2 is titled "Strategies for positive risks or opportunities." We don't typically think in terms of positive risk; risk by nature seems to be negative. The PMBOK has three strategies for dealing with positive risk, or emerging opportunities. These are to exploit the opportunity (i.e. to take actions to ensure the risk event does occur), share the opportunity (i.e. to bring in another party who might be better positioned to capitalize on the opportunity), or enhance the opportunity (i.e. recognize why it is an opportunity and maximizing the positive impact or increasing the probability of it arising). While some might say this is just being "lucky," the sustained leader recognizes that it takes hard work to identify such opportunities and to position the team to capitalize on them.

This sounds like me

| A lot | somewhat | just a little | not at all |

Additional Resources:

Russell Conwell, *Acres of Diamonds*.

James Collins and Morten T. Hansen, *Great by Choice*.

Denis Waitley, *Timing Is Everything*.

Ken Blanchard, *Leading at a Higher Level*.

Personal Objective:

Specific Actions:

Due Date:

2.3.17 Measured by Contribution

WBS Dictionary: A leader is most commonly measured by the results they produce. Depending on how you define the goals, the leader's role is to contribute toward the accomplishment of those goals. Activities not related to the goals, or distracting to those organizational goals, detracts from the leader's ability to lead. The leader's contribution can come in the form of both tangible and intangible benefits. Certainly locating financing for a new expansion or soliciting contributions for a nonprofit are tangible results. Creating greater shareholder value is also tangible. Demonstrating leadership traits, however, is often more intangible. Being crystal clear about the expected ethical standards for the organization, and enforcing them, are somewhat less tangible, but no less important to the organizational mission. Promoting the organization to its various stakeholders, dealing effectively with crisis, making appropriate managerial changes, and guiding the organization to adapt to inevitable changes and market dynamics are all areas where a leader is measured. The sustained leader understands the importance of these contributions and ensures that they are performed and documented.

Application: Roberto Goizueta earned a reputation as a hard worker with great attention to detail. Having escaped Cuba when Castro came into power, he rose through the ranks at Coca-Cola, starting as a chemical engineer in Cuba and later for its Latin American operations. By 1979 he was its vice-chairman, and in 1980 he was named president. It was under his watch that "New Coke" was introduced. Despite meticulous research and testing that concluded the new product was more palatable, i.e. it tasted better, it was a public relations disaster. No one was prepared for the immediate and vociferous response from the public that was so loyal to the old formula. Had this been an irreversible decision, Goizueta would have been remembered as a leader who failed to rise to the occasion and most likely would have been removed from his position. Instead he immediately brought "old" Coke back as a "classic" edition. He continued a pattern of success despite this massive "failure," and under his guidance Coke grew from a $5 billion operation to one over $150 billion. Those are impressive results by anyone's measurement. Both new Coke and classic Coke contributed to this growth.

The leader must contribute in two tangible manners. They must actually lead—providing the vision and mission and gathering the resources necessary for the team to succeed. This includes attracting the right team and properly guiding them. Further, the leader, through their competence, should bring a tangible contribution to the team's efforts. Whether the team succeeds or fails, the strongest reflection will fall on the leader. Sustained leaders understand that any success belongs to the team while all setbacks belong to the leader. Accepting the responsibility for setbacks reflects many aspects of leadership, including character (1.0), which the team will remember and appreciate. Compare this to the many situations reported on the daily news where the ostensible leader blames the lack of success on others. This is not an attractive attribute, but it is well locked into our human psyche.

This element suggests that there is continual action. The entire team must be in action and not resting on its laurels. The sustained leader knows that action must be continuous. Even if some of the action is misdirected and leads into blind alleys, that information is then recycled into the team efforts and new, more promising avenues explored. A complete lack of action yields a complete lack of measurable results. The sustained leader understands that activity in a positive direction is a primary imperative. It is the results of that action that will form the basis of measurement of the leader.

The sustained leader produces. They will establish a vision and mission for the team and select the team members. They will then guide the team to successful completion. There will be results. There will be progress. There will be improvement in whatever sphere the team is working. There will be *measurable* results that demonstrate the outcome as being positive against the metrics established by the vision.

This sounds like me

A lot   **somewhat**   **just a little**   **not at all**

Additional Resources:
Jeffrey H. Gitomer and Paul Hersey, *The Little Book of Leadership*.
David Ulrich, Jack Zenger, and Norman Smallwood, *Results-Based Leadership*.
Roger Connors, Tom Smith, and Craig Hickman, *The Oz Principle*.

Personal Objective:

Specific Actions:

Due Date:

2.3.18 Audacity

WBS Dictionary: A person with audacity has a level of boldness and confidence that exceeds the norm. This element calls on the sustained leader to be bold, and audaciously so. This does not include recklessness or hubris, but combines the traits of daring with confidence approaching, but not exceeding, arrogance. This boldness may go against conventional thought, qualifying the actor as a contrarian. It does not permit the violation of ethical norms or other societal standards that would reflect a poor or weak character. It is practical; it has measurable and high potential rewards. It considers the risks associated with the action and encourages additional levels of boldness without, again, passing an appropriate level of collective risk. There is a clear need for discretion and discernment in exercising audacity, but memorable sustained leaders are often characterized as audacious in their behavior.

Application: Audacity implies a boldness that borders on rudeness. It is acting in a daring manner with extreme confidence, almost an arrogance toward others' feelings or even societal conventions. When we speak of a sustained leader being audacious, it is not suggesting that you take actions that violate any other element of the WBS. Kindness, caring, effective communication and other such traits must always guide a leader's actions. Audacity of the sustained leader should be tempered and not be in a rude or insolent manner. And sometimes bold action will need to be followed by an apology for unintended consequences. The point is that the sustained leader should never fear taking action—bold action, definitive action—when the situation calls for it. They should not, however, go out of their way to be rude or offend the sensibilities of the team.

Grace Hopper, rear admiral in the US Navy, has said, "[Leaders], when in doubt, don't ask, just do; many times it is easier to apologize than to get permission. The big rewards go to the people who take the biggest risks. A ship in port is safe, but that's not what a ship is built for."[292]

Gary Dahl had an idea one night while out drinking with friends. The conversation turned to their pets and how much trouble they could be. After all, when you have to leave a good gathering of friends to go home and let the dog out, that can ruin a fun evening. Gary observed that his pet was no trouble at all since he had a pet rock. As men often do, he regaled his friends with stories of his pet rock, pretty much made up on the fly during the gathering. Feeling that he was on to something, he wrote a book about tending to a pet rock, borrowing significantly from other resources on pets. "Some Pet Rock owners have found that the ticking of an alarm clock placed near the box has a soothing effect, especially at night," he wrote.

His book got some favorable press and he decided to actually package rocks in small cage-like boxes and market them during the upcoming holiday season. He correctly surmised that his created craze would last only one buying season, and

---

292 Quoted in Alan C. Elliott, *American Dream*, 174.

he worked tirelessly to package and distribute his novelty toy. He was correct. Had he not acted quickly and decisively to capitalize on his crazy (inebriated?) idea, the opportunity would have been lost. As it was, he created something that has become part of our pop culture that is still remembered forty years later. Audacity can, among other things, be very profitable.[293]

This sounds like me

A lot   **somewhat**   **just a little**   **not at all**

Additional Resources:

Martin Blumenson, *Patton.*

Norman Schwarzkopf and Pete Petre, *It Doesn't Take a Hero.*

Susan Scott, *Fierce Leadership.*

Personal Objective:

Specific Actions:

Due Date:

2.3.19 Avoids Needless Activity and Procrastination

WBS Dictionary: Some needless activity is mischaracterized as "work." It is at best "busy work," meaning that it keeps you busy but does not work toward the achievement of a proper goal. Another form of this is simple procrastination—performing any task, even meaningful ones, in lieu of a significant task that is being avoided. Some people attempt to justify this behavior on the basis that pushing up against a deadline forces them to do their best work. Studies

---

293 As described in Alan C. Elliott, *American Dream*, 169.

suggest otherwise, but not without some exceptions. The sustained leader avoids unnecessary activities and overt procrastination. This does not mean the sustained leader does not engage in hobbies or other activities not directly associated with the performance of "work."[294] Failure to pay attention to your health and failing to engage in diversionary activities can have harmful effects. Where team activities predominate, however, the sustained leader focuses on those designed to produce the most significant results, whether tangible or intangible. The sustained leader avoids things that waste time without any productive benefit, and prioritizes remaining tasks such that the most important ones are achieved first.

Application: In *The 7 Habits of Highly Effective People*, Stephen Covey speaks of putting our activities in one of four quadrants defined by Important-Unimportant and Urgent-Not Urgent. He urges successful people to concentrate on quadrant two: Important and Not Urgent. If we are forced to engage primarily in quadrant I activities, Important and Urgent, which he characterizes as fire drills, we never prepare properly for other important matters. He also suggests that those who spend most of their time in quadrant I will spend the majority of their remaining time in quadrant IV—Not Important and Not Urgent. This is why solitaire exists on most computers.

Thomas Edison observed that "Being busy does not always mean real work. The object of all work is production or accomplishment and to either of these ends there must be forethought, system, planning, intelligence, and honest purpose, as well as perspiration. Seeming to do is not doing."

Henry Ford also admonished that "You can't build a reputation on what you are going to do."

Whether your hardest tasks should be allocated to first thing in the workday or later in the workday is not relevant. Different people have different circadian rhythms related to when their most productive hours might be. A popular procrastination technique is to tell yourself that you will tend to the task later in the day, then later in the day you tell yourself that you will tackle it in the morning when you are fresh. Stop lying to yourself.

---

294 "Work" here is defined in the manner of Mark Twain in *The Adventures of Tom Sawyer*: "that Work consists of whatever a body is *obliged* to do, and that Play consists of whatever a body is not obliged to do."

In *Getting Things Done*[295] David Allen speaks to optimizing your work space by simplifying and removing clutter and distractions. His ideas are good and proven to be useful in getting control of the multitude of inputs with which we are barraged every day. The caution, however, is this: reorganization can simply be another form of procrastination, especially if it occurs often. It can make you feel productive when in fact it is simply an avoidance action (see 2.3). Many good ideas and useful tools and techniques can be good in moderation and extremely destructive in excess. The sustained leader understands that most things need to be handled in moderation. An excess of anything can be destructive to your goals and plans. Remove unnecessary things and avoid unnecessary work.

Automating the things you do can lead to greater efficiency, but usually not right away. Depending on your ability to adapt to new technologies (2.2.6), you may have a steep learning curve. The story is told of two friends at work. The one says to his friend, "I saw you today on the way to work. You were running beside your bike. Why would anyone run beside their bike?" His friend replies, "Man, I was so late I didn't have time to get on it." While we may laugh at that story, how often do you fail to stop long enough to simply get on the bike? The short time it takes to get on the bike is more than made up by riding the bike rather than walking or running beside it. Many efficiencies can be achieved by making use of the tools available to you. Yes, you must take the time to learn new systems. And you must be on constant guard against simply automating your inefficiencies. This will only assist you in making the same mistakes faster. Apply wisdom and discretion to the approach. Avoid needless work; avoid procrastination. Be efficient in all you do even if you must take a step or two backwards to "get on the bike."

This sounds like me

A lot   **somewhat**   **just a little**   **not at all**

Additional Resources:
Stephen Covey, *The 7 Habits of Highly Effective People.*
Ken Blanchard and Steve Gottry, *The On-Time, On-Target Manager.*
Brian Tracy, *Eat That Frog!*

---

295 David Allen, *Getting Things Done* (New York: Penguin Group, 2001), 104-12.

Personal Objective:

Specific Actions:

Due Date:

3.0 Compassion

WBS Dictionary: Compassion is a deep empathy for people. It is not soft-hearted or weak; it is a strength that allows leaders to connect with people of all types and backgrounds. It uses principles of natural law (1.2.2.4) to recognize that people are not tools but unique individuals with dreams, goals, and capabilities of their own. The leader connects with others through compassion and knows how to develop them into new leaders (3.2). The sustained leader takes their role quite seriously in leading followers. The trust and loyalty (1.1) engendered from the relationship establishes a bond that the leader respects and shares with their followers. Compassion is also not Machiavellian. Followers are treated with respect. The temptation to abuse compassion or to corrupt it is strong, and weak leaders either do not master this, or worse, learn it too well and abuse it. It is a form of power. Followers observe closely how it is used. Used well, the leader grows stronger; misused and the followers abandon the leader. This element is all about personal human relationships. The sustained leader understands that in all matters, relationships must always come before transactions.

Application: General Charles Henry has observed:

I have learned that if the leaders are going to make permanent, important changes to the organization, they must exhibit a genuine concern for the well-being of the employee. It is one thing to be appointed the leader, it is another to be truly the leader. People will follow effective leadership.

People will tolerate for some time the ineffective appointed leader. While you should not pamper or be passive to the work force, great leaders will genuinely presume that their decisions are predicated on what is good for the individual. The synergy that comes about when the workforce senses a leader is concerned about them is extremely valuable.[296]

Author and trainer Bob Pike notes that "People are hired for their technical skills or their managerial skills, but they are fired for their lack of interpersonal skills."[297] The same is true for sustained leaders. They may have many of the necessary skills and traits as defined here, but without a sense of compassion for their followers, without the ability to relate to people one-to-one, their tenure in a leadership position will be short-lived.

Albert Einstein

Concerns for man and his fate must always form the chief interest of all technical endeavors. Never forget this in the midst of your diagrams and equations.

The sustained leader takes care of their team. These people come with a full package of capabilities, talents, flaws, personalities, and every other human dimension. The sustained leader can segregate these attributes and see the human soul that lies beneath this surface, and then can treat each individual as the individual they are. Certainly our various attributes allow us to be grouped sociologically according to those attributes, whether they be physical, psychological, or societal. In the final analysis, however, we are each a minority of one. The sustained leader gets that.

In many companies the responsibility for dealing with employees is relegated to an HR department. Too many functional leaders, not believing that they are "people" persons, allow all such interpersonal matters to be handled by a resident bureaucrat in HR. This is wrong for so many reasons, not the

---

296 Maj. Gen. Charles R. Henry, *A General's Insight into Leadership and Management* (Batelle Press, 1996), 37.
297 *Training* (periodical), May/June 2014, 84.

least of which is the abdication of responsibility for caring for the team by the functional/ostensible leader. Sustained leaders don't permit that to occur. Sustained leaders understand that employees do not leave companies—they leave bosses.[298] The loss of a key team member is the responsibility of the leader, not the HR manager. While there are many administrative responsibilities for an HR department, the fact is that the care and feeding of the team is primarily the responsibility of the leader. As one leader has noted, "Leadership is ultimately *about* people, not just sterile objectives and strategies that can be written on paper."[299]

This sounds like me

A lot   somewhat   just a little   not at all

Additional Resources:

Les Giblin, *How to Have Confidence and Power in Dealing with People.*

Richard E. Boyatzis, et al., *Resonant Leadership.*

Personal Objective:

Specific Actions:

Due Date:

3.1 Defines Roles

WBS Dictionary: When a leader attracts followers behind a vision, they must understand the importance of using those human resources to the maximum

---

298 This concept has been often stated and explored. One such source is Victor Lipman, *The Type B Manager: Leading Successfully in a Type A World* (Prentice Hall, 2015).

299 MacArthur, John. *The Book on Leadership.* (Thomas Nelson, 2006), 73.

advantage of the team's objectives. This must take into consideration what the team members bring to the accomplishment of the mission and realization of the vision. On the one hand the leader must consider the applicable systems and the needs of the programs, and then consider the talents of the team members. Different leaders will structure identical projects differently based on their experience and preferences and the specific mix of talents and capabilities of the team members which will change over time. Effectively the sustained leader is doing their best to put the round peg in the round hole and the square peg in the square hole. Unfortunately, people and mission roles do not usually align in a very precise fashion. This element considers this dilemma and requires the sustained leader to configure the team and the project in the most compatible (and ultimately successful) fashion possible. Defining the roles of those you wish to have as followers is essential to sustained leadership.

Application: One of the more popular expressions of this concept is from Jim Collins in *Good to Great* where he talks about getting the right people on the bus, the wrong people off the bus, and then getting those travelers in the right seats. Collins places the need to get the right people on board before even setting the vision and mission. Occasionally you will find talent that wishes to join your team that is just so good you bring them on board before you have fully defined their proposed contribution. Sustained leaders do this in appropriate circumstances. These circumstances should be carefully considered. Too often it is based more on friendship or past relationships than on a conscious thought about the current enterprise or organization. When a seat on the bus is no longer appropriate for a particular individual, a sustained leader knows to promptly get the person either in a more appropriate seat or completely off the bus. Jack Welch has noted that his motivation in pushing to remove the bottom 10 percent of performers was that "There's no cruelty like waiting and telling people late in their careers that they don't belong."[300]

Defining roles must be based on the systems proscribed by the organization or enterprise (2.2.7). Everyone in the organization is expected to have a role and to fulfill that role. Any organization has tasks that must be accomplished and thus the

---

300 Jack Welch and John A. Byrne, *Jack: Straight from the Gut* (Business Plus, 2001), 163-64.

people who can perform these tasks.[301] In smaller organizations people tend to wear a lot of different hats; in larger organizations the roles and responsibilities are more focused. It is the responsibility of the sustained leader to define the roles necessary for the organization to achieve its mission and vision. This requires the attraction of the right team members (3.1.2) and then getting them in the right seats on the bus (3.1.1).

As technology advances, the sustained leader must also consider whether the tasks to be performed are better performed by people, by technology, or by a combination of both. As advocates for minimum wages press their position and minimum wages rise, consideration of the business dynamics (see 2.1) could tip the scales toward more automation. While this might seem less than compassionate for the employee who loses their job to technology, the capitalistic system within which we operate demands that such trade-offs be made. Even in these situations, when roles are redefined, when tasks are completed, when people outgrow their jobs, or any other situation that calls for the removal or reassignment of personnel, the sustained leader knows to do so with compassion. By properly defining the roles, putting people into the positions that best use their skills and allow them room to grow, when the time comes to remove them from the team, the sustained leader has prepared them for a next assignment where the same benefits can continue.

This sounds like me

A lot	somewhat	just a little	not at all

Additional Resources:
Jim Collins, *Good to Great*.
Tom Rath, et al., *Strengths Based Leadership*.

Personal Objective:

---

301 The team will in many cases include subcontractors, suppliers, volunteers, and others, not just employees.

Specific Actions:

Due Date:

3.1.1 Attracts Talent

WBS Dictionary: The sustained leader understands at a fundamental level that a leader without followers is not, by definition, a leader at all. A leader without followers must in some fashion attract (or invent) followers. The sustained leader appreciates what it takes to attract the talent necessary for the organization. The sustained leader keeps people challenged and engaged. The sustained leader has influence (1.1.2.5) to attract followers. In large measure this is getting talented people on board and then giving them the freedom to meet challenges. This includes granting them permission to fail (3.17). It also involves effective use of your network (1.1.1.1) and communication (4.0). You can force people into followership positions through the use of power or coercion, but that is not a legitimate use of power or leadership. Talent is attracted not solely by a leader's charisma or the organizational vision and mission, although those things are important, but by those things that provide a personal sense of satisfaction and worth: a positive work environment, appealing tasks, appropriate placement, development in both personal and professional arenas, the elimination of negative traits (5.2), and having worthy team players with whom to interact who also work well with others and don't run with scissors. The sustained leader obtains and retains talented individuals.

Application: The story of Michael Dell and the creation of what became Dell Computers is widely known. Being somewhat forced by his parents into college at the University of Texas in Austin, his heart lay elsewhere and after dismantling a computer down to its chips, Dell determined that he could buy the parts and assemble computers to match customers' specific needs. He outgrew his dorm room and built his business into an operation making over $100 million annually. Knowing that such an operation was outgrowing his significant business acumen, he began recruiting talent from other high-tech companies to ensure that his business model was sustainable. He was able to attract the talent he needed because he had first demonstrated the leadership skills necessary to build a sustainable business. Others were drawn to him and continued the success he had started as a reluctant college student from his dorm room.

Niccolo Machiavelli

The first method for estimating the intelligence
of a ruler is to look at the men he has around him.

The sustained leader knows themselves (1.3) and looks for talent that fills in their gaps wherever they may appear. No leader can escape personal responsibility for the essential leadership journey checklist elements, but beyond that others can pick up the slack where the leader is still developing their skills, talents, and abilities. This is what is meant when it is said that a sustained leader must first lead themselves. Like Michael Dell, personal dissatisfaction with your own status in life may cause you to reinvent yourself into someone of whom you are proud.

Several examples related to attracting the right people have been evident in political environments. We elect each individual to a specific office, and the higher the office the more opportunity each leader has to construct the team that surrounds them. A question that seems to be too seldom asked is, can the candidate attract the right quality of people around them as a support team? Whoever briefed and rehearsed Sarah Palin in her infamous interview with Katie Couric should have been summarily fired. The team let her down—and this is regardless of what you might have thought of the candidate. She likewise failed to prepare herself, which demonstrates a personal failure in element 1.3.1.3. Richard Nixon had people he could trust, but too few of high character. When asked to violate the law or the constitutional rights of some, a few of them resigned. That demonstrated great strength of character. Nonetheless the Watergate scheme was carried to completion, including the cover-up that followed. Carter had poor support in almost every respect. His domestic, foreign, and economic policies were so deficient that the country was plunged into a deep recession, while the sycophants around him signed off on each failed decision. In each case, these leaders of the free world failed to get the right people on the bus.

As Goffee and Jones have noted, "Subordinates may not decide who their bosses are, but it is the followers who will ultimately decide who the leaders are."[302] If you are not striving to become a sustained leader, your ability to attract quality followers will be hindered.

John Maxwell postulates five levels of leadership. Jim Collins has a similar model. In each case they provide a roadmap to the gradual elevation of the leader as they proceed on their leadership journey. Maxwell makes the further point that you cannot attract leaders who are above you in the leadership hierarchy. Thus, the sustained leader must constantly strive to be the best leader they can be since it will have a direct impact on the quality of the team they can attract. The sustained leader understands this dynamic and will make sure they attract the mentors they need (1.3.12). This will assist their growth and encourage those on the team to do likewise, thus elevating the entire team.

This sounds like me

A lot   **somewhat**   **just a little**   **not at all**

Additional Resources:

John Maxwell, *The 5 Levels of Leadership*.

Jim Collins, *Good to Great*.

Rob Goffee and Gareth Jones, *Why Should Anyone Be Led by You?*

Personal Objective:

Specific Actions:

Due Date:

---

302 Rob Goffee and Gareth Jones, *Why Should Anyone Be Led by You? What It Takes to Be an Authentic Leader* (Harvard Business Review Press, 2006), 198.

3.1.2 Fills the Seats

WBS Dictionary: To use the Jim Collins metaphor of an organization being a bus headed in a proper direction, the sustained leader is responsible for getting the right people on the bus, and then to get them in the right seats on the bus. The sustained leader defines what those seats are (3.1) and attracts the talent necessary to fill those seats (3.1.1). The sustained leader must then get the team aligned with the organizational goals, being informed by the personal goals, attributes, and talents of those they have attracted. The sustained leader will assess the team members, provide them opportunities to succeed or fail, and make the adjustments that are necessary for the good of the organization, its vision, and its mission. This assessment must be devoid of personal attachment and nepotistic sentiments. These choices may be difficult and occasionally unpopular. There is simply, however, no excuse for keeping a person on the bus who is not performing (or even worse is disruptive to the good performers) or who is in the wrong seat. The sustained leader makes the necessary adjustments without delay.

Application: Kenny had served as the general counsel for an organization for more than three years. The business manager of the organization got himself into a conflict situation and had to be let go. The general manager came to Kenny and asked him to take over the business operations. "But I'm a lawyer," he protested. "What do I know about business?" The GM's reply was direct and concise. "More than you even recognize," she responded. "What you are is an excellent leader, and that is what that team needs right now. It is full of good talent. Just let them do their jobs that they know so well. You just apply your leadership skills to the organization and it will be successful." And as Kenny learned over the next two years, she was right. Not every leader, however, inherits a situation where the team already has the right people in the right seats.

With the roles defined and the ability to attract good talent, the sustained leader must align the organizational needs with the needs and desires of the team members. This will often not be clear-cut and may involve a fair degree of assessment, and even some trial and error. Clear communication (4.0) is critical, and in appropriate circumstances placing people in seats where they have room to grow is a leader's responsibility.

James C. Hunter offers the following anecdote:

Most of you have heard of Lou Holtz, the famous former Notre Dame Football coach. Holtz is renowned for his ability to generate great enthusiasm on the teams he coaches. And not just enthusiasm with the players alone. His entire staff—coaches, secretaries, assistants, even the water boys—are filled with this enthusiasm wherever he has coached in his amazing career. Anyway the story goes he was once asked by a reporter, "How are you able to get everyone to be so enthusiastic on your team?" Lou Holtz replied, "It's really quite simple. I eliminate the ones who aren't."[303] That's getting the right people on the bus and in the right seats!

Every person has skills and talents. Every task the team is to complete will require a specific set of skills and talents. The sustained leader must assess the team and the tasks and make sure they assign the right people to the right tasks. They assign multiple people where a mix of skills and talents are required. They provide coaching and mentoring to help people grow into tasks and assignments. When necessary, they move people to different seats, and occasionally off the bus entirely.

This sounds like me

A lot **somewhat** **just a little** **not at all**

Additional Resources:
Jim Collins, *Good to Great*.
Marcus Buckingham, *StandOut*.

Personal Objective:

---

303 James C. Hunter, *The Servant: A simple story about the true essence of leadership* (Rocklin, CA: Prima Publishing, 1998), 146.

Specific Actions:

Due Date:

Essential Leadership Journey Checkpoint
3.2 Develops Leaders

WBS Dictionary: The development of other leaders is often perceived as the most important role of a leader. Jack Welch, John C. Maxwell, and others have emphasized this aspect of leadership over many others. It is not enough that you have trained and disciplined yourself for the role of leader; it is imperative that you also find ways to develop those around you. The organization will typically have a permanent life. You will not. It is your obligation to make sure the organization has the requisite number and level of leaders to carry it forward. To not do so is an incredibly selfish act. This element is an essential leadership journey checklist item because a significant failure of those in leadership positions is to hoard the authority and power, failing to grow and develop other members of the team.

Application: There is often the question of why it is appropriate to develop people if they are just going to leave. Andy Stanley has observed that eventually everyone leaves anyway, so "I've simply decided that it is better to launch people than to lose them."[304] A popular posting in social media asks the question, "What if we train all our people and they leave?" The answer is, "What if we don't train them and they stay?" Another popular bumper sticker says, "If you think training is expensive, try ignorance." The point is that all the perceived down-sides to training and development are illusory. It is ALWAYS appropriate to develop those around you.

---

304 *Next Generation Leader*, 40.

---●---

Walter Lippmann

The final test of a leader is that he leaves behind him
in other men the conviction and the will to carry on.

---●---

John Maxwell speaks to the five levels of leadership, the top level of which is the creation of more leaders. Jack Welch has said that the development of new leaders is the highest priority of a leader. Mel Ziegler, founder of banana republic, has said that "A leader discovers the hidden chasm between where things are and where things would better be, and strings up a makeshift bridge to attempt the crossing. From the other side he guides those who dare to cross his rickety traverse until the engineers can build a sturdier span for all."[305]

John Maxwell and his co-author, Jim Dornan, make the following observation:

We believe that our country is experiencing a leadership crisis today. Once, we saw an article in the New Republic that addressed the issue. In part it read "Two hundred years ago, a little republic on the edge of the wilderness suddenly produced people like Jefferson, Hamilton, Madison, Adams, and others. Yet the total population was only 3,000,000 people. Today we have over 300 million. Where are the great people? We should have 60 Franklins in a cover story on leadership. The search was in vain."

Today, producing leaders isn't a priority for many people. Besides, developing other leaders isn't always easy or simple, especially for people who are natural leaders.

That's why it's important for a person who wants to raise up other leaders to be committed to the task. We've said it before and we'll repeat it here: Everything rises and falls on leadership. When you raise up and empower leaders, you positively impact yourself, your organization, the people you develop, and all the people their lives touch. Reproducing leaders is the most important task of any person of influence. If

---

305 Maxwell, *How to Influence People*, 117, citing an advertisement in *Esquire*.

you want to make an impact, you have got to be committed to developing leaders.[306]

Chronologically, a leader that is relatively new in their journey might easily dismiss this element as something the "big kids" do. Two thoughts: 1) any journey is better enjoyed with company. This includes the encouragement that comes from the teamwork associated with any long journey. And 2) if you are a leader on any part of the journey (and this might come as a shock to you), you already are one of the "big kids." The point is that sharing your leadership experiences whether formally or informally helps inform other leaders. You are contributing to their development as you develop your own leadership capabilities.

Bob Hope, the legendary comedian, loved America and especially its service men and women. He once said, "America's greatest natural resource has always been her people. In times of crisis, this nation always finds the leaders to guide her through." The political environment of recent decades suggests that someone is falling down on the job. Where are the political leaders? In the corporate world, crony capitalism is rampant and many significant businesses fail or are forced into mergers to save what is left of them. Where are the corporate leaders? Society is becoming more and more polarized on religious matters with greater intrusion into religious matters by the government and gross misconduct by those who should be religious leaders. Where are the religious leaders? Perhaps the more important question to ask is what are you doing to develop yourself as a sustained leader and to likewise develop others into sustained leaders? Whatever your answer might be, these data points suggest that we are not doing enough.

This sounds like me

A lot	**somewhat**	**just a little**	**not at all**

Additional Resources:
John Maxwell, *Developing the Leaders around You.*
Jim Collins, *Good to Great.*
John C. Maxwell, *The 5 Levels of Leadership.*
Lee Iacocca, *Where Have All the Leaders Gone?*

---

306 Maxwell, *How to Influence People*, 169.

Personal Objective:

Specific Actions:

Due Date:

3.3 Loyalty

WBS Dictionary: Loyalty is the process of being faithful to someone or something. It recognizes obligations and commitments made to others and works strenuously to ensure the fulfillment of these commitments. It is sometimes referred to as fealty, allegiance, or devotion. It reflects a desire to stand by someone and to vigorously adhere to central principles. The sustained leader is loyal to their organization and its team, but even more so to their own fundamental principles of morality. The sustained leader has a strong sense of right and wrong and incorporates those principles into the vision and mission of the organization they lead. Consistency is a key element of true loyalty. When loyalty is tested, or when commitments previously made begin to conflict with each other, the sustained leader assesses the conflict and applies the embedded principles of right and wrong to reconcile, adjust, or make amends. In no case does the sustained leader abandon the commitments completely.

Application: Past generations grew up with the notion that a good life was had by finding a good job with a good company and staying with that company until retirement. The pursuit of the gold watch was the ultimate goal. In turn, companies prided themselves on being able to sustain their employment levels and never engaging in a layoff to reduce the staff. IBM was famous for this, even though many joked that in order to stay with the company you had to accept the notion that IBM stood for "I've been moved."

Over time these notions faded. IBM began conducting layoffs. Many companies stopped referring to the departments assigned responsibility for the care of its people from "Personnel" to "Human Resources." People were merely resources, not individuals to whom and from whom loyalty was expected. This was often justified on the basis of economic conditions and necessity. But more than that was going on.

Under criminal law, the rule always was that you had to have two elements proven beyond a reasonable doubt. Those were the *mens rea* (the mental intent to commit a crime) and the *actus rea* (the act of committing the crime.) Society began to modify this approach and created some vicarious liability rules such as the felony murder rule which makes every participant in the commission of a felony responsible for any death that occurs in the commission of the felony. This is true *even if* the criminal team agreed that "no one would be hurt" and the person convicted of felony murder was merely the getaway driver. No intent, no action, but a lawful conviction. Over time more and more crimes were identified as not requiring either the intent or the act. In today's corporate world, companies are enticed by law enforcement (and the laws passed by Congress) to "give up" their employees in order to avoid more serious punishment for any discovered misconduct. It has, in many cases, become illegal to act in a historically ethical manner. We have effectively worked to destroy traditional perceptions of loyalty.

The sustained leader knows what they believe and why they believe it. This level of confidence permits them to establish loyalty to those principles. As Shakespeare said, "This above all: to thine own self be true, and it must follow, as the night the day, thou canst not then be false to any man." Loyalty requires the sustained leader to keep their word, to fight injustice, and to support and protect their team. It is absolutely a two-way street and must start with the leader.

This sounds like me

A lot	somewhat	just a little	not at all

Additional Resources:
John Hasnas, *Trapped.*
Patrick Lencioni, *Getting Naked.*

Personal Objective:

Specific Actions:

Due Date:

3.4 Empathy

WBS Dictionary: The sustained leader develops the ability to identify with others, not necessarily in agreement with, but to understand the perspective of others. Empathy is the result of actually or figuratively walking a mile in their shoes to fully appreciate what current experiences are affecting the individual and how. The sustained leader develops the ability to vicariously experience what others are experiencing and feeling. While the attitudes of the two people will differ, the empathetic person seeks to understand, again even if not agreeing with, the attitudes and feelings of the other person. The empathetic leader listens actively to the other person and views them as unique individuals deserving of respect and, occasionally, tough love.

Application: The sustained leader understands empathy as the ability to consider other people—their feelings, moods, culture, and sentiments, in appropriate measure—when making decisions. Empathy is genuine and sincere; it cannot be faked.

Dana Perino tells a story of President Bush addressing a group of SEALS, including SEAL Team Six, about to be deployed. He thanked them for their service and the missions they had completed after the events of 9/11.

He spoke without notes and from the heart. He finished with 'God bless you, and may God continue to bless America,' and they cheered for a long time ignoring his pleas to stop. That was an order they didn't have to obey. The President had tears in his eyes, and so did I.

After his speech, President Bush shook hands with every one of them and posed for pictures they could send to their families and friends. All of the young men had really long beards, so it wasn't hard to figure out where in the world they were about to be deployed (and it wasn't Indiana). The jackets and ties they were wearing for the President's visit would soon be switched out for their combat uniforms.[307]

Management texts often discuss the 8/24 syndrome. What this means is that a member of the team may only be physically present with the team for eight hours a day. While the leader would certainly prefer that those eight hours be dedicated solely to the team's goals and objectives, with human beings this is simply not possible on all occasions. Every member of the team brings all twenty-four hours of their day to the team efforts. Anything else that is happening in any other aspect of their life is with them while working with the team. Whether that is an elderly parent, an errant child, a sick family member, a commitment to a charity, maintenance on their home, financial stress, or a problem with a pet—every aspect of the person's life is embodied in them while working with the team. Sustained leaders are no different and will recognize that we are all twenty-four-hour people. By setting priorities and helping team members do the same, while also providing external resources when appropriate, the sustained leader can demonstrate genuine empathy with the team. The same is true when significant disasters affect the team, such as a workplace violence event or local disaster. In those cases, bringing external help in to the team may be necessary since the empathy of the entire team may be depleted.

This does not suggest that the sustained leader must coddle the employees or allow a particular team member to take advantage of the empathy shown by not performing their assigned tasks, having an excessive number of absences, or distracting the team with lengthy stories of their miseries. Each situation must be assessed on its own merits.

---

307 Dana Perino, *And the Good News Is…: Lessons and Advice from the Bright Side* (New York: Hachette Book Group, 2015), 16-17.

Interestingly, this is an area where US law has legislated certain aspects and standards of empathy. This includes leaves of absence for a new child (both men and women) and the Family and Medical Leave Act, which permits time off to care for a sick family member. The sustained leader will, of course, make themselves aware of such applicable laws and follow them. They will do so in a spirit of cooperation rather than rigid compliance. More importantly, the sustained leader does not need such laws in the first place.

This sounds like me

A lot	somewhat	just a little	not at all

Additional Resources:

Jeffrey Pfeffer, *The Human Equation*.

Adrian Gostick et al., *The 24-Carrot Manager*.

Dale Carnegie, *How to Win Friends & Influence People*.

Personal Objective:

Specific Actions:

Due Date:

3.4.1 Active Listener

WBS Dictionary: Too often things that are heard are not properly registered by the listener. This may be due to distraction or even intentional disregard. The sustained leader develops a strong sense of active listening. This improves the leader's understanding of what is being said, provides a basis to ask outstanding questions (4.4.1), and encourages the speaker to continue until the situation under discussion is fully understood. If a person feels they are being ignored, they will keep quiet and less information will flow to the leader. An uninformed, or even misinformed, leader will not lead well. Maintaining eye contact, offering positive and encouraging body language (e.g. leaning forward, nodding), and paraphrasing are all effective techniques.

Active Listening

Most people do not listen with the intent to understand;
they listen with the intent to reply.
—Stephen Covey

The best leaders are very often the best listeners. They have an open mind.
They are not interested in having their own way but in finding the best way.
—Wilfred Peterson

Listening builds trust, the foundation of all lasting relationships.
—Brian Tracy

Listening is one of the key characteristics of exemplary leaders.
—Kouzes and Posner

Leaders who don't listen will eventually be
surrounded by people who have nothing to say.
—Andy Stanley

No man ever listened himself out of a job.
—Calvin Coolidge

One of my favorite sayings from [Dick] Cheney was,
"You never get in trouble for something you didn't say."
—Dana Perino

Don't shoot the messenger. It dries up the supply of messengers.
—Norm Augustine

———————— ● ————————

Application: A person can think far faster than anyone can speak. Most commonly the listener is structuring in their mind what they are going to say next, as Stephen Covey notes in the sidebar. This is compounded when there are more participants in the conversation. Active listening sends constant signals and feedback to the speaker that effective communication is occurring. It is simple, but difficult.

———————— ● ————————

President Bill Clinton

*Being president is like running a cemetery; you've got
a lot of people under you and nobody's listening.*

———————— ● ————————

Active listening is explained well in *How to Influence People* by John C. Maxwell. He notes several critical benefits to listening carefully. Listening, he says, shows respect, builds relationships, increases knowledge, generates ideas, builds loyalty, and tends to help others and yourself.[308]

Active listening is not passive. On the contrary, the "active" part is very active. It is more than smiling, nodding, and looking the person in the eye—all of which are important parts of active listening. It requires that you fight the urge to interrupt and focus on really understanding what the person is saying—untainted by the prejudices and biases that you bring to the conversation. Periodically you should take the opportunity to paraphrase and sum up what you are hearing to make sure that you are communicating effectively. Learning to ask excellent questions is also part of active listening (4.4.1). Like any skill, it improves with practice. So practice active listening at every opportunity. When listening, it is acceptable to make notes, but make them brief so that you do not have extended times of broken eye-contact. If you ever have the opportunity to observe a great reporter you will see that they

---

308 Maxwell, *How to Influence People,* 62-65.

ask excellent questions and then have the learned ability to continue writing while maintaining eye-contact with the interviewee. And they write clearly. It is not the chicken scratch that you might imagine. In this way, they record impressions while being sure not to miss any nonverbal cues.

Listening is also not letting things go in one ear and out the other. It requires that you absorb and retain what is being said. When you paraphrase it back to the speaker, you must have a reservoir from which to draw. When you are listening to things that are either contrary to your beliefs, or are on a subject with which you have no prior experience, it is often difficult to absorb and synthesize. In the former case, you must construct a parallel matrix in your mind to match what is being said with your pre-existing sensibilities. In the latter case, you have no pre-established frame of reference and thus must temporarily construct one within your thought patterns until you can understand the overall structure of what is being presented. Only then can you conduct a proper assessment of the message and compare it to your underlying values in order to properly understand the position being presented. Active listening is very active.

It is important to understand that men and women both speak and listen differently. Deborah Tannen has written extensively on communication in a variety of contexts, including between the sexes. While strict generalities cannot be made, there are identifiable tendencies in the way men and women both speak and listen. After reading Dr. Tannen's work, you might wonder how we procreate as a species!

Dorothy Leeds, in her outstanding work *The 7 Powers of Questions*, notes that you should listen with a purpose, and by listening well you can formulate better questions that elicit even better answers and information. She includes extremely good advice on how to *start* listening better and how to assess your listening skills. Weak listeners would do well to start here.

One common complaint about managers and leaders is that they do not listen. And even if this is completely wrong (it's not!), that fact would not be relevant. The critical measure is whether people feel or perceive that bosses are listening to them. Only through careful attention to listening skills will a leader be able to convince others that they are listening. It is not a mechanical act; it includes actually understanding what is being said. Both Daniel Goleman[309] and William Ury[310] have written extensively on the importance of truly understanding the other party's interests—not just what they are saying with their words. You must listen in the spaces to grasp what is really behind the message.

When you listen attentively you open up the circuits in your brain that permit empathetic interactions. Unless you allow the message to seep into those areas of your brain, you may be perceived as cold or even heartless. Clearly, if you allow your emotions to totally control your reaction you will be a less effective leader, possibly perceived as one who is too emotional to deal effectively with situations. Attentive listening allows you to control which part of your brain will control your reaction. A lack of attentive listening might cause a more visceral reaction that may or may not be appropriate for the situation. When practicing active listening, be certain that you are listening to understand and not listening to reply.

Stephen Covey has noted that a key habit of successful people is they seek first to understand and only after that to be understood. Providing signals such as paraphrasing ("Let me see if I understand…"), moving from principle to conclusion (doing it in reverse is rationalization, not comprehension), and learning the great value of silence are all part of an active listening repertoire. Find someone you respect, perhaps a mentor or current leader, and observe their listening style. Observe body language, listen from the heart, and listen for content. Then ask their honest assessment of your listening skills.

This sounds like me

A lot	somewhat	just a little	not at all

Additional Resources:

Deborah Tannen, *Talking from 9 to 5.*

Stephen R. Covey, *The 7 Habits of Highly Effective People.* Note Habit #5.

John Maxwell, et al., *How to Influence People,* chapter 4, "A Person of Influence… Listens to People," 59-78.

Dorothy Leeds, *The 7 Powers of Questions,* 131-56.

---

309 See e.g., Daniel Goleman, *Focus: The Hidden Driver of Excellence* (New York: HarperCollins, 2015), 226-27.

310 William Ury, *Getting Past No: Negotiating with Difficult People* (Bantam, 1991).

Personal Objective:

Specific Actions:

Due Date:

3.4.2 Views People as Ends Not Means

WBS Dictionary: People in an organization are often referred to as "human resources." In that way they are not personable human beings, they are merely tools to be used in the accomplishment of some end. People become the means. If, however, you begin to view other team members as an end unto themselves, then the tools take on character and personalities. They appear as the 24/7 people that they are (3.7). They have talents, families, goals, ambitions, hobbies, struggles, and health and money concerns. Simply stated, they are human beings with all the baggage that entails. The sustained leader understands that the team members have their individual goals and abilities. If they are just laborers, perhaps not much more than slaves, then neither they nor the team will achieve their highest levels. Thus, they cannot be viewed as simply the means to an end. Developing each of them into the best "them" they can be certainly helps them as individuals, but also makes the entire team stronger. The sustained leader understands this.

Application: Many managers are more devoted to achieving a goal at any cost than to the people involved in reaching the goal. Management metrics more commonly relate to quarterly sales and profit or rises in stock prices than to how happy the workforce might be. One adage suggests that you should be kind to the people you step on when climbing the ladder to success since those are the same people who will choose whether to cushion your fall. When you view people as tools to be used to promote yourself, you are not acting with empathy. This does not mean that the other extreme of being so empathetic toward others that you become incapable of experiencing your own feelings is appropriate either. There is a balance that must be struck between being empathetic toward your team members and losing yourself in another. Many social relationships are destroyed by people who are unable to draw that distinction.

The sustained leader must train themselves to be able to identify the legitimate needs of each team member. Keep in mind that in most cases the team member will be oblivious to their true needs and will express themselves in terms of "wants." If we were to give children everything they wanted they would not grow into mature, rational adults. They would remain spoiled brats. The sustained leader must look past the expressed wants to what the person truly needs.

In a military setting, there are often choices that must be made, recognizing that there will be losses of personnel. Any loss is unfortunate, yet the leader must still have empathy for the troops. Gen. George Patton struggled with this when he said, "I consider it no sacrifice to die for my country. In my mind we came here [the burial ground of troops he had lost in battle] to thank God that men like these have lived rather than to regret that they have died."[311]

Jon Gordon delves into an area that is so often misunderstood in leadership development—love. He says, "[Love is] a process not a goal. Love is something that needs to be nurtured. But if there is one thing I urge you to start immediately it's focus on bringing out the best in each person on your team. When you love someone you want the best for them. You want them to shine. And the best way to do this is to help them discover the value inside them."[312]

This sounds like me

A lot	somewhat	just a little	not at all

Additional Resources:

Stephen R. Covey, *Principle Centered Leadership*. Note especially Principle #4. Martin Blumenson, *Patton*.

---

311 Martin Blumenson, *Patton: The Man Behind the Legend, 1885-1945* (William Morrow, 1985), 214.
312 Jon Gordon, *The Energy Bus* (Hoboken, NJ: John Wiley, 2007), 117.

Personal Objective:

Specific Actions:

Due Date:

3.4.3 Respect

WBS Dictionary: A person who shows empathy earns the respect of others. It is an attracting quality that helps in drawing talent to the leader. Much of a leader's responsibility deals with building relationships. A person who cannot identify with their team, or who is extremely standoffish, will not foster positive relationships. They will earn no respect. Such people also tend to have excessive egos and an inability to share credit. They become, if they are not already, selfish and possibly greedy. Demonstrating positive character, having strong principles which others can see being lived, and relating personally to the various team members earn their respect. Certainly, fulfilling the other leadership traits, attributes, and roles as described elsewhere in this WBS contribute to earning the respect of others as well, but it is the attitude of empathy that makes the leader seem more human and not sitting upon a pedestal. Knowing where people are struggling, what they have already overcome, and appreciating their goals makes the sustained leader someone that others wish to follow. The completely non-empathetic leader may see some aspects of success in leadership, but they will never obtain the role of sustained leader. The leader who demonstrates genuine respect and empathy toward the team will earn their respect, with emphasis on the concept of "earn." Respect must be a shared sentiment, and both parties to the relationship must ultimately earn it.

Application: Everyone has a story. Telling it makes them more human. The sustained leader listens to these stories and reacts to the protagonist as an important person. John Maxwell relates that Fred Rogers, star of the popular kids' TV show

Mr. Rogers' Neighborhood, kept a quote in his wallet that said, "There isn't anyone you couldn't learn to love once you've heard their story." Maxwell continues, "It's hard to remain self-centered when your focus is on others. Hearing people's stories is a great way to get outside of yourself. Not only will their stories inspire you to help them, but they will show you *ways* you can help them."[313]

Leaders in many organizations have access to information that is not generally known about the team members. For example, the personnel file may reflect certain military service. Not everyone is comfortable talking about or even acknowledging everything about themselves. If the leader were to disclose this information, no matter how benign the leader perceives it to be, the trust would be broken and the respect lost. Even if it were in the context of attempting to build up the individual, if the information was not made public by the person, no one else has a right to disclose it. Letting the person know that you are aware of such information privately and asking their permission to disclose it is more appropriate. And if the person declines, then the information is to remain private.

Respect reflects a sense of esteem or worth of the person—as a person, not a resource tool. The sustained leader accords a high level of respect to everyone, regardless of position or status. Even in bearing bad news, the sustained leader honors the respect deserved of all people. Jack Welch speaks often of his philosophy that the bottom 10 percent of any organization should be removed. He also emphasizes that this separation should be done compassionately and with respect. You don't just walk people to the door and slam it behind them. You arrange for outplacement; you provide them with severance. You respect them as an individual who, for whatever reasons, will not be able to find success within your organization.[314]

This sounds like me

A lot	**somewhat**	**just a little**	**not at all**

Additional Resources:

Dale Carnegie, et al., *How to Win Friends & Influence People.*

Stephen Covey, *Principle Centered Leadership.*

---

313 John C. Maxwell, *Intentional Living: Choosing a Life That Matters* (New York: Center Street, 2015), 120-21 (emphasis in original).

314 Jack Welch and John A. Byrne, *Jack: Straight from the Gut* (Business Plus, 2001), 163-64.

Personal Objective:

Specific Actions:

Due Date:

3.4.4 Tough Love

WBS Dictionary: The sustained leader is not always perceived as nice. There are times when the leader must be firm to the point of insistence. This is true absolutely whenever the fundamental principles or values of the leader or the organization are threatened. It is also true when the leader judges or ascertains that the employee's development is being hindered by a flaw that can and must be corrected, but the follower simply cannot or will not acknowledge the issue or recognize the necessary remedy. Similar to a parent, the sustained leader develops the necessary toughness and sensitivity that is appropriate for the situation. The leader must make the necessary balance between steel and velvet in leading their team. While the goal will be to make the team member and the entire team more productive, it might destroy the relationship between the leader and the team member. Not everyone can handle such criticism, and some may refuse to acknowledge the necessary change. If the impact is to the entire team, however, the leader has no choice but to address the issue and, if necessary, remove the team member from the team. This requires that the sustained leader have enough self-confidence and empathy to deal effectively with the particular issue and to be as certain as possible of the required change even when it might be unpopular or particularly detrimental to a team member.

Application: There are times when leaders need to be firm, harsh even. Selectively used, extreme firmness can be motivating and instructional. As noted by Vince Molinaro, "…there's a difference between selectively being harsh when the situation demands it and being a jerk all the time. One's a tactic; the other is a personality trait."[315]

Tough love requires a strong adherence to principle; it is the principle that is being enforced. If the leader cannot or chooses not to adhere to any principles, there will never be a reason to exercise tough love. Such events are unpleasant for both the leader and the recipient. Like an intervention, the goal is to express sincere and deep concern for the individual while insisting on the cessation of the destructive behavior. Thus, even when the leader discerns that a tough love situation exists, there will still be resistance to taking the necessary action.

Gen. Colin Powell (Ret.)
Being responsible sometimes means pissing people off.

Ideally the leader will alert the person to the issue and in appropriate circumstances develop an improvement plan with which the person participates and agrees. If the person can be rehabilitated and can change the behavior that manifests the undesirable trait, then both parties win. If not, then further, more definitive action must be taken, thus prolonging the unpleasant task even further. Even great leaders are affected by the distaste of some tasks. That provides no excuse for avoiding it.

As a boy growing up in Virginia, George Washington wrote often in his journal and made notes that served him well throughout his life. Among the rules he noted was #45, which says, "Being to advise or reprehend any one, consider whether it ought to be in publick or in Private; presently, or at Some other time in what terms to do it & in reproving Shew no Sign of Cholar but do it with all Sweetness and Mildness."[316] In other words, even difficult tasks can and should be done with kindness and consideration of the individual. As a man, Washington took many difficult actions which he perceived would preserve the new country, but his caring

---

315 Vince Molinaro, *The Leadership Contract: The Fine Print to Becoming a Great Leader* (Wiley, 2013), 45.

316 George Washington and L. Baldrige, *George Washington's Rules of Civility & Decent Behaviour in Company and Conversation* (Mount Vernon Ladies Association of the Union, 1989).

for his troops and the citizens of his country always tempered his actions no matter how difficult those actions were to take.

This sounds like me

A lot   **somewhat**   **just a little**   **not at all**

Additional Resources:

Jack Welch, et al., *Winning.*

Tony Dungy, et al., *The Mentor Leader.*

Personal Objective:

Specific Actions:

Due Date:

3.4.5 Social Conscience

WBS Dictionary: A social conscience can be displayed in a number of ways and in a variety of dimensions. Essentially this means having a caring sentiment toward the society as a whole, apart from its distinct members. It may also mean that a personal sacrifice must be made for the good of the society. It might have a focus on a particular societal segment and can be shown as a respect for minorities, education, having minimal environmental impact, adopting policies that support such things as recycling and alternative energy, or a sense of history. It practices the motto reflected in the Hippocratic Oath that, first, you shall do no harm. Or the Scout approach to leave a place better than you found it. Society is the construct within which we all live, and its stability and continuation are critical for the survival of the species. To ignore it is irresponsible. The sustained leader understands the obligation we all have to society and respects that obligation in their decisions and actions.

Application: A social conscience comes with a sense of balance among competing interests. Diane Blair died in 2000. She had served in several political capacities during her life and was considered a close friend of Hillary Clinton. After Blair's death, her papers were given by her husband to the University of Arkansas. Peggy Noonan, in *The Wall Street Journal*,[317] characterized her as "smart and loyal, an intimate," and then says, "some of what she wrote casts her friend in a poor light." Noonan does not perceive this as being disloyal to her friend, but being loyal to history and society at large.

Some perceive a social conscience as requiring severe steps in developing alternative energy sources. Wind is popular, but in order to generate electricity from wind large blades must be turned by the wind. Unfortunately, these large blades are extremely hazardous to birds—some of them endangered species. Is it more socially conscious to develop alternative energy or to preserve endangered species? Reasonable people can differ, but it reflects the choices that sometimes must be made. More importantly, the sustained leader chooses to consider these issues and actively consider the policy decisions that must be made. They do not simply ignore the facts (1.2.1.2) and do not choose to be willfully ignorant (5.2.8). The sustained leader considers the waste stream that their activities create, the public support or lack of support for a particular political issue or candidate, the plight of the homeless or unemployed, and the conditions of employment or engagement of the team. The sustained leader does not see their activities in a vacuum but as a part of society at large.

Many companies encourage employees to engage in some organized effort to help society. Perhaps they adopt a section of highway to clean up or a secret Santa effort during the holidays. Perhaps they sponsor a day at a local soup kitchen or invest in retraining efforts for those without current work or the skills to get work. All of these are worthy endeavors, and people are well advised to participate. What the sustained leader understands is that these activities can never be coerced, even by peer pressure, or count as fulfillment of this element by proxy. If you encourage everyone else to donate to a charity and then give nothing yourself, you are not being honest. If you arrange for a day of help on a Habitat

---

317 February 15-16, 2014, page A17.

for Humanity project and then fail to roll up your sleeves and get dirty as well, you are a fraud in this element.

The sustained leader considers the effect on society of the decisions being made. Sometimes these will be tough decisions, such as closing a plant and increasing unemployment in a particular area. These effects do not make the decision wrong, but failing to even consider the social ramifications is not indicative of a sustained leader.

This sounds like me

A lot	**somewhat**	**just a little**	**not at all**

Additional Resources:

Jean-Jacques Rousseau, et al., *The Social Contract.*
John Mackey, et al., *Conscious Capitalism.*
Harvard Business School Press, *Harvard Business Review on Corporate Ethics.*

Personal Objective:

Specific Actions:

Due Date:

3.5 Inspiring

WBS Dictionary: Inspiration is the ability to dream big dreams and to cause others to rise to the occasion. It involves the ability to influence or impel another to a higher level of performance or thought. The sustained leader will produce or arouse in others a desire to excel. The inspirational leader will fill others with a higher level of influence. Inspiration is an effect on someone's beliefs. It causes them to believe in making what appeared impossible possible. While often related to spiritual beliefs, it also has an impact on capabilities and performance levels. More can be accomplished by those who are inspired. The sustained leader understands this concept and works toward inspiring the team toward greater objectives. The sustained leader is able to do this because they believe that higher achievement is possible and that some of this effort must be drawn out of the performer. Through words, deeds, actions, and relationships the sustained leader can inspire the team to perform at a level never before achieved.

Application: Inspiration is the companion to perspiration. Hard work means nothing if it is not focused on a worthy goal. And having a great idea, what Jim Collins refers to as a BHAG (big hairy audacious goal), is meaningless if no action is ever taken to achieve the goal. It is only when someone is inspired to achieve that real action takes place. In looking back at such achievements, they are often described as being "inspired."

Inspiration is always a positive trait. It allows no room for negativity, self-doubt, or dealing with naysayers. It is the combination of desire, vision, and action all coming together. It creates a synergy that, working alone, people could not achieve. People can be inspired on their own and can accomplish amazing work through inspiration. Sometimes it comes from a life event; other times it just seems to sneak up on you. Other times you have to work very hard to generate inspiration. Interestingly, hard work often is one of the keys to gaining inspiration. As noted elsewhere, (see 2.3), you can't steer a ship that is dead in the water. A ship must be moving for the rudder to have any effect. Very often the key to inspiration is simply to dive in and see where your hard work takes you.

Many feel that inspiration applies only to the creative arts—writing, painting, poetry, woodworking (for a few examples)—and it is true that much creative work is truly inspired. What is not recognized in such situations is how many hours of "less inspired" work preceded the "inspired" result.

Jack and Suzy Welch make the following observation:

Your people give their days (and sometimes their nights) to you. They give their hands, brains, and hearts. Sure, the company pays them. It fills their wallets. But as a leader, you need to fill their souls. You can do that by getting in their skin, by giving the work meaning, by clearing obstacles, and by demonstrating the generosity gene. And you can do it, perhaps more powerfully, by creating an environment that's exciting and enjoyable.[318]

Inspiration is the sustained leader touching the soul of the team members. It is understanding them well enough to know what types of stimuli will inspire them. Typically inspiration is a personal endeavor. It is possible to inspire whole teams if they share a sufficient bond, such as loyalty to country or a shared view of a charitable endeavor. Even then, each person will find something specific on which to latch their inspiration.

The sustained leader also understands that inspiration, when it exists, is always genuine. It cannot be faked.

This sounds like me

| A lot | somewhat | just a little | not at all |

Additional Resources:
Jeffrey Gitomer, et al., *The Little Book of Leadership*.
John MacArthur, *The Book on Leadership*.

Personal Objective:

Specific Actions:

Due Date:

---

318 Jack and Suzy Welch, *The Real Life MBA: Your No-BS Guide to Winning the Game, Building a Team, and Growing Your Career* (New York: HarperCollins, 2015), 21.

3.6 Disciplines and Rewards

WBS Dictionary: In the classic sense, recognition and correction are the carrot and the stick. Different team members will respond differently to both the nature and intensity of rewards or demerits. The sustained leader calibrates well with each individual to ascertain the proper level of reward and punishment that is required to improve the individual. Unless the leader studies the nature and temperament of the team members, they will not know how best to calibrate on the appropriate level of discipline and reward. The sustained leader must therefore work on the relational aspects and gain an increased understanding of what makes each team member tick. The nature and scope of both punishment and reward must also be calibrated to the age, gender, work experience, and future aspirations of the team member. This is absolutely *not* a case of one-size-fits-all. Each event must be custom tailored to the individual while still meeting the sense of fairness collectively held by the team. This cannot be managed in a carefree manner; the leader must be decisive and act accordingly. The sustained leader knows not to withhold either reward or punishment and how important it is to be as consistent as possible in distributing both.

Application: Certainly the level and nature of discipline differs considerably as between children and adults. The sustained leader is not in a parent-child relationship with the team members, and it would be inappropriate for the relationship to be considered in that context alone. Showing appreciation is one of the key rewards leaders can give team members. It is important to remember that the appreciation must be specific and sincere. General statements of "good job," while useful, do not engender the same positive response as those that are specific. See also 4.2.15.

The sustained leader must maintain a proper environment for development of the team (3.9) and a key aspect of that is a system of rewards and discipline that is perceived as fair and effective. A lack of perceived fairness (3.15) of the leader will hinder the team's development. Even so, the nature of each individual must be considered. Studies show that appreciation means more than money to most people. MOST people. There are those who measure their value solely via the dollars received. The sustained leader must identify these differences and act accordingly. It was former Secretary of Defense and World Bank President

Robert McNamara who said, "Brains are like hearts—they go where they are appreciated."[319]

Some people respond well when given specific criticism, and take it to heart. Others become petulant and rebel further. Certainly this is a measure of the maturity level of the team member, and the sustained leader must be able to assess this with each stakeholder.

In the governmental arena, the rigidity of a sense of fairness has made it more difficult to treat people differently since each such example of different treatment will be used to demonstrate favoritism or discrimination. The more rigid strictures of such an environment must be followed by a leader in that environment, but that does not change this element and the need for the sustained leader to mete out both rewards and punishment where appropriate. Such environments do not prohibit either; they merely require more detailed record keeping and consistency to enforce either.

Religious discipline also has its unique aspects. Corporal punishment was widely accepted in parochial schools until fairly recently. The Judeo-Christian precept of "spare the rod spoil the child" permitted spanking and the smack of a ruler across the hand.

To the degree that rewards and discipline must be administered, it is the leader's responsibility to do so in a fair, equitable, and productive manner—and when there are external guides or principles that must also be followed, to understand those requirements and adhere to them.

This sounds like me

A lot	somewhat	just a little	not at all

Additional Resources:

Adrian Gostick, et al., *The 24-Carrot Manager.*

Jeffrey Gitomer, *Customer Satisfaction Is Worthless, Customer Loyalty Is Priceless.*

Personal Objective:

---

319 Quoted in John Maxwell, *How to Influence People*, 27.

Specific Actions:

Due Date:

3.7 Understands 24-Hour People

WBS Dictionary: We are an accumulation of our life experiences. People who work on a team do not simply work on your team. They are all 24-hour people. This means that whatever else is going on in their lives in the 16 hours a day they are away from the team comes with them during the 8 hours they are participating with the team. Whatever else is going on in their family, their church, with their kids, with their spouse, with their dreams, goals, and ambitions is as much a part of them while they are with the team as when they are not. People lose focus; they respond psychologically to stress or depression or even excitement. They think about things in their subconscious and in their conscious brains. They lose focus. All 24 hours of their day is with them, and all 168 hours of their week, and all 722 hours of their month, and all 8,760 hours of their year. Every year. The good, the bad, the relevant, and the irrelevant. It's all part of them, all the time.

Application: Frank Irving Fletcher, we are told by John Maxwell, noted that "No man can deliver the goods if his heart is heavier than his load."[320] We never know what is going on in a person's head, and since we have all made mistakes, we all have skeletons of one type or another in our full walk-in closets, and there are constantly distracting thoughts on which we wish to focus. We sometimes call this "baggage," but it is not the sort of thing from which we can simply set down and walk away. It is attached to us; it is part of what makes us who we are today. The leader has to ask, however, does this help frame my future vision, goals, and aspirations? To the degree the leader can keep those aspects separate, and draw on the strength of those experiences without allowing the downside to taint the progress, the better equipped they are to help others do the same.

---

320 John Maxwell and Jim Dornan, *How to Influence People: Make a Difference in Your World* (Nashville, TN: Thomas Nelson, 2013), 118.

There are some events and conditions, over which people have limited or no control. Wounded veterans who return from war with missing limbs, mental disruptions, and other serious physical and mental issues struggle with this in the most extreme fashion. And, sadly, they do not all survive the experience. The sustained leader understands this about themselves as well as those they lead. Some people have strong religious convictions. They attempt to live up to those beliefs and conduct their lives accordingly. Others are burdened with strong egos, disrupted home lives, past mistakes whether generally known or unknown, regrets, memories, and a thousand other life events from which they cannot escape. The point is that *everyone* has these as part of their life. Different people deal with them in different ways, and such misfortune is not evenly distributed. As our parents tried to caution us—life is not fair. Thus, each individual has their own sense of personal justice and creates their own scenario for dealing with it. Some achieve this fairly well; others do not. It is not the role of the sustained leader to solve all the issues of everyone in the world. It is the role of the sustained leader to understand their team and what makes them successful. If a team member needs professional help, then this may be something with which the leader can assist. Not being a trained professional in the majority of such situations, however, the sustained leader never makes the mistake of taking ownership of any team member's personal issues. They merely acknowledge that each team member, including the leader, has their own set of baggage and remains sensitive to how this affects the overall team performance. A good phrase to keep in mind is, "Always be kind. You have no idea the battles others are waging."

This sounds like me

A lot   **somewhat**   **just a little**   **not at all**

Additional Resources:
Adrian Gostick, et al., *The Invisible Employee.*
Jon Gordon, et al., *The Energy Bus.*

Personal Objective:

Specific Actions:

Due Date:

3.8 Delegates Effectively

WBS Dictionary: No person is good at everything; some people are good at only a very few things. When a leader believes they have "everything" under control, they are exhibiting the trait of hubris, or a lack of humility. They are prideful. The simple fact is that no matter how many good traits a person holds, no matter how experienced they are, no matter what level of education or even enlightenment they may have achieved, they cannot singlehandedly do everything that needs to be done. Similarly, asking others for help takes a special level of humility since it is tacit acknowledgment that some things are beyond their ability. This is the primary reason that weak leaders fail to delegate effectively. An inability to delegate is also a sign that the weak leader cannot trust others. Perhaps it is because they know *they* cannot be trusted and they project that onto others. In any case, delegation must be to those who can be trusted, who are responsible, who have the appropriate level of ability to accomplish the task, who have been developed to an appropriate level of competence, who have also been delegated the appropriate level of authority, who can be held accountable for accomplishing the task and (this is important) agrees to accept the delegation. In other words, the leader must develop the person to whom tasks are delegated and then gain their permission for the delegation. Effective delegation includes all these aspects, and the sustained leader understands these requirements—authority, responsibility, and accountability. Any failure by the leader in meeting each of these requirements with each delegation is the fault of the leader, not the performer. Sustained leaders do not make such mistakes.

Application: In 2.1.3 we discussed the management concepts of POSDCoRB. Recall that the "D" stands for delegation. It is usual and customary for a leader to both receive and give delegations. In larger organizations, specific delegated authority is often documented in policies and procedures containing Delegations of Authority (DOA). This assigns approval authority to people in specific positions, thus a change in personnel maintains the authority at the same level, barring organizational changes that modify the hierarchical structure or change the position titles.

Delegation requires that the aspects of leadership be retained regardless of who is personally exercising the authority or making the decision. All the elements of leadership—character, competence, compassion, communication, and commitment—must be maintained by the delegator and the person who receives the delegation. The empowerment delegated often helps the person receiving the delegation to grow. Delegation is an excellent tool for growing new leaders. Delegation does not transfer the ultimate responsibility, however. The sustained leader understands that even after delegating they remain responsible for the outcome.

Delegation should never be simply busy-work or menial tasks. It has to have substance and meaning to the person receiving the delegation or it will fail to be effective. It must, in fact, be part of a goal that the person has personally accepted. If they are merely performing tasks that further another person's goals, they are not likely to complete it well, or on time. John Maxwell has provided an excellent delegation checklist that should be used by the inexperienced delegator until it becomes second nature.[321]

Theodore Roosevelt said, "The best leader is the one who has sense enough to pick good men to do what he wants done, and the self-restraint to keep from meddling with them while they do it." The sustained leader learns to delegate effectively.

This sounds like me

A lot	somewhat	just a little	not at all

Additional Resources:
Frank Huppe, *Successful Delegation*.
D. Michael Abrashoff, *Get Your Ship Together*.

---

321 John Maxwell, *How to Influence People*, 161.

Personal Objective:

Specific Actions:

Due Date:

3.9 Develops Team Members

WBS Dictionary: People are in a constant state of change. Ideally this change is an improvement and yields positive results. Backsliding is common, however, and constant reinforcement is usually necessary to maintain improvements. Even using the *Sustained Leadership WBS* will require constant attention and regular reinforcement. Leadership development requires development across the entire spectrum of *Sustained Leadership WBS* elements. Future leaders need to be prepared to address all the elements of character, competence, compassion, communication, and commitment. Just as anyone using this WBS will require that attention be given to each essential leadership journey checkpoint element, the same is true for anyone being developed by the sustained leader.

Application: There is always room for improvement. Not everyone is willing to be "improved," and in many cases those trying to do the "improvement" are basing their assessment on their own value system and sense of "right." Such things cannot be imposed on others. The sustained leader understands that the development of the team members must be tailored to their specific needs. In many, if not most, cases people are not in complete agreement with what type of improvement might be necessary. Some people are sufficiently self-aware that they see the need and work to fill it. Others must be guided in doing their own self-assessment to reach a point where they are willing to undertake the improvement process. Others still must be persuaded, and such persuasion is often not well received. There are some who believe they are already fully improved. Not everyone can be reached, and it is sometimes impossible to convince them otherwise.

This is where the *Sustained Leadership WBS* can be an extremely useful tool in illustrating with specificity the improvement that is necessary. The development should minimally and initially span the five Level 1 elements of the *Sustained Leader WBS* and the essential leadership journey checkpoints. As a minimum the team member should be developed in competence to facilitate their next assignment when the current team's objectives have been met. Character, compassion, communication, and commitment likewise should be addressed in a formal and informal manner to maintain balance among the many elements (5.2.14).

The sustained leader struggles when they see a need for improvement that the team member will not acknowledge. The sustained leader also recognizes that they cannot act without permission. The proposed improvement may be rejected in its entirety. The sustained leader meets each team member where that team member currently exists and offers guidance in that person's development. The question is whether the leader has the true best interests of the team member at heart and whether the team member holds sufficient trust in the leader to consider their advice and assessment of the needed improvement. The sustained leader knows how to engender that trust and provide an accurate assessment of the team member's needs. They are also willing to invest their own time, talent, and treasure to help the team member.

Every person has a different set of innate skills and talents. Some have developed their talents; for others they remain latent. Thus, for each individual their further development must be individually tailored. Such development might include formal education, specific training, on-the-job experience, or some combination of all three. The sustained leader understands this about their team and seeks out the specific needs of each team member. Remember that one key role of a leader is to help each team member become the best "them" they can be. Setting the proper behavior that is to be modeled is an excellent first step.

In today's society, such individualized tailoring might be considered a form of discrimination, and a leader must understand all of the applicable laws related to such situations (2.1.2.2). Nonetheless, the sustained leader must conduct the necessary assessments and provide the appropriate opportunities for each team member to develop their talents to the fullest. Recognizing that people are differently motivated (3.13), the sustained leader must also determine what motivation is necessary and appropriate to encourage personal development. As noted above, this cannot be forced on a person. They have to be receptive to continuous learning (1.3.1).

Whether to develop is a personal choice. The leader cannot force a person to engage in development activities. They can perhaps demand their attendance at a class, but it is the individual who chooses whether to put the lesson to use and make a personal improvement. About the best the sustained leader can do is to create the proper environment within which team members can develop and become the best "them" they can possibly be. Like tending a garden, you cannot force the vegetables to grow. That is all part of natural law. All you can do is tend the garden and provide the right mixture of fertilizer, good soil, water, sun, and ambient temperatures. The growth is usually a natural result of that effort, but you cannot force larger pumpkins. The sustained leader is responsible for creating the environment that is conducive to the development of the individual team members, including their ability to function as a team. The sustained leader cannot force a team member to improve.

This sounds like me

A lot	somewhat	just a little	not at all

Additional Resources:
Patrick Lencioni, *The Five Dysfunctions of a Team*.
John Maxwell, *Developing the Leaders around You*.
Tony Dungy, *The Mentor Leader*.

Personal Objective:

Specific Actions:

Due Date:

3.10 Accountable

WBS Dictionary: The sustained leader accepts their role and is willing to be held to account for their actions, activities, progress, and results. Accepting the responsibility to serve as the lead for a team, the sustained leader knows they will be constantly tested across all the elements of sustained leadership. This includes being ultimately accountable for the team results. Being accountable means that the sustained leader accepts the duty, indeed the obligation, to report on these results, to explain what they mean (without "spin"), and to justify the results. The sustained leader needs to consider the audience and to communicate (4.0) these important assessments effectively. The sustained leader owes this accountability to all stakeholders, but all stakeholders are not identically situated. This requires that the sustained leader adjust the communication to the situation and the audience (4.2). Whether the results are positive or negative makes no difference. The sustained leader accepts their role as the accountable individual on any team they lead.

Application: The sustained leader must have the competence (2.0) to effectively communicate relative to their area of accountability. If you do not understand the nature of the task, it is difficult to establish appropriate accountability metrics. Thus, the description of the standard and the applicable metrics must precede the acceptance of the accountability. Many entities use a document, while variously called, which sets forth an individual's responsibility, authority, and accountability (see 1.1.2.2 and 1.2.1.1). In this context, the accountability needs to align with the responsibility and authority. Too often a boss tries to hold people accountable without having fully defined the responsibility and authority portions of the equation (3.8). A sustained leader makes sure that their superiors have done this for them, and in turn makes sure this is done for each member of their team. As Arnold Glasow has reminded us, "A good leader takes a little more than his share of the blame, a little less than his share of the credit."

Napoleon Hill

Make excuses for the shortcomings of others, if you wish, but hold yourself to a strict accountability if you would attain leadership in any undertaking.

Accountability requires the acceptance of the responsibility. When things go wrong, it is imperative that the leader identify where their leadership failed and what was learned from the experience. If there are problems with the team that need to be addressed, then the sustained leader will deal with them in an appropriate context—not in front of the leader's bosses. (And, yes, the term "boss" is being used intentionally here. Not every leader is managed by a leader.) It is the *leader* who is accountable. It is the *leader* who is responsible. And it is the *leader* who will ensure that the appropriate levels of authority and responsibility are obtained *before* accepting the accountability.

There are often circumstances where portions of the authority are divided among different organizations outside the sustained leader's span of control. If you have accepted the accountability, then you should assess beforehand where those situations might exist. Remember the concept of the negative stakeholder (3.11.2). There really are those who will seek your failure. This doesn't change the accountability equation. The sustained leader will use their capabilities of persuasion, competence, and determination to work with even the most recalcitrant of peers. Learning how to get along with and work collaboratively with even difficult people can be a key skill for the sustained leader to develop. Leadership might sometimes feel like playing dodgeball, given the directions from which challenges and attacks might come. The accountable leader accepts the good and bad that come with exercising authority. It is critical to the success of the sustained leader.

This sounds like me

A lot   **somewhat**   **just a little**   **not at all**

Additional Resources:

Douglas Stone, et al., *Difficult Conversations.*

Robert I. Sutton, *The No Asshole Rule.*

Personal Objective:

Specific Actions:

Due Date:

3.11 Manages Conflicts

WBS Dictionary: The sustained leader is not called upon generally to help when things are going well. In most cases the sustained leader is called upon to use their leadership skills when things are going less than optimally. In such situations, there typically exists some conflict with part of the team or stakeholders. The sustained leader must be adept at identifying and resolving the problems that arise. Conflicts arise for a variety of reasons, and the resolution of conflicts often entails a more detailed understanding of the various positions or interests that are in conflict. Many such conflicts have a natural course that runs to their final resolution, but not always without some help and guidance. The exploration of the divergent interests often leads to a greater understanding of the conflict and its root cause. The specific conflict may or may not deal directly with the team mission or vision and might be on the periphery of relevance to the team effort. Nonetheless conflict between or among team members will affect the team performance. The sustained leader engages with the conflicting parties to help manage the conflict to a successful conclusion—for the individuals and the team. This does not include the irrational emotional outbursts, or those that escalate to violence among the combatants, but does include the constructive development of their interests and an understanding of a proper reconciliation. Constructive conflict can be very useful to team dynamics, and the sustained leader captures those benefits for the good of the team and its members. Situational awareness (2.1.6) plays a significant role here since the dynamics within a conflict might not be readily apparent. As a result, the sustained leader also needs to gather as much information, data, and facts (1.2.1.2) as possible in order to lead effectively.

Application: There is an old technique that was derived from Dale Carnegie and more recently described by John Maxwell.[322] It is the "feel, felt, found" approach to resolving conflict or addressing objections. It creates a common ground and identity and makes the person to whom you are talking more receptive to listening. In its simplest form, you say, "I know how you feel and I understand it. I felt that way previously. Let me share with you what I've found." In this way you create identity with the person, establish both empathy and sympathy, and then share what wisdom you have on the subject. It provides a structure that is easy to remember and commonly leads to a positive outcome.

Elbert Hubbard

The man who has no more problems to solve is out of the game.

The sustained leader also learns how to use constructive conflict. Letting members of the team "battle it out" can provide a dialogue that is instructive for everyone. Certainly you do not let it escalate to violence, nor do you leave unresolved conflict at the table. Encouraging the free flow of ideas, even crazy or unpopular ones, almost invariably promotes better decision making (2.3.6). Sometimes it is less important what the answer to a question might be than it is that someone actually asked the question and forced the team to think about it. There should always be rules to such constructive conflict or constructive criticism (that truly is "constructive"), and everyone has to feel that they are being heard and not being abused or singled out. The leader must make sure the discussion is not dominated by the extroverts or those with more dominant personalities. Make sure the introverts have their say as well. Often in such situations the newer team

---

322 John Maxwell, *How to Influence People*, 137.

members will sit quietly, especially if they are unfamiliar with this management technique, or have only seen it done poorly. Encourage them as well, and invite questions to improve their understanding.

There are many different techniques that can be used to manage conflict. Exploring the parties' interests, rather than their emotional reactions, is advocated in the extremely useful negotiation book *Getting to Yes* and several follow-up books by the authors. What this suggests is that the sustained leader has to educate themselves on human nature. They need not be full-blown psychologists (that is probably a hindrance), but they should be well versed in personality types and traits and how people interact in productive ways. Understanding the warning signs of trouble within the team or even in the higher bosses in the organization will serve the sustained leader well.

This sounds like me

A lot   **somewhat**   **just a little**   **not at all**

Additional Resources:

Stephen Covey, *The 3rd Alternative*.

William Ury, *Getting Past No*.

Roger Fisher, et al., *Beyond Machiavelli*.

Kerry Patterson, et al., *Crucial Conversations*.

Otto Kroeger, et al., *Type Talk at Work*.

Personal Objective:

Specific Actions:

Due Date:

3.11.1 Difficult Conversations

WBS Dictionary: Difficult conversations may involve a variety of topics. They might include a disciplinary matter, or a termination of employment or other engagement, or matters that are deeply personal. They frequently involve emotional attachments and reflect the resolution of conflicts that may not be immediately accepted by one of the parties. They involve the transmission of "bad news" to at least one of the parties. There is a tactful way to approach difficult conversations, and no two situations are identical in nature or emotional engagement. The sustained leader is sufficiently versed in these variations to be able to engage in the necessary transmission of information that constitutes the "difficulty" of the conversation. The sustained leader is tactful, empathetic, perceptive, discerning, and insightful to the situation. This permits the sustained leader to lead the conversation through the difficult nature of the topic or situation to a conclusion that is acceptable to those participating. This does not mean that everyone gets everything they want out of the conversation, but that, as a minimum, a higher level of understanding occurs among the parties. Minimizing residual antagonism is also a worthy, but not always achievable, goal.

Application: Litigation often fits this paradigm. Lawyers are often considered the instigators of litigation. Many people are surprised that a significant portion of a lawyer's training is actually focused on helping people resolve disputes short of litigation. The pattern used, however, is instructive. The first step is the recognition of a problem. Sometimes the circumstances reveal this; other times it occurs when a suit is filed, or more commonly a complaint is registered. Each side then expresses their view. (In litigation this is called the complaint and the answer.) The dispute then moves on to "discovery" or the ascertainment of the facts as viewed by each party. Sustained leaders always work from the facts (1.2.1.2). In almost all litigation once the parties begin to come together on the facts an amicable solution is reached, even if it occurs "on the courthouse steps." Sometimes the facts are not in dispute. The parties simply disagree on the proper interpretation of the facts, or what principle should be followed. In a trial the jury is charged with ascertaining the facts and the judge decides the law that applies. This pattern of litigation serves as a model for resolving disputes in a less formal manner. In difficult conversations, the sustained leader plays the role of both judge and jury.

Once the parties have had a chance to see that they have been heard, even if they cannot agree with the resolution, they can accept it. It is human nature to try to avoid conflicts, and many managers fail because they just "try to stay out of it." Letting problems fester, or not taking definitive action to fix a situation confronting the team, is not the appropriate response from a sustained leader. Have a bias for action (2.3). Certainly the leader should not jump in prematurely. Judges do not go looking for cases to decide; they have to wait until a party brings it to their court. Sustained leaders should generally follow this model. If the situation has escalated quickly, however, or if persons or property are likely to be harmed without intervention, then the sustained leader should take immediate action. The sustained leader develops the discretion and judgment to know the difference and learns the skills necessary to conduct difficult conversations.

This sounds like me

A lot   **somewhat**   **just a little**   **not at all**

Additional Resources:

Douglas Stone, et al., *Difficult Conversations.*

Les Parrott, *The Control Freak.*

Personal Objective:

Specific Actions:

Due Date:

3.11.2 Deals Effectively with Negative Stakeholders

WBS Dictionary: Regardless of the project or the team endeavor there are always those who will benefit from its failure or lack of success. These adversaries are known as negative stakeholders. They have an interest in the endeavor, but they are hoping that the expressed mission does not meet with success. Whether they are looking to be the market leader, or to minimize their loss in an investment, or to displace the current market holder, or to capture the budget, personnel, or other asset of the project if it is cancelled, or any of a great variety of other motivations, negative stakeholders always exist, although not always in an obvious manner. A sustained leader recognizes the existence of a negative stakeholder and deals with them in a manner that is effective in terms of the ultimate project success. Learning to deal with these negative stakeholders is an important trait for the sustained leader to develop, and while the situations are greatly varied, certain techniques and tactics have been found to be useful when dealing with negative stakeholders.

Application: The first step is to be able to identify those who have an agenda contrary to the vision and mission of the team. They are not always obvious, and given the many different motivations they might have, they will not all give the same signals. Certainly if someone has suggested you "watch your back with Joe" that's a pretty good indicator. Past conduct can also reflect those who oppose you. Occasionally the problem is one of jealousy—they resent your position, your success, your comradery with "higher-ups," or they hold a more specific bias or prejudice. The possible reasons are limited only by the imagination of the negative stakeholder. Their reason for animosity might not be found in logic at all. The sustained leader must continually hone their ability to assess situations quickly and accurately (2.1.6). Don't be oblivious or remain willfully ignorant of the facts (1.2.1.2). These stakeholders will not just go away. They must be dealt with affirmatively.

The direct method of dealing with such parties is to simply confront them in a private non-adversarial fashion. The goal is to gather the facts behind the sentiment. It should be in private so as not to put the person on the defensive in a public setting, or to embarrass them. That would only lead to escalation of the problem, making it worse. And you do not start the conversation with, "You got a problem with me?" While many approaches can work, finding one with which you are comfortable is important. It is likely to be a tense situation, and you want it to remain as calm and focused as possible. Share the vision and mission of the team—what you are trying to accomplish and why it is good for the organization. Ask for their thoughts, their views, their opinions. They may immediately tell you why they hope your team fails. If not, probe by asking great questions (4.4.1) to see where their real issue lies.

From there, you must use your best negotiation skills (4.2.10) to diffuse the issue. In a best-case solution, you manage to co-opt them or accommodate their concerns in a way that will include them in the team's success. The discussion might engage them in such a way as to demonstrate that there are other possible benefits to the stakeholder, possibly intangible benefits.

Despite your best efforts, there are those who will simply never be satisfied, and this requires a different approach from the sustained leader. If they are disruptive to the team, remove them. If they report to a different organization, discuss the issue with their supervisor, or ask your supervisor to hold that conversation peer-to-peer. At a minimum, document your attempt to ameliorate the situation and find some resolution to the conflict. Keep your management chain informed and, to the degree appropriate, the team informed as well.

This sounds like me

A lot	somewhat	just a little	not at all

Additional Resources:

Robert Greene, *The 48 Laws of Power*.

Project Management Institute, *A Guide to the Project Management Body of Knowledge*.

Aaron James, *Assholes*.

Personal Objective:

Specific Actions:

Due Date:

3.11.3 Resolves Conflicts

WBS Dictionary: The sustained leader is adept at recognizing the root causes of problems between or among people and finding peaceful solutions to the conflict. They are peacemakers and strive to be objective in their views. They have an appreciation of psychology and the things that motivate people. They also understand the nature of alternative dispute resolution (ADR) and can use the tools of ADR to bring people to a resolution. It is important that the leader not impose their solution on the parties unless absolutely necessary for the overall good of the organization. Rather the sustained leader seeks to allow the people to work through their differences and come to a mutually agreeable solution with which they both (or all) have buy-in. This does not require the Wisdom of Solomon or even the use of unique solutions. In many cases the solution to conflicts resides within a more effective communication technique. The sustained leader needs a full quiver of solutions since the nature of conflicts are extremely varied. The sustained leader also must have good command of several other key elements including decisiveness (2.3.6), compassion (3.0), and empathy (3.4).

Application: Conflict comes in every conceivable size and shape. It might be a matter of who didn't empty the hole-punch, who drank the last cup of coffee without making fresh, or food disappearing from the community fridge. Or it might be whose responsibility certain project tasks might be. Some people are very conscious of their "turf" and resent others playing in their sandbox. Other times there are "negative turf-wars" based on the dilemma when no one wants the task and so everyone tries to foist it off on someone else. Rarely does the sustained leader get confronted with issues of workplace violence or external violence that intrude into the workspace, but being prepared for those eventualities is a wise investment in training resources.

As noted in 3.11, Managing Conflict, the first step is to identify the precise existence and nature of the conflict. Use your negotiation and persuasive capabilities, and continue to hone them. Allow all the interested parties to have their say, and maintain decorum and respect in all communications and from all participants—or remove them and their abusiveness from the discussion. Like a judge in a courtroom, the rules are yours—it is YOUR courtroom. As a sustained leader you know not to abuse the power you have and to treat everyone fairly.

One thing that the sustained leader must always keep in mind: some people are their own worst enemy in that they seem to engender conflict wherever they go. They are never happy, and most commonly it is everyone else's fault (5.2). These people either have a very significant issue affecting their twenty-four-hour day (3.7) or they are dealing with a more clinical problem that may require professional attention. In these cases it is often best to refer the matter to a professional either within the organization who is equipped to deal with such matters (such as an internal or external Employee Assistance Program), or to medical or paramedical professionals. The sustained leader knows when a matter is outside of their competence (2.0) or experience and will require other resources. It might be fun to play sit-com superhero and be able to solve any problem in thirty minutes or less, but it is not reality. Getting in over your head will most likely disrupt the situation even further and can cause blow-back on you, negatively affecting your leadership journey.

Any resolution reached should have universal acceptance by the parties, be documented, and have timelines to revisit the situation to ensure the resolution is being fulfilled.

This sounds like me

A lot	somewhat	just a little	not at all

Additional Resources:
Roger Fisher, et al., *Getting to Yes.*
Roger Fisher, et al., *Beyond Machiavelli.*
Mark Gerzon, *Leading Through Conflict.*

Personal Objective:

Specific Actions:

Due Date:

3.12 Team Builder

WBS Dictionary: A leader has nothing to lead without followers. A leader must be able to gather followers—to attract the right people with the right talent, time, and treasure to contribute to the vision and mission of the team. Without this, the leader becomes an individual contributor and not a sustained leader. The sustained leader has completed a comprehensive self-assessment (1.3.3.1) and has determined what skills and traits are necessary for the achievement of the team's mission and vision. They have assessed the available talent and chosen those who are best suited to help achieve the vision and mission, those who can best collaborate to achieve the vision. They build a team that can best optimize the results. The well-established sustained leader develops their own reputation and begins to attract the necessary, and the best, talent. Team building is not a haphazard activity and must be done with proper analysis and deliberation. The sustained leader develops the skill of identifying the appropriate talent and attracting them to the team. Similarly, the sustained leader works to avoid those who would disrupt the effective performance of the team and removes those who are not positive contributors.

Application: Assume that you have been chartered to create a cross-functional team to solve a specific problem. As you assess the team needs you see that you will need a representative from Logistics. So you go to Old Bill, the curmudgeon that runs Logistics, and ask him for a "volunteer" to participate on your team. Who do you think he will assign to your team, Go-Getter Gil who does the work of three people and keeps the Logistics department looking good in the eyes of the senior executives, or Lazy Lou who hasn't contributed anything positive for years? (Put aside the lack of leadership demonstrated by Old Bill in keeping Lazy Lou on the payroll.) Of course, you are going to get Lazy Lou, who will not enhance your team performance. Old Bill has just passed his leadership failure to you. How does the sustained leader avoid this predicament?

T. Boone Pickens

Leadership is the quality that transforms good intentions into positive action; it turns a group of individuals into a team.

Suppose you did a little homework to learn a few things about Old Bill, Go-Getter Gil, Lazy Lou, and the other members of the Logistics team. Now consider how different the conversation would be with Old Bill if it started with a statement of your team charter, a review of the team needs, the benefits to Logistics if your team successfully solves the problem addressed in its charter, and then specifically requests the support of Go-Getter Gil? The sustained leader prepares (1.3.1.3), communicates effectively (4.0), and acts decisively (2.3.6).

The second part of this is being the kind of leader who draws the talent of Go-Getter Gil to their teams. Are you recognized as a sustained leader? Do you have a track record of success and recognition? Success, as is said, breeds success. Demonstrating the characteristics of a sustained leader draws others toward you, giving you a higher quality slate of candidates from whom to choose.

Another thought is worth mentioning. In the 1980s Martin Marietta, an aerospace contractor that went on to later merge with Lockheed, got involved in a government investigation concerning a travel-agent subsidiary it had established. The investigation had revealed that certain employees of Martin Marietta made some bad choices and ignored certain rules involved in government contracting. Since Martin Marietta relied almost exclusively on government contracts for its business, the risk of being disqualified from entering into such business would be devastating. Norm Augustine was then the chairman of Martin Marietta and was interviewed extensively by the press. On at least one occasion he responded to a question about the "bad apples" in his organization. He observed that he would be interested in seeing the town of over sixty-thousand people that did not contain a jail. While every effort was made to prevent such elements from working for his company, some portion of the population is inclined to engage in improper conduct. When they are identified, and to the degree they cannot be screened out in the hiring process, they must be removed. The sustained leader knows what people to attract to the team; the sustained leader also knows what elements to remove from their team. Putting the right people on the team is important. Getting the wrong people off the team is equally important.

Woodrow Wilson

A man is not as big as his belief in himself; he is as big as the number of persons who believe in him.

Getting a set of diverse personalities to work together as a team is a feat of collaboration. It is difficult to get any number of people to work in the same direction. As our ability to communicate around the globe instantaneously continues to shrink the world, there are ever-increasing opportunities to collaborate. With some generational segments of our population such collaboration has been a given since their birth. Thus, even as the world absorbs more and more knowledge, becoming ever so much more complex, it continues to shrink and require more intense collaboration among team members. Kouzes and Posner note that "Collaboration is a social imperative."[323] They go on to note that companies will continue to fail, not because of technology. "It'll be a failure of relationships. In the Old, New, or Next Economy learning to work well together was, is, and always will be a critical success factor."[324]

---

323 Kouzes and Posner, *The Leadership Challenge*, 242.
324 Ibid., 243.

This sounds like me

| A lot | somewhat | just a little | not at all |

Additional Resources:

Stephen R. Covey, *Principle-Centered Leadership*. Note especially Principle #7. Patrick Lencioni, *The Five Dysfunctions of a Team.*

Personal Objective:

Specific Actions:

Due Date:

3.13 Motivates

WBS Dictionary: People do not tend to act unless something compels them to do so. And most actions taken by people are to further their own interests. Thus, the sustained leader understands what causes people to act in certain ways and understands that most people act primarily in their own self-interest. It is the responsibility of the leader to get the team moving in a single direction toward the accomplishment of its mission. This has been often referred to as herding cats. It is a difficult task. The sustained leader identifies similar motivational techniques that affect the entire team (recognition, professional fulfillment, etc.) and also identifies the specific motivational factors of each team member. By combining these motivational incentives, the sustained leader spurs the team on toward greater accomplishments than might otherwise be achievable. This requires a bit of sociology, psychology, and business acumen. It requires a level of "people skills" that must be developed for the sustained leader to be successful and to duplicate that success.

Application: James C. Hunter provides the following definition: "Motivation is any communication that influences choice."[325] It pushes toward a decision. It drives action, progress, and advancement.

What causes people to act in the way they do has been the subject of much study since the dawn of man. People choose to act in one way or another for reasons that, as of yet, remain a mystery to science. They can document trends and tendencies. They can argue over nature or nurture aspects, and certainly some stimuli may cause a portion of society to act in a consistent way. The sustained leader understands that, under natural law (1.2.2.4), the fact remains that people have free will. They can be coerced in some respects to act in a given way. Financial rewards and punishments have been shown to be strong motivators, and certainly indoctrination, whether religious or educational or political, can cause people to act in defined ways. Even so, people will always find a way to act against the predicted way. Why? Because they can. That's what free will is.

In leading a team, sustained leaders know there will never be a single specific motivator for all members of the team. Certainly the team has been attracted to the leader for reasons that are usually personal to the leader—strong vision, strong character, charisma, or any of the specific elements of leadership that draw people together. Establishing trust and maintaining that trust are important.

Gen. Colin Powell (Ret.) has noted that "Leadership is the art of accomplishing more than the science of management says is possible." This is accomplished through the motivation of the team. A study of Maslow's Hierarchy of Needs can be helpful to calibrate on the team members. In most cases, however, safety and security are not the real issues. Ideally the team members are at the stage of self-actualization, and this is where the variety of things that people will find motivational becomes incredibly diverse. It is the leader's responsibility to assess each team member and determine what best motivates them. One-on-one discussions can be helpful, but you may find that people are not certain what their own motivations truly are. If they have not found a dream or purpose for their lives, they may just be marking time and be genuinely uncertain of what would motivate them once they found a dream and a goal to follow. It is the leader's role to assist the team in making good choices and in finding their purpose. Developing them as leaders (3.2) can

---

325 James C. Hunter, *The Servant: A Simple Story about the True Essence of Leadership* (Rocklin, CA: Prima Publishing, 1998), 144.

help them focus and make good choices. As Eleanor Roosevelt has noted, "We all create the person we become by our choices as we go through life. In a real sense, by the time we are adults, we are the sum total of the choices we have made." It is never too late to start making good choices and finding what motivates you. The sustained leader guides the team and each of its members to finding their personal version of self-actualization and being motivated toward achieving it.

This sounds like me

A lot	**somewhat**	**just a little**	**not at all**

Additional Resources:

Warren Bennis, *Managing People Is Like Herding Cats*.

Adrian Gostick, et al., *The 24-Carrot Manager*.

Personal Objective:

Specific Actions:

Due Date:

3.14 Views Diversity as a Strength

WBS Dictionary: In today's society it seems that many people preach diversity solely for the sake of diversity. Very often these preachers (used in the colloquial sense) have a specific agenda and want to promote people solely because of a particular physical attribute. This would include race and gender. There are occasions when physical traits are crucial for team success. Basketball teams seek people who are tall. Football teams need large, brawny, strong linemen for the team to be successful. The sustained leader pays no attention to such traits unless they are directly relevant to the team's mission. The sustained leader looks for those who carry the necessary traits that will make the team successful. If that person happens to be tall or short, slender or obese, or white or brown or black (or purple!), or gay or straight, or religious or agnostic or atheist, or Russian or Arab or Asian, or natively speaks English or Spanish or French, or dresses stylishly, or dresses like an engineer, or any other physical trait that is completely irrelevant to the goals of the team, the sustained leader does not care. The sustained leader looks for people who bring a diversity of views to the table, who will help the team define its goals and contribute to the success achieved by the team. The sustained leader wants team members who will provide different and objective perspectives to the issues before the team. Unless the particular trait is relevant to team success, the sustained leader does not concern themselves with irrelevancies.

Application: Diversity brings many strengths. Ask any geneticist and they will tell you that successive generations of inbreeding produce and accentuate weaknesses in the gene pool. The greater the diversity, the greater strength of the species. When certain species have become endangered, one of the key concerns is the extremely limited genetic diversity of the surviving members of the species. In any team situation, the sustained leader must be similarly concerned.

Groups that are too similar engage in group-think and become unreasonably polarized. The sustained leaders seeks to prevent this. Each situation must be assessed on its own merits; the necessary traits represented by the team must be as diverse as is appropriate to the situation. The sustained leader remains cognizant of the available pool of talent and perspectives that can be gathered on the team (3.12) and draws the necessary skills, talents, and traits to the team.

Sustained leaders will seek people with diverse work backgrounds, diverse Meyers-Briggs® types, different strengths as defined by Strength Finders®, and other traits that will bring broad diversity of thought and experience to the team.

Laws in most countries prohibit discrimination. The sustained leader understands this but is not concerned about violating it because they would never make a decision based on biases that discriminate against a particular gender or religion or race, or any other factor not relevant to the success of the team. The sustained leader honors the laws, as is appropriate (2.1.2.2), and works to prevent any semblance of discrimination by any member of the team.

Many managers hire, intentionally or unintentionally, people just like themselves. This can create an imbalance in views and perspectives and ultimately destroy an organization. If for no other reason (and there are many), an organization requires diversity to prevent a lack of constructive confrontation and to provide a proper balance to its decisions. Face it: if there are two people in your organization who agree with each other on every issue, one of them is unnecessary.

This sounds like me

| **A lot** | **somewhat** | **just a little** | **not at all** |

Additional Resources:

Daniel Goleman, *Emotional Intelligence.*

Thomas Sowell, *The Thomas Sowell Reader.*

Personal Objective:

Specific Actions:

Due Date:

3.14.1 Generations

WBS Dictionary: The workforce consists of a continuum of ages. It always has and always will. Diversity in generational attributes is a natural condition. The specific percentages might vary, but there is, represented within the entire workforce, the full range of working ages. Certain jobs and activities attract a specific segment of the workforce. Many got their first job at a fast food establishment. Many food servers remain with the younger generations. Some jobs are more appealing to older workers, some of whom return to the fast food establishments. College graduates tend to have a broader choice of job opportunities, but economic conditions can affect these opportunities. The sustained leader understands that individual team members will have their own reasons for seeking certain positions. Employers might try to hire a younger workforce in an effort to hold down wages, while older workers who have a retirement income and some form of medical coverage could be more attractive for such positions.

Regardless of the numerous dynamics affecting the workforce, the sustained leader recognizes that generally speaking different generations have different needs and expectations. They cannot assume that everyone on the team has identical employment or activity interests. Nor can they assume that people of the same general generation have identical desires or needs. The sustained leader must recognize that the team members are to be treated as individuals and that their reasons for wanting to be part of the team will vary. It would be inappropriate to assume that *all* members of a particular generation have identical interests, but that is often the assumption made and is supported by much of the literature on leadership. The sustained leader stays familiar with that literature since it may reflect certain traits of any generation of which the leader is not a member. Even so, only the inexperienced leader makes gross-level assumptions about any individual within any specific generation.

Application: Discrimination is wrong and illegal on many levels. When age comes into play, some employers intentionally try to remove older workers so that the retirement either doesn't begin or even vest. This too is illegal. But it happens. The sustained leader respects the team members regardless of age and acts in the best interests of the team without regard to age. The leader who betrays the loyalty of a team member, or who acts *solely* because the law compels it, will never become a sustained leader.

Younger generations grow up with technology that is foreign to older generations. It is often wise for an older member of the team to seek out a younger mentor to help with technology. While the press likes to make broad generalizations about the generations, the fact is that they are not easily compartmentalized. People are being born every day. Each person grows up in an environment unique to the family unit. Thus, the generations are a continuous spectrum. The sustained leader understands that each individual must be treated as an individual and not necessarily as part of a group that may or may not define them as an individual.

This sounds like me

| A lot | somewhat | just a little | not at all |

Additional Resources:

Eric Chester, *Employing Generation Why?*
Haydn Shaw, *Sticking Points.*

Personal Objective:

Specific Actions:

Due Date:

3.14.2 Ethnicity and Gender

WBS Dictionary: There is much press about both gender and ethnic issues in society. In many cases it is less a matter of genuine discrimination than it is a matter of ignorance and inconsiderate actions. It is also true that very few people act in a discriminatory manner intentionally; it is more often based on certain values which are deeply imbedded in our upbringing. Conversely, those who fail to perform and are called out on this failure too often allege that it was a form of discrimination. Such false allegations do not further the discussion. It is illegal and improper to discriminate on the basis of ethnicity or gender. It is equally illegal to allege discrimination when it does not exist. It is not illegal or improper to discriminate on the basis of failure to meet legitimate job requirements or for failure to perform. The sustained leader understands both the legal and moral implications of discrimination. This is not to say that discrimination never exists—it clearly does. It is not, however, the only excuse for inappropriate or even discourteous treatment. The sustained leader understands the difference and treats people with appropriate respect, denying them rights or privileges only when based on a legitimate team-related performance reason.

Application: Kenny, a white male, went into a popular chain restaurant for breakfast one morning. The hostess seated him, asked if he wanted coffee, and left him at the table. Kenny took out his *Wall Street Journal* and began reading. As he completed his review of the day's news, about forty-five minutes later, it dawned on him that he had not received his coffee. He also had not had his order taken. It was as if he didn't exist. As he gathered up the sections of newspaper and headed to the door, the hostess asked if he had enjoyed his meal. Kenny told her that he never even got his coffee let alone a meal. He went down the street to a competing restaurant and had breakfast. A few months later a pair of black men filed suit against the first restaurant chain for their failure to be served in a restaurant. Kenny had to wonder—should he have sued the restaurant for his failure to get served? Was it because he was white? Or was it just a case of bad customer service, having nothing whatsoever to do with discrimination on any level?

In current American society, there is an increasing move to respect a person's "identity" as the person chooses to express it. A woman who was clearly white led an NAACP chapter for many years. While genetically she was white, she identified with the black culture. Olympic champion Bruce Jenner decided to identify as a woman and went through various procedures to alter his appearance so that he could be a she. Some people found this courageous. Others found it disgusting. Even very young children are being encouraged to "identify" in these fashions. Some states have recognized a right of a person who is biologically one gender to adopt the traits and practices of the opposite gender. This apparently entitles them to use the opposite sex bathrooms and locker rooms. This right seems to trump the rights of those who are biologically identified as that gender to any sense of privacy. This is all quite confusing to many very intelligent and reasonable people. What is the sustained leader to do in these circumstances?

The sustained leader will be focused on the needs of the team. The sustained leader will hold their own personal views and values, and their character will be reflected in the choices they make. These choices will never be based on group prejudices—i.e. they will never pre-judge a situation or a person solely because of their race or gender. They will educate themselves and their team on the biases that can negatively affect team performance, and will search themselves for latent prejudices. They will tolerate no discrimination and will mold the team and its individuals into fair-minded, free-thinking people. They will discipline the team as appropriate and without regard to any race or gender issues. This is difficult with prejudices and excuses too often displayed in society, but the sustained leader learns to deal with it all effectively.

This sounds like me

A lot   **somewhat**   **just a little**   **not at all**

Additional Resources:

Thomas Sowell, *Intellectuals and Race.*

Michael Gurian, and Barbara Annis, *Leadership and the Sexes.*

Personal Objective:

Specific Actions:

Due Date:

3.14.3 Myers-Briggs and Strength Finders

WBS Dictionary: The Myers-Briggs Type Indicator (MBTI) is a statistically validated assessment of certain aspects of people's tendencies in the manner and style with which they receive and process information. It is a questionnaire that allows the person to determine what their preferences are regarding their perceptions and decision making. This analysis is based on Jungian theories that suggest we all experience the world on the basis of sensation, intuition, feeling, and thinking. While the differences among people do not establish a "better" or "worse" standard by which to measure individuals, it does reflect differences in the way that people react. The Strengths Finder survey, developed by the Gallup organization, looks to ascertain those specific areas, among thirty-five defined topics, where a person demonstrates particular strength. The Gallup position is that people perform best in areas of their strength and thus should be assigned tasks within those areas. Regardless of the tool used, and there are many others, these two are especially popular and will most likely yield data that are relevant to the sustained leader's leadership role. The sustained leader appreciates these differences and capitalizes on the abilities that each team member brings into the team.

Application: Having a wide diversity of the sixteen Myers-Briggs types on the team provides a more balanced approach to a team's assessment of issues and solutions. It provides a diversity of approaches to the mission of the team and strongly suggests how the solution will be perceived and implemented by the organization at large. It also has some predictive tendencies when presenting information to certain MB types. While people can learn behaviors that run counter to their preferences, in times of stress they are more likely to revert to their preferences.

The sustained leader assigns tasks that play to the preferences of the individual. If a scientific measurement must take place a "senser" might be a better choice than an "intuitive." If an unpopular personnel action must be undertaken, then a "feeler" might perform better than a "thinker." These broad generalizations are not absolute and do not do the MBTI proper service or credit, but they do provide an illustration of the distinction among the various types. The sustained leader gains a proper understanding of the theories that underlie MBTI and can apply them in the pragmatic manner in which they were intended.

Likewise, assigning tasks within a person's area of strength as identified by the Strengths Finder tool will yield the most effective and efficient team performance. The sustained leader makes themselves aware of these assessment tools and uses the information for the better performance of the team. It is also worth noting that as the sustained leader seeks to develop other leaders (3.2), encouraging team members to conduct self-assessments (1.3.3.1) as reflected by these tools furthers both their development as team members (3.9) and leaders (3.2).

This sounds like me

A lot   **somewhat**   **just a little**   **not at all**

Additional Resources:

Otto Kroeger, et al., *Type Talk at Work.*

Marcus Buckingham, et al., *Now, Discover Your Strengths.*

Tom Rath, et al., *Strengths Based Leadership.*

Personal Objective:

Specific Actions:

Due Date:

3.15 Fair

WBS Dictionary: Fairness is a concept that we learn at a very young age. Children on the playground understand justice sufficiently to cry out "That's not fair!" when their sense of justice has been violated. Some even learn to make that claim whenever they simply do not get their way. Fairness means that the decision or action is made or taken without any bias or predetermination concerning the outcome. Fairness avoids injustice. The sustained leader learns to manage by fact (1.2.1.2) and to assess situations without bias. Decisions (2.3.6) are made on the basis of equity and reasonableness. Fairness is objective, not subjective, and some level of inequity, perceived or real, may be present in a fair decision. Fairness seems to be part of our human DNA as every individual grasps the concept innately. Some later try to manipulate situations or facts in order to get their way while appealing to a false sense of fairness. The sustained leader avoids such situations and such people, calling them out on their hypocrisy and demanding that fairness, in the true sense, prevails.

Application: The etymology of the word stems from the old English word for beauty. There is something beautiful to a fair decision or outcome. It might remind us of the biblical story reflecting the Wisdom of Solomon. It is true, however, that life in general is not fair. Resources are not distributed evenly; personal attributes and capabilities vary greatly. Some people are "beautiful," some are "smart," and some are born with specific biological handicaps that will affect their lives. Misfortune falls inequitably. The forest fire burns one house and leaves the one next door untouched. Floods wipe out entire communities and leave one house standing.

How is any of this "fair"? It's not. And there is nothing you can do about it *except* to make the best decisions you possibly can based on the information that is available to you. Some people get "lucky" in the market, and others have their entire life's savings wiped out by misfortune or illegal conduct of others. It's just not fair.

In some situations there simply is not a solution that will appease all the parties, and allegations of a lack of fairness will ring out. It is sometimes difficult to be the decision-maker in those situations. Leadership is not always easy and will call on the leader to make those tough decisions. We all can, and do, criticize some judges when we feel that a criminal sentence that has been handed out is either too strict or too lenient. And there are great injustices in our justice system that lead to eminently unfair results. Fairness is an amorphous concept sometimes, and the leader must appeal to their character and values to make the best decision.

The sustained leader will seek out the most equitable solution in all cases and strive to make the best decisions possible. They will not always be correct, and disproportionate inequity might result. In those cases, the sustained leader will make reparations as appropriate and extend a sincere apology (4.2.15). And next time they will attempt to make a better decision. As difficult as it may be to be fair in all cases, the sustained leader never stops trying to implement the fairest of decisions in all cases while refining their own character and further developing their values.

This sounds like me

A lot   somewhat   just a little   not at all

Additional Resources:

William J. Bennett, *The Moral Compass*.

Robert Heller, *Essential Managers: Making Decisions*.

Personal Objective:

Specific Actions:

Due Date:

3.16 Patient

WBS Dictionary: Patience is a virtue, we are told. So exhibiting patience reflects a virtuous person. A patient person bears slights or provocations; they do not have a quick trigger to their anger. Patience does not respond to being provoked, or petty annoyances. A patient person controls their irritation with people and circumstances. Misfortune, delay, or "bad luck" produces no complaint. In its simplest terms, patience means that sometimes you just have to wait. A patient person perseveres in the face of obstacles and maintains an even temper toward situations that provoke, whether intentionally or by happenstance. The sustained leader is expected to be this patient person.

Application: Children are particularly impatient. Some never outgrow that tendency, especially in today's "microwave society." As technology allows us to move ever faster and create more time- and labor-saving devices, we increasingly lose our capacity for patience. Fifty years ago, even a TV dinner had to bake for twenty-five to thirty-five minutes in the oven. When all you have known is our current microwave society, patience seems like a quaint anachronism. Nonetheless, the sustained leader recognizes that many factors control the timing of events, and they do not control all these variables (as much as they might prefer that they did!).

Joyce Meyer

Patience is not simply the ability to wait—
it's how we behave while we're waiting.

A popular wine company uses the slogan that they will "serve no wine before its time." Until we solve the constraints of the space-time continuum, we will have to live with the fact that processes consume time. People mature and develop at different rates. Political, social, and corporate situations evolve over time. There is simply no escaping the fact that everything does not happen on a timetable that we prefer or to which we attempt to plan.

Edith Sitwell

I am patient with stupidity but not with those who are proud of it.

Procrastination is the extreme of patience, and it is not a good trait for a sustained leader. The sustained leader does not confuse the two or use the excuse of patience to rationalize inaction (2.3). There are times when simply waiting around is not the best course of action. The sustained leader must know when to inject a catalyst into the situation to motivate (3.13) the team to act. This must be balanced with a bias for action (2.3) and consider all the various aphorism guidance that applies. Haste makes waste. Early bird gets the worm. A good idea implemented now is better than a perfect idea never implemented. Certainly these can be used to rationalize a future outcome, but generally it is important to act now from wherever you are and not wait for some external factor or event.

When is the best time to plant a tree? Thirty years ago. When is the second-best time to plant a tree? Today. Soren Kierkegaard observed that not making a decision is in fact a decision. Not making a choice is a choice, and "We create ourselves by our choices" whether done in patience and proper consideration or in haste or by default.

Another aspect of patience is Maxwell's Law of the Farm. Too often it seems a lack of patience causes us to pull the plant up by its roots to see how it is doing. This of course destroys the plant and you get nothing. And yet we see examples of this frequently. In many cases you must allow nature (and the natural law, 1.2.2.4) to take its course. The sustained leader will create an environment that is conducive to development, but cannot force the development—whether that is the progress of a project, the development of a future leader, or the changing of the seasons. The sustained leader will remove the true time-wasters (2.3.4) and patiently wait as other aspects of the goal come together while working diligently toward the accomplishment of the goal.

This sounds like me

A lot	somewhat	just a little	not at all

Additional Resources:
Seth Godin, et al., *The Dip*.
Chip Heath, et al., *Made to Stick*.

Personal Objective:

Specific Actions:

Due Date:

3.17 Encourages Failure as a Learning Tool

WBS Dictionary: A person who never experiences setbacks is a person who never tries. If you are not experiencing setbacks you are not attempting enough challenging things. When you fail in your attempt or in achieving your goal, do not treat it as a true failure since that only occurs when you stop trying. View it instead as a setback, not as a defeat, and create an opportunity to learn from the experience. Leaders encourage their followers to do likewise. Making a mistake or experiencing a failure of any magnitude is a normal part of life. It is not a serious problem unless you fail to learn from the experience, or if you keep repeating the same mistake or continue to create the circumstances for failure. When dealing with people it is important not to let them feel defeated beyond recovery. The sustained leader approaches failed opportunities not as a defeat, but as a setback from which things can be learned. Regardless of the person, the magnitude of the perceived failure, and the consequences to the team of the apparent failure, each situation can be a source of lessons for others on the team. The sustained leader takes advantage of these teaching opportunities for the benefit of the entire team.

Application: How do you develop good business judgment? The most common answer is education and experience. What is interesting about that answer is that education and training can only take you so far. Eventually you must actually perform—you must apply the education and training to the project at hand. The only other way to gain good business judgment is by exercising, or learning from others who have exercised, bad business judgment. You can't live long enough to make every possible mistake. You must therefore learn from the mistakes of others. Reading biographies, reviewing case studies in your field, and gaining whatever knowledge you can from lessons learned are excellent methods to learn from others' mistakes.

Tom Watson Sr. was the leader of IBM for many years and understood business like few of his peers. An often-told story is of one of his executives who was given the green light on a project that cost the company over $10 million. It failed. Prepared to tender his resignation, he was told by his boss, "You can't be serious. We've just spent $10 million educating you." Watson understood the value of capturing the lessons that could be learned from failures—even monumental ones.

Denis Waitley has advised: "Failure should be our teacher, not our undertaker. Failure is delay, not defeat. It is a temporary detour, not a dead end." Thus, we prefer to refer to these situations as setbacks rather than failures.

William Voit was another example. His rubber business, especially rubber balls, was seriously undone by cheaper Japanese models and then the 1929 economic crisis. He persevered and learned from his hard lessons. By 1946, Voit balls were a standard in schools across America. But for his earlier setbacks, from which he learned, he might not have been the ultimate success that he was.

Often the misfortune that befalls us is a product of our own doing. Whether it is lack of preparation, a bad decision, failing to shape the team properly, or any other element of this WBS, these lessons can be the most valuable and memorable. And everyone will experience them. The critical success factor is how you respond. Acknowledge the mistake, make amends and apologies, and capture the lesson to be learned. As Caroline Gascoigne has advised, "An error gracefully acknowledged is a victory won."

This sounds like me

A lot	somewhat	just a little	not at all

Additional Resources:

John Maxwell, *Failing Forward*.

Warren Bennis and Steven B. Sample, *The Art and Adventure of Leadership*.

Personal Objective:

Specific Actions:

Due Date:

3.18 Servant-Leader

WBS Dictionary: A leader who understands what it means to serve others is better qualified to lead others. Being a servant to those you lead means that you can distinguish between the team members' wants and needs, providing them what they need and helping them to better calibrate their wants. This includes providing the proper environment, the proper encouragement, and the proper challenges. It includes proper development of the team members and working diligently to develop the relationship with each one. The servant-leader models the appropriate behavior rather than lecturing, preaching, or demanding compliance.

Application: Robert Greenleaf is a significant influence in the servant-leader school, often credited as its founder.

> The servant-leader is servant first... It begins with the natural feeling that one wants to serve, to serve *first*. Then conscious choice brings one to aspire to lead... The difference manifests itself in the care taken by the servant-first to make sure that other people's highest priority needs are being served. The best test, and difficult to administer, is: do those served grow as persons; do they, *while being served*, become healthier, wiser, freer, more autonomous, more likely themselves to become servants?[326]

Greenleaf understood that the mission of the organization defined the nature of the service that was required and that the servant-leader's responsibility was to help the organization get its work done.

It is important that the sustained leader distinguish between a team member's wants and their needs. It is not the role of the sustained leader to give in to the wants of any individual. Like an indulgent parent, the only outcome of giving into a person's wants will be to spoil them like a small child and only encourage them to express further wants. Those who give in to the wants of individuals is no better than a slave. A servant properly addresses the needs whether the recipient recognizes it or not. Even so, it is not the servant-leader's role to force-feed the team member. It is still the responsibility of the individual to accept the service. As

---

326 Robert K. Greenleaf, *The Servant as Leader*, (Indianapolis, IN: The Robert K. Greenleaf Center, 1991), 7. Emphasis in original.

Colleen Barrett has noted, "I think you finally become an adult when you realize you're not here to get, but to give—to serve, not to be served."[327]

A servant mindset is in a constant giving mode. Servant-leaders do not neglect their own needs but are willing to sacrifice for the good of others. This was the model provided by Saint (previously Mother) Teresa. Her life of giving to the poor and under-served led to her sainthood by the Catholic Church. She noted that "The miracle is not that we do this work, but that we are happy to do it." Servant leadership is a joyful experience. It is not a chore or merely a duty; it is an act of joyful service. Elsewhere she said, "If you can't feed a hundred people, then feed just one." Do what you can do where you are, but never stop serving.

Ken Blanchard is well known for his leadership wisdom. As regards servant leadership he notes, "Self-serving leaders think they own their position. Most of their leadership time is spent protecting their position—what they think they own. They want to make sure everyone knows who the boss is. They run bureaucracies and believe the sheep are there for the benefit of the shepherd."[328]

The sustained leader understands their role as a servant-leader and the necessary loyalty to the team—to make their lives easier and more productive, to develop them to achieve their best, and to encourage each team member to be the best they can be.

This sounds like me

A lot　　　　**somewhat**　　　　**just a little**　　　　**not at all**

Additional Resources:

Stephen R. Covey, *Principle-Centered Leadership*. Note especially Principle #2.
Robert K. Greenleaf, et al., *The Power of Servant-Leadership*.
James C. Hunter, *The Servant*.
Kenneth H. Blanchard and Phil Hodges, *Servant Leader*.

Personal Objective:

---

327 Ken Blanchard and Colleen Barrett, *Lead with Luv: A Different Way to Create Real Success* (Upper Saddle River, NJ: FT Press, 2011), 119. (Colleen Barrett comment.)
328 Ibid. 131 (Ken Blanchard comment).

Specific Actions:

Due Date:

4.0 Communication

WBS Dictionary: Communication comes in four parts. The style (4.1) speaks to the forums where communication takes place. Every communication also has specific content (4.2), usually tailored to the audience. When communicating, the speaker relies on whatever charisma they may hold (4.3). The excellent speaker perfects the various techniques that make communication more effective (4.4) Communication includes the non-verbal component of communication as well; body language, first impressions, and general physical appearance all contribute to the message received by the listener or observer. Whether or not a person chooses to become a team member and follow a particular leader has a great deal to do with their perception of how well the leader has mastered the element of communication. The sustained leader tends to embody these attributes and maximizes their positive influence.

Application: President Reagan observed that "In America, we believe everyone has the right to speak. But even in a free society, you have to earn the right to be heard."[329] He was often referred to as "the great communicator." His prior career as an actor and his position as head of the actor's union allowed him to hone this trait more than other people. His incredible strength in this area compensated for his perceived weaknesses in other areas.

Communication *will* occur in an organization. The issue for the sustained leader is whether that communication will be managed or whether unmanaged communication will destroy the organization. A failure to communicate (with apologies to Cool Hand Luke) a desired message will cause the void to be filled with other inaccurate communications. At best, they may be frivolous and waste time; at worst, they will involve rumor and innuendo and be destructive to the organization's dynamics. The sustained leader never communicates with rumor or

---

329 Maxwell, John C. *The 5 Levels of Leadership: Proven Steps to Maximize Your Potential* (New York: Center Street, 2011), 235.

innuendo; in fact, the sustained leader will work diligently to quell rumor and clarify explicitly any innuendo.

Max DePree suggests the following: "At the root, communication in one of its forms, language, are commitments to a convention, a culture. Dishonest or careless communication tells us as much about the people involved as it does about anything else. Communication is an ethical question. Good communication means a respect for individuals."[330]

Some people speak in "code." This takes many forms and formats and could be as simple as simply "spinning" the story, being deliberately ambiguous, or speaking in euphemisms. In politics, some statements are supposed to be interpreted by friendly audiences as "dog whistles"—phrases that are code words for what is really intended that will be understood by the listeners. For example, a politician may be seeking the votes of a particular union constituency; however, they also need to suggest to the electorate that they do not really support the union. All of this tends only to obfuscate the issues and is often an attempt to permit the speaker plausible deniability regarding the statements—the ability to pretend they did not "really" say that. This is deliberate falsehood and is not a practice of the sustained leader.

Another form of this is "loaded language," which also comes in a variety of forms. Loaded language carries meanings beyond the specific words and the usually accepted definitions of those words, usually by implication. This typically appeals to emotion and is intentionally designed to draw upon those specific emotions, whether positive or negative. Critics will say the speaker is pandering to the audience. Eventually, the language may achieve mainstream use. For example, progress is generally considered as a good thing. Certain political parties adopted the word "progressive" to capture this good will. After all, who would be against progress? Over time, those who promoted progressive government generally supported increasing growth of government, even when it might infringe on certain rights of some groups of citizens. Similarly, if you claim to be "pro-choice" you backhandedly accuse your opponents of being "non-choice" while those who claim to be "pro-life" are alleging that those who oppose them are "pro-death." These are all examples of loaded language.

There is some similarity to the lawyer who asks a leading question—one in which the questioner assumes the answer and builds it into the question.

---

330 Depree, Max. *Leadership is an Art*. (New York: Dell, 1989), 102-03.

Circular language bases its premise on the conclusion and then justifies the conclusion on the basis of the premise. It is a false rationale. An example: I argue that it's wrong to kill animals because they have a right to live like any person does, therefore killing them is wrong because they have a right to life, which means it is wrong to kill them.[331]

A sustained leader communicates with graciousness and kindness. They have manners that they demonstrate at every opportunity, without exception. They communicate with dignity without stealing the dignity of those with whom they speak. In a word, they have "class." They leave others feeling better about themselves than they did before speaking. This takes a great deal of self-discipline and practice, but it can be learned. A sustained leader never has need for profanity, dirty jokes, or offensive statements. This is one of the key outward manifestations of a sustained leader. This attribute also helps to ameliorate the sensitivities of some who might be excessively, even unreasonably sensitive. Dana Perino quotes her co-worker Charles Krauthammer, who has observed that "manners are the keys to civility. Without them, we're hopeless. Manners make everything else work."[332]

Sarcasm is another dangerous communication technique. Most people don't appreciate it. Dana Perino says that "Sarcasm is like cheap wine—it leaves a terrible aftertaste."[333] It can bring attention to you that is not positive, as the line between funny and rude is finely drawn and not easily seen.

A popular meme offers the following perspective: *When I talk to managers, I get the feeling that they are important. When I talk to leaders, I get the feeling that I am important.* Which view matches the way you leave people after speaking with them?

There are several techniques you can use to improve your communication. As a self-study, take a company policy or an agency regulation. Consider how it could be improved if it were rewritten. You may or may not choose to share this within your organization; the important part is that you conducted an exercise to improve your writing. If you do not share it internally, share it with a trusted mentor who can write well.

Another excellent approach is to join Toastmasters, where you will learn to speak in a variety of contexts—both extemporaneously and formally prepared.

331 Ingram, David Bruce, Ph.D. and Jennifer A. Parks, Ph.D., *The Complete Idiot's Guide to Understanding Ethics* (Indianapolis, IN: Alpha Books, 2002), 7.
332 Dana Perino, *The Rest of the Story*, 209-10.
333 Dana Perino, *The Rest of the Story*, 219.

Your communication must also consider your audience, especially when there are language barriers. Language, customs, and idioms or dialects can be major obstacles to clear communications.

This sounds like me

A lot	**somewhat**	**just a little**	**not at all**

Additional Resources:

Deborah Tannen, *The Argument Culture*.

Harry G. Frankfurt, *On Bullshit*.

Harry G. Frankfurt, *On Truth*.

Anthony J. Alessandra, et al., *People Smarts*.

Personal Objective:

Specific Actions:

Due Date:

4.1 Style

WBS Dictionary: Communication occurs in many formats and forums. This element pertains to the various forums in which communication may occur and the variations to the objectives of each communication style. For example, when teaching opportunities arise, the nature and tone of the communication will differ from the opportunities where constructive criticism might be in order. The approach, the amount of preparation, the tone of the conversation, and the level of detail necessary will always vary. The sustained leader must understand all of the nuances of the various styles of communication and be able to draw on the appropriate set of characteristics for each one. Writing, whether a hand-written note or an email, or speaking, whether to individuals or groups, always demand their own styles. Using the wrong style demonstrates that the leader does not have a proper sense of perspective in communicating. Examples include writing when speaking directly to the person would be more appropriate, or providing a training session when a status meeting was the occasion. The sustained leader calibrates to the appropriate style in all communications.

Application: The use of different communication styles has much in common with entertainment styles and techniques.[334] Communication style, in turn, relates to the use of power. It's like a comedian who says "I had them eating out of my hands." In effect, his communication style held sway over the audience and he was able to lead them through his story to the point of the punch line. The best leaders also tell stories. Leaders must persuade and to do so they must have an audience—an audience who listens voluntarily and surrenders some portion of their power to the speaker. To have legitimate power, the leader must exercise influence; however, individuals have complete power over who they choose to allow to have influence over them. Those who hold false power, such as dictators, govern (note: they do not lead) on the basis of rules, punishments, and controls. It is intimidation and force that welds the power, not influence.

The sustained leader understands the need for voluntary influence. The sustained leader understands the power of a story. The sustained leader understands that communication style is a powerful tool that can lead to powerful influence. Using skills of an entertainer, the sustained leader can adjust their style to the audience and exercise influence. Without a proper moral compass, the evil leader can lead people astray via this misappropriated influence. This element does not concern itself with that moral compass since the skills are the same regardless of whether they are used for good or evil.

The best speaker does not want to speak over the heads of their audience or down to their audience. Kouzes and Posner note that "Words matter. They're as much a form of expression for leaders as they are for poets, singers, and writers. Words send signals, and, if you listen intently, you may just hear the hidden

---

334 "General George Marshall observed that in a democracy, a leader must be an entertainer."
   Bennis, Warren and Stephen B. Sample (with Rob Asghar) *The Art and Adventure of Leadership; Understanding Failure, Resilience, and Success.* John Wiley & Sons, Inc. (Hoboken, NJ: 2015), 34.

assumptions about how someone views the world."[335] For example, the person who texts a breakup message with their current significant other is clearly not using the appropriate style.

Long ago in the Greek theater or forum, there were no microphones or amplifiers. The speaker had to speak loudly and clearly to be heard. The same is true for the most famous debates and speeches in American political history. Such events required a great deal of yelling! Both Lincoln and Douglas were probably hoarse after their public debates. Even today, some speakers feel the need to speak loudly, even when they are using a microphone. For every speaker (yes *every* speaker; those who say otherwise are not being truthful), when they are called upon to speak to an audience, (whether a group of co-workers around the staff room table or to an audience of thousands in a large arena) they will tense up. Their vocal cords tense and lose much of their elasticity. Their throat goes dry and, in an extreme case of stage fright, their mind goes blank. This can prompt volume issues, causing the speaker to offer either a whisper or a shout. Sometimes both.

Shouting, EVEN IN WRITING, is offensive. People shut down and stop listening. Similarly, if you speak very quietly your audience will have to work too hard to hear you and will disengage. The speaker must calibrate across all these dimensions.

This sounds like me

A lot	somewhat	just a little	not at all

Additional Resources:
Dorothy Leeds, *Powerspeak*.
Dale Carnegie, *The Quick and Easy Way to Effective Speaking*.

Personal Objective:

---

335 Kouzes and Posner, *Leadership Challenge*, 57.

Specific Actions:

Due Date:

4.1.1 Speak

WBS Dictionary: Some people are naturally more articulate than others. Some people think well on their feet while others are not comfortable being asked to speak extemporaneously. There is a great variety of both natural talent and desire in this element. Nonetheless, a great deal of a leader's communication will come in the form of speech—whether in a one-on-one setting with a meeting of direct reports, or as the keynote speaker at an industry conference. As difficult as it can be to get in front of a crowd and give a strong presentation, it is an important skill for the sustained leader. Speaking well includes both content and fluency in presentation. It requires that there be a defined message and that it provide a variety of tools to permit the listeners, each of whom has their own learning style, to capture the salient points and instill them into their own thinking. Regardless of your starting point, this is a skill that *can* be learned and should be practiced regularly. Considerations of the audience, the environment, the content, and the appropriate techniques to use (4.2 through 4.4) will filter into how the spoken presentation occurs. Despite these variables, the sustained leader must become comfortable in presenting their views (and especially their vision (5.1.2)) in a cogent and compelling fashion.

Application: Seth Godin has offered some of the best advice on this element and is therefore quoted at length:

Fear of public speaking

Very few people are afraid of speaking.

It's the public part that's the problem.

What makes it public? After all, speaking to a waiter or someone you bump into on the street is hardly private.

I think we define public speaking as any group large enough or important enough or fraught enough that we're afraid of it.

And that makes the solution straightforward (but not easy). Instead of plunging into these situations under duress, once a year or once a decade, gently stretch your way there.

Start with dogs. I'm not kidding. If you don't have one, go to the local animal shelter and take one for a walk. Give your speech to the dog. And then, if you can, to a few dogs.

Work your way up to a friend, maybe two friends. And then, once you feel pretty dumb practicing with people you know (this is easy!), hire someone on Craigslist to come to your office and listen to you give your speech.

Drip, drip, drip. At every step along the way, there's clearly nothing to fear, because you didn't plunge. It's just one step up from speaking to a schnauzer. And then another step.

Every single important thing we do is something we didn't use to be good at, and in fact, might be something we used to fear.

This is not easy. It's difficult. But that's okay, because it's possible.[336]

Speaking in public can be scary. "According to research done by a nationwide communication training and consulting firm, many people are more afraid of having to give a speech than they are of dying."[337] With a little practice, even if you need to borrow Seth's pooch, anyone can become a comfortable and fluent speaker.

This sounds like me

A lot	**somewhat**	**just a little**	**not at all**

Additional Resources:

http://www.toastmasters.org/

Chris Anderson, *TED Talks*.

Chris Brady, *Splash*.

---

336 Seth's Blog 01/26/15 http://sethgodin.typepad.com/seths_blog/2015/01/fear-of-public-speaking.html Accessed 10/11/16

337 Kouzes, James M. and Barry Z. Pozner. *The Leadership Challenge*. Josey-Bass, (San Francisco, CA: 2002), 184. Citing B. Decker, *You've Got to Be Believed to Be Heard* (New York: St. Martin's Press, 1993).

Personal Objective:

Specific Actions:

Due Date:

4.1.2 Teach

WBS Dictionary: The sustained leader brings a great deal to the table. To keep this hidden is inappropriate and hinders the overall performance of the team. Thus, the leader assumes the role of teacher in many circumstances. Teaching requires the cognitive ability to structure lessons and to present them in a manner that the audience can absorb. The elementary school child has a fundamentally different learning method than the college student or the adult learner. The sustained leader must assess the environment and the audience to be able to teach effectively. The leader must be perceived as possessing more knowledge than the class and the sustained leader must know how to get the class to humble themselves (1.3.3) to be in a position to learn. If the student holds too much hubris, there is very little the teacher can teach. It simply will not be absorbed. The sustained leader also knows that people, especially adults, have very different learning styles and must present in a manner, sometimes repeatedly, that induces the student to learn and accept the lesson. Whether the class is one of substantive knowledge or what has become known as the "soft skills," teaching is still the same process. The sustained leader also knows that more is learned through observation and interaction than in a formal presentation format.

Application: In order to teach anyone anything, the learner must be receptive and willing to learn. Without that crucial ingredient, any lesson, whether it is considered education or training, will fail. While the decision of whether to even try to learn is that of the student, there is a great deal the speaker can do to facilitate that learning.

Everyone knows more than someone else. In other words, everyone has the ability to teach something to any other particular person. No one person knows everything (despite what some would like you to believe). Thus, there are always teaching opportunities. The sustained leader is both a constant teacher and a constant learner (1.3.1). The senior member of the team might need to learn a new computer tool. The mid-career team member might need to develop their management or leadership skills. The new hire may simply need some guidance on developing a proper work ethic. Every member of the team should be in a constant learning mode, whether that is cross training, general education, process training, lessons learned material, or leadership training and education.

Simply presenting material and expecting that it will be understood is a flaw of many instructors. The practiced teacher will use a variety of techniques to convey a lesson, especially with adults who have pretty well locked in their learning techniques. Visual representations, videos, group discussions, case studies, and auditory presentations are all part of the arsenal of the experienced instructor. As Ben Franklin said, "Tell me and I forget, teach me and I may remember; involve me and I learn." As a final step, the leader must ensure that the intended lesson was actually learned and can be applied when the student returns to the job. This is true in all teaching situations, including mentoring or coaching. The sustained leader ensures that the message was received and is properly applied.

This sounds like me

A lot	somewhat	just a little	not at all

Additional Resources:
Malcolm S. Knowles, et al., *The Adult Learner*.
Benedict Carey, *How We Learn*.
Spencer Johnson, *The One Minute Teacher*.

Personal Objective:

Specific Actions:

Due Date:

4.1.3 Mentor/ Coach

WBS Dictionary: The sustained leader recognizes that leadership is sorely lacking in most areas of society. From business, to family, to politics, to church, to service organizations, there seem to be too few leaders and too many pretenders. The sustained leader puts effort into mentoring others in various disciplines and leadership skills. This is in addition to their own continued development and constant learning (1.3.1). As a sustained leader, you have a strong sense of social consciousness (3.4.5) and a strong desire to give back to society and the profession (5.1.8). The sustained leader also knows the importance of the development of current team members (3.9) into new leaders (3.2). All of these elements require some institutional acumen on how to mentor others. This includes the necessary skills for mentoring and the devotion to the necessary effort to be a good mentor. It includes the establishment of ground rules and enforcing them with the mentee. It also includes the development of mentee specific tasks and goals, as well as the appropriate level of coaching to achieve the goals. It does not create a "boss-employee" relationship and does not seek to create a protégé that is a clone of the mentor. It seeks to take the mentee from wherever they are now to where they are the best they can possibly be in relation to their goals, personal vision, and mission. It should make them the best "them" they can be.

Application: The word "mentor" is derived from the man left behind by Odysseus to teach his son Homer during the Trojan War. Yet the concept has a name in all cultures. As noted by John Maxwell, "sensei," "guru," "lama," "maestro," and "tutor" all express the same idea.[338] There is another word that is NOT a synonym for mentor, and that word is "cicerone." A cicerone is one who serves as a tour guide for sight-seers. You must not serve solely as a tour guide. A proper mentor lives a life that models proper behavior. The true mentor is already a sustained leader.

---

338 Maxwell, *The 15 Invaluable Laws of Growth*, 219-20.

This does not suggest that you should defer serving as the best mentor you can be while you work to become the ideal mentor. You will continually learn as you teach. Most people who teach, instruct, or mentor on a regular basis will tell you that they learn as much from the process as the students do. "For many people, just because they want to enlarge others doesn't necessarily mean they are ready for the task. They usually need to do some work on themselves first. As in most instances, if you want to do more for others, you have to become more yourself. That's never more valid than in the area of mentoring. You can teach what you know, but you can reproduce only what you are."[339]

Good mentors often use the Socratic method of asking questions to help the mentee think through issues on their own. Rather than make assumptions about what the mentee is saying, a good mentor probes much more deeply in order to elicit a more detailed and thought-through response. As noted by Ms. Leeds, such questions illustrate the responder's reasoning skills and mental maturity.[340]

Mentoring is hard work. It is a skill that requires significant development. Not everyone is good at it. As important as mentoring is, there seems to be too little of it and much of that is not done well. The sustained leader hones their mentoring skills. It is critically important to the development of other leaders.

This sounds like me

A lot	somewhat	just a little	not at all

Additional Resources:
David Cottrell, et al., *Monday Morning Leadership*.
Tony Dungy, et al., *The Mentor Leader*.
John Maxwell, et al., *How to Influence People*, Chapter 6, pp. 97—111.

Personal Objective:

---

339 Maxwell, *How to Influence People*, 101.
340 Leeds, Dorothy. *The 7 Powers of Questions: Secrets to Successful Communication in Life and Work*, Berkely Publishing (New York: 2000), 204-06.

Specific Actions:

Due Date:

4.1.4 Criticism

WBS Dictionary: People seem to love giving criticism. They sometimes think that calling it "constructive" criticism it takes some of the sting out of the expression. The sustained leader appreciates the importance of true constructive criticism and the importance of criticism in communicating with others in a manner that effectively provides useful advice and commentary. Good criticism is almost always delivered in private and with as little emotion as possible. Corrective actions might be offered if the person being criticized is receptive. The sustained leader knows that a person has to personally desire to change before any change can take place. While the leader can mandate certain conduct, they cannot change a person's heart. To be taken seriously, the sustained leader must come from a position of moral authority, i.e. they must be respected and their advice must be based on sound experience. Correcting behavior is just the first step. Changing habits and deeply held sentiments takes much longer. It is all part of developing proper character (1.0).

Application: Communicating criticism is risky. It can be misunderstood, it can be taken very personally, and it can be wrong. There is often a large dose of opinion in most criticism and thus it must be rooted in a moral center, as perceived by the hearer, to be considered valid. The more serious the perceived need for the criticism, the riskier the exchange might be. The greater the moral centers of the two people differ, the less valid the criticism will seem.

Even so, the sustained leader cannot leave things that need to be corrected go unaddressed. Any failure in the team results will fall squarely at the feet of the leader and, as difficult as correcting behavior might be, correction must be undertaken for the good of the team. More importantly, it must be undertaken for the good of the individual.

Criticism received is a gift. It's not always a welcome gift, but it's a gift nonetheless. When you receive a gift, you say "Thank you." You might later decide to return the gift or tuck it on a closet shelf without using it; that choice is solely the choice of the recipient. At the time, a simple "thank you" is far preferable to an immediate emotional or visceral reaction.

When giving criticism, you must modulate what you say to the severity of the action causing the criticism, the immediacy of the problem and the need for the change, and the sensitivities of the person receiving the criticism. There is never an excuse to be rude, vindictive, or to engage in any ad hominem statements. The situation must be handled with sensitivity and compassion.

To criticize a person indicates that you believe that they need to change. Whether it is behavior, attitude, or any other perceived failure, the person expressing criticism must firmly believe that a change is necessary. It is, at heart, a sincere expression of caring. Here is a critical key, though: unless and until a person is ready to change, until they actively agree that a change is necessary— they won't. This is one of the principles espoused by Alcoholics Anonymous. You cannot change a person; only they can change themselves. You may have the power and authority to control their behavior, for example, at work, but you cannot change their heart.

In some situations people will question the person offering criticism and not take them seriously unless they have been through a similar life experience. That is often not realistic. There are some situations as well that are beyond the usual capabilities of the layman and the assistance of a trained professional might be necessary. The sustained leader also knows not to get too personally intimate with the person being corrected. Some situations invite mischief in this regard. Be scrupulous in such dealings.

It was Martin Luther King, Jr. who observed that "It may be true that the law cannot make a man love me, but it can keep him from lynching me, and I think that's pretty important." He knew that you can't change a person's heart; only they can make that change. You can, however, force a modification in their behavior, and that might be enough. Criticism can be tricky. Even so, it is an important skill for the sustained leader.

This sounds like me

| A lot | somewhat | just a little | not at all |

Additional Resources:

Marshall Goldsmith, et al., *Coaching for Leadership*.

Kerry Patterson, et al., *Crucial Conversations*.

Personal Objective:

Specific Actions:

Due Date:

4.1.5 Meetings

WBS Dictionary: Meetings are necessary and important means of communication. They are also a horribly abused method of wasting time and conveying the wrong message. Every meeting, by definition, becomes part of the corporate culture. How an organization's meetings are perceived will be a significant input to all stakeholders' views of the corporate culture. All meetings must have an agenda, a list of attendees, and minutes—what happened. Very often these minutes include action items and methods of accountability. The attendance list sends a message to both attendees and non-attendees—you are either "in" or you are not. This is a powerful message. Wasting peoples' time with unnecessary (or worse, boring) meetings also sends the message that attendees' time is not worth anything. Poor planning by a meeting organizer will result in a poor meeting. The attendees will feel (and become more) disengaged. The sustained leader holds only necessary meetings and only for so long as is needed to cover the agenda.

Application: The next time you are in a meeting, look around the room. While you might not be able to gauge it exactly, you often have at least some insight to what the attendees make on an hourly basis. Calculate the length of the meeting, the average salary, and the number of attendees. You will quickly see how amazingly expensive meetings can be. Ask yourself—were the accomplishments from the meeting worth the cost? You will find that most are not.

Ask yourself a few key questions about any meeting. What are the objectives? What do you expect the outcome of the meeting will be? A plan? A decision? An informed team? If you do not know what you are trying to achieve, it becomes very difficult to plan. Would a different format be more effective? Is the meeting just an ego builder for the boss where all of their minions come to pay homage and allow the boss to gaze upon them? In one organization, the employees often joked about the semi-annual weekly staff meeting. The boss was so often unavailable for the meeting he had scheduled that it was commonly cancelled after everyone showed up. The employees viewed the boss with appropriate disdain. Determine ahead of time if a different activity might be more effective.

The format of the meeting can be critical. Will you go around the room and make everyone participate? Will you just let those attendees talk who choose to, resulting in rewarding extroverts and diminishing the contribution of introverts? Is it a specific presentation? If so, what is the required outcome? Meetings should be scheduled with an appropriate amount of time to accomplish the objectives. If there are no objectives, there should be no meeting.

No meeting should ever be held that does not have an agenda. The meeting leader must adhere to that agenda. Diversions and distractions will prevent the accomplishment of the meeting objectives. If you expect someone to present or speak at the meeting, make sure they are well aware of the expectations. Every meeting should be viewed as an opportunity to educate, enlighten, or entertain. When appropriate, introduce some creativity. Use guest speakers (again with clearly defined expectations), audio visual, and sometimes a positive surprise. Your attendees will *never* get the time they spend in a meeting back. You owe it to them to make it worth their time.

The atmosphere of a meeting should also be planned and structured. All-day negotiations will require a more comfortable setting and possibly refreshments. Some organizations hold a daily "stand-up" meeting which, as the name implies, requires everyone to stand during the meeting. It has the tendency to keep people alert, move the meeting along, and help the meeting to end on time. People get tired of standing. All meetings should have minutes and, in the best circumstances, a defined list of action items and responsibilities.

If the meeting is designed to reach a decision, it will be important to make it clear how the decision will be made. Will it be majority? Will it be by the leader after input? Has the decision already been made with the meeting designed to rubber-stamp the decision? Ask appropriate questions and practice active listening (See 4.4.1 and 3.4.1). Close with a genuine thank you to attendees.

The sustained leader respects the time of the team and communicates efficiently and effectively when meetings are the style of communication that should be used. Limit attendance to those who truly need to attend. Manage the time; start on time and finish on time. Make sure everyone has an opportunity to participate and make sure minutes and action items are distributed in writing after the meeting concludes. Meetings can be a valuable tool for the sustained leader. They can also demonstrate a considerable lack of leadership acumen.

This sounds like me

A lot	somewhat	just a little	not at all

Additional Resources:

Chris McChesney, et al., *The 4 Disciplines of Execution*.

Patrick Lencioni, *Death by Meeting*.

Susan Cain, *Quiet*.

Personal Objective:

Specific Actions:

Due Date:

4.1.6 Write

WBS Dictionary: Everyone has applied for a job where one of the requirements was "proficient writing skills." It may seem odd that people with a strong educational background still cannot write well, but it is surprisingly common. The sustained leader must be able to express themselves in a manner that will be read and understood. Whether the purpose of the writing is to persuade, inform, direct, delegate, or otherwise affect the thinking of the team members, a sustained leader works hard to hone their writing skills. Unsurprisingly, writing is best honed by actually writing. Many authors report that they arise in the morning and write for a given number of hours, every single day. It is clearly a discipline. This element covers the critical skill of being able to express cogent thoughts in written form that are appropriately targeted to a specific audience. Clear, concise, cogent, and comprehensive writing is a discipline that the sustained leader gains and practices constantly.

Application: Writing skills are improved, among other methods, by reading a broad variety of materials. This not only educates you on the subject about which you are reading, but it exposes you to various writing styles. Some of these are good examples, while others are bad; however, they all contribute to your understanding of what constitutes good writing. What have you read that you remember? Who presented a particular argument that you found compelling? What have you read that actually changed your view on a particular subject? These indicators reflect good writing. Have you ever read something and suddenly found that you were a page or two beyond what you last remember without any cognizance of what was on those last pages? It is easy for your mind to wonder, and while it may be a function of your personal distraction, it is more commonly a function of bad writing. If, on the other hand, your distraction is due to a particular thing you read that caused your mind to wander more deeply into that subject, this may be a sign of excellent writing—it made you think.

Chris Widener

Writing is the gold standard of communication.
Learn to do it well and see more gold.

The other thing that improves your writing is, of course, actually writing. In many respects, it doesn't matter what you write so long as you are writing. Professional writers—authors, copywriters, screenplay writers, bloggers—hone their craft by writing in a disciplined manner. Perhaps they arise at 5 AM and write for two hours, or they start writing at 10 PM and write until they run out of ideas. Very often the writing will be terrible. That's OK. That will all be taken care of in the editing. Some people carry a pen and paper with them and make notes during down time. Others wake up in the middle of the night and make notes of some brilliant flash that came to them. The person who wishes to improve their writing will be prepared to write at any time and will engage in the constant practice of actually writing.

It does not matter what tools you use. Pen and paper, a pencil, a typewriter, a computer, and even a cell phone are all good tools if you can use them to write. Don't ignore the freedom that comes from using crayons.

Writing skills are not emphasized in schools, just as critical thinking skills are often ignored. This is unfortunate for many reasons, but especially because people with a high school education too often do not write well. Some cannot even read. Even those who are functionally literate fail to hone their writing skills and thus fail to communicate effectively in writing. Hiring managers will tell you that it is amazing how many resumes they get that do not use proper spelling or grammar. Those resumes are, of course, immediately discarded. Interestingly, hiring managers also opine that the one skill most lacking in many applicants and new hires is the ability to engage in critical thinking (1.3.9.1). The two skills are closely linked.

Clear writing and clear thinking go hand in hand. Muddled thinking leads to muddled writing. Muddled writing reflects muddled thinking. Whether you intend to write the next great masterpiece or simply write tweets and blogs, continuously hone your writing skills. Take a class at the local community college. Expand the types of materials you read. Practice writing. Make use of good writing handbook.

Marilyn Vos Savant, reportedly the smartest person on earth based on IQ test scores, has a fascinating book on proper spelling.[341] She reports that there is actually no correlation between those who spell well and the person's intelligence. Smart people can spell poorly and less equipped people can spell fabulously. But here is her

---

341 Vos Savant, Marilyn. *The Art of Spelling: The Madness and the Method*. (W.W. Norton & Company, New York, 2000).

point—when people include misspellings in their work, the reader **perceives** them as being less intelligent and will be reflected in the way they treat the person. Bad spellers, regardless of absolute IQ, will often be denied advancement opportunities and leadership positions due to these erroneous perceptions. Sustained leaders learn how to spell, make use of spellcheck on their computers, and watch very carefully for the traps that can be laid by autocorrect systems. The same is true regarding the use of good grammar. The writing should be your thoughts, not what the computer substitutes for your words. Learn to write well.

This sounds like me

| **A lot** | **somewhat** | **just a little** | **not at all** |

Additional Resources:
Henry Ramsey, et al., *The Little, Brown Handbook.*
William Strunk, et al., *The Elements of Style.*

Personal Objective:

Specific Actions:

Due Date:

4.2 Content and Audience

WBS Dictionary: When a sustained leader communicates, he or she must remain conscious of the specific message they intended to convey (content) and who will hear the message (audience). An unfocused message will cause confusion, and attempting to convey information that is inappropriate (as regards content, method, or level of complexity) to the audience will likewise lead to confusion or, worse, miscommunication and unnecessary activity. In addition to the audience acting on its misunderstanding, the entire process may have to be repeated, the prior work un-done, and the correct actions taken. Clarity of communication in the first instance avoids these types of time-wasting activities. Lack of clarity in communication also suggests that the speaker is unclear in their thinking. A sustained leader understands that clear thinking leads to clear communication. Conversely, muddled communications suggest that the thinking behind it is likewise muddled and will mislead and confuse your audience.

Application: A CEO speaking on a conference call to a group of investors will approach the subject in terms of things about which investors care. When speaking to their direct reports, there may be information that is important to them but not to others. When speaking to a group of new employees and welcoming them to the organization, the message should, again, consider the content and audience. The first step is always to determine what the message should be and then phrase it appropriately for the audience. It is said that most newspapers are written to a 6th grade level. Attempting to explain to the average 6th grader the intricacies of higher mathematics or detailed political philosophy is probably not useful. Speaking to these issues with a college professor seems more appropriate. On the other hand, a 6th grader can and should understand math principles communicated at their level of understanding.

When the goal of the communication is to encourage the listener to remember a principle, the most effective way (perhaps the ONLY effective way) is to couch the principle in a story. Whether the story is real or fictional, people remember stories. They become, at least on some level (even if only a visceral level), emotionally attached to the actors. This is one reason that biographies are such excellent books for leaders to read (1.3.1.1). Think back to your parents reading you Aesop's fables and Mother Goose nursery rhymes. Those lessons are still with you today. There is just something about a story that registers with the human mind.

The sustained leader learns to tell a story; one with a beginning, a middle, and an end. In many situations, it is the soundbite that is paramount. Whether witty, poignant, sarcastic, deprecating, or just barbed, the soundbite can also communicate effectively (4.2.14). One of the best ways to learn this is to learn to tell jokes—clean, wholesome ones with a sardonic point or a humorous twist.

Jokes may be corny, but they are a story nonetheless. They have a beginning, a middle, and an end. The punchline might make people laugh or groan, but that is not the point. The point is that storytelling is memorable. Often, a story is not something you can always tell off the top of your head unless you have studied it, memorized it, and practiced it to be able to present it without backtracking, leaving something out, or just totally butchering it.

Anonymous

I know you think you understood what you thought I said, but what you don't understand is that what you heard is not what I meant to say.

Mark Twain was a great story teller. Read his short stories or one of his many biographies where many of his pithy quotes are recorded. To tell a good story, you must read many good stories. When the time comes to relay a story of importance to the sustained leader's vision, you will be well versed in the technique and will be able to effectively communicate the specific message you are seeking to convey. Story-telling is a skill that can be learned by any aspiring leader and will be one more arrow in their quiver for demonstrating sustained leadership.

When considering your communication and its audience, consider the variety of delivery devices. Each might require adjustments to your usual communication technique. For example are you texting, tweeting, emailing, or placing a phone call? Is this a formal or informal communication? Is the message solely for the recipient or would it be OK if they share it?

A pitcher has a variety of pitches they can use even though one of them typically is their best one. Before each pitch, the catcher and pitcher communicate so that the catcher knows which one to expect. This variety keeps the batter on their toes. If a pitcher has only one pitch, the batter will always know which way the ball will be spinning and how it will travel to the plate. The batter's average should go way up, along with the pitcher's ERA! Likewise, you need to have a variety of communication styles and techniques. Just like the pitcher who considers the batter's stance, position, average, favorite pitch, etc., you can modify your communication style to your audience. It helps people listen more attentively and better retain what you are communicating.

This sounds like me

| A lot | somewhat | just a little | not at all |

Additional Resources:

Eric Harvey, et al., *The Leadership Secrets of Santa Claus.*
Dorothy Leeds, *Powerspeak.*

Personal Objective:

Specific Actions:

Due Date:

4.2.1 Values and Mission

WBS Dictionary: When a sustained leader communicates their values and mission, they are expressing the most fundamental part of their humanity. They are expressing the things that make them rise each morning and to which they choose to devote their time, talent, and treasure. It is easy to see where a person's values reside, as their actions are so clear on the matter, even if their words conflict. Actions will always speak louder than words in this area. A person with no values and no direction in life is not destined for success, at least in any contemporary measure. They might achieve financial success by some fashion, but they cannot be considered a success on a human level. A person's values reflect whether they are self-centered or other-centered. It reflects what their goals and desires are for themselves and others. Their mission explains how they have thought through these values and their plan to get there. Communicating that to those who need to know these important matters is a key role for a leader (See 5.1.2). A sustained leader must know their values and where they are headed. Those they lead have a right to know what values will be promoted and where the organization is headed. Unless the leader communicates this effectively and consistently in both words and actions, the team will become confused and disoriented.

Application: When a leader accepts the mantle of "leader," there is nothing, not one single thing, more important than their ability to convey to the team a clear vision and mission based on their values and character. The expressed vision and mission must clearly communicate the expected values of the organization, and a firm insistence that these values be honored by every team member.

Many members of the senior management of organizations often express amazement that the "troops" "just don't get it." It is true that many team members, like any cross section of people, will have both short and selective memories. The sustained leader accepts that as a given and pronounces the values and mission of the organization again and again. And again. And again. Pretty much without ceasing. Constant reminders, effectively communicated, are indispensable, ensuring that each and every team member "gets it." It is the responsibility of the management and leadership team, not the "troops," to make sure that everyone "gets it."

Values should not be expressed in a complex way. In most cases, values are very simple to express. They might be a bit more difficult to implement due the many vagaries of situations and people. Their expression, however, is simple. The sustained leader appreciates the importance of clearly expressing the values and mission to the team. He or she works diligently to express them in both word and deed. The team is watching. The team is *always* watching. The sustained leader is not fooled into a lax attitude. They model the behaviors that they want each and every member of the team to model. Did they wake up one morning, discover they were a leader, and began to model the values? Of course not. Their values are so fundamental to their being (1.2.1) that they have always exhibited those values, long before they were ever placed in a leadership role. When you live the values every day, your deeds communicate them. Your words are confirmation. That's the easy part.

This sounds like me

A lot   somewhat   just a little   not at all

Additional Resources:

William Bennett, *The Book of Virtues.*

Jeffrey Abrahams, *The Mission Statement Book.*

Personal Objective:

Specific Actions:

Due Date:

4.2.2 Positions and Persuasion

WBS Dictionary: The sustained leader will often find that specific positions must be taken and defended. This will usually require that others be persuaded to view the situation in the same way that the leader does. It includes the concept of building the team, attracting the necessary talent, determining various aspects of implementation of the strategic plan (1.3.9.3), and pushing toward completion of the project. In negotiations, there are times when positions must be defended; however, positional bargaining is not always the most conducive method to achieving win-win success. The preferable approach is to explore the underlying interests of all parties and seek solutions to meeting the maximum level of interests of both parties. This is usually referred to as win-win negotiation. The sustained leader will be called upon to exercise their persuasive skills to help others understand why these interests, or principles, are so important. This will require the use of logic, emotion, and clarity of words to present the argument (in the Greek forum sense) in a manner that persuades. The sustained leader seeks opportunities to hone this skill and to learn more about the logical and emotional processes used by people to reach decisions. This is not to suggest that the leader should be manipulative or inappropriately use their sources of power. Furthermore, the leader should never use their persuasive abilities to convince people to act in a manner that is against their own best interests. While there are exceptions to this when operating in a formal command structure, those situations must be truly exceptional.

Application: Experienced speakers understand that technique is important when imparting information. When you seek to persuade or to establish a position, word choice can produce an almost subliminal effect on the listener. The sustained leader will speak with affirming tones and language. Speaking with confidence, enthusiasm even, has a positive effect on the listener; push that too far, however, and you will be speaking hyperbolically. This extreme can turn people off and can lead them to assume an opposite perspective due to the breach of trust. Drama can be persuasive; excessive drama can produce the opposite result.

Thomas Jefferson

Amplification is the vice of modern oratory.

Booker T. Washington was born a slave in 1856. Leaving the Deep South at 9, he grew up in West Virginia. He worked in a mine and attended school at night. At 16, he attended school in Hampton, VA and, upon graduation, earned a position on the faculty. He was later invited to become the principal of a school in Tuskegee, AL for African Americans. One of his jobs was to raise funds for the school building. While his arguments were persuasive one member of the community, Collis Huntington, offered him a mere $2. By holding fast to his position that it was important for all races to "invest in the Negro race", Washington persuaded Mr. Huntington to ultimately donate $50,000, as well as money for new building later that was named Huntington Hall.[342] A black man persuading a rich white man to donate significant funds for the education of Negros in Alabama in that era was truly a feat of persuasion.

---

342 Elliott, *American Dream*, 178.

––––––––––– ● –––––––––––

Napoleon Hill

It will make a big difference to you whether you are a
person with a message or a person with a grievance.

––––––––––– ● –––––––––––

Aristotle proposed that there must be three related elements to be persuasive. As described by John Dickson, these are "*logos*, the intellectual dimension; *pathos*, the emotional or personal dimension; and *ethos*, the social and ethical dimension of persuasion"[343] (See 4.2.7 where this same concept is used in the area of credibility). Dickson continues: "*The perceived character of the persuader is central to his powers of persuasion.*"[344] Persuasion is powerful. It moves people to act. It is not enough to have beautiful speech; you must also be trusted. If you have not moved someone to act, you have not persuaded.

This sounds like me

A lot   **somewhat**   **just a little**   **not at all**

Additional Resources:

Jeffrey Gitomer, *Little Green Book of Getting Your Way*.
Robert Cialdini, *Pre-Suasion*.
Kathleen Kelley Reardon, *It's All Politics*, Chapter 5, Persuasion.

Personal Objective:

Specific Actions:

Due Date:

–––––––––––––

343 Dickson, John. *Humilitas: A Lost Key to Life, Love, and Leadership*. (Grand Rapids, MI: Zondervan, 2011), 137.
344 Ibid. at 140. Emphasis in original.

4.2.3 Proposals

WBS Dictionary: Leaders are often called upon to present proposals. These proposals may be related to internal operations, business restructuring (including mergers and acquisitions), modifications to the company vision or mission, or the process of seeking additional business opportunities or grants. A proposal is an act of offering something that is different from the current status quo. It introduces change, and many followers are naturally resistant to change. The sustained leader understands the pros and cons of introducing such a change, and delivers a message to the team that suggests that the change should be accepted or adopted. The message must encourage the team to implement the change or accept the business proposal, then perform in a manner that supports the change. Proposals are, therefore, a unique set of content addressed to a specific audience to encourage acceptance of the change.

Application: Proposals, it has been said, are the lifeblood of a business. No matter the purpose, the proposal is the starting point for persuading one or many people of the wisdom of the decision they are about to make in your favor.

Proposals are, therefore, a very critical and specialized form of communication. In some cases, the proposal is a written document or a "term sheet." In other cases, the proposal is a verbal presentation. Occasionally, it is both. There might be several rounds of discussions, negotiations, and revised proposals, and each one is an opportunity to further persuade the decision makers.

Politicians and some business speakers fail to articulate their policy choices. For many politicians, the argument seems to be "Vote for me because I'm not my opponent." Business people seem to preach the following: "We create jobs (when we feel like it) so trust us and give us more tax breaks." These are very weak messages. They offer neither policy choices, nor do they identify benefits to all of the involved parties.

Proposals must be concise and comprehensive. They should not assume the reviewer has any prior knowledge of the project. In some contexts, especially for publicly-funded contracts and grants, if the point is not addressed within the proposal itself, it cannot be considered in the evaluation. Proposals and grant requests must also follow the instructions and requirements of the issuer. These can be very detailed and have rigid requirements such as page limitations or items to submit with the initial submission. It takes a communicator with good persuasive skills, good argumentative skills, and great attention to detail to avoid being disqualified from the start. Being able to say the most with the fewest words is a key ability of proposal writers, and sustained leaders will develop this skill or find those who have it, as proposals are the life-blood of any organization.

This sounds like me

A lot   **somewhat**   **just a little**   **not at all**

Additional Resources:
David G. Pugh, et al., *Powerful Proposals.*
Jane C. Geever, et al., *The Foundation Center's Guide to Proposal Writing.*

Personal Objective:

Specific Actions:

Due Date:

4.2.4 Clarity

WBS Dictionary: The sustained leader communicates with the highest level of clarity. In some circles, there is a motivation to be obscure or to cloud the information. The sustained leader eschews obfuscation. That means that the sustained leader seeks clarity in all situations and does not permit political issues (5.2.3), hidden agendas (5.2.7), arrogance (5.2.6), or deception (5.2.5) to have any role whatsoever in communication. The sustained leader presents the truth as they perceive it without reservation. They further seek to make sure that there is no loss of clarity through the omission of pertinent data. In other words, they tell the truth, the whole truth, and nothing but the truth, to borrow a well-known phrase. Clarity demands that the word choice is appropriate for the audience and the content. The logic must be well presented, and the emotional factors that concern the audience must be addressed. Though bad news, or perceived bad news, is rarely well received, the sustained leader hones their communication skills to ensure that, while the audience may not like the message, there is no lack of clarity in understanding the message. This also demands that the sustained leader understand the appropriate use of an apology (4.2.15). A lack of clarity in expression strongly suggests that there is a lack of clarity in the thinking behind the communication. Unless the intent is to confuse the issues (a practice in which the sustained leader never engages), the message must always be as clear as possible for the intended audience.

Application: The sustained leader always seeks clear communication. It is always easier to get the correct message into circulation from the outset than to have to return to the topic and provide further clarification. In those instances, the speaker must also generally work to undo the misinterpretation and reconfirm the intended message. This unnecessary effort can be avoided with initially clear communications.

Sadly, there are often intentionally unclear communications, or communications that are absolutely clear—just false. Promises were made that everyone would be able to keep their insurance and keep their doctor under the US Affordable Care Act. There was no lack of clarity to these statements. They were simply incorrect, and led to greater confusion and lack of clarity overall. On another subject, while testifying before Congress, Federal Reserve Board Chairman Alan Greenspan was heard saying "I guess I should warn you, if I turn out to be particularly clear, you've probably misunderstood what I've said."[345]

When testifying in court, it is critical that all witness answers are completely clear. Sometimes the witness must ask the lawyer conducting the examination to clarify the question in order to avoid confusion. The court is seeking the facts and it is only with crystal clarity in the process of gathering the clear and correct facts that the court can be certain of reaching the right resolution of the case. Clarity is paramount, and all speakers should seek the utmost level of clarity in their communications.

---

345 Parietti, Jeff. *Stupid Business Quotes*, 103.

Clarity must also consider the audience. Explaining the intricacies of a new theoretical physics discovery to a room full of theoretical physicists will have a different approach to clarity than welcoming first graders to their first day of school. The sustained leader will always adjust the required level of clarity to the audience, neither talking down to nor over the heads of their audience.

A lack of clarity will muddle your goals, your vision, your writing, and your thinking. It will confuse your followers and result in considerable re-work, re-direction, and possibly failure of the mission. It is the responsibility of the sustained leader to ensure beyond any shadow of a doubt that they are communicating clearly and that the listener is clearly receiving the message. Care in communicating clearly will save countless hours and even relationships that become stressed when misunderstandings occur.

Brian Tracy once said that "The clearer you are about the consequences of your actions and the more intensely you desire to enjoy the consequences that your behaviors may lead to, the more motivated you will be." GE CEO Jeffrey Immelt is more emphatic: "Every leader needs to clearly explain the top three things the organization is working on. If you can't, you are not leading well." Finally, cleric and educator Theodore Hesburgh offered this astute metaphor on the subject: "The very essence of leadership is that you have to have a vision. It's got to be a vision you articulate clearly and forcefully on every occasion. You can't blow an uncertain trumpet."

The importance of clarity in communication is essential for successful leadership results. The sustained leader ensures that they are thinking clearly, communicating clearly, and expressing their expectations clearly. Anything less is a failure in leadership.

This sounds like me

A lot	somewhat	just a little	not at all

Additional Resources:
William Bennett, *Death of Outrage*.
Robert Bly, *Elements of Business Writing*.
Peggy Noonan, *On Speaking Well*.

Personal Objective:

Specific Actions:

Due Date:

4.2.5 Conviction

WBS Dictionary: The sustained leader always speaks with conviction. This means that they are personally convinced of the veracity of their communication and that it is the best choice among all available options. Whether it is a change, a proposal, or a statement of values or of mission, the sustained leader is fully convinced that the message being delivered is correct on all levels of consideration. It is a belief that is firm or fixed. There may still be room for alternative choices based on a standard of reasonableness; however, for the current time and situation, the sustained leader communicates with conviction. If they are not yet to that point in their own mind, then it is clear that a decision has not been made and further discussion or research must be conducted. Conviction involves moving the audience through argument, evidence, or emotion to a point of agreement, or at least consent. It calls for a consensus on a course of action. Without conviction on the part of the sustained leader, no one will be convinced.

Application: The sustained leader is unequivocally convinced that the vision that has been set for the organization or team is absolutely correct. There is no doubt, second-guessing, or deviation from that vision. This is what it means to hold conviction.

Walter Lippman has suggested that "The final test of a leader is that he leaves behind him in other men, the conviction and the will to carry on." The sustained leader must not only feel that level of conviction, but be able to transfer it to the other team members. How? By developing strong relationships and capitalizing on their persuasive ability. Jack and Suzy Welch have noted that "Socialization takes intentionality"[346] This type of socialization requires that the sustained leader fill people in, stay in touch, and keep the lines of communication open. It does not happen by accident. Instilling a sense of conviction in the team, and in the sustained leader, takes directed and concerted effort.

Many other WBS elements are dependent on the leader's level of conviction. Perseverance, integrity, goal-setting, motivation, and others depend on the sustained leader's level of conviction to the vision and mission. If you do not believe that your team or organization holds a vision and mission that you can unequivocally support, you should not be leading that group. Fashion designer Ralph Lauren suggested that "A leader has the vision and conviction that a dream can be achieved. He inspires the power and energy to get it done." If you do not hold that belief, move to another leadership position. It becomes a matter of integrity.

When a lawyer writes a brief for a court case, they must adopt the perspective that their client is correct and has a right to receive the relief requested. There is no room for equivocation in this belief. The lawyer must be fully convinced at this point. Only then can they write clear and convincing arguments that fulfill that belief.

A sustained leader's conviction must be absolute. Any chink in that armor can prove disastrous to the leadership objectives.

This sounds like me

A lot   **somewhat**   **just a little**   **not at all**

Additional Resources:
Girvan Peck, *Writing Persuasive Briefs*.
Albert Mohler, *The Conviction to Lead*.

Personal Objective:

---

346 Welch, Jack and Suzy. *The Real Life MBA: Your No-BS Guide to Winning the Game, Building a Team, and Growing Your Career*, (New York: Harper Collins, 2015), 166.

Specific Actions:

Due Date:

4.2.6 Consistency of Message

WBS Dictionary: The sustained leader does not shift as the sands on the shore do. There is always, of course, room for re-direction, mid-course corrections, or a well-considered change in the vision or mission of an organization. Such major shifts are undertaken only after due consideration and ultimate buy-in from those affected. Even then, the process of decision making must be well communicated and disciplined, leading to a consistency in the messaging process. Once a decision has been reached, consistency in the message from a sustained leader is critical to engaging the team in the effort. Inconsistency damages credibility (4.2.7). Consistency is the steadfast adherence to principles, even in the face of opposition. The sustained leader is consistent in the content of their messaging, regardless of the audience.

Application: In trials, opposing attorneys will often enlist the aid of expert witnesses. These are people who hold special expertise or credentials related to the issues in the trial. Their role is to help others who are not so well-versed in the technology or subject matter to better understand the legal issue in the context of the laws of physics, a body of regulations, or the usual practice within a profession. If the expert, or any witness for that matter, tells the court one thing in the first instance and then changes their story in the second instance, their message has become inconsistent. They have damaged their credibility and the audience is unsure which version, if either, they should believe. Their lack of consistency makes almost everything they have or will say suspect.

Along with gossiping about subordinates to each other, another leadership "don't" that really kills trust is having different stories about the business for different audiences. The fact is, every leader is called upon to deliver status reports to different constituencies. It doesn't make any difference if you're a team leader and your constituents consist of (a) your boss, (b) three colleagues, and (c) a handful of clients, or if you're a CEO and your constituents include the board, Wall Street analysists, journalists, and so on. For any leader at any level, having multiple "concerned parties" is perfectly routine. What can't be routine is a substantive jiggering of the story for each group—a jiggering in emphasis, level of optimism, or data shared. Trust-building leaders tell the same story to everyone all the time. To do otherwise is a killer, especially now, when information has no boundaries or walls. Everyone hears everything, and variations or discrepancies or attempts to spin loom large indeed. So peddle in consistencies only, and enjoy the confidence in you that blows back at you from all quarters because of it. [347]

Sustained leaders never communicate inconsistently. The message is always essentially the same, adjusted only for the specific audience. Whenever an inconsistency is perceived, the first thing the sustained leader must do is remain quiet and reconsider their thinking. It is possible that they have not thought the situation through to a definitive conclusion. In such circumstances, saying nothing is better than being inconsistent. In some cases, the sustained leader may have to admit that they don't know something. The sustained leader is not afraid to admit that they either need to gather more facts or need to reconsider some elements of their thought process. It's even OK to admit that you just don't know or can't recall—if that's the truth. A sustained leader is always honest. At the earliest opportunity, clarify the inconsistency or the misperception and move on.

This sounds like me

A lot	somewhat	just a little	not at all

Additional Resources:

Robert Cialdini, *Pre-Suasion*.

Deborah Tannen, *Talking from 9 to 5*.

---

347 Welch, Jack and Suzy. *The Real Life MBA: Your No-BS Guide to Winning the Game, Building a Team, and Growing Your Career*, (New York: Harper Collins, 2015), 136-37.

Personal Objective:

Specific Actions:

Due Date:

4.2.7 Credible

WBS Dictionary: It was previously noted that competence contributes to credibility (2.0), but it takes more than competence to engage the team in accepting the leader as credible. Credibility is dealing honestly with the facts and acknowledging weakness in their positions. Credibility is rooted in truthfulness without any carelessness or reckless disregard for the truth. As additional facts come to light, the level of truthfulness of the message is tested and it should stand up. Credible people keep their word; they become known for truthfulness and reliability. It is relatively easy to destroy your own credibility with one small lapse of attention to the details of the truth. As the saying goes, "One 'oh shoot' destroys a thousand 'atta boy's'." The sustained leader does not let this happen. Credibility is in the details. Credibility never stretches or strains the truth. Credibility dictates that when your word is given, you follow through. Credibility is ultimately a question of character.

Application: People can (and do) stand up in front of others and spout all sorts of nonsense. It is possible that they actually believe what they are saying, but they are wrong. They have been selective with their facts; they use linguistic ploys like the strawman fallacy or they speak in generalities, lumping disparate groups together. What these people lack is credibility.

Aristotle suggested that the persuasive speaker holds three attributes: logos, pathos, and ethos. By using the right words, with the correct level of passion, all within a proper ethical framework, credibility is established and people can be persuaded. You can still ruin your own credibility, however, even if you hold all three, through a variety of missteps. Some may be flagrant, such as denying that you have an objective and later having emails that reveal a hidden objective disclosed (5.2.7). Others are less obvious; for example, when you tell a "little white lie" and those you told later find out the truth. Even with the best of intentions, an inattention to truth will be your undoing. Recall the fable of the boy who cried wolf. He did it several times just to see the townspeople come running. Then when the wolf appeared, he cried "wolf" and no one responded. He lost his credibility.

When the sustained leader is uncertain, he or she says nothing or openly admits that they don't know. There is no shame in not knowing; if you feel such shame, consider the element on humility (1.3.3). Such pride and hubris has no place in the sustained leader. In fact, the wisest of men is more likely to discover that the more they learn, the more they discover how much is unknown to them.

Consider the oath that a witness takes in a court of law. "I promise to tell the truth, the whole truth, and nothing but the truth." These are the major elements of credibility, as the court wants only credible witnesses. As a sustained leader you will pay close attention to the truth in all of its details. You will communicate only the truth and be the credible witness in all situations.

This sounds like me

A lot　　　　　　**somewhat**　　　　　　**just a little**　　　　　　**not at all**

Additional Resources:
James M. Kouzes, et al., *Credibility*.
Bill George, et al., *Authentic Leadership*.
Robert Goffee, et al., *Why Should Anyone Be Led by You?*

Personal Objective:

Specific Actions:

Due Date:

4.2.8 Feedback

WBS Dictionary: Communicating feedback is an important, yet frequently neglected, role of a leader. Both people and projects require feedback, both positive and negative. Too often evaluators focus only on the negative. Feedback is more of a continuous loop of information that permits real-time, mid-course corrections of tasks or a person's activities. It is best delivered close in time to the activity being evaluated and in a consistent fashion. Feedback must be calibrated against the standards under which the activity was initiated. Providing consistent feedback has a great deal to do with the team's overall success. By providing feedback to the team or any individual in the team, each participant can adjust the performance outcome and improve it. This is particularly true in repetitive cycles of performance, but that is not the only way it can enhance results. Consistent feedback shows that the leader is paying attention. Frederick Taylor demonstrated in his management experiments of the 1900's that performance improves simply when someone is paying attention. Feedback provides assurance and encourages greater performance by the team and its members.

Application: Feedback is the oft-forgotten last step in any system, and its purpose is to improve the system and move the team forward. In any system diagram, there will be a planning stage, an execution stage, and a closeout stage. The closeout stage is the stage to inject feedback, or lessons learned, back into the planning cycle. It permits continuous improvement. Without that closing of the loop, the same process will be repeated over and over without any change. Since circumstances will change and the environment of any system will change, failing to account for process improvements and efficiencies will make the process less useful, and perhaps even harmful.

The same is true with people. Without feedback, sometimes coupled with tough love (3.4.4), people will often remain unaware of a need to change or of options to change their behavior. The sustained leader practices effective feedback communication techniques that are customized to the individual receiving the feedback. This requires a certain sensitivity to the perceptions of the person receiving the feedback, even if those sensitivities are extreme or perhaps unreasonable. Typically, many organizations require a periodic review that provides feedback. Unfortunately, too often these are delayed or, worse, drafted by the person being reviewed. Providing feedback is exclusively the role of the leader; team members should not be denied that benefit.

Communicating feedback can often be difficult when the feedback is related to an individual's performance and not an inanimate system. Even then, systems are run by people, so criticizing some aspect of the system invariably criticizes a person. When a particular adjustment (i.e. change) must be made, the recipient of the precipitating feedback might not be receptive. The process by which the news is delivered is crucial.

Many organizations attempt to collect feedback or lessons-learned into a database. The goal is to make relevant information available for similar projects in the future in order to improve its performance. Unfortunately, these are databases that can't be searched or are improperly indexed. Data that are formatted inconsistently prevents proper indexing. That data is useless if it cannot be located and wastes time if the relevancy cannot be easily identified. Such lessons-learned data also must be identified to clarify whether the lesson relates to a failure in the plan or in the execution. Additionally, some events are anomalous and might have minimal influence on future efforts, even if the projects are remarkably similar.

The sustained leader maintains consistent attention to what is happening with the people and the projects under their leadership. They will conduct detailed analysis of these situations (2.1.6) and offer constructive feedback. They will also record events and progress in order to assist in informing future leaders of possible errors or pitfalls of their projects.

This sounds like me

| A lot | somewhat | just a little | not at all |

Additional Resources:

Marcus Buckingham, et al., *Now, Discover Your Strengths.*

Harvard Press, *Motivating People for Improved Performance.*

Personal Objective:

Specific Actions:

Due Date:

4.2.9 Tactful

WBS Dictionary: Tact is the use of words and phrases in your communication that reflects a keen sense of what to say so as to avoid offending the audience. It is true that some people are very easily offended and that some feign offense for political or tactical advantage. The sustained leader develops the skill of dealing with delicate situations in a manner that works through the sensitivities of the participants. Tact includes the concepts of proper taste for the audience and sensitivity to their perceptions. It includes poise, diplomacy, and the fostering of good will. It is often couched in what might be called "window dressing" that makes the acceptance of news, data, or information that might be perceived as negative to some of the audience more acceptable. The sustained leader learns to express himself or herself with the skill and judgement that is necessary to handle delicate situations.

Application: An old bumper sticker said "Tact is being able to tell someone where to go in such a way that they actually look forward to the trip." Leaders often must present sensitive data or what will be perceived by the audience as bad news. This may be in groups or one-on-one. Each situation will require a slightly modified approach. Each audience member, or audience of one, will have different sensitivities and cultural backgrounds that will affect their perceptions. The sustained leader is sensitive to these differences.

The sustained leader develops a very keen sense of their audience (4.2.12) in order to calibrate on what might offend them. Using words that are appropriate and tasteful to the situation requires that the sustained leader understand that the toast at the bachelor party is different than the one delivered at the wedding, or that eulogies are generally not the appropriate forum for a stand-up routine. While these are extreme examples, most people can think of situations where the speaker violated this basic requirement of tact.

In today's society, where people often feign offense, this can be a difficult challenge. Language that just a few years or decades ago was acceptable has now become inappropriate, and as soon as you think you have learned the rules—they change. This can be very dangerous ground. At the opposite extreme, some conduct or speech should be confronted, but as William J. Bennet has noted, we seem to have lost our ability to be outraged at egregious conduct.[348] It is up to the sustained leader to re-establish the appropriate baseline for both outrage and offense. The appropriate use of tact can facilitate that return to normalcy.

This sounds like me

A lot	**somewhat**	**just a little**	**not at all**

Additional Resources:

William Bennett, *Death of Outrage.*

Anne B. Hendershott, *The Politics of Deviance.*

Deborah Tannen, *That's Not What I Meant!*

Personal Objective:

---

348 Bennett, W. *Death of Outrage: Bill Clinton and the Assault on American Ideals,* (US: Free Press, 1988).See also Hendershott, Anne B. *The Politics of Deviance,* (US: Encounter Books, 2002).

Specific Actions:

Due Date:

4.2.10 Negotiator

WBS Dictionary: A sustained leader often exhibits their communication skills most demonstrably when they are negotiating. Many people do not realize, however, that negotiations are constantly going on around them. A negotiation over a lunch location, quite obviously, is much different than a negotiation over a multi-billion dollar merger. Fruitful negotiations employ all the best communication skills of the parties involved. This is seen more obviously when there are multiple parties to a transaction, or when the native languages of the participants vary. Communications that are negotiations require the framing of appropriate questions (4.4.1), expressing and understanding each party's interests, sharing possible solutions to the inevitable impasses that arise, identifying and addressing the use of inappropriate negotiation tactics, and interpreting body language (4.4.5). The adept negotiator learns to speak the language of the other parties, literally or figuratively, in order to solidify the relationship. The expert negotiator understands that all negotiations involve three aspects—the substance of the negotiation, the relationship, and the negotiation process. All three are constantly being negotiated until the matter or the deal is settled. A sustained leader works to improve their communication skills in a negotiation environment to maximize the fulfillment of their interests in the negotiation. The entire team will be affected by the skill of the negotiator.

Application: Without realizing it, people are involved in negotiations constantly. When the spouse calls to ask if you will pick up the children, that is a negotiation. The outcome might be foreordained, yet it is still a negotiation. When two or more people are meeting for lunch, the time and location are both matters of negotiation. And, of course, buying a car, a house, or a business are all obvious and different types of negotiations. When the team lead assigns a task or charters a new team, the parameters of the assignment, the team members, the schedule, the specific tasks, the level of authority, and the accountability are all matters to be negotiated. They must all be defined, and all of the participants must have buy-in with each element. The larger the team, or the broader the impact, the more sensitive these negotiations might be. Depending on the perceived relative negotiating power of the participants, the ultimate project definition might differ greatly from the leader's initial projections.

Businessman Donald Trump has been involved in his share of negotiations. "Another important skill is negotiation. I receive many requests asking me about my negotiation skills, and there's a balance to successful negotiation that many people fail to see. The best negotiation is when both sides win. There's a compromise involved, which means careful listening, and when that is achieved you'll see results that work. Business is an art in itself, and powerful negotiation skills are one of the techniques necessary to facilitate success."[349]

Kathleen Kelley Reardon tells us that "Research indicates that negotiators who use cooperative strategies more frequently have higher joint gains than those who don't. Those who rely on such competitive strategies as demands and threats fail to achieve optimal outcomes. Threats are acts of desperation and desperation does not demonstrate power."[350]

The sustained leader recognizes the incredible importance of being a skillful negotiator and should never turn down an opportunity to receive additional training in this important area or to participate in a negotiation. A proper perspective and objectives must be identified and implemented. The sustained leader always seeks win-win solutions and never takes unfair advantage of the other parties. Negotiations are rarely one-off events; they form the basis of the on-going relationship. Take unfair advantage and when the relative power of the participants shifts, (and it will) the party who felt abused previously will be sure to return the compliment.

This sounds like me

A lot	somewhat	just a little	not at all

---

349 Trump, Donald with Meredith McIver. *Think Like a Champion*, (New York: Vanguard Press, 2009), 186.

350 Kathleen Kelly Reardon, *It's All Politics: Winning in a World Where Hard Work and Talent Aren't Enough* (New York: Currency Doubleday, 2005), 171 (citation omitted).

Additional Resources:

Roger Fisher, et al., *Getting to Yes.*

William Ury, *Getting Past No.*

Personal Objective:

Specific Actions:

Due Date:

4.2.10.1 Concessions and Compromise

WBS Dictionary: When negotiating, a sustained leader understands that lofty goals (and sometimes goals that are not lofty at all) will not be acceptable to the other party or parties to the transaction. Not everything that the sustained leader hopes to achieve through the arrangement will be achieved. Thus, the various goals and objectives must be prioritized, and consideration must be given to that which might be foregone in the negotiation process. The person who is not prepared (1.3.1.3) for the negotiation will not find that the negotiated agreement protects their interests as well as it may have if they had properly prepared, understood the interests of the respective parties, and honed their negotiation skills so as to obtain a favorable outcome. The sustained leader recognizes the negotiation process as an exploration of interests and the creation of what is usually called a "win-win" outcome. At the same time, the sustained leader recognizes that not everyone seeks "win-win" outcomes, instead viewing all negotiations as originating from a zero-sum position. For everything they gain, someone else loses (and vice versa). The sustained leader rejects this premise and negotiates on the basis of interests that can often create greater value for all parties involved.

Application: Rather than view any negotiation as a win-lose proposition, the sustained leader seeks opportunities to make the pie larger for everyone's benefit. In almost all situations, the environment can be defined within three primary constraints. These are cost, schedule, and technical (or quality) requirements. If you view those as sides of a triangle, you begin to see that you cannot change any one of them without having an effect on the other two. For example, if the budget is absolutely limited, you might need to modify the schedule or reduce the desired quality or scope to fit within that budget. If the schedule is fixed, you might need to come up with more money to accomplish the task in the allotted time or, again, reduce the quality to get the work finished.

Each situation is unique and unless you fully grasp the relative importance of the constraints, you will not be prepared to make appropriate concessions and compromise. Even if you try to argue that they are *all* equally important, the fact is that this is never the case. One of them is the most important, if even by the smallest of margins. The point is that you want to make concessions or find a compromise in the areas of least importance to your project.

Some negotiation classes teach win-lose negotiations and suggest the use a variety of gambits, occasionally including blackmail and fraud. The sustained leader's moral center (1.2.2.1) will never permit such an approach; however, the sustained leader should thoroughly study these techniques and the defenses against them. They will eventually confront someone who believes this is an appropriate negotiation approach and will attempt to use these tactics against them. The sustained leader must learn to both identify and defend against them.

All negotiations involve three elements that are in constant flux. These include the substance of the deal (obviously), the ongoing relationship (even when you believe this is a one-off deal), and the negotiation process itself. For example, you will occasionally encounter the table pound. It is done to intimidate. One of the best defenses is to pound the table right back. When you get their look of surprise, you simply respond, "Oh! I thought that was the process you wanted to use for these negotiations. Perhaps we should set some ground rules for respectful behavior." It will quickly defuse their attempt to intimidate.

Sustained leaders hone their negotiation skills. They understand the priorities of their projects and remain acutely aware of where trade-offs and concessions can be made. They are not drawn into the false dichotomy of "I gave in there, so you have to give in here" and defend against unfair or unethical tactics and ploys. Remember that leaders are most often measured by results and a great deal of measurable results flow directly from successful negotiations.

This sounds like me

A lot	somewhat	just a little	not at all

Additional Resources:

Roger Fisher, et al., *Getting to Yes.*

William Ury, *Getting Past No.*

William Ury, *The Power of a Positive No.*

Personal Objective:

Specific Actions:

Due Date:

4.2.10.2 Alliances

WBS Dictionary: Negotiating alliances allows an organization to expand its capabilities by borrowing the talent and treasure of another organization without a major investment. These arrangements should be mutually beneficial to the parties seeking alignment; of course, the profits, or benefits, or losses are shared as well. The interests of other affected stakeholders must be considered. For example, unless benefits flow to any clients or customers, the purpose of the alliance should be questioned. Forging alliances is often a method to assist in the management of risk (1.3.15 and 2.1.4). The sustained leader understands that establishing such alliances is similar to a marriage, in that they are often long term and divorces are messy. The reputation of both organizations become linked and failures or false steps in leadership of one will reflect on the other. Partners must be selected very carefully. These types of negotiations, therefore, involve different and often greater issues than the routine business negotiation. These arrangements are less complicated than a merger where one of the organizations end up in full control, and more sophisticated than a simple supplier relationship governed by standard commercial contracting practices. They are contracts, but of a stronger flavor than more common transactions and carrying consequences that are often orders of magnitude greater than most contracts. The sustained leader develops the ability to engage in the "big deal" and to protect their interests while learning how to best serve the interests of the other party or parties. Be careful with whom you hitch your wagon—your fates are frequently inextricably entwined from that point forward.

Application: Linking with other partners involves a great deal of trust between or among the parties. Once linked, a failure or misstep by one reflects on the other. Many advertising agencies and their clients have discovered this, much to their chagrin. Jared Fogle was a spokesperson for Subway sandwich shops from 2000 to 2015. He lost a great deal of weight, ostensibly because he had eaten primarily Subway sandwiches (coupled with some level of exercise) for a considerable period of time. He was very popular, and was even satirized in an episode of South Park. He became a celebrity due to his association with Subway.

In 2015, however, he was arrested for child pornography and soliciting sex with minors. He was sentenced to 15 years in prison. Subway, of course, survived and immediately severed all ties with Mr. Fogle. The damage, however, was done. This lengthy association had a very bad end for both parties and both paid a hefty price for the misdeeds of only one of them.

Sustained leaders are very circumspect when forming alliances with other parties. Major contracts, while carrying the potential for considerable profits, will require considerable investment and support from a variety of other contractors. It is estimated that 60% to 80% of all project dollars flow to subcontractors and suppliers. Lower level suppliers and subcontractors can often be managed through the contracting process. Teammates, on the other hand, often have a level of management responsibility for the overall project. They will have face-time with the customer and, under legal principles (2.1.2), will often share what is known as joint and several liability. This means that even if only one of the parties is guilty of misconduct, the other party will be held fully responsible for any damages or unfortunate consequences. In many cases, the truly guilty party will have absconded or otherwise disappeared, leaving only the deep pockets of the innocent party to pay the damages.

Associations and alliances thus require a much deeper level of analysis and a thorough understanding of the risk profiles. Great trust must exist between the parties, and significant failures by one of them will reflect on the perceived leadership of the other. Great discretion and discernment is required of the sustained leader, with proper due diligence in understanding whether sustained leaders represent the other party as well. When Jack Welch and Norm Augustine met to discuss aligning GE Aerospace with Martin Marietta, the deal closed relatively quickly because of the trust and mutual respect of these two aerospace sustained leaders. Many, if not most, other mergers or partnerships tend to be far less successful.

This sounds like me

A lot	**somewhat**	**just a little**	**not at all**

Additional Resources:

Robert Porter Lynch, et al., *Business Alliances Guide.*

Mike Mutek, *Contractor Team Arrangements-competitive Solution or Legal Liability.*

Personal Objective:

Specific Actions:

Due Date:

4.2.11 Enthusiasm

WBS Dictionary: Some people never seem to get very excited about anything. While it might not always be obvious to the casual observer, there is real excitement in leadership. There is an appropriate level of emotionalism in accomplishing goals, in doing what has perhaps never been done before, in celebrating a team's success, and in demonstrating financial success. The personal sense of accomplishment is invigorating. Enthusiasm is contagious and typically spurs people on to better performance. Every person in advertising understands this "Buy it Now!" mentality. In part, this is dependent on the confidence shown by the leader. People cannot get excited about a weak vision, a boss of low character, or a company that has no sense of urgency in its operations. As cleric and educator Theodore Hesburgh has noted, "You can't blow an uncertain trumpet." The sustained leader is enthused about their vision (5.1.2) and is passionate (5.1.1) about achieving the goals of the organization. While these attributes are often related and sometimes even conflated, they are distinct in terms of their impetus and direction of action. For those aspects of enthusiasm related to positive attitudes, see 4.3.2.1.

Application: When you truly care about something, truly, truly CARE, it engenders an emotional response that you can't really control. You express this enthusiasm in the only way you know how—by doing all the things necessary to bring the thing you care about to final fruition. You want the dream you hold to be the reality you see. You talk about it, you encourage others, you knock down roadblocks, and you make steady progress toward the goal. Your communication is perceived as authoritative and authentic. You are perceived as committed (5.0) and are automatically given more respect. You draw followers to you. Charles Schwab once said that "A man can succeed at almost anything for which he has unlimited enthusiasm."

Enthusiasm, like leadership itself, cannot be scientifically measured. Its only measure is results.

Edward George Bulwer-Lytton

Nothing is so contagious as enthusiasm, it moves stones, it charms brutes. Enthusiasm is the genius of sincerity and truth accomplishes no victories without it.

Without a scientific standard, it tends to receive minimal attention in the literature. Motivational speakers will try to inspire you (often to be enthused about what THEY are enthused about rather than getting you enthused about your own dreams), but that inspiration will not translate into enthusiasm unless YOU hold the dream. Enthusiasm is a singlemindedness of purpose coupled with a determination to see the dream become a reality. Enthusiasm can even overcome a lack of innate skill. Reaching significant goals is arduous work. It can become frustrating and people and situations will seem to continually work against you. Only enthusiasm will break down these impediments and set you back on the path of achievement.

Most business metrics can be precisely measured; enthusiasm is more nebulous. It tends to evolve through the culture of the organization, and the sustained leader learns how to imbue each member of the team with a desire to win, a desire to achieve, and a desire to see the dreams become goals that become reality. It is a form of excitement, like a child waking up on Christmas morning. It provides purpose. The sustained leader crafts a vision (5.1.2) that draws out the enthusiasm of the team. Just being enthused about a goal, however, will not automatically transfer that enthusiasm. Certainly, the sustained leader must demonstrate enthusiasm to the team, but the personal enthusiasm trigger of each team member will vary. The sustained leader seeks that out and finds a way to flip the specific switch for each member of the team. (3.5). Enthusiasm is a trait that many biographers point out in telling the story of successful subjects. The word derives from the Greek *entheos,* which means "filled with the divine." This creates a natural attraction from others to what they perceive as divine energy. The truly successful always seem to have a strong dose of enthusiasm. They care. They care intensely. They share that sense of caring. They draw others around them and they achieve amazing things.

Og Mandino

Every memorable act in the world is a triumph of enthusiasm. Nothing great was ever achieved without it because it gives any challenge or any occupation, no matter how frightening or difficult, a new meaning. Without enthusiasm you are doomed to a life of mediocrity but with it you can accomplish miracles.

Jim Henson, creator of the Muppets advises the following: "Follow your enthusiasm. It's something I've always believed in. Find those parts of your life you enjoy the most. Do what you enjoy doing." Sustained leaders learn how to follow their heart and gather a team around themselves. Enthusiasm makes the difference.

This sounds like me

A lot   **somewhat**   **just a little**   **not at all**

Additional Resources:

Stephen Covey, *Principle-Centered Leadership*, (Principle #3).

Zig Ziglar, et al., *See You at the Top*.

Dr. Norman Vincent Peale, *Enthusiasm Makes the Difference*.

Marsha Sinetar, *Do What You Love, the Money Will Follow*.

Personal Objective:

Specific Actions:

Due Date:

4.2.12 Deals Effectively with Diverse Audiences

WBS Dictionary: The sustained leader often does not get to choose their audience. They are subject to surprise visitors and critics from every direction. Occasionally, they may be able to plan the message and separate the audiences from each other in a way that makes their dealings with the various stakeholders more effective. Often, any given message will be heard by all stakeholders, many with divergent interests. The sustained leader has to be able to communicate in such a way that all of these various interests, or as many as are practical, can be addressed. This is often not possible. The constant stress of attempting to do this can wear on the leader, and their ability to maintain composure can be tested. This is often seen during strenuous political campaigns. The candidate begins to perform badly while their message and health suffers. Meanwhile, they are trying to get the support across a great diversity of interests. The sustained leader assesses the audience, then adjusts the message to the appropriate level and content. They do not get "confused" or fatigued and end up conveying the wrong message. Every speaker will feel that they may have done better, or wished they had not forgotten a certain point—that is human nature. There will never be a perfect speech, whether in content or delivery. The sustained leader understands this, but tries to do so anyway.

Application: When the sustained leader reads anything—a book, a memo, a position paper, a transcript, or a scientific paper—he or she can readily gauge the level of writing. It is said that newspapers are written at a 6th grade level, with no big words and simple sentences. Newspapers are designed to reach the broadest audience. Newspapers like the Wall Street Journal speak to a more educated audience and are more careful in their editorial style to use proper grammar. Most TV shows today, especially sitcoms and dramas, do severe violence to proper grammar, but they are speaking to a broad audience and use language more familiar to the listener.

On social media, we find the same dynamic. People write the way they speak and, very often, they do not have a firm grasp of the rules of grammar. In much writing, misspellings are endemic, even with the use of spell-check and grammar-check software tools. Marilyn Vos Savant, the person who has scored the highest on standard IQ tests, wrote about spelling and determined that studies show that those who spell poorly or even carelessly are *not* statistically dumber than those who spell well. Even so, she notes, people who do not spell well are *perceived by others* to be less intelligent. This diminishes their ability to be heard. In communicating with others, it is important to speak to the audience. The level of writing, word choice, sentence complexity, and even flow of logic will change depending on the audience. Lawyers giving a closing argument where the whole story needs to be told in terms the jury understands, scientists writing a report on the results of clinical tests that will be read by other highly-educated scientists, writers of children's' books, and doctors writing prescriptions to be followed by pharmacists should all communicate, whether spoken or in writing, to the level of their audience.

Billy Sunday was a hard-drinking, hard-driving baseball player who, amidst a round of drinking with friends, ran into a group of evangelists who had a profound impact on his life. He turned his life over to Jesus and began a new career of preaching. Being a man of the earth, he spoke an earthy language that often would not be accepted in "higher" society. He wasn't talking to high society. He was talking to others who spoke as he did, and without great attention to rules of grammar. He spoke clearly and plainly, and his audience understood him well. Thousands upon thousands of lives were likewise changed by adopting the Christian faith.

As a counterpoint, during a recent election cycle, a highly educated candidate (a lawyer, in fact) gave a speech in the American South and adopted a southern accent with the drawl familiar to her audience. Many mocked her for being pretentious, and perhaps she was. She was making an effort to sound credible to her audience. The point is that speaking to your audience can be important in effective communication. Not being your authentic self or sounding pretentious can be detrimental to the message. And sometimes when a person tries too hard to speak above their level of experience, they end up looking foolish, making errors of fact, introducing sometime unintentionally humorous malapropisms, and not getting their message across. The sustained leader is always true to themselves, and trains themselves in a variety of styles, methods, and modes of communication to have a full arsenal of tools to improve the effectiveness of their communications to as diverse an audience as possible.

This sounds like me

| A lot | somewhat | just a little | not at all |

Additional Resources:
Jeffrey Gitomer, *Little Black Book of Connections*.
Deborah Tannen, *That's Not What I Meant!*

Personal Objective:

Specific Actions:

Due Date:

4.2.12.1 Employees

WBS Dictionary: Employees are in a unique position in an organization. Though in various contexts the proper title might be volunteer or team member, this element pertains more directly to employees—those who earn their livelihood from the organization and support themselves and their family by trading their time, effort, energy, or intelligence with the organization in exchange for money. There is a bind between the organization and the employee that is, in many respects, mutually dependent—the organization needs what the employee brings, and the employee is dependent on the organization for their income.

Application: The employee-employer relationship, however, is not typically so straightforward. In American society, labor laws at the federal, state, and local levels make the relationship much more complicated than a straight transaction of services for fees. Minimum wage laws, discrimination laws, workplace safety rules, and work schedules (including vacation and holidays) are all heavily regulated in most western democracies. Thus, communications with employees take on a unique nature. Both parties are extensively invested in the good faith and honesty of the other. While the employee seeks an honest wage for an honest day's work, the employer easily adopts the inverse statement that they only seek an honest day's work for an honest day's wage. So long as everyone acts in good faith and fairness, there are no need for the burdensome laws and regulations covering the workplace. Clearly, history does not support this premise. The sustained leader, when communicating with employees, must recognize the inherent nature of the relationship, as well as the various rules and regulations superimposed on the relationship—quite often with many unintended consequences. Communicating in that environment can be dicey. The sustained leader recognizes this unique relationship with this audience and adjusts their communication message and delivery accordingly.

Some studies have shown that effective communication must be based first and foremost on trust and loyalty. As suggested by Aristotle, without ethos, pathos, and logos, there can be no argument that the audience will find persuasive. From this trust in the speaker's character, employees must then be informed of the overall organizational strategy and the individual contribution each is expected to make toward that strategy. Stated differently, people want work that has meaning and it is the sustained leader's role to provide that meaning. The employee is then entitled to honest feedback (4.2.8). This feedback should include both the individual and organizational performance against the stated goals.

The sustained leader understands that effective communication is critical to maintaining the trust and loyalty that initiated the relationship. The non-communicative leader will not likely remain in a leadership position. The followers will simply stop following.

This sounds like me

A lot   **somewhat**   **just a little**   **not at all**

Additional Resources:
John Hasnas, *Trapped.*
James A. Belasco, and Ralph C. Stayer, *Flight of the Buffalo.*

Personal Objective:

Specific Actions:

Due Date:

4.2.12.2 Press

WBS Dictionary: Communicating with the press becomes increasingly important to the leader who has responsibility for a public company, charity, or other high-profile organization. The sustained leader understands that the press is not necessarily their friend, and that bad news, even tragedy, draws in readers. The press is not the leader's public relations department. The well-honed leader will know how to tell a compelling story (4.4.2) that makes the job of the press much easier. The sustained leader will adjust their presentation style and delivery to match the needs of the press. A well-scripted story delivered well is the leader's goal, but the press works to its own agenda. They may ask leading and aggressive questions; they may have their own agenda; they may not have done their homework and ask amazingly stupid questions; and they may ask questions in such a manner and order that prevents the telling of the leader's story. The sustained leader will be able to think on their feet, adjust to the reporter's style and tone, and still present a compelling story. Effectively communicating with the press can be the riskiest task a leader tackles; they can come out of it a hero or a joke.

Application: Speaking to the press can be more unnerving than speaking to an arena full of people. Entire classes are built around the skills and disciplines necessary to convey a leader's story to the press effectively. Often the reporter is not as well versed in the subject matter as the leader and will frequently have an agenda that diverges from that of the leader. The reporter's agenda may well be diametrically opposed to the leader's story. The reporter may have a genuine desire to learn; more frequently, they are looking for the big "scoop" that will help their career. Understanding the facts is far less important once they have made up their mind on the story they wish to tell. This is not to disparage all reporters and interviewers. Many are true professionals and a credit to their craft. The sustained leader, however, will not necessarily know which flavor of reporter with whom they are dealing and thus must assume and prepare for the worst.

The dynamics of an in-person interview and a phone interview are dramatically different. There is no reading of body language on the phone. Going to a TV studio with its bright lights and unfamiliar activities places the leader out of their normal environment—they are "out of their element." In either case, the leader is often not given the time needed to tell their story the way they would prefer. Being questioned disrupts the logical flow of the story the leader would like to tell.

Hostile or leading questions can disrupt the well-rehearsed thought processes the leader brings to the interview or press conference.

When talking to the press, the sustained leader should stick to the basic key points and practice relating them in the simplest of terms and language. This often gives rise to the sound-bite (4.2.14). The more simply the leader can package their story for the reporter, the more likely the reporter is to buy into it, making the reporter's job easier. The key points should be conveyed regardless of the circumstances or time constraints imposed. More importantly, the sustained leader knows their facts, know what facts they don't know, and, when appropriate, aren't afraid to say, "I don't know."

Most business communications, and especially those issued by a Public Relations department or firm, are highly edited and reviewed. This will not happen with the reporter's story. It is, in fact, a breach of etiquette to even request the opportunity to review the story before it goes to print. Occasionally there might be a request by the reporter to verify certain facts, and things that are clearly reported in error will generally receive a "correction" in a small back-page note in a future issue of the publication. Similarly, nothing said in the presence of a reporter is ever "off the record." There are some reporters who recognize the importance of having an "inside" source and will report the things they are told "on background" without attribution. Many organizations actually prohibit employees and others who are not official spokespeople from even talking to the press as an official statement of the company. Whistleblower laws, freedom of speech, and interference with on-going investigations often hinder strict enforcement of such policies, so both premature and erroneous information will often find its way to the press and be reported as "official."

The New York Times once noted that "Almost every day, the Internet demands a head on a platter."[351] In order to sell the news, it has to be juicy. Finding corruption, even if only perceived corruption, sells. After all, the public relishes the metaphorical head on a platter. As a sustained leader, there are several cautions to take from this. First, treat the press with respect. They can hurt you even when you (or those you lead) have done nothing wrong. Second, do not betray the trust others have put on you as their leader. Do not use scapegoats or sacrificial lambs.

---

351 Quoted in Welch, Jack and Suzy. *The Real Life MBA: Your No-BS Guide to Winning the Game, Building a Team, and Growing Your Career*, (New York: Harper Collins, 2015), 111.

And third, your press will never be consistently kind or fair. Do the best you can to cooperate; however, some days you are the windshield and other days you are the bug. Deal with it. The sustained leader will.

This sounds like me

A lot   **somewhat**   **just a little**   **not at all**

Additional Resources:
Jeffrey Gitomer, *Social BOOM!*
Mark E. Mathis, *Feeding the Media Beast.*

Personal Objective:

Specific Actions:

Due Date:

4.2.12.3 Other Stakeholders

WBS Dictionary: There are many stakeholders in any situation where leadership is required. Some of them are obvious, such as the employees, shareholders, bankers, and management in a company; volunteers, financial experts, executives, and benefit recipients in a charitable organization; taxpayers, Congress, executive agencies, the courts, and benefit recipients in many government entities. Regardless of the situation, many people will lay claim to a stake in the game even if that stake is tenuous, marginal, or imaginary. The sustained leader understands that any endeavor has a variety of stakeholders, including negative stakeholders—those who have an interest in the failure of the leader and the team they lead. It is not possible to address all the other "miscellany" that may exist. The sustained leader must understand, however, that they exist, they will arise from unexpected places with surprising agendas, and they will demand a seat at the table. The sustained leader cannot be oblivious to their existence.

Application: In communicating with stakeholders of all stripes, the sustained leader researches their claims, assesses their legitimacy, and communicates appropriately. When an illegitimate stake is pressed, the sustained leader identifies the falsity of the claim. When a marginal claim is pressed, the sustained leader puts it in context among all stakeholders and addresses it appropriately. Each situation and each stakeholder must be dealt with in a fashion that matches their interest in the team effort. If there is none, that needs to be explained. Unlike a democracy, not everyone is entitled to a vote.

In the 2010's, a movement arose called "Occupy Wall Street." Loosely organized with little to no apparent leadership, there was a significant "mob mentality" in the participants. They engaged in acts of civil disobedience such as refusing to disband and setting up camps on public and private property. According to contemporary press reports, they were rebelling against the "big corporations." Even so, they communicated on social media and used their Apple iPhones and Samsung smartphones to communicate. They were apparently oblivious to the irony. Whether or not the movement was truly organized by some centralized interest group may never be known, but for a period of time they demanded to be heard, disrupted traffic and business, and gave the police a very difficult time. Reports of urination and defecation on police cars and other public places were common. Destruction of private and public property occurred. Were they legitimate stakeholders? Did they have legitimate complaints that deserved a public hearing? Were their means and methods the most effective way to accomplish their ends? Many of these answers were unimportant. Civic, business, and charitable leaders had to work together to stop the disruption and civil unrest. The Occupy Wall Street movement was, nonetheless, comprised of self-described stakeholders who demanded to be heard. The sustained leader must be prepared for such stakeholders, legitimate or not, and learn effective ways to communicate with them.

This sounds like me

A lot somewhat **just a little** not at all

Additional Resources:
Steven F. Walker, et al., *Stakeholder Power.*
Ram Charan, *What the Customer Wants You to Know.*

Personal Objective:

Specific Actions:

Due Date:

4.2.12.4 Regulators

WBS Dictionary: Some entities are formally regulated, such as airlines and banks. Others are less formally regulated, such as the American Bar Association for lawyers or the American Medical Association for doctors. Even for the entities that may experience no direct formal regulation, there are still many rules to follow. Examples include tax law compliance, or local ordinances related to their business, or general regulatory environments such as the Occupational Health and Safety Administration, the Equal Employment Opportunity Commission, and the Consumer Product Safety Commission. Everyone is regulated in many aspects of their lives, even if it is simply through the process of obtaining a driver's or marriage license. Dealing with regulators and the usual cadre of lawyers that tend to accompany them often requires a different type and form of communication than might apply in any other situation. The sustained leader adjusts to these situations, seeks the counsel of those more experienced in these matters, and learns to follow the advice of these advisors. It is a specialized type of communication that the sustained leader seeks to master.

Application: Regulators tend to have discretion. Regulators and prosecutors have the ability to make your life miserable or to grant you a free pass based on their discretion. This power, whether perceived as legitimate or not, sets the relationship between the parties. The leader may have little to no control over the situation. For these reasons, the sustained leader seeks to understand this unnatural relationship and to communicate effectively with those who have power over the situation.

America and many other western societies today have become very polarized in regard to how much control the government should exercise. Special interest groups also weigh in on the subject to protect their interests. For example, many states regulate cosmetology services but the degree of regulation varies immensely. In some states, you must be licensed in all aspects, including nails and makeup, when all you want to do is cut hair. Lawyers similarly must be licensed in any state in which they wish to practice and engage in continuing legal education. So long as they take the required number of hours of CLE, they retain their license, even if the classes they took bear no relation to the area of law they practice. Again— regulations vary greatly and the regulators have great discretion. Thus, the means to communicate effectively will vary considerably.

Sustained leaders must have sufficient competence (2.0) to manage the affairs of the team they lead. That competence must include the nature and extent of regulation, as well as the nature of the individuals who wield discretion in interpreting and enforcing the regulations. Communications with regulatory bodies tend to be very formal and contain a great deal of jargon, including acronyms, that defines the field. Administrative bodies are required to maintain records of their actions, including discussions, enforcements, prosecutions, and resolutions. Their rules are usually subject to a formal rule-making process, and the sustained leader understands how those rules are made. They communicate with the regulatory body during that process, respond promptly to any communication from the regulators, file all appropriate reports and filings, and work to avoid unnecessary entanglements caused by ineffective communications. The sustained leader might work independently to petition the government concerning regulations and the rule-making process. They will, however, comply with the law and communicate effectively, even if that entails hiring experts knowledgeable about the process. (2.1.2.3)

This sounds like me

| **A lot** | **somewhat** | **just a little** | **not at all** |

Additional Resources:
Ernest Gellhorn, et al., *Administrative Law and Process in a Nutshell.*

Personal Objective:

Specific Actions:

Due Date:

4.2.12.5 Customers and Beneficiaries

WBS Dictionary: Customers are never an interruption to a business; they are the reason for it. Beneficiaries are not an interruption to an organization's raison d'etre; they are, obviously, the reason for it. Governments that ignore their constituents are soon replaced by election or revolution. The communication expected by these important stakeholders is one of helpfulness and respect. As customers, they are voting for you and your activities with every dollar they spend or contribute. They expect a certain level of loyalty in return. They sometimes, however, have perceptions that are possibly not based in reality; furthermore, their expectations may also hale from that same unreal universe. Nonetheless, the importance of the customers, clients, beneficiaries, constituents, or parishioners of any organization makes communications with them crucially important. Many such communications are driven by a particular problem the customer experiences. The customer does not seek explanations; they seek solutions. There are many communication techniques that assist in this effort, increasingly including social media, and the sustained leader takes advantage of opportunities to learn and practice them. The leader cannot alienate the people who ultimately pay their salary or who are designed to benefit from their efforts. Doing so leads to very short-term leadership roles. The sustained leader learns the appropriate customer relationship management techniques. The sustained leader also recognizes the customer is a source of revenue. This is not based solely on the present interaction; it considers the value of the client or customer over the lifetime of the relationship.

Application: There is a popular slogan seen in some businesses: "If we don't take care of our customer, someone else will." Customers come in many shapes, sizes, and titles. For convenience, we will refer to them all as "customers." Customer care is a core function of any entity. Without customers, the entity ceases to exist. The communications must be tactful and fact based. They must be sympathetic, perhaps even empathetic. The customers must be spoken to at a level they understand, but never condescendingly. Under no circumstances should they be quoted "company policy." That is the most insulting thing a person who has given you money can hear.

American Family Publishers is widely known due to its spokesperson of many years, Johnny Carson's sidekick, Ed McMahon. Their operation is highly automated and when they find a potential target to whom to pitch their magazine subscriptions, they load the data into a database. Out prints a very personalized letter to John, or Mary, or Sue. Glitches do occur, however, as was reported by a church that had adopted the name "Bushnell Assembly of God Church." It appears that the database was fed the name "God Church" and promptly sent off a letter that began, "We've been searching for you, God!"[352] Ah yes. Haven't we all? While many forms of communication MUST be automated to cut costs and improve consistency, the sustained leader understands the principle best articulated by Dale Carnegie in *How to Win Friends and Influence People*. A person's name is the sweetest sound they can hear. Mess that up and any attempt to communicate after that is wasted energy. Customers can be particularly fickle about that.

Customers might choose any number of ways to communicate. They may write a letter or call the corporate offices. They might show up at a store and be very vocal. They might post reviews on any number of internet review sites. They may also use Twitter, Facebook, or other social media platforms. One author suggests that a happy customer tells 3 people while an unhappy one tells 3000. Most communications with customers will not come directly from the leader. Other team members will actually handle the compliment or concern. It is the leader, however, who sets the tone and imposes discipline on the systems under their

352 Parietti, Jeff. *The Book of Truly Stupid Business Quotes*, 130.

control that manage these communications. Recognizing the importance of these interactions, the sustained leader will practice excellent communication techniques and drive them down through the entire organization.

This sounds like me

| A lot | somewhat | just a little | not at all |

Additional Resources:

George J. Thompson, et al., *Verbal Judo.*

Dale Carnegie, *How to Win Friends & Influence People.*

Pete Blackshaw, *Satisfied Customers Tell Three Friends, Angry Customers Tell 3,000.*

Personal Objective:

Specific Actions:

Due Date:

4.2.12.6 Suppliers

WBS Dictionary: Most projects (and therefore leadership roles) require the support of other entities. For communication purposes, any entity or person that provides such support and is not directly part of the organization of which the leader is aligned is considered a supplier. They may be called vendors, subcontractors, or other similar terms. Suppliers are teammates and should be working toward the same ends as the leader. These teammates are integral to the success of the mission of the organization and must be selected with great care. The relationship must also be nurtured as the operational process between the two entities is worked out and accepted. This process is often referred to as a "dance," and requires that the parties decide early on who leads and who follows. Market dynamics, whether transitory (such as a fluctuating price of oil) or more institutional (such as a market that is characterized as a monopsony), will drive the power equation. The sustained leader understands that these business partners can greatly assist or greatly hurt the leader's organization. Thus, the sustained leader nurtures the relationship so that the relationship remains strong in both good times and bad. Communication with suppliers entails many of the same techniques used for other communications, including negotiation.

Application: Power is often present in disproportionate levels between suppliers and those they supply. Communications are often more vernacular, and especially when the trade has its own terms of art. While the buyer, or prime contractor, is usually perceived as holding the power since that is the source of funds, it is often the case that a particular supplier provides a key technology or critical skill that absolutely must be maintained for success of the project. Throughout the life of the project, these power relationships will shift. The sustained leader fosters a positive relationship designed to out-live the project. Clear, consistent communication is a key element of such a relationship.

Neither party likes surprises. Mishaps and accidents will happen. In these cases, the adage that "bad news is best served fresh" applies. The more informed each party is, the more time there is to work around issues. Letting problems or issues fester only compounds them and makes future communications even more difficult

The supplier relationship can take many forms depending on the needs of the parties. It may be a straight commodity purchase of fungible goods. It might be a custom designed product or a commercial item. It might be a piece of technology that is proprietary to the supplier. It might even be a device for manned space flight that must include redundancies and 100% reliability. None of this matters in terms of the consistent need for clear communication (4.2.10.2).

Whenever possible, the sustained leader will only seek suppliers and enter into relationships when the other entity is also run by a sustained leader. Honesty and integrity will guide the relationship, communications will be based in fact, and when issues arise they will be addressed in an upright and ethical manner. When sustained leaders team up, they are pretty much unbeatable.

This sounds like me

| A lot | somewhat | just a little | not at all |

Additional Resources:

David Simchi-Levi, et al., *Managing the Supply Chain*.

Jeffrey Gitomer, *Little Teal Book of Trust*.

Personal Objective:

Specific Actions:

Due Date:

4.2.13 Diplomatic

WBS Dictionary: The sustained leader is diplomatic in their communications. Diplomacy is similar to tact (4.2.9), but is used in different contexts. A tactful communication is more directive, such as, for example, when a leader must terminate the relationship with another party (supplier, employee, etc.). The decision has been made and the message must be communicated with tact. Diplomacy reflects a greater balance of power between or among the parties. While tact might be used when a decision is imposed, diplomacy is involved when relatively equal parties must come to a consensus. Diplomacy reflects a greater balancing of interests. Seeking possible solutions requires a different set of skills and approaches than merely communicating a decision. Diplomacy is most often used in relation to interactions among governments. While that is a key platform for exercising diplomacy, diplomacy can be used in any situation where people differ and none of the parties have sufficient power to force a particular solution. Diplomacy might also involve a measure of cunning, but being too Machiavellian will damage the relationship. Out-maneuvering other parties is not inherently a bad thing, but it can be when taken to extremes. Diplomatic communications must balance opposing interests in such a way as to reach consensus. It will involve tact, but it requires something more.

Application: Diplomacy is involved in a variety of possible scenarios since it such a multi-faceted concept. While its most common use is between governments, it can appropriately be used in many other situations. Diplomacy appreciates the sensitivities that exist among parties, between parties, or are isolated to only one of the parties. For example, the political situation in a negotiator's home country might require certain sensitivities and appearances. Certainly, a level of discretion is required, even to the point of using euphemisms in certain discussions. This is not intended to imply any deception, but rather appreciates the perspective of others. For example, you would not say "your government is full of communist pigs." Rather, you might refer to "the form of government selected by your country's rulers."

Finesse and delicacy are also part of this concept. Agility with language and the ability to express yourself in a way that will be understood, but is not blunt, bold, or brash is critical. The judicious use of discretion plays well with diplomacy, as does an acute ability to discern subterfuge and ill intent.

The sustained leader adopts these various techniques and attitudes when exercising diplomacy. There is always a goal associated with the use of diplomacy and there is sometimes no assurance that both parties will fulfill the deal once agreed to. The methods of resolving these disputes, short of warfare (literally or figuratively), include setting an enforceable schedule for compliance, and determining the result when a different ruler or elected individual replaces the individuals engaged in the current arrangement. Again, while this might sound most appropriate in international relations, diplomacy applies in many less consequential matters. Mergers and acquisitions can involve deep personal attachment to the status quo. Bet-the-company negotiations, bankruptcy workouts, and dealing with regulators, can also require great levels of diplomacy.

In some respects, diplomacy is most useful for the most sensitive of negotiations. The true diplomat (by skill, not position) will find that the effective use of diplomacy will yield many long-term benefits. Being a diplomat is a proper aspiration for the sustained leader.

This sounds like me

A lot   **somewhat**   **just a little**   **not at all**

Additional Resources:

Kelly-Kate S. Pease, et al., *International Organizations.*

Roger Fisher, *Getting Together.*

Kathleen Kelly Reardon, *It's All Politics.*

Personal Objective:

Specific Actions:

Due Date:

4.2.14 Understands Importance of a Sound Bite

WBS Dictionary: The sound bite has become a mainstay of communication with broad audiences. It is typically a short, pithy statement expressed by a public figure with the intent that it will be picked up by national broadcasters as a key element of a short news story. It is usually witty or striking in some way, and may be derived from a longer speech or a quick "man-on-the-street" type of news reporter ambush. Such statements fit well with the short news stories typical in the 24-hour news cycle embraced by most news broadcasts, and mirrors the societal view of the microwave society in which we live—people will not wait for the punchline. Everyone is in too much of a hurry, so all messages must be packaged into sound bites in order to get the attention of re-broadcasters and so as to not lose the attention of the short-attention-span listener. The best sound bites are memorable and tend to stick with the listener or become a message within themselves and thus get shared across various mediums. Not everything can be communicated in a sound bite, but a good slogan or catchphrase can accent the key points of a longer argument or presentation. Sustained leaders appreciate the impact of a sound bite and package their communications accordingly. It is often a function of popular culture and typically involves the ability to stay tech-savvy. Detriments can occur if the phrase is "too cute" or is considered derogatory to a particular group. The sound bite is powerful whether it generates positive or negative feelings toward the speaker. The sustained leader knows the difference and works to ensure that captured sound bites are positive.

Application: Great leaders often capitalize on a specific slogan or motto. They find a way to take a complex, often emotionally charged, issue and distill it into a simple phrase or acronym. Battle cries such as "remember the Alamo" or "remember the Maine" are designed to inspire and motivate people to action. Advertising slogans attempt to accomplish the same thing, encouraging people to buy a product through pithy slogans like "we will serve no wine before its time," or "lower your insurance rates in 15 minutes," or "you're in good hands." President Harry Truman had a plaque on his desk that said "the buck stops here." Ronald Reagan once said to the world "Mr. Gorbachev, tear down this wall." In the 24-hour news cycle of today's world, the sound bite often drives the story. Occasionally they get repeated so often (after testing positively with a sample audience) that they become trite mantras rather than informative points.

The social media site Twitter was ridiculed for having a 140 character limit to any message posted on its site. While perceived correctly as limiting to those who felt such postings needed more context, they stuck to their rules and forced people to be concise in what they said. It also gave rise to greater use of emoticons to express emotions in a fewer characters and the resurgence of what was known as "text-speak" where the word "are" was reduced to the letter "r" and "your" reduced to "ur". Yes, it is improper spelling, but it is effective in communicating using fewer characters in an informal setting.

Some hand gestures have long been used to express a thought. Certainly, there are those that are intended to be vulgar, and sustained leaders should never stoop to the level of using them. Others convey a sense of hope and optimism. The two finger "V" originally stood for victory and later was adopted to indicate "peace." Everyone understands a thumb up, yet in certain societies it has the opposite meaning than it does in America. Quick, short phrases can be used effectively and often are the only thing the news stations will capture out of a two-hour speech, presentation, or debate. Sustained leaders understand the importance of a sound bite, both from the perspective of conveying a positive message and the use that will be made by others for the errant words or "open mic" situations where such words are captured inadvertently to the speaker's detriment. The sustained leader guards their words and offers up positive sound bites for broad consumption by their audience.

Society has adopted a variety of aphorisms that reflect the person who is full of hot air without any substance to what is being said. Texans say a person is all hat and no cattle. Being all bark and no bite is often heard along with all talk and no action. A fancy word for this is "prolix." The sustained leader is not wordy or tedious in their speech. Not everything should be a sound-bite however. An overuse of the sound bite permits no substance of thought and masks a lack of critical thinking (1.3.9.1). The sustained leader understands when a brief, tight thought can be expressed in a sound bite and when greater development of the thought is appropriate. They are never unnecessarily lengthy, but also never unnecessarily brief.

This sounds like me

A lot	somewhat	just a little	not at all

Additional Resources:

Mark E. Mathis, *Feeding the Media Beast.*

Dorothy Leeds, *Powerspeak.*

Peggy Noonan, *On Speaking Well.*

Personal Objective:

Specific Actions:

Due Date:

4.2.15 Saying "Sorry" and "Thanks."

WBS Dictionary: Showing genuine appreciation and genuine remorse is a skill that can be developed. Few people come by it naturally. Thank-yous tend to be perfunctory and sorrys tend to be gulped down. Too often people try to explain things away, suggesting perhaps the listener misunderstood or is being too sensitive. In the law, there is the principle that you take your plaintiff as you find them. If you happen to accidently hit a person with a pre-existing medical condition and that hit causes extraordinary damage, you are responsible for the full damage. The fact that another person might have laughed it off is not relevant. The same is true with appreciation and apologies. In today's society, the politically correct among us find offense at everything. There is a considerable loss of sense of humor in society. There are also those who apologize more as a figure of speech than with any genuine remorse. We also see those who have made major blunders that seem far less than sincere in making a public apology. Everyone makes mistakes, and occasionally these mistakes hurt others. Leaders must be prepared to acknowledge their mistakes and make amends. Conversely, they must also be prepared to express sincere gratitude for courtesies extended.

Application: William Ury, who co-wrote *Getting to Yes*, notes that "There may be no better gateway to happiness than cultivating our gratitude."[353] He goes on to quote the research of Dr. Robert A. Emmons that demonstrably indicates the psychological benefit that derives from a thankful attitude. Dr. Emmons writes, "I've concluded that gratitude is one of the few attitudes that can measurably change peoples' lives."[354]

Just saying "thanks," while important, is not genuine appreciation. Like a heart-felt apology, a sincere thank you requires a bit of thought and planning; in fact, it might well include a celebratory event (1.3.17). "Sorry," "Thank you," and even "I love you" are expressions of genuine sentiment and should not be tossed around cavalierly.

Gratitude, like apologies, tend to be accepted without question. If you offer one, it will be accepted, even by strangers on the street. A voiced "Thank you" or "I'm Sorry" will most commonly be responded to with "no problem" or "you are very welcome." Service members are becoming more receptive to being thanked for

---

353 Ury, William, *Getting to Yes with Yourself,* 83.
354 Ibid, 84.

their service because, thankfully, so many people are now doing so in an unsolicited manner. The same is true for sympathy, as when someone says, sincerely, "I'm sorry for your loss."

Apologies are effective at diffusing tense situations. There is even research that says an apology is more accepted than monetary compensation.[355]

Dana Perino observed: "I don't ever want to apologize for something I've said, but I want to be gracious enough to be ready to apologize if I ever need to."[356] The sustained leader will apologize when appropriate and will even apologize for failures of the team for which the leader is not directly responsible. They accept the responsibility because they are the leader. Leaders are often asked to say a few words on more solemn occasions to express the sympathy of the entire team. Such requests, as hard as they may be personally to deliver, are appropriate for the sustained leader; communicating them in a heartfelt manner is expected. The leader who laughs it off or expresses the sentiment poorly will be viewed in a less positive light. This can be extremely difficult for "sensitives"—those who easily choke up in emotional situations (even if only a movie). Controlling that can be extremely difficult for some.

Many people use the non-apology and believe that it will suffice. Note the difference between "I am truly sorry for making such statements that offended you" and "I'm sorry if you were offended by what I said." The point is the direction of the action. If what I did caused harm—I owe an apology. If what I said or did caused a reaction from you, then perhaps the apology is not due. Consider this in the context of discipline or tough love (3.6 and 3.4.4). There are many ways to give a false apology and the sustained leader avoids them all. For example, making an apology too general and not addressing the specifics of the offense (everyone knows it would be wrong…), being too conditional (If what I did…), speaking in the passive voice rather than the active (effectively removing the actor), hiding behind legal technicalities (my lawyer has advised…), and deflecting responsibility (as a victim of these circumstances…). None of these are true, heart-felt apologies. The sustained leader never offers such excuses and expresses only *sincere* appreciation or regret.

---

355 Barking Up the Wrong Tree (website), November 15, 2015 citing "The Power of Apology" from Economics Letters, Volume 107, Issue 2, May 2010, Pages 233-235.

356 Perino, Dana. *And the rest of the story…*, 209.

This sounds like me

A lot   **somewhat**   **just a little**   **not at all**

Additional Resources:

Susan Cain, *Quiet.*

Lauren M. Bloom, *Art of the Apology.*

Ken Blanchard, et al., *The One Minute Apology.*

Eric Mosley, et al., *The Power of Thanks.*

Personal Objective:

Specific Actions:

Due Date:

4.3 Charisma

WBS Dictionary: Charisma is a term used to describe a person who carries an aura of personal warmth and seems to have the ability to draw people toward them with minimal effort. This natural attraction often causes a large number of people to gather around a person who displays charisma. In religious history, the word was used to describe a special blessing from heaven. People who are considered charismatic exude charm and are said to have a "presence." They attract positive attention and have a great depth of social adeptness. Charisma is one of the more difficult elements of leadership because it is extremely difficult to fake a natural tendency. In some respects, you either have it or you don't; however, to a degree, you can learn to express enthusiasm or develop the devotion of your followers. Through various actions you perform and attitudes you display, you can begin to foster a more natural sense of charisma. Charisma is also sometimes referred to as having a natural magnetism that draws people in. The sustained leader understands the importance of exhibiting whatever natural charisma they may have while developing and accentuating those traits that exhibit whatever authentic charisma they possess.

Application: It can be dangerous to treat charisma as a "fake it 'til you make it" trait because if you are "found out" you will be labeled a phony and lose whatever respect you may have gained. Some mistake egoism with charisma, and while there is an element of confidence in charisma, over-confidence or misplaced confidence (thinking you are more than you are, or thinking you are something that you are not to others) will damage your credibility. Charisma is in large part modesty and humility coupled with confidence. It is appearing comfortable in a variety of social settings and being able to engage people on a personal level. It is implementing the elements discussed in Dale Carnegie's *How to Win Friends and Influence People* to their maximum utility. You remember peoples' names and significant facts. You might use "cheat sheets" to record various personal details like birthdays, status of children and spouse, and current activities so that you can address those topics the next time you meet. This impresses people and causes them to perceive that you hold a level of charisma. So long as you are working on a genuine interest in others, you will not typically be perceived negatively.

The word "charisma" has been both overused and misused. According to Bernard Bass, "In the popular media, charisma has come to mean anything ranging from chutzpah to Pied Piperism, from celebrity to superman status. It has become an overworked cliché for strong, attractive, and inspiring personality."[357]

Kouzes and Posner further observe that social scientists have determined that charisma is a function of animation. Charismatic people "smile more, speak faster, pronounce words more clearly, and move their heads and bodies more often. They are also more likely to reach out and touch or make some physical contact with others during greetings. What we call charisma, then, can better be understood as nonverbal (and very human) expressiveness."[358]

---

357 B.M. Bass, Leadership and Performance Beyond Expectations (New York: Free Press, 1985), 35, cited in Kouzes, James M. and Barry Z. Pozner, *The Leadership Challenge*, (San Francisco, CA: Josey-Bass, 2002), 158.
358 Ibid, 158-59.

They also note the following: "What we have discovered, and rediscovered, is that leadership is not the private reserve of a few charismatic men and women. It is a process ordinary people use when they are bringing forth the best from themselves and others. What we've discovered is that people make extraordinary things happen by liberating the leader within everyone."[359]

Research at UCLA has determined that specific vocal control and inflection, traits that can be learned, are shared by those around the world who are perceived as charismatic leaders. This vocal command will "strongly affect how people respond to them, independent of the meaning of the words they say or the ideas they express."[360]

The confidence that is embedded within charisma is rooted in competence. Charisma without competence is flamboyance reflecting a high degree of undeserved egoism. This can lead to the negative trait of arrogance (5.2.6). Arrogance deflates charisma and can permanently disqualify a person from any leadership role. The sustained leader takes a genuine interest in people, develops their competence and the competence of those around them, and instills confidence while dealing with people in a very personable way. You can't "claim" charisma falsely. You must demonstrate it and earn the respect of others to truly be considered charismatic.

This sounds like me

A lot	somewhat	just a little	not at all

Additional Resources:

Dale Carnegie, *How to Win Friends & Influence People*.

Napoleon Hill, *Think and Grow Rich*.

Personal Objective:

---

359 Ibid. xxiii.

360 "Hear, Hear!! Scientists Map What Charisma Sounds Like." Wall Street Journal, 12/2/14, page D.1.

Specific Actions:

Due Date:

4.3.1 Personal Warmth

WBS Dictionary: Warmth is a difficult trait to describe. Justice Potter Stewart's often quoted comment when reviewing a Supreme Court case concerning pornography summarizes it well. He stated that he could not define it, but he knew it when he saw it. Likewise, we recognize people who have a personal warmth, and, conversely, recognize those who do not. Personal warmth comes from a pleasant attitude, even in the face of adversity, and a focus on those around you. Self-centered and self-focused people are not perceived as warm individuals. People generally react to a visceral feeling about the leader and how interacting with them makes the person feel. Such things defy logic, as they are emotionally based. Warmth is a moderated form of heat; it is neither extreme in heat nor lacking in heat. Personal warmth is moderate, neither shunning people nor causing them to huddle too close. It can be a sense of tenderness or compassion, and is usually expressed as a form of kindness or attraction. It can also be characterized as more intimate or attached, but that level of warmth is for appropriate relationships. Keep in mind, this is an emotional sense of the recipient. Too much familiarity when expressing warmth can be misinterpreted. Too much warmth can get a leader burned. A strong and consistent positive attitude toward everyone is an appropriate way to exhibit personal warmth.

Application: Warmth is the adept practice of interpersonal skills. It involves varying levels of affection, compassion, and kindness. It is demonstrated through the interactions you have with others and is easily the toughest part of charisma to fake. People can tell if you are feigning warmth. Nonetheless, you can learn to demonstrate warmth by interacting with others in a positive and encouraging way. Regardless of the circumstances, think of yourself as the host or hostess in the setting. Welcome people. Shake their hand with care and enthusiasm. Be obvious in your pleasure at seeing someone. Regardless of your personal sentiment or current mood, avoid appearing cool and detached or distracted. Make eye contact. Listen actively. Call people by their name.

Warmth must also be balanced with a sense of confidence. Without confidence and comfort with power, excessive warmth may cause others to perceive you as a Casper Milquetoast character. Do not be stiff. Be relaxed and comfortable with yourself. Avoid limp handshakes, verbal hesitations, and staring at the floor.

Warm people express gratitude. They compliment people and encourage them. They thank people for their contribution, no matter how small, and express the contribution in terms of the big picture. Warmth in a sustained leader is affirming (1.2.2.6). Warm people show empathy and an appropriate level of curiosity about the person, their life events, and their accomplishments. They are cordial in all respects and call to mind past events and interactions with the individual. The warmer you act toward others, the warmer you will feel. Make introductions to help others expand their networks and follow up to make sure both people saw some value.

Open your body language to be welcoming and above all else, SMILE! Some people are uncomfortable with their smile. It might be due to issues with their teeth, or perhaps their facial structure is such that a typical smile tends to squint their eyes. Both insecurities can be addressed through a proper dental hygiene or orthodontic correction and with practice in teaching your facial muscles to compensate. It sounds odd, perhaps, but a warm smile, however achieved, is critical to a warm appearance.

There are also many sources that strongly state the importance of a positive attitude. In fact, they suggest that it is the *sine qua non* of success and a very clear indicator of personal warmth. People like to be around positive people. "A smile changes the way you feel, the way you think, and how you interact with others. The energy you fuel the ride of your life with is entirely up to you. As the driver, you're the one who must also choose your vision of where you want to go."[361]

The sustained leader must in all cases be authentic. Warmth is not necessarily something that comes naturally and when faked, it will be perceived as being contrived and have the exact opposite effect of what is intended. The sustained leader takes a genuine interest in people and express it openly. They smile, shake hands, and encourage those they encounter.

---

361 Gordon, Jon, *The Energy Bus*, (Hoboken, NJ: John Wiley, 2007), 29.

This sounds like me

| A lot | somewhat | just a little | not at all |

Additional Resources:

Harvey Mackay, *Dig your Well Before you're Thirsty.*
Cynthia D'Amour, *Networking.*
Dale Carnegie, *How to Win Friends & Influence People.*

Personal Objective:

Specific Actions:

Due Date:

4.3.2 Direct

WBS Dictionary: The sustained leader seeks clarity of communication and the single best way to accomplish this is to communicate directly. This means communicating directly (not through an intermediary) to the intended audience and presenting the intended message in as clear and direct a manner as possible. Certainly, an appropriate level of both diplomacy and tact must be considered, but more importantly, for the sake of clarity, the leader should speak as directly as possible to avoid confusion or misunderstanding. The sustained leader avoids euphemisms, spin, loaded language, and inappropriate metaphors. People also consider those who speak their mind directly, but not obnoxiously, to hold a level of charisma due to their ability to communicate clearly. Speaking directly provides a sense of confidence, a key contributor to charisma. Misused, this type of communication can be hurtful and counterproductive. Used appropriately, the sustained leader will hasten understanding and avoid time-wasting errors in communication.

Application: Beating around the bush, as the saying goes, may seem to be a tactful way to communicate a difficult thought. More commonly, however, a direct approach that immediately frames the issue is a far better way to communicate. This does not mean that you are offensive or intentionally cruel; rather, you are coming straight to the point and moving the conversation on to a further discussion of contributing issues and resolutions.

Direct communicators use simple words and as few words as possible to convey the thought. They do not belabor the context and when asked the time do not proceed to tell you how to build a watch. This does not mean that all "small talk" is avoided, since some level of informal interaction can humanize the situation. When the time comes to "get down to business," the sustained leader does so with confidence and poise. Similarly, when making presentations or expressing a particular viewpoint, the sustained leader does not hesitate and introduce other distracting information. They give the facts, express their view and the rationale behind it, and, if appropriate, request a decision.

Being direct does not mean that you avoid being warm (4.3.1) but it does suggest that charisma requires a balance of both warmth and being direct. The sustained leader grasps that and displays the proper balance. To ensure understanding from the other party, they follow the old teacher's mantra: tell them what you are going to tell them, tell them, then tell them what you told them. Extraneous material is left out. Relevant and pertinent material is all that is provided, without fluff or other distractions.

This sounds like me

A lot	somewhat	just a little	not at all

Additional Resources:

Kerry Patterson, et al., *Crucial Conversations*.

Deborah Tannen, *Talking from 9 to 5*.

Personal Objective:

Specific Actions:

Due Date:

4.3.3 Socially Adaptable

WBS Dictionary: The sustained leader is comfortable in a variety of social settings and remains continually conscious of the setting, even if it is subject to rapid change. Social adeptness also mandates certain inviolate restrictions on conduct. Vulgar language or jokes and humor that is derogatory to any particular class of people (lawyers being the one possible exception), is never acceptable. In other words, always keep it clean and courteous. There is never an excuse for ill manners or a basic lack of understanding of appropriate social protocols. The sustained leader is aware of the social setting, anticipates new or unique settings, and prepares for them. They consciously take advantage of opportunities to expose themselves to new social settings.

Application: Being socially adept means that the leader assesses the situation and approaches it with the appropriate level of formality and dignity as appropriate. A meeting with the Queen of England, the Pope, or any other head of state requires that a high level of formality and respect for decorum be exhibited. A golf game with a few college buddies is less formal than a golf game with a client. A dinner party at a neighbor's house is different than a dinner party with a Congressman.

Appropriate dress, proper manners, and complete avoidance of excessive imbibing are also important aspects of being socially adept. Not everyone, is naturally comfortable in a variety of social situations. This is especially true for introverts. The sustained leader will find themselves in such variable situations on a very regular, if not constant basis. These social skills can be learned, even if it requires a mentor specifically for such training. This was the purpose of what was known in an earlier era as "finishing schools."

Ben Franklin was as comfortable at the pub in downtown Philadelphia as he was meeting with the King of France. Even so, he had quite a bawdy side and often had to restrain his natural tendencies based on the social situation.

Many businesses are global and must conduct their businesses in a great variety of cultures and languages. Politics is, by its nature, international. Most religions have a global reach as well. Each of the three major societal institutions expose their leaders to international situations, and many of them are quite unique. Steven Traylor is an executive with an international investment group. After visiting a popular Russian location for conducting business meetings he observed that "Being naked with a bunch of guys in a sauna and being beaten with a bunch of beech leaves is not for me. But that's part of the Russian way of doing business."[362]

Stay alert to the changing environment and upcoming unique (to you) situations. Prepare for them and behave appropriately. As one advisor said, "Stay classy."

This sounds like me

A lot   **somewhat**   **just a little**   **not at all**

Additional Resources:

Benjamin Franklin, Silverman, K. (ed.), *The Autobiography and Other Writings*. Harry G. Frankfurt, *On Bullshit*.

Personal Objective:

Specific Actions:

Due Date:

---

362 Parietti, Jeff, *The Book of Truly Stupid Business Quotes*, 197.

4.4 Techniques

WBS Dictionary: Within the genre of communication, there are a great number of techniques that can be used. The sustained leader works to develop an ability to use all of them in the appropriate circumstance. Certainly yelling, cursing, and berating are possible communication techniques, but not ones used by sustained leaders. This element is composed of five specific techniques that are most useful to the sustained leader. Developing skill in each of these will prepare the sustained leader to meet a great number of variable situations with aplomb. Proper use of these techniques will instill confidence in the followers, improve outcomes in dealing with people, and contribute to the development of charisma. The sustained leader becomes more effective in each of these techniques through continued practice.

Application: Techniques in communication are tools that facilitate effective communication. By developing strong capabilities in a variety of techniques, the sustained leader brings greater control to the communication and can work toward the best outcome from the conversation. The ability to craft outstanding questions elicits better information and can help the other parties engage in much-needed critical thinking. Being able to tell a memorable story ensures that the desired point is the real take-away and that the point will be better remembered by the audience. Being able to adjust to unexpected situations shows flexibility and works toward achieving the communication objective despite any setbacks or surprises. Understanding body language will permit the sustained leader to convey the appropriate unspoken messages and read the audience to better understand how the message is being received. The ability to simplify ensures that a broader audience will be reached and, more importantly, that the sustained leader truly understands the substance of the message.

General George C. Patton was an extremely effective fighting general. He was very firm in his beliefs about warfare and the fighting soldier. He was, however, less political than his superiors believed he should be. He was coarse, direct, and opinionated. The story is told of a reporter who asked him if he prayed. Patton responded with "Every God-Damned day!" Upon further inquiry about his use of profanity, he reportedly told the reporter that there were (damn) few words in the English language that everyone understood, and he intended to use every (damn) one of them. Reportedly his language was bit more colorful than reflected here. In that era, in his position, and in that environment, this may have been an appropriate communication technique. Clearly, given the trouble his mouth caused him in his career, he might have benefited from more effectively using the communication techniques suggested here. Still, while it seemed to have worked for him in reviewing his entire career, such situations are extremely rare. The sustained leader is advised to follow this guidance in lieu of the communication techniques used by General Patton.

This sounds like me

A lot	somewhat	just a little	not at all

Additional Resources:

Martin Blumenson, *Patton*.

John Maxwell, *Everyone Communicates, Few Connect*.

Nido Qubein, *How to be a Great Communicator*.

Annette Simmons, *Whoever Tells the Best Story Wins*.

Personal Objective:

Specific Actions:

Due Date:

4.4.1 Good Questions

WBS Dictionary: Questions are a source of power. The sustained leader develops the ability to ask probing and insightful questions. Questions allow the sustained leader to guide the conversation. They reflect an interest in what the other person has to say. Coupled with active listening, questions allow the sustained leader to gather great multitudes of information, and very often without disclosing a great deal about themselves. The entire Socratic method of education is based on the ability of the instructor to ask good questions. The best litigators know how to ask great questions and how to guide the story-telling of others. Similarly, the sustained leader appreciates the power over the situation that careful questioning can create. Questions can show interest, create warm relationships, and challenge others to think critically. Questions are a powerful communication technique for the sustained leader.

Application: Good questions fall into one of several categories, each designed to elicit a specific type of response. Direct questions can often be answered with a "yes" or a "no." Factual questions seek specific data or information. Leading questions presuppose the answer and should be used in very limited and defined circumstances. They are generally not desirable in normal conversation. Explanatory questions ask the responder to tell a story. They can also be in the form of non-questions that encourage the speaker to continue what they are saying. An explanatory question might take the form of, "Then what happened?" while the non-question seeking a similar response might grammatically be in the form of a command, such as "Tell me more."

Sales guru Jeffrey Gitomer is a big fan of questions and encourages their use as an integral part of the sales technique. He calls the best ones "power questions," questions that are useful for gathering information when the initial response is, "No one ever asked me that before."[363] The aphorism is variously stated that "knowledge is power," or "information is power." Both lead to the same conclusion—gathering knowledge or information is useful. There are both ethical and unethical ways to gather this information. Questions should to be neutral, in that they do not force a response and any response given is considered voluntary. Perhaps the better aphorism is the one that says, "It never hurts to ask." The key is, you have to ask. That starts the process. People fear asking questions under the mistaken idea that it might reflect their lack of knowledge, or more vernacularly, because it makes them feel stupid. It was Mark Twain who once said that "It is better to remain silent and be thought a fool, than to open your mouth and remove all doubt." Fear of embarrassment will often hinder good questions.

---

363 Gitomer, J., Little *Red Book of Selling: 12.5 Principles of Sales Greatness*, (US: Bard Press, 2004), 112.

Dorothy Leeds has a very instructive book on questions where she notes that the best questions are what she calls Super Probes. She describes these as open-ended questions that are directive, i.e. guide the person's answers to a thoughtful, careful, and detailed response. This is compared to those questions that are general and permit a non-focused answer. Many such questions are not really questions so much as commands using such words as describe, compare, distinguish, or explore the subject of the question.[364] Since the sentence does not end in a question mark, they are called implied questions. Ms. Leeds also cites a question that is certainly a candidate for the best question of all time. It comes from Laura Weinstock, age six, who asked "Does the Fairy godmother know she's make-believe?"[365]

Good starter questions are factual questions that reflect what a reporter might ask—who, what, where, why, when, and how. This will often set the stage and open the dialog. Other good questions are open-ended questions that ask the person to open up about themselves. Asking about feelings ("How did that make you feel?") is a technique useful to counselors. Asking for confirmation is also useful. Such questions might take the form of, "I'm not sure I understood that; could you go over it again?" or, "Let me see if I understood you…" followed by a paraphrase of what you believe you heard.

Questions can also serve specific purposes. Well-phrased questions can seek out hidden agendas and lead people who intend to deceive to trap themselves. Different versions of a story may suggest deception, as will recitation of rote memorization, particularly when different participants say the exact same thing. Making notes on the timeline of a story will often reveal such deception as well.

Certain questions are inappropriate in almost all situations. Ambiguous questions are those that are subject to more than one interpretation. Misuse of pronouns can often indicate an ambiguous question, and such situations can lead to extended misunderstandings. The ambiguity might not be immediately apparent. The parties may or may not realize that they are taking different, yet reasonable, interpretations of the ambiguity. If asked an ambiguous question, always seek clarification.

Controversial questions can also create problems. Such questions typically solicit opinions, and stating your opinion first can make you vulnerable. This

---

364 Leeds, Dorothy, *The 7 Powers of Questions: Secrets to Successful Communication in Life and Work*, (New York: Berkely Publishing, 2000), 188.
365 Ibid, 226.

is why it is often said that you never discuss religion or politics on a first date. Such questions can polarize the parties before any real progress or understanding has occurred. Some questions are both controversial and leading, in that they presuppose agreement with the questioner's opinion. Often, there is no data involved in the opinion. Social convention might prevent the sustained leader from completely avoiding or ignoring such a question, especially when dealing with the press (4.2.12.2). A better approach might be to redirect it to the questioner. Get them to express their opinion first, or at least clarify what it is they seek.

Questionable Quotes

To ask the right question is already half the solution of a problem.
—Carl Jung

*It is much harder to ask the right question than
it is to find the right answer to the wrong question.*
—E. E. Morison

*The important thing is not to stop questioning.
Curiosity has its own reason for existing.*
—Albert Einstein

Even "good" questions can have their traps for the unaware. A direct question may get an appropriate "yes" or "no," but it will not typically elicit any further response. Direct questions also assume a context that is usually not stated, probably not understood, and may very well be wrong. In team situations, an outside party might pose a direct question to one of the team members. The sustained leader knows to reassert control over the situation and guide the response, or take the response away from the person to whom the question was directed. The person to whom it was directed may not have all the necessary information, or may already be known by the leader to not understand the context in which it is asked. This may seem "controlling," but the sustained leader knows when to assert such control.

Factual questions, although seemingly benign, can still cause problems. Factual questions deal with provable data. There is typically no opinion or interpretation of data included. This might leave things unsaid that are important for the context. When asked a factual question, the sustained leader knows to be certain of the facts they are presenting. The sustained leader also knows when to say, "I don't know" and, depending on the circumstances, will agree to find the answer or solicit a further response from someone who does know the facts.

Questions should always be worded clearly, concisely, and courteously. Avoid using deliberately ambiguous, controversial, or leading questions. Be careful of your tone of voice and word choice. Practice active listening (3.4.1) and paraphrase or ask for clarification. Acknowledge the point being made without necessarily agreeing or disagreeing with it. It is also useful to acknowledge the speaker's feelings about the subject. Allowing free-running emotions can lead to a breakdown in the communication. Try to agree whenever you can and, if a misunderstanding has occurred, it is often useful to offer an apology regardless who created the misunderstanding. Project confidence in your questions.

Vince Molinaro in his work *The Leadership Contract* speaks to the culture of an organization as reflected in its leadership. He identified the one question that he can ask and immediately discern from whatever answer he is given, what the culture of the organization really is. That question is "How is asking for help viewed in this organization?"[366] Andy Stanley posed this question in the context of leaders needing to have the courage to act. "What do I believe is impossible to do in my field . . . but if it could be done would fundamentally change my business?"[367] These are great power questions. Learn to ask such questions.

As a final note, work diligently to remove the word "but" from your vocabulary. Whenever you use the word it suggests that you are negating everything that came before the word. If that content came from the other party, you are expressing disagreement. A far better approach is to use the word "and" instead. It acknowledges their point and adds yours to the discussion without being disagreeable. If the context does not permit the eradication of that word (most likely because you DO disagree), simply end the sentence and start a new one without using either "but" or "and."

366 *Leadership Contract*, 148.
367 *Next Generation Leader*, 66. This question was a driving factor behind the book you are holding.

"Questions frame the issue and set the agenda," say leadership researchers Kouzes and Posner. Never underestimate the importance of language in communication. Word choice has a very specific result. The use of loaded language is often intentional, simply to get a reaction or to package a statement with greater innuendo. Politicians understand this all too well. The sustained leader is aware of this tendency and avoids its use for purposes of manipulation. Conversely, people will also use loaded language in the presence of leaders, so it is important to understand its ramifications. Kouzes and Posner continue:

> Leaders understand and are attentive to language. They know the power of words. The words we choose to use are metaphors for concepts that define attitudes and behaviors, structures and systems. Our words evoke images of what we hope to create and how we expect people to behave....
>
> Questions, too, are quite powerful in focusing attention. When leaders ask questions, they send constituents on mental journeys—"quests"—in search of answers. The questions that a leader asks send messages about the focus of the organization, and they're indicators of what's of most concern to the leader. They're one more measure of how serious we are about our espoused beliefs. Questions provide feedback about which values should be attended to and how much energy should be devoted to them. What questions should leaders be asking if they want people to focus on integrity? On trust? On customer or client satisfaction? On quality? On innovation? On growth? On personal responsibility?[368]

Frances Hesselbein reminds us of another Drucker quote on the subject: "The leader of the past tells. The leader of the future asks. Ask, don't tell."[369]

John Maxwell also emphasizes the importance of asking yourself good questions. "Whenever I take time to pause and reflect, I begin by asking myself a question. Whenever I'm thinking and reflecting and I feel like I have hit a roadblock, I ask myself questions. If I'm trying to learn something new or delve deeper into an area so I can grow, I ask questions. I spend a lot of my life asking questions. But that's

---

368 Kouzes, James M. and Barry Z. Posner. *The Leadership Challenge*, (San Francisco, CA: Josey-Bass, 2002), 91. See also pages 101-02.
369 Hesselbein, Frances. *My Life in Leadership* (San Francisco: Josey Bass, 2011), 135.

a good thing." As author and speaker Anthony Robbins says, 'successful people ask better questions, and as a result, they get better answers.'"[370]

This sounds like me

| A lot | somewhat | just a little | not at all |

Additional Resources:
Dorothy Leeds, *The 7 Powers of Questions*.
Dale Carnegie, *How to Win Friends & Influence People*.
Jeffrey Gitomer, *Little Red Book of Selling*.
John Maxwell, *Good Leaders Ask Great Questions*.

Personal Objective:

Specific Actions:

Due Date:

4.4.2 Good Story Teller

WBS Dictionary: People engage with stories. Stories have a beginning, or set-up, followed by a description of events, usually, but not always, in chronological order, with a conclusion or ending. A joke, a parable, a fable, and most nursery rhymes are all forms of stories. People tend to have difficulty remembering facts. Facts put into the context of a story, or even a mnemonic device, are much more memorable. Sustained leaders know how to tell stories. The use of parables or example stories that are not necessarily based on real events can be an effective technique. It is also

---

370 Maxwell, John C. *The 15 Invaluable Laws of Growth* (Center Street: New York, 2012), 58-9.
    See also Maxwell, John C. *Good Leaders ask Great Questions*.

very useful to use quotes from recognized sources. Being able to recall a pithy quote can make your point more memorable.

Application: Learning to tell good stories requires three major steps. The first is to read as many stories of a wide variety of types as you can. Become familiar with the layout and tempo of a story. Don't be the person who, when asked what time it is, proceeds to tell the person how to build a watch. Knowing what to leave out can be more important than what you leave in. There are excellent story-tellers including Mark Twain, John Steinbeck, Stephen King, and Joyce Carol Oates. Read them, not just to enjoy the story, but to understand the structure, technique, and pace of the story.

The second step is to practice telling stories. Whether it is around the water cooler, while out for a beer with friends, or in a staff meeting, sustained leaders should learn to practice the skill and techniques. To start, it might be useful to memorize short stories and even jokes. Have you ever had someone start to tell a joke and then forget the punchline? You never remember the story they were telling, only that they totally bungled it and most likely embarrassed themselves. Learn a few good jokes and share them with a variety of audiences.

The third step is to rehearse story-telling. Whether it is in a public forum or private, there is nothing wrong with video or audio recording what you are practicing and playing it back for yourself. You will be amazed at how you both look and sound, and you will usually become your own worst critic. Seek others whose opinions you trust to critique your presentation as well. Nothing beats practice; practice builds confidence. Confident story tellers are considered credible, memorable, and competent. Sustained leaders learn to tell great stories.

Vince Molinaro suggests that every leader should tell their own leadership story. Within his consulting practice, he has participants develop their leadership timeline and then tell their story. This is an excellent exercise. Both your positive and negative experiences are outlined and reviewed to provide insight to the leader you are today. As Vince says, "experiences can only be the best teacher if we take the time to reflect on them and consider how they have shaped us."[371] The full exercise has each participant review their experiences, identify themes and patterns, and then *share it*. In other words, you must find a way to share your own light. This is a great story. It is *your* story. You need to tell it. As you do, your ability to tell other

---

371 *Leadership Contract* p.185.

stories will improve. To this end, have you read (1.3.1.1) any biographies? These are stories of leaders.[372]

The phrase "corporate memory" usually relates to the company operations and the employees who carry out those operations. High turnover of employees can diminish the retention of that memory. Younger, smaller companies where the founder is still around or not far removed retain the corporate lore that goes with all companies. This lore is part of the character of the company. It builds camaraderie and inspires people to follow the leaders of these companies. Stories are things people retain. Stories build legends. Whenever a sustained leader communicates, they should do so with stories.[373]

How important are the stories we tell? Max DePree offers the following thought:

> We work to maintain these values. Yet a system of beliefs is always threatened by change, and change is something no one can avoid. Successful entrepreneurships tend to become corporations. Successful corporations tend to become institutions. Institutions foster bureaucracy, the most superficial and fatuous of all relationships. Bureaucracy can level our gifts and our competence. Tribal storytellers, the tribe's elders, must insistently work at the process of corporate renewal. They must preserve and revitalize the values of the tribe. They nourish a scrutiny of corporate values that eradicates bureaucracy and sustains the individual. Constant renewal also readies us for the inevitable crises of corporate life.[374]

This sounds like me

A lot	somewhat	just a little	not at all

---

372 For a contemporary example, read Carson, B., and Murphey, C. *Gifted Hands: The Ben Carson Story*, (US: Zondervan, 1996).

373 For those who are biblically inclined, consider Matthew 18 (et al.) where Jesus spoke in parables—stories that people remember. For the historians among us, consider how oral traditions existed long before the written word. It is the story that we remember. And as a final example, do you remember the nursery rhymes and fables that were read to us when we were small? Of course you do. They were memorable stories.

374 DePree, Max. *Leadership is an Art*. (New York: Dell, 1989), 90-91.

Additional Resources:

Annette Simmons, *Whoever Tells the Best Story Wins.*

Boyd Clarke, et al., *The Leader's Voice.*

https://www.toastmasters.org/

Mark Twain, *The Signet Classic Book of Mark Twain's Short Stories.*

Personal Objective:

Specific Actions:

Due Date:

4.4.3 Able to Adjust Message to Audience Level

WBS Dictionary: A person who communicates well appreciates that different audiences require a different message. This does not mean that you are duplicitous and provide conflicting answers, however. One simply would not answer the question "Where do babies come from?" in the same way for a four-year-old that they would for a 12 year-old. Similarly, an employee whose livelihood depends on the viability of the company is entitled to more information than a member of the public at a cocktail party. Even when a professional presentation is expected, an outstanding communicator will adjust if the audience is expected to be for working professionals or a group of high school students on a class tour. The sustained leader can perceive the audience before and during the presentation, and determine how to adjust the message to ensure that it is being received. Different audiences have different agendas, collectively and individually. The sustained leader recognizes these attitudes and adjusts accordingly. This is not to say that the speaker should just cave-in to audience whims. It may require a level of dominance and control to make sure the message is delivered, even if unpopular or ill-received. The sustained leader maintains their situational awareness (2.1.6) and their decorum, and responds accordingly.

Application: Classrooms, training sessions, shareholder meetings, and other routine communications usually begin with an expectation of the audience level of comprehension, background knowledge, and an agenda to listen rather than disrupt. Every accomplished speaker knows too well that such expectations are not always realized. Adjustments, sometimes real-time adjustments (often referred to as "thinking on your feet"), must be made. This may be due to questions from the audience, a sense of restlessness from the audience, or outright rudeness expressed by the audience.

It has been said that if you do enough public speaking, everything will have happened. Late breaking news might completely redirect the intended message. Disrupters may infiltrate the presentation. A perceived friendly audience member might be preparing to embarrass the speaker to discredit them. Audio/video equipment has an amazing ability to fail at the most inopportune time. Unexpected things will happen. These are all real-time events that will require adjustment.

The sustained leader will work to understand the message that is intended and the audience to whom he or she is speaking. While some of this can be managed through prior preparation, it can just as readily happen during the presentation. These events will require the leader to adjust and respond. The purpose of the communication is to convey specific information, to motivate, to inspire, to mentor, to educate, or to build the relationship. Regardless of the message, there will be a need to adjust the message in terms of delivery, style, or technique. Content should not change, however. The overarching message should be the same.

Kenny was asked to teach a class to experienced professionals. He prepared the topic and went to the venue to present the material. When he arrived, he polled the audience, as he always does, to ascertain their expectations of the class. The class, as it turned out, contained many people who were very new to the profession and they had been told that the class would be to help them understand the basics. Their supervisors, who were supposed to attend the class, had decided to send more junior people. Kenny realized that his original presentation would be inappropriate for this audience. Using the same presentation charts, however, he reduced the level of complexity and sophistication to meet the audience expectations. His speaking ability and subject matter knowledge allowed him to provide a useful class that got extremely high ratings from the participants. As a sustained leader, he adjusted the message to the audience level.

This sounds like me

A lot　　　　　**somewhat**　　　　　**just a little**　　　　　**not at all**

Additional Resources:
Dorothy Leeds, *Powerspeak.*
Jay Heinrichs, *Thank You for Arguing.*

Personal Objective:

Specific Actions:

Due Date:

4.4.4 Able to Simplify

WBS Dictionary: There are many things which, by their nature, are complex. The world itself seems to become more complex every day yet, in order to effectively transmit information, the message must be simplified as much as possible to ensure the maximum comprehension. If a speaker uses large words, intending to impress, it is more likely that many in the audience will not understand. Those who do understand may even dismiss the message as pompous and irrelevant. They may perceive that the speaker is using hyperbole inappropriately, which will diminish the speaker's credibility. There are some who are so used to communicating to a specific audience of their peers that they lose the ability to simplify. Both good speakers and writers hone the skill of simplification. This is not to say that you must "dumb down" the message to a level that insults your audience (See 4.4.3) since that will simply alienate them. Even so, it is not necessary to show off your abilities by speaking above your audience's comprehension. Simplify to the point of maximum comprehension; retain complexity only when absolutely necessary and when the audience can at least stretch their understanding to grasp the gist of the message. The sustained leader understands both sides of these extremes and adjusts accordingly.

Application: Albert Einstein, who admittedly was rather smart, observed this: "If you can't explain it simply, you don't understand it well enough." The ability to simplify the complex is a skill that can be developed and requires that one thoroughly and completely understands the subject. Often, it takes more time to make things simple than to construct the message initially. Sustained leaders take the time to consider the audience and the appropriate level of complexity for the message. Any failure in communicating falls to the speaker, not the audience.

Businessman and TV reality show host Donald Trump notes that brevity is crucial for effective communications. "We don't have time for loquacious colleagues, and ... longwinded diatribes...."

He continues, "Simple as it sounds, there is great wisdom in the short, fast, and direct route. Knowing where you're going in your conversation and demonstrating to others you know where you're going by being concise, is a big step toward leadership and respect. Hone these skills in every situation and with every opportunity you have.... Learn to economize. People appreciate brevity in today's world."[375]

Franklin Roosevelt gave similar advice much more succinctly. He said, "Be sincere; be brief; be seated." Wise words.

Simplicity in communication crosses from the spoken word to the lyric. Despite a complete lack of formal musical training and very little formal education at all, Irving Berlin learned to sing in bars through one-fingered piano playing. Even so, in his own simplistic way, he gave us "God Bless America," "White Christmas," and "I Hate to get up in the Morning." He eventually wrote music for the Marx Brothers, the Ziegfeld Follies, and Broadway shows. His music was never complex, but his simple, memorable tunes have become part of the American musical tradition. In

---

375 Trump, Donald with Meredith McIver, *Think Like a Champion*, (New York: Vanguard Press, 2009), 63.

their simplicity, they hold a staying power that makes some of his songs best sellers to this day.

When Russell Conwell visited with Abraham Lincoln, he reported that when the president turned his attention to him, Lincoln's first words were, "I am a very busy man and have only a few minutes to spare. Now tell me in the fewest words what it is you want."[376]

Brevity and simplicity are key for the sustained leader. Never say more than is needed and always reduce the message to its simplest terms. If your message is still muddled or hard to understand, this suggests that you do not understand the subject as well as you should.

This sounds like me

A lot	somewhat	just a little	not at all

Additional Resources:

Caryl Rae Krannich, *101 Secrets of Highly Effective Speakers.*
Dorothy Leeds, *Powerspeak.*

Personal Objective:

Specific Actions:

Due Date:

4.4.5 Body Language

WBS Dictionary: Displaying appropriate body language for any occasion is necessary for the sustained leader to communicate effectively. This includes both

---

376 Conwell, Russell, *Acres of Diamonds*, 49.

dress and demeanor. There are times for postures of dominance and for those of submission. There are appropriate facial expressions for different occasions, and the sustained leader understands that others will judge them based on their own interpretation of these subconscious indicators. This includes both the "sending" and the "receiving" of such signals. The sustained leader not only portrays the appropriate countenance, but learns to appropriately interpret the countenance of others. This can be an extremely useful tool in negotiations, in managing people, and in dealing with people generally. Making people feel warm and comfortable in your presence will cause others to be drawn toward you. You attract followers, which substantiates you as a leader. As an additional dimension, the sustained leader understands that their attire and hygiene are also part of their body language. As touched on in 1.1.2.4, being socially adept includes a sense of proper fashion and attire. Certainly, your clothes, hair style, piercings, hair color, and breath can have a significant impact on what others perceive about you, especially in a first impression.

Application: Posture tells a great deal about the person. Doctors use it as an indicator of certain health conditions. The elderly person with a walker who is hunched over may have osteoporosis and might not have had sufficient calcium in their diet. Scoliosis can alter the body profile, and certain diseases like muscular dystrophy and polio can also affect the body appearance. Stephen Hawking, the great physicist, suffers from amyotrophic lateral sclerosis (ALS), yet his mind remains sharp and he continues to contribute to his field of science. In these situations, there is very little the person can do to alter their appearance. Whether that elicits sympathy or disdain from those they encounter is totally beyond their control. What the sustained leader understands is that there are many things that can be controlled regardless of the circumstances. To the degree these things *can* be controlled and they are *not*, the audience will pass judgement.

Some body stances are aggressive while others are subdued. Some hand gestures can be threatening while others can be calming. Some gestures are clearly a function of habit and are repeated endlessly. Nervous tics and what poker players call "tells" are clear signals to the careful observer what is going on inside the head of the person. We are constantly sending signals to those around us through our body language.

Students of body language can learn to modify their unconscious signals. The more Machiavellian among us can even alter our signals to the point of deceiving, thus the science of body language cannot be more than generalities since there are so many variables that go into it. Leaning toward a person shows interest; however, leaning too close and invading their personal space can be threatening. Open arms show a welcoming stance; crossed arms, however, reflect a closed, non-receptive stance. Facial expressions from smiles to sneers actually transcend species, suggesting how built-in the body language cues are. Experts have studied the act of picking non-existent lint from your clothes, fiddling with glasses or car keys, and a variety of hand positions, especially when touching the head and face. There are definite signals that we send. The sustained leader learns to both control their signals and read those of others.

As George Washington noted as a young boy, "The Gestures of the Body must be Suited to the Discourse you are upon."[377]

This sounds like me

A lot	**somewhat**	**just a little**	**not at all**

Additional Resources:

Ricardo Bellino, *You Have Three Minutes!*

Allan Pease, *The Definitive Book of Body Language.*

Personal Objective:

Specific Actions:

Due Date:

---

377 Washington, G., & Baldrige, L. *George Washington's Rules of Civility & Decent Behaviour in Company and Conversation,* (US: Mount Vernon Ladies Association of the Union, 1989) (Rule 20)

5.0 Commitment

WBS Dictionary: Everyone is committed to something. It might be to your own entertainment or edification, but part of life is acting on our priorities, and thus it is relatively easy to determine what it is to which we are committed. When you are committed you devote your resources to that objective. You feel passionate and consistently seek to make a difference. Whether it is your talent, your time, or your treasure, when you track where those are being expended you can determine your levels of commitment.

Commitment includes your vision, your contribution to society, and your industry. Commitment understands when it is appropriate to pull the plug on certain activities and put them on your "don't do" list. When you are passionate about your vision, it is easy to devote resources consistently toward that objective. When you focus (2.3.11) your effort you can achieve more. When your resources are dispersed and unfocused, goals (2.3.1) become more difficult to achieve.

Your commitment demonstrates your capacity to lead and draws followers to you. If your followers do not feel that your commitment toward the team's goals is sufficiently powerful, they will not continue as followers. Commitment reflects what you are willing to do and where you draw the line, beyond which exist the things you will not do. This will also include those situations where you must expend considerable effort in "fixing," which may entail removing or unlearning certain traits or habits. This element also involves a level of character (1.0) in that once you have given your word you are committed to seeing whatever it is you have promised to its timely conclusion. Thus, this element melds many other elements of leadership into the place where the rubber meets the road in determining whether you truly have what it takes to be a sustained leader.

Application: To some, it might seem that this element should come first. A WBS does not necessarily place elements in chronological order—that is the role of the scheduling function. It is fair to say, however, that unless you have mastered the elements of character (1.0), competence (2.0), compassion (3.0), and communication (4.0), your commitment toward a particular objective is unlikely to be achieved. It is also important to recall that a WBS provides ALL of the elements necessary to achieve a unique end-product. In this case this is you as a sustained leader. In that regard, this element is no more or less important than any other.

Even so, there are certain elements within this WBS whereby a failure to master them will result in your ultimate failure as a leader.

It is probably not humanly possible to master every element of this WBS. Everyone will discover a natural ability for certain elements, but each person's inventory will be very different from everyone else's. It is not reasonable to assume that every leader must master every element. Choices will have to be made and tradeoffs will occur. Again, some will find this easier than others, but it is important to recognize that the more completely you master every element, the stronger your leadership will be. Perhaps your commitment to becoming a sustained leader will entail an initial effort on elements where you perceive a particular weakness, or where you or your mentors feel that your lack of mastery is hindering your progress. As you grow in your leadership abilities you will want to reassess your progress and renew your commitment to becoming a sustained leader. It will become a lifetime commitment to your continued progress and success.

Clearly you cannot do everything all at once. You will be forced to make choices relative to your progress. Perhaps a lesson might be drawn from the life of Benjamin Franklin as discussed in Chapter 2 in explaining why a self-improvement program is not really a project because it never ends. You might find that useful in your pursuit of sustained leadership. Do not try to achieve all elements at one time. That is not practical, and no one has that level of resources to devote to it. Be committed, however, to continuous improvement and review this WBS at least annually to assess your progress. A lifetime of leadership improvement will enhance your life personally and professionally.

When thinking of your commitment to leadership and the principles explained in each element of this WBS, one helpful question to ask yourself is this: If everyone in my team (or tribe, or family, etc.) were to act *exactly* like me, would this be a better or weaker team? Your behaviors and attitudes will be modeled and mimicked. People are watching. Parents understand this, sometimes much too late, when they realize that their children are amazingly like them. How many of us have woken up one morning, looked in the mirror, and asked, "When did I become my mother (or father)?" We all do this. Babies throughout the animal kingdom mimic their parents and strive to be like them. Are you a positive role model or a negative one for your team? Is the world better because others follow your example, or are we worse off? Your strength of commitment is crucial to this part of the process.

A side note to students. Your role in life right now is to prepare for the future. While it may not seem to be true, you have more time to devote to developing your sustained leadership right now than at any time in your life to come. Devoting effort to developing your leadership capabilities *now* will pay huge dividends throughout your life. You are encouraged to do so. And if you are not currently a student in the formal sense (sustained leaders are committed to constant learning) you might find yourself voluntarily or involuntarily with more time on your hands. Use it wisely. Whether you have elected to take a sabbatical or are "currently seeking new opportunities," spending time on developing your leadership abilities is an excellent use of your time regardless of your current station or situation in life.

This sounds like me

A lot   **somewhat**   **just a little**   **not at all**

Additional Resources:

Benjamin Franklin, *The Autobiography of Benjamin Franklin & Selections from His Other Writings*.

Brian Tracy, *No Excuses!*

Personal Objective:

Specific Actions:

Due Date:

5.1 Do

WBS Dictionary: As noted in 2.3 Bias for Action, a leader is measured by results. There are certain things on which a leader must focus (2.3.11) to achieve the goals

(2.3.1) required for the leadership role. When a person is committed to achieving results, they focus their attention and effort on the actions necessary to create those results. There is a great difference between knowing what must be done and actually being sufficiently motivated to act toward those objectives.[378] There are many well-intentioned people who, sadly, achieve little. Within this element of commitment (5.0) we distinguish between those things that must be done and those things that must be avoided. This element focuses specifically on what the sustained leader does and includes the sub-elements of passion and vision among others. It includes consistency and adaptability. It also deals with maintaining your health and knowing the difference between true failure and simply adjusting your goals to eliminate certain efforts that will not yield the desired results. These are the things that a sustained leader does to provide the driving force behind team accomplishments. Ignore them at your peril.

Application: Mahatma Gandhi has been quoted as saying:

Your beliefs become your thoughts,
Your thoughts become your words,
Your words become your actions,
Your actions become your habits,
Your habits become your values,
Your values become your destiny.

This stream of thought suggests that what you are inside will eventually translate to what you do on the outside. Thus, a sustained leader must control all aspects of their life, from their beliefs, to their thoughts, to their words, to their actions, habits, values, and ultimately even their destiny. And people are watching.

Parents understand this all too well. It is amazing to discover that the smallest of your actions or words—things to which you gave no thought before the act and almost none after the fact—become your child's firmest memory.

Thus, what you do is a direct reflection of who you are and has a direct impact on the quality of leadership you will display. Holding the proper beliefs leads you

---

378 Pfeffer, Jeffrey, and Robert I. Sutton. *The Knowing-Doing Gap.* (Boston: Harvard Business School Press, 2000).

through the path described by Gandhi. Practicing good habits, on foundational beliefs, prepares you for leadership opportunities and events.

Similarly, as a leader you will be judged by your results. And your actions will speak volumes more than your words—again a concept parents understand in raising children. The entire chain of "do" items, therefore, is critical for the sustained leader to maintain. A wise man said, "Don't say things. What you are stands over you the while, and thunders so that I cannot hear what you say to the contrary."[379] The sustained leader will hold firm beliefs that will be reflected in all they do and think. Their leadership will be judged by the results of these actions. The sustained leader is committed to understanding the natural law (1.2.2.4) as it relates to our thoughts and beliefs being reflected in who we are and what we do. The sustained leader is then committed to maintaining all aspects of this natural order, or, in other words, keeping their heart pure. It is a difficult path that requires constant attention.

This sounds like me

| A lot | somewhat | just a little | not at all |

Additional Resources:

Jeffrey Pfeffer, et al., *The Knowing-Doing Gap*.

Ken Blanchard, et al., *Know Can Do*.

Personal Objective:

Specific Actions:

Due Date:

_____

379 From an essay titled "Social Aims" by Ralph Waldo Emerson published in 1875.

5.1.1 Passion

WBS Dictionary: Passion is emotional. It might often defy logic because it is so intensely emotional. Some perceive that passion is one of those "touchy-feely" or "warm and fuzzy" things with which true leaders never concern themselves and is perceived as an unimportant aspect of leadership. This has occasionally caused others to treat a passionate leader in a diminished light. These attitudes are *not* the ones held by the sustained leader.

Passion is powerful and compelling. It is often used in the context of romantic or sexual love because of its power to cause some people to "lose their mind" over the situation. The passion of the sustained leader should hold that level of intensity. The sustained leader should be extravagantly enthused about the goals of the organization. Anything less is not sustainable, nor will it cause others to join the team. Passion includes enthusiasm, focus, and direction. It can be exhausting. It is critically important to the organization. Unless the leader feels such passion, the achievement of the organization's goals is jeopardized. Passion connects with people and becomes contagious. It causes the focus of time, talent, and treasure toward the object of the passion. When a leader is passionate they are perceived as being tough minded and reasonably assertive. Passion might raise the competitiveness level of the leader, but it will also tend to enhance their creativity.

Application: The concepts of passion and vision are often conflated because they are very interdependent. It is difficult to feel passionately about an ill-defined vision. Likewise, a strong vision will engender passionate response from the team and will maintain the leader's ambition toward the goals set by the team. Passion can be demonstrated in a variety of ways. Your overall enthusiasm toward a particular goal or vision will infect every aspect of your leadership journey. This passion is a direct indicator of the degree to which you will go to overcome obstacles. And every leader confronts obstacles, often with ever-increasing size and complexity. If your passion cannot sustain you through this journey, you are trying to lead the wrong team to the wrong vision.

Howard Schultz

When you are surrounded by people who share a passionate commitment around a common purpose, anything is possible.

Passion is internally and volitionally generated. "No matter what term is used—whether *purpose, mission, legacy, dream, goal, calling,* or *personal agenda*— the intent is the same: leaders want to do something significant, to accomplish something that no one else had yet achieved. What that something is—the sense of meaning and purpose—has to come from within. No one can impose a self-motivating vision on you. That's why, just as we said about values, you must first clarify your own visions of the future before you can expect to enlist others in a shared vision. To create a climate of meaningfulness, first you must personally believe in something yourself. Before you can inspire others, you have to be inspired yourself."[380]

———————— • ————————

Martin Luther King Jr.

Human progress is neither automatic nor inevitable... every step toward the goal of justice requires sacrifice, suffering, and struggle; the tireless exertions and passionate concern of dedicated individuals.

———————— • ————————

W. Edward Demming is known as the master of quality improvement. After WWII American manufacturers, having been devoted to the war effort for so many years, could make most anything and find a market for it. Quality was not a big concern; it was not really a concern at all. Not finding a quality-focused audience in America, Demming found an eager audience in Japan. Japan had already developed a reputation for cheap shoddy products. Demming was passionate about his idea that quality was not to be inspected into the product at the end, but built into it from the very beginning. He never did get American companies to listen—until they were being soundly beaten in the marketplace by the Japanese.

Businessman Donald Trump states that "if you want to get rich, two important considerations are passion and efficiency: Have passion for what you do and be efficient about it at the same time. That combination has worked for me."[381]

---

380 James M. Kouzes and Barry Z. Posner, *The Leadership Challenge* (San Francisco: Jossey-Bass, 2002), 112.
381 Donald Trump with Meredith McIver, *Think Like a Champion* (New York: Vanguard Press, 2009), 179.

This sounds like me

A lot   **somewhat**   **just a little**   **not at all**

Additional Resources:
Chris Widener, *The Angel Inside.*
Mark Sanborn, et al., *The Fred Factor.*

Personal Objective:

Specific Actions:

Due Date:

Essential Leadership Journey Checklist
5.1.2 Vision

WBS Dictionary: A leader's vision provides direction for the organization. It defines a clarity of purpose. It was Yogi Berra who said that if you do not know where you are going, you will probably end up somewhere else. He's right. The primary role of a leader is to set a vision for the organization. A vision assesses where the organization is today and anticipates what will (or even may) come to pass. It involves a level of discernment of a multitude of facts and variables in order to determine both what COULD be and what SHOULD be.

John F. Kennedy said, "Many people see things as they are and ask 'why?' I see things as they could be and ask 'why not?'"[382] That is vision. It is a proper sense of perception of what is possible. Grand visions are aggressive. They inspire. They provide a point around which a team can rally and adopt the passion of the leader to work toward achievement of that vision. It is also a function of the

---

382 See also quote from George Bernard Shaw in 5.1.4.

imagination since a vision that merely sees things as they are is called sight. The sustained leader creates in their imagination a sense of what can be accomplished, effectively communicates that to the team, and inspires the team to work toward the same vision, focusing their energy toward that end.

Application: Kouzes and Posner make the appropriate link between "possibility thinking" and the creation of an inspiring vision. They define vision as "an ideal and unique image of the future for the common good."[383] Unless the common good is the objective, rather than the leader's selfish interests, it will not attract the necessary following.

Theodore Hesburgh

The very essence of leadership is that you have to have a vision. It's got to be a vision you articulate clearly and forcefully on every occasion. You can't blow an uncertain trumpet.

William Ury tells the following story of his work with Richard Fisher in the 1980s on *Getting to Yes*. He says, "Our goal was to help people shift from adversarial approaches to cooperative methods for dealing with differences at work, at home, and in the community. But our dream was bigger than that. It was to help the world take a step toward peace. We were concerned about humanity itself, whose fate in an age of mass destruction ultimately rests on our abilities to resolve disputes in a cooperative fashion."[384] To the cynic this might recall memories of all the beauty pageant contestants who said that if selected they would work for world peace. A properly channeled vision can be powerful. The body of knowledge collected by Roger Fisher before his death, the work of Bill Ury that continues, along with Bruce Patton (a later contributor), and Robert Mnookin, who took over the Harvard Negotiation Project from Fisher and Ury, have all contributed toward seeking solutions to global problems, disputes, and aggressions. Even when some of the parties involved believed that a solution was impossible, this bold vision has contributed measurably to world peace—as best it exists today. *That* is a vision.

---

383 Kouzes and Posner, *Leadership Challenge*, 125.
384 Ury, *Getting to Yes with Yourself*, p. 175.

John Maxwell tells the story of an experiment that was conducted using rats in water deep enough for them to swim. When placed in water in utter darkness, the rats swam for only about three minutes before giving up. When placed in the same water with a single ray of light shining in, the rats continued to swim for thirty-six hours before giving up. "Each time you cast a vision for others and paint a picture of their future success, you build them up, motivate them, and give them reasons to keep going."[385]

Once a leader can express a vision, there is some general consensus within the literature that the leader must have a strategy (1.3.9.3) for achieving that vision. Daniel Goleman says that strategy derives from the battlefield and means "the art of the leader."[386] Strategy is how you deploy, or position, your resources. The greatest wisdom on strategy comes from Jack Welch, who said that strategy is simple—"pick a general direction and implement like hell."[387]

Thus, the strategic choices link directly to the vision. The more important aspect then becomes the tactical choices of specific actions that will be taken to achieve the goals (2.3.1), or as Welch would say, the implementation. Once positioned (strategy) within a system (systems thinking), actions (tactics) are taken to maximize the return on the effective use of available resources. This is where the sustained leader leads, and the measure of success will be from the results of those actions.

The Importance of Having a Clear Vision

Where there is no vision people perish
—Proverbs 29:18.

Vision is the art of seeing things invisible.
—Jonathan Swift

---

385 John Maxwell and J. Dornan *How to Influence People: Make a Difference in your World.* (Nashville: Thomas Nelson, 2013), 52-53.

386 Daniel Goleman, *Focus: The Hidden Driver of Excellence* (New York: Harper Collins, 2015), 213.

387 Jack Welch, and Suzy Welch, *Winning.* (New York: Harper Business Publishers, 2005), 165.

> *Teaching people skills without giving them a vision for a better future—*
> *a vision based on common values—is only training.*
> **—Nido Qubein**

> *Vision is the ability to see what is not yet, so you can create what never was.*
> **—Doug Firebaugh**

> *A decision is made with the brain. A commitment is made with the heart.*
> *Therefore, a commitment is much deeper and more binding than a decision.*
> **—Nido Qubein**

———————— • ————————

Team members seek two primary things. The first is to be engaged in interesting work. This desire comes in higher than making a lot of money. Another desire that ranks higher than income is "working for a leader with vision and values."[388]

Kouzes and Posner make the following observation:

> By the ability to be *forward-looking*, people don't mean the magical power of a prescient visionary. The reality is far more down-to-earth: it's the ability to set or select a desirable destination toward which the company, agency, congregation, or community should head. Vision reveals the beckoning summit that provides others with the capacity to chart their course toward the future. As constituents, we ask that a leader have a well-defined orientation toward the future. We want to know what the organization will look like, feel like, be like when it arrives at its destination in six quarters or six years. We want to have it described to us in rich detail so that we'll know when we've arrived and so that we can select the proper route for getting there.[389]

They go on to note that people perceive forward-looking as a positive trait in a leader 95 percent of the time, while the percentage of those perceived to hold the

---

388 Kouzes and Posner, *Leadership Challenge*, 151. Elsewhere the authors note that venture capitalist Geoff Yang seeks out those with "great vision." These are people who "are able to recognize patterns when others see chaos in the marketplace." Ibid. at 113.

389 Kouzes and Posner, *Leadership Challenge*, 29. (Emphasis in original).

trait falls around 60 percent. The logical conclusion, they note, is that this "suggests a major developmental need for individuals as they move into roles that are more strategic in nature."[390]

Greg Mckeown emphasizes the role of a clear vision on the team. "The results of [my] research were startling: when there was a high level of clarity of purpose, the teams and the people on it overwhelmingly thrived. When there was a serious lack of clarity about what the team stood for and what their goals and roles were, people experienced confusion, stress, frustration, and ultimately failure. As one senior vice president succinctly summarized it when she looked at the results gathered from her extended team: 'Clarity equals success.'"[391]

The idea of a vision was summarized by Blanchard and Barrett. "A compelling vision tells you who you are (your purpose), where you're going (your picture of the future), and what will guide your journey (your values)."[392] This provides a very useful formula for creating your vision. If you are not experienced in doing so write down these three elements, or even just possible candidates for each of the elements. If you are still stuck, try this exercise. Write down a list of "Ten Things I Believe." These should be truly heartfelt beliefs. Many people end up with lists of fifty or one hundred, but start with ten. From this list you can begin to discern your values and your purpose. For any of the things you believe that do not seem to match the world as you see it today, describe what the world *should* look like to match your values and beliefs. You now have a vision.

Kouzes and Posner provide a step-by-step process for developing a vision, which includes the words of a vision statement.[393]

Napoleon Bonaparte said, "A leader is a dealer in hope."[394] It is often said that hope is not a strategy, but a vision contains a high level of hope. A dream envisions the hope that the team, working together and consistently, can achieve the vision. And then they can create a new, bigger vision and continue to work toward it.

---

390 Ibid.
391 Greg Mckeown, *Essentialism: The Disciplined Pursuit of Less* (New York: Crown Business, 2012), 240.
392 Ken Blanchard and Colleen Barrett, *Lead with Luv: A Different Way to Create Real Success* (Upper Saddle River, NJ: FT Press, 2011), 63.
393 Kouzes and Posner, *Leadership Challenge*, 130-39.
394 Orrin Woodward, *The Leadership Train* (Cary, NC: Obstacles Press, 2014), 126, quoting Napoleon Bonaparte, *Napoleon in His Own Words: From the French of Jules Bertaut*, as translated by Herbert Edward Law and Charles Lincoln Rhodes (Chicago: A.C. McClurg & Co., 1916), 52.

The vision of a sustained leader does not exist as a real tangible place. It is a distant shore that the leader seeks, enlisting others to go along, sometimes as ballast, but hopefully as oarsmen, or cooks, or navigators, or coxswain, or whatever talent and treasure the person has to contribute to the cause.

It is interesting that every corporate vision has been expressed in words. This is curious since the human memory does not function in words, but in images. Rather than a dry description, a vision must be a picture of the future as we see it in our mind's eye. The leader who can articulate a clear picture of the future they seek to achieve will be able to draw a following of people who see that same vision. Words are great and a wonderful way to communicate; pictures provide a vision.

"Every great dream begins with a dreamer. Always remember, you have within you the strength, the patience, and the passion to reach for the stars to change the world."[395]

This sounds like me

A lot　　　　　**somewhat**　　　　　**just a little**　　　　　**not at all**

Additional Resources:

James Kouzes, et al., *The Leadership Challenge*.

John Lukacs, *Churchill*.

Personal Objective:

Specific Actions:

Due Date:

---

395 Harriet Tubman, quoted in Blanchard and Barrett, *Lead with Luv*, 145.

5.1.3 Consistency in Vision

WBS Dictionary: The sustained leader stays the course. They have their vision and mission in clear focus and work day in and day out toward the accomplishment of that vision. Their passion drives them forward and creates a path of continued success on the journey of realizing the vision. And they do so on a consistent and constant basis. Consistency is firmness in conviction and steadfast if not rigid adherence to the values of the organization. The same principles are adhered to in a uniform pattern. Consistency is predictable; it conforms to previous behaviors, attitudes, and actions rooted in the sustained leader's moral anchor (1.2.2.1). The sustained leader is not swayed by the prevailing winds of the day. He or she will so clearly see the vision and so passionately desire the projected outcome that they will modify their behavior to be persistent in achieving the goals. Consistency does not extend to the point of being ridiculous, and the sustained leader knows when to quit (5.1.9). In the performance of their leadership duties, however, the sustained leader is consistent in their pursuit of excellence. The principle of consistency is the same as is found in consistency of message (4.2.6), and in this element the concept pertains to consistency of commitment.

Application: When your actions are consistent, they reflect the fact that you are consistent in your beliefs and values. The sustained leader must recognize, however, that if their value system is not firmly rooted in their spiritual anchor, they will be acting consistently wrong. Sometimes this is reflected in a series of decisions that have bad outcomes. Or decisions that cause harm to others that was unnecessary. Being consistent in such ways is not a hallmark of a sustained leader. Likewise, a person who acts inconsistently on a regular basis, or, in more colloquial terms, is "all over the place," cannot instill confidence in their team. It will appear that the person is only guessing at the correct action and is not guided by a strong value system and moral code or genuinely has no idea what they are doing. It is important that the sustained leader apply discernment to this element. Being consistent is a positive trait, and many developing leaders need to be more consistent in their actions. If, however, such consistency is based on the wrong values, or is at variance with the organizational vision, the consistency will tend to produce the wrong results. In those cases, the sustained leader must alter their actions to better conform to a more fully developed value system. These actions will appear at first to be inconsistent, and they are—to past actions based on misplaced values. Over time, the consistency based on a proper moral code will become evident and draw team members to the leader.

This is difficult. It requires a great deal of soul searching and often extensive mentoring. It can be the most difficult action a developing leader ever takes. The earlier in life that this occurs, the more productive the leader will be over time. This midcourse correction, if taken earlier in life, alters the trajectory in significant ways over time. Later in life such corrections are more difficult since they militate against very entrenched habits, but they are nonetheless critical to sustained leadership success. If you find that you are acting inconsistently it might suggest that you are adopting a system of relative morality—applying a different moral standard to each action based on the situation. Moral relativity is a recipe for disaster. Strive for more consistency in your actions, but make sure that the "new" consistency is rooted in a strong moral character.

A caution is appropriate. Rigid consistency when you are proven wrong is just stubbornness and pigheadedness. It is not positive; it has a very negative impact on your leadership. The sustained leader must continually strive to improve. Thus, being consistent with your old bad habits is *not* useful. It is not what this element intends to address. Those who maintain such rigid consistence cannot improve themselves. Rigid consistency can infect an organization in many ways, one of which is called malicious compliance. When a team resorts to malicious compliance they rigidly follow a process or procedure which they know will cause harm. There are always variations in any process. The positive variations can lead to improvements; the negative ones, if allowed to persist, will become deviance—ultimately negative results. The leader that permits this level of rigidity is failing in their leadership responsibility. Consistency is *not* rigidity.

This sounds like me

A lot	**somewhat**	**just a little**	**not at all**

Additional Resources:

Chip Heath, et al., *Made to Stick*.

Seth Godin, et al., *The Dip*.

Personal Objective:

Specific Actions:

Due Date:

5.1.4 Creates a Legacy

WBS Dictionary: The sustained leader is conscious of their legacy (1.3.8) and recognizes that their very existence will create a legacy, or at least a reputation. In this element the focus is on having a commitment to creating a positive legacy and making a difference in the world. A sustained leader's commitment is so strong that it affects those with whom they interact—those they lead, those they follow, and those on the same team. They seek to make a positive difference. Boy Scouts know that when they visit nature they are to leave the location better than when they found it. Or, to use the medical doctor's Hippocratic Oath, the first rule is to do no harm. The sustained leader finds ways along their journey to extend their positive influence. This might be through formal or informal mentoring, or by just being a consistently positive influence.

Sustained leaders are respected because they have earned the respect. They are not takers but givers. Sustained leaders give constantly and generously. Their legacy might be a library like Mister Pratt's (1.3.8) or simply a weekly offering at their place of worship. Their legacy may result in the form of a college classroom or hospital wing being named after them, or it might be providing food to the local pantry. The magnitude is not crucial, and givers do have to maintain their sense of humility (1.3.3). The sustained leader makes a difference by modeling the best of behaviors and encourages goals and aspirations of other members of the team. They create an environment where people seek to excel and become the best person they can be. The legacy of the best sustained leaders is a string of new leaders (3.2).

Application: It has been said that everyone brightens up a room—some by entering and others by leaving. One legacy that some leaders fail to recognize is their own legacy as a leader and whether they have developed other leaders around them. The legacy can be negative, and without a string of leaders to step in, the departure of one key hero-leader can leave a legacy of destruction and failure. No leader "plans" for that, but given how often it happens, it does seem that sustained leaders should be conscious of such shortcomings and therefore work hard to prevent the lack of future leadership from becoming the legacy they leave behind.

Edward Gardner

*It's not what you take with you but what
you leave behind that defines greatness.*

Very often a legacy is created simply by finding a void and filling it. George Bernard Shaw (1856–1950) said, "You see things; and you say 'Why?' But I dream things that never were; and I say 'Why not?'"[396] The sustained leader seeks out things that are needed and fills that need. Much culture and art seems to follow this pattern. The latest direction of art and culture follows a path of creating the "new" and moving away from the "old." Many of the great masters in art saw no purpose in simply creating more of the same and struck out into a new style.

Henry Wadsworth Longfellow

*Lives of great men remind us we can make our lives sublime,
and departing, leave behind us footprints on the sands of time.*

The sustained leader creates their own legacy, and this is often done by filling voids. "Most people are afraid to break so boldly with tradition, but they secretly admire those who can break up the old forms and reinvigorate the

---

396 See also John F. Kennedy quote in Chapter 1 and 5.1.2.

culture. This is why there is so much power to be gained from entering vacuums and voids."[397]

Sustained leaders recognize that they will be remembered—whether fondly or not. Aside from being conscious of their legacy after they are gone (see 1.3.8), the sustained leader works actively and diligently to create the legacy they desire. A fully developed sustained leader will automatically create the atmosphere and motivation for success. A strong record of repeated success (strong positive results) and the further success of those they have led can be the greatest legacy a leader creates.

This sounds like me

A lot   **somewhat**   **just a little**   **not at all**

Additional Resources:
John Maxwell, *The Difference Maker.*
Malcolm Gladwell, *The Tipping Point.*

Personal Objective:

Specific Actions:

Due Date:

5.1.5 Adaptable

WBS Dictionary: No two situations are identical, and even those who train constantly for unexpected situations, such as airline pilots, know that there will always be subtle differences in each situation. The sustained leader has developed

---

397 Robert Green and J. Elffers, *48 Laws of Power*, (US: Penguin Books, 2000), 354.

their leadership skills and traits to such a level that it does not matter what circumstances are encountered—they will be able to lead effectively. Leadership is a discipline within itself and when properly nurtured can be applied in any situation. Many leaders are called upon to change fields or focus, say a CEO who is hired away by a company in a completely different field of commerce. Or a business leader who pursues a political position. Leadership is leadership is leadership, and generally speaking there is far too little of it demonstrated by those who are named to head organizations.

The sustained leader has confidence in their leadership abilities and works to enhance them. While they may not be as technically proficient in a new field, they have demonstrated *some* level of proficiency (2.2.1) and can apply their leadership skills in most any environment. The sustained leader is a constant learner and can change fields readily. They can adapt to most any situation, whether planned or unplanned and whether large or small. The adaptability here pertains to being able to apply leadership skills and principles in any environment that requires leadership.

Application: Paul was the CEO of a medical device company and had led the company to a series of successes in development and deployment of several cutting-edge devices that improved the lives of many patients. When he sought a change, he obtained a position as CEO of a company that designs and builds high-precision, high-reliability components for the space program. His leadership was fully transferable with a few adjustments in the technology. He was adaptable and was able to find considerable success in the new environment.

Sustained leadership is fungible. This means that a sustained leader can apply sustained leadership in any environment. You cannot, of course, ignore the requirements of 2.0 related to competence. Cost accounting as applied to manufacturing can be quite different when applied to services, and different still as may be required in government cost accounting. Thus, new environments will always place a level of responsibility on the newly assigned sustained leader to improve by learning the specifics of the new assignment. As a constant learner (1.3.1) this should not be difficult, and many sustained leaders have demonstrated competence outside of their primary field before being reassigned. This level of "other knowledge" often is the very thing identified elsewhere in the organization that gives rise to the offer to assume a different leadership role. So whether it occurs before the new assignment or after, it must occur. In today's environment of rapid technological advances, any leader who does not constantly improve their skills will soon be relegated to the ranks of resident dinosaurs. A failure to learn, a failure to adapt, and a failure to grow are not indicators of a sustained leader.

There is an old adage in business that you should never make yourself indispensable. While it suggests the indispensable employee can never be fired, it also says they can never be promoted. The sustained leader will actively seek new opportunities, new challenges, and sometimes just a change in environment. If you are not adaptable, or have not properly developed leaders to replace you, these opportunities will not become available to you and your development as a sustained leader can be stilted.

This sounds like me

A lot   **somewhat**   **just a little**   **not at all**

Additional Resources:

Stephen C. Lundin, et al., *Fish! Sticks*.

Zig Ziglar, et al., *Top Performance*.

Personal Objective:

Specific Actions:

Due Date:

5.1.6 Physically Fit

WBS Dictionary: The sustained leader achieves such status through hard work and discipline. While some aspects may come more naturally to certain individuals, the sustained leader is a complete package, and everyone has to work on some things to achieve success across all defined elements. Being physically fit reflects a discipline of character that is visible for all the world to see. This does not mean that only marathon runners are qualified to be leaders, but it does suggest that a complete lack of attention to this element will cause a widespread perception of a lack of attention to personal health and hygiene. The perception of a lack of physical fitness can also stem from certain medical conditions, which *never* disqualify the sustained leader. Nonetheless, there are some who would attribute their lack of fitness to such uncontrollable circumstances when that is not in fact the primary reason. While the traditional trait theory of leadership has long been discredited, its discredit does not obviate the obvious perception many hold toward those who are, to one degree or another, "out of shape." The sustained leader knows that for purposes of personal health, demonstration of discipline, and the perhaps unfair assessment of the team toward an out-of-shape leader that it would be better to give physical fitness a higher priority than might naturally be the case.

Application: Many leaders find their daily routine disrupted by travel commitments, restaurant dinners, eating on the run, not being able to stick with a fitness routine, or simply overindulgence due to stress or seeking some level of comfort. As a result, keeping fit is an even greater challenge than for their less stressed, less traveled compatriot.

In reading biographies of General George Patton, you quickly see that he was demanding on his troops and insisted on physical training. Long before jogging became a "thing," he insisted that his troops run at least a mile every day. As a result his troops could outlast the enemy in endurance. He also matched physical fitness with mental fitness, believing that the mind should control the body rather than the other way around. Mental discipline was one of his key principles, urging his troops to read every day and preferably from the Bible (when such things were allowed in the American military.) Dr. Kenneth Cooper, another military man (Air Force), published his book *Aerobics* in 1968. The knowledge necessary to stay fit has been known for a very long time. Why then is heart disease our number one killer? It seems that even with the knowledge, we lack the necessary self-discipline (2.3.11) and bias for action (2.3).

The sustained leader cannot achieve their maximum level of performance if they are not physically and mentally fit. Dealing with issues of poor health that could have been avoided with better care of your mind and body is a foolish tradeoff. And whether people will personally admit it or not, a certain level of bias and discrimination against those who are excessively obese is still prevalent. The vestiges of the trait theory of leadership (Chapter 1) still exist in the minds of many. The sustained leader cannot control the bias of others against them, but they can remove the triggers of such bias in some cases. Physical fitness is one of them. Don't feed the prejudice beast. Keep yourself physically and mentally fit. The self-discipline required to do so will serve the sustained leader well in many different areas and aspects of life.

Reports suggest that Americans have never been more obese than they are now and, sadly, that trend does not seem to be diminishing. When you consider the significant failures in leadership across the major institutions of our society (government, industry, and religion) there seems to be a correlation. The less care we take of ourselves, the less care we seem to take of our other responsibilities. While this may be a chicken-and-egg situation where there is no documented cause-and-effect relationship, there does seem to be, at least anecdotally, a strong link between the two.

Some people are said to "age well." It is interesting to see the statistics related to the surprisingly short time between retirement and death for many. People require a purpose to keep living. It is important for the sustained leader to stay active. Certainly you will restrict heavy contact sports, and certain body parts like knees, hips, and shoulders may need some medical attention. Manage your life and your finances to be able to take care of such things. Sabstiaoe Ferraz de Camargo Penteado, who at eighty was still active as head of Brazil's largest construction firm, once said, "Life is like a bicycle. Whoever stops pedaling will fall over."[398]

This sounds like me

A lot   **somewhat**   **just a little**   **not at all**

Additional Resources:

Jim Karas, *The Business Plan for the Body*.

Anthony Robbins, *Awaken the Giant Within*.

Arianna Huffington, *Thrive*.

---

398 Parietti, Jeff *The Book of Truly Stupid Business Quotes*. (US: Harper Paperbacks, 1997), 87.

Personal Objective:

Specific Actions:

Due Date:

5.1.7 Deals Effectively with Setbacks

WBS Dictionary: Failure is the lack of success. It is therefore imperative to properly define success before you characterize any endeavor as a failure. Everyone will encounter setbacks—things that do not turn out as planned. The sustained leader does not confuse such circumstances with failure. The sustained leader seeks to understand the root causes of the lack of success and improve in those areas or aspects that contributed to the shortcoming. One aspect of that is to reassess whether the goal or endeavor was even a proper one to be seeking in the first place. As Thomas Alva Edison is so quoted as saying (perhaps anecdotally) in response to a reporter's questions concerning his failure to find a better filament for his new light bulb invention, "I have not failed. I've just found ten thousand ways that won't work." Ultimately, as we are all aware, he invented a light bulb that was both bright and long lasting. The sustained leader will use temporary failure as a training device (3.17), but more importantly the sustained leader knows how important it is to not make the same mistake twice. Repeated lack of success can drain an organization of resources. Effectively dealing with setbacks preserves those assets and prepares the organization to continue in its mission. Setbacks are inevitable and especially so in any audacious endeavor (2.3.18). The sustained leader prepares for them, works diligently to avoid them, strategizes to minimize their impact, learns from them, and ultimately prevails over them. To do otherwise is to truly fail.

Application:

Thomas Sowell has said, "You cannot tell whether someone is failing or succeeding without knowing what they are trying to do."[399]

Setbacks Are Not Failures

Forget past mistakes. Forget failures. Forget everything
except what you're going to do now and do it.
—William Durant

Failure is only the opportunity to more intelligently begin again.
—Henry Ford

Failure should be our teacher, not our undertaker. Failure is delay, not
defeat. It is a temporary detour, not a dead end. Failure is something we
can avoid only by saying nothing, doing nothing, and being nothing.
—Denis Waitley

I am not judged by the number of times I fail, but by the number
of times I succeed; and the number of times I succeed is in direct
proportion to the number of times I can fail and keep on trying.
—Tom Hopkins

---

399 Patriot Post 11/11/14 http://patriotpost.us/opinion/30828

You can tell how big a man is by observing
how much it takes to discourage him.
—Francois Fenelon

Success is stumbling from failure to failure with no loss of enthusiasm.
—Winston Churchill

Far better it is to dare mighty things, to win glorious triumphs
even though checkered by failure, than to rank with those poor
spirits who neither enjoy nor suffer much because they live in
the gray twilight that knows neither victory nor defeat.
—Theodore Roosevelt

To maintain maximum attention, it's hard to beat a good, big mistake.
—David D. Hewitt

―――――――――――― ◦ ――――――――――――

A word that is often used to describe a leader is "resilient." Leaders know how to bounce back and turn any temporary setback into a learning event (3.17). They understand that persistence is critical to long-term success (2.3.3). The resilient leader has a firm grasp of their values and can adhere to them even in the toughest of times. They are emotionally mature and do not allow such things to cloud their judgment. They maintain their focus and optimism regardless of what is going on around them. Failure is, in large measure, a state of mind—how you react or respond to events. Confucius said that you have never failed until you quit trying. The sustained leader learns from any setback and adjusts their course going forward. They do not perceive such events as "failures." And this is not simply a viewpoint that ignores realities. It simply refuses to let such events control their reaction or impede their goals.

A similar word attributed to leaders is "resolve." While resilience is your ability to "bounce back," resolve "is your ability to dig deep and push forward in the face of adversity."[400] Both pertain to how a leader deals with perceived failure. On a

―――――――――――

400 *Leadership Contract*, 127.

personal level, resolve will dictate whether you stick to your resolutions, lose those last ten pounds, get to the gym three days a week, and all of the other things that you know you should do and yet allow other things to consume the time allotted to these important tasks. Personal leadership (or the lack thereof) is sometimes there for all the world to see.

Many people have confronted numerous setbacks. Through perseverance (2.3.3) they ultimately met with great success, but as the old adage says, "When you are surrounded by alligators it is difficult to remember that the task was to drain the swamp." The primary issue is always what you learn from the experience and how you will apply these lessons in the future. That is why these events are merely setbacks and not failure. Failure occurs only when you give up or fail to learn. Kouzes and Posner modify a well-known phrase when they more accurately say, "Success does not breed success. It breeds failure. It is failure which breeds success."[401]

---------- ◆ ----------

Wisdom of Napoleon Hill

You cannot become a power in your community nor achieve
enduring success in any worthy undertaking until you become big
enough to blame yourself for your own mistakes and reverses.

"Yes, he succeeded—but—he almost failed!" So did Robert Fulton and
Abraham Lincoln and nearly all the others whom we call successful. No man
ever achieved worthwhile success who did not, at one time or other, find
himself with at least one foot hanging well over the brink of failure.

You are fortunate if you have learned the difference between temporary defeat
and failure; more fortunate still, if you have learned the truth that the very
seed of success is dormant in every defeat that you experience.

---------- ◆ ----------

401 Quoted in Kouzes and Posner, *Leadership Challenge*, 214, (citations omitted). The authors provide an impressive list of people perceived as major success, listing all the times they failed before they reached the point of success for which they are remembered.

As a general rule, a failure in tactics is not truly a failure. It might not be considered a success in a monetary sense (or whatever the specific goal was intended to be), but it is not a failure. You've merely found something that didn't work. And it is worth analyzing the reasons for this lack of success. A failure in strategy may result in a devastating and even fatal situation, such as when a company is forced out of business for not recognizing the next generation of products. Please note this is not a fatal failure in the sense of leadership even when it results in a loss of the leadership position. The only *true* failure is one of morality or character. When a person in a position of leadership demonstrates a lack of character or morality, that person has failed. Can they recover? Perhaps. It is not easy and it requires a deep moral realignment, along with reparations and seeking genuine forgiveness. At a minimum it should remove the person from consideration as a leader at least for some period of time if not permanently.

Consider the "mistakes" that people have made. Dr. Percy Spencer invented the microwave oven after he melted a candy bar in his pocket. Fleming discovered penicillin when he failed to clean up a "failed" experiment. Post-it notes came out of 3M when it "failed" to make the glue as sticky as they had planned. And Federal Express was based off of a college business plan that got a grade of C for its author, Fred Smith.

Milton Hershey failed in his business in Philadelphia, then Denver, then New York. When this man with a fourth-grade education returned home to Lancaster, PA, he finally began to succeed making caramel. That success led to what became the town of Hershey, PA.

The sustained leaders should deal with forgiveness in the same fashion whether it is a personal setback or a setback by one of the team members. It requires assertive behavior to address the shortcoming. It should tend neither toward excessively passive "ignore it" response nor excessively aggressive behavior that is personally damaging to the individual. With respect, the sustained leader is open and honest with the person, dealing directly and specifically with the shortcoming. Rather than "forgive and forget" as is often advocated, the sustained leader forgives and then never forgets that it has been forgiven. This is an attitude bereft of resentment or lingering animosity. It's history. It has been used as a lesson and now life has moved on. See also 3.4.4.

This sounds like me

A lot   somewhat   just a little   not at all

Additional Resources:
John Maxwell, *Failing Forward.*
David G. McCullough, *The Wright Brothers.*

Personal Objective:

Specific Actions:

Due Date:

5.1.8 Gives Back to Profession / Industry / Society

WBS Dictionary: The sustained leader understands that they have achieved their status through the help of others. Perhaps teachers, past team members, past leaders, mentors, or coaches (whether paid or volunteer) gave their time and attention to the development of the sustained leader. Even if the sustained leader is a "self-made" person, there has been some interaction with others through books or directly that have influenced the leader. The leader gathers lessons from everywhere as they develop their leadership capabilities. As a consequence of this, and even for the totally unicorn-esque self-made individual (if such a creature exists), the sustained leader finds a way to give back to their profession, their industry, or to society at large. A failure to do so is a transgression of the preservation of the total memory of society since their contribution will be forever lost. The sustained leader finds ways to apply their leadership to a variety of situations for the improvement of those with whom they have interacted, and for the benefit of those who follow behind.

Application: Many leaders get involved in a professional organization or an industry association. Others are active in their church, with the YMCA/YWCA, Boys or Girls clubs, or some other charitable entity. Various charities that cater to the needs of wounded veterans, victims of child abuse or human trafficking, and many other worthwhile endeavors can be appropriate and popular eleemosynary entities that sustained leaders chose to support. The need for volunteers in our society is ubiquitous. Excuses such as waiting until you have time, waiting until the kids are grown, or any other excuse is really no excuse at all—it is just a reason.

Developing other leaders is an Essential Leadership Journey Checkpoint for the sustained leader. Many volunteer efforts can be directed here as well. Leadership is one of the goals of the youth group mentioned above, Junior Achievement, and even high school science fairs. The sustained leader is generous with their time, treasure, and talent in all of these areas.

Mentoring opportunities are also widely available, and everyone, including sustained leaders, have a constant need for good mentoring. One irony of mentoring is the incredible amount the mentor learns from the process as well. One excellent program was initiated by Dana Perino and is described in her book *And the Good News is....*[402] It is called Minute Mentoring.

Sometimes a worthy way to give back is to make sure that records are clearly kept. John James Audubon made significant contributions to ornithology from the drawings of birds he produced. Fleming discovered penicillin quite by accident, but was scientifically curious enough to document the odd mold. Many feel the need to write books. The point is that the person who does not give back to society in some way is just plain selfish and does not exhibit the traits of a sustained leader. With the time, treasure, and talent that the sustained leader holds, it is a breach of the trust given to leaders *not* to use them for the greater good.

A caution to those who tend to have more compulsive personalities. While charity is a wonderful thing, it can be overdone causing an imbalance in life. Such imbalances will impede your progress as a sustained leader. As with all things, you must consider your overall demands for your time, talent, and treasure. Despite your good intentions, you can put yourself in a position of not honoring your

---

402 Perino, D. *And the Good News Is...: Lessons and Advice from the Bright Side.* (US: Twelve, 2015), 159-61. www.minutementoring.com.

word because you have become over-extended. Measure carefully your ability to contribute to worthwhile endeavors.

This sounds like me

A lot   **somewhat**   **just a little**   **not at all**

Additional Resources:
Dana Perino, *And the Good News Is....*
John R. Vile, *The Men Who Made the Constitution.*

Personal Objective:

Specific Actions:

Due Date:

5.1.9 Knows When to Pull the Plug

WBS Dictionary: Commitment is important and its power should never be underestimated. Conversely, there are times when it is necessary to change direction, and sometimes dramatically. The sustained leader knows when it is appropriate, or even necessary, to cease the current effort. Circumstances may have changed; goals may have shifted; investment targets may have been exceeded. Persistence likewise is crucial to success, but chasing false goals, failing to recognize realities, and not saving enough seed corn for next season are all fool's errands. Companies enter and exit various business lines every day. Some of these are wise decisions; others are premature; others are long overdue. Only the results bear witness to these decisions. The sustained leader plans appropriately and sets signposts to provide early trip wires to guide decisions. The sustained leader can dissociate the emotional attachment from a project or prior decision, and can further assess the loss of sunk costs in a business endeavor and make a proper decision going forward.

Application: Business tie-ups appear almost every day in the business press. Companies believe that they are better together and agree to join forces to better exploit a particular market. Some of these arrangements progress to a closing, and while research suggests that the majority of them don't reach the initial goals, they are maintained until market conditions change again and new decisions to join or split are made. Sometimes regulators step in and challenge the arrangement as detrimental to competition. These governmental reviews can take a very long time and cost the merging companies considerable sums in both direct and indirect costs, not to mention the delay in capturing the projected savings, if ultimately permitted at all.

Very often these initial agreements contain a provision that if the deal does not go through, say the target company finds a new suitor, they must pay the other partner a sum as a break-up fee. So there are considerable costs in arranging the deal, considerable costs in implementing the deal, and potentially greater costs in ending the arrangement—often measured in the billions. Nonetheless, despite these sunk costs, deals must be ended—the plug must be pulled—and the sustained leader must know when that is appropriate.

Decisions (2.3.6) are based on the best evidence available at the time. New evidence might become available, or situations will change that lead to the consideration of new or different evidence. With many decisions less than half of the information that is desired is available. If the situation permits later adjustments, then a future decision can adjust the trajectory. Other times a single direction has been chosen and it is not practicable to modify that direction. The only solution is to completely pull the plug and stop the effort. The sustained leader must develop discernment and study situations to be sure of making the right decision, even if that decision is to abandon considerable sunk costs and start over. These are not easy decisions, and the sustained leader must become comfortable with measuring the commitment against the opposing forces to make the best decision for the team under the present circumstances. Even the Founding Fathers recognized the value of being able to pull the plug when they included in the Constitution provisions related to bankruptcy.

Situations are never the result of a single decision; they are a compilation of many, many decisions that converge. A series of bad decisions does not mandate that they continue.[403] Changing direction might not be considered a "pull the plug" situation, but it is similar and reflects the same decision process. Consider the young adult who makes a series of decisions that places them in a car with a drunk driver. Any number of decisions by this young adult may have helped to create this situation, along with the decisions of others. Nonetheless, the young adult is confronted with the decision, "Do I get into a car with an impaired driver behind the wheel, and probably show up at home before curfew, or do I find another mode of transportation home that will make me late?" The young adult must learn that it makes no difference how many bad decisions contributed to the current situation. The current situation is new and it is now. A new decision must be made and it can and should be a good decision. It is never too late to stop making bad decisions and start making good decisions. When do you pull the plug on the current trajectory and take action to alter it? The sustained leader knows that it is never too late to start making good decisions.

This sounds like me

A lot	somewhat	just a little	not at all

Additional Resources:

Anthony L. Iaquinto, et al., *Never Bet the Farm*.

Chip Heath, et al., *Decisive*.

George Bush, *Decision Points*.

Personal Objective:

---

403 Studies of major disasters such as the Challenger Space Shuttle, Bhopal, and others reflect that one good decision within the chain that led to the disaster would have altered the result dramatically. There are always numerous opportunities to change the direction, and thus the outcome, of any situation.

Specific Actions:

Due Date:

5.2 Don't Do

WBS Dictionary: Many who seek to be leaders have too many self-destructive traits, habits, thoughts, or attitudes. Amidst all of the things that a leader must do, it is wise to consider the things that a leader should not do. Many of these can simply be the opposite of the other WBS elements or an extreme example of one. Even a positive attribute in extreme is bad. Consider this the "don't do" list as compared to your "to do" list. If you remove these things from your life, you will increase your productivity, demonstrate better character, and attract a higher caliber follower. Many who were considered great leaders at one time fell from grace by failing to take care not to engage in these traits or habits. President Nixon was respected for his intellect, but his lack of personal warmth and communication skills ultimately resulted in his disgrace and downfall. This mandates that the sustained leader develop strong traits of discretion, discernment, and judgment and learn how and when to use them.

Application: Turning again to Kouzes and Posner:

> In making it safe for people to experiment, you must also make sure it's safe for them to challenge authority. Be aware of certain 'boss' behaviors that create a sense of fear and apprehension Abrasive and abusive conduct—such as glaring eye contact ('the look'), silence, brevity or abruptness, snubbing or ignoring people, insults and put-downs, blaming, discrediting or discounting, aggressive mannerisms, job threats, yelling and shouting, angry outbursts, and physical threats—whether these behaviors are intentional of not—erect very thick walls of antagonism and resentment. You also generate tension by creating ambiguity—by, for example, making decisions behind closed doors or failing to acknowledge or respond to

people's input and suggestions. People simply won't share ideas unless they feel there's a safe, open place for them to do so.[404]

Harvard Business Professor Abraham Zeleznik has said, "I think if we want to understand the entrepreneur, we should look at the juvenile delinquent."[405] Many professions such as lawyers, congressmen, and journalists, for some typical examples, are perceived as being deceptive, manipulative, and opportunistic—in a bad way. As one lawyer noted, "It's the 98 percent of the lawyers out there who are giving the other 2 percent of us a bad name." Monty Python alum John Cleese, who has spent a significant part of his illustrious career portraying businessmen and executives in both training films and commercials, has said, "I find it rather easy to portray a businessman. Being bland, rather cruel, and incompetent comes naturally to me." Even if certain traits or behaviors are considered "typical" within a class or a profession, the sustained leader works against the stereotype. If you see yourself in any of these "don't do" elements, set your sights on removing them as quickly as possible.

These "don't do" examples are included in this portion of the WBS, Commitment, because in nearly every case developing the habit that prevents you from doing certain things will go against what you perceive to be your nature and is most likely an engrained habit. It is much harder to break old habits than to develop new ones. Unless you are deeply committed to making these changes, any of the "don't do" items will hinder your development as a leader. If you are like most people, you will also discover that as you correct past bad habits, there are others standing in line to fill the void. It is a constant struggle to dismiss an old habit and keep it gone. Your commitment will be tested and it must be constantly strengthened. Your commitment to be the best leader you can possibly be—to become a sustained leader—will be tested. Expect that. And then recommit to making the necessary adjustments to become a sustained leader.

The Wall Street Journal looked at the situation where the office "jerk" seems to get the promotion. Psychologists, says the report, refer to a set of traits as the

---

404 Kouzes and Posner, *Leadership Challenge*, 227, citing K.D. Ryan and D.K. Oestreich, *Driving Fear Out of the Workplace: Creating the High-Trust, High-Performance Organization*, 2nd ed. (San Francisco: Jossey-Bass, 1998).
405 Jeff Parietti, *Stupid Business Quotes*, 10.

"'dark triad': manipulativeness, a tendency to influence others for selfish gain; narcissism, a profound self-centeredness; or an antisocial personality, lacking in empathy or concern for others." Noting that these personality types are also known as Machiavellians, they "can also be charismatic leaders and forceful negotiators… And while antisocial personalities lack empathy or concern for others, they can be creative because they often enjoy testing the limits."[406]

The point is that these tendencies can lead to a temporary, often flamboyant rise in some organizations, but they are not sustainable. In isolated circumstances they can appear wildly successful, but each contains a fatal flaw that will result in the ultimate undoing of the leader's trajectory.

"The careers of people with these characteristics tend to derail over time, in part because they tend to focus on short-term benefits for themselves rather than long-term results for their organizations. Colleagues may come to view them as hostile, harsh or arrogant, Dr. Spain says. And when present at extreme or clinical levels, these traits disrupt lives. What eventually trips people up, Mr. Ratley says: 'They think the rules don't apply to them.'"[407]

Sadly, part of the personality disorder appears to be an inability to identify it as a problem. On the contrary, they are proud of their accomplishments despite the collateral damage. The article goes on to review the events surrounding Health-South Corp. CEO Richard Scrushy, who ultimately served time in prison. He acknowledged that certain illegal activities happened under his watch, yet failed to take any personal responsibility, believing his style to be effective with those he led. "You don't manage 120 people by being a pansy…Any CEO worth his salt has to be a bit strong… I don't think it's a 'dark side.' It's a skill, to be able to build a business from scratch."[408]

These "don't do" items are important for the sustained leader to fully understand how some extremes do violence to the underlying principles of sustained leadership. Whether exhibited as bullying or the opposite extreme of being "too nice," these are the "dark side" of leadership, and being able to identify them in yourself or others is crucial for *sustained* success as a leader.

---

406 Sue Shellenbarger. "Ever thought, 'How Did He Get Promoted?' Here's How" *Wall Street Journal*, July 9, 2014. Page D1.

407 Ibid. at D2, citing researchers identified in the article. See also, Pfeffer, Jeffrey, *Leadership BS: Fixing Workplaces and Careers One Truth at a Time*, (New York: Harper Collins, 2015).

408 Ibid.

This sounds like me

| A lot | somewhat | just a little | not at all |

Additional Resources:

Marshall Goldsmith, et al., *What Got You Here Won't Get You There.*
John MacArthur, *The Quest for Character.*
David Allen, *Getting Things Done.*

Personal Objective:

Specific Actions:

Due Date:

5.2.1 Rigidity

WBS Dictionary: A popular military aphorism is that it is important to know the rules so that you know when you are breaking them. There are times when strict adherence to a set of rules or procedures is absolutely necessary, such as building nuclear weapons, or conducting a complicated surgery. Outside of public safety, or the need to have complete consistency in a process (such as McDonald's making a Big Mac™ or Starbucks making a caramel latte), excessive rigidity fails to consider the constancy of change, stifles innovation, and can bore your followers into complacency. Rigidity also fails to permit the use of discretion and the appropriate use of judgment. It effectively stunts progress.

The sustained leader understands the circumstances where rigidity is appropriate and where it is not. It is a matter of judgment where reasonable people might differ. Making clear to the team when rigidity will be applied and when it will not is effective for addressing these situations. It's like honoring the "no ex post facto" clause of the Constitution. Make the rules clear first, then enforce them evenly and with discretion. Excessive rigidity is the hallmark of a small thinker.

Application: In the 2000s we saw an increasing use of "zero tolerance" situations. Not permitting random guns in schools is a good thing. Suspending a child because he broke his Pop-Tart into the shape of a gun, or made a gun figure out of his fingers, seems, to many, to be excessively rigid. Or disciplining a high school student who failed to take a hunting knife out of his pickup truck after a weekend of hunting, after he voluntarily self discloses the presence of the weapon, seems, again to many, to also be excessively rigid.

Conversely when a person of strong religious faith states an absolute based on the moral teachings of their religion, they are labeled zealots and intolerant. Those who oppose such faithful beliefs resort to ridicule and begin to modify the language, thereby introducing a sense of moral relativity. At what point is the sustained leader to adopt a path of rigidity or one of relativity? The simple answer is one of principle. The sustained leader should never compromise on their foundational principles. If your upbringing was within the Judeo-Christian construct, right and wrong have very definite meanings. Many situations, however, are not so clear cut, and over time we have allowed these "tough cases," which are actually few and far between, to become the norm. Rather than remaining clear that as to moral issues black is black and white is white, we have allowed the small gray area between them to dominate.

> The process of redefining deviance is a subtle one, and the changes in language we have discussed are so incremental and innocuous that the new meanings appear almost invisibly. Social philosopher Alasdair MacIntyre implores us all to examine this process more closely when he writes, "Ours is a culture dominated by experts, experts who profess to assist the rest of us, but who often instead make us their victims." MacIntyre says that we must be able to identify the particular set of precepts that will help us achieve that which contributes to the common good. Most of us know that there are unwritten, morally based "laws" that tell us what kind of behavior is deviant. They have not necessarily been codified within the legal system, but are nonetheless binding.[409]

409 Anne Hendershott, *The Politics of Deviance* (San Francisco: Encounter Books, 2002), 154 (citations omitted).

The sustained leader has this sense of the "common good" and respects the true nature of natural law (1.2.2.4). The sustained leader knows these "unwritten, morally based laws" and follows them, even without threat of civil legal entanglements. At some point, this requires that they become rigid in upholding these rules. Until that point, so long as it is not a path down a slippery slope, more flexibility might be appropriate. Distinguishing between the two can be difficult, especially to those unfamiliar with moral codes. The sustained leader has the appropriate spiritual underpinning (1.2.2) and moral compass (1.2.2.1).

This sounds like me

A lot   **somewhat**   **just a little**   **not at all**

Additional Resources:

Michael Treacy, et al., *The Discipline of Market Leaders.*

Anne B. Hendershott, *The Politics of Deviance.*

Personal Objective:

Specific Actions:

Due Date:

5.2.2 One-Dimensional Thinking

WBS Dictionary: Some people prefer to think of things linearly like a timeline. Others prefer to think holistically. Mechanics think about how a mechanical system works; lawyers might analyze everything in terms of litigation. Doctors often do not think of people as persons so much as they think about the target, such as a gall bladder or a tonsillectomy. A sustained leader can be trapped by thinking only in one dimension—usually the dimension that comes most naturally to them. By failing to think about the myriad dimensions of a problem, critical solutions will be missed. People are complex and leaders lead people not things. While some people might be focused, perhaps excessively so, they still have multiple dimensions. Some people compartmentalize. Others expand a "How are you?" question into a life history. Failing to appreciate the multiple dimensions of your team, your stakeholders, your constituency, your clients, your employees, or whatever will cause you to fail in assessing the totality of the circumstances, which means a failure in your risk or situational assessment and setting up potential disaster under your leadership.

Application: Many one-dimensional thinking traits are found within the "isms." Racism, sexism, ageism, and various faith-isms all fit within this arena. To many, this pitfall is unconscious and thus the sustained leader must search themselves to see if the insidious trait lies within. Have you noticed how men are often addressed by their last name, but women are always addressed by their first? Have you ever heard someone refer to a man as assertive, yet a woman exhibiting the same traits is called "bitchy"? Is a person being "slow" or "thorough"? Have you listened to, or told, a joke where the punchline disparaged a particular faith or sex or race or hair color? When someone violates rules are they a lawbreaker or someone who thinks outside of the box? When you do something to please a superior are you a brown-noser or being cooperative? When a woman gets a promotion is it because of merit or because she is "sleeping her way to the top"? See how insidious this shortcoming can be?

In simplest terms those who think in one dimension are often trapped within the construct they create. They lose the ability to see people as individuals. They believe that the rules apply to everyone but them, since their violations are for the presumed greater good. Their single-dimension construct also causes them to lie. They say things that are patently false, and provably so because those who wish to believe them will. It is a case of fooling some of the people all of the time. They are blind to the illogic of their thinking.

Sustained leaders celebrate diversity in all its dimensions. The obvious ones are self-evident such as race and sex. Have you considered that different Meyers-Briggs types also reflect diversity? Have you considered that people from different professions are trained to look at things a particular way? In an effort to simplify, it is normal to remove things that might be distractions to our natural or trained tendencies. This is often the starting point for one-dimensional or, as a minimum, limited-dimensional thinking. Sustained leaders train themselves to think more broadly and consider all the dimensions. Sustained leaders are on the lookout to remove thinking that considers less than all the dimensions and variables and seek to actively broaden the aperture. They also never forget that a stopped clock is right twice a day. Just because one-dimensional thinking may have been right on one occasion, it is dangerous to consider it as a trend or precedent. As Abraham Maslow noted, "I suppose it is tempting, if the only tool you have is a hammer, to treat everything as if it were a nail."[410]

This sounds like me

A lot	somewhat	just a little	not at all

Additional Resources:
Morgan D. Jones, *The Thinker's Toolkit*.
M. Neil Browne, et al., *Asking the Right Questions*.

Personal Objective:

Specific Actions:

Due Date:

---

410 The concept seems to predate Maslow, but this iteration is directly attributable to him in a 1966 publication, *The Psychology of Science: A Reconnaissance*.

5.2.3 Playing Politics

WBS Dictionary: The phrase "playing politics" is most often used with a negative connotation. It can be used by those who are simply on the losing end of a situation as a rationalization. In leadership it means that the person is not exhibiting leadership traits; rather they are engaging in various games of deceit, subterfuge, and obfuscation. Occasionally it involves direct lying. They are relying on personal connections and "favors" rather than merit. Nepotism is a form of playing politics. It has the air of essential unfairness in the transaction or activity. Even as children we learn early when something is just "not right," and we complain, "But that's not fair!" We feel harmed and express that from our most basic core. The sustained leader does not permit the falseness of politics to affect their judgment or decisions. They discern when and where it is occurring and work to thwart it. The sustained leader *never* initiates a game of politics.

Application: It is a sad indictment that we have adopted the phrase "playing politics" to connote such a negative trait. Even sadder, those who have engaged in the political process are less and less morally centered and more and more practicing a relativism that allows them to play all the political games that bring in the donations to pay for the massive expense of winning a political contest. Lobbyists are paid huge amounts by their employers in order to have "access" to politicians—who will then pass laws that have a direct impact on those very same employers. These laws are the same ones that do NOT continue to reflect the moral underpinnings of our founding documents, but adopt a more rights-based concept, expanding rights and finding new ones in the penumbras of those documents. Simultaneously they further restrict the rights that are guaranteed in those documents without using the process that the documents themselves provide for making changes. Why? In simplest terms because they cannot get the necessary majority to agree with their view of what the rules "ought" to be. This is the game that is played when "playing politics." Couple that with similar actions by the judiciary where the laws are not interpreted as written, but are rewritten to suit their political views. This is politics in a different suit and called judicial activism.[411] It is what Reardon calls "pathological politics."

411 These statements might seem politically charged in their own right by those who disagree with the characterization. Those who feel this way are encouraged to conduct a deeper study of the concepts of the "Rule of Law" and the judicial restraint doctrines related to "political

The political arena does not require that a person's moral center be compromised in order to appeal to the masses necessary to win an election, yet that seems to be a common perception. It was Daniel Patrick Moynihan who noted that our sense of deviance had been "defined down" such that what was once reprehensible is now acceptable. Much of this has been done using the "language of politics" rather than the language of leadership. For example, the North American Man/Boy Love Association has advocated for a "normal erotic continuum" and describe their activities not as pedophilia but as "intergenerational intimacy." Similar redefinitions have occurred in the area of drug abuse, euthanasia, assisted suicide, and abortion—all for political gain, and completely outside of any moral center.

The sustained leader does not fall into these traps of "political correctness," nor do they play the "political game." While this may at times hinder their career progress or place them outside of certain so-called "mainstream" lines of thought, the sustained leader adheres to the principles of leadership that are required to sustain their leadership role. With a proper moral compass, they recognize these things as the subterfuge they are and avoid them.

This sounds like me

| **A lot** | **somewhat** | **just a little** | **not at all** |

Additional Resources:
Anne B. Hendershott, *The Politics of Deviance.*
Sylvan Barnet, et al., *Critical Thinking, Reading, and Writing.*
Jay Heinrichs, *Thank You for Arguing.*
Kathleen Kelly Reardon, *It's All Politics.*

Personal Objective:

---

questions." Sustained leaders can hold whatever political leanings they choose, but they cannot violate natural law and the necessary things that flow from that recognition.

Specific Actions:

Due Date:

5.2.4 Negativity and Cynicism

WBS Dictionary: The traits of negativity and cynicism are joined as two parts of the same trait. The two are nearly the same, with the primary difference being one of degree. Cynicism involves the assumption that things are not as they seem, but worse. Negativity suggests that regardless of the circumstances, the most negative outcome will be expected. The rationalization that being negative or cynical makes you happy when things do not turn out as badly as anticipated is a false logic. Too often the negative view taints the situation and becomes nearly a self-fulfilling prophecy. When you focus on the negative, your subconscious adopts that as the normal situation and works to achieve it. This element specifically addresses the attitude of negativity whether exhibited as cynicism or as a personality trait of constant doomsday predictions.

Application: It has been said that it's better to shoot for the stars and only hit the moon than to have aimed for the ground and hit it. Negative and cynical views are choices we make. You can just as easily choose positive views of the outcome and assume the best from people. When you put those views into the public scene, most often people will rise to the occasion and work to not disappoint. When you pose the negative, people will also likely serve so as to not disappoint. The sustained leader recognizes the power of expectations and positive reinforcement with their team. The sustained leader chooses to keep things in a positive view and encourages the team to do likewise.

Napoleon Hill

Every line a man writes, and every act in which he indulges, and every word he utters serves as unescapable evidence of the nature of that which is deeply imbedded in his own heart, a confession that he cannot disavow.

For many the negative and cynical perspective has become a habit. If so, this habit needs to be broken and a conscious decision made to accentuate the positive. Some hide this habit by posing their cynicism as humorous. Some even get a reputation for being humorous people based on their expressed cynicism. This is a false perspective since, in the final analysis, cynicism is not a positive trait.

------ ● ------

Anonymous

"Cheer up," they said. "Things could be worse."
So I cheered up and, sure enough, things got worse.

------ ● ------

A dry sense of humor is often based in cynicism. Very few people can pull it off. The safer approach is to modify your behavior. Another form of humor is self-deprecating where a person puts themselves down in anticipation of someone else doing it for them. Certainly admitting your own failures can serve as examples and can serve to express genuine humility. It can also be used as a false humility, egging people on to say something nice just so the first speaker can hear it. This is similar to the person who, when they hear a compliment, have trained themselves to pretend they did not, prompting the person to repeat the compliment.

As Napoleon Hill has so artfully said, your self-talk is the most important part of maintaining your self-esteem.

This sounds like me

A lot	somewhat	just a little	not at all

Additional Resources:
Napoleon Hill, *The Law of Success in Sixteen Lessons*.
Norman Vincent Peale, *The Power of Positive Thinking*.

Personal Objective:

Specific Actions:

Due Date:

5.2.5 False Promises and Deception

WBS Dictionary: If you were a student of Machiavelli, or engaging in activities like warfare, then deception may be a normal part of your toolkit. Using such tactics with those you lead, however, breaks the trust and loyalty parts of your relationships and thus reflects poorly on your character. Although war analogies are often used in business, it is a mistake for the sustained leader to confuse the adversary with their followers. Tell the truth; be honest; manage by fact not rumor; understand power; and deal directly with people. Your character is at stake.

Application: Turning to Robert Greene, Law #31 is "Control the Options: Get Others to Play with the Cards You Deal." The goal here is to limit the choices. This often involves setting up a straw-man which no one has advocated or would choose and juxtaposing that with the choice you want the person to select. Says Greene, "This supplies the clever and cunning with enormous opportunities for deception. For people who are choosing between alternatives find it hard to believe they are being manipulated or deceived; they cannot see that you are allowing them a small amount of free will in exchange for a much more powerful imposition of your own will. Setting up a narrow range of choices, then, should always be part of your deceptions."[412]

Deceit, or making false promises, is an intentional act. The deceiver is intentionally concealing the truth. A milder form, but truly as egregious, is intentionally distorting the truth. Other words that come to mind include duplicity or fraud. Regardless of the degree of the falsity or deceit, the key element is the intent. People make mistakes. Leaders are people. Therefore leaders make mistakes. This element is never a mistake; it requires an intent to deceive. Sustained leaders don't do this.

---

412 Robert Greene, *48 Laws of Power*, 259.

Wisdom that is nearly twenty-five hundred years old was stated by Sun Tzu when he said, "All war is based on deception."[413] More colloquially it is said that all is fair in love and war. Leaving love aside for the moment, it is always difficult to see reality from false perception in times of war. What is important is that the sustained leader knows the difference between war and not war. You will often hear business men and women attempt to create a metaphor between business and war, especially against the competition. And perhaps there are some similarities, but the point is that you cannot fight any battle in an immoral way. Defeating oppressors who deny the basis of human dignity is appropriate. Using subterfuge to find out a competitor's pricing in order to win a competition is not.

When perception is manipulated it affects the decision-making process. Thus, people can be manipulated to act against their best interests if you alter their perception. If you have convinced them that you will perform your side of the bargain, they will readily perform theirs. If, in fact, you created a false impression through falsehood or deception, they will act against their own interests without realizing it.[414]

Another form of this is competency extrapolation. As described by John Dickson, this is a failure to know the limits of your competency. If you are smart in physics, some might perceive that you are smart in politics as well. There is no relationship whatsoever. Certainly demonstrated competency in an area might demonstrate critical thinking, critical reading, and a greater capacity to understand abstract concepts, but it does not mean that you know everything about everything.

You are encouraged to acknowledge the limits of your competence and not be too full of hubris, deceiving those around you with your false claims of knowledge. "Humbly acknowledging limitations and refusing to engage in competency extrapolation are not signs of weakness. They demonstrate realism and are therefore strengths."[415]

False denial is related to this element since it hides the "real" or the truth. It creates a false impression; it manipulates perception of others. Deception

---

413 Sun Tzu, *The Art of War* 1:18.
414 The law refers to this as "detrimental reliance" and provides a remedy for the aggrieved against the oppressor.
415 John Dickson, *Humilitas: A Lost Key to Life, Love, and Leadership* (Grand Rapids, MI: Zondervan, 2011), 56.

is likewise related in that it shows what is fake, thus implicitly denying what is real. Either way, false promises and deception are not the tools of the sustained leader except in very limited circumstances such as war where your fundamental principles are threatened. The sustained leader is expected to know the difference.

This sounds like me

A lot   **somewhat**   **just a little**   **not at all**

Additional Resources:

Niccoli Machiavelli, *The Prince.*

Robert Greene, et al., *The 48 Laws of Power.*

Ken Blanchard, *Leading at a Higher Level.*

Personal Objective:

Specific Actions:

Due Date:

5.2.6 Arrogance

WBS Dictionary: Arrogance is a form of self-pride displayed in words and actions. The sustained leader, while quite capable and adept at leading, can never become arrogant about their skills, talents, and attributes. The sustained leader knows that despite their many fine qualities and vast improvement from times past, there is always significant room for improvement and they are by no means perfect in every respect. They remain humble (1.3.3). Their attitude must be tempered by this self-knowledge. Arrogance gives rise to a false sense of invincibility, creating many who would seek to dethrone this self-proclaimed king. Arrogance destroys relationships and taints your legacy. It alters communication and quite simply reflects a poor character. Arrogance destroys many of the favorable elements that contribute to the sustained leader. Avoid arrogance. Learn to identify it in yourself and others.

Application: Arrogance has unseated many a king. In the era of 600-500 BC, Cyrus solidified Persia and defeated the Medes, Croesus of Lydia, Ionia, and Babylon. He became known as Cyrus the Great. Feeling himself invincible, if not god-like, he failed to solidify his conquests and instead sought more to conquer. When he went up against Queen Tomyris of the Massagetai, he sought a bridge too far. She defeated his army, cut off his head, and stuffed it in a wineskin of human blood, giving him, as she had promised before Cyrus arrogantly attacked her kingdom, to give him his "fill of blood."

Greek mythology gives us the example of Icarus whose wax wings could not fly so close to the sun as Icarus desired. He arrogantly flaunted his father's wisdom and fell to his death. Napoleon met his Waterloo. Arrogance seems to eventually undo so many leaders. Both actions and words can display arrogance. You may hear someone say that they are the smartest person in the room, or they are the "adults" in the room. Throwing chairs across a basketball court, slapping things down on a counter, or a speaker walking off stage when they were supposed to be available for questions are all examples of arrogant behavior.

John Elway retired at his peak. Johnny Unitas stayed too long. Arrogance? Perhaps, but certainly not the last memory they probably hoped the fans would have. The arrogant leader is not sustainable.

Arrogance is a form of pride, the most insidious of the deadly sins since those who hold it are the least capable of identifying it in themselves. Consider asking a trusted friend to assist you in your assessment of this element.

This sounds like me

A lot	somewhat	just a little	not at all

Additional Resources:
John P. Dickson, *Humilitas*.
Charles R. Swindoll, *Elijah*.

Personal Objective:

Specific Actions:

Due Date:

5.2.7 Hidden Agenda as a Strategy

WBS Dictionary: There are times when it is important to keep your agenda or ultimate goals a secret. In some negotiations, this can be a proper and ethically appropriate tactic. To use it as a continuous strategy, however, will quickly cause your reputation to suffer. People will learn not to trust you and will believe you to be dishonest. Some pathological liars rationalize such behavior on the belief that a failure to disclose is not a lie. Catholics may understand this concept as a dichotomy between sins of commission and sins of omission. Both are still sins. A hidden agenda is the failure to disclose something that would be considered material to some who are engaged in the activity or transaction. Having a hidden agenda is the opposite of transparency. The right and wrong times to use a hidden agenda are matters of discernment, and reasonable people may differ. The sustained leader develops their level of discernment on such matters.

Application: The use of a hidden agenda is a power play. It is hiding an important piece of information. As noted in the WBS Dictionary, it can be an acceptable tactic in a specific circumstance. The sustained leader, however will never use it as a strategy. When used repeatedly or in a manner to gain power that is intentionally designed to be malicious, the person who uses it will be seen, appropriately, as duplicitous and not to be trusted. They will not create a following and will instead create an army of enemies. Their leadership will not be sustained.

Hidden agendas reflect a diversion of interests. It might be a matter of self-dealing (5.2.15.1), self-protection (5.2.5.2), or self-righteousness (5.2.15.4). In any of these, the fundamental motivation is selfishness. In the Project Management Body of Knowledge there is a role identified as a "negative stakeholder." This is a person who desires to see your project fail. Perhaps they want your budget, or your resources. Perhaps they want to discredit you so that you are eliminated from consideration in the next promotion in which the negative stakeholder is competing against you. This negative stakeholder might seek a key role on your team. Abiding by the adage to keep your friends close and your enemies closer, this negative stakeholder does not have the success of your project as their goal. In fact, their goal is specifically the failure of your project. The negative stakeholder has a hidden agenda.

Any time a person has a hidden agenda, they are failing to disclose some part of the story. Why is Joe strongly recommending a supplier who is not the lowest cost? Joe may be getting a kickback. Why is Sally pushing a less senior person for the promotion? Perhaps Sally has an undisclosed family relationship with the person. Not all hidden agendas are so nefarious, but they are all rooted in selfishness—a trait of which the sustained leader has no need.

This sounds like me

A lot   **somewhat**   **just a little**   **not at all**

Additional Resources:

Robert Greene, et al., *The 48 Laws of Power*.

Deborah M. Kolb, et al., *Everyday Negotiation*.

Wess Roberts, *Leadership Secrets of Attila the Hun*.

Personal Objective:

Specific Actions:

Due Date:

5.2.8 Willful Ignorance

WBS Dictionary: No one can know everything. Nonetheless the sustained leader works hard to be competent (2.0) and to excel in at least one key discipline. Through self-assessment the sustained leader is well aware of what they know and the things they know they don't know. In any organization, it is the things you don't know and of which you are not aware you don't know (the so-called unknown unknowns) that will most often trip you up. Within that construct, however, are many degrees of ignorance. In society today there is the concept of "plausible deniability." The idea is that you inform the boss just a little, keeping them in the dark sufficiently so that after the fact (when the project has fallen apart) the boss can claim to have known nothing about the project, when in fact the initial information should have prompted them to dig deeper to fully understand what was going on under their watch. Of course they knew; they simply pretend that they don't so their denial is plausible.

The sustained leader should be naturally curious and a constant learner, absorbing data and information in quantities and qualities that best suits them. To be aware of known unknowns and not work to move them into the category of known knowns is a complete dereliction of a leader's duty. To remain ignorant of facts, situations, information, or data willfully or intentionally will derail a leader and disqualify them from leadership roles. Mistakes will happen. Accidents are called that *because* they are unplanned and unexpected.

No leader can or will know everything, but to remain willfully ignorant is inexcusable.

Application: An old adage asked the question of which was worse—ignorance or apathy. The correct answer is "I don't know and I don't care." Unfortunately, the humor here stems from the statement's truth. It is reminiscent of the statue of the three monkeys, each covering its eyes, ears, and mouth, reflecting another adage of "see no evil, hear no evil, speak no evil." Or perhaps the image is from Colonel Klink from the old *Hogan's Heroes* TV show where the colonel would say in his deep (though fake) German accent, as the prisoners engaged in various escapades, "I know nothing!"

It is not possible for any one person to know everything all the time, and as a constant learner the sustained leader seeks to know as much as possible. Even so, there will be gaps in the knowledge base for any leader. This element, however, addresses the situation where the leader has the opportunity to make themselves more aware and simply fails to do so. It would be like a judge preparing to rule on a case without having read the briefs provided by the parties or the law that should be applied. We would view that as gross incompetence, yet leaders fail to prepare (1.3.1.3) or choose to remain ignorant at their peril. Decisions (2.3.6) will always be made on incomplete information; that does not excuse the sustained leader from trying to know as much as they can about the decision to be made. It is said that ignorance of the law is no excuse. There is no excuse for willful ignorance.

This sounds like me

| A lot | somewhat | just a little | not at all |

Additional Resources:
C.S. Lewis, *The Inspirational Writings of C.S. Lewis.*
Ernest Rhys, *Aesop's and Other Fables.*

Personal Objective:

Specific Actions:

Due Date:

5.2.9 Authoritarianism

WBS Dictionary: There are various theories of jurisprudence and leadership. One such theory is known as the "command theory." In certain environments, such as the military, the command structure is important to effective operations. In simplest forms this is a recognition that the person in charge will make the rules and all others must follow them. Given that a leader typically must draw others around them as followers, thus providing the basic definition of a leader as one who has followers, an autocratic or authoritarian approach might not necessarily attract anyone, let alone the best team members. Authoritarianism is reflected in such sayings as "My way or the highway," or through the use of a micro-management approach where a person feels a need to control even the minutest details of the performance of a task. Ultimately there must be a single focal point of responsibility, and there are occasions where an autocratic management approach may be necessary. But those are relatively rare. Neither situation provides an excuse for authoritarianism. Often it is just a vain attempt to hold on to power; the most common result is the loss of power and the leadership position because followers will not stand for it. Sustained leaders do not engage in such practices.

Application: Those who hold a position of royalty in societies where such a government exists perhaps have an ability to rule in an authoritarian manner. In all civilized societies today, even royalty is, in many respects, subject to their people. Authoritarian rule today is found predominantly in dictatorships. This is not to say that authoritarian elements can't be found in all models of leadership. Whether it is in the form of an executive order by the US president or the invasion of countries by the Russian leader, authoritarianism exists to some degree.

 ⊛

Napoleon Hill

*No man can become a great leader of men unless he has
the milk of human kindness in his own heart, and leads by
suggestion and kindness, rather than by force.*

 ⊛

Considering the three major institutions in our society—government (including politics), religion, and industry—the true autocrat tends to have a short tenure as leader. People don't like it. Being treated as a tool or a resource rather than as a person is humiliating and dehumanizing. They won't put up with it. Certainly there are command structures such as the military where the use of authoritarianism might be necessary in certain situations to preserve property or life. But these are rare. Sustained leaders are never heard to say, "My way or the highway," or "You'll do it if you know what's good for you." Parents certainly have that prerogative as they train up the next generation. In other leadership environments, however, authoritarianism will not get the best out of the team. Lee Iacocca said, "I hire people brighter than me, and then I get out of their way." The sustained leader knows not to micromanage the team or deal with them like a parent. It will not get the most out of your team.

This sounds like me

A lot   **somewhat**   **just a little**   **not at all**

Additional Resources:
Sarah Myers McGinty, *Power Talk*.
Allan R. Cohen, et al., *Influence without Authority*.

Personal Objective:

Specific Actions:

Due Date:

5.2.10 Sense of Privilege

WBS Dictionary: Sustained leaders understand their role and that it may not include them being the sole face of the organization. Some leaders lose their sense of identity, thinking that the organization is simply their own personal alter ego. The non-sustained leader often develops a sense of entitlement that attempts to set them apart. They feel insulated and perhaps invulnerable. They begin to believe they are entitled to the lion's share of the rewards for success in the organizational mission and objectives, not the least of which is often the generation of great wealth.

Application: Actress Reese Witherspoon was a passenger in a car stopped by the police.[416] As the encounter unfolded she got out of the vehicle and confronted the policeman. Obviously, the police officer retained control of the situation, and Ms. Witherspoon ended up in cuffs, causing her to say, "Do you know who I am?" The officer appropriately said, "I don't care." To the policeman she was of no particular consequence and was interfering with the performance of his duty. The police are to administer the laws fairly and equitably. Under the Rule of Law principles fostered under our republic form of government, the law knows no favorites. Congressmen, company presidents, actors and actresses, and even national presidents have succumbed to this failure in their character. Certainly when you work hard to create a successful lifestyle you are entitled to enjoy the fruits of your labor. You are not, however, entitled to be worshiped simply due to your position. You are not, in fact, entitled to be worshiped at all! When you attempt to lead from a perspective of "them" versus "us" you set up a dynamic that leads to the formation of labor unions, sit-ins, protests, and sometimes violence. That is not leading. Anyone who tries to lead in this fashion will lose their leadership position. They will never earn the legitimate power of a leader.

---

416 http://gawker.com/5995177/reese-witherspoon-arrested-shouts-do-you-know-my-name-at-police Accessed 11/20/16

Robert Greene relates the story of Genghis Khan, who attempted to open trade with Muhammad, the shah of Khwarezm. He was rudely rebuffed by Muhammad, who "did not know this upstart from the east, who, it seemed to him, was extremely arrogant to try to talk as an equal to one so clearly his superior." A second attempt met with failure when a governor under Muhammad attacked the gift-laden caravan and killed its leaders. On a third attempt, Muhammad himself had the caravan leader beheaded. Genghis Khan responded by attacking the governor's capital city, seizing the governor, and executing him by pouring molten silver into his eyes and ears. He then proceeded against Muhammad, ultimately destroying his kingdom and leaving Khan in sole control of the Silk Route he had hoped to exploit and share with Muhammad. Greene provides this analysis:

> Never assume that the person you are dealing with is weaker or less important than you are. Some men are slow to take offense, which may make you misjudge the thickness of their skin, and fail to worry about insulting them. But should you offend their honor and their pride, they will overwhelm you with a violence that seems sudden and extreme given their slowness to anger. If you want to turn people down, it is best to do so politely and respectfully, even if you feel their request is impudent or the offer ridiculous. Never reject them with an insult until you know them better; you may be dealing with a Genghis Khan.[417]

Whether you are Muhammad or Reese Witherspoon, a sustained leader never responds with the "do you know who I am?" argument. Your arrogance will become your undoing. And if this is a habit you have intentionally or inadvertently developed, work tirelessly to break it and remove all arrogance, including any sense of privilege or entitlement, from your repertoire of responses.

This sounds like me

A lot	**somewhat**	**just a little**	**not at all**

417 Robert Greene, *48 Laws of Power*, 139-40.

Additional Resources:

Patrick Lencioni, *The Five Temptations of a CEO.*

Tom Rusk, et al., *The Power of Ethical Persuasion.*

Laurie Beth Jones, *Jesus CEO.*

James C. Hunter, *The World's Most Powerful Leadership Principle.*

Personal Objective:

Specific Actions:

Due Date:

5.2.11 Gossip and Rumor

WBS Dictionary: A communication void will always be filled. Most commonly, team members will fill the void with gossip and rumor. It becomes the leader's responsibility to, in the first instance, not permit communication voids and, secondly, never participate in the spreading of gossip or rumors. Other times managers will try to "float a trial balloon" to see what sort of reaction it receives. Whether gossip and rumor seeps into an organization through a void or through false information, it is still wrong. A sustained leader works with facts. A sustained leader can have doubts and function with less than full information, but they do not fly blindly. This element demands that leaders do not engage in rumor or gossip—whether permitting a void to be filled with rumors, circulating rumors as an originator, or circulating rumors as an intermediary. There are many times that a leader might be mistaken, but to intentionally lie or be willfully ignorant is a disqualifying attribute for a leader. Included here would be the political talking points, or the "party line," where a falsehood or half-truth is repeated at various levels of the organization in the hopes that the false idea will gain traction. This is just another flavor of gossip and is an unacceptable form of manipulation (5.2.7).

Application: Eleanor Roosevelt noted that "great minds discuss ideas; average minds discuss events; small minds discuss people." People will always talk—about something. The sustained leader knows the importance of keeping the team informed, because a failure to inform will result in the team talking anyway. Without the facts, people will make up their own. As is often heard during investigations, "The people who are talking don't know and the people who know aren't talking." If the sustained leader does not keep the team informed with the facts, the default mode will be management by rumor and innuendo. In a discussion where such practices are permitted you will begin to see the false arguments as well. The use of straw-men, false dichotomies, and other logical fallacies will predominate, and the less well informed will believe them.

Napoleon Hill

No man may become an accurate thinker until he learns how to separate mere gossip and information from facts.

George Washington, at a very young age, cataloged a list of precepts that served him well throughout his life. One of those was, "Be not Curious to Know the Affairs of Others neither approach those that Speak in Private" (Rule 81). He knew that rumor, innuendo, and gossip were not useful pieces of information. They are not reliable and may be being spread by those with a specific agenda to unfairly discredit others. A fable best illustrates this point.

The Eagle, the Cat, and the Wild Sow

AN EAGLE made her nest at the top of a lofty oak; a Cat, having found a convenient hole, moved into the middle of the trunk; and a Wild Sow, with her young, took shelter in a hollow at its foot. The Cat cunningly resolved to destroy this chance-made colony. To carry out her design, she climbed to the nest of the Eagle, and said, "Destruction is preparing for you, and for me too, unfortunately. The Wild Sow, whom you see daily digging up the earth, wishes to uproot the oak, so she may on its fall seize our families as food for her young." Having thus frightened the Eagle out of her senses, she crept down to the cave of the Sow, and said, "Your children are in great danger; for as soon as you go out with your litter to find food, the Eagle is prepared to pounce upon one of your little pigs." Having instilled these fears into the Sow, she went and pretended to hide herself in the hollow of the tree. When night came she went forth with silent foot and obtained food for herself and her kittens, but feigning to be afraid, she kept a lookout all through the day. Meanwhile, the Eagle, full of fear of the Sow, sat still on the branches, and the Sow, terrified by the Eagle, did not dare to go out from her cave. And thus they both, along with their families, perished from hunger, and afforded ample provision for the Cat and her kittens.[418]

Gossip and rumor will destroy. The sustained leader thrives on facts and seeks them whenever they can.

This sounds like me

A lot   **somewhat**   **just a little**   **not at all**

Additional Resources:
John Maxwell, *Everyone Communicates, Few Connect.*
Nido Qubein, *How to be a Great Communicator.*

Personal Objective:

Specific Actions:

Due Date:

---

418 http://aesopfables.com/cgi/aesop1.cgi?2&TheEagletheCatandtheWildSow Accessed 9/8/16

5.2.12 Celebrity

WBS Dictionary: Being a leader is hard work. A successful leader is often the face of the organization, and to the degree it gets public recognition, the leader will be the one to appear on TV or radio in support of the organization. Appearing on TV is a big deal, with production schedules, makeup, hitting your "spot," getting your sound-bite just right—it treats the person doing the talking like a celebrity. A weak leader will succumb to this attention and eventually believe they are entitled to such treatment all the time. They will see the trappings of success as the goal itself to be sought and will allow their leadership responsibilities to become inconsequential to them. They will begin to believe that their "people" (as in "have your people call my people") are the ones who must do all the work while they rest on their laurels and receive the accolades of an adoring public. This sense of celebrity is anathema to the sustained leader. It is the opposite of humility and relationship building. It has no role or place whatsoever with the sustained leader.

Application: In Hollywood and to somewhat the same degree in TV, a commonly heard phrase is, "Don't believe your own press." The caution is designed to prevent people from getting a "swelled head" over their own popularity. If you read all the wonderful things that the press is saying, you will become too prideful and will not dedicate yourself to the improvement you surely need. There is nothing wrong with being proud of your accomplishments, but that is a private pride. Pride should never be boastful. If you ever hear yourself saying, "Do you know who I am?" (5.2.10), you can be assured that you have gone too far in believing in your own self-importance.

There is a profound difference between leaders, heroes, and celebrities. Leaders may be perceived by others as heroes or celebrities but should never perceive themselves as such. A hero is one who has stepped forward at a time of crisis to preserve life or property. Heroes are the human version of the cartoon superheroes (those who have some type of superpower). Yes, people have been known in time of extreme emergency to demonstrate superpowers such as lifting cars off of people. Adrenalin is a powerful drug. And celebrities are those who, for whatever sociological reason, are widely known throughout society. Local TV personalities might be celebrities in their hometown. Wartime gives rise to too many opportunities for people to demonstrate heroic actions. And mass media makes celebrities of others. Perhaps the celebrity is a talented actor, business leader, or even a religious leader. But none of this has *anything* to do with being a sustained leader.

If others wish to celebrate you in some fashion, maintain your humility (1.3.3). The true leader understands that the victories belong to the team; the setbacks belong to the leader. Those who seek celebrity status are misguided and risk becoming celebrities simply for the sake of celebrity. Consider what tangible contribution some celebrities have made, if you can find any contribution at all beyond a leaked sex tape.

This sounds like me

A lot	somewhat	just a little	not at all

Additional Resources:

Jon M. Huntsman, *Winners Never Cheat.*

Robert I. Sutton, R. *The No Asshole Rule.*

Aaron James, *Assholes: A Theory.*

Personal Objective:

Specific Actions:

Due Date:

5.2.13 Anger / Emotional Extremes / Instability

WBS Dictionary: Displays of anger, emotional outbursts, or other indicators of instability are always negative events. The person to whom such emotion is directed may well have "deserved it," yet the result tends to reflect more negatively on the speaker than on the target. In past times some leaders believed that the only viable leadership model was the "command and control" model. You did not earn the respect or loyalty of your subordinates; you merely got them to obey. This demand for blind obedience was a significant factor in the development of labor unions. Positional leaders have been known to yell, scream, intimidate, throw things, threaten bodily harm, and worse just to get their way. While such actions *might* engender obedience to their will, they destroy whatever relationship there may have been and more often create sentiments of vengeance. This vengeance can be demonstrated in a number of ways including sabotage, embezzlement, pilfering, and even malicious compliance. All people are prone to display emotion from time to time. The sustained leader knows where the time and place might exist, if at all, and constrains their emotions to prevent these destructive behaviors from hindering their growth as a leader.

Application: It was January of 1809 when Napoleon hurried back from his conquests in Spain, because word had reached him that certain of his ministers were plotting against him. Much of his anger was directed to his foreign minister, Talleyrand. As Napoleon ranted about treason, loyalty, and trust, he expected his staff, and especially Talleyrand, to begin to tremble from fear. Talleyrand smiled and seemed bored. As Napoleon's attacks became more direct and personal, Talleyrand continued to seem unfazed. The anger continued to mount as Napoleon seemed unable to comprehend how someone could remain so nonplussed in light of charges that could get him hanged. Talleyrand continued to respond calmly. As Napoleon rested his voice and bulging eyes, Talleyrand walked across the room filled with other ministers of the court, put on his coat, and remarked, "What a pity, gentlemen, that so great a man should have such bad manners." Napoleon did not have him hanged but stripped him of his authority, apparently believing that it would be more humiliating to him. Unfortunately, the tirade became the talk of the town. By maintaining his composure, Talleyrand had humiliated the little emperor. He would later remark, "This is the beginning of the end."[419]

---

419 Robert Greene, *48 Laws of Power*, 326.

---·---

Dwight D. Eisenhower

You do not lead by hitting people over the head—that's assault, not leadership.

---·---

In her book *And the Good News Is...* Dana Perino reviews the events surrounding the publication of a book by her predecessor as President Bush's press secretary. Scott McClellan's book was less than kind to the president. Perino was extremely upset about the book and felt a great sense of betrayal by someone she had considered a mentor. Amid her stress over the book, the president said, "I'd like you to try to forgive him." Perino was incredulous and expressed a desire to throw McClellan under the bus first. Her boss responded like a leader, teaching Perino an important lesson. "I don't want you to live bitterly like he is. Nobody will remember this book three weeks from now. And we can't let a book like this take us away from the important work we have to do here on behalf of the American people."[420]

Anger can push people to do very uncharacteristic things. A sustained leader knows how to deal with anger and exercise emotional control. It's not that things don't make the sustained leader angry or prone to other emotions; it merely means the sustained leader has developed a variety of coping mechanisms so that their emotions do not get completely out of control.

In large measure anger is a visceral reaction to facing the unexpected. When a person cuts you off in traffic, you don't expect that and it stimulates anger. People, likewise, do what is to you unexpected and "they" make you angry. In reality *you* make you angry. Only you can control these visceral reactions. Only you can stew over people and situations and allow the anger to eat at you. The sustained leader controls their anger and trains themselves *not* to respond immediately and viscerally. They take the unexpected and add it to their database of how people act and respond. They learn from the experience and work very hard not to be confronted with the unexpected. They learn to expect anything and everything and identify situational awareness (2.1.6). The unexpected should not generate anger; it should generate greater awareness.

---

420 Dana Perino, *And the Good News Is...: Lessons and Advice from the Bright Side* (New York: Hachette Book Group, 2015), 125.

When you allow external stimuli to trigger reactions, you are not demonstrating emotional control. Many people, either by nature or lack of self-discipline, react very negatively to a variety of stimuli. Daniel Goleman reviews a game developed for children to assist them in being aware of certain triggers as reflected in their breathing. The game, *Tenacity*, is a relatively simple app, but it reflects where future mind-training opportunities for leaders might reside.[421] By being aware of the triggers you can more readily assess the situation (1.3) and calibrate your reaction to an appropriate level. Sustained leaders understand this need for self-control and never, absolutely never, allow the situation to control them.

> Learning the game of power requires a certain way of looking at the world, a shifting of perspective. It takes effort and years of practice, for much of the game may not come naturally. Certain basic skills are required, and once you master these skills you will be able to apply the laws of power more easily.
>
> The most important of these skills, and power's crucial foundation, is the ability to master your emotions. An emotional response to a situation is the single greatest barrier to power, a mistake that will cost you a lot more than any temporary satisfaction you might gain by expressing your feelings. Emotions cloud reason, and if you cannot see the situation clearly, you cannot prepare for and respond to it with any degree of control.

Anger is the most destructive of emotional responses, for it clouds your vision the most. It also has a ripple effect that invariably makes situations less controllable and heightens your enemy's resolve. If you are trying to destroy an enemy who has hurt you, far better to keep him off-guard by feigning friendliness than showing your anger.[422]

This sounds like me

A lot	somewhat	just a little	not at all

---

421 Daniel Goleman, *Focus*, 183-5.
422 Robert Greene, *48 Laws of Power*, xix.

Additional Resources:

Daniel Goleman, et al., *Primal Leadership*.

Charles F. Stanley, *Emotions*.

Personal Objective:

Specific Actions:

Due Date:

5.2.14 Imbalance in Positive Traits

WBS Dictionary: The sustained leader must be balanced. It is not expected, and is probably not humanly possible, to be the perfect leader who fully embodies all elements of the *Sustained Leadership WBS* and does not embody any of the undesirable tendencies as described in element 5.2. Another trap for some who strive to be leaders is to be extremely unbalanced in their positive traits. If, for example, they worked toward *only* achieving the Essential Leadership Journey Checkpoints, many important traits and tendencies would be overlooked and set them up for failure. Or perhaps the leader exhibits many of the necessary elements to be a sustained leader but completely ignores certain aspects that are included in the WBS. In either case the leader will exhibit an imbalance in the positive traits. Such an imbalance creates blind-spots that might be exploited by those seeking to remove them as a leader. These are risks to the leader. The sustained leader reviews the *Sustained Leadership WBS* frequently and maintains a continual self-assessment of their progress on the journey toward sustained leadership.

Application: A Renaissance man (or woman) is a person who is broadly educated and trained; they are knowledgeable and proficient in a wide range of fields. Being a sustained leader does not require that the person be a polymorph, yet the more broadly trained the leader is, the better leader they are likely to be. The danger, however, is for the leader to become *too* focused on just a few of the many elements. If the overall approach to addressing the elements is not balanced, the leader will be unbalanced in their approach and will eventually begin to confront situations for which they are not properly prepared. In the ideal setting, the leader should be able to perform all of the tasks of those on their team. This is not realistic in most situations, and so the second-best approach is to be able to understand what the various members of the team are doing in sufficient detail that they can ask intelligent questions and use that information to make good decisions.

Frances Hesselbein reminds us that we must see our life as a "whole." It is not the role of our jobs or the government; we must do this for ourselves. "We continually strive to find enough time for family, friends, the people we love and who love us, and the colleagues who share our passion for the mission and vision of the future of the enterprise. And then we try to make room for that further dimension, where we try to make a difference, work to change lives in the organizations we choose to serve, volunteer in community efforts to move beyond the walls and build the healthy, inclusive community that cares about all its people."[423] Finding balance in all aspects of our life is a continual effort for everyone. We too often tend toward extremes and try to do everything. Too late we realize that trying to do everything results in us doing everything poorly. Psychologists suggest that, to some degree, we all have certain compulsive aspects to our personality. The sustained leader fights these compulsions and maintains balance among their many admirable traits.

William J. Bennett continues this line of thought.

The founders [of America] (like the ancient Greeks) believed it was important that the head of the good polity be a man of good character, and they advocated that the office of the presidency be filled by persons whose "reputation for integrity inspires and merits confidence." The intimate connection between private and public character was understood as a form of integrity, whose root word is *integer*, meaning "whole." The leader must be whole; he cannot have his public character be honest and his private character be deceitful. "The purity of his private character gave effulgence

---

423 Frances Hesselbein, *My Life in Leadership* (San Francisco: Jossey-Bass, 2011), 190.

to his public virtues" were the beautiful words said of George Washington upon his death.[424]

A particular caution was highlighted in the Harvard Business Review by noting that it is inappropriate to promote promising young talent out of fear that you will lose them. "Promoting talented young managers too quickly prevents them from developing key emotional competencies."[425] This becomes a forced and avoidable imbalance. As a leader, avoid this; as an aspiring leader, recognize that you may still lack certain emotional intelligence maturities.

This sounds like me

A lot	somewhat	just a little	not at all

Additional Resources:
Tom Rath, et al., *How Full is Your Bucket?*
Mark Sanborn, et al., *The Fred Factor.*
Harvard Business Review, *HBR's 10 Must Reads on Emotional Intelligence.*

Personal Objective:

Specific Actions:

Due Date:

---

424 William J. Bennett, *The Death of Outrage: Bill Clinton and the Assault on American Ideals* (New York: Free Press, 1998), 37.
425 Harvard Business Review, *HBR's 10 Must Reads on Emotional Intelligence* (Boston: HBR Press, 2015), 141. "The Young and the Clueless" by Kerry A Bunker, Kathy E. Kram, and Sharon Ting.

5.2.15 Integrity Enemies

WBS Dictionary: There are some traits that leaders have developed over the course of their life to which they may be blind. Some of these may be initially perceived as self-preservation and directly related to the flight-or-fight nature of all mankind. They may be "justified" on a very base level. Nonetheless, for the sustained leader, some of these natural traits and tendencies must be overcome and suppressed. These traits are grouped within this heading of integrity enemies because giving into them, however naturally, can derail a leader's progress. Overcoming these impediments may require the unlearning of some things and the relearning of others. This requires a large measure of humility and self-analysis. Not everyone can do this effectively, and the failure to do so will cause continued blindness to these shortcomings. They will affect your credibility and call your integrity into question. They may have been developed with intent and with the highest of moral objective. Yet taking such actions will negatively affect your integrity from both a personal viewpoint and from those viewing you externally. Character, it is said, is who you really are; reputation is how others perceive you. The sustained leader gets this and makes sure that their character and reputation remain consistent and accurate. Defeat these enemies to your integrity to maintain your status as a sustained leader.

Application: One such enemy is greed or avarice. Maximizing your desire to make more money might be rationalized on the basis of "taking care of my family." And certainly the sustained leader must meet their obligations. Heinrich Steinway was orphaned at an early age. Ultimately settling in New York, he began to make very high-quality pianos. Production was low, and Heinrich insisted that his pianos be the best, not that he make as many as he can. He curtailed his income in order to maintain the quality, and given his impoverished beginnings, who would blame him for seeking a higher income? When the American economy became more difficult, he was offered royalties to allow other companies to capitalize on his name. He refused since he would be unable to oversee the quality of the products that bore his name. He turned down significant income and refused to allow greed to affect the integrity of his product and his family name.

Some would say that Mr. Steinway would have been justified in capitalizing on his reputation for quality. He understood, however, as any sustained leader does, that when you cannot control the quality that is attached to your name, you are ill advised to permit others to do so. The same is true for all areas of integrity. When a sustained leader provides a recommendation for another, the expected response should be that such a letter really means something. Only by maintaining your integrity to the highest level can you be assured of not discounting it to others.

The book of Proverbs provides the Wisdom of Solomon for all ages. "Whoever puts up security for a stranger will surely suffer harm, but he who hates striking hands in pledge is secure" (Proverbs 11:15).

Protect your name. Protect your integrity. Protect your path on your journey to becoming a sustained leader.

This sounds like me

A lot   **somewhat**   **just a little**   **not at all**

Additional Resources:
Michael Van Dyke, *Radical Integrity*.
John MacArthur, *The Power of Integrity*.

Personal Objective:

Specific Actions:

Due Date:

5.2.15.1 Self-Interest / Self-Dealing

WBS Dictionary: In its simplest form this trait is simply greed. Greed is one of the seven deadly sins; its existence within your character will taint all of your actions. You will constantly be asking "What's in it for me?" You will position yourself for maximum gain regardless of the impact on others. You might accumulate great wealth, or the most valuable collection of baseball cards, or any other earthly collection of anything. You will seek to obtain the items regardless of cost, including the cost to those you hurt or "step on" along the way. Everything you do is designed to satisfy your own impulses, be they ego, power, excessive safety or security, or the excessive need to "win" at any cost. The sustained leader respects the property and interests of others and does not manipulate situations to maximize their personal gain.

Application: There are rare occasions when a form of self-dealing may be beneficial to all of the interested parties. The sustained leader avoids these situations when possible, but if not possible then the action should be taken only after full disclosure to all the parties. Only after disclosure and permission may you even begin to think about such activities. The far better approach is to avoid such entanglements altogether. Simply do not engage in self-dealing, and honestly assess where your interests truly lie. We may want to think that everything we do is based on altruistic sentiments, but that is more generally not the motivating force behind our actions. Wouldn't it be an interesting world if in fact all of our actions were solely for the benefit of others? What if everyone was actively traveling on their path toward sustained leadership?

Financial managers have gotten into considerable trouble by failing to adhere to this principle. In the management of funds belonging to a client, often very considerable sums, it can be tempting to appropriate some of it for yourself. Acting on information not generally available to the public is another form of this self-deception, and people have gone to prison for doing so or lying about it to investigators.

As P.J. O'Rourke noted, "No drug, not even alcohol, causes the fundamental ills of society. If we're looking for the source of our troubles, we shouldn't test people for drugs, we should test them for stupidity, ignorance, greed, and love

of power." The sustained leader understands that these are the key discriminators between those who are eligible to lead others and those who are not. The self-centered greed that is part of any form of self-dealing is simply unacceptable in a leader, disqualifying them for such service.

This sounds like me

A lot   **somewhat**   **just a little**   **not at all**

Additional Resources:

Ken Blanchard, et al., *Self-Leadership and the One Minute Manager.*
Richard E. Boyatzis, et al., *Resonant Leadership.*

Personal Objective:

Specific Actions:

Due Date:

5.2.15.2 Self-Protection

WBS Dictionary: In a natural disaster you would like to hear the call for "women and children first." Sadly, that is rarely the approach taken. It becomes a situation of "every person for themselves." Certainly we have a natural tendency to preserve our own lives. Every creature in nature has this instinct, yet some will not win this battle or the food chain would be irreparably damaged. This does not mean that you are to throw yourself to the wolves, and it is not necessary to play the role of the superhero. You do not have superpowers. You are human, with all the frailties that encompasses. Even so, when you constantly watch out for number one (i.e. *you!*), those who follow you see this. It weakens you in their eyes. They learn not to trust you or your judgment. They will never be sure whether you have the organization or yourself at the forefront. This natural tendency must be fought and properly calibrated. Discretion, it is said, is the greatest part of valor. This is where that adage finds a home.

Application: Kenny had to attend an offsite meeting where one of his peers did a presentation with an opening page in German. No one at the conference spoke German. The presenter then proceeded to praise his new boss and all he had learned from him. On his last chart he provided the interpretation of the first chart. The most important lesson he had learned from his new boss was, "Always keep someone else between you and the problem." He was not an employee of the company at the next conference, despite his accurate assessment of his new boss.

In Robert Greene's *The 48 Laws of Power*, Law #26 is Keep Your Hands Clean. The opening explanation says, "Our good name and reputation depend more on what we conceal than on what we reveal. Everyone makes mistakes, but those who are truly clever manage to hide them, and make sure someone else is blamed. A convenient scapegoat should always be kept around for such moments."[426]

Elsewhere in this WBS we have discussed the Machiavellian nature of this work from Mr. Greene. Whether he was speaking tongue-in-cheek or not, the sustained leader clearly understands that such an attitude will destroy whatever loyalty their team might have for them. These are not the actions or attitudes of a sustained leader. Don't do this.

This sounds like me

A lot	somewhat	just a little	not at all

Additional Resources:
Brian Tracy, *No Excuses!*
William Ury, *Getting to Yes with Yourself.*

Personal Objective:

---

426 Robert Greene, *48 Laws of Power*, 201.

Specific Actions:

Due Date:

5.2.15.3 Self-Deception

WBS Dictionary: Humans have a very bad tendency to lie. It seems to come naturally to many people. Sadly, we are also very adept at lying to ourselves. We want to believe the best of ourselves and so we rationalize and justify our actions. We remain intentionally blind (or ignorant) of the truth that those around us see. We attempt to deceive others by deceiving ourselves. If we believe the lie strongly enough, we tell ourselves, others will buy into our web of deceit. Lying to others is despicable. Lying to ourselves is beyond despicable. We are not all pretty pictures. We all have a past and we all have done wrong. To continue to deceive yourself about such truths is a fatal flaw for the sustained leader. This does not mean that we must wallow in an endless pit of guilt. Forgive yourself, which includes the personal commitment to *never* do such things again, and move on with your life. You will make mistakes and act inappropriately. We all do. The question is whether you will forgive yourself, commit to continued self-improvement, and move on to better behavior. The sustained leader will do so.

Application: Believing lies, whether emanating from yourself or others, is not the path to sustained leadership. As Thomas Jefferson said, "He who permits himself to tell a lie once, finds it much easier to do it the second time." When you choose a path of believing falsehoods, it becomes easier and easier until you convince yourself of the truth of what is demonstrably false. You become a habitual liar and lose the ability to trust anyone. Often this includes yourself.

If you have a habit of making bad decisions, or if you believe your "luck" has run out, you may be suffering from self-deception. People can be a victim of their circumstances, but more accurately you are a victim of the decisions you have made that have created those circumstances. When you find yourself consistently bumping your head against the same wall, it's a pretty good guess that you are lying to yourself about that wall—what it is, where it came from, and what it will take to truly break it down. You can make midcourse corrections, and like any flight trajectory, the earlier you make that correction the easier it is, and the smaller the required correction. Waiting until the situation has deteriorated to the point that only a massive effort will overcome the inertia is very unwise. It does not make the course correction impossible, but it does increase the challenge to improve.

This sounds like me

A lot　　　　　**somewhat**　　　　　**just a little**　　　　　**not at all**

Additional Resources:
The Arbinger Institute, *Leadership and Self-Deception*.
Harry Frankfurt, *On Truth*.

Personal Objective:

Specific Actions:

Due Date:

5.2.15.4 Self-Righteousness

WBS Dictionary: Leaders who hold an inappropriate level of self-righteousness are those who believe that the means always justify the ends. This is to say that it matters not how you got to the objective, only that you achieved the objective. The sustained leader views things from a vastly different perspective. The ends might be fully justified, but the means must also be appropriate and not tread on others in the process of seeking the objective. Objections to these tactics are met with the justification that the goal was achieved, and thus the damage along the way was acceptable. While this may be an appropriate assessment in military conflicts, as with other traits, the sustained leader always distinguishes between their followers and the adversary in an armed conflict.

Self-righteousness is most commonly rooted in pride. Those with excessive pride tend to justify their actions solely on the basis of the ends achieved. They seek adulation for achieving the success. The means are promptly ignored. Look at any political campaign season and you see this incredible lack of leadership in candidates of all stripes. Lie, cheat, and steal, but win the election. Stuff the ballot box if you must, or let those not eligible cast ballots. Take the opponent's comments out of context, or create a straw-man argument that you allege your opponent supports. Create false dichotomies, and as a final resort, appeal to ad hominem arguments. Whatever it takes to then turn to your constituents and claim that you will lead honorably in this elected position. It is often ironic, even humorous if not so sad, that these politicians actually perceive this as leadership. It is not.

Application: In American society today there are several "mentalities" that seem to be prevalent. There is the "welfare mentality" where people believe they are entitled to things they have never earned. There is the "bully mentality" where some believe they can simply push others around to get their way. This is nothing but a throw-back to the might-makes-right form of leadership related more to Cro-Magnon societies than modern societies. And even more prevalent is the "victim mentality" where the slightest of offenses give rise to extreme reactions. It is another way to psychologically shift blame to the offender rather than accept the blame yourself. It is personality trait that is learned, or acquired, from those with whom a person associates. By regarding themselves as a victim of the actions of others, whether genuinely negative or objectively offensive, the "victim" perceives it as such and behaves accordingly. The victim requires no evidence and in many cases will make up a false narrative even when the falsity of that narrative can be clearly demonstrated to be false. They adopt the view that they have made up their mind and will not be confused by the facts. Thus, the definition of this as a personality disorder. It results from habitual thought processes, and thus recovery is possible. People with a victim mentality feel trapped and powerless. They also often attribute their circumstances to luck, or more accurately bad luck, again accepting no personal responsibility for their situation. It was Ayn Rand who said, "We can evade reality, but we cannot evade the consequences of evading reality." Playing the victim is evading reality. And it ruins your credibility when you truly are the victim.

―――― ● ――――

Napoleon Hill

If you can run a losing race without blaming your loss on someone else, you have bright prospects of success further down the road in life.

―――― ● ――――

Sustained leaders do not succumb to these "mentalities." They recognize that they are entitled to nothing, they get what they earn, and petty offenses or political correctness can never interfere with sustained leadership. Being politically correct and being factually correct are mutually exclusive. Deal with the facts (1.2.1.2). This does not require that you be rude and run roughshod over others' feelings. Another person's decision to never grow up and continually find offense, or to shift blame for the outcome of their own decisions, is not leadership material. They do not make good team members, and they need more than simple mentoring. Self-righteousness has no place in the sustained leader. It must be both avoided and discouraged. It has no positive outcomes. "It will make a big difference to you whether you are a person with a message or a person with a grievance."[427]

This sounds like me

| A lot | somewhat | just a little | not at all |

Additional Resources:
Warren Bennis, *On Becoming a Leader*.
Ed Catmull, et al., *Creativity, Inc.*

Personal Objective:

---

427 Napoleon Hill, *The Law of Success*, Lesson Six Imagination (Chatsworth, CA: Wilshire Book Company, 1928, 2000).

Specific Actions:

Due Date:

CONCLUSION

As the various elements of the *Sustained Leadership WBS* have demonstrated, becoming a sustained leader is a choice. We are called to be the best we can be. The *Sustained leadership WBS* is a tool that can help you improve and achieve your leadership goals.

Only you can decide whether you need to improve in any particular area. It would be helpful to gather your mentors and solicit their views. Like Ben Franklin, choose just a few areas to start. Improve in those and then select a few others. Life events may sometimes direct you to a particular area. And don't be surprised if you need a refresher on an area where you initially scored yourself highly. There is a lot here and, with apologies to all of the Type "A" individuals reading this, you will never be perfect in all of the areas. And that is not even the point. The point is simply to have a tool and a plan to generate self-improvement and begin your leadership journey.

Emerson said, "An institution is the lengthened shadow of one man." If you ever felt that one person can't seem to accomplish much against the tide of the world rushing against them, keep in mind that every major institution, every major accomplishment ever achieved succeeded because an idea started with one person and they accepted the role of leader to cast their shadow across the accomplishments of all mankind. How long of a shadow will you choose to cast?

The world needs better leaders. It needs leaders at all levels. It needs you to be a leader. Whether you choose to lead a country, or a company, or a religion, or a PTA, or a charitable institution, or your neighborhood watch, or your family—the skills are the same. The difference is only in how you apply them. Regardless of those choices, you are the leader of yourself and the starting point for any leader is to accept that level of responsibility and make the most of it. Only you can make you the best "you" that you can possibly be. Greater leadership opportunities will arise from that.

Let us re-quote a point that was made in Chapter one:

> We have tried to resist a recipe—and we have included in our book men and women in very different places, all over organizations. Our central contention, then, is that leadership is *situational, nonhierarchical, and relational*. You might feel this is almost common sense, but you would be surprised how often it is forgotten.[428]

There are no easy answers. You may have made a sincere effort to assess your leadership traits and capabilities. You may have even embarked on a process to improve your leadership, either by using this book or other resources. What you must recognize, however, is that you may still not be a sustained leader. Unless and until you have learned to lead with your heart, your leadership will be mechanical and unappealing. You will not attract followers. Your life will be full of empty works—deeds without meaning. While many societal standards may measure you as a "success" it is not the type of success that this book is designed to elicit from you. Care. Have feelings. Be empathetic. Be human. Maintain your character. Make mistakes. Apologize. Move forward. Only then will you appreciate what it really means to be a sustained leader.

Oliver Wendell Holmes noted that "Man's mind, once stretched by a new idea, never regains its original dimensions." We hope that we have sufficiently stretched your mind to more broadly and deeply cover the concepts of leadership. How much more encouragement do you need? We have taken away one of your biggest excuses for NOT improving yourself, namely, where to start. You hold all the tools

---

428 Goffee, Rob, and Gareth Jones. *Why Should Anyone Be Led by YOU?* (Boston: Harvard Business School Press) 2006 p.204. Emphasis in original.

necessary to begin your leadership journey. It was Max DePree who said, "We cannot become what we need to be by remaining what we are."

You cannot rewrite your past, but you can grab a clean sheet of paper today and write your future. Make a decision (2.6) Decide to lead (1.3.5.2). Take action (2.3). Lead well.

A work that attempts to cover an entire area of thought can never do the topic complete justice, and we make no assertions that this one does. We do hope that it contributes materially to the literature on the subject and prompts others to carry the torch further. Friedrich A. Hayek made the following assertion in the preface to one of his significant works.

> I believe I have made honest use of what I know about the world in which we live. The reader will have to decide whether he wants to accept the values in the service of which I have used that knowledge. The apology concerns the particular state at which I have decided to submit the results of my efforts to the reader. It is perhaps inevitable that the more ambitious the task, the more inadequate will be the performance. On a subject as comprehensive as that of this book, the task of making it as good as one is capable of is never completed while one's faculties last. No doubt I shall soon find that I ought to have said this or that better and that I have committed errors which I could myself have corrected if I had persisted longer in my efforts. Respect for the reader certainly demands that one present a tolerably finished product. But I doubt whether this means that one ought to wait until one cannot hope to improve it further. At least where the problems are of the kind on which many others are actively working, it would even appear to be an overestimate of one's own importance if one delayed publication until one was certain that one could not improve anything. If a man has, as I hope I have, pushed analysis a step forward, further efforts by him are likely to be subject to rapidly decreasing returns.[429]

Amen.

---

429 Von Hayek, F. (1960). *The Constitution of Liberty*. Chicago: Regnery (1972) (Preface).

ABOUT THE AUTHOR

 Tom Reid is an attorney and consultant based in Broomfield, Colorado, near Denver and the majestic Rocky Mountains. He has served in many roles in his extensive career following several sustained, and many not so sustained, leaders. He developed his leadership abilities while serving as a federal attorney, an attorney and business manager for large, medium, and smaller businesses, and operating his consulting firm since 2002. He presently serves as a consultant to businesses seeking to do business with the government, as President of the Subcontract Management Institute, and as an expert witness, assisting in the administration of justice while helping the various participants understand the highly regulated and complex arena of government contract law. His previous writings include four books, chapters contributed to the work of others, and more than two dozen articles on business, leadership, management, and government contracting.

ACKNOWLEDGEMENTS

A work of this magnitude is never a solo effort. While recognizing that any errors that remain are totally those of the author, appreciation is extended to my editors, Angie Kiesling, Vanessa Gonzales, Mallie Rust, and Mia Konstantakos who provided amazing guidance and input to vastly improve the original text. Through the development of the manuscript the constant review, encouragement, criticism, and constructive input from Dan Jacobs, Dave Stameshkin, Ron Sipiora, and Len Vincent, sustained leaders I have always respected, was truly invaluable. The graphic and website support from Chris Hansen and Rod Campos was incredibly important to the book's development. And a special thanks to Oti whose caring encouragement helped move this project along.

As reflected in the bibliography, there are many legendary leaders and authors who have substantially contributed to the concept of leadership as we understand it today.

Finally, appreciation must be expressed to all of the leaders at all levels that I have encountered in my career. While many were excellent examples, there were those who, as Mark Twain would note "can always serve as a bad example." Both types contributed significantly to the development of this work and in the case of the latter group, convinced me of the great need for this book.

BIBLIOGRAPHY

Abrahams, J. (1994) *The Mission Statement Book: 301 corporate mission statements from America's top companies*. Berkeley, CA: Ten Speed Press.

Abrashoff, D. Michael. (2004) *Get Your Ship Together: How Great Leaders Inspire Ownership from the Keel*. US: Portfolio Hardcover.

Alessandra, Anthony J., O'Connor, M., and Dyke, J. (1994) *People Smarts— Bending the Golden Rule to Give Others What They Want*. US: Pfeiffer.

Allen, David. (2000) *Getting Things Done: The Art of Stress-Free Productivity*. New York: Penguin Group.

Allen, James. (1991) *As a Man Thinketh*. US: Barnes and Noble Books.

Anderson, Chris. (2016) *TED Talks: The Official TED Guide to Public Speaking*. US: Houghton Mifflin Harcourt.

Anderson, Walter. (1990) *Read With Me*. US: Houghton Mifflin.

The Arbinger Institute. (2002) *Leadership and Self-Deception: Getting Out of the Box*. US: Berrett-Koehler Publishers.

Barnet, Sylvan, and Bedau, H. (1998) *Critical Thinking, Reading, and Writing: A Brief Guide to Argument*. US: St. Martin's Press.

Belasco, James A. and Ralph C. Stayer, (1993) *Flight of the Buffalo: Soaring to Excellence, Learning to Let Employees Lead*. US: Warner Books.

650

Bellino, Ricardo. (2006) *You Have Three Minutes! Learn the Secret of the Pitch from Trump's Original Apprentice.* US: McGraw-Hill.

Bennis, Warren. (1994) *On Becoming A Leader: Revised Edition.* US: Perseus Books.

Bennis, Warren and Robert Townsend. (1994) *Reinventing Leadership: Strategies to Empower the Organization.* US: William Morrow and Co.

Bennis, Warren. (1996) *Managing People Is Like Herding Cats.* US: Covey Leadership Center.

Bennis, Warren, Kouzes, J., and Tunney, J. (2003) *Taking Charge Lessons in Leadership.* US: Insight Publishing / David Wright.

Bennis, Warren, and Stephen B. Sample (with Rob Asghar). (2015) *The Art and Adventure of Leadership: Understanding Failure, Resilience, and Success.* Hoboken, NJ: John Wiley and Sons.

Bennett, William J. (1993) *The Book of Virtues: A Treasury of Great Moral Stories.* US: Simon and Schuster.

Bennett, William J. (1995) *The Moral Compass: Stories for a Life's Journey.* US: Simon and Schuster.

Bennett, William J. (1998) *The Death of Outrage: Bill Clinton and the Assault on American Ideals.* New York: Free Press.

Berra, Yogi, Berra, L., Berra, T., Berra, D., and Garagiola, J. (1998) *The Yogi Book: "I Really Didn't Say Everything I Said."* US: Workman Publishing Company.

Blackshaw, Pete. (2008) *Satisfied Customers Tell Three Friends, Angry Customers Tell 3,000: Running a Business in Today's Consumer-Driven World.* US: Crown Business.

Blanchard, Ken, (1999) *The Heart of a Leader: Insights on the Art of Influence.* US: David C. Cook.

Blanchard, Ken, McBride, M., & McBride, M. (2003) *The One Minute Apology: A Powerful Way to Make Things Better.* US: William Morrow.

Blanchard, Kenneth H. and Phil Hodges. (2003) *Servant Leader: Transforming your Heart, Head, Hands, and Habits.* US: Thomas Nelson.

Blanchard, Ken and Steve Gottry, (2004) *The On-Time, On-Target Manager: How a "Last-Minute Manager" Conquered Procrastination.* US: William Morrow.

Blanchard, Kenneth H. and Marc Muchnick. (2004) *The Leadership Pill: The Missing Ingredient in Motivating People Today.* New York: Free Press.

Blanchard, Ken, Fowler, S., Hawkins, L., and Hawkins, L. (2005) *Self-Leadership and the One Minute Manager: Increasing Effectiveness through Situational Self-Leadership.* US: William Morrow.

Blanchard, Ken, Meyer, P., and Ruhe, D. (2007) *Know Can Do!: Put Your Know-How into Action.* US: Berrett-Koehler Publishers

Blanchard, Ken. (2009) *Leading at a Higher Level, Revised and Expanded Edition: Blanchard on Leadership and Creating High Performing Organizations.* US: FT Press.

Blanchard, Ken, and Colleen Barrett. (2011) *Lead with Luv: A Different Way to Create Real Success.* Upper Saddle River, NJ: FT Press.

Bloom, Lauren M. (2013) *Art of the Apology: How, When, and Why to Give and Accept Apologies.* US: Fine and Kahn.

Blumenson, Martin. (1985) *Patton: The Man behind the Legend, 1885-1945.* US: William Morrow.

Bly, Robert. (1992) *Elements of Business Writing: A Guide to Writing Clear, Concise Letters, Memos, Reports, Proposals, and other Business Documents.* US: Longman.

Boss, Judith A. Boss, (2004) *Analyzing Moral Issues.* US: McGraw-Hill College.

Bossidy, Larry, Ram Charan, and Charles Burck. (2001) *Execution: the discipline of getting things done.* New York: Crown Business.

Bossidy, Larry and Ram Charan. (2004) *Confronting Reality: Doing What Matters to Get Things Right.* US: Crown Business.

Boyatzis, Richard E., and McKee, A. (2005) *Resonant Leadership: Renewing Yourself and Connecting with Others Through Mindfulness, Hope, and Compassion.* US: Harvard Business Review Press.

Brady, Chris, and Orrin Woodward. (2007) *Launching a Leadership Revolution: Mastering the Five Levels of Influence.* US: Business Plus.

Brady, Chris. (2014) *Splash: A Leader's Guide to Effective Public Speaking.* US: Obstaclés Press.

Brandon, Rick. (2004) *Survival of the Savvy: High-Integrity Political Tactics for Career and Company Success.* US: Free Press.

Browne, M. Neil, and Keeley, S. (2006) *Asking the Right Questions: A Guide to Critical Thinking.* US: Prentice Hall

Buckingham, Marcus, and Curt Coffman. (1999) *First, Break All the Rules: What the World's Greatest Managers Do Differently.* US: Simon and Schuster.

Buckingham, Marcus, and Donald O. Clifton. (2001) *Now, Discover Your Strengths.* US: Free Press.

Buckingham, Marcus. (2005) *The One Thing You Need to Know: ... About Great Managing, Great Leading, and Sustained Individual Success.* US: Free Press.

Buckingham, Marcus. (2007) *Go Put Your Strengths to Work: 6 Powerful Steps to Achieve Outstanding Performance.* US: Free Press.

Buckingham, Marus. (2011*) StandOut: The Groundbreaking New Strengths Assessment from the Leader of the Strengths Revolution.* US: Thomas Nelson.

Burkett, Larry, (1992) *Financial Freedom Library Vol 1, Boxed Set of 6 Paperback Books: Personal Finances; Financial Freedom; Giving and Tithing; Insurance Plans; Sound Investments; and Major Purchases.* US: Moody Press.

Bush, George. (2010) *Decision Points.* US: Crown Publishers.

Buss, Dale. (2005) *Family Man: The Biography of Dr. James Dobson.* US: Tyndale House Publishers, Inc.

Cain, Susan. (2012) *Quiet: The Power of Introverts in a World That Can't Stop Talking.* US: Crown.

Carey, Benedict. (2014) *How We Learn: The Surprising Truth About When, Where, and Why It Happens.* New York, N.Y.: Random House.

Carnegie, Dale. (1962) *The Quick and Easy Way to Effective Speaking.* Garden City, NY: Dale Carnegie and Associates, Inc.

Carnegie, Dale. (1970) *How to Develop Self-Confidence.* US: Pocket Books.

Carnegie, Dale. and Pell, A. (1998) *How to Win Friends and Influence People.* US: Pocket Books.

Carson, Ben, and Murphey, C. (1996) *Gifted Hands: The Ben Carson Story.* US: Zondervan.

Carson, Ben, and Lewis, G. (2007) *Take the Risk: Learning to Identify, Choose, and Live with Acceptable Risk.* US: Zondervan.

Catmull, Ed, and Wallace, A. (2014) *Creativity, Inc.: Overcoming the Unseen Forces That Stand in the Way of True Inspiration.* US: Random House.

Charan, Ram. (2001) *What the CEO Wants You to Know: How Your Company Really Works.* US: Crown Business.

Charan, Ram. (2007*) What the Customer Wants You to Know: How Everybody Needs to Think Differently About Sales.* US: Portfolio Hardcover.

Chester, Eric. (2002) *Employing Generation Why?* US: ChesPress.

Chester, Eric, (2010) *Bring Your A Game to Work (Teen Version).* US: ChesPress.

Cialdini, Robert. (2016) *Pre-Suasion: A Revolutionary Way to Influence and Persuade.* US: Simon and Schuster.

Coffin, Christina, managing ed. (2002) *Business: The Ultimate Resource.* US: Basic Books.

Coffman, Curt, and Gabriel Gonzalez-Molina. (2002) *Follow This Path: How the World's Greatest Organizations Drive Growth by Unleashing Human Potential.* US: Business Plus.

Clarke, Boyd, Crossland, R., and Peters, T. (2002) *The Leader's Voice: How Your Communication Can Inspire Action and Get Results!* New York: Select Books.

Clarke, Colleen S. (2006) *Networking: How to Build Relationships that Count.* US: Colleen Clarke and Associates

Cohen, Allan, and Bradford, D. (1991) *Influence without Authority.* US: Wiley.

Collins, James C., and Jerry I. Porras. (1994) *Built to Last: Successful Habits of Visionary Companies.* New York: HarperCollins.

Collins, Jim. (2001) *Good to Great: Why Some Companies Make the Leap…And Others Don't.* New York: Harper Business.

Collins, James, and Morten T. Hansen. (2011) *Great by Choice: Uncertainty, Chaos, and Luck--Why Some Thrive Despite Them All.* US: Harper Business.

Connors, Roger, Tom Smith, and Craig Hickman. (2004) *The Oz Principle: Getting Results through Individual and Organizational Accountability.* US: Portfolio.

Conwell, Russell. *(1968) Acres of Diamonds.* Kansas City, Mo.: Hallmark.

Corrigan, Paul. (2000) *Shakespeare on Management: Leadership Lessons for Today's Management.* US: Kogan Page Business Books.

Cottrell, David, Adams, A., and Baldwin, J. (2002) *Monday Morning Leadership: 8 Mentoring Sessions You Can't Afford to Miss.* US: CornerStone Leadership Institute.

Covey, Stephen R. (1991) *Principle-Centered Leadership: Teaching Timeless Principles of Effectiveness.* US: Summit Books.

Covey, Stephen R. (1996) *Rethinking the Future: Rethinking Business, Principles, Competition, Control and Complexity, Leadership, Markets and the World.* US: Nicholas Brealey.

Covey, Stephen. (1997) *The 7 Habits of Highly Effective Families: Building a Beautiful Family Culture in a Turbulent World.* US: Golden Books.

Covey, Stephen R. (1989) *The 7 Habits of Highly Effective People: Powerful Lessons in Personal Change.* New York: Simon and Schuster.

Covey, Stephen R. and Breck England. (2011) *The 3rd Alternative: Solving Life's Most Difficult Problems.* US: Free Press.

Crainer, Stuart. (2001) *The 75 Greatest Management Decisions Ever Made: ...and 21 of the Worst.* New York, NY: MJF Books.

D'Amour, C. (1996) *Networking: The Skill the Schools Forgot to Teach.* US: Jump Start Books.

Danzig, Robert J., and Kaplan, H. (1997) *The Leader Within You: Master 9 Powers to Be the Leader You Always Wanted to Be!* US: Lifetime Books.

DeCandido, Keith R. (2014) *The Klingon Art of War.* US: Pocket Books/Star Trek.

DePree, Max. (1993) *Leadership Jazz: The Essential Elements of a Great Leader.* US: Dell.

DePree, Max, (1997) *Leading without Power: Finding Hope in Serving Community.* US: Jossey-Bass.

DePree, Max. (2004) *Leadership Is an Art.* US: Crown Business.

Dickson, John. (2011) *Humilitas: A Lost Key to Life, Love, and Leadership.* Grand Rapids, MI: Zondervan.

Droms, William G. (1990) *Finance and Accounting for Nonfinancial Managers.* US: Perseus Books.

Drucker, Peter. (1973) *Management: tasks, responsibilities, practices.* US: Harper and Row.

Duke Corporate Education. (2005) *Translating Strategy into Action (Leading from the Center).* US: Kaplan Business.

Duggan, William. (2013) *Strategic Intuition: The Creative Spark in Human Achievement.* US: Columbia University Press.

Dungy, Tony and Nathan Whitaker. (2009) *Uncommon: Finding Your Path to Significance.* US: Tyndale Momentum.

Dungy, Tony, and Nathan Whitaker. (2010) *The Mentor Leader: Secrets to Building People and Teams That Win Consistently.* US: Tyndale Momentum.

Engstrom, Theodore Wilhelm, and Larson, R. (1987) *Integrity.* US: W Pub Group.

Elliott, Alan C. (1998) *A Daily Dose of the American Dream: Stories of Success, Triumph, and Inspiration.* US: Thomas Nelson.

Ferrazzi, Keith. (2009) *Who's Got Your Back: The Breakthrough Program to Build Deep, Trusting Relationships That Create Success--and Won't Let You Fail.* US: Crown Business.

Fine, Debra. (2005) *The Fine Art of Small Talk: How to Start a Conversation, Keep it Going, Build Networking Skills- and Leave a Positive Impression.* NY: Hyperion.

Fisher, Donna. (1995) *People Power: How to Create a Lifetime Network for Business, Career, and Personal Advancement.* US: Bard Press.

Fisher, Roger. (1988) *Getting Together: Building a Relationship That Gets to Yes.* US: Houghton Mifflin.

Fisher, Roger, Bruce Patton, and William Ury. (1991) *Getting to Yes: Negotiating Agreement without Giving In.* US: Penguin Books.

Fisher, Roger, Kopelman, E., and Schneider, A. (1996) *Beyond Machiavelli: Tools for Coping with Conflict.* US: Penguin Publishing Group.

Fisher, Roger, and Sharp, A. (1997) *Getting It Done: How to Lead When you're Not in Charge.* US: Harper Business.

Forbes, B.C. (1976) *The Forbes Scrapbook of Thoughts on the Business of Life.* New York: Forbes, Inc.

Frankfurt, Harry. (2005) *On Bullshit.* US: Princeton University Press.

Frankfurt, Harry. (2006) *On Truth.* US: Knopf.

Franklin, Benjamin. (1950) *The Autobiography of Benjamin Franklin and Selections from His Other Writings.* US: The Modern Library College Editions.

Freed, Richard C., Romano, J., and Freed, S. (1994) *Writing Winning Business Proposals: Your Guide to Landing the Client, Making the Sale, Persuading the Boss.* US: McGraw-Hill Trade.

Freiberg, Kevin, and Jackie Freiberg. (1996) *NUTS! Southwest Airlines' Crazy Recipe for Business and Personal Success.* US: Bard Press.

Friedman, Jack P. (1986) *Dictionary of Business Terms (Barron's Business Guides).* US: Barron's Educational Series.

Gabor, Don. (1997) *Talking with Confidence for the Painfully Shy: How to Overcome Nervousness, Speak-Up, and Speak Out in Any Social or Business Situation.* US: Harmony.

Garten, Jeffrey. (2001) *The Mind Of The CEO: The World's Business Leaders Talk About Leadership, Responsibility The Future of the Corporation, and What Keeps Them Up at Night.* US: Basic Books.

Geever, Jane, and P. McNeill. (1997) *The Foundation Center's Guide to Proposal Writing.* US: Foundation Center.

Gellhorn, Ernest, and Barry B. Boyer. (1987) *Administrative Law and Process in a Nutshell (Nutshell Series).* US: West Publishing Co.

George, Bill, and Warren Bennis. (2003) *Authentic Leadership: Rediscovering the Secrets to Creating Lasting Value.* US: Jossey-Bass.

George, Michael L., David Rowlands, and Bill Kastle. (2003) *What is Lean Six Sigma?* US: McGraw-Hill.

Gerzon, Mark. (2006) *Leading Through Conflict: How Successful Leaders Transform Differences into Opportunities.* US: Harvard Business Review Press.

Giblin, Les. (1985) *How to Have Confidence and Power in Dealing with People.* US: Prentice Hall Press.

Gilbert, Thomas F. (1996) *Human Competence: Engineering Worthy Performance (ISPI Tribute Edition).* US: Pfeiffer.

Gitomer, Jeffrey. (1998) *Customer Satisfaction Is Worthless, Customer Loyalty Is Priceless: How to Make Customers Love You, Keep Them Coming Back and Tell Everyone They Know.* US: Bard Press.

Gitomer, Jeffrey. (2004) *Little Red Book of Selling: 12.5 Principles of Sales Greatness.* US: Bard Press.

Gitomer, Jeffrey. (2006) *Little Black Book of Connections: 6.5 Assets for Networking Your Way to Rich Relationships.* US: Bard Press.

Gitomer, Jeffrey. (2007) *Little Green Book of Getting Your Way: How to Speak, Write, Present, Persuade, Influence, and Sell Your Point of View to Others.* US: Financial Times Press.

Gitomer, Jeffrey. (2008) *Little Teal Book of Trust: How to Earn It, Grow It, and Keep It to Become a Trusted Advisor in Sales, Business and Life.* US: FT Press.

Gitomer, Jeffrey. (2011) *Social BOOM!: How to Master Business Social Media to Brand Yourself, Sell Yourself, Sell Your Product, Dominate Your Industry Market, Save Your Butt, … and Grind Your Competition into the Dirt.* US: FT Press.

Gitomer, Jeffrey, *and Paul Hersey. (2011) The Little Book of Leadership: The 12.5 Strengths of Responsible, Reliable, Remarkable Leaders That Create Results, Rewards, and Resilience.* US: Wiley.

Giuliani, Rudolph W., and Ken Kurson. (2002) *Leadership.* US: Hyperion.

Gladwell, Malcolm. (2002) *The Tipping Point: How Little Things Can Make a Big Difference.* US: Back Bay Books.

Gladwell, Malcolm. (2005) *Blink: The Power of Thinking without Thinking.* US: Little, Brown and Company.

Gladwell, Malcolm. (2008) *Outliers: The Story of Success.* US: Little, Brown and Company.

Godin, Seth, and Hugh Macleod. (2007) *The Dip: A Little Book That Teaches You When to Quit (and When to Stick).* US: Portfolio Hardcover.

Godin, Seth. (2008) *Tribes: We Need You to Lead Us.* US: Portfolio Hardcover.

Godin, Seth. (2010) *Linchpin: Are You Indispensable?* US: Portfolio Hardcover.

Goffee, Rob, and Gareth Jones. (2006) *Why Should Anyone Be Led by YOU?* Boston: Harvard Business School Press.

Goldsmith, Marshall, Lyons, L., and Freas, A. (2000) *Coaching for Leadership: How the World's Greatest Coaches Help Leaders Learn.* US: Pfeiffer.

Goldsmith, Marshall, and Reiter, M. (2007) *What Got You Here Won't Get You There: How Successful People Become Even More Successful.* US: Hyperion.

Goleman, Daniel. (2000) *Working with Emotional Intelligence.* US: Bantam.

Goleman, Daniel, McKee, A., and Boyatzis, R. (2002) *Primal Leadership: Realizing the Power of Emotional Intelligence.* US: Harvard Business Review Press.

Goleman, Daniel, (2006) *Emotional Intelligence: 10th Anniversary Edition; Why It Can Matter More Than IQ.* US: Bantam.

Goleman, Daniel. (2015) *Focus: The Hidden Driver of Excellence.* US: Harper Paperbacks.

Gongwer, Todd G. (2011) *LEAD . . . for God's Sake!: A Parable for Finding the Heart of Leadership.* US: Tyndale House Publishers, Inc.

Gordon, Jon. and Ken Blanchard. (2007) *The Energy Bus: 10 Rules to Fuel Your Life, Work, and Team with Positive Energy.* US: Wiley.

Gostick, Adrian, and Chester Elton, (2003) *24-Carrot Manager: A Remarkable Story of How a Leader Can Unleash Human Potential.* US: Gibbs Smith.

Gostick, Adrian, and Chester Elton. (2006) *The Invisible Employee: Realizing the Hidden Potential in Everyone.* US: Wiley.

Greene, Robert, and Elffers, J. (2000) *The 48 Laws of Power.* US: Penguin Books.

Greenleaf, Robert K. (1991) *The Servant as Leader.* Indianapolis, IN: The Robert K. Greenleaf Center.

Greenleaf, Robert K., Larry C. Spears, and Peter B. Vaill. (1998) *The Power of Servant-Leadership.*US: Berrett-Koehler Publishers.

Grint, Keith. (2010), *Leadership: A Very Short Introduction.* New York: Oxford University Press.

Gurian, Michael, and Annis, B. (2008) *Leadership and the Sexes: Using Gender Science to Create Success in Business.* US: Jossey-Bass.

Hansen, Mark Victor, and Batten, J. (2004) *The Master Motivator: Secrets of Inspiring Leadership.* US: Barnes and Noble Books.

Harris, B. and Norris, C. (2008) *Do Hard Things: A Teenage Rebellion Against Low Expectations.* US: Multnomah.

Harvard Business School Press, (2003) *Harvard Business Review on Corporate Ethics (Harvard Business Review Paperback Series).* Boston: Harvard Business Press.

Harvard Business Review. (2015) *HBR's 10 Must Reads on Emotional Intelligence.* Boston: Harvard Business Review Press.

Harvard Press, (2005) *Motivating People for Improved Performance (Results Driven Manager).* Boston: Harvard Business Press.

Harvey, Eric, Lucia, A., and Hourigan, M. (2003) *The Leadership Secrets of Santa Claus.* US: The WALK THE TALK Company.

Hasnas, John. (2006) *Trapped: When Acting Ethically is Against the Law.* US: Cato Institute.

Heath, Chip, and Dan Heath. (2007) *Made to Stick: Why Some Ideas Survive and Others Die.* US: Random House.

Heath, Chip, and Dan Heath. (2013) *Decisive: How to Make Better Choices in Life and Work.* US: Crown Business.

Hedges, Burke. (2000) *Read and Grow Rich: How the Hidden Power of Reading Can Make You Richer in All Areas of Your Life!* US: International Network Training Institute.

Heinrichs, Jay. (2013) *Thank You For Arguing, Revised and Updated Edition: What Aristotle, Lincoln, And Homer Simpson Can Teach Us About the Art of Persuasion.* US: Three Rivers Press.

Heller, Robert. (1999) *Essential Managers: Making Decisions.* US: DK Adult.

Hendershott, Anne B. (2002) *The Politics of Deviance.* US: Encounter Books.

Herman, Mark L., Mark D. Frost, and Robert Kurz, (2008) *Wargaming for Leaders: Strategic Decision Making from the Battlefield to the Boardroom.* New York: McGraw Hill.

Hersey, Paul. (1983) *The Situational Leader.* US: Center for Leadership Studies.

Hesselbein, Frances, and Jim Collins. (2011) *My Life in Leadership: The Journey and Lessons Learned Along the Way.* US: Jossey-Bass.

Henry, Charles R. (Maj. Gen. ret). (1995) *A General's Insights into Leadership and Management: Reorganizing, Consolidating, Downsizing.* US: Battelle Press.

Hill, Napoleon. (1987) *Think and Grow Rich.* US: The Ballantine Publishing Group.

Hill, Napoleon. (2000) *The Law of Success in Sixteen Lessons (2 Volume Set).* US: Wilshire Book Co.

Hillman, James. (1995) *Kinds of Power: A Guide to its Intelligent Uses.* US: Doubleday Business.

Horwath, Rich. (2009) *Deep Dive: The Proven Method for Building Strategy, Focusing Your Resources, and Taking Smart Action.* US: Greenleaf Book Group Press.

Hsieh, Lawrence. (2010) *The Small-Business Contracts Handbook: Understand, negotiate, and avoid problems. (Self-Counsel Legal).* US: Self-Counsel Press, Inc.

Huffington, A. (2014) *Thrive: The Third Metric to Redefining Success and Creating a Life of Well-Being, Wisdom, and Wonder.* US: Harmony.

Hunter, James C. (1998) *The Servant: A simple story about the true essence of leadership.* Rocklin, CA: Prima Publishing.

Hunter, James C. (2004) *The World's Most Powerful Leadership Principle: How to Become a Servant Leader.* US: Crown Business.

Huntsman, Jon M. (2005) *Winners Never Cheat: Everyday Values We Learned as Children (But May Have Forgotten).* US: Pearson Prentice Hall.

Huppe, Frank. (1993) *Successful Delegation: How to Grow Your People, Build Your Team, Free Up Your Time, and Increase Profits and Productivity.* Hawthorne, NJ: Career Press.

Iacocca, Lee. (2007) *Where Have All the Leaders Gone?* US: Scribner.

Iaquinto, Anthony L. and Stephen Spinelli Jr., (2006) *Never Bet the Farm: How Entrepreneurs Take Risks, Make Decisions—and How You Can, Too.* US: Jossey-Bass.

Ingram, David Bruce, Ph.D. and Jennifer A. Parks, Ph.D., (2002) *The Complete Idiot's Guide to Understanding Ethics.* Indianapolis, IN: Alpha Books.

Jacobs, Daniel M. (2010) *The Art of the Possible: Create an Organization with No Limitations.* US: CreateSpace Independent Publishing Platform.

James, Aaron. (2014) *Assholes: A Theory.* US: Anchor.

Jennings, Marianne. (2005) *Business: Its Legal, Ethical, and Global Environment.* US: South-Western College/West.

Jenson, Ron. (2001) *Achieving Authentic Success.* San Diego, Ca: Future Achievement International.

Jensen, Doug, McMullen, T., & Stark, M. (2006) *The Manager's Guide to Rewards: What You Need to Know to Get the Best for -- and from -- Your Employees.* US: AMACOM

Johnson, Dwight, and Nelson, D. (2001) *The Transparent Leader.* US: Harvest House Publishers.

Johnson, Spencer. (2003) *The Present: The Gift That Makes You Happier and More Successful at Work and in Life, Today!* US: Crown Business.

Johnson, Spencer. (1985) *The One Minute Teacher: How to Teach Others to Teach Themselves.* New York: W. Morrow.

Jones, Charlie. (1981) *Life Is Tremendous.* US: Tyndale Momentum.

Jones, Laurie Beth. (1995) *Jesus, CEO: Using Ancient Wisdom for Visionary Leadership.* US: Hyperion.

Jones, Morgan D. (1998) *The Thinker's Toolkit: 14 Powerful Techniques for Problem Solving.* US: Crown Business.

Josephson, Michael, and Hanson, W. (1998) *The Power of Character: Prominent Americans Talk About Life, Family, Work, Values, and More.* US: Jossey-Bass.

Kahneman, Daniel. (2013) *Thinking, Fast and Slow.* US: Farrar, Straus and Giroux.

Kanter, Rosabeth Moss. (1994) *World Class: Thriving Locally in the Global Economy.* New York: Simon and Schuster.

Kaplan, Robert S., and David P. Norton. (1996) *The Balanced Scorecard: Translating Strategy into Action.* US: Harvard Business Review Press.

Karas, Jim. (2001) *The Business Plan for the Body.* US: Harmony.

Keirsey, David, and Bates, M. (1983) *Please Understand Me: Character and Temperament Types.* US: B and D Books.

Keller, Gary, and Jay Papasan. (2013) The *ONE Thing: The Surprisingly Simple Truth behind Extraordinary Results.* US: Bard Press.

Keller, H. (2010) *The World I Live In and Optimism: A Collection of Essays.* US: Dover Publications.

Kelman, Steven. (2005) *Unleashing Change: A Study of Organizational Renewal in Government.* US: Brookings Institution Press.

Kendrick, Tom. (2003) *Identifying and Managing Project Risk: Essential Tools for Failure-Proofing Your Project.* US: AMACOM.

Kilmeade, Brian, and Yaeger, D. (2013) *George Washington's Secret Six: The Spy Ring That Saved the American Revolution.* US: Sentinel HC.

Kiyosaki, Robert T., and Lechter, S. (2000) *Rich Dad's Rich Kid, Smart Kid: Giving Your Child a Financial Head Start.* US: Warner Business.

Knowles, Malcolm. (1998) *The Adult Learner, Fifth Edition: The Definitive Classic in Adult Education and Human Resource Development (Managing Cultural Differences).* US: Gulf Professional Publishing.

Koch, Richard. (1998) *The 80/20 Principle: The Secret to Achieving More with Less.* New York: Currency/Doubleday.

Kolb, Deborah M., and Williams, J. (2003) *Everyday Negotiation: Navigating the Hidden Agendas in Bargaining.* US: Jossey-Bass.

Kotter, John P. (1990) *A Force for Change: How Leadership Differs from Management.* US: The Free Press.

Kotter, John P. (1996) *Leading Change.* Boston, MA: Harvard Business School Press.

Kotter, John P. (1998) *On What Leaders Really Do.* Boston: Harvard Business School Press.

Kotter, John P., Holger Rathgeber, and Spencer Johnson, (fwd). (2004) *Our Iceberg is Melting: Changing and Succeeding under any Conditions.* New York: St. Martin's Press.

Kotter, John and Holger Rathgeber. (2016) *That's Not How We Do It Here!: A Story about Organizations Rise and Fall--and Can Rise Again.* US: Portfolio.

Kouzes, James M. and Barry Z. Posner. (1992) *Credibility: How Leaders Gain and Lose it, Why People Demand it.* San Francisco: Jossey-Bass Publishers.

Kouzes, James M. and Barry Z. Posner. (2002) *The Leadership Challenge: How to Make Extraordinary Things Happen in Organizations.* San Francisco: Jossey-Bass.

Kouzes, James M. and Barry Z. Posner. (2005) *A Leader's Legacy.* San Francisco: Jossey-Bass.

Kouzes, James M. and Barry Z. Posner. (2010) *The Truth about Leadership: The No-Fads, Heart-Of-The-Matter Facts you Need to Know.* San Francisco, CA: Jossey-Bass.

Krannich, Caryl Rae. (2002) *101 Secrets of Highly Effective Speakers: Controlling Fear, Commanding Attention.* US: Impact Publications.

Kroeger, Otto, Thuesen, J., and Rutledge, H. (2002) *Type Talk at Work (Revised): How the 16 Personality Types Determine Your Success on the Job.* US: Delta.

Krogerus, Mikael, Tschäppeler, R., Earnhart, P., and Earnhart, P. (2012) *The Decision Book: 50 Models for Strategic Thinking.* US: W. W. Norton and Company.

Kubicek, Jeremie. (2011) *Leadership Is Dead: How Influence Is Reviving It.* US: Howard Books.

Kuzmeski, Maribeth. (2010) *...And the Clients Went Wild!: How Savvy Professionals Win All the Business They Want.* US: Wiley.

Kyne, Peter, & Ramsey, D. (2011) *The Go-Getter: The Timeless Classic That Tells You How to Be One.* Brentwood, TN: Lampo Press

Laborde, Genie Z., (1984) *Influencing with Integrity: Management Skills for Communication and Negotiation.* US: Syntony Publishing.

Leeds, Dorothy. (1988) *Powerspeak: The Complete Guide to Persuasive Public Speaking and Presenting.* US: Prentice Hall Trade.

Leeds, Dorothy. (2000) *The 7 Powers of Questions: Secrets to Successful Communication in Life and Work.* New York: Berkely Publishing.

Lencioni, Patrick. (1998) *The Five Temptations of a CEO: A Leadership Fable*. US: Jossey-Bass.

Lencioni, Patrick. (2002) *The Five Dysfunctions of a Team: A Leadership Fable*. US: Jossey-Bass.

Lencioni, Patrick. (2004) *Death by Meeting: A Leadership Fable…About Solving the Most Painful Problem in Business*. US: Jossey-Bass.

Lencioni, Patrick. (2006) *Silos, Politics and Turf Wars: A Leadership Fable about Destroying the Barriers That Turn Colleagues into Competitors*. US: Jossey-Bass.

Lencioni, Patrick. (2007) *The Three Signs of a Miserable Job: A Fable for Managers (And Their Employees)*. US: Jossey-Bass.

Lencioni, Patrick. (2010) *Getting Naked: A Business Fable About Shedding The Three Fears That Sabotage Client Loyalty*. US: Jossey-Bass.

Lewis, C.S. (1996) *The Inspirational Writings of C.S. Lewis*. US: Thomas Nelson.

Lipman, Victor. (2015) *The Type B Manager: Leading Successfully in a Type A World*. Prentice Hall,

Liu, Lan. (2010) *Conversations on Leadership: Wisdom from Global Management Gurus*. US: Jossey-Bass.

Loehr, James E., and Tony Schwartz. (2002) *The Power of Full Engagement: Managing Energy, Not Time, is the Key to High Performance and Personal Renewal*. New York: Free Press.

Lohrenz, Carey. (2014) *Fearless Leadership: High-Performance Lessons from the Flight Deck*. US: Greenleaf Book Group Press.

Lukacs, John. (2002) *Churchill: Visionary. Statesman. Historian*. US: Yale University Press.

Lundin, Stephen C., Christensen, J., and Paul, H. (2002) *Fish! Sticks: A Remarkable Way to Adapt to Changing Times and Keep Your Work Fresh*. US: Hachette Books.

Lynch, Robert Porter, and H. Lynch. (1992) *Business Alliances Guide: the Hidden Competitive Weapon*. New York: J. Wiley.

MacArthur, John. (1997) *The Power of Integrity: Building a Life without Compromise*. US: Crossway.

MacArthur, John. (2005) *The Fulfilled Family: God's Design for Your Home*. US: Thomas Nelson.

MacArthur, John. (2006) *The Book on Leadership*. US: Thomas Nelson.

MacArthur, John. (2006) *The Quest for Character.* US: Thomas Nelson.

McCarthy, Dennis G. (1997) *The Loyalty Link: How Loyal Employees Create Loyal Customers.* US: Wiley.

Maccoby, Michael. *Narcissistic Leaders,* Harvard Business Review, January 2004, PP. 92-101.

Machiavelli, Niccolo, and Daniel Donno. (1984) *The Prince.* US: Bantam Classics.

Mackay, Harvey. (1999) *Dig Your Well before you're Thirsty: The Only Networking Book You'll Ever Need.* US: Currency Books.

Mackey, John, Sisodia, R., and George, B. (2013) *Conscious Capitalism: Liberating the Heroic Spirit of Business.* US: Harvard Business Review Press.

Mandino, Og. (1983) *Og Mandino's University of Success.* US: Bantam.

Mandrou, Robert, and Pearce, B. (1979) *History of European Thought: from Humanism to Science, The Pelican: 1480-1700; Volume 3.* US: Penguin Books.

Martin, Roger L. (2001) *The Responsibility Virus: How Control Freaks, Shrinking Violets-and The Rest of us-Can Harness the Power of True Partnership.* New York, NY: Basic Books.

Mathis, Mark E. (2002) *Feeding the Media Beast: An Easy Recipe for Great Publicity.* US: Purdue University Press.

Maxwell, John C. (1993) *Developing the Leader within You.* Nashville, TN: Thomas Nelson.

Maxwell, John C. and Dornan, J. (1997) *Becoming A Person of Influence: How to Positively Impact the Lives of Others.* US: Thomas Nelson.

Maxwell, John C. (1999) *Failing Forward: Turning Mistakes into Stepping-Stones for Success.* Nashville, TN: Thomas Nelson Publishers.

Maxwell, John. (2000) *Developing the Leaders around You.* Nashville: Thomas Nelson Publishers.

Maxwell, John C. (2003) *There's No Such Thing as "Business" Ethics: There's Only One Rule for Making Decisions.* US: Center Street.

Maxwell, John C. (2004) *Ethics 101: what every leader needs to know.* New York, NY: Warner Books.

Maxwell, John C. (2006) *The 360 Degree Leader: Developing Your Influence from Anywhere in the Organization.* US: Thomas Nelson.

Maxwell, John C. (2006) *The Difference Maker: Making Your Attitude Your Greatest Asset.* US: Thomas Nelson.

Maxwell, John C. (2007) *Talent Is Never Enough: Discover the choices that will take you beyond your talent.* Nashville, TN: Thomas Nelson.

Maxwell, John C. (2008) *How Successful People Think: Change Your Thinking, Change Your Life.* New York: Center Street.

Maxwell, John C. (2009) *Put Your Dream to the Test: 10 Questions that Will Help You See It and Seize It.* US: Thomas Nelson.

Maxwell, John C. (2009) *Everyone Communicates, few Connect: What the most Effective People do Differently.* Nashville, Tenn.: Thomas Nelson.

Maxwell, John. (2011) *The 5 Levels of Leadership: Proven Steps to Maximize Your Potential.* New York: Center Street.

Maxwell, John C. (2012) *The 15 Invaluable Laws of Growth: Live Them and Reach Your Potential.* US: Center Street.

Maxwell, John C. and J. Dornan. (2013) *How to Influence People: make a difference in your world.* Nashville: Thomas Nelson.

Maxwell, John C. and Wooden, J. (2013) *Sometimes You Win--Sometimes You Learn: Life's Greatest Lessons Are Gained from Our Losses.* US: Center Street.

Maxwell, John C. (2013) *How to Influence People: Make a Difference in your World.* Nashville, TN: Thomas Nelson.

Maxwell, John C. (2014) *Good Leaders Ask Great Questions: Your Foundation for Successful Leadership.* US: Center Street.

Maxwell, John C. (2015) *Intentional Living: Choosing a Life That Matters.* New York: Center Street.

McChesney, Chris, Sean Covey, and Jim Huling. (2012) *The 4 Disciplines of Execution: Achieving Your Wildly Important Goals.* US: Free Press.

McChrystal, Stanley, Collins, T., Silverman, D., and Fussell, C. (2015) *Team of Teams: New Rules of Engagement for a Complex World.* US: Portfolio.

McCullough, David G. (2015) *The Wright Brothers.* US: Simon and Schuster.

McGinnis, Alan. (1979) *Friendship Factor: How to Get Closer to the People You Care for.* US: Augsburg Fortress Pub.

McGinty, Sarah Myers. (2001) *Power Talk: Using Language to Build Authority and Influence.* US: Warner Business Books.

Mckeown, Greg. (2012) *Essentialism: The Disciplined Pursuit of Less*. New York: Crown Business.

Murphy, James D. and Murphy, J. (2014) *The Debrief Imperative*. US: FastPencil Premiere.

Meyer, Joyce. (2001) *A Leader in the Making: Essentials to Being a Leader After God's Own Heart*. US: Harrison House Inc.

Mohler, R. Albert. (2012) *The Conviction to Lead: 25 Principles for Leadership That Matters*. US: Bethany House Publishers.

Molinaro, Vince. (2013) *The Leadership Contract: The Fine Print to Becoming a Great Leader*. US: Wiley.

Mosley, Eric, and Irvine, D. (2015) *The Power of Thanks: How Social Recognition Empowers Employees and Creates a Best Place to Work*. US: McGraw-Hill Education.

Mutek, Mike, (2006) *Contractor Team Arrangements-Competitive Solution or Legal Liability*. US: ABA.

Nierenberg, Gerald. (1996) *The Art of Creative Thinking*. US: Barnes & Noble Books.

Noonan, Peggy. (1999) *On Speaking Well: How to Give a Speech With Style, Substance, and Clarity*. US: William Morrow Paperbacks.

Oakley, Ed, and Doug Krug. (1994) *Enlightened Leadership: Getting to the Heart of Change*. US: A Fireside Book.

Orwell, George. (1949) *1984*. New York: Penguin Group.

Page, Rick. (2003) *Hope Is Not a Strategy: The 6 Keys to Winning the Complex Sale*. US: McGraw-Hill.

Parrott, Les. (1999) *The Control Freak*. US: Tyndale House.

Patterson, Kerry, Grenny, J., McMillan, R., Switzler, A., and Covey, S. (2002) *Crucial Conversations: Tools for Talking When Stakes Are High*. US: McGraw-Hill.

Patterson, Kerry, Grenny, J., McMillan, R., and Switzler, A. (2004) *Crucial Confrontations: Tools for Resolving Broken Promises, Violated Expectations, and Bad Behavior*. New York: McGraw-Hill.

Peale, Norman Vincent, (1989) *Inspirational Writings of Norman Vincent Peale*. US: Bristol Park Books.

Peale, Norman Vincent, and Ken Blanchard. (1989) The *Power of Ethical Management*. US: Fawcett

Peale, Norman Vincent. (2003) *The Power of Positive Thinking*. US: Touchstone.

Peale, Norman Vincent. (2003) *Enthusiasm Makes the Difference*. New York: Fireside.

Pease, Kelly-Kate S. and Reviews, C. (2002) *International Organizations: Perspectives on Governance in the Twenty-First Century (2nd Edition)*. US: Prentice Hall.

Pease, Allan. (2006) *The Definitive Book of Body Language*. US: Bantam.

Peck, Girvan. (1984) *Writing Persuasive Briefs*. US: Little Brown and Co. Law and Business.

Perino. Dana. (2015) *And the Good News is…: Lessons and Advice from the Bright Side*. New York: Hachette Book Group.

Peter, Laurence J. and Raymond Hull. (1968) *The Peter Principle*. New York, NY: Bantam Books.

Peters, Tom, and Waterman, R. (1982) *In Search of Excellence: Lessons from America's Best-Run Companies*. US: Harper and Row.

Pfeffer, Jeffrey. (1993) *Managing With Power: Politics and Influence in Organizations*. Boston: Harvard Business Review Press.

Pfeffer, Jeffrey. (1997) *The Human Equation: Building Profits by Putting People First*. Boston: Harvard Business School Press.

Pfeffer, Jeffrey, and Robert I. Sutton. (2000) *The Knowing-Doing Gap*. Boston: Harvard Business School Press,

Pfeffer, Jeffrey. (2015) *Leadership BS: Fixing Workplaces and Careers One Truth at a Time*. New York: Harper Collins.

Pirsig, Robert. (2006) *Zen and the Art of Motorcycle Maintenance: An Inquiry into Values*. US: HarperTorch.

Pugh, David G., Bacon, T.R. (2005) *Powerful Proposals: How to Give Your Business the Winning Edge*. US: AMACOM.

Qubein, Nido. (1996) *How to be a Great Communicator: The Complete System for Communicating Effectively in Business and in Life*. US: Creative Services, Inc.

Project Management Institute. (2013) *A Guide to the Project Management Body of Knowledge, 5th Edition (PMBOK Guides)*. US: Project Management Institute.

Rachels, James. (2002) *The Elements of Moral Philosophy.* US: McGraw-Hill College

Radin, Margaret Jane. (2012) *Boilerplate: The Fine Print, Vanishing Rights, and the Rule of Law.* US: Princeton University Press.

Ramsey, Henry, and Aaron, J. (1988) *The Little, Brown Handbook.* US: Scott Foresman and Co.

Ramsey, Dave. (2003) *Financial Peace Revisited.* US: Penguin Group.

Rath, Tom, and Clifton, P. (2004) *How Full is Your Bucket?* US: Gallup Press.

Rath, Tom. (2006) *Vital Friends: The People You Can't Afford to Live Without.* US: Gallup Press.

Rath, Tom. (2007) *StrengthsFinder 2.0.* US: Gallup Press.

Rath, Tom, and Conchie, B. (2009) *Strengths Based Leadership: Great Leaders, Teams, and Why People Follow.* US: Gallup Press.

Rath, Tom. (2013) *Eat Move Sleep: How Small Choices Lead to Big Changes.* US: Missionday.

Rath, Tom. (2015) *Are You Fully Charged?: The 3 Keys to Energizing Your Work and Life.* US: Silicon Guild.

Reardon, Kathleen Kelly. (2005) *It's All Politics: Winning in a World Where Hard Work and Talent Aren't Enough.* New York: Currency Doubleday.

Rhys, Ernest. (1979) *Aesop's and Other Fables.* US: Dutton Adult.

Rice, Charles E. (1993) *50 Questions on the Natural Law: What it is and why we Need it.* US: Ignatius Press.

Robbins, Anthony. (1992) *Awaken the Giant Within: How to Take Immediate Control of Your Mental, Emotional, Physical and Financial Destiny!* US: Free Press.

Robbins, Anthony, and McClendon, J. (1997) *Unlimited Power: The New Science of Personal Achievement.* US: Free Press.

Roberto, Michael A. (2009) *The Art of Critical Decision Making.* Chantilly, VA: The Teaching Company.

Roberts, Wess. (1989) *Leadership Secrets of Attila the Hun.* US: Grand Central Publishing.

Rosener, Judy B. (1997) *America's Competitive Secret: Women Managers.* US: Oxford University Press.

Rousseau, Jean-Jacques, and Cranston, M. (2006) *The Social Contract*. US: Penguin Books.

Rusk, Tom, and Miller, D. (1993) *The Power of Ethical Persuasion: From Conflict to Partnership at Work and in Private Life*. US: Viking Adult.

Sanborn, Mark, and Maxwell, J. (2004) *The Fred Factor: How Passion in Your Work and Life Can Turn the Ordinary into the Extraordinary*. US: Currency.

Sanborn, Mark. (2006) *You Don't Need a Title to Be a Leader: How Anyone, Anywhere, Can Make a Positive Difference*. New York: Currency Doubleday.

Sanborn, Mark. (2008) *The Encore Effect: How to Achieve Remarkable Performance in Anything You Do*. US: Crown Business.

Schwarzkopf, Norman, and Petre, P. (1992) *It Doesn't Take a Hero: The Autobiography*. US: Bantam Books.

Scott, Susan. (2009) *Fierce Leadership: A Bold Alternative to the Worst "Best" Practices of Business Today*. US: Crown Business.

Senge, Peter M. (1990) *The Fifth Discipline: The Art and Practice of the Learning Organization*. New York: Doubleday Business.

Shaw, Haydn, and Covey, S. (2013) *Sticking Points: How to Get 4 Generations Working Together in the 12 Places They Come Apart*. US: Tyndale House Publishers, Inc.

Shim, Jae, Joel G. Siegel, and Abraham J. Simon. (1986) *The Vest-Pocket MBA*. US: Prentice-Hall, Inc.

Shim, Jae, and Joel G. Siegel, (2000) *Dictionary of Accounting Terms*. US: Barron's Educational Series, Inc.

Simchi-Levi, David, and, Simchi-Levi, E. (2003) *Managing the Supply Chain: The Definitive Guide for the Business Professional*. US: McGraw-Hill.

Simmons, Annette. (2007) *Whoever Tells the Best Story Wins: How to Use Your Own Stories to Communicate with Power and Impact*. US: AMACOM.

Sinek, Simon. (2011) *Start with Why: How Great Leaders Inspire Everyone to Take Action*. US: Portfolio.

Sinetar, Marsha. (1986) *Do What You Love, the Money Will Follow*. US: Dell.

Sowell, Thomas. (2011) *The Thomas Sowell Reader*. US: Basic Books.

Sowell, Thomas. (2013) *Intellectuals and Race*. US: Basic Books.

Stanley, Andy. (2003) *The Next Generation Leader: Five Essentials for Those Who Will Shape the Future*. Sisters, OR: Multnomah.

Stanley, Charles F. (2013) *Emotions: Confront the Lies. Conquer with Truth.* US: Howard Books.

Stone, Douglas, and Bruce Patton. *Difficult Conversations: How to Discuss What Matters Most.* US: Viking Adult.

Stout, Martha. (2006) *The Sociopath Next Door.* US: Harmony.

Strunk, William, and White, E. (1978) *The Elements of Style.* US: Macmillan Publishing Co.

Sutton, Robert I. (2007) *The No Asshole Rule: Building a Civilized Workplace and Surviving One That Isn't.* US: Business Plus.

Swindall, Clint. (2007) *Engaged Leadership: Building a Culture to Overcome Employee Disengagement.* US: Wiley.

Swindoll, Charles R. (2000*) Elijah: A Man of Heroism and Humility.* US: Word Publishing—Thomas Nelson.

Takash, Joe. (2008) *Results through Relationships: Building Trust, Performance, and Profit through People.* US: Wiley.

Tannen, Deborah. (1991) *You Just Don't Understand: Women and Men in Conversation.* US: Ballantine Books.

Tannen, Deborah. (1992) *That's Not What I Meant!: How Conversational Style Makes or Breaks Relationships.* US: Ballantine Books.

Tannen, Deborah. (1994) *Talking from 9 to 5: How Women's and Men's Conversational Styles Affect Who Gets Heard, Who Gets Credit, and What Gets Done at Work.* US: William Morrow and Company.

Tannen, Deborah. (1998) *The Argument Culture: Moving from Debate to Dialogue.* US: Random House.

Tannen, Deborah. (2006) *You're Wearing That?: Understanding Mothers and Daughters in Conversation.* US: Ballantine Books.

Terry, Robert W. and Cleveland, H. (2001) *Seven Zones for Leadership: Acting Authentically in Stability and Chaos.* US: Nicholas Brealey America.

Thompson, George J. and Jenkins, J. (1994) *Verbal Judo: The Gentle Art of Persuasion.* US: Quill.

Tichey, Noel M. and Sherman, S. (1994) *Control Your Destiny or Someone Else Will.* US: HarperPB.

Towers, Mark. (1994) *Reinventing Your Self: 28 Strategies for Coping with Change.* US: Skillpath Publications.

Tracy, Brian. (1999) *Success Is a Journey: Making Your Life a Grand Adventure*. US: Executive Excellence Publishing.

Tracy, Brian. (2001) *Focal Point: A Proven System to Simplify Your Life, Double Your Productivity, and Achieve All Your Goals*. US: AMACOM.

Tracy, Brian. (2002) *Eat That Frog!: 21 Great Ways to Stop Procrastinating and Get More Done in Less Time*. US: Berrett-Koehler Publishers.

Tracy, Brian. (2011) *No Excuses! The Power of Self-discipline*. US: MJF Books.

Treacy, Michael and Fred Wiersema. (1997) *The Discipline of Market Leaders: Choose Your Customers, Narrow Your Focus, Dominate Your Market*. US: Basic Books.

Truitt, Wesley B. (2010) *Power and Policy: Lessons for Leaders in Government and Business*. US: Praeger.

Trump, Donald, with Meredith McIver. (2009) *Think like a Champion: An Informal Education in Business and Life*. New York: Vanguard Press.

Twain, Mark. (1985) *The Signet Classic Book of Mark Twain's Short Stories*. New York: Penguin Books.

Tzu, Sun, Galvin, D., and Giles, L. (2004) *The Art of War*. US: Barnes and Noble Classics.

Ulrich, David, Jack Zenger, and Norman Smallwood. (1999) *Results-Based Leadership*. US: Harvard Business Review Press.

Ury, William. (1993) *Getting Past No: Negotiating in Difficult Situations*. New York: Bantam Books.

Ury, William. (2007) *The Power of a Positive No: How to Say No and Still Get to Yes.* US: Bantam Books.

Ury, William. (2015) *Getting to Yes with Yourself: And Other Worthy Opponents*. US: HarperOne.

Vilas, Sandy, Fisher, D., and Vilas, S. (1992) *Power Networking: 55 Secrets for Personal and Professional Success*. US: Bard Press.

Van Dyke, Michael. (2012) *Radical Integrity*. US: Barbour Publishing.

Ventrella, Scott W. and Norman Vincent Peale. (2001) *The Power of Positive Thinking in Business: Ten Traits for Maximum Results*. US: Free Press.

Vile, John R. (2013) *The Men Who Made the Constitution: Lives of the Delegates to the Constitutional Convention*. US: Scarecrow Press.

Von Hayek, F. (1972). *The Constitution of Liberty*. Chicago: Regnery.

Vos Savant, Marilyn. (1996) *The Power of Logical Thinking: Easy Lessons in the Art of Reasoning…and Hard Facts About Its Absence in Our Lives.* US: St. Martin's Press.

Waitley, Denis. (1992) *Timing Is Everything: Turning Your Seasons of Success into Maximum Opportunities.* US: Thomas Nelson Inc.

Waitzkin, Josh. (2007) *The Art of Learning: A Journey in the Pursuit of Excellence.* US: Free Press.

Walker, Steven F. and Marr, J. (2001) *Stakeholder Power: A Winning Plan for Building Stakeholder Commitment and Driving Corporate Growth.* US: Basic Books.

Wallace, Les, and Trinka, J. (2007) *A Legacy of 21st Century Leadership: A Guide for Creating a Climate of Leadership Throughout Your Organization.* US: iUniverse, Inc.

Washington, George. (1989) *Rules of Civility and Decent Behaviour in Company and Conversation.* Mount Vernon, VA: Mount Vernon Ladies Association.

Weisinger, Hendrie. (1997) *Emotional Intelligence at Work: The Untapped Edge for Success.* San Francisco: Jossey-Bass Publishers.

Welch, Jack, and John A. Byrne. (2001) *Jack: Straight from the Gut.* US: Business Plus.

Welch, Jack, and Suzy Welch. (2004) *Winning.* New York: Harper Business Publishers.

Welch, Jack and Suzy Welch. (2015) *The Real Life MBA: Your No-BS Guide to Winning the Game, Building a Team, and Growing Your Career.* New York: Harper Collins.

Widener, Chris. (2007) *The Angel Inside: Michelangelo's Secrets For Following Your Passion and Finding the Work You Love.* US: Currency Doubleday.

Wolgemuth, Robert. (2009) *She Still Calls Me Daddy: Building a New Relationship with Your Daughter After You Walk Her Down the Aisle.* US: Thomas Nelson.

Woodward, Orrin. (2014) *The Leadership Train.* Cary, NC: Obstacles Press.

Woodward, Orrin. (2015) *The Financial Matrix.* Cary, NC: Obstacles Press.

Ziglar, Zig, and Savage, J. (1985) Top *Performance.* Old Tappan, N.J.: F.H. Revell.

Ziglar, Zig, and Mayton, A. (2000) *See You at the Top.* US: Pelican Publishing.

Morgan James
Speakers Group

We connect Morgan James published authors with live and online events and audiences who will benefit from their expertise.

Morgan James makes all of our titles available
through the Library for All Charity Organization.

www.LibraryForAll.org

CPSIA information can be obtained
at www.ICGtesting.com
Printed in the USA
LVHW04s2232090518
576606LV00002B/15/P